ZHITOMIR-BERDICHEV

GERMAN OPERATIONS WEST OF KIEV
24 DECEMBER 1943–31 JANUARY 1944

Volume 1

Stephen Barratt

Helion & Company Ltd

This volume is respectfully dedicated to those whose lives were affected by the events described herein; particularly those whose voice was taken from them as a result.

Helion & Company Limited
26 Willow Road
Solihull
West Midlands
B91 1UE
England
Tel. 0121 705 3393
Fax 0121 711 4075
Email: info@helion.co.uk
Website: www.helion.co.uk

Published by Helion & Company 2012

Designed and typeset by Farr out Publications, Wokingham, Berkshire
Cover designed by Farr out Publications, Wokingham, Berkshire
Printed by Gutenberg Press Limited, Tarxien, Malta

Text and maps © Stephen Barratt 2012
Photographs © as credited

Front cover: A German infantryman on a *Sturmgeschütz*, the Ukraine, 1943/44. (Bundesarchiv, Bild 101I-709-0339-19A, photo: Gerhard Gronefeld)

ISBN 978-1-907677-66-3

British Library Cataloguing-in-Publication Data.
A catalogue record for this book is available from the British Library.

All rights reserved. No part of this publication may be reproduced, stored in a retrieval system,or transmitted, in any form, or by any means, electronic, mechanical, photocopying, recording or otherwise, without the express written consent of Helion & Company Limited.

The right of Stephen Barratt to be identified as the author of this work has been asserted by him in accordance with the Copyright, Designs and Patents Act 1988.

For details of other military history titles published by Helion & Company Limited contact the above address, or visit our website: http://www.helion.co.uk.

Contents

List of Illustrations	4
List of Maps	5
List of Tables	9
Acknowledgements	10
List of Terms and Abbreviations	11
Introduction and Note on Sources	13

Part I: The Initial Situation
1	The Soviet Situation – Planning and Deployment	21
2	The German Situation	43

Part II: The Start of the Soviet Offensive
3	The Initial Breakthrough	81
4	The Offensive Widens	101
5	The *4.Panzerarmee* Falls Back	128
6	The Front is Split Apart	154

Part III: The Arrival of the *1.Panzerarmee*
7	Hube Assumes Command	185
8	The *1.Panzerarmee* Splits into Three	202

Part IV: The *4.Panzerarmee* Front Begins to Stabilise
9	The Offensive Slows	231
10	Preparing the Counterstrike	260

Photographs of Commanders	
German	296
Soviet	297
Index	298

List of Illustrations

German   296

Generalfeldmarschall Erich von Manstein, commander of Army Group South (left) in conversation with *Generalleutnant* Theodor Busse, Chief of Staff of Army Group South (centre). Photo taken in summer 1943. (Bundesarchiv, Bild 101I-219-0579A-21)

Generaloberst Erhard Raus, commander of the *4.Panzerarmee*. (Bundesarchiv, Bild 146-1984-019-28, photographer: Wolff/Altvater)

General der Panzertruppen Hans-Valentin Hube, commander of the *1.Panzerarmee*. (Bundesarchiv, Bild 146-2009-0114, photographer: Hoffmann)

Soviet   297

Army General Nikolai Vatutin, commander of the 1st Ukrainian Front.
Lieutenant General Nikolai Pukhov, commander of the 13th Army.
Lieutenant-General Ivan Chernyakhovskii, commander of the 60th Army.
Colonel-General Andrei Grechko, commander of the 1st Guards Army.
Colonel-General Konstantin Leselidze, commander of the 18th Army.
Major-General of Artillery Kirill Moskalenko, commander of the 38th Army.
Lieutenant-General Fillip Zhmachenko, commander of the 40th Army.
Colonel-General Sergei Trofimenko, commander of the 27th Army.
Lieutenant-General of Tank Forces Mikhail Katukov, commander of the 1st Tank Army.
Colonel-General of Tank Forces Pavel Rybalko, commander of the 3rd Guards Tank Army.

List of Maps

Maps are in separate map book. Page references given are for those in the map book.

1. Soviet objectives	10
2. Overall situation evening 23 December 1943	11
3. Situation evening 23 December 1943 – *XXIV.PzK*	12
4. Situation evening 23 December 1943 – *VII.AK*	13
5. Situation evening 23 December 1943 – *VII.AK* left wing	14
6. Situation evening 23 December 1943 – *XXXXII.AK*	15
7. Situation evening 23 December 1943 – *XIII.AK*	16
8. Situation evening 23 December 1943 – *XXXXVIII.PzK*	17
9. Situation evening 23 December 1943 – *LIX.AK*	18
10. Overall situation evening 24 December 1943	19
11. Situation evening 24 December 1943 – *XXXXII.AK*	20
12. Situation evening 24 December 1943 – *XIII.AK*	21
13. Situation evening 24 December 1943 – *XXXXVIII.PzK*	22
14. Overall situation evening 25 December 1943	23
15. Situation evening 25 December 1943 – *VII.AK* left wing	24
16. Situation evening 25 December 1943 – *XXXXII.AK*	25
17. Situation evening 25 December 1943 – *XXXXIII.AK*	26
18. Situation evening 25 December 1943 – *LIX.AK*	27
19. Overall situation evening 26 December 1943	28
20. Situation evening 26 December 1943 – *VII.AK* left wing	29
21. Situation evening 26 December 1943 – *XXXXII.AK*	30
22. Situation evening 26 December 1943 – *XXXXVIII.PzK*	31
23. Situation evening 26 December 1943 – *XIII.AK*	32
24. Overall situation evening 27 December 1943	33
25. Situation evening 27 December 1943 – *VII.AK* left wing	34
26. Situation evening 27 December 1943 – *XXXXII.AK*	35
27. Situation evening 27 December 1943 – *XXXXVIII.PzK*	36
28. Situation evening 27 December 1943 – *XIII.AK* right wing	37
29. Situation evening 27 December 1943 – *XIII.AK* left wing	38
30. Overall situation evening 28 December 1943	39
31. Situation evening 28 December 1943 – *VII.AK* left wing	40
32. Situation evening 28 December 1943 – *XXXXII.AK*	41
33. Situation evening 28 December 1943 – *XXXXVIII.PzK*	42
34. Situation evening 28 December 1943 – *XIII.AK* right wing	43
35. Situation evening 28 December 1943 – *XIII.AK* left wing	44
36. Situation evening 28 December 1943 – *LIX.AK*	45
37. Overall situation evening 29 December 1943	46
38. Situation evening 29 December 1943 – *VII.AK* left wing	47
39. Situation evening 29 December 1943 – *XXXXII.AK*	48

40. Situation evening 29 December 1943 – *XXXXVIII.PzK* right wing   49
41. Situation evening 29 December 1943 – *XXXXVIII.PzK* left wing   50
42. Situation evening 29 December 1943 – *XIII.AK*   51
43. Situation evening 29 December 1943 – *LIX.AK*   52
44. Overall situation evening 30 December 1943   53
45. Situation evening 30 December 1943 – *VII.AK* right wing   54
46. Situation evening 30 December 1943 – *VII.AK* left wing   55
47. Situation evening 30 December 1943 – *XXXXII.AK*   56
48. Situation evening 30 December 1943 – *XXXXVIII.PzK*   57
49. Situation evening 30 December 1943 – *XIII.AK*   58
50. Overall situation evening 31 December 1943   59
51. Situation evening 31 December 1943 – *VII.AK* left wing   60
52. Situation evening 31 December 1943 – *XXXXII.AK*   61
53. Situation evening 31 December 1943 – *XXXXVIII.PzK*   62
54. Situation evening 31 December 1943 – *XIII.AK*   63
55. Situation evening 31 December 1943 – *LIX.AK*   64
56. Overall situation evening 1 January 1944   65
57. Situation evening 1 January 1944 – *VII.AK* left wing   66
58. Situation evening 1 January 1944 – *17.Panzer-Division*   67
59. Situation evening 1 January 1944 – *XXIV.PzK*   68
60. Situation evening 1 January 1944 – *XXXXVIII.PzK*   69
61 Situation evening 1 January 1944 – *XIII.AK*   70
62. Situation evening 1 January 1944 – *LIX.AK*   71
63. Overall situation evening 2 January 1944   72
64. Situation evening 2 January 1944 – *VII.AK* right wing   73
65. Situation evening 2 January 1944 – *VII.AK* left wing   74
66. Situation evening 2 January 1944 – *17.Panzer-Division*   75
67. Situation evening 2 January 1944 – *XXIV.PzK*   76
68. Situation evening 2 January 1944 – *XXXXVIII.PzK*   77
69. Situation evening 2 January 1944 – *XIII.AK*   78
70. Situation evening 2 January 1944 – *LIX.AK*   79
71. Overall situation evening 3 January 1944   80
72. Situation evening 3 January 1944 – *VII.AK*   81
73. Situation evening 3 January 1944 – *6.Panzer-Division*   82
74. Situation evening 3 January 1944 – *17.Panzer-Division*   83
75. Situation evening 3 January 1944 – *XXIV.PzK*   84
76. Situation evening 3 January 1944 – *XXXXVIII.PzK*   85
77. Situation evening 3 January 1944 – *XIII.AK*   86
78. Situation evening 3 January 1944 – *16.Panzer-Division*   87
79. Situation evening 3 January 1944 – *LIX.AK*   88
80. Overall situation evening 4 January 1944   89
81. Situation evening 4 January 1944 – *VII.AK* right wing   90
82. Situation evening 4 January 1944 – *VII.AK* left wing   91
83. Situation evening 4 January 1944 – *6.Panzer-Division*   92
84. Situation evening 4 January 1944 – *17.Panzer-Division*   93
85. Situation evening 4 January 1944 – *XXIV.PzK* right wing   94

LIST OF MAPS

86. Situation evening 4 January 1944 – *XXIV.PzK* left wing	95
87. Situation evening 4 January 1944 – *XIII.AK/XXXXVIII.PzK*	96
88. Situation evening 4 January 1944 – *16.Panzer-Division*	97
89. Situation evening 4 January 1944 – *LIX.AK*	98
90. Overall situation evening 5 January 1944	99
91. Situation evening 5 January 1944 – *VII.AK* right wing	100
92. Situation evening 5 January 1944 – *VII.AK* left wing	101
93. Situation evening 5 January 1944 – *6.Panzer-Division*	102
94. Situation evening 5 January 1944 – *17.Panzer-Division*	103
95. Situation evening 5 January 1944 – *XXIV.PzK* right wing	104
96. Situation evening 5 January 1944 – *XXIV.PzK* left wing	105
97. Situation evening 5 January 1944 – *XIII.AK/XXXXVIII.PzK*	106
98. Situation evening 5 January 1944 – *16.Panzer-Division*	107
99. Situation evening 5 January 1944 – *LIX.AK*	108
100. Overall situation evening 6 January 1944	109
101. Situation evening 6 January 1944 – *XXXXII.AK*	110
102. Situation evening 6 January 1944 – *VII.AK* right wing	111
103. Situation evening 6 January 1944 – *VII.AK* left wing	112
104. Situation evening 6 January 1944 – *III.PzK* right wing	113
105. Situation evening 6 January 1944 – *III.PzK* centre	114
106. Situation evening 6 January 1944 – *III.PzK* left wing	115
107. Situation evening 6 January 1944 – *XXIV.PzK* right wing	116
108. Situation evening 6 January 1944 – *XXIV.PzK* left wing	117
109. Situation evening 6 January 1944 – *XXXXVIII.PzK*	118
110. Situation evening 6 January 1944 – *16.Panzer-Division*	119
111. Situation evening 6 January 1944 – *LIX.AK*	120
112. Overall situation evening 7 January 1944	121
113. Situation evening 7 January 1944 – *XXXXII.AK*	122
114. Situation evening 7 January 1944 – *VII.AK*	123
115. Situation evening 7 January 1944 – *III.PzK* right wing	124
116. Situation evening 7 January 1944 – *III.PzK* left wing	125
117. Situation evening 7 January 1944 – *XXIV.PzK* right wing	126
118. Situation evening 7 January 1944 – *XXIV.PzK* left wing	127
119. Situation evening 7 January 1944 – *XXXXVIII.PzK*	128
120. Situation evening 7 January 1944 – *16.Panzer-Division*	129
121. Situation evening 7 January 1944 – *LIX.AK*	130
122. Overall situation evening 8 January 1944	131
123. Situation evening 8 January 1944 – *XXXXII.AK*	132
124. Situation evening 8 January 1944 – *VII.AK*	133
125. Situation evening 8 January 1944 – *III.PzK* right wing	134
126. Situation evening 8 January 1944 – *III.PzK* left wing	135
127. Situation evening 8 January 1944 – *XXIV.PzK* right wing	136
128. Situation evening 8 January 1944 – *XXIV.PzK* left wing	137
129. Situation evening 8 January 1944 – *XXXXVIII.PzK*	138
130. Situation evening 8 January 1944 – *LIX.AK* right wing	139
131. Situation evening 8 January 1944 – *LIX.AK* left wing	140

132. Overall situation evening 9 January 1944 — 141
133. Situation evening 9 January 1944 – *XXXXII.AK* — 142
134. Situation evening 9 January 1944 – *VII.AK* — 143
135. Situation evening 9 January 1944 – *III.PzK* right wing — 144
136. Situation evening 9 January 1944 – *III.PzK* left wing — 145
137. Situation evening 9 January 1944 – *XXXXVI.PzK* right wing — 146
138. Situation evening 9 January 1944 – *XXXXVI.PzK* left wing — 147
139. Situation evening 9 January 1944 – *XXIV.PzK* — 148
140. Situation evening 9 January 1944 – *XXXXVIII.PzK* — 149
141. Situation evening 9 January 1944 – *LIX.AK* right wing — 150
142. Situation evening 9 January 1944 – *LIX.AK* left wing — 151

List of Tables

Table 1: Numerical comparison of units deployed by the 1st Ukrainian Front — 40
Table 2: Categories shown in *4.Panzerarmee* weekly combat strengths returns — 70
Table 3: Maximum and minimum combat strengths of *4.Panzerarmee* at 5 December 1943 — 70
Table 4: Maximum and minimum combat strengths of *4.Panzerarmee* at 8 January 1944 — 71
Table 5: Maximum and minimum combat strengths of *1.Panzerarmee* at 8 January 1944 — 72
Table 6: Summary of *4.Panzerarmee* armour strength on 20 December 1943 — 72
Table 7: *4.Panzerarmee* Armour Strength at 20 December 1943 — 76

Acknowledgements

I wish to express my thanks to the many people and organisations that in one form or another have assisted in the preparation of this book, a few of which deserve special mention.

First of these is the American Historical Association for arranging the microfilming of captured German records after the Second World War. Their work all those years ago still provides scholars and historians with easy access to a rich archive of primary source material for any history of the war between Germany and the Soviet Union. Without their foresight this book would not exist.

Acknowledgement is also due to the Army Map Service of the Corps of Engineers in the US Army which compiled revised cartographic material on the basis of sheets originally published by the Red Army during the war. This material has been used as the underlying background for the detailed maps in this book.

I should also like to thank Gary Wright, a good friend of mine for longer than either of us probably cares to remember. It was he who introduced me all those years ago to the subject of military history and he must therefore bear at least some of the responsibility for this book.

I would also like to mention Simon Alderson at DA Archive Solutions Ltd for getting me started again when I ran into problems with my microfilm equipment and it seemed as if I might have to give up any hope of completing what I had started.

Most of all though, I owe an immense debt of gratitude to my wife Carol for her enduring support and good humour while I was spending my time with events and people long since passed. Without her unfailing patience and encouragement, it is entirely possible that none of this would have seen the light of day.

Stephen Barratt
Kington St Michael
2012

List of Terms and Abbreviations

Abt.	*Abteilung*	Battalion
AOK	*Armeeoberkommando*	Army Headquarters
Arko	*Artillerie-Kommandeur*	Artillery commander
Aufkl.	*Aufklärungs*	Reconnaissance
	balka	Ravine
Begl.Kp.	*Begleit-Kompanie*	Escort company
Btl.	*Bataillon*	Battalion
BvTO	*Bevollmächtigter Transport Offizier*	Authorised Transport Officer
DG IV	*Durchgangsstrasse IV*	Through road or major highway IV
FEB	*Feld-Ersatz-Bataillon*	Field replacement battalion
	Flammpanzer	Flamethrower Tank
Geb.	*Gebirgs*	Mountain
Geb.Jäg.	*Gebirgsjäger*	Mountain infantry
Gr.W.	*Granatwerfer*	Mortar
H.Pi.Btl.	*Heeres-Pionier-Bataillon*	GHQ or Army engineer battalion
Ia	*Führungs-Abteilung*	Operations Section
Ic	*Feindnachrichten-Abteilung*	Intelligence Section
Jäg.	*Jäger*	Light infantry
Kav.	*Kavallerie*	Cavalry
KG	*Kampfgruppe*	Battle group
KK	*Kampfkommandant*	Combat commandant
Kolkhoz	*Kollektivnoe khozyaistvo*	Collective Farm
Korück	*Kommandant des rückwärtigen Armeegebiet*	Commander of an Army rear area
Lds.Btl.	*Landesschützen-Bataillon*	Local Defence Battalion
	Lehr	Demonstration
	Marschbataillon	March battalion
Nbl.	*Nebelwerfer*	Rocket launcher
	oblast	A higher political administrative area in the Soviet Union
OFK	*Oberfeldkommandantur*	Higher Field Commandant
OKH	*Oberkommando des Heeres*	Army High Command
	panje	A breed of horse capable of working in extreme cold
Pi.	*Pionier*	Engineer
Pi.B.Btl.	*Pionier-Bau-Bataillon*	Construction battalion
Pz.	*Panzer*	Armour
PzAOK	*Panzerarmeeoberkommando*	Tank Army Headquarters
Pz.Aufkl.	*Panzeraufklärungs*	Armoured reconnaissance

Pz.Pi.	*Panzerpionier*	Armoured engineer
Pz.Zers.	*Panzer-Zerstörer*	Tank destroyer
Pzgr.	*Panzergrenadier*	Armoured infantry
	Panzerzug	Armoured train
	raion	A lower political administrative area in the Soviet Union
Sich.	*Sicherungs*	Security
Sovkhoz	*Sovetskoe khozyaistvo*	State Farm
	Sturm-Bataillon	Assault battalion
StuG	*Sturmgeschütz*	Assault gun
	Süd	South
	Waffen-Schule	Weapons School
WBU	*Wehrmachtbefehlshaber Ukraine*	Armed Forces commander in Ukraine

Introduction and Note on Sources

The Zhitomir-Berdichev operation is the one which Soviet military historians describe as the first of the 1943/1944 Winter Strategic Offensive, although planning for it actually began whilst the preceding operations around Kiev were still running their course. It began on 24 December 1943 and continued well into the New Year, and although the Soviets brought the offensive to an end on 14 January 1944, the series of German counterstrokes which followed only came to a close at the end of the month when emphasis was shifted towards relieving the Korsun' pocket. By virtue of its timing therefore, it was something of a transitional operation, falling between the strategic offensives of summer/autumn 1943 and winter/spring 1944. The Soviet high command had taken the decision to undertake the Zhitomir-Berdichev offensive at a time when the Kiev defensive operation was still underway, and as a result, planning was heavily influenced by those events. In the Kiev offensive operation, the Soviets had aimed to push out the Dnepr bridgehead at Lyutezh into one of strategic importance, striking towards Berdichev and Vinnitsa to the south-west, while at the same time expanding the flanks towards Korosten' in the north-west and Belaya Tserkov' in the south-east. The offensive had begun on 3 November 1943 and had initially pushed past Fastov before being intercepted by the defending Germans, who then managed to bring the advance to a halt by 11 November. The *4.Panzerarmee* had then launched a series of counterattacks, led by the *XXXXVIII.PzK*, in an attempt to eliminate the now considerably wider bridgehead.

The first of these had struck the Soviet 3rd Guards Tank Army south of Fastov, and although it brought the Soviet advance to a standstill, the counterattack made no real progress in pushing the Russians back.[1] Following the stalling of this first counterattack, the *XXXXVIII.PzK* began a second on 12 November, this time aiming northwards between Fastov and Zhitomir. The attack struck through Brusilov before wheeling westwards towards Zhitomir which was recaptured by the Germans on 20 November. With this success behind it, the *XXXXVIII.PzK* wheeled to face eastwards, aiming towards Kiev itself. The renewed counterattack reached as far as Brusilov by 25 November, but stiff resistance and mounting casualties forced the *Korps* to break off the attack and regroup. By 5 December it was ready again and jumped off from position just north of Zhitomir, this time heading towards Radomyshl' and Malin to the north-east. It made good initial progress, effectively clearing the area between the Teterev and Irsha rivers, but the Soviets began to commit more and more reserves to the fighting, and eventually the operation ground to a halt. By 15 December, the *Korps* was making little progress, and two days later the *PzAOK 4* called off the attack in order to regroup. The next counterattack began on 19 December, this time further west, against Soviet forces deployed south-east of Korosten'. Again the attack faltered after only a few days' fighting, and the *Korps* had been brought to a standstill by 22 December.

---

1   For the purposes of this book, the terms 'Soviet' and 'Russian' have been used interchangeably when applied as an adjective to describe forces of the Red Army. This is no more than a stylistic convenience and use of the term 'Russian' in this context is not intended to imply any particular nationality.

This was the situation in which the 1st Ukrainian Front would launch its devastating new offensive against the left wing of Army Group South; one which would very nearly bring the German northern wing in Ukraine to the point of collapse; one which would inflict irreplaceable casualties upon the German troops; and one which would create the immediate preconditions for the next German disaster in Ukraine, the Korsun' pocket, and the longer term expulsion of Axis forces from the region.

This book is a description of the military operations conducted by the *4.Panzerarmee* and the *1.Panzerarmee* in response to the Soviet Zhitomir-Berdichev offensive operation from late December 1943 to the end of January 1944. It is being published in two volumes to reflect the major stages of the operation and the German response. This is the first volume and it covers operations from the start of the Soviet offensive on 24 December 1943 until 9 January 1944. Although the Soviets continued to press the attack until 14 January 1944, the offensive had effectively reached its high water mark by the time the Germans began the first of their counterstrokes on 10 January. This date marked a distinct change in emphasis and initiative, and it therefore provides a suitable point to end the first volume. The second volume will cover operations from 10 January to the end of the month, and will include the appendices.

The account given in these volumes is based largely on the records created and maintained by the Operations Sections (the *Ia* staff) of those two armies, including the war diaries, the orders received and issued by the respective headquarters, and the situation reports submitted by the subordinate *Korps* headquarters. The history here presented is therefore the view of operations as seen, understood and recorded by the German army staffs. Although it represents the official record, it should be remembered that it is still a one-sided view. Official records provide no guarantee of accuracy in every respect, and as in all walks of human life mistakes are made. They remain the official record nonetheless. It may also be pointed out that while many of the documents in the records were compiled by junior officers, these were usually checked and signed off by more senior staff. The source material itself is now held by the Bundesarchiv (Abteilung Militärarchiv) of the Federal Republic of Germany, although it has also been reproduced on microfilm by the US National Archives as part of Publication T-313. Individual roll and frame numbers for each reference quoted have not been given in the footnotes, although it may be noted that all the records concerned are located on Rolls 69-73 for the *PzAOK 1* and on Rolls 372-399 for the *PzAOK 4*. These primary sources have been supplemented in places by published material, and, as the number of these is not large, full details of the relevant publications have been provided in the footnotes rather than as a separate bibliography. Use has also been made of Soviet primary sources where these have been published, and details of those publications have also been given in the footnotes. As this book is an account of German operations, the use of Russian material has generally been restricted to discussions of higher level planning.

This book contains no significant analysis of, or commentary on, either the papers or the operations themselves, except insofar as the records themselves include analyses and comment made by the participants at the time. Any detailed and objective analysis can only really be carried out with the benefit of access to the corresponding records created by the Soviet units participating in the operation, but this lies outside the scope of this book.

INTRODUCTION AND NOTE ON SOURCES 15

The description of a series of simultaneous military operations, sometimes more connected, sometimes less so, carries its own difficulties, particularly when they are all a response to a single planned offensive. To address the problem as a chronological one, in effect to present a diary of operations for the *Panzerarmee*, means to risk losing any real sense of continuity at the *Korps* or division level; to miss the changing developments as they happen at the lower command levels. On the other hand, a description based on sectors, either *Korps* or division, presents its own problems, since every sector is essentially dependent upon the actions of its neighbours. Nevertheless, the purpose of this book is to present an account and description of German operations from the viewpoint of the controlling army headquarters, so the diary option has been chosen as offering the best solution. If, as a result, the narrative sometimes feels disjointed or overstretched, this is the price which has to be paid for a day-by-day account of military operations. The information will all be there, it may simply require from the reader a greater degree of recall to understand, and place in context, operations at any given time. The accompanying maps should assist in this respect. This level has been selected on grounds of scale, to give the best overall view of events within the scope of the operation. For the most part, the Zhitomir-Berdichev operation involved the two German army level headquarters stated above, although for the first week, the *PzAOK 4* held the whole sector on its own. By concentrating on army level documents, we are permitted a description of operations within manageable proportions, whilst retaining sight of the essential decision making process. Looking at *Korps*, or even division, level records would afford a greater glimpse of tactical matters, but would force the undertaking to assume too great a bulk. Similarly, concentrating on army group records would permit an understanding of how decisions and operations on the left wing fitted in with the campaign in western Ukraine as a whole, but the cost would be a consequent lack of detail which would reduce the book to little more than a resumé of German operations in the area. Thus, the army level papers provide an ideal scale for the description of the German response to the Soviet offensive.

Within the army level records, the most important sources may be conveniently divided into three categories: the *Ia Kriegstagebuch* (the war diary maintained by the operations staff); the *Morgen-* and *Tagesmeldungen*, the reports submitted by the various subordinate *Korps* level headquarters during the morning and evening respectively; and the actual orders and directives issued by the respective *Panzerarmee* headquarters. Of these, perhaps the second category requires some explanation. At the end of each day, the respective *Korps* headquarters would compile a brief report of events on their respective sectors, known as the '*Tagesmeldung*' (daily report), this being submitted to the *Panzerarmee* during the evening, some time between about 18.00 and 20.00 hours, but on occasion as late as 21.00 hours. At the beginning of each day, usually between about 05.00 and 07.00 hours, they would also submit a similar report to cover the events of the previous evening and night, everything in fact which had happened since the previous *Tagesmeldung*. This was called the '*Morgenmeldung*' (morning report). When used as the source for a description of events, such reports will be described in an appropriate footnote. The *Ia Kriegstagebuch*, and the operational orders, will be similarly footnoted, as will any other documents not falling within these three main categories. The methodology used in footnote numbering also requires explanation. A footnote will generally be inserted at the end of the first sentence which introduces a new documentary source, so, for example, the first sentence in a new paragraph describing an order issued by the *PzAOK 4* will carry a footnote to give the date and reference of that document. The remainder of that paragraph, or occasionally more than that paragraph, will also be derived from the same source, but the reference will appear only once, in the initial footnote.

In an effort to standardise reporting within the *4.Panzerarmee*, its chief of staff, *Generalmajor* Fangohr, found it necessary to write to his counterparts in the subordinate *Korps* headquarters on 15 December 1943, reminding them of the necessity of accurate tactical reporting.[2] In the paper, Fangohr indicated that many of the reports being received at *Panzerarmee* headquarters were not in accordance with established directives, and resulted in the army staff having to ask supplementary questions in order to gain a full picture. Again and again, terms such as 'strong', 'strongest' and 'superior', were used to describe enemy attacks, whilst artillery fire was inevitably described as 'drum fire' or 'heavy barrage'. These words had, in effect, become bywords or catchphrases, regardless of the actual situation being reported, with the result that it was proving impossible to determine with any accuracy the current state of affairs anywhere. He cited examples. A few weeks earlier, one of the *Korps* headquarters had described a Soviet artillery barrage as 'drum fire', following which Fangohr had himself discussed the matter with one of the regimental commanders on that sector. This man, who incidentally had participated in the First World War and had experienced true 'drum fire' at first hand, told Fangohr that although the enemy had certainly not been sparing with their artillery ammunition, the end result could not be compared to 'drum fire'. In another incident a 'strong' infantry assault had been reported, only to be shown later as a company strength attack intended for reconnaissance purposes.

Fangohr reminded the chiefs of staff that all tactical reporting should be dispassionate and free from ambiguous opinion, and to assist in this regard he imposed a new regime of reporting terminology and standards. Enemy attacks, for example, were to be broken down and categorised as follows:

Number of enemy attacking	Description
1-50	in the strength of 'x' men
51-100	company strength
101-200	1-2 company strength
201-300	battalion strength
301-500	about 2 battalions
501-1,000	regimental strength

Any attacks made in what seemed to be greater than regimental strength were no longer to be reported by the estimated headcount, but rather only on the basis of statements taken from prisoners of war, or captured material. Moreover, any attack reported to be involving more than 300 men was to be accompanied by an estimate of the possible scale of the assault. Fangohr requested that in future, all the *Korps'* chiefs of staff were to use this terminology, and refrain from just using words such as 'strong' and 'superior'. This terminology will feature heavily in the account of operations which follows, and readers will find it useful to recall these figures when assessing the scale

---

2   *PzAOK 4*, Ia unreferenced paper dated 15 Dec 43.

of individual assaults described during the course of this book. All attacks have been described as reported by the defending units, and should therefore coincide with these instructions from the *PzAOK 4*.

Throughout the book, German military nomenclature has been used when describing German units and offices. The purpose of this is twofold. The first reason is to retain the correct titles of such units and offices in what is essentially an account of their operations, whilst allowing the reader the opportunity to see those titles in their original form. The second is to provide a simple contrast with Soviet units and offices which are translated into their English equivalents. For those not familiar with such German terminology, a list of terms and abbreviations, together with translations, has been provided.

A word on place names will also not be out of place. Perhaps the first point to make is that the operations described in the book took place in regions where towns and villages enjoy different names depending on the language being used. The concept of this is actually quite common, and as an example for those whose mother tongue is English, the example of Germany is an apt one. The Germans refer to their own state as *Deutschland*, very different from the word in English usage. In the context of this book, Rovno may serve as an example to illustrate the point. Rovno is a direct transliteration from the Russian Cyrillic. The Ukrainian name transliterates as Rivne, while in Polish the town is known as Rowne. It is inevitable that there are instances where the use of the Ukrainian or even Polish version of place names might be more correct or appropriate, but this book will use the Russian version in an effort to achieve both simplicity and consistency. This may not be ideal when consulting the most up-to-date indigenous maps of the region, but should allow easier reference to the Russian military maps available. It may also be noted that in transliterating Russian place names for use on their military maps, the Germans were not entirely error free, so entries in reports and war diaries often resulted in misspellings. This is also true of Russian maps of the area which, based on earlier maps, in some cases Polish or even Austro-Hungarian, contain transcription errors or just plain spelling mistakes. All of this means that any given place name might be spelled in any number of different ways, and this gives rise to difficulties or frustrations in reconciling the records with the maps. Some place names are more prone to this than others. It may also be noted at this point that many Ukrainian and Polish place names have simply changed since the 1940s, meaning that the names found in the German records no longer appear on modern maps. This of course makes the action difficult to follow on more recent mapping. In other cases, some settlements are simply not marked on some maps, either contemporary or modern. Notwithstanding these issues though, the place names used throughout the text are generally those which appear on the US Army cartography employed as background material to the maps in the book, although some spelling mistakes have been corrected where necessary. In any case where something is still not clear, a footnote has been added for clarification, but it is regrettably inevitable that some inconsistencies remain.

Part I
The Initial Situation

1

The Soviet Situation – Planning and Deployment

Soviet planning for the Zhitomir-Berdichev operation began as part of a wider concept for a series of winter offensives to liberate western Ukraine. In November and December 1943, the *Stavka* and the General Staff began to draw up operational plans for these offensives, and during this period Stalin discussed the subject on a number of occasions with both Vatutin, the commander of the 1st Ukrainian Front, and Zhukov, who was co-ordinating the activities of the 1st and 2nd Ukrainian Fronts.[1] Within the wider context, it was now recognised that, since they had been engaged in active operations since July 1943, the forces of the 1st Ukrainian Front were no longer strong enough to continue their offensive mission.[2] The *Stavka* therefore assigned new forces to Vatutin's command, the main components of which were the 18th Army under Leselidze, the 1st Tank Army under Katukov, and the 4th Guards and 25th Tank Corps. Following this reinforcement the 1st Ukrainian Front deployed a total of seven all-arms armies, two tank armies, one air army, and two fortified regions by 24 November 1943.[3]

Recognising the weakening of the Front's combat power, and taking into account both the plans for the wider winter offensive and the time it would take to transfer the new forces to Vatutin's command, the primary concern of the Soviet planners at this stage was to prevent any further attempt by the Germans to re-capture Kiev. On 28 November therefore, Vatutin received new orders from the *Stavka*.[4] These acknowledged that the 1st Ukrainian Front no longer possessed sufficient strength to conduct a major offensive, and Vatutin was therefore ordered to go over to the defensive with immediate effect. Apart from allowing the Front commander to concentrate his resources for the defence of Kiev, if such proved necessary, the object of this was to wear down the German forces with the assistance of artillery and air support. The order went on to state that with the arrival of the 18th Army and the 1st Tank Army, as well as other forces, the 1st Ukrainian Front would be required to organise a major offensive with the aim of destroying the German forces on its sector and pressing forward to the reach the Southern Bug river. Vatutin was reminded that the plans should be prepared as thoroughly as they had been for the Belgorod operation earlier in the year, and was instructed to present his operational plan in due course.

---

1   A M Vasilevsky, *A Lifelong Cause*, Moscow, Progress Publishers, 1981, p. 307.
2   A N Grylev, *Dnepr-Karpaty-Krym: Osvobozhdenie Pravoberezhoi Ukrainy i Kryma v 1944 gody*, Moscow, Nauka, 1970, p.238.
3   These were the 1st Guards, 13th, 18th, 27th, 38th, 40th and 60th Armies, the 3rd Guards and 1st Tank Armies, the 2nd Air Army, and the 54th and 159th Fortified Regions.
4   Archive MO of the USSR. F. 148a. Op. 3763. D. 74. L. 111. Quoted in *Russkii Arkhiv: Velikaya Otechestvennaya. Stavka BGK: Documenty i Materialy 1943*. Vol. 16 (5–3). —Moscow: Terra, 1999, p.241.

On the basis of this new order, Vatutin issued revised operational orders to his commanders on 29 November 1943, instructing the 13th, 60th, 1st Guards, 38th and 40th Armies to go over to a static defence with the primary objective of preventing any German advance towards Kiev.[5] Having thus instructed his armies to establish new defensive positions, Vatutin started assembling his reserves in the rear area. The 18th Army was moved to the region north-west of Kiev to concentrate in the Borodyanka-Gostomel' area, while the 1st Tank Army assembled south-west of the city in the Svyatoshino-Tarasovka-Zhulyany area. The 3rd Guards Tank Army was meanwhile pulled out of the front line and moved to the Byshev-Chernogorodka area north of Fastov, while the 5th Guards Tank Corps was transferred from the 38th Army to the Front reserve and moved to the Teterev-Peskovka area north-west of Borodyanka. The 1st Guards Cavalry Corps meanwhile was to assemble in the Zauryad'e-Byrva area, while the newly arriving 4th Guards Tank Corps was to re-group in the Malin area. The order also instructed the armies to reinforce their infantry units and to stockpile reserves of fuel, ammunition, and foodstuffs, while the Front headquarters began the task of developing the plan for the forthcoming offensive.

Vatutin's basic plan of operations was to place the main point of effort in the centre of the Front, on the sectors held by the 1st Guards Army and the 38th Army, with the 1st Tank Army and the 3rd Guards Tank Army in the second echelon. The offensive was planned to begin on 24 December 1943, with the initial objective being the defeat of the German forces in the Brusilov area.[6] Having achieved the first stage of the operation, this central assault group was then to advance over 130 kilometres to a line running from Lyubar on the river Sluch' through Vinnitsa to Lipovets on the river Sob. Two days later, the offensive was to be widened to the north, with the 60th Army striking out from the Malin area in conjunction with the 4th Guards Tank Corps, its initial objective being the defeat of the German forces in the Radomyshl' area. Following this, it was to advance 120 kilometres westwards to the river Sluch' between Rogachov (28 kilometres south-east of Novograd-Volynskii) in the north and Lyubar in the south, a sector of 55 kilometres. Further north still, the 13th Army, with the 1st Guards Cavalry Corps and the 25th Tank Corps attached, was given the task of covering the Front right wing. It was to advance westward through Korosten' and Novograd-Volynskii to reach a line running from Tonezh far to the north, through Olevsk to Rogachov. This would give it responsibility for a sector of 160 kilometres. On the Front left wing, the 40th Army and the 27th Army would meanwhile strike southwards, initially towards Belaya Tserkov' and then further towards Khristinovka where it was planned that they should link up with troops of the 2nd Ukrainian Front to destroy the German forces operating in the area south of Kanev. The 5th Guards Tank Corps and the 1st Czechoslovak Infantry Brigade would operate with the 40th Army. Overall, the offensive would be supported by the 2nd Air Army. In preparing for the operation, the Front command paid great attention to disinformation activities. To divert German attention away from the main point of effort, a concentration of large forces of infantry, tanks and artillery were

---

5   A N Grylev, *Dnepr-Karpaty-Krym: Osvobozhdenie Pravoberezhoi Ukrainy i Kryma v 1944 gody*, Moscow, Nauka, 1970, p.39.

6   Soviet intelligence had correctly identified this group as the *8., 19.,* and 25.Panzer-Divisions, together with the *SS Panzerkampfgruppe 'Das Reich'*.

THE SOVIET SITUATION – PLANNING AND DEPLOYMENT

simulated in the areas around Korosten' on the right wing, and the Bukrin bridgehead on the river Dnepr on the left.[7]

To strengthen the right wing of the forthcoming operation, the *Stavka* issued orders on 9 December for the 1st Belorussian Front to transfer six rifle divisions to the 13th Army, together with a corps headquarters.[8] Three of the divisions were to be transferred by 15 December and the remaining three by 18-19 December. On 14 December, Vatutin conducted a briefing for his subordinate army commanders and the members of their military councils.[9] He informed them of the general situation and of the tasks given to the 1st Ukrainian Front, and let them know that the decision to proceed with the Zhitomir-Berdichev operation had now been made. He briefed them on the overall concept, informing them that the immediate aim was to break through the German lines of defence and, by the end of the second day, to have destroyed the German forces in the Brusilov area, including the 8., 19., and 25.*Panzer-Divisions*, as well as the SS *Panzerkampfgruppe 'Das Reich'*. After achieving this initial objective, the offensive was to be developed in the general direction of Berdichev and Kazatin. The main blow was to be supplemented by two secondary attacks; one on the right wing by the 60th and 13th Armies, and the other on the left wing around Belaya Tserkov' by the 40th and 27th Armies. Vatutin assigned the task of breaking through the German defences on the main sector to his all-arms armies, keeping his tank armies back to exploit any success or advantage achieved. The general plan was for the tank armies to be committed only once the German defences had been broken through to a depth of about five or six kilometres, something which was planned to be achieved by the middle of the first day. Thus, once the German defences around Brusilov had been defeated, the 3rd Guards Tank Army would advance to the north-west, into the rear of the German Radomyshl'-Malin grouping, while the 1st Tank Army was to advance south-westwards to divide the German forces facing the Front into two separate groups, one around Zhitomir and the other around Belaya Tserkov'.

To give a more detailed idea of Soviet planning on the main axis of attack, it may be useful to at this point to consider the approaches taken by the 38th Army and the 1st Tank Army, both deployed on the main sector, one in the first echelon and the other in the second. Following the issue of Vatutin's order of 29 November, Moskalenko's 38th Army was responsible for the defence of a line from Negrebovka south-east of Radomyshl' in the north, through Stavishche on the main Kiev-Zhitomir road, and from there through Yastreben'ka to Sushchanka just east of Kornin, a total of 42 kilometres. Its primary task at that time was to prevent the Germans from trying to break through towards Kiev, but it was also to prepare its forces for the forthcoming operation. It was also to arrange for replenishment, training, and stockpiling of supplies.[10] On 16 December, the plan for the Zhitomir-Berdichev operation had been signed off by the Front military council,

---

7   A N Grylev, *Dnepr-Karpaty-Krym: Osvobozhdenie Pravoberezhoi Ukrainy i Kryma v 1944 gody*, Moscow, Nauka, 1970, p.41.
8   Archive MO of the USSR, F. 148a. Op. 3763. D. 143. L. 304. Quoted in *Russkii Arkhiv: Velikaya Otechestvennaya. Stavka BGK: Dokumenty i Materialy 1943*. Vol. 16 (5–3). —Moscow: Terra, 1999, p.246.
9   A.Kh. Babadzhanyan, N.K. Popel', M.A. Shalin, I.M. Kravchenko, *Liuki Otkryli v Berline: Boevoi Put' 1-i Gvardeiskoi Tankovoi Armii*, Moscow, Voenizdat, 1973.
10 Moskalenko K S, *Na Yugo-Zapanom Napravlenii, 1934-1945*. Vospominaniya Komandarma. Kniga II – Moscow: Nauka, 1973, p.207ff.

and as we have seen, the basic concept was to deliver an overpowering blow which would permit the Russians to advance all the way to the river Southern Bug, removing once and for all any possibility that the Germans might threaten Kiev again. The timing of the preparation for this new operation was such that it needed to be conducted while the right wing of the Front still had to deal with the *XXXXVIII.PzK* counterattack towards Malin.

The 38th Army conducted aggressive patrolling, sending small groups as much as 10 kilometres into the German rear, and this, together with intelligence received from prisoners of war, allowed the Russians to piece together a picture of the German defences. This included the identification of troop deployments, the system of defensive fire, and weak points in the defence, such as unit boundaries. Commanders at all levels, including division and corps commanders, together with their artillery chiefs, involved themselves personally in this activity on a daily basis. In this way, the Soviets believed they had identified areas where artillery was concentrated and where the German armour was located. The results of this intelligence gathering allowed Moskalenko to plan his attack carefully, exploiting for example the fact that the Germans had not reinforced the areas around Soloveevka, Ozera, and Krivoe as expected. It was the same story in the Mokhnachka area, which allowed the army to concentrate on this sector too and plan an advance on Kornin in conjunction with the 40th Army to its left.

The day after the Front briefing on 16 December, Moskalenko called together his corps and division commanders, as well as the commanders of his independent units, and briefed them on the orders received from Vatutin before outlining his proposals for fulfilling these. During the morning of 19 December, the 38th Army issued its formal instructions, setting out the plan to break through the German defences in conjunction with troops from the 1st Tank Army. The army was to advance on the Khomutets-Khodorkov axis with the objective of defeating the German forces in the Brusilov-Khodorkov-Kornin area and pressing on towards Brovki. The main breakthrough was to be achieved on the right wing, where two rifle corps were to drive past Brusilov from the south, while a secondary assault was to be made on the left wing by a single rifle corps. Both corps on the main sector were to be split into two echelons. By the end of the first day, the attack was to have advanced about eight kilometres to reach a line from Brusilov to Divin, thereby allowing the 1st Tank Army to be committed to drive the advance forwards to achieve the large-scale breakthrough. At the end of day two, the attack was to have advanced about 30 kilometres, while the objective after that was to advance a total of 60 kilometres into the German rear. To the right, the 18th Army, together with the 3rd Guards Tank Army, was to strike north of Brusilov, while on the left, elements of the 40th Army were to strike in the Mokhnachka area, bypassing Kornin from the south.

Moskalenko even went so far as to provide guidance to his commanders on the manner in which the Germans could be expected to react. He pointed out the great manoeuvrability of German forces, being based on small armoured units with attached motorised infantry, and referred to the German method of deploying small groups of tanks in villages to provide greater flexibility in counterattacks. He also made specific reference to the German self-propelled artillery and their manoeuvrability, as well as the fact that infantry tended to be deployed in small groups. The Germans, he said, would be most likely to react to the offensive with a series of counterattacks made by small

THE SOVIET SITUATION – PLANNING AND DEPLOYMENT

groups of tanks with infantry armed with automatic weapons, and with attacks made by reserves of tanks and infantry in the depth of the defensive position. The assaulting Soviet units would therefore have to be ready to counter any such counterattacks and make sure they stifled any attempt by the Germans to go over to the offensive.

In detail, the 38th Army assault was to be conducted in accordance with the following principles. Both assault corps, the 74th and the 17th Guards, were to be deployed in two echelons, with each division in the first echelon having two regiments forward and one held in reserve. Units in the second echelons were to advance behind the first, moving in combat formation behind the initial lines of assault taken by the first echelon units, and all units were to move off road if at all possible. Tank destroyer regiments and battalions were to move in bounds, going from high ground to high ground to try and prevent the advancing troops from being taken by surprise by counterattacking tanks. Mounted groups of submachine gunners were to move in combat formation with the tanks, without dismounting to engage enemy tanks and self-propelled artillery. Anti-tank assets were to be concentrated on the flanks to counter possible armoured counterattacks from the directions of Brusilov, Vodoty, Khodorkov, Soloveevka, and Kornin. Motor vehicles operating in divisions and corps were to maintain a stock of anti-tank mines with them. Leading troops were to be supported by tank destroyer artillery regiments and allocated units armed with anti-tank mines. Each assault battalion was to have obstacle-clearing groups attached, including one or two snipers with the engineers. The activities of the obstacle-clearing groups were to be covered by all available fire. Assault groups were to work in close co-operation with the obstacle-clearing groups in destroying any German weapon emplacements which had not been suppressed by artillery fire. All units were to be ready to repel armoured counterattacks, keeping on hand all available anti-tank means, including mines. Infantry and tanks were to be prepared for co-operation and co-ordinated actions at the detachment/platoon level, and infantry units were to be provided with the means of raising the alarm, especially tracer bullets and rockets. An anti-tank system was to be defined in advance along the planned lines of attack, with anti-tank assets being deployed along the most likely axes of counterattack. Strongly defended villages were to be bypassed, and assaults from the rear and flank were always to be the preferred method of attack, irrespective of the strength of enemy resistance. In the event there was a need to increase the front line combat strength in rifle companies, men were to be taken from the 50mm mortar units. Detailed planning was to be conducted such that the division commanders issued instructions to the regiment commanders by no later than 20 December, with these briefing their respective battalion commanders by the following day. Battalion commanders in turn were to issue orders to their company commanders on 22 December. Instructions were to be handed out to individual soldiers just two hours before the assault was due to commence.

In order to ensure that planning and preparation was being conducted properly by all the armies involved, Zhukov issued orders for the process to be checked by external auditors. The check on the 38th Army preparations was conducted by a group of generals headed by Lieutenant-General Vasilii Golubovskii, who had been appointed to Zhukov's staff in September 1943. The group spent two days at the army headquarters on 17 and 18 December, as a result of which Moskalenko was essentially given a clean bill of health. Golubovskii first looked at the manpower issue, noting that between 1 and 15 December, the 38th Army had received approximately 18,000 replacement personnel between the ages of 18 and 45, the majority of these having been mobilised from recently liberated territory. He also confirmed the numerical strengths of the individual divisions concerned, reporting that those of the 74th Rifle Corps had an average of 6,900 men each, the 17th Guards Rifle Corps an average of 5-6,000 men each, and the 21st Rifle Corps, on the secondary axis, having between 4,500 and 5,000 each[11]. Despite the relative weakness of the latter two, he reported that the measures in place to bring them up to strength were acceptable. The artillery units too were all reported to be satisfactory. The availability of winter clothing was reported to be around 60%, with a particular issue regarding footwear for officers. One of the main concerns related to the lack of motor transport for the units in the army, and Golubovskii reported that the Front should provide additional resources in this regard.

At the start of the offensive, the 38th Army deployed three rifle corps, the 21st on the left, the 17th Guards in the centre, and the newly arrived 74th on the right. This latter had been attached to the army as replacement for the 52nd Rifle Corps, which had just been transferred to the neighbouring 18th Army on 19 December. Each corps had three rifle divisions, and in total the army sector was some 25 kilometres wide. The main assault was to be delivered on the right by the 74th and 17th Guards Rifle Corps, where each had a breakthrough sector of just 3.5 kilometres. Moskalenko concentrated the bulk of his artillery and other supporting arms on this sector, and behind the 74th Rifle Corps there was an average of over 190 artillery pieces and mortars per kilometre of front, with over 175 per kilometre behind the 17th Guards. Additionally, the assault infantry were supported by three tank regiments, the 7th, 9th Guards and the 39th, while further to the rear the armour of the 1st Tank Army waited for the breakthrough to be achieved. On the army left wing, the 21st Rifle Corps held a sector of some 18 kilometres, supported by an average of only 18 artillery pieces and mortars per kilometre.

With the arrival of the 74th Rifle Corps, it was necessary for the 17th Guards Rifle Corps to shift its front to the left, both to vacate what would become the former's assault sector and also to narrow its own front prior to the attack. This was carried out between 20 and 23 December, and whilst it was going on it offered an opportunity to the Germans not only to detect the troop movement but also to try and disrupt it. In the event, the Soviets believed they had carried out the movements undetected, primarily because it had all been done at night-time and there had been strict *maskirovka* discipline as well.

In preparation for the assault, the 38th Army also conducted reconnaissance in force in accordance with instructions issued by Front headquarters. This was carried out at the same time as the troop movements, and began at 15.00 hours on 21 December. That day, all divisions in the front line conducted reconnaissance in force along the secondary sectors, using reinforced rifle companies. The following day, the activity was increased, with reconnaissance being carried out by reinforced battalions and now extending the scope to include both secondary and main sectors. It was repeated again on 23 December, the day before the main offensive began. This reconnaissance confirmed that the Germans continued to occupy a forward defensive position but kept their mobile armour reserves at tactical depth. As soon as the Russian troops went over to the defensive during these preliminary actions, the Germans immediately launched counterattacks with tanks and assault guns, reinforced by small groups of infantry. From this, Moskalenko concluded

---

11   The full manpower complement of a rifle division would have been over 9,600.

that the Germans lacked the necessary infantry to hold a strong forward defence, but instead relied on counterattacking from depth. The reconnaissance also allowed the Russians to plot the German forward positions accurately, permitting the artillery to be used more effectively.

Meanwhile, the task given to Katukov's 1st Tank Army was to exploit the breach to be made by Moskalenko's 38th Army.[12] Once Moskalenko's troops had made the breakthrough and advanced to a depth of about five or six kilometres, Katukov was to commit his army to battle and begin his advance south-westwards. By the end of the second day of the operation, the 1st Tank Army was expected to have crossed the river Irpen' and reached a line between Khodorkov and Krivoe, an advance of between 30 and 40 kilometres, and be prepared to advance further towards Kazatin.[13] At the same time, Vatutin instructed Katukov to keep his lead brigades ready to provide assistance to the rifle divisions to complete the breakthrough of the main German defensive sector. The objective for the first and second days of the operation was to achieve a penetration 15 kilometres in depth. This relatively modest task reflected the Soviet view that the Germans maintained a large armoured grouping on this sector, including the *19. and 25.Panzer-Divisions* which were both deployed in the main defensive position. In order to increase the density of the army and corps artillery on the main attack sector, the heavy self-propelled artillery regiments of the 1st Tank Army took part in the preparatory artillery activities in the assault sector of the 38th Army. Reconnaissance was undertaken at all levels covering both the planned march routes and the wider area where studies were also made of German defences and forces. Katukov's plan called for the 1st Tank Army to be committed to battle on four routes. The 11th Guards Tank Corps was to operate on the right flank, and the 8th Guards Mechanised Corps on the left, while he retained an army reserve made up of the 64th Guards Tank Brigade, the 81st Motorcycle Battalion, the 79th Guards Mortar Regiment, and an anti-tank reserve made up of two tank-destroyer artillery regiments. Each corps was in turn to enter the battle on two separate routes in two echelons. The first echelon of the 11th Guards Tank Corps was made up of the 45th and 44th Guards Tank Brigades, together with reinforcements attached, whilst that of the 8th Guards Mechanised Corps comprised the 21st and 19th Guards Mechanised Brigades. Each brigade of the first echelon was allocated a special radio-equipped tank in order to maintain better contact with the artillery of the 38th Army to allow them to provide closer support to the 1st Tank Army operations. These vehicles included artillery officers and were attached to brigade headquarters where they requested and corrected the fire of supporting artillery when instructed to do so by the brigade commanders. Two tank-destroyer artillery regiments were assigned to secure the flanks from German armoured counterattacks, and overall the army's operations were be supported by the 291st Ground Attack and 8th Guards Fighter Divisions. On 20 December, Katukov received orders to move his forces into their starting positions for the offensive, being in the Gruzkoe-Byshev-Motyzhin areas and along the river Irpen', a tributary of the Dnepr,

---

12 A.Kh. Babadzhanyan, N.K. Popel', M.A. Shalin, I.M. Kravchenko, *Liuki Otkryli v Berline: Boevoi Put' 1-i Gvardeiskoi Tankovoi Armii*, Moscow, Voenizdat, 1973.
13 Archive MO of the USSR, F. 299, Op. 37805, D. 1, Ll, 2. Quoted in A.Kh. Babadzhanyan, N.K. Popel', M.A. Shalin, I.M. Kravchenko, *Liuki Otkryli v Berline: Boevoi Put' 1-i Gvardeiskoi Tankovoi Armii*, Moscow, Voenizdat, 1973.

about 45 kilometres west of Kiev.[14] By the night of 23-24 December 1943, the forces of the 1st Tank Army were deployed in their starting positions, about five kilometres behind the front line, and ready to go over to the offensive. As the assault began, the army deployed 42,300 officers and men, 546 tanks and self-propelled artillery guns, 585 artillery guns and mortars, 31 rocket launchers and 3,432 motor vehicles.[15]

The Soviet forces that would take part in the Zhitomir-Berdichev operation came under the command of the 1st Ukrainian Front. This field headquarters had been formed on 20 October 1943 on the basis of orders issued by the *Stavka* on 16 October 1943 re-naming the Voronezh Front. This had in turn been formed on 9 July 1942 following orders issued by the *Stavka* on 7 July 1942 to improve the command and control of forces operating under the Bryansk Front in response to the German summer offensive. As a result, a little over a week into that major German offensive, the new Front headquarters assumed command over what had previously been the southern wing of the Bryansk Front. It participated in the remaining weeks of the defensive Voronezh-Voroshilovgrad operation before adopting a defensive posture for much of the rest of the year. In December 1942, forces of the Front took part in the Soviet counterattack in the Stalingrad region, and between January and March 1943 it participated in the series of Voronezh-Khar'kov offensive operations. The first of these was the Ostrogozhsk-Rossosh operation, which it successfully concluded between 13 and 27 January with the co-operation with the 6th Army operating under the Southwest Front. Between 24 January and 2 February, forces of the Front undertook the Voronezh-Kastornoe operation, together with troops from the left wing of the Bryansk Front, liberating Voronezh on 25 January and surrounding a total of nine Axis divisions. In conjunction with forces from the Bryansk and Southwest Fronts, the Front then launched Operation *Zvezda*,[16] the major offensive operation to take Khar'kov. The attack began on 2 February and continued until 3 March 1943, by which time the Soviets had retaken Kursk, Belgorod, and Khar'kov. By the beginning of March, as the Germans began their counterattack, the Front was deployed on the approaches to Sumy and Poltava. From 4 to 25 March, the Front was engaged in trying to counter the German response to Operation *Zvezda*, but was unable to prevent the loss of both Khar'kov and Belgorod. Together with troops from the Steppe Front, the Front was instrumental during July 1943 in the successful defence of the German southern thrust during the battle for Kursk, and on 3 August it went over to the offensive. During the ensuing Belgorod-Khar'kov operation, it inflicted a heavy defeat on the German army between 3 and 23 August, before advancing towards the river Dnepr throughout the months of September and October 1943. Then, on 20 October 1943, the Front was re-named the 1st Ukrainian Front, and its first major operation was the Kiev offensive to break out of the Lyutezh bridgehead and push back the German forces away from Kiev. This began on 3 November 1943 and continued until 13 November, by which time it

---

14   Katukov M E. *Na Ostrie Glavnogo Udara*. Moscow: Voenizdat, 1974, p.273.
15   Archive MO of the USSR, F. 299, Op. 76784, D. 1, Ll. 76—78. Quoted in A.Kh. Babadzhanyan, N.K. Popel', M.A. Shalin, I.M. Kravchenko, *Liuki Otkryli v Berline: Boevoi Put' 1-i Gvardeiskoi Tankovoi Armii*, Moscow, Voenizdat, 1973.
16   Star.

had liberated Kiev on 6 November and advanced about 150 kilometres westwards from the Dnepr. Then, between 13 November and 22 December, it was involved in the Kiev defensive operation as the *4.Panzerarmee* tried to shore up the left wing of Army Group South and re-stabilise its positions.

The Front was under the command of Army General Nikolai Vatutin. He had been in charge since March 1943, although he had also had an earlier spell in command the previous year, between July and October 1942. He had just turned 42 years old and was a career soldier. He had joined the ranks of the Red Army in 1920, and served during the civil war before attending the infantry school in Poltava during 1922. He later studied at the Frunze Military Academy in 1929, before joining the teaching staff there in 1934 and going on to the Joint Staff Academy in 1937. Before the outbreak of the war, he had served as chief of staff of a division, deputy chief of staff of a military district, chief of staff of the Kiev Military District, and chief of the operational administration of the Joint Staff. Following the German invasion, he had been posted to the Northwest Front where he took up the post of chief of staff, staying in that role until May 1942. At that point, he was transferred to the Bryansk Front until July 1942 where he acted as first deputy of the Chief of the Joint Staff and the *Stavka* representative. In July 1942, he was given his first field command and appointed to take control of the newly-forming Voronezh Front, staying in post until October that year when he was moved to take charge of the Southwest Front instead. He remained there throughout the winter campaigns until March 1943, when he returned to take command of the Voronezh Front again, staying in that position throughout the rest of the year. He had therefore served at different Front headquarters in different capacities since the start of the war, and had a lot of experience of operating at that level. He also had 18 months of direct command experience, and had led his troops through a number of major operations, both defensive and offensive.

On the right wing, on the northern flank of the Front, holding the line to a point midway between Korosten' and Malin, was the 13th Army.[17] It had been established during May 1941, just before the German invasion, and had been formed in the Western Special Military District on the basis of instructions issued by the General Staff on 24 April 1941. When the war began, it was attached to the Western Front and was deployed in the Minsk area. By the end of June 1941, the army was already engaged in heavy defensive fighting against the German *Panzergruppe 3*, defending the Minsk fortified area. It was first forced to retreat to the river Berezina, in the area around and to the south of Borisov, and then to the river Dnepr where it held a line south of Orsha, between Kopys' and Novyi Bykhov. From 10 July to 10 September, the army took part in the fighting around Smolensk and on 24 July, it was transferred first to the Central Front, and then on 15 August to the Bryansk Front, during which time it was involved in the defensive fighting on the rivers Sozh, Sudost' and Desna. From 30 September to 23 October 1941, the army took part in the Orel-Bryansk defensive operation, and by the beginning of November it was on a line running between Maslovo and Tim, covering the Livny-Yelets direction. On 11 November 1941, the army was attached

---

17 Much of what follows is drawn from two main sources. Information relating to the different armies and their histories comes from *Velikaya Otechestennaya Voina 1941-1945: Deistvuyushchaya armiya*. Moscow, Animi Fortitudo, 2005. Data relating to their commanders is drawn from *Velikaya Otechestvennaya. Komandarmy. Voennyi Biograficheskii Slovar'*. Moscow, Zhukhovskii, 2005.

to the Southwest Front, conducting defensive operations north of Voronezh, and by 5 December it had withdrawn to a line from a point south-east of Yefremov, running east of Yelets, to Volovo. When the major Soviet counterattack around Moscow began, the 13th Army took part in the Yelets offensive operation between 6 and 16 December 1941. On 24 December, it was transferred to the Bryansk Front and re-captured Livny on 25 December as part of the general advance towards Orel. By the end of the year, it was holding a line south-east of Orel, running from Skorodnoe to Kolpny, at which point it went over to the defensive, holding the same positions until the middle of 1942. Beginning on 28 June 1942, it played a role in the Voronezh-Voroshilovgrad defensive operation, being caught up on the northern edge of the German drive towards Stalingrad as the *4.Panzerarmee* drove towards Voronezh, but the front line soon stabilised again as the Germans concentrated their efforts further south. It held its new line until late January 1943 when it took part in the Voronezh-Kastornoe offensive, driving down from the north into the left wing of Army Group B. This was only a brief operation, beginning on 24 January and lasting until 2 February, and by the end of the month the army had pushed out to the west to form what would become the Kursk salient, and was holding a line from Maloarkhangel'sk to Rozhdestkvenskoe. It maintained this line for the next few months, being transferred to the Central Front on 13 March 1943, and conducted an aggressive defence throughout in order to improve its positions. Starting from 5 July 1943, it was caught up in the battle of Kursk under the Central Front, and, in co-operation with troops of the 70th Army, frustrated the main German effort to break through southwards on the Orel-Kursk direction. On 12 July, it went over to the attack as part of the Orel offensive operation to drive back the northern wing of the German position, continuing the assault until 18 August. After a short pause, it then took part in the Chernigov-Pripyat' offensive operation which began on 26 August and lasted until 30 September. On 6 October 1943, it was transferred to the Voronezh Front, renamed as the 1st Ukrainian Front with effect from 20 October. It went over to the defensive throughout the month, but then participated in the Kiev offensive operation, which lasted between 3 and 13 November, before establishing a fairly static defence on the right wing of the Front. The army was commanded by Lieutenant General Nikolai Pukhov, who had led the army since January 1942. He was a 48-year old career soldier who had joined the Russian army in 1916 during the First World War, serving on the northern front as a cavalry reconnaissance officer. He joined the Red Army in 1918, and during the civil war he fought against the White Guards on the southern, western and Karelian fronts. He later rose to become chief of staff of a rifle brigade and then a rifle division, before commanding a rifle regiment between 1924 and 1929. In 1930 he was assigned to teaching work before being transferred in July 1932 to become assistant to a head of department in the Directorate of Armour. He continued in this specialism, first studying, and then teaching, at the Red Army academy for mechanisation and motorisation. In July 1936, he was appointed as assistant to the head of the Khar'kov tank school, becoming the head himself in March 1938. From April 1939, he served as a teacher in the Red Army Military-economic Academy, before moving in January 1941 to take up an appointment as head of the educational department of the Red Army Logistics Academy. During the war, he was given command of the 304th Rifle Division, before being appointed as commander of the 13th Army in January 1942, a post which he then held for the rest of the war. He was promoted to Lieutenant-General on 14

THE SOVIET SITUATION – PLANNING AND DEPLOYMENT

February 1943. He was therefore a very experienced commander, having operated at that level for nearly two years through a series of major offensive and defensive operations, reaming with the same headquarters throughout.

To the left of the 13th Army was the 60th Army, holding the line from near Chopovichi to a point north-east of Radomyshl'. This had been formed on 7 July 1942 by renaming the 3rd Reserve Army, which had been held in the *Stavka* reserve at the time. The army was allocated to the Voronezh Front on 9 July 1942 in response to the German 1942 summer offensive, and took part in the defensive Voronezh-Voroshilovgrad operation. It remained in the area until the end of 1942, conducting defensive actions on left bank of the river Don, in the area north of Voronezh. During the first part of 1943, it took part in the series of Soviet counterattacks following the battle for Stalingrad, beginning on 24 January 1943 with the Voronezh-Kastornoe operation. During this it re-captured Voronezh on 25 January and took Kastornoe four days later. Immediately following this operation, the 60th Army took part in the Khar'khov offensive which started on 2 February 1943. During this, the army formed the right wing of the Voronezh Front's drive towards Khar'kov in the south and Kursk in the north, liberating the latter on 8 February before driving westwards to take L'gov on 3 March. By the beginning of March 1943, the army had advanced to the river Seim and was deployed in the area around Ryl'sk. On 23 March 1943, it was transferred to the newly formed and short-lived Kursk Front, before being allocated to the Central Front just 3 days later. It remained on defensive duties until July 1943 when the Germans began their offensive at Kursk. It fought during this operation and then participated in the drive towards the Dnepr and the liberation of the left bank of Ukraine. In doing so, it took Glukhov on 30 August, followed by Konotop on 6 September, and liberated Vakhmach on 9 September, in conjunction with the 13th Army, and Nezhin on 15 September. By the second half of September, the army had reached the eastern bank of the Dnepr north of Kiev, and forced a crossing off the march, establishing bridgeheads at Strakholes'e and Yasnogorodka, east of Dymer. On 6 October, the army was transferred to the Voronezh Front. It then took part in the Kiev offensive which began on 3 November, driving westwards to liberate Malin on 12 November, before going on to take Korosten' as well five days later. By this time though, the *4.Panzerarmee* had begun its series of counterattacks, and the army was obliged to fall back and give up Korosten' again on 27 November. By 23 December, the 60th Army was still fighting off the *XXXXVIII.Panzerkorps* attacks east of Korosten'. The army was commanded by Lieutenant-General Ivan Chernyakhovskii, who had held the post since July 1942, just after the army's initial formation. At 37 years, he was one of the younger army commanders, and he had originally intended to work on the railways like his father. However, he joined the Red Army in 1924, attending the cadet school in Odessa until October 1925. He studied at the artillery school in Kiev in 1928, before being given the command of a platoon the same year. He held a number of varied posts throughout the years that followed including head of a mapping section in a rifle regiment, and assistant to an artillery battery commander. He graduated from the Red Army academy for mechanisation and motorisation in 1936, and was subsequently appointed chief of a staff to a tank battalion before assuming command of one himself. Between May 1938 and July 1940, he served as commander of a tank regiment and assistant to the commander of a tank division, and in March 1941, at the age of just 35, he became the commander of the 28th Tank Division in the Baltic Special Military

District, a post he still held at the outbreak of the war. He led the division throughout the first year of the war, even after it had been re-organised as the 241st Rifle Division in December 1941. The following year, he was promoted to Major-General on 5 May 1942, before being posted very briefly to take charge of the newly formed 18th Tank Corps in July 1942. Almost immediately he was re-assigned to take charge of the newly forming 60th Army, in which post he was promoted to Lieutenant-General on 14 February 1943.

To the south was the 1st Guards Army, holding positions from north-east of Radomyshl' across the Teterev to Negrebovka, a short distance south-east of Radomyshl'. This army had been created on 8 December 1942, on the basis of orders issued by the *Stavka* on 5 December 1942. It had been established using operational troops from the Southwest Front, with the headquarters staff coming from the headquarters of the 4th Reserve Army. Its first active operations were conducted under the Southwest Front as a part of the Soviet counterattack around Stalingrad. During January and February 1943, it took part in the general advance in the Donbas region, and between 17 and 27 July 1943 it participated in the Izyum-Barvenkovskaya offensive operation, before being involved in the general offensive operations to clear the left bank of Ukraine during August and September. During October 1943, the units attached to the army were transferred to the 46th Army, and the army headquarters was allocated to the 3rd Ukrainian Front with effect from 20 October. It did not remain there long however, and on 26 October the headquarters were taken out of the active field army and assigned to the *Stavka* reserve in the Konotop area, east of Kiev. It was released again from the reserve on 12 November 1943, being returned to strengthen the 1st Ukrainian Front with the 74th, 94th, and 107th Rifle Corps. It arrived just in time to take part in the Kiev defensive operation as Army Group South tried to build a new defensive position on its left wing. The army had been commanded by Colonel-General Vasilii Kuznetsov since its formation, but on 14 December 1943, command had been passed instead to Colonel-General Andrei Grechko, following Stalin's dissatisfaction with the way the 1st Ukrainian Front had handled the recent German counterattack.[18] Grechko was a 40-year old cavalry officer and had been a member of the Red Army since 1919. He had served during the civil war with the 11th Cavalry Division, going on to study at the cavalry school in 1926 before being given command of a platoon, and then a squadron, in the 1st Independent Cavalry Brigade in the Moscow Military District. In 1936 he passed out of the Frunze Military Academy, and in October 1938 was appointed chief of staff of the Special Cavalry Division in the Belarus Special Military District. The following year he took part in the offensive into eastern Poland, and by the first half of 1941 he had passed out of the Military Academy of the Joint Staff. He was working in the Joint Staff when the war broke out, but requested a field command very quickly. As a result, he was transferred in July 1941 to the Southwest Front to take command of the 34th Independent Cavalry Division, remaining in that post until January the following year and fighting under the 26th, 38th, and 6th Armies in the retreat through Ukraine. On 18 January 1942, Grechko was appointed to take command of the 5th Cavalry Corps in the Barvenkovo-Lozovaya offensive operation south of Khar'kov, and on 12 March that year he was transferred to lead an operational group of forces under the Southern Front where he was engaged in defensive fighting in

---

18 Kuznetsov's dismissal was largely due to the fact that during the course of the German counterattack, troops of the 1st Guards Army had withdrawn from the Radomyshl' bridgehead over the river Teterev which they had occupied since 11 November.

THE SOVIET SITUATION – PLANNING AND DEPLOYMENT

the Donbas. A month later, on 15 April 1942, he was given command of the 12th Army, then defending positions on the Voroshilovgrad direction, and during the following summer he led the army as it pulled back into the Caucasus. In September 1942 he was appointed to command the 47th Army whose forces had prevented the Germans from advancing along the Black Sea coast, denying them access to the port of Novorossiisk. On 19 October, he was moved again, this time assuming command of the 18th Army which was then conducting the successful Tuapse defensive operation, preventing the German from reaching the Black Sea coast over the Caucasus mountains. On 5 January 1943, Grechko was transferred to assume command of the 56th Army under the Black Sea Group of Forces of the Transcaucasus Front, and shortly afterwards the Soviets went over to the offensive, beginning the Krasnodar offensive operation on 9 February. The army participated in the operation under the North Caucasus Front being engaged until it was completed on 16 March. Grechko remained with the army throughout the summer of 1943, taking part in the Novorossiisk-Taman' operation during September that year, until on 16 October, he was appointed as deputy commander of forces under the Voronezh Front. In this capacity, he participated in the Kiev offensive and defensive operations before being given command of the 1st Guards Army on 15 December 1943.

To the left of the 1st Guards Army was the 18th Army. This had been formed in June 1941 using the headquarters of the Khar'kov Special Military District, together with troops from the Kiev Special Military District. It was sent into action almost immediately, being released from the *Stavka* reserve on 25 June and allocated to the Southern Front where it was deployed west of Chernovtsy. Through the period June to August 1941, the army fell back in the face of the German offensive, being pressed back from the river Prut' across western Ukraine until by late August it had fallen back to the east bank of the Dnepr in the area north-west of Melitopol'. Throughout the next couple of months, it continued to fall back through southern Ukraine before taking part on the right wing of the Soviet counterattack around Rostov. This began on 17 November 1941 and ended on 2 December, with new positions being established along the river Mius. The army remained in this static defence throughout the spring of 1942 before being caught up in the German summer offensive through the Donbas and into Kuban'. It was then pushed back into the foothills of the Caucasus, being transferred to the North Caucasusian Front on 29 July 1942. As a part of the Coastal group of armies under the Front, the army then took part in the Armavir-Maikop defensive operation between 6 and 17 August, falling back across the mountains towards Tuapse on the Black Sea coast. On 4 September, it was transferred to the Black Sea group of armies under the Transcaucasian Front, and during the period from 25 September to 20 December 1942, it participated in the Tuapse defensive operation. Following the withdrawal of German forces into the Kuban' bridgehead after the battles around Stalingrad, the 18th Army began to move forwards again, and by the beginning of February 1943 it was deployed opposite Krasnodar where, starting on 9 February, it played a role in the Krasnodar offensive, helping to liberate the town on 12 February. The operation continued until 16 March, but the 18th Army headquarters played no further part. On 11 February 1943, the commander of the North Caucasian Front issued orders for the staff to be transferred to the Tuapse area where, with effect from 15 February, it began to form the 18th Landing Army. It subsequently took over responsibility for the southern wing of the front on the Black Sea coast, and on 6 April 1943, it was renamed as the 18th Army again. The front remained relatively stable throughout the summer of 1943, but beginning on 9 September it took part in the Taman offensive to push the Germans back into the Crimea. The operation began with an assault landing against German positions around Novorossiisk on the coast, and by 16 September the town had been liberated, allowing the army to move up the coast. The operation drew to a close on 9 October, with the 18th Army having cleared the town of Taman six days earlier. At the end of the month it took part in the Soviet attempt to force the Kerch' straits as part of the Kerch'-Eltigena assault operation, which began on 31 October and lasted until 11 December 1943. As part of this operation, troops of the army landed in the Eltigena area, south of Kerch', on 1 November and managed to seize a bridgehead and hold it for 40 days before being obliged to give it up. In the middle of the wider operation, the army was withdrawn from the front and transferred to the *Stavka* reserve on 20 November 1943, after which it was moved to the Kiev area, where on 30 November it was assigned to the 1st Ukrainian Front as part of the build-up of forces for the forthcoming Zhitomir-Berdichev operation. Before the offensive began, the army was inserted into the front between the 1st Guards Army and the 38th Army to the south, and held the sector between Negrebovka and a point north-east of Brusilov. It was commanded by Colonel-General Konstantin Leselidze, who had held the post since March 1943. He was 40 years old, and had been a member of the Red Army since 1921. In 1922 he graduated from the military school in Georgia, before passing through the artillery school in Tiflis during 1925, and the artillery staff course in 1929. From 1922, he served in Transcaucasia in various positions, rising from platoon commander to become assistant to a battery commander and then battery commander himself. Thereafter, he received command of first a battalion and then a regiment, before being appointed as chief of artillery in a rifle division in June 1938, taking part in the campaign against eastern Poland in 1939. In February 1941, he was appointed to become the chief of artillery of the 2nd Rifle Corps in the Belorussian Special Military district, a position he still held at the outbreak of the war. He was later transferred to become chief of artillery of the 50th Army, taking part in the battle for Moscow and conducting the artillery in the defence of Tula. In June 1942, he was given command of the 3rd Rifle Corps under the Transcaucasus Front, serving under the 46th Army in the defence of the Caucasus. Two months later, he was given command of the 46th Army itself, keeping the post until January 1943 as the forces of the army were engaged in heavy defensive fighting trying to deny access to the central part of the Caucasus range to the Germans. He led the neighbouring 47th Army between January and March 1943, as it conducted a series of offensive actions Novorossiisk. In March 1943 he took over the 18th Army, and led it through the remainder of the year before it was transferred to reinforce the 1st Ukrainian Front for the forthcoming Zhitomir-Berdichev operation.

In the second echelon behind the 18th Army was the 3rd Guards Tank Army. This had been formed on 14 May 1943 in the *Stavka* reserve, and by the middle of July it was concentrated around Novosil', about 70 kilometres east of Orel. With the German summer offensive around Kursk failing, the Soviets went over to the attack on 12 July 1943, and two days later, the army was released from the reserve and assigned to the Bryansk Front to take part in the Orel offensive operation. During the course of the operation, the army was transferred to the Central Front on 27 July, although just before this ended it was withdrawn from the front and returned to the *Stavka* reserve on 15 August. It remained there for almost a month until 10 September when it was allocated to the Voronezh Front for the drive to the river Dnepr. Elements of the army were the first to reach the Dnepr south of Kiev, forcing a crossing of the river on 22 September 1943 in the vicinity of Velikii Bukrin. As the Soviets closed up to the Dnepr, the 1st Ukrainian Front began planning for the Kiev offensive operation, and in preparation for this the 3rd Guards Tank Army was transferred northwards on 26 October, moving from the Velikii Bukrin area to take up new positions in the Lyutezh bridgehead just north of Kiev. The operation began on 3 November, and in conjunction with troops from the 38th Army, the army liberated Kiev on 6 November and the town of Fastov the day after. During the second half of November and most of December, the army was heavily engaged in defending against the *PzAOK 4* counterattacks from the area south-west of Fastov. During the latter half of December, the army was pulled out of the front line and moved into the 1st Ukrainian Front reserve. The 3rd Guards Tank Army was led by Colonel-General of Tank Forces Pavel Rybalko, who had held command of the army since its creation back in May 1943. Rybalko was 49-years old and had joined the Russian Army as an enlisted man in 1915, serving as a career soldier ever since. He served on the Russian Western Front during the First World War and joined the Red Guards in 1917 after the October revolution, becoming an assistant to the commander of a guerrilla group during the occupation of Ukraine by the German army in 1918. He joined the Red Army in 1919 and participated in the Russian civil war, acting as commissar of a regiment and then a brigade in the 1st Cavalry Army, operating on the southern front. He also served in the Soviet-Polish war of 1920, before going on various staff training courses. After graduating from the Frunze military academy in 1934, he served in different posts, commanding a squadron, a regiment, and a brigade, before becoming assistant to the commander of a mountain cavalry division. Between 1934 and 1936 he also spent some time as a military adviser in China in the fighting against Uigur insurgents. From 1937 to 1940, he served as military attaché in Poland and China, before moving into teaching work. On 4 June 1940 he was promoted to Major-General of Tank Forces, a rank he still held when the war broke out. He was teaching at the Frunze Military Academy in June 1941 and did not receive a combat posting until he was appointed as deputy commander of the 3rd Tank Army, before receiving command the 5th Tank Army from June to until September 1942. He was then transferred back to take command of the 3rd Tank Army from September 42, being promoted to Lieutenant-General of Tank Forces on 18 January 1943. He held the position until April 43 when he was transferred to take over the new 3rd Guards Tank Army in May 1943. He had therefore led the army since its formation, and despite his lack of field command in the first year of the war, was an experienced officer at that level.

South of the 18th Army was the 38th Army, holding the line from north-east of Brusilov to Sushchanka on the river Irpen'. It had been created on 3 August 1942 under the Bryansk Front on the basis of the 4th Reserve Army and operational forces commanded by Lieutenant-General Chibisov. It was deployed in the Voronezh area where it was engaged in both defensive and offensive operations for the rest of the year, being transferred to the Voronezh Front on 2 September 1942. Following the major Soviet offensives around Stalingrad, the army took part in the Voronezh-Kastornoe operation during the period 24 January to 2 February 1943, along with many other armies that would participate in the Zhitomir-Berdichev offensive. As that operation drew to a close, the 38th Army then took part in the much larger Soviet operation towards Khar'kov and

Kursk which began on 2 February. During the course of this attack, it drove across the river Tim, taking the town of the same name on 5 February before advancing further westwards to liberate Oboyan' on 18 February. By the time the operation ended on 3 March 1943, the army had advanced far as the area north-east of Sumy on the river Psel. For the following three weeks, it was engaged in the ensuing defensive operations as the Germans counterattacked to re-capture Khar'kov and Belgorod, forming the great salient around Kursk. By the end of the operation on 25 March, the army was established on a line running from Korenevo (about 25 kilometres south-east of Ryl'sk) to Vyazovoe (about 26 kilometres south-east of Sumy), and it held this position until the beginning of the German Kursk offensive in July 1943. Just before the end of the operation, on 23 March, the army was transferred to the Kursk Front, but was re-assigned three days later to the Voronezh Front. It was not directly involved in the main fighting during the battle of Kursk, but provided assistance and troops to the 40th and 69th Armies defending the southern strike towards Oboyan and Prokhorovka. When the Russians went over to the counterattack, the 38th Army extended its right wing to the area south of Sumy, providing the link between the Voronezh and Central Fronts. During September 1943, the troops of the army took part in the clearing of the left bank of Ukraine as the Soviet forces advanced towards the Dnepr, liberating Sumy on 2 September, followed by Romny on 16 September and Priluki on 18 September. It reached the Dnepr on 27 September and forced a crossing north of Kiev, securing a bridgehead in Lyutezh-Novo-Petrovtsy area and holding this throughout October. Beginning on 3 November 1943, it participated in the Soviet Kiev offensive operation, providing the main attacking force in conjunction with the 3rd Guards Tank Army, and liberating the city of 6 November before going on capture Zhitomir on 12 November, the day before the offensive drew to a close. Thereafter it withdrew under pressure from the *4.Panzerarmee*, falling back to positions either side of Brusilov. The army was commanded by Major-General of Artillery Kirill Moskalenko, who had been given command of the army in October 1943, taking over from Lieutenant-General Nikandr Chibisov. He was 41 years old and had served in the Red Army since 1920, participating in the civil war. He worked through various command appointments in the artillery branch until in 1934 he was appointed as commander of an artillery regiment. With effect from June 1935 he became the artillery commander in the 23rd Mechanised Brigade stationed in the Far East, and in September 1936, he returned to the Kiev Military District to take up a position in the 133rd Mechanised Brigade. In 1939 he passed through a staff course at the Dzerzhinsky Military Academy and was appointed as artillery commander in the 51st Rifle Division, and in this capacity, he participated in the Soviet-Finnish war during 1939 and 1940. He was then transferred to become the artillery commander of the 35th Rifle Corps, and subsequently, between August 1940 and May 1941, the artillery commander of the 2nd Mechanised Corps based in the Odessa Military District. In May 1941 he was appointed as the commanding officer of the 1st Motorised Anti-tank Artillery Brigade, and was serving in this post when the war began. In September 1941 he was posted to take command of the 15th Rifle Corps, then operating under the 5th Army as part of the Southwest Front. He was later given command of a Cavalry-Mechanised Group under the 13th Army as part of the Southwest Front, and by the end of 1941, he was appointed as deputy commander of the 6th Army, before going on to take command of the 6th Cavalry Corps on 12 February 1942. He was given his first full command of an

THE SOVIET SITUATION – PLANNING AND DEPLOYMENT

army in March 1942 when he was transferred to lead the 38th Army. He had a brief spell commanding the 1st Tank Army during July and August 1942, before being transferred to the command of the 1st Guards Army, a post he held for only three months before being transferred to take charge of the 40th Army on October 1942. He held this post for the following year, before re-assuming command of the 38th Army in October 1943. As an army commander therefore, he had fought through the defensive battles on the southern front in 1942, including the Khar'kov, Don and Stalingrad battles, before leading his forces in the offensive which followed, including the Ostrogozhsk-Rossosh operation, the Voronezh-Kastornoe operation and the Belgorod-Khar'kov operations. From the summer of 1943, he had led the 40th Army through the Kursk battles and the subsequent drive towards and crossing of the Dnepr.

Behind it, in the second echelon, was the 1st Tank Army. This had been established on 7 February 1943 on the basis of orders issued by the *Stavka* on 30 January 1943. Its headquarters was formed by renaming the headquarters of the 29th Army, then in the *Stavka* reserve. On 15 February the new army had been released from the reserve and allocated the Group of Forces under General Khozin as part of the operation to reduce the German pocket around Demyansk. It remained in the area until 12 March 1943 when it was returned to the *Stavka* reserve. On 28 April 1943, it was transferred to the Voronezh Front as part of the Soviet defensive preparations on the southern side of the Kursk salient, being held in Front reserve when the German offensive began. It was released into the fighting on 6 July and remained in the front until the operation ended on 23 August. On 10 September, with the Soviet forces advancing towards the Dnepr, the army was pulled out of the front and returned to the *Stavka* reserve. It remained in reserve for nearly 2 months before being assigned to the 1st Ukrainian Front on 30 November 1943 during the Kiev defensive operation. The army was commanded by Lieutenant-General of Tank Forces Mikhail Katukov. He was a 43-year old armour specialist and had been appointed to the post in January 1943. He had taken part in the October rebellion in St Petersburg and subsequently joined the Red Army in 1919, before serving on the southern front during the civil war. In 1922 he completed the infantry course in Mogilev, and senior officer courses in 1927, before going on to attend training courses at the Red Army Military Academy of Motorisation and Mechanisation in 1935. Between 1922 and 1940 he held different command positions at platoon and company level, before becoming head of a regimental school and the commander of a training battalion. He was later promoted to become chief of staff of a brigade, before being appointed as commander of a tank brigade. In November 1940, he was given command of the 20th Tank Division, and by the outbreak of the war he was still leading the division as a colonel under the 9th Mechanised Corps. He commanded the division through the initial defensive operations on the southern front, taking part in the fighting around Lutsk, Dubno, and Korosten' under the 5th Army. In September 1941, he was transferred to take command of the newly forming 4th Tank Brigade, and led the brigade during the battles on the Volokolamsk highway as part of the defence of Moscow. Following this, the brigade was given Guards status, being re-designated as the 1st Guards Tank Brigade on 11 November 1941. In 1942, he was transferred to take command of the 1st Tank Corps, which he led through the defensive battles on the Kursk-Voronezh axis during that summer. In September 1942 he was moved again to take over the new 3rd Mechanised Corps, leading the unit under the 22nd Army in the final months of the year, and taking part in Operation 'Mars', the unsuccessful attempt by the Soviets to reduce the German salient around Rzhev-Sychevka. In January 1943, he was designated as commander of the newly forming 1st Tank Army, a post he then held throughout the rest of the year, leading his new army through the successful defensive and offensive operations which finally led to it being assigned to the 1st Ukrainian Front at the end of November 1943. During this time, Katukov was promoted on 23 September 1943 to become Colonel-General of Tank Forces.

To the left of the 38th Army, holding the line from the river Irpen' to a point south of Vasil'kov, was the 40th Army. This army had been created on 26 August 1941 on instructions from the *Stavka* of the same day. It was formed by the Southwest Front in the area north and north-west of Konotop on the basis of the 27th Rifle Corps which had previously been attached to the 5th Army. It was thrown into combat immediately, and over the next few months was engaged in heavy defensive fighting until, by the beginning of December 1941, it had fallen back to the line of the river Tim, east of Kursk. From the end of December until February 1942, the army was involved in a couple of local offensives towards Kursk and Belgorod. On 3 April 1942, it was transferred to the Bryansk Front, and between 28 June and 24 July it was caught up in the fighting on the right wing of the Voronezh-Voroshilovgrad defensive operation during the German 1942 summer offensive. On 9 July, during the course of the operation, the army was transferred to the newly formed Voronezh Front, and by the end of the month it had withdrawn behind the line of the river Don south of Voronezh. It maintained this position until the end of the year when it then took part in the Ostrogozhsk-Rossosh offensive between 13 and 27 January 1943, meeting up with the 15th Tank Corps under the 3rd Tank Army on 18 January to trap the troops of the Hungarian 2nd Army and the Italian 8th Army. On 20 January, the army also liberated the town of Ostrogozhsk, before going on to wipe out the remaining pockets of enemy resistance in conjunction with the 18th Independent Rifle Corps and elements of the 3rd Tank Army. Having achieved this, it then participated on the southern wing of the Voronezh-Kastornoe operation between 24 January and 2 February 1943. No sooner had it completed this operation than it participated in the major operation to recapture Khar'kov which began on 2 February, and during which it liberated Stary Oskol, Belgorod, Khar'kov, Akhtyrka and Gadyach, advancing almost 200 kilometres in fewer than four weeks. The Germans then counterattacked and the army was engaged in defensive fighting throughout March 1943 before the front stabilised towards the end of the month. It was heavily engaged during the defensive Kursk operation, but took part in the subsequent Soviet counterattack and the drive towards the Dnepr which cleared the left bank of Ukraine. On 24 September 1943, its forces crossed the Dnepr south of Kiev in the Staiki and Rzhishchev areas, establishing bridgeheads which it was then obliged to defend in heavy fighting. During October, it was engaged in the defensive fighting in the Bukrin bridgehead, before taking part in the Kiev offensive on the southern wing between 3 and 13 November. The commander of the army was Lieutenant-General Fillip Zhmachenko, who had assumed command only recently, during October 1943. He was 48 years old and had originally worked on the railways before being called up to fight in the First World War. In November 1917 he had joined the Red Guards, later joining the Red Army in 1918. He participated in the civil war and completed a military commissars course in Khar'kov during 1922, before attending tactical courses in 1923 and 1926. Thereafter he served as deputy commander of a regiment, commander and military commissar of a regiment, before being given command of the 92nd Rifle Division in 1937. He also served as a head of department in the Khar'kov Military District before being posted to take command of the 67th Rifle Corps in March 1941. He was still in charge of the corps when the war broke out, and shortly afterwards, on 2 July 1941, it was transferred from the *Stavka* reserve to the 21st Army where it fought in the defensive battles around Rogachev, Zhlobin and Gomel' under the Central Front before being disbanded on 1 October 1941. On 13 October 1941, Zhmachenko was appointed deputy head of the garrison in Khar'kov, before being transferred in November to take command of a group of forces on the right wing of the Bryansk Front. In February 1942 he was appointed as commander of 3rd Army, holding the post until May 1942 while the army was in stable defensive positions along on the river Zusha, east of Orel. In September 1943, he was transferred to take command of the 47th Army under the Voronezh Front, holding the post for only two months before moving to take control of the 40th Army in October 1943. He had been in charge of the army for just two months then when the offensive began.

Holding the left wing of the 1st Ukrainian Front was the 27th Army, maintaining positions from south of Vasil'kov to the river Dnepr. The army had been formed on 1 June 1942 on the basis of orders issued by the *Stavka* on 22 May 1942. It had been established using units taken from the 11th Army under the Northwest Front, and until January 1943 it was deployed in defensive operations on the line of the river Lovat, east of Staraya Russa. In February 1943, it took part in the Demyansk offensive operation, which lasted from 15 to 28 February. On 9 April 1943, the army was withdrawn from the front and placed in the *Stavka* reserve, although by 20 April it had been transferred to the Gzhatsk area while still remaining in the reserve. On 25 May, it was allocated to Steppe Military District as part of the defensive preparations before the Kursk battles, before being returned to active operations when the whole military district was renamed as the Steppe Front on 9 July 1943. The whole Front was released by the *Stavka* on 19 July to reinforce the Soviet counterattack which had begun on 12 July, and the 27th Army was transferred to join the Voronezh Front the day after, taking part in the drive towards Belgorod and Khar'kov. By 23 July, the attack had pushed the Germans back to their starting positions before proceeding to drive towards the river Dnepr. By the end of September 1943, the army had advanced to the Kanev area and crossed to the west bank of the river, before pushing on to expand the Bukrin bridgehead. During the Kiev offensive operation, from 3 to 13 November 1943, the army played a subsidiary role on the southern wing, helping to pin down German forces which might otherwise have been deployed to strengthen the defence against the main attack. It was commanded by Colonel-General Sergei Trofimenko, who had assumed control at the beginning of the year, in January 1943. He was 44 years old and another professional solider, having been in the Red Army since 1919. He had participated in the civil war, serving on the southern, western and south-western front, rising from private to command a platoon. In 1924 he had been appointed as military commissar to the 132nd Rifle Regiment in the Ukrainian Military District, before going on to command a battalion in the 133rd Rifle Regiment during 1926. He undertook a number of training courses, graduating from the Frunze Military Academy in 1932 before being posted as chief of staff to the 61st Rifle Division in May that year. In December 1935, he was appointed as head of the operations section in the Volga Military District, before moving on the Kiev Military

District. He attended the General Staff Military Academy during 1937, before being transferred in July 1938 to become chief of a staff of the Zhitomir group of forces within the same district. In September 1939, he was appointed to the command of the 5th Army, taking part in the invasion of eastern Poland later that month. He then moved on to become deputy chief of staff of the 7th Army and as such took part in the Soviet-Finnish war of 1939-40. In August 1940 he moved again, this time becoming chief of staff in the North Caucasus Military District, and in January the following year he became commander of forces in the Central Asian Military District. On 29 August 1941, he was transferred to take command of the 51st Army, newly formed for the defence of the Crimea, remaining in post until 30 October that year. In December 1941, he took command of the Medvezh'egorsk operational group of forces assigned to the 7th Army on the Karelian front, before taking command of the newly forming 32nd Army, created from the Medvezh'egorsk and Massel'sk operational groups on the same front in March 1942. In June 1942, he transferred to take command of the 7th Independent Army, then deployed on static defensive operation along the river Svir between Lake Onega and Lake Ladoga. He retained this position until January 1943 when he was transferred to take over the 27th Army under the Western Front, staying with the army until the Zhitomir-Berdichev operation began.

☆

Such were the forces and commanders who would undertake the Zhitomir-Berdichev operation, and as the attack began the 1st Ukrainian Front deployed a total of 63 rifle divisions (including one airborne infantry division), three cavalry divisions, two fortified areas, one infantry brigade (Czechoslovak), six tank and two mechanized corps, together with five independent tank brigades. In total, the Front comprised 831,000 infantry, 11,387 guns and mortars (excluding 50mm mortars), 1,230 antiaircraft guns, 297 rocket launchers, 738 tanks, 387 self-propelled artillery guns, and 529 planes.[19] In the absence of information to the contrary, it has to be assumed that this figure represents the total manpower complement, and that the Front's actual front line combat strength was considerably smaller. Since the beginning of the Kiev offensive operation on 3 November 1943, the 1st Ukrainian Front had been significantly reinforced. At the start of that operation, the Front had deployed 671,000 men,[20] meaning that it had received at least another 160,000 men in terms of replacements and additional units, and maybe as many as 253,300. However as can be seen from Table 1 below, most of the additional forces had already been attached by the beginning of December, either as a precautionary measure against the Germans trying to re-capture Kiev, or a part of a longer-term build-up of forces for the Zhitomir-Berdichev operation. Opposing them, Soviet intelligence had identified that German forces in the region comprised 30 infantry divisions under the *4.Panzerarmee*, with 574,000 infantry, 6,960 guns and mortars (excluding 51mm mortars), and 1,200 tanks and assault guns. In this sector, they believed the Germans

---

19 *Grylev* p.23. However, another more recent source gives the total strength of the Front at 924,300 – see Krivosheev G. F., *Rossiya i SSSR v Voinakh XX Veka – Poteri Voorruzhennykh Sil*, Moscow: Olma-Press, 2001.
20 Krivosheev G. F., *Rossiya i SSSR v Voinakh XX Veka – Poteri Voorruzhennykh Sil*, Moscow: Olma-Press, 2001.

THE SOVIET SITUATION – PLANNING AND DEPLOYMENT

could deploy up to 500 aircraft from the *VIII.Fliegerkorps* under the *Luftflotte 4*, and could also call upon additional aircraft from the *IV.Fliegerkorps*. As a whole therefore, the Soviets believed they held the advantage in forces, with the exception of tanks and self-propelled guns where they believed there was approximate parity. In contrast, the records of the *PzAOK 4* indicate that 19 divisions were deployed in the front line, seven of which were armoured. In reserve were an infantry division and an artillery division, with a *Panzergrenadier* division being refitted in the rear. Its total manpower strength was reported as 359,000, although many of that number would not have been in front line combat units.[21] Indeed, as will be seen in the next chapter, the German figures suggest that the *PzAOK 4* deployed as few as 50,000 men in front line combat strength. In terms of armour, the *4.Panzerarmee* reported a total of 936 armoured vehicles just before the offensive began, of which 432 were actually operational.[22]

Table 1: Numerical comparison of units deployed by the 1st Ukrainian Front

Unit	1 Nov 43	1 Dec 43	1 Jan 44
Army HQ	5	7	7
Tank Army HQ	1	2	2
Rifle Corps HQ	13	18	20
Rifle Division	42	60	62
Airborne Division	3	3	1
Rifle Brigade	1	1	1
Cavalry Corps	1	1	1
Cavalry Division	3	3	3
Fortified Region	-	1	2
Artillery Corps	1	1	1
Breakthrough Artillery Division	2	2	3
Artillery Division	1	1	1
Independent Artillery Brigade	3	3	3
Independent Artillery Regiment	10	12	12
Tank Destroyer Artillery Brigade	6	8	8
Independent Tank Destroyer Artillery Regiment	27	34	39
Independent Mortar Brigade	1	1	1
Independent Mortar Regiment	12	15	15
Guards Mortar Division	1	1	1
Independent Guards Mortar Brigade	-	-	2
Guards Mortar Regiment	11	14	13
Anti-aircraft Division	7	6	7
Anti-aircraft Regiment	10	11	12

21 *PzAOK 4*, O.Qu./Qu.1 Nr.53/44 geh. dated 8 Jan 44.
22 See Tables 6 and 7.

Unit	1 Nov 43	1 Dec 43	1 Jan 44
Independent Anti-aircraft Battalion	2	2	2
Tank Corps	5	5	6
Mechanised Corps	1	2	2
Independent Tank Brigade	4	5	5
Independent Tank Regiment	3	6	6
Self-propelled Artillery Regiment	4	7	9
Motorcycle Regiment	1	1	1
Independent Armoured Battalion	-	-	1
Independent Motorcycle Battalion	-	-	1
Independent Armoured Train	4	4	4
Engineer Brigade	6	7	7
Pontoon Bridging Brigade	2	2	2
Engineer Battalion	11	15	16
Pontoon Bridging Battalion	6	6	6

2

The German Situation

Towards the end of 1943 German forces in western Ukraine came under the command of two Army Groups. Army Group A was responsible for the southern sector, covering the Crimea and about 100 kilometres or so of the coastal strip adjoining the Black Sea, while Army Group South, somewhat perversely, held the northern part, covering the area between the left wing of Army Group A and a line running along the approximate southern edge of the Pripyat' marshes. Army Group South was under the command of *Generalfeldmarschall* Erich von Lewinski, known as von Manstein, a post he had held since 22 November 1942. At that time he had been transferred together with his staff of the *Armeeoberkommando 11*, from the Leningrad area into the maelstrom caused by the Soviet offensive around Stalingrad. The *11.Armee* had been re-designated as Army Group Don, to be re-designated once more on 12 February 1943 when the then Army Group headquarters was disbanded. Von Manstein's headquarters was re-designated as Army Group South, a name which it bore until 25 March 1944 when it was renamed as Army Group North Ukraine. Command of the Army Group lay with von Manstein throughout this entire period. His chief of staff in December 1943 was *Generalleutnant* Theodor Busse, himself a member of von Manstein's staff since his first arrival at *AOK 11*, and his *Ia* or Operations Officer, was *Oberst* Schulze-Büttger.

The southern wing of Army Group South, in the Dnepr bend as far north as Kirovograd, was held by the *1.Panzerarmee*, whilst the centre was covered by the *8.Armee* from that point to Kanev on the river Dnepr. It fell to the *Panzerarmeeoberkommando 4* to hold the northern, left wing of Army Group South, where the impending Soviet Zhitomir-Berdichev operation was about to be launched. It covered a sector running from Kanev in the east, running broadly north-westwards along the west bank of the Dnepr, past the Soviet bridgehead in the river bend known as the 'knee', to a point just south of Rzhishchev. From there, the front bent back westwards, running north of Grebenki, and turning north just past Trilesy, passing to the east of Kornin. It continued northwards to a point east of Brusilov before turning to the north-west again, across the main Kiev-Zhitomir road, and running as far as Radomyshl' on the river Teterev. At that point, it turned northwards again, heading for Malin on the river Irsha, but bending back north-west about six kilometres south of the river. It ran parallel to the south bank of the Irsha for another 15 kilometres or so before bending south-westwards as part of a wide arc covering the Soviet bridgehead over the Irsha south of and either side of Chopovichi. Where the front crossed the Irsha once more, about 12 kilometres south-west of Chopovichi, it turned northwards again, past the only area where the *4.Panzerarmee* was engaged in active operations, and on east of Korosten'. Just north of the town, the front bent back westwards, marking the left wing of both the *Panzerarmee* and also Army Group South. North of Korosten', there was a wide expanse of Soviet territory, about 90 or so kilometres through forest and swamps, to the right wing of Army Group Centre in the vicinity of El'sk. This gap between the two Army Groups was known to the *OKH* as the "*Wehrmachtsloch*"[1], and in it there were no major German or Axis combat units. This was a dangerous situation, and one in which neither Army Group had any real chance of addressing the problem. It was, however, accepted with due pragmatism in the *OKH*, hence the term, but this in itself implied a certain semi-permanence to the feature.

Command of the *4.Panzerarmee* was held by *General der Panzertruppen* Erhard Raus, an experienced armour commander who had nevertheless only held the post since 1 November 1943. He was 54 years old and had originally enlisted in the Austro-Hungarian army in 1909, but on 19 December 1936 he had transferred as an *Oberst* to the German *Reichsheer*. He first saw action under the *6.Panzer-Division* when he assumed command of the *Schützen-Regiment 4* on 15 July 1940 during the campaign in France, but on 15 April the following year he given greater responsibility and handed command of the *Schützen-Brigade 6* prior to the beginning of the war in the East. He remained with the *6.Panzer-Division* throughout the first years of the campaign, being promoted to *Generalmajor* in September 1941, before going on to command the division from 1 April 1942. Shortly afterwards, in May 1942, the *6.Panzer-Division* was transferred to France for rest and refitting. It returned to the East in December 1942 where it was thrown into the southern sector following the Soviet counterattack at Stalingrad. Raus stayed with the division during these difficult times, and on 1 January 1943, he was promoted to *Generalleutnant*. On 7 February 1943, he was transferred into the *Führerreserve* and posted onto the staff at Army Group Don under which he took over the *Generalkommando z.b.V. Cramer* three days later, it being re-named *Generalkommando z.b.V. Raus* as a result. With this command, he took part in the re-capture of Khar'kov in the spring of 1943. With effect from 1 May 1943, he was promoted to *General der Panzertruppen*, and on 20 July he was appointed as commanding officer of the newly formed *XI.Armeekorps*.[2]

Throughout this time, the *Korps* was deployed on the southern sector, taking part in the fighting retreat across the eastern part of Ukraine, first under the *Armee-Abteilung* Kempf and later under the *8.Armee*. He was transferred to take command of the *XXXXVII. PzK* on 5 November 1943 and held this post for less than a month before being returned to the *Führerreserve* by the end of the month. He was then given temporary command of the *4.Panzerarmee* with effect from 30 November 1943, replacing *Generaloberst* Hermann Hoth who had been sacked by Hitler following the retreat to the river Dnepr. He was confirmed in his new post on 10 December 1943. Despite only holding his position for little more than a month therefore, Raus was a very experienced officer, having held commands in armoured units at all levels from regiment upwards. Apart from a few months resting and refitting with the *6.Panzer-Division* in France, he had been continually assigned to the Eastern Front, and therefore possessed the experience of a soldier with 3½ years first-hand knowledge of warfare against the Soviet Union. The chief of staff at the *PzAOK 4* was *Generalmajor* Friedrich Fangohr who at least had been in post since 15 July 1942, and his *Ia* was *Oberst* Müller. Now in charge of the *PzAOK 4*, Raus had command of six *Generalkommandos*, two of which were *Panzerkorps* and four

---

1   Meaning literally 'armed forces hole', and intended to describe the gap which had opened up between the two Army Groups.
2   This was essentially the same headquarters of the *Generalkommando z.b.V. Raus* re-designated. The original *XI.Armeekorps* had been destroyed at Stalingrad.

of which were *Armeekorps*. These headquarters in turn commanded six *Panzer-Divisions*, ten *Infanterie-Divisions*, two *Korps-Abteilungs*, one *Sicherungs-Division*, and a brigade-size *Panzerkampfgruppe*. The *4.Panzerarmee* itself retained direct control of a further *Sicherungs-Division*, an *Artillerie-Division*, a *Panzergrenadier-Division* and elements of a *Reserve-Division*. At the beginning of December 1943, the total manpower of the Panzerarmee had been about 359,000, but many of that number would not have been in frontline combat units.[3]

The right wing of the *4.Panzerarmee's* sector was held by the *Generalkommando XXIV.Panzerkorps* under *General der Panzertruppen* Walther Nehring, a post he had held since 10 February 1943. Nehring was a vastly experienced officer who had served under both Guderian and Rommel in his time. He had served as chief of staff in Guderian's *XIX.Armeekorps* in both the Polish and French campaigns, remaining in the post when the *Korps* was upgraded to the status of *Panzergruppe* Guderian in June 1940. In October 1940 he had been given command of the newly forming *18.Panzer-Division*, a post which he held during the opening stages of the Russian campaign, again under Guderian's *Panzergruppe* 2. He left the Soviet Union when he was transferred to take command of the *Deutsche Afrika Korps* on 9 March 1942, this time under another of the *Wehrmacht's* greater exponents of armoured warfare, *Generaloberst* Erwin Rommel. He kept this position until November that year when he was elevated briefly to the post of *Befehlshaber in Tunesien*, Commander in Tunisia, before returning to Germany in December 1942. After a spell of two months he returned to active service on 10 February 1943 as commanding officer of the *XXIV.Panzerkorps*, then involved in the wake of the Stalingrad fighting under Army Group B. He had been in command of the *Panzerkorps* since that time, leading it as it withdrew from the eastern Ukraine, towards and across the Dnepr. He had considerable experience therefore, having served as both chief of staff and commander of major armoured formations and fighting alongside both Guderian and Rommel. He also had recent knowledge of conditions on the Eastern Front and had been in post for almost a year. He was a valuable asset for the *4.Panzerarmee*. His chief of staff was *Oberstleutnant* Karl Giese, an experienced staff officer who had served with the headquarters of the *16.Panzer-Division* and more recently with the *Generalstab des Heeres*. He had joined Nehring on 5 November 1943 for his first post as a *Korps* chief of staff. The *Panzerkorps* deployed a total of three *Infanterie-Divisions*, or equivalent, these being, from right to left, the *Korps-Abteilung B*, the *34.Infanterie-Division* and the *82.Infanterie-Division*. Of these the *Korps-Abteilung B* perhaps warrants special mention. Following the failure of Operation *"Zitadelle"*, the Kursk battle, in the summer of 1943, the Soviet counteroffensive had forced the Germans to fall back along the whole front in Ukraine until the whole of the left bank had been cleared. The fighting had been desperate in many places and losses had been severe, and many German divisions had been reduced to little more than regimental strength *Kampfgruppen*. Some degree of re-organisation had clearly been necessary, but the measure adopted by the *OKH* was one of expediency, and one which was not without its opponents. During the course of November and December 1943 the remnants of these divisions were brought together at the front to form new *Korps-Abteilungen*. A *Korps-Abteilung* was organised essentially as an *Infanterie-Division n.A. 44* (the new style 1944 infantry division), its three *Grenadier-Regiments* being designated instead as *Divisionsgruppen*. Each *Divisionsgruppe* was formed

3   PzAOK 4, O.Qu./Qu.1 Nr.53/44 geh. dated 8 Jan 44.

as the name suggests from one of the existing, badly depleted, frontline divisions. As a rule, each division pooled its remaining combat infantry into a *Divisionsgruppe* bearing the number of the disbanded division, with the *Divisionsgruppe* then being organised as a *Grenadier-Regiment* from the *Infanterie-Division n.A.44*. The *Divisionsgruppe* itself comprised of a headquarters, the *13.* and *14.Kompanie*, and two *Regimentsgruppen*, each of battalion strength and numbered after two of the disbanded division's regiments. In Army Group South's area alone, fifteen *Infanterie-Divisions* were disbanded during the final three months of 1943, with just fourteen *Divisionsgruppen* being formed from the forty regiments dissolved. Nine of these *Divisionsgruppen* were used to form three new *Korps-Abteilungen*, designated as "A", "B", and "C", the remainder being allocated to existing frontline divisions to replace regiments which had been disbanded following heavy casualties. In essence then, the equation was three new division-equivalents (the *Korps-Abteilungen*), in exchange for fifteen divisions, and two of these new *Korps-Abteilungen*, B and C, were attached to the *4.Panzerarmee*.

The *Korps-Abteilung B* had been formed on the basis of the *112.*, the *255.*, and the *332.Infanterie-Divisions*, each providing a *Divisionsgruppe* of the same number. The headquarters was provided by the former *112.Infanterie-Division* staff, and the other units of the *Korps-Abteilung* were all numbered 112 as a result. The only exception to this was the *Artillerie-Regiment 86* which had been made available by the disbandment of the *86.Infanterie-Division* under Army Group Centre. The *Korps-Abteilung B* held a sector running from Kanev on the Dnepr roughly north-westwards as far as Vedmedevka, a width of some 20 or so kilometres. Its commander was *Generalleutnant* Theobald Lieb, an officer with limited combat experience. He had served as commander of an Infantry Regiment in the Polish and French campaigns but, apart from a brief spell of two months in 1941 as deputy commander of an *Infanterie-Division* under Army Group North, most of his time had been spent in Germany. He did not receive his first command of a division until February 1943. This was the *306.Infanterie-Division*, a unit which had only previously been engaged in occupation duties in Belgium, but which had been rushed to Army Group Don in the aftermath of the Soviet Stalingrad offensive. Lieb held the post only until the end of March 1943 before being recalled to Germany. This had been his last tour on the Eastern Front for he spent the next six months without an active service post before assuming command of the *112.Infanterie-Division* on three September 1943. In all, Lieb had just three months experience as a divisional commander on the Eastern Front.

The *34.Infanterie-Division* had been a division in the peacetime army, and although it had served on the western front during the Polish campaign, it had taken an active part in the subsequent Campaign in the West. It had then participated in the attack against the Soviet Union from the outset, initially being deployed under Army Group Centre. It had remained on the central sector until September 1943 when it was transferred southwards to the *XXIV.Panzerkorps* during the retreat to the Dnepr. It now held the sector to the left of the *Korps-Abteilung B*, from Vedmedevka northwest to Rzhishchev and then along the Dnepr to a point just north of Yushki. Its front then bent back westwards to the eastern edge of Chernyakhov, a total front of about 35 kilometres. The commanding officer was *Generalleutnant* Friedrich Hochbaum, and he had served with the division since July 1940, first as a commander of *Infanterie-Regiment 253*, and subsequently as division commander since 2 November 1942. Although relatively new to the sector, both he and the division were well acquainted with conditions on the Eastern Front.

The remaining division under the *XXIV.Panzerkorps* was the *82.Infanterie-Division*. This unit had been begun forming on 1 December 1939 as part of the 6.*Welle* (or 6th Wave) of the *OKH* infantry division mobilisation. Following a brief involvement in the Campaign in the West under Army Group A, the division was '*beurlaubt*' during August 1940, being granted special leave of absence during which time it was in effect dissolved. It was recalled during March 1941 for occupation duties in the Netherlands and remained there until June 1942 when it was transferred to Army Group South in the Soviet Union prior to the German summer campaign. It had remained in the area north-west of Voronezh until caught up in the Kastornoe pocket during the Soviet 1942/43 winter offensives. Having broken out of the encirclement, the division was refitted during the spring in the Army Group Centre rear area, before being sent to the front once more in the same sector. It then participated in the general withdrawal to the Dnepr following the failure of the German Kursk offensive, moving on the Sumy-Kiev axis before taking up its positions south of Kiev with the *XXIV.Panzerkorps*. It now held the westernmost sector belonging to the *Korps*, between Chernyakhov and Germanovka, a total frontage of about 20 kilometres. The division was commanded by the newly promoted *Generalleutnant* Walter Heyne, an artillery specialist. He had commanded artillery battalions in the Polish and French campaigns, before joining the division as the commander of *Artillerie-Regiment 182* in March 1942. His first experience of the Eastern Front had come therefore when the division was transferred during the summer of that year, but he had remained there ever since, taking command of the division on 15 March 1943. Again, both division and commander were experienced in combat on the Eastern Front.

In *XXIV.PzK* reserve was the *168.Infanterie-Division*. This division had also been formed on 1 December 1939 but as part of the 8.*Welle*. It had taken part in the second stage of the campaign in the West, but only as a reserve unit with no active combat operations. In July 1940 it had been transferred to Poland where it continued in training until the invasion of the Soviet Union. At that point, it was attached to the *6.Armee* under Army Group South and it remained on the southern sector thereafter. It fell back through 1943 under the *Armee-Abteilung Kempf* participating in the retreat through Belgorod, Khar'kov and Kiev, being temporarily re-organised and designated in September 1943 as *Kampfgruppe 168* owing to the severe losses it had incurred. In November 1943 the *Kampfgruppe 168* was attached to the *XXIV.PzK* where it was placed into reserve to begin a process of re-formation and refitting. At this time, the division was re-built according to the revised tables of organisation and equipment for the '*Infanterie-Division n.A. 44*, incorporating two infantry battalions from the *223.Infanterie-Division* which was disbanded at around this time. The division was led by *Generalmajor* Werner Schmidt-Hammer, a 49-year old infantryman. At the outbreak of the war, he had been assigned to the *168.Infanterie-Division* where he was appointed to command the *Infanterie-Regiment 417*. He held the post until December 1940 when he took over the *Infanterie-Regiment 456* under the *256.Infanterie-Division* where he gained his first combat experience in the central sector of the Eastern Front. On 1 December 1943 he had been promoted to *Generalmajor* and appointed to command the *168.Infanterie-Division*, his old unit. It was his first post as a divisional commander, but both he and his troops were seasoned veterans of the war in the East.

To the left of the *XXIV.Panzerkorps*, holding the line from Germanovka onwards was the *VII.Armeekorps*, commanded by *General der Artillerie* Ernst-Eberhard Hell. Hell had assumed command of the *Korps* on 8 January 1942, and was therefore an experienced *Korps* commander on the Eastern Front. Before that he had commanded two *Infanterie-Divisions*, one of these in the campaign against the Soviet Union. His first command at the outbreak of war had been the *269.Infanterie-Division*, a unit which had been stationed in the west during the Polish campaign, but which Hell commanded during the assault in the West. Just before the division transferred to Denmark for occupation duties, Hell was moved, on 12 August 1940, to take command of the *15.Infanterie-Division*, earmarked for occupation duties in France, a deployment which it maintained until its transfer to the Eastern Front the following summer. The division was initially attached to Guderian's *Panzergruppe 2* under Army Group Centre, and it stayed on the central sector before being transferred back to France in May 1942. Before this, on 8 January 1942, Hell had been transferred to take command of the *VII.AK*, also on the central sector, receiving his promotion to *General der Artillerie* the following month. He oversaw the *Korps* refit during May 1942 before it was re-assigned to the northern wing of Army Group South during the summer. There it held positions on the river Don near Voronezh before pulling back to the general Sumy area during the winter of 1942/43. Beginning in August 1943, the *Korps* was attached to the *4.Panzerarmee* and pulled back behind the Dnepr along with the rest of Army Group South, and by the middle of December it was in defensive positions north of and either side of Belaya Tserkov'.

On the *Korps* right wing, adjoining the left wing of the *XXIV.Panzerkorps*, was the *75.Infanterie-Division*. This had been formed on 26 August 1939 as part of the *2.Welle*, passing the Polish campaign in a defensive role on the western front under Army Group C, before having a fairly passive part to play on the same sector in the campaign against France. The division was then transferred to occupied Poland and the Eastern Front. It received its effective baptism of fire during the assault against the Soviet Union as part of Army Group South, remaining on the northern end of the southern sector with the *VII.AK* throughout 1942 and the first half of 1943. With the rest of the *Korps*, the division fell back through northern Ukraine during the autumn of 1943, and by this time it was holding a sector running westwards from Germanovka to a point just east of Stepanovka, a distance of about 20 kilometres. Commanding the division was *Generalleutnant* Helmuth Beukemann, another experienced division commander, who had been in post since 15 September 1942. He knew his division well and he knew conditions on the Eastern Front. Before taking up his command, Beukemann had been the commanding officer of *Infanterie-Regiment 382* since 13 January 1940. The regiment had belonged to the *164.Infanterie-Division*, and as such Beukemann had missed out on the campaign in the West, but had seen action in the Balkans, before settling down to occupation duties on Crete. Indeed, in January 1942 the division was re-designated as the *Festungs-Division 'Kreta'*, the Fortress Division "Crete". But Beukemann was due for promotion, and he left the regiment in August 1942, just before it was converted to a *Panzergrenadier-Regiment* and transferred to North Africa along with the rest of the division. The *75.Infanterie-Division* had been in continuous action on the Eastern Front since the start of the campaign, and Beukemann had been in command for over a year. Both were well experienced.

Holding the centre of the *VII.AK* sector was the *198.Infanterie-Division*. This unit had been formed in December 1939 and had taken part in the occupation of Denmark the following year, effectively missing the campaign against France, although it was transferred to eastern France in July 1940 to take up occupation duties. It remained there until moved to Rumania the following spring as part of the *Heeresmission Rumänien*, the German Army Mission to Rumania. It was attached to Army Group South for the attack against the Soviet Union, driving through southern Ukraine in 1941, and further on into the Caucasus the following year. Following the German reverses at Stalingrad, the division then withdrew through the Kuban' peninsula before being refitted in the Zaporozh'e area and transferred back to the area south of Khar'kov during the summer of 1943. It had fallen back to the Dnepr with the *8.Armee* before being transferred to the *4.Panzerarmee* in November. The following month it had been attached to the *VII.AK*, where it now held the sector running westwards from Stepanovka, passing north of Grebenki, to the railway line linking Belaya Tserkov' to Fastov. It therefore covered the main road heading south from Kiev towards Belaya Tserkov', and its sector was correspondingly narrower, being only 14 kilometres wide. The division commander was *Generalleutnant* Hans-Joachim von Horn, an officer who had been in the west during the Polish campaign, as chief of staff with the *XII.AK*, and in the *OKH* reserve, as chief of staff with the *X.AK*, during the latter half of the campaign in the West. He had thus managed to avoid any serious action during the early stages of the war, but was later attached to the staff of the *7.Panzer-Division* in September 1942. However, he had taken up his appointment as commanding officer of the *198.Infanterie-Division* on 5 February 1943 as it was pulling back from the Caucasus into the Kuban', and he had been with the division ever since, building up considerable experience of both his troops and the conditions of the war against the Soviet Union. Despite his initial lack of experience therefore, he was still a veteran of the Eastern Front.

To the left of von Horn's division, guarding the left wing of the *VII.AK*, was the *88.Infanterie-Division*, another unit which had been blooded in the Soviet Union. It had been formed as part of the *6.Welle*, on 1 December 1939, part of the same series as the *82.Infanterie-Division* fighting to its right. It, too, had taken no effective part in the campaign against France, and had been similarly "*beurlaubt*" between August 1940 and February 1941. The division was recalled for occupation duties in France, but in January 1942 it was transferred to Army Group South in the Soviet Union, where it was deployed on the left wing in the general area around Kursk. It stayed on that general sector throughout 1942 and the first half of 1943, being attached to the *VII.AK* in June of that year. From that point on it shared the fate of its parent *Korps*, falling back to the Dnepr, through Kiev south-westwards until, by the last week in December, it was holding the sector to the west of the *88.Infanterie-Division*. Its right wing was anchored on the Fastov-Belaya Tserkov' railway, running westwards from there along the river Kamenka as far as Trilesy, before turning more north-westwards to Volitsa station on the Fastov-Zhitomir railway line, near Dmitrievka. That marked the left wing of the *VII.AK*, and gave the division a sector of about 23 kilometres to defend. Commanding the division was *Oberst* Graf von Rittberg, another artillery specialist. Von Rittberg had only assumed command of the division on 12 November 1943, and before that his only infantry combat command had been that of the *Grenadier-Regiment 2* for a few months in the spring and summer of the same year. That had been under the *11.Infanterie-Division* under Army Group North, and other than that, he had held only artillery commands. Two of these had been divisional *Artillerie-Regiments*, one in the French campaign and the other in the Russian campaign under Army Group Centre. In December 1942 he had been given command of a *Korps* level *Artillerie-Kommandeur*, a post he held for 4 months before assuming command of the *Grenadier-Regiment 2*. He had seen no active service between summer 1943 and taking up his post with the *88.Infanterie-Division*, so overall he lacked the experience of many of his colleagues, but at least the division itself had been tempered.

Also in the *VII.AK* sector, and deployed in the area around Grebenki behind the *198.Infanterie-Division* was the *18.Artillerie-Division*. This was a unique formation in the *Wehrmacht*, and represented the first and only real attempt by the Germans to create a standard divisional-level organisation for the concentration of artillery firepower for major offensive or defensive operations. It is likely that the concept was copied from the Soviet Army which deployed several artillery divisions throughout the Great Patriotic War, but the Germans seemed ultimately to have judged the experiment to have been a failure and the division was formally disbanded after only a few months. It was formed in the field under Army Group Centre on 1 October 1943 on the basis of the recently disbanded *18.Panzer-Division*. Its planned organisation was not actually put into place, and on 26 October the *OKH* formally changed its structure to comprise three artillery regiments (*Artillerie-Regiment 88*, *Artillerie-Regiment 288*, and *Artillerie-Regiment 388*), each of which possessed three artillery battalions. These were supported by the *Sturmgeschütz-Batterie 741*, the *Heeres-Flak-Abteilung 280*, as well as observation, fire control, and other service troops. For infantry support, it deployed the *Schützen-Abteilung 88*, established on the basis of the former *Panzeraufklärungs-Abteilung 18* of the *18.Panzer-Division*. The division was commanded from its formation by *Generalmajor* Karl Thoholte, a 50-year old artillery specialist who had been the *Höher-Artillerie-Kommandeur 301* since February 1943. This position had been the artillery commander under Army Group D in France and he had been promoted to *Generalmajor* whilst in post there. Thoholte saw no combat action whilst on the Western Front, but previously he had held the position of *Artillerie-Kommandeur 101* which had been deployed in different sectors in the Soviet Union. Before this, he had also seen active service on the Eastern Front as commander of the *Artillerie-Regiment 36* under the *36.Infanterie-Division*. He held this position from January 1941 until he was appointed *Arko 101*, and so, although he had been absent from the East for over 6 months, he had previously gained experience in the campaigns of both Army Group North and Army Group Centre. Although the division had been formed under Army Group Centre, it had seen no combat as a distinct formation, and the Zhitomir-Berdichev operation would be its baptism of fire.

Left of the *VII.AK*, and holding the sector which was bear the full force of the Soviet offensive was the *Generalkommando XXXXII.Armeekorps*. This was commanded by *General der Infanterie* Franz Mattenklott, a 59-year old infantry specialist. He had been a career soldier, having first entered service in 1903. He already held the rank of *Generalmajor* at the outbreak of war in 1939 when he was in command of the *72.Infanterie-Division*. This division had remained on the Western Front throughout the campaign in Poland, and had moved into the *OKH* Reserve in May 1940. It subsequently served under the *6.Armee* and the *4.Armee* during the fighting in France before being deployed on occupation duties in Brittany. Mattenklott had meanwhile been promoted to *Generalleutnant* on 1 February 1940, and was appointed *Kommandant* in Metz in July the same year. Just over a year later, on 1 October 1941, he was promoted again and made *General der Infanterie*. Three months later he was given his first field command as a *Korps* commander when he was appointed to lead the *XXXXII.AK* with effect from 1 January 1942. At that point, the *Korps* was attached to the *11.Armee* and deployed in the Crimea, where with effect from August 1942 Mattenklott was simultaneously designated as the *Befehlshaber Krim*, or territorial commander in the Crimea. The *XXXXII.AK* remained in the Crimea until May 1943 when it was transferred northwards to the area east of Khar'kov to join the *Armee-Abteilung Kempf* under Army Group South. It was subsequently attached to the *8.Armee* during the retreat to the river Dnepr following the failed Kursk offensive, before being transferred to the *4.Panzerarmee* in October 1943. By this time, Mattenklott had been on the Eastern Front for nearly two years, but he had served on quiet sectors for most of this time, and it was really only during the previous few months that he had experienced serious combat.

On the right wing of the *XXXXII.AK* was the *25.Panzer-Division*. This was a relatively new unit, having been formed on 25 February 1942 in Norway on the basis of the *Schützen-Verband Oslo*, which was simultaneously renamed as the *Schützen-Regiment Oslo*. This unit had originally been formed in July 1940 as a guard battalion for the city on the basis of a parachute battalion from the *163.Infanterie-Division*. At that stage the *25.Panzer-Division* only comprised the *Schützen-Verband* (re-named the *Schützen-Regiment 146* from 19 May 1942), the *Panzer-Abteilung 214*, and a 100mm motorised canon battery. With effect from November 1942 however, the division was gradually brought up to strength, and by June the following year it was re-organised as a full *panzer-division*. In August 1943, it began transferring to northern France, only to learn on 19 October that it was to be transferred to the Eastern Front. It was originally to be moved to the Kirovograd area where it would remain as *OKH* reserve in the Army Group South area, but the deteriorating situation around Kiev led to it being re-routed to the Berdichev-Kazatin-Skvira region instead. With no combat experience and short of both training and equipment, the division was thrust into a fluid situation where it took part in the effort to re-stabilise the front following the Soviet Kiev operation. It remained in the area until the beginning of the Zhitomir-Berdichev operation. On 24 December 1943, its right wing was on the boundary between the *XXXXII.AK* and the *VII.AK*. It was anchored on Dmitrievka where it met with the left wing of the *88.Infanterie-Division*, and from there it passed almost northwards, taking in Mokhnachka and Luchin before passing to the east of Divin and on to Vil'shka. This gave the division a sector of 30 kilometres to secure, a task for which it was neither prepared nor equipped given that this was the sector where the Soviets would choose to develop their main assault. To add to the difficulties, the division had only recently had a change in commanding officer. Until 15 November 1943, it had been commanded by *Generalleutnant* Adolf von Schell, a post he had held since 1 January 1943, but he had been taken ill in recent weeks and had left the division to return to Germany. His place was taken by *Generalmajor* Hans Tröger, a 47-year old career soldier who had specialised in mobile warfare. As an *Oberstleutnant*, he had commanded the motorcycle battalion in the *3.Panzer-Division* during the campaign in France, before being promoted to *Oberst* in June 1941 and transferred to take on the same role in the *14.Panzer-Division* during the early stages of the war in the East. In December 1941 he was given the command of the *Schützen-Regiment 103* in the same division, before being recalled to Germany some time in 1942 to take command of the School for Battalion Commanders in Ohrdruf. On 30 November 1942, he was transferred back to the Eastern Front to take command of the newly formed *27.Panzer-Division* just as it was sent into the desperate situation created following the Soviet offensive around Stalingrad. He was promoted to *Generalmajor* with effect from 1 January 1943, but saw his division reduced to a *Kampfgruppe* in a matter of weeks. It was officially disbanded on 15 February 1943, and most of its elements were incorporated into the *7.Panzer-Division*. Meanwhile, Tröger had been transferred back to Germany where he took up post as commander of the School for Panzer Troops on 28 February 1943. This was his final post before being ordered to take command of the new *25.Panzer-Division* with effect from 20 November 1943. He had therefore had a varied career, much of it specialising in mobile warfare, but his actual experience of combat operations on the Eastern Front was quite limited, particularly as a senior officer. His division on the other hand was without any combat experience of any kind, other than that it had gained in the previous 6 weeks or so.

To the left of the *25.Panzer-Division* was the *19.Panzer-Division*. This unit had been formed on 1 November 1940 on the basis of the former *19.Infanterie-Division* which had originally been a peacetime division. It had participated in the Polish campaign in 1939, and also the campaign in the West in 1940 before being returned to Germany for conversion to a *panzer-division*. It was attached to *Panzergruppe 3* under Army Group Centre during the invasion of the Soviet Union, and it stayed on the central sector until December 1942 when it was transferred to Army Group Don during the Stalingrad operations. It took part in the retreat across eastern Ukraine during the spring of 1943 under the *1.Panzerarmee*, before being transferred to the *4.Panzerarmee* in August of the same year and joining the retreat to the river Dnepr during September. It remained in the general Kiev region for the next three months, participating in the defence and counterattacks mounted by the *4.Panzerarmee* in that area. On 24 December 1943, it was deployed in the central part of the sector held by the *XXXII.AK*, having its right wing just north of Vil'shka and running from there almost north-westwards to include Yastreben'ka, Staritskoe and Mestechko to a point about three kilometres south-east of Vysokoe on the main Kiev-Zhitomir road. It therefore held a sector of about 15 kilometres, considerably less than its southern neighbour, but it would have been seen as holding a more dangerous sector given its proximity to the main road. The division was commanded by *Generalmajor* Hans Källner, a 45-year old career soldier with a background in the cavalry. He had commanded the *Aufklärungs-Abteilung 11* at the outbreak of the war, being promoted to *Oberstleutnant* on 1 November 1939, and remaining with that unit until August 1941 at which point he was posted to the *19.Panzer-Division* to take command of the *Panzergrenadier-Regiment 73*. On 1 July the following year, he was placed in charge of the *Panzergrenadier-Brigade 19*, a brigade headquarters in command of the two panzergrenadier-regiments under the *19.Panzer-Division*. On 28 October 1942, orders were received for this headquarters to be disbanded, but the *4.Panzerarmee*, to which the division was attached at the time, resisted the instruction and instead re-deployed the staff as an independent headquarters, first as the *Stossgruppe*[4] Källner and

---
4   Strike Group.

later as the *Stossgruppe* von Manteuffel, before it eventually became the headquarters of the *1.Ski-Division* in June 1944. Källner meanwhile had been given command of the *19.Panzer-Division* on 18 August 1943, and was subsequently promoted to *Generalmajor* on 1 November 1943. He had therefore been with his division for over two years in various positions of command, and throughout this time had served all his time in the campaign against the Soviet Union. Both he and his division therefore had considerable experience of conditions on the Eastern Front.

To the north, the sector was held by the *8.Panzer-Division*. This division had been formed on 16 October 1939 on the basis of the former *3.leichte-Division*, with the addition of the *I./Panzer-Regiment 10* from the *Armeetruppen Ostpreussen*. It took part in the campaign in the West before being allocated to occupation duties in France. It returned to Germany towards the end of 1940 for refit and re-organisation, receiving a third *Panzer-Abteilung*, a second *Panzergrenadier-Regiment*, and a third *Artillerie-Abteilung*. In March 1941 it returned to France for a brief spell before being transferred to Yugoslavia for a few weeks. During May and June 1941 it came under the commander of the Replacement Army before being attached to *Panzergruppe 4* under Army Group North for the campaign against the Soviet Union. It remained on the northern sector until the end of 1942 when it was transferred to Army Group Centre, serving under different armies for the next nine months. In October 1943, the division was transferred to the *4.Panzerarmee* to try and bolster the defence in the Kiev region. When the Soviets began the Zhitomir-Berdichev offensive, the division was responsible for the sector which lay astride the main Kiev-Zhitomir road. This ran from a point about three kilometres south-east of Vysokoe along the eastern edge of Stavishche before bending back north-westwards along the road to Rakovichi and continuing along and past the northern edge of that village to Negrebovka on the Belka stream about three kilometres further on. The total length of its sector was a little less than 15 kilometres. The *8.Panzer-Division* was under the command of *Generalmajor* Gottfried Frölich, another career soldier who had joined up in August 1914 just after the outbreak of the First World War. By the time of the start of the Second World War, he had progressed to become an *Oberstleutnant* in command of an artillery battalion in the *1.leichte-Division*, soon to be used to form the *6.Panzer-Division*. On 1 November 1939 he was appointed to take command of the *Panzerartillerie-Regiment 78* in the newly-forming *7.Panzer-Division*, where he would later serve under Rommel. He held the post for over 3½ years, during which time he served in the campaign in the West and the first 12 months of the campaign in the East where the division was deployed in the central sector. He stayed with the division while it refitted in France during the second half of 1942 and returned with it to the southern sector of the Eastern Front in January 1943. Here he served in the Stalingrad and Kursk operations before being transferred to take up temporary command of the *36.Infanterie-Division* in August 1943 after it had taken heavy losses in the Kursk operation. On 20 September 1943, Frölich took command of the *8.Panzer-Division* and was promoted to *Generalmajor* on 1 December 1943. Although he had spent almost two years on the Eastern Front, he was an artillery specialist by trade and had little experience as a division commander. His division though was more experienced in conditions in the Soviet Union, having fought there continuously since the beginning of the campaign.

On the left wing of the *XXXXII.AK* was the *SS Panzerkampfgruppe 'Das Reich'*. This was the remnant of the *2.SS Panzer-Division 'Das Reich'* which had suffered heavy losses since its transfer to the Eastern Front in February 1943. The division belonged to the *Waffen-SS* and had been formed in April 1940 from a number of independent *SS-Standarten* which had seen action in the Polish campaign. It had originally been known as the *SS-Division Verfügungstruppe* or *SS-V*, in which guise it had served in the campaign in the West, seeing action in the Netherlands and France before taking up occupation duties in France under the *1.Armee*. In December 1940 it had been re-organised and re-named as the *SS-Division (mot.) Reich*, before it took part in the Balkans campaign in April 1941. Following that it returned to Austria for refit prior to being sent to take part in the invasion of the Soviet Union. It was initially assigned to the *2.Panzerarmee* under Army Group Centre, but was later transferred to the *4.Panzerarmee* and then the *9.Armee* where it spent months on the Rzhev sector. By the summer of 1942, the division was in need of refitting and it returned to France in August 1942, being attached to the *15.Armee* for the purpose. Whilst there it was re-organised as well, before being sent back to the Eastern Front in January 1943 as part of the German reinforcement of the southern sector in the wake of the Stalingrad disaster. During its stay in northern France, the division was re-named again in November 1942, this time becoming the *SS-Panzergrenadier-Division 'Das Reich'*. It then fought through the winter campaign before playing an important role in the Kursk battle prior to taking part in the retreat to the Dnepr under the *8.Armee*. On 22 October 1943, it was re-named as the *2.SS Panzer-Division 'Das Reich'*, and by November 1943 it was attached to the *4.Panzerarmee*, participating in the counterattack in the area west and south-west of Kiev. As a result of the Kursk fighting and the subsequent retreat, the *'Das Reich'* had been severely weakened, and by the middle of December it had been decided to pull what was left of the division out of the front line and return it to Germany for refitting and reorganisation. Nevertheless, those elements which were deemed to be still combat-capable were to remain with the *4.Panzerarmee* and be brought together to form a single *Kampfgruppe*. This comprised the *SS Panzergrenadier-Regiment 'Das Reich'* (with two *panzergrenadier* battalions), the *Panzer-Abteilung 'Das Reich'* (with two companies), an artillery battalion (with two batteries of *lFH* 105 mm and one battery of *sFH* 155 mm), a *Werfer* battalion (with two batteries), a reconnaissance company, an engineer company, a heavy weapons company, two *Sturmgeschütz* companies and an anti-aircraft battery, as well as the usual support and service units. In total it was about 5,000 strong. Initially, it was also given extra reinforcement, including the *Panzer-Pionier-Bataillon 87* and the *Panzeraufklärungs-Abteilung 25* from the *25.Panzer-Division,* and the *Panzer-Pionier-Bataillon 19* from the *19.Panzer-Division*.[5] The last elements of the rest of the division rolled out of the station in Zhitomir on 24 December, just as the Soviets began their offensive. By this time, the remaining *SS Panzerkampfgruppe 'Das Reich'* was deployed on a line running from the Belka stream at Negrebovka along the road running north-west towards Radomyshl', taking in the villages along the road and ending on the eastern bank of the river Teterev, a distance of just over 10 kilometres in total. The *'Das Reich'* was by this time under the command of *SS Obersturmbannführer* Sommer, the former *Ia* of the division, although he too would be replaced on 28 December, moving on to take up post as the chief of staff to the planned *IV.SS Panzerkorps*. At this point, *SS Oberführer* Heinz Lammerding assumed command of the *Kampfgruppe*. Shortly after the start of the war, Lammerding had been serving as the commander of the engineer

---

5 Weidinger, *Division Das Reich*, (Osnabrück: Munin Verlag, 1982), Volume V, page 18ff.

battalion in the *SS-Totenkopf-Division*, having been promoted to *Sturmbannführer* in October 1939. He served with the battalion through the campaign in the West until he took over as the division *Ia* in December 1940. He served in that capacity when the division took part on the invasion of the Soviet Union on the northern sector, initially under the *4.Panzerarmee* and later the *16.Armee*. After only a couple of months, he was promoted to *Obersturmbannführer* in September 1941 and continued to serve with the division until June 1942 when he was flown out of the Demyansk pocket. Back in Germany he worked organising the division's replacements until, in early October 1942, the rest of the division was pulled out of the Eastern Front and transferred to south-western France for rest and refit. Around this time he commanded the *SS Infanterie-Regiment 9 'Thule'* whilst it was being incorporated into what was by this time the re-organised *SS Panzergrenadier-Division 'Totenkopf'*. He was promoted again at the end of January 1943, this time rising to the rank of *Standartenführer*, before being transferred temporarily to the *II.SS Panzerkorps* to act as the chief of staff at the beginning of May 1943. In late July 1943 he was moved to become chief of staff to *Obergruppenführer und General der Polizei* von der Bach, then acting as the *Chef der Bandenkampfverbände*[6] operating against partisans in the Eastern Front rear area. Lammerding was promoted again on 9 December 1943, and it was in his new rank of *Oberführer* that he assumed command of the *SS Panzerkampfgruppe 'Das Reich'*. He therefore had considerable experience of operating in divisional and equivalent level headquarters on the Eastern Front, but much of this had been in a different operating environment to the one he and the remnants of the *'Das Reich'* would now face.

Also attached to the *XXXXII.AK* was the *20.Panzergrenadier-Division*. This had originally been a peacetime *Infanterie-Division*, but had been motorised as early as the autumn of 1937, becoming the *20.Infanterie-Division (mot.)*. It participated in the Polish campaign in September 1939 before being moved to the Western Front in December that year. In spring 1940 it gave up one of its three *Infanterie-Regiments* to the newly forming *10.Panzer-Division*, before taking part in the campaign in France. It returned to Germany for re-organisation in November and December the same year, before going back to France for occupation duties throughout the spring of 1941. It was transferred to the east in May 1941 and participated in the invasion of the Soviet Union as part of the *Panzergruppe 3* under Army Group Centre. By September 1941, the division had been transferred to the *16.Armee* under Army Group North where it remained until withdrawn to Army Group Centre reserve in December 1942. It was back in the front line in February 1943 under the *3.Panzerarmee* in the Velizh area where, on 23 July 1943, it was re-organised as the *20.Panzergrenadier-Division*, receiving the newly-formed *Panzer-Abteilung 8* and the *Heeres-Flak-Abteilung 284*. It remained on the central sector until October 1943, when it was transferred to the *XXXXVIII.PzK* under the *8.Armee*. It also served under the *VII.AK* during November that year, before being transferred to the *XXXXII.AK*. By 13 December 1943, the division had been placed in the reserve where it was being rested and refitted in the area west of Berdichev. It was commanded by *Generalleutnant* Georg Jauer, a 47-year old professional soldier who first joined the army as a volunteer in August 1914, serving in a number of different artillery appointments. When the war started, Jauer had been working as an *Oberstleutnant* in the *Heeres-Personal-Amt*, receiving promotion to *Oberst* on 1 October 1940. He was

---

6   Head of Anti-Partisan Units.

first transferred to a combat position in March 1941 when he took up the position commanding the *Artillerie-Regiment 29* in the *29.Infanterie-Division*. He remained with the division throughout the first nine months of the campaign in the East, fighting on the central sector under the *Panzergruppe 2* and then the *2.Panzerarmee*. On 15 March 1942, he returned to Germany to take command of the newly forming *Artillerie-Regiment Grossdeutschland*, as part of the *Infanterie-Division (mot.) Grossdeutschland*, a post he held for another 10 months. During this time, he returned to the Eastern Front with the new division in June 1942, fighting on the southern sector under Army Groups South and A, before returning to the central sector in September 1942. He stayed there for a couple of months before being transferred to the officers' reserve pool on 28 November 1942. On 20 January 1943 he was transferred back to Army Group Centre to take command of the *20.Infanterie-Division (mot.)*. He was promoted to *Generalmajor* in April that year and again to *Generalleutnant* in October, remaining with the division until it finally joined the *4.Panzerarmee* the following month in November 1943. He therefore had some experience of combat on the Eastern Front, but much of it as artillery commander and much of it on the quieter sectors. Nevertheless, he had commanded a division for almost a year, even if this had not been heavily involved in major operations for much of the time. The division itself though had been on the Eastern Front since the beginning of the war against the Soviet Union, and had built up a lot of experience of conditions in the East.

To the left of the *XXXXII.AK* was the *Generalkommando XIII.Armeekorps*. This was commanded by the newly promoted *General der Infanterie* Arthur Hauffe who had only taken up the post on 7 September 1943. He was another professional solider, having joined the army in the summer of 1912, and served with the *Infanterie-Regiment 171* during the First World War. He had been posted mainly to staff positions, serving as an operations officer and chief of staff between the wars. Just after the outbreak of the Second World War, Hauffe was an *Oberst* serving as chief of staff with the *XXV.Armeekorps*, a position he held until February 1940 when he was transferred to become the chief of staff of the *XXXVII.Armeekorps*. Just before the invasion of the Soviet Union, he was promoted to *Generalmajor* and took up the post of chief of staff to the German military mission in Rumania, where he remained for a year and a half until January 1943. At that time, he was promoted to *Generalleutnant* before taking command of the *46.Infanterie-Division* on 7 February 1943, staying with it until August that year, before being transferred to take charge of the *XIII.AK* the following month. In recognition of his new posting, he was promoted to *General der Infanterie*, and when the Soviet offensive began, Hauffe was 52 years old, having just celebrated his birthday on 20 December.

There were four divisions operating under Hauffe's command, and on the right wing was the *68.Infanterie-Division*. This division had been formed on 26 August 1939 as part of the *2.Welle* and had taken part in the Polish campaign under Army Group South before being transferred to the Western Front in December 1939. It then served in the campaign in the West before returning to Poland in July 1940 for occupation duties. By the time the invasion of the Soviet Union began the division was stationed on the southern sector with the *17.Armee* under Army Group South. It remained on that sector throughout the rest of 1941 as the Germans advanced through Ukraine, serving under both the *17.Armee* and the *6.Armee*. During the first four months of 1942, the division served under the *17.Armee* during the defensive operations in the

Donets basin, before being transferred to the *1.Panzerarmee* during its fighting on the river Mius sector. From August 42, it was transferred northwards to the *2.Armee* under Army Group B where it served with the *XIII.AK* during the defensive battles around Voronezh. By early February 1943 the division had been transferred to the *VII.AK* under the *2.Armee*, and had been moved to the Sumy area on the southern side of the Kursk salient by March 1943. Following the failed German offensive at Kursk during July 1943, the division was transferred to the *4.Panzerarmee* as part of the *VII.AK* in August 1943 as the retreat to the river Dnepr began. It remained with the same *Korps* until December 1943 when it found itself attached to the *XIII.AK*. It had therefore been on the Eastern Front continuously since 1941, but despite this it had seen prolonged spells on quieter sectors and had escaped the worst of the fighting. When the Russian offensive began, the division had its right wing anchored on the river Teterev in the northern suburbs of Radomyshl', across the river from the *SS Panzerkampfgruppe 'Das Reich'*. Its front ran north-westwards from there, taking in Lutovka and Malaya Racha before turning north to run through the eastern edge of Krasnoborka and the tiny village of Krasnoselka where its left-hand boundary lay. It held a front of approximately 12 kilometres. The division was commanded by *Oberst* Paul Scheuerpflug, who had only been appointed two months previously on 25 October 1943. He was 47 years old at the time, having joined the army as an 18-year old on the outbreak of the First World War. By the time of the Second World War, he had risen to become an *Oberstleutnant*, and was serving as an adjutant with the *35.Infanterie-Division* on 1 September 1939. On 1 February 1940 he was transferred to the *I.AK* where he also served as an adjutant during the Campaign in the West, before being appointed as the corps chief of staff in September the same year. On 1 April 1941 he was transferred again, this time to take command of the *Infanterie-Regiment 116* of the *9.Infanterie-Division*. He fought with the division on the southern sector of the Eastern Front, initially with the *6.Armee* and then the *17.Armee* from September 1941. The division then stayed with the *17.Armee* throughout the operations in the Donets basin and the subsequent advance into the Caucasus during 1942. Following the Stalingrad battles, the division fell back into the Kuban bridgehead where it remained until September 1943, at which point it was transferred to the Melitopol' area under the *6.Armee*. By this time, Scheuerpflug had commanded the *Infanterie-Regiment 116* for a period of almost 2½ years, having been promoted just once in that time, becoming *Oberst* on 1 January 1942. Shortly after the *9.Infanterie-Division* had been pulled out of the Kuban bridgehead, Scheuerpflug was transferred to take command of the *68.Infanterie-Division* then holding a sector on the southern edge of the Soviet Lyutezh bridgehead, north of Kiev. He commanded the division throughout the Russian breakout from Kiev and the subsequent German counterattack, but by 24 December 1943 he still had only two months' experience, both with his new unit and also as operating as a division commander.

North of the *68.Infanterie-Division* was the *213.Sicherungs-Division*.[7] This had been formed in March 1941 as one of nine such divisions to be raised in preparation for the campaign against the Soviet Union where they were planned to perform security duties in the army rear areas. It was to be formed on the basis of the headquarters of the former *213.Infanterie-Division* together with the *Infanterie-Regiment 318* and the *I./Artillerie-Regiment 213* from that division. Following a re-organisation in April 1943, the division

7   Security Division.

comprised the *Infanterie-Sicherungs-Regiment 177*, the *Infanterie-Sicherungs-Regiment 318* (each of which had three battalions), the *III./Polizei-Regiment 6*, and the *Kosaken-Abteilung 213*. Its artillery battalion was taken away in September 1943 to join the 320. Infanterie-Division. The division had operated in Ukraine since June 1941, serving in the rear area of Army Group South and Army Group B, and engaged in security and anti-partisan operations. It was caught up in the general retreat to the river Dnepr, and by October 1943 it had been called into front line duties, being attached to the *VII.AK* in the Kiev area. From that time it remained under the *4.Panzerarmee* though transferring between different *Korps* commands, before being finally attached to the *XIII.AK* in December 1943. The division was still in the front line at the beginning of the Zhitomir-Berdichev offensive, although in recognition of its status as a security unit, it held a sector of less than 5 kilometres, stretching northwards from the left wing of the *68.Infanterie-Division* at Krasnoselka to a point just beyond Mircha. The division was commanded by *Generalleutnant* Alex Goeschen, one of the oldest senior commanders at 59 years old. He had joined the army in 1906 and served as a cavalry officer, commanding the *Reiter-Regiment 2* under the *Reichswehr* between the wars. At the outbreak of the war, he was in charge of the *Remonteschule* in Bamberg as an *Oberst*, and he stayed in this post until February 1942, having been promoted to *Generalmajor* in August 1941. He was posted in August 1942 to take command of the *213.Sicherungs-Division*, leading it through the rear area operations of the Stalingrad campaign and the subsequent retreats through 1943. In August 1943, a few months before he would find himself having to lead his division in the front line, he was promoted to *Generalleutnant*.

To the left was the *340.Infanterie-Division*. This had been formed in November 1940 as a static division in the *14.Welle*, on the basis of elements taken from the *68.Infanterie-Division* and the *170.Infanterie-Division*, together with a battalion from the *290.Infanterie-Division*. Once its initial formation had been completed, the division was transferred to northern France in June 1941 for occupation duties, and it remained there until May the following year. During the next couple of months it was transferred into the *OKH* reserve and moved to the southern sector on the Eastern Front. By August 1942 it had been assigned to the *2.Armee* and deployed in the front line near Voronezh where it remained in a static defence for the rest of the year. In January and February 1943, the division was caught up in the Soviet Voronezh-Kastornoe operation, being encircled before breaking out and retreating to the Ryl'sk area. Following the failure of the German Kursk offensive in July and August 1943, the *340.Infanterie-Division* fell back to the Dnepr with the rest of Army Group South, coming under the *4.Panzerarmee* for the first time when the *XIII.AK* was transferred there from the *2.Armee*. It was then involved in the Soviet offensive to liberate Kiev, falling back before finally taking up new defensive positions south of Malin in December 1943. By this stage, the division had suffered considerable casualties and had a rather fluid organisation. As early as March 1943, it had incorporated the remnants of the *377.Infanterie-Division* when the latter had been severely mauled during the Voronezh-Kastornoe operation, and by early November 1943 it had also incorporated the remnants of the *327.Infanterie-Division*. Its reorganisation would continue during the period of the Zhitomir-Berdichev operation when the *XIII.AK* would be pulled out of the front for rest and refit. Given its condition, the division also held a relatively short sector of the front line, running a total of seven kilometres from the left wing of the *213.Sicherungs-Division* just north of Mircha, heading first north and then north-west to cross the river Voznya north of Vorsovka to reach a point about two kilometres north-west of the town. *Oberst* Werner Ehrig was in command of the division and had been only since 25 October 1943. He was 46 years old and joined the army just after the outbreak of First World War, serving as a *Leutnant* in the *Infanterie-Regiment 108*. He served as the *Ia* of the *22.Infanterie-Division* during the *Reichswehr* period, being promoted to *Oberstleutnant* on 1 April 1939. He was still serving in the same post when the Second World War broke out, but remained in post only until 26 August 1939 at which point he was transferred into the *Führer* reserve, taking no active part in the Polish campaign. On 25 October 1939 he was transferred to take command of the *II./Infanterie-Regiment 216* under the *86.Infanterie-Division*, with which he remained on the Western Front until March the following year. At that time he was transferred to become *Ia* of the *164.Infanterie-Division*, then still in the process of forming up near Dresden. On 15 January 1941 he was transferred to become *Ia* of the newly forming *15.Armee* in France, being promoted to *Oberst* whilst there. He remained in that post for almost two years until 15 November 1942 when he took up post as chief of staff to the *LXXXVII.AK*, then forming up in Brittany in north-western France. On 10 June 1943, before the *LXXXVII.AK* moved to Italy to take part in the defence against the allied invasion there, he was transferred back to the *Führer* reserve, before being tasked with leading the *340.Infanterie-Division* on 25 October. His first experience of the Eastern Front came in July 1943 when he was transferred to Army Group Centre as part of its pool of reserve officers, and it was only three months later when he had to take command of the division. He was therefore inexperienced both with the Eastern Front and the command of a division.

On the left wing of the *XIII.AK* was the *208.Infanterie-Division*. This had been formed in August 1939 as part of the *3.Welle*, prior to taking part in the Polish campaign and spending a few weeks on occupation duties there. By December 1939, the division had been transferred to the west, being deployed along the lower Rhine under first the *6.Armee* and later the *18.Armee*. It took part in the campaign in the West, moving first through southern Holland towards Antwerp as *18.Armee* reserve before joining the encirclement of Dunkirk. It took no part in the second part of the campaign, spending its time on the Belgian coast. It remained there on occupation duties until December 1941 when it was transferred to central sector of the Eastern Front under Army Group Centre. It was assigned to the *2.Panzerarmee* in the Zhizhdra area where it was engaged static defence north-west of Orel until the middle of 1943. In July 1943, the division was involved in heavy defensive fighting in the Bolkhov area, suffering heavy casualties before being transferred to the *2.Panzerarmee* reserve. Three of its infantry battalions were disbanded around this time. In August, it was transferred to Army Group South where it was allocated to the *VII.AK* under the *4.Panzerarmee*, and involved first in the defensive fighting following the Kursk battle and then in the long withdrawal to the river Dnepr. The division formed the left wing of the *XIII.AK*, holding a sector of about 7 kilometres length, running to the north-west from a point just north-west of Vorsovka through Zybin and Elevka to the edge of Berezino. The *7.Panzer-Division* was operating beyond that point, but the front line was no longer contiguous. The *208. Infanterie-Division* was commanded by *Generalmajor* Hans Piekenbrock, a 50-year old career soldier. He had joined the army in September 1914, serving in a hussar regiment and ending the war as a regimental adjutant. He served in the Reichswehr between the wars, and by September 1939, he was an *Oberstleutnant* serving as head of *Abteilung 1* in the *OKW* intelligence department under Canaris, where he was responsible for espionage. In all he served 6½ years in the same office, being promoted to *Oberst* in December 1940 whilst there, before being given the command of an infantry regiment in March 1943. On 22 June 1943, Piekenbrock was transferred to take command of the *208.Infanterie-Division*, being promoted to *Generalmajor* on 1 August 1943. He had taken over just as the division became involved in heavy fighting, and he remained with it during the defensive battles over the following months. Together, Piekenbrock and his division were not a strong combination. Not only did he lack experience of operating at that level, but he also had little experience of command in the field, and had less than a year's familiarity with conditions on the Eastern Front. The division itself had recent and bitter experience of the Eastern Front, but it was a severely weakened unit.

Left of the *XIII.AK* was the *XXXXVIII.PzK*, still leading the counterattack to restore the German front line following the Soviet offensive to break out of the Kiev bridgehead. The *Korps* was led by the newly promoted *General der Panzertruppen* Hermann Balck who had only assumed command as recently as 15 November 1943. Balck had just turned 50 years old and had been a professional soldier since he joined the army in 1913. He reached the rank of *Oberstleutnant* on 1 February 1938, and at the outbreak of the war he was serving with the *Inspektion der Schnellen Truppen* in the *OKH (In 6)* office. On 23 October 1939, following the Polish campaign, he was posted to the *1.Panzer-Division* where he assumed command of the *Schützen-Regiment 1*. He led the unit through the campaign in the West, including the action to break through the Maginot line at Sedan for which he was awarded the Knight's Cross of the Iron Cross. He was promoted to *Oberst* on 1 August 1940 and gave up his command on 23 October 1940 before being transferred to the *2.Panzer-Division* to take command of the *Panzer-Regiment 3* on 15 December 1940. He led this unit through the Balkan campaign during the spring of 1941 before taking charge of the *Panzer-Brigade 2* on 15 May 1941. Following the conclusion of the campaign, Balck was transferred back to the *OKH* on 7 July 1941 where he initially worked in the department responsible for army equipment and the replacement army. After a few days though, he was given a special task to look into the serious losses being incurred by German armour in the Soviet Union, and on 1 November 1941 he was appointed as the *General der Schnellen Truppen* in the *OKH*.

On 16 May 1942 he was returned to active duty, taking command of the *11.Panzer-Division* and holding the post until March 1943 as the division fought on the southern sector in the East throughout the campaigns around the rivers Don and Donets. Whilst in charge of the division, he was promoted twice, first becoming *Generalmajor* on 1 August 1942 and then rising to *Generalleutnant* on 1 January 1943. He left the *11.Panzer-Division* on 4 March 1943 having by then received the Oak Leaves and Swords to the Knight's Cross. He was initially transferred to the *Führerreserve*, but after a few weeks he was moved to take command of the *Infanterie-Division (mot.) 'Grossdeutschland'* on three April 1943. He remained there for only a short time, being transferred back into the *Führerreserve* on 30 June 1943. On 2 September 1943, he was sent to Italy as acting commander of the *XIV.PzK*, but was involved in a plane crash which left him unable to continue in post. He was promoted shortly afterwards, becoming a full *General der Panzertruppen* on 1 November 1943, and within two weeks he was given temporary command of the *XXXX.PzK* on 12 November, remaining there for only three days before transferring to take up full command of the *XXXXVIII.PzK* on 15 November 1943. Balck was therefore an experienced officer who had specialised in mobile warfare, and had participated in a number of successful operations and been highly decorated as a result. Notwithstanding this, most of his experience of the Eastern Front was drawn from his time as commander of the *11.Panzer-Division*, and his experience as a *Korps* commander was limited.

On the right wing of the *XXXXVIII.PzK* was the *7.Panzer-Division*. It had been formed in October 1939 on the basis of the *2.leichte Division* and took part in the campaign in the West during 1940 before being transferred back to Germany in early 1941 for re-organisation. It took part in the invasion of the Soviet Union as part of *Panzergruppe 3* on the central sector, almost reaching as far as Moscow. It remained on the central sector throughout most of the first half of 1942, participating in the defensive battles around Rzhev before being transferred to France for rest and refit. It stayed in the West until the end of the year before being returned to the southern sector on the Eastern Front where it was thrown into the fighting following the major Soviet offensive around Stalingrad. It remained on that sector throughout the spring of 1943, absorbing the remnants of the *27.Panzer-Division* during February, and was deployed in the Izyum and Khar'kov areas before taking part in the German Kursk offensive during July that year. Following the successful Soviet counterattack, the division fell back with the *4.Panzerarmee* and the *8.Armee* to the river Dnepr. It then participated in the defence of the Soviet offensive to breakout of the Kiev bridgehead and the subsequent German counterattack to re-capture Zhitomir. As part of the final attempt of this operation to restore the German front line, the division had just gone over to the defensive in the area to the south-west of Malin, and when the Zhitomir-Berdichev offensive began, it was strung out in a series of defensive positions, holding a loose line between the left wing of the *208.Infanterie-Division* and the rest of the *Korps* nearly 25 kilometres away at Shershni. The line ran in a concave arc running from a point west of Berezino through Fortunatovka, Budilovka, Guta Potievka, and Dobryn' to Zabrannoe, a distance of some 35 kilometres in all. At the time, the division was commanded by *Generalmajor* Hasso von Manteuffel, a 56-year old professional soldier, but he was due to leave before the end of the year being replaced by *Oberst* Adalbert Schulz, then the commander of the division's *Panzer-Regiment 25*. Schulz had only just turned 40 on 20 December 1943, and had not been a professional solider all his working life. He had initially worked in a bank, but later joined the police force before joining the army as a young officer in 1935. On 12 October 1937 he was appointed as company commander in the newly-forming *Panzer-Regiment 25*, a position he still held when the war began. The regiment was later incorporated into the *7.Panzer-Division* in October 1939, and as part of that unit, Schulz led his company through the campaign in the West, being given the command of a battalion in the regiment on 6 June 1940. In September of that year he was awarded the Knight's Cross to the Iron Cross in recognition of his achievements. He took part in the invasion of the Soviet Union with the division, receiving the Oak Leaves to the Knight's Cross for his part in a German withdrawal in the Klin area. He assumed command of the whole regiment on 5 March 1943 and was promoted *Oberstleutnant* on 1 April 1943 in recognition. Following the Kursk operation, he also received the Swords to the Knight's Cross and was promoted again later in the year, becoming *Oberst* on 1 November while still in command of the *Panzer-Regiment 25*. The following month he was awarded the

Diamonds to the Knight's Cross, and on 1 January 1944 he would be given command of the division, being promoted to *Generalmajor* after having held the rank of *Oberst* for only two months. Schulz was unusual in that he had not been a career soldier, only joining the army at 32 years of age, and he had learned his trade in the space of 8 years, all spent with the same unit, rising from commanding a company to the whole division in that period. Despite this, he was an experienced and highly decorated officer, and although he had been in command of a panzer-regiment for nearly ten months, it was his first test as a division commander.

In the centre of the *XXXXVIII.PzK* was the *1.SS Panzer-Division 'Leibstandarte-SS-Adolf Hitler'*. This unit had initially been constituted as a full division on 15 July 1942 when the former *Leibstandarte SS-Adolf Hitler* was reorganised to become the *SS-Division (mot.) 'Leibstandarte-SS-Adolf Hitler'*. In November the same year, it was re-organised again to become the *SS-Panzergrenadier-Division 'Leibstandarte SS Adolf Hitler'* before being re-organised again in October 1943 as a full panzer-division, now with the title *1.SS Panzer-Division 'Leibstandarte-SS-Adolf-Hitler'*. Before being organised as a full division, the *'Leibstandarte'* had participated in the campaign in Poland and also taken part in the campaign in the West, fighting in the Netherlands, Belgium and France. It remained in eastern France until early March 1941 when it was transferred eastwards to Bulgaria and Romania prior to taking part in the invasions of Yugoslavia and Greece in April 1941. By May 1941, it had been transferred to Czechoslovakia for reorganisation and refit before being sent to Poland in preparation for the attack on the Soviet Union. It was attached to the *Panzergruppe 1* under Army Group South and advanced through Ukraine before finding itself on defensive duties along the Mius and Donets rivers beginning in November 1941. It later spent a short time on coastal defence duties around Mariupol' in June 1942, before returning to France in July 1942 to be re-organised as a division. It returned to the Eastern Front in January 1943 to the region around Khar'kov, where it took part first in the defence against the Soviet operation 'Star' to capture that city, and then the German counterattack to re-take it after it had been lost. By the end of March 1943, the division had been withdrawn to the rear area where it took part in anti-partisan operations before preparing for the forthcoming German offensive at Kursk. Following the failure of this operation, the division was transferred to northern Italy towards the end of July 1943 where it was re-organised as a full panzer-division with effect from 22 October 1943. Just a week later, it was returned to the southern sector of the Eastern Front where it was attached to the *XXXXVIII.PzK*. The division initially unloaded in the Kirovograd area, but after only a few days it was ordered northwards with the *Korps* to try and counter the Soviet operation which had begun on 3 November to break out of the Kiev bridgehead. Since that time, it had remained with the *Korps* as it first defended and then counterattacked in a number of successive actions to try and restore the German line. It was still in the middle of the last one of these when the Soviet offensive began, holding a line beginning from the north-western part of Shershni and heading through the eastern edge of the wood west of Meleni. From there the attached *Reserve-Grenadier-Regiment 212* held the line east of Graby to a point three kilometres south of Dubrova, at which point it swung away to the east along the southern edge of the wooded area south of Bolyarka. In all, its sector was about 12 kilometres long. The division was commanded by *SS Brigade-Führer und Generalmajor der Waffen SS* Theodor Wisch. Born in December 1907, Wisch was then 36 years old and had been a member of the *NSDAP* and the *Allgemeine SS* since 1930. He had transferred to the *SS Sonderkommando Berlin* in 1933, and was still serving with the unit in November 1933 when it was re-named the *Leibstandarte SS-Adolf Hitler*. He had assumed command of its *1.Kompanie* in October the same year, and was still its commanding officer at the outbreak of the war, when he led the unit through the Polish campaign, winning the Iron Cross in the process. In November 1939 he was transferred to take command of the newly forming *IV.(Wach)Bataillon* of the '*Leibstandarte*', with which unit he then took part in the campaigns in the West and the Balkans. At the end of May 1941, following the conclusion of the latter campaign, he had been transferred to take command of the *II./Leibstandarte SS-Adolf Hitler*, a post he then retained until July 1942. In this role, he took part in the Russian campaign from the outset, receiving the Knight's Cross on 15 September 1941 for his part in the heavy defensive fighting west of Zhitomir during July. He was wounded in February 1942, but returned to the division in the beginning of July 1942 to take command of the *Infanterie-Regiment 2 'Leibstandarte SS-Adolf Hitler'*. He was promoted to *SS Standartenführer* on 30 January 1943 and took over command of the 'LSSAH' on 4 July 1943, the day before the start of the Kursk offensive. In recognition of this new command, he was promoted again, this time to *SS-Oberführer*. Wisch was therefore unusual in much the same way as Schulz, the commander of the *7.Panzer-Division*, in that he had served with the same unit throughout the war. He was therefore an experienced commander, despite his years, having served at different levels, but importantly both he and his division had been on the Eastern Front throughout the previous 12 months.

The right wing of the *Korps* was held by the *1.Panzer-Division*, one of the five original peacetime armoured divisions formed by the Germans in 1935. It had taken part in the campaign against Poland before returning to its home bases in Germany in early October for rest and refit. At the end of November 1939, the division was transferred to the Dortmund area as part of the preparations for the campaign in the West. In February 1940 it was moved the western bank of the river Rhine, and then in March it was sent to the southern Eifel and the river Mosel. It took part in the invasion of France, heading through Luxembourg and Belgium under the *XIX.Panzerkorps*. At the end of the campaign, the division remained for a while in France until it was transferred to East Prussia during early September 1940. It remained there until June 1941 when it participated in the invasion of the Soviet Union as part of *Panzergruppe 4* under Army Group North. Having reached the outskirts of Leningrad by the end of September, it was transferred southwards to join the *Panzergruppe 3* for the final drive on Moscow. By February 1942, it was under the *9.Armee* in the area west and south-west of Rzhev where it remained until the end of the year, involved in a series of major defensive operations. During the first half of January 1943, the division was transported back to northern France where it was re-built and re-fitted. On 20 May 1943 it received instructions to head east again, but this time to Greece where it was to secure the Peloponnese and the Greek mainland from the threatened Allied invasion. Following the surrender of Italy in September that year and the subsequent occupation by German forces of the Peloponnese, the division was given orders to transfer back to the Eastern Front. The main transport began to arrive in Kirovograd on 2 November just before the Soviets began their operation to break out of the Kiev bridgehead away to the north. A week later the division was heading north to shore up the front of the *4.Panzerarmee* south of Kiev, and on 12 November 1943 it was attached to the *XXXXVIII.PzK*. It too participated in the subsequent operations throughout November and December as the *PzAOK 4* struggled to restore its front line west of Kiev, and by 23 December it was holding the northern wing of the *XXXXVIII.PzK* salient which was trying to push forward along the road towards Malin. It was deployed in a salient projecting south-eastwards either side of the Korosten'-Kiev railway with its lead elements around Pristantsionnoe[8] north of Chopovichi, and its left flank running back towards Stremigorod where it maintained contact with the right wing of the *291.Infanterie-Division* under the *LIX. AK*. Its sector was almost 15 kilometres in length, but given the nature of its offensive operations, the front line was not manned continuously. The division was commanded by *Generalleutnant* Walter Krüger, although he would remain in charge only until the end of the year. At that time, command would pass to *Generalmajor* Richard Koll, a 46-year old career soldier. During the First World War he had served in a number of different signals-related positions, a specialism he retained for a short period after the war. Later he served in a series of posts with responsibility for motor transport before being transferred to the *2.Panzer-Brigade* as adjutant in October 1935. On 12 October 1937, Koll was transferred to the *1.leichte Division* as commanding officer of the *II./Panzer-Regiment 11*, a position he still held at the outbreak of the war, having risen to the rank of *Oberstleutnant*. He took part in the campaign in Poland, commanding the battalion before the division was re-organised as the *6.Panzer-Division* on 18 October 1939. He was given command of the *Panzer-Regiment 11* on 1 January 1940, leading the unit through the campaign in the West before the division returned to Germany in July 1940. By December that year, it had been moved to East Prussia, remaining there until it took part in the invasion of the Soviet Union. Koll had meanwhile been promoted to *Oberst* back in December 1940, and now led his regiment through the first year of the campaign in the East, serving under the *6.Panzer-Division*. The division was initially deployed under *Panzergruppe 4* on the northern sector, but was later transferred to Army Group Centre where it took part in the drive against Moscow in December 1941. Following the failure of the German offensive, the division remained on the central sector and took part in the defensive battles in the Rzhev area during the spring of 1942 before being transferred to France at the end of April 1942. Koll left the division during its period of rest and refit, moving to the *OKH Führer-Reserve* on 1 July 1942. In September 1942 he moved to the *OKH* where he served as head of the office responsible for vehicle repairs, remaining there until July the following year, at which point he took on a similar role under the *OKW*. On 20 November 1943 he returned to the *OKH Führer-Reserve*, attending the division commanders' course until 14 December 1943. A week after the Zhitomir-Berdichev operation began, Koll was transferred to take temporary command of the *1.Panzer-Division* when Krüger left to take command of the *LVIII. Reserve-Panzerkorps* in France. Both division and commander had previously fought on the Eastern Front, though neither had recent experience. Koll had no experience as a division commander, and had not seen action in the Soviet Union since the spring of 1942. Nevertheless, he did have 18 months' experience commanding a *Panzer-Regiment*, about nine of which had been served in the East. The division too was lacking recent experience, and although it had previously spent 18 months in the Soviet Union, it had been involved in no major operations for almost a year.

---

8   Referred to as Bahnhof Tschepowitschi (or Chopovichi station) in the German records.

THE GERMAN SITUATION

Holding the far right wing of the *4.Panzerarmee* was the *LIX.AK*, commanded by *General der Infanterie* Kurt von der Chevallerie, a post he had held for a long time, since 28 December 1941. He was another career soldier, and had turned 52 years old on 23 December 1943. He had joined the army in 1910 and served through First World War in a number of appointments, initially as an infantry company commander, but later in a number of different staff positions after having been wounded in July 1915. After the war, he was again appointed to the command of different infantry companies, before rising through the ranks to command first a battalion and then in October 1934 a regiment. By October 1937 he was back in a staff position, serving in the army General Staff and being promoted to *Generalmajor* in March 1939. He did not serve in the Polish campaign, but assumed command of the newly-forming *83.Infanterie-Division* on 1 December 1939, leading the division through the campaign in the West in the summer of 1940. A year later, on 1 December 1940, he was transferred to take command of the *99.leichte Infanterie-Division*, then forming up as a new division of the *12.Welle*. Newly promoted to *Generalleutnant*, he led the unit briefly during the invasion of the Soviet Union, where it was deployed as part of the *6.Armee* on the southern sector, but by November 1941 it was back in Germany to be re-organised into the *7.Gebirgs-Division*. Von der Chevallerie was moved into the *OKH Führer-Reserve* for a few weeks before being transferred to France to take temporary command of the *Höheres Kommando z.b.V. LIX* on 28 December 1941. This headquarters was formally re-designated as the *LIX.Armeekorps* on 20 January 1942, and on 1 February 1942 von der Chevallerie was given formal command of the headquarters, in recognition of which he was promoted to *General der Infanterie*. At the same time, the new headquarters was transferred to the Eastern Front where it was attached the *3.Panzerarmee* under Army Group Centre, and deployed in the Velikiye Luki and Velizh areas. It remained in the same area until October 1943 following the battle of Kursk when it was attached to the *4.Panzerarmee* as Army Group South fell back towards the river Dnepr. Apart from a couple of spells, first between June and July 1942 and again between January and March 1943, von der Chevallerie had remained the *Korps'* commander through almost two years of fighting on the Eastern Front, and both he and his staff had considerable experience as a result.

On the right wing of the *LIX.AK* was the *291.Infanterie-Division*, formed in February 1940 as part of the *8.Welle*. It was transferred to the Western Front as the campaign began, moving through the Netherlands and Belgium into France by the end of May 1940. It took part in the second phase of the battle for France, before securing the newly-established demarcation line by the end of June. Towards the end of July, the division was ordered to East Prussia where it passed the winter in training and constructing field fortifications. It spent the spring of 1941 training and preparing for the forthcoming invasion of the Soviet Union, and was attached to the *18.Armee* under Army Group North when the campaign began. It remained on the northern sector, taking part in the Leningrad campaign before remaining on the defensive Volkhov front throughout nearly all 1942. In November that year, the division was transferred to Army Group Centre where it took part in the operation to relieve Velikiye Luki. It remained on that sector until September 1943 when it was transferred further south to the Kiev area where it was allocated to the *LIX.AK* under the *4.Panzerarmee*. It took part in the defence against the Soviet offensive to break out of the bridgehead north of Kiev, falling back towards Korosten' before participating in the re-capture of the town on 27

November. It was then involved in the *XXXXVIII.PzK* counterattack south-east of the town until, by 24 December, it held a line running along the railway from the south-eastern edge of the town towards Khotinovka, a sector of about six kilometres. The division was commanded by *Generalleutnant* Werner Göritz, a 51-year old career soldier who had first joined the army in 1911. He had been promoted to *Oberst* on 1 October 1937, before being appointed to take command of the *Infanterie-Regiment 134* under the *44.Infanterie-Division* on 10 November 1938. He was still serving in this post when the war broke out, and led the regiment through the campaigns in Poland and the West. On 18 June 1940, he was moved into the *Führer-Reserve* of the *OKH* before being appointed as the *Wehrmachts-Verkehrsdirektor*[9] in Paris on 29 June 1940. He held the post for just a few months before being transferred to become the head of the *Eisenbahn-Transport-Abteilung Ost*[10] on 15 November 1940. He stayed in this post for over two years, taking on additional responsibilities for the north-east in September 1941 and being promoted to *Generalmajor* on 1 December 1941. On 1 March 1942, he was transferred to the Eastern Front where he took up post as the *General des Transportwesens*[11] under Army Group Centre. He remained in this post for only two months before returning to the *Führer-Reserve*. On 19 June 1942 he was given temporary command of the *291.Infanterie-Division* while it was engaged on the Volkhov front, being confirmed as permanent commander of the division on 1 August 1942. In recognition of his command position, he was promoted to *Generalleutnant* on 1 January 1943. He had therefore been in charge of the division for 18 months, and shared a common experience with it since its days on the Volkhov front. Much of this experience had been on a fairly static front, but both unit and commander did have considerable knowledge of conditions of the Eastern Front.

On the left of the *LIX.AK*, and therefore holding the northern wing of Army Group South, was the *Korps-Abteilung C*. This was the second *Korps-Abteilung* deployed by the *PzAOK 4*, and had been formed on 2 November 1943 by the amalgamation of the *183.*, the *217.*, and the *339.Infanterie-Divisions*. The *183.Infanterie-Division* had served on the Eastern Front since August 1941, predominantly under Army Group Centre, on the Moscow, Gzhatsk and Spas-Demensk sectors. During the course of the retreat to Gzhatsk in March 1942, its *Infanterie-Regiment 343* had been disbanded and the division was left with seven infantry battalions. In August 1943 it was transferred southwards to the Bakhmach sector, being attached to the *XIII.AK* in September and the *LIX.AK* the following month. The *217.Infanterie-Division* had been on the Eastern Front since June 1941, serving under Army Group North until September 1943 when it was transferred to *LIX.AK* to bolster the northern wing of the *4.Panzerarmee* in the retreat to the Dnepr. The *339.Infanterie-Division* had first been transferred to the Eastern Front in August 1941 when it was deployed in the rear area of Army Group Centre. It was primarily engaged against partisan units for the rest of the year, before being attached to the *2.Panzerarmee* in the Bryansk area in January 1942. It remained on that sector until September 1943 when it too was transferred south to join the *LIX.AK* as it pulled back to the Dnepr. At the start of the Soviet Zhitomir-Berdichev operation, the *Korps-Abteilung* was holding the line east of Korosten', from its south-eastern edge near the

---

9   The Armed Forces Traffic Director.
10 The Railway Transport Section (East).
11 General for Transport Affairs.

railway junction running northwards on the western side of Grozino and Nemirovka, across the river Uzh and on to Bekhi. At this point, the front turned north-westwards to run to Solovy, although outside the villages the line was only really held as strongpoints on the road and railway to Ignatpol'. In total the sector was about 22 kilometres long. The *Korps-Abteilung* was under the command of *Generalleutnant* Wolfgang Lange, the previous commander of the *339.Infanterie-Division*. Lange was 45 years old and had joined the German army during the First World War. By 1938 he was serving as a *Major* and working as a lecturer in the *Kriegsakademie*, being promoted to *Oberstleutnant* in March 1939. At the outbreak of the war, he was appointed to the staff of Army Group C, then responsible for the Western Front before moving on 5 February 1940 to become the *Ia* for the newly formed *XXXVIII.AK*. He remained with the *Korps* until May 1940 before being posted on 1 August 1940 to an inspectorate with the *OKH*. Nearly two years later he was given a field command for the first time during the war, taking up the post of commanding officer of the newly-formed *Infanterie-Regiment 145* on 20 July 1942. In this position, he served with the *65.Infanterie-Division* for seven months, during which time it was stationed on occupation duties in the West under the *15.Armee*. He left the division in February 1943 to take command of the *Grenadier-Regiment 880* which was to be used to re-build the *305.Infanterie-Division* following its destruction in Stalingrad. On 25 April 1943, Lange left the regiment to begin the training course for division commanders, and following this, he was posted on 1 October 1943 to take command of the *339.Infanterie-Division*, just after it had been transferred south to join the *4.Panzerarmee*. He therefore had little experience of command at division level and no experience of the Eastern Front. His new division was also of limited experience, as, despite having been in the East since 1941, it had been primarily engaged on static fronts or behind the lines in operations against partisans. It was moreover severely weakened, and would soon be used to form part of the *Korps-Abteilung C*.

The *147.Reserve-Division* was also deployed in the region, but it was not a combat unit and was never committed as a complete division. It was however caught up in the Zhitomir-Berdichev operation, as many of its subordinate units were attached to other divisions at different times. The division had been formed in October 1942 when the German Replacement Army decided the previous month to split the replacement and training functions for which it was responsible. This functional split became a physical split when, beginning in October 1942, the existing replacement and training battalions were divided, with the replacement elements remaining in Germany while the training battalions were transferred into the occupied territories around Europe. At this point, the former *Division Nr.147*, which had been based in Augsburg in Germany as the second replacement division for *Wehrkreis VII*, was re-named the *147.Reserve-Division* and moved to the Novograd-Volynskii area in north-western Ukraine. Here it was attached the *LXII.Reservekorps*, itself newly established on 15 September 1942 and based in Dubno to control the reserve divisions in the area under the command of the *Wehrmachtsbefehlshaber Ukraine*. It had remained in the region since that time, and by early December 1943, the division was deployed as follows:

- *Reserve-Grenadier-Regiment 212* based at Korosten'
  - *Reserve-Grenadier-Bataillon 63* at Borodyanka
  - *Reserve-Grenadier-Bataillon 316* at Korosten'
  - *Reserve-Grenadier-Bataillon 320* at Malin
  - *Reserve-Grenadier-Bataillon 423* at Belokorovichi
  - *Reserve-Grenadier-Bataillon 468* at Olevsk[12]
- *Reserve-Grenadier-Regiment 268* based at Novograd-Volynskii
  - *Reserve-Grenadier-Bataillon 91* at Korets
  - *Reserve-Grenadier-Bataillon 488* at Novograd-Volynskii
- *Reserve-Artillerie-Abteilung 27*
- *Reserve-Pionier-Bataillon 27*

As the Soviets pushed westwards out of the Kiev bridgehead throughout November 1943, elements of the division were committed to strengthen the front line troops, and by the end of December 1943 the *Reserve-Grenadier-Regiment 212* was deployed with the *XXXXVIII.PzK* holding the line west of Meleni between the *7.Panzer-Division* and the *1.SS Panzer-Division 'LSSAH'*. Most of the remainder of the division was assembled in the vicinity of Novograd-Volynskii and comprised the following:

- HQ *Reserve-Grenadier-Regiment 268*, together with the 13th and 14th Companies
- *Reserve-Grenadier-Bataillon 488* (less one company)
- *Reserve-Grenadier-Bataillon 320* (depleted)
- *Reserve-Grenadier-Bataillon 423* (depleted)
- Three companies of the *Reserve-Pionier-Bataillon 27*
- Two batteries of the *Reserve-Artillerie-Abteilung 27*.

At about this time, the division was also in the middle of a re-organisation which had been ordered by the *OKH*, and its situation regarding weapons and equipment was far from satisfactory. There were on average just six light machine-guns available to each company, and overall the division possessed just five heavy anti-tank guns and no close-range anti-tank weapons at all. As far as artillery was concerned, there were no modern weapons available, and the only guns on the establishment were of an older type. In command of the division was *Generalleutnant* Otto Matterstock, a 54-year old professional soldier. He had joined the army back in 1909 and fought during the First World War before transferring to the Bavarian State Police in April 1920. He transferred back to the army in October 1935, being promoted to *Oberst* on 1 January 1937 prior to becoming *Kommandant* in Würzburg in 1938. Just before the outbreak of the war, he was transferred to become commanding officer of the newly formed *Infanterie-Ersatz-Bataillon 73*, holding the post until 1 December 1939 when he was appointed as commander of the new *Infanterie-Regiment 330* under the *183.Infanterie-Division*. He remained with the division throughout 1940, taking part in the campaign in the West and the subsequent occupation. In July 1940, the division was transferred to occupied Czechoslovakia where it continued its training for the remainder of the

---

12 This battalion was transferred from the division on 28 December 1943 and used to form the *Grenadier-Regiment 957*.

year. In April 1941, the division took part in the invasion of Yugoslavia, but Matterstock was transferred on 3 May 1941 to take command of the *716.Infanterie-Division*, then forming up ready for transfer to occupied France. On 1 September 1941, he was finally promoted to *Generalmajor*, and he went on to command the division for almost two years, being promoted again on 1 November 1942 to *Generalleutnant*. He was finally posted to take charge of the *147.Reserve-Division* on 17 September 1943, just as the Army Group South began its retreat towards the Dnepr. Neither he nor his division had the experience to face the forthcoming Soviet offensive, but they would be dragged into it nonetheless.

Also deployed in the rear areas was the *454.Sicherungs-Division*. This was a security division not intended for front line combat, and was one of nine formed for use of the Eastern Front. It had originally been formed in March 1940 on the basis of a normal infantry regiment, the *Infanterie-Regiment 375* from the *221.Infanterie-Division*, but had undergone a number of organisational changes by the end of 1943. It had served under Army Group South since the beginning of the invasion of the Soviet Union, operating under a number of different headquarters, depending on the circumstances at the time. Although it predominantly operated in the rear area, it had sometimes been attached forward to different *Korps* level headquarters, being involved in actions as various as security duties, mopping up, anti-partisan operations, and front line offensive and defensive manoeuvres. Throughout the summer of 1943, it had been deployed in the Army Group South rear area, before being transferred in September to the Kiev area where it was attached to the *XXXXII.AK* under *PzAOK 4*. By this time it comprised:

- *Sicherungs-Regiment 360*
- *Sicherungs-Regiment 375*
- *Ost-Reiter-Regiment 454*
- *Artillerie-Abteilung 454*
- *Ost-Pionier-Bataillon 454*

Elements of the *Sicherungs-Regiment 375* were deployed on the left wing of the *LIX.AK*, protecting the left flank of the *Korps-Abteilung C* on a line running from from Solovy through Bovsuny to Luginy and Glukhova. The division was under the command of *Generalleutnant* Hellmuth Koch, then 52 years old. He had joined the army in 1909, serving through the First World War, before transferring in 1920 to the police. On 1 October 1935, he had transferred back to the army as an *Oberstleutnant* in command of the *II./Infanterie-Regiment 84*. In June 1937 he was posted to the office of the *Ausbildungs-Leiter* 2 in Glatz, and was still charge of the unit on 26 August when it was used to form the *Infanterie-Regiment 350*. He therefore commanded this regiment when the war broke out, and took part in the Polish campaign under the *221.Infanterie-Division*. He remained with the division in Poland on occupation duties throughout the winter and spring of 1940, being promoted to *Oberst* on 1 December 1939, before being transferred to the West where he took part in the latter part of the campaign against France. Following this the division was sent on leave in July 1940, before being reconstituted in March 1941 and used to form a number of security divisions, including the *454.Sicherungs-Division*. Koch was posted to take command of the division on

9 December 1941, and had been in charge ever since that time, seeing it through all different campaigns it had seen throughout the southern Soviet Union.

☆

These then were the units with which the *4.Panzerarmee* would try and oppose the forthcoming Soviet offensive, and it will be interesting to review how well prepared they were to deal with the assault in terms of personnel and equipment. At the outset of the campaign against the Soviet Union, each German *Infanterie-Division* had comprised three regiments, each of three battalions. However, the large number of re-organisations and disbandments that had taken place in the field since 1942 had effectively caused the original scheme to be redundant. In general, the infantry component had been reduced to six battalions from the original nine, although where manpower allowed, a seventh battalion was sometimes retained either as a cycle battalion or just a spare infantry battalion acting as a divisional component. As a result of these re-organisations, many divisions had converted to a two-regiment structure, each retaining three battalions, although others had still managed to retain the original three-regiment structure, but only with two battalions each. All these necessary *ad-hoc* arrangements were later formalised in an instruction issued by the *Oberkommando des Heeres* (*OKH*) in October 1943.[13] This introduced a new organisation, for almost all areas of the army, known as the '*Infanterie-Division neuer Art*' (*Inf.Div. n.A.*), or 'Infantry Division New Type'. According to the new tables, each division was now to re-organise with three infantry regiments; each comprising a headquarters staff, two infantry battalions, a howitzer company and an anti-tank company. Divisions which had previously disbanded their third regimental HQ were to re-establish them, and the battalions of the new third regiment were generally formed by re-numbering the respective *III.Battalion* from each of the other two regiments. According to the new tables of organisation and equipment, the infantry regiment should have a total strength of 2,008 men, with 48 officers, 316 non-commissioned officers, and 1,644 other ranks. Each of its two infantry battalions should have deployed 708 men, comprising 15 officers, 113 NCOs, and 580 other ranks. Similarly, each battalion was to have three infantry companies of 142 men, with two officers, 21 NCOs, and 119 other ranks. This was the official establishment of an *Infanterie-Division* by December 1943 when the Zhitomir-Berdichev operation began, but as might be expected the situation in the field was markedly different. By this time, German manpower had fallen significantly, and units at every level were seriously under strength compared to the standard tables of organisation and equipment. The *4.Panzerarmee* submitted weekly combat strength returns to the *OKH*, and these may be used to gain an insight into the strengths of these units around this time. In compiling these returns, the divisions were instructed to classify their constituent battalions according to a five-point scale, depending on their actual combat strength, as shown in Table 2.[14]

---

13 *OKH*, GenStdH/Org.A Nr. I/3197/43 dated 2 October 1943.
14 'Combat strength' in this context is a translation of the German word *Kampfstärke*, which was intended to include those soldiers who would be either engaged directly in the fighting or forward of a battalion command post and in immediate support of those engaged directly in the fighting. See *OKH/Gen. St.d.H. Org Abt. 1/2000/44 g.*, dated 25 Apr 44.

THE GERMAN SITUATION

Table 2: Categories shown in *4.Panzerarmee* weekly combat strengths returns

Rating	Equivalent	Combat strength
Stark	Strong	> 400
Mittelstark	Medium strong	300 – 400
Durchschnittlich	Average	200 – 300
Schwach	Weak	100 – 200
Abgekämpft	Exhausted	< 100

From these figures in can be seen that an infantry battalion at anything over 56% strength was considered strong, whilst a figure of around 250 men was viewed as average and a battalion was only regarded as 'weak' once its combat manpower had been reduced to the equivalent of a single company. Unfortunately, there are no *PzAOK 4* returns available for the last week in December 1943, and the latest relates to 5 December almost three weeks before the start of the offensive. Summarised, this return indicates that the divisions of the *4.Panzerarmee* deployed maximum and minimum combat strengths as shown in Table 3.[15]

Table 3: Maximum and minimum combat strengths of *4.Panzerarmee* at 5 December 1943

Unit	Minimum	Maximum
25.Panzer-Division	2,800	4,900
2.Fallschirmjäger-Division	2,700	4,600
1.Panzer-Division	2,700	4,600
75.Infanterie-Division	2,900	4,300
198.Infanterie-Division	2,900	4,100
112.Infanterie-Division	2,500	3,900
168.Infanterie-Division	2,600	3,700
1.SS Panzer-Division 'LSSAH'	2,200	3,700
291.Infanterie-Division	1,900	3,000
34.Infanterie-Division	1,700	2,500
Korps-Abteilung C	1,310	2,400
8.Panzer-Division	1,310	2,400
82.Infanterie-Division	1,500	2,300
340.Infanterie-Division	1,200	2,100
68.Infanterie-Division	930	1,900
208.Infanterie-Division	710	1,400
7.Panzer-Division	810	1,400
19.Panzer-Division	610	1,300
2.SS Panzer-Division 'Das Reich'	800	1,200
213.Sicherungs-Division	600	900
88.Infanterie-Division	200	300

15 *PzAOK 4*, unreferenced table dated 5 December 1943. It should be noted that the relative strengths of some the divisions is skewed by the cross attachment of battalions between them.

Unit	Minimum	Maximum
Totals	34,880	56,900

These figures are based upon the standard component infantry units, together with other infantry-based elements such as reconnaissance, engineer, and replacement units, but exclude manpower in supporting elements such as artillery and anti-tank units. Taking the mean of the minimum and maximum figures, the *PzAOK 4* probably deployed a combat strength of something around just over 46,000 men. In contrast, a standard *Inf. Div n.A.* would have deployed a total of 7,352 men in its comparable units, and a standard regiment a total of 2,008. Over half these infantry divisions were therefore operating at a combat strength equivalent to a single regiment or less, and even the strongest of them could probably not deploy the equivalent of two regiments. The next available returns are dated from 8 January 1944, and show a similar picture – see Table 4.[16]

Table 4: Maximum and minimum combat strengths of *4.Panzerarmee* at 8 January 1944

Unit	Minimum	Maximum
4.Gebirgs-Division	3,600	6,300
1.SS Panzer-Division 'LSSAH'	1,730	2,900
1.Panzer-Division	1,610	2,600
1.Infanterie-Division	1,700	2,600
168.Infanterie-Division	1,710	2,500
16.Panzer-Division	1,600	2,500
Korps-Abteilung C	1,310	2,200
18.Artillerie-Division	1,300	2,000
7.Panzer-Division	1,100	1,800
454.Sicherungs-Division	800	1,400
19.Panzer-Division	460	1,400
291.Infanterie-Division	530	1,100
20.Panzergrenadier-Division	520	1,000
25.Panzer-Division	110	300
Totals	18,080	30,600

Using the mean again, this produces a combat strength of around 24,500 men, although since the *1.Panzerarmee* had assumed responsibility for much of the sector by this time, its totals need to be added to gain a complete picture of the German forces opposing the 1st Ukrainian Front. On the basis of the weekly return for 8 January 1944,[17] the formations of the *PzAOK 1* deployed combat strengths as set out in Table 5.

16 *PzAOK 4*, Ia Nr. 198/44 geh. dated 10 Jan 1944, and *PzAOK 4*, Ia Nr. 295/44 geh. dated 12 Jan 1944. The picture is incomplete as it excludes those divisions which had been pulled out of the front line for refit, including the *68.*, *208.*, and *340.Infanterie-Divisions* as well as the *213.Sicherungs-Division*. However, the fact that these units were no longer capable of sustained front line operations suggests strongly that their combat strength would have been negligible by this time.

17 *PzAOK 1*, Ia Nr.32/44 g.Kdos dated 10 Jan 44 and 12 Jan 44.

THE GERMAN SITUATION

Table 5: Maximum and minimum combat strengths of *1.Panzerarmee* at 8 January 1944

Unit	Minimum	Maximum
34.Infanterie-Division	1,500	2,400
75.Infanterie-Division	1,600	2,500
82.Infanterie-Division	1,400	1,900
88.Infanterie-Division	1,100	2,200
198.Infanterie-Division	1,600	2,400
Korps-Abteilung B	2,400	3,600
6.Panzer-Division	700	1,100
17.Panzer-Division	900	1,500
Totals	11,200	17,600

This produces a mean figure of around 14,500 which, when added to the *PzAOK 4* totals, suggests a combined combat strength of about 39,000 men at the end of the first week in January 1944, a drop of about 7,000 from the figure of 46,000 in early December.

Notwithstanding this obvious weakness in infantry strength, much of the combat power of a *Panzerarmee* might ordinarily be expected to be provided by its armoured components. In this context it may be noted here that at this stage of the war a German *Panzer-Division* generally deployed a single armoured regiment comprising two armoured battalions, one with *Panzer V 'Panther'* and the other with the older and less capable *Panzer IV*. Each battalion in turn comprised three *Panzer* companies, each of which should have been equipped with 14 tanks, two in a headquarters platoon, and four in each of three platoons. With an additional six tanks for its headquarters, each armoured battalion should therefore have deployed a total of 48 tanks. A few days before the offensive began, the *4.Panzerarmee* collected returns from its subordinate units, setting out the status of their armoured vehicles.[18] These figures are summarised in Table 6 and indicate that the *PzAOK 4* deployed a total of 936 armoured vehicles, of which 429 (or around 46%) were actually operational.

Table 6: Summary of *4.Panzerarmee* armour strength on 20 December 1943

Vehicle	Operational/Total	% operational
Panzer I	2/2	100
Panzer II	9/17	53
Panzer III	22/55	40
Panzer IV	143/329	43
Panzer V 'Panther'	28/139	20
Panzer VI 'Tiger'	11/58	19
Sturmgeschütz	131/207	63
Panzerjäger (Sfl.)	83/129	64

18 These returns were submitted separately by the units concerned, using the common date of 20 December 1943, so there is no single reference containing the information summarised here.

A more detailed breakdown of these figures is shown in Table 7, and from this data it will be seen that of the 507 unserviceable vehicles, 386 were undergoing forward repair with their respective units, while the other 121 were in depth repair at maintenance depots in the rear area. All other things being equal, there would have been a reasonable expectation that the number of operational armour would increase as vehicles were returned to serviceability by their own units. Despite this, it can be seen that the whole of the *PzAOK 4* could not muster the equivalent of a single operational *Panzer V* battalion, whilst at the same time it could put no more than the equivalent of three *Panzer IV* battalions into the field.

At the headquarters of Army Group South, von Manstein was only too well aware of the problems facing many of his divisions. Just before the middle of December, the commanding officers of the *1.Panzerarmee* and the *8.Armee* had both submitted reports regarding the condition of individual units, and von Manstein had passed these to the office of the *Generalstab des Heeres* (the Chief of the army General Staff) to put before Hitler as examples of the poor condition of the troops.[19] In informing his respective army commanders that he had done this, von Manstein repeated that the Army Group was well aware of the condition of the troops, and knew only too well that they were continually called upon to give more than should be expected. The Army Group had repeatedly brought this to the attention of the *OKH*, and von Manstein himself had seized any opportunity which presented itself to inform Hitler personally. But the fact remained that Army Group South would only have been in a position to assist the army commanders if it had reserves of its own, and even this would only permit a short period of rest and recuperation for individual divisions. The situation at the time however, with the lack of available forces and the already stretched front line, meant that even this small measure was impossible. The only other real possibility was the formation of strong reserves by an effective shortening of the frontline, but this had been rejected out of hand by Hitler, on spurious operational grounds. It remained to be seen whether the troops, in their existing condition, would prove able to conduct a wide-ranging withdrawal. On the other hand, as von Manstein pointed out, it was likely that the Soviet formations facing the Army Group were also more or less at the end of their strength, particularly since they too had been engaged in continuous offensive operations for five months. They must have suffered heavy casualties over this period, and he hoped that they would not be able to carry on much further, at least in the short term. In this, he appears to have seriously misjudged the ability of the Soviet military to maintain and even increase its resource levels while simultaneously conducting large-scale offensive operations. As events would soon indicate, von Manstein's assessment was over-optimistic. Though he acknowledged that the demands made upon the troops were hard, he also made it clear that, for the foreseeable future, there was no alternative if the continuing Soviet offensives were ever to be brought to a halt. Although the situation for the German divisions was extremely difficult, he reminded his troops of how the Russians would be viewing the same situation. Despite the expenditure of huge human, armour and ammunition resources in unrelenting attacks over a number of weeks, in conditions which von Manstein compared to some kind of sacrifice, he believed that they had still not managed to achieve their objectives, in spite of gaining considerable ground. This too seemed optimistic, and it is difficult to agree with this assessment, almost irrespective of

---

19 *H.Gr.Süd*, Ia Nr.4205/43 g.Kdos. dated 15 Dec 43.

which measure is used. In the absence of any more tangible benefit though, von Manstein was left with only one option. He could do no more than encourage his commanders, and exhort them to pass on these thoughts to their subordinates to try and prevent them from coming to the conclusion, however understandable, that there was no point in continuing. His final request was for the commanders to check again and again for any weakening of Soviet forces on any sectors, or even for any change to a defensive posture, to see if there was any chance of pulling units out of the front, to form reserves and give the troops some chance for recovery.

☆

Such was the German situation towards the end of December 1943, and in the meantime, the Soviets had been making their final preparations for the forthcoming offensive while the Germans were still struggling to shore up the left wing in the area east of Korosten'. On 19 December 1943, as the majority of the *4.Panzerarmee* front lay relatively quiet, Raus began what would be the last of a series of counterattacks to restore the German front line following the success of the Soviet offensive which had begun back in early November. The *XXXXVIII.PzK*, supported by elements of the *LIX.AK* to its left, went over to the offensive east of Zlobichi, and following a planned artillery barrage, the *Korps* edged its way into the Soviet defences. It broke the initial resistance and pressed on quickly through a number of minefields, making good progress to the north and north-east. The first day's objectives were reached and passed. The sector appeared to be defended by only the Soviet 112th Rifle Division, recently strengthened with the arrival of a large number of recently recruited local civilians, with a few tanks in support. Away to the south-east, the *7.Panzer-Division* was opposed by the 2nd Guards Airborne Division which put up a stiff resistance, but which nevertheless began to fall back northwards. For the following day, 20 December, it was intended that the *XXXXVIII.PzK* would wheel to the south-east towards Malin and destroy the Soviet forces on the north bank of the river Irsha, particularly in the Chopovichi area. The strike was to meet up with an attack northwards by elements of the *7.Panzer-Division* which would cross the Irsha to reach the area north of Slobodka. On the left, the *LIX.AK* would continue to support the attack, moving up to the Gnidovka stream.

The 20 December proved to another quiet day for the *PzAOK 4*, the only action continuing to be on the left wing where the *XXXXVIII.PzK* was still pressing ahead with its attack. The *Korps* ran into pre-prepared Soviet defensive positions, held amongst other units by elements of the 4th Guards Tank Corps and the 25th Tank Corps. Although the *XXXXVIII.PzK* had managed to break into the positions between the road and railway north of Chopovichi, it was difficult to foresee any further major progress. A planned assault seemed to provide the only chance of success, but this would not be helped by the tank-supported attacks now being made against the *Korps'* northern flank. The *LIX.AK* too made little progress, with the defending Soviet units standing firm in the Singai area, just north-east of Korosten'. But despite the lack of any real success in the first two days' fighting, the *4.Panzerarmee* decided to press ahead with the *XXXXVIII.PzK* attack on 21 December, although south of the Irsha the *7.Panzer-Division* was ordered to go over to the defensive until such time as the main assault looked more promising.

But instead of providing the success which had been hoped for, 21 December proved to be a turning point for the *PzAOK 4*. Over on the left flank, the Soviets went over to the counterattack against the leading units of the *XXXXVIII.PzK* north-west of Chopovichi, attacking from the south-east, east and north-east. In addition to elements of the 4th Guards Tank Corps and the 25th Tank Corps, units identified now included the 140th and 143rd Rifle Divisions; and these were in addition to those which had previously been established in the area. Despite the extra reinforcement though, the Russians proved unable to dislodge the *XXXXVIII.PzK*, and despite its original intentions the *Korps* judged the day to have been a complete defensive success. To the right, in the area south of the river Irsha, where the *7.Panzer-Division* had gone over to the defensive, the Soviets left only weak screening troops, including the 1st Guards Cavalry Corps and the 248th Rifle Brigade. During the day, these troops even pulled back northwards about three or four kilometres. Elsewhere on the *4.Panzerarmee* front, things were again beginning to happen. Opposite the *XXXXII.AK* sector, Soviet forces closed up to the German defensive positions on a broad front, conducting reconnaissance patrols in anything up to company strength. The *Korps* had however not been able to establish the presence of any major Soviet armoured units, so it was difficult to assess whether the preparations were just pinning attacks or were preparation for a major offensive, in which case the Russian 1st Tank Army was a likely candidate.

The 22 December was a cloudy, misty day with a light frost covering the frozen ground. Along the whole of the *PzAOK 4* front from the Dnepr in the east to the Irsha in the north-west, the Soviets conducted lively reconnaissance, but particularly on the Radomyshl'-Kornin sector between the rivers Teterev and Irpen. On that sector alone there were a total of no fewer than 15 attacks, in anything up to battalion strength. Reconnaissance had shown the arrival of two new Soviet units, the 316th Rifle Division opposite the southern wing of the *XIII.AK*, and the 129th Guards Rifle Division opposite the *XXXXII.AK*, with both new units having been transferred from the Kuban. Over on the left wing, the *XXXXVIII.PzK* continued to fight it out with counterattacking Soviet units, and by the end of the day neither side had made any real advance. The *4.Panzerarmee* decided to call off the attack.

The 23 December proved in many ways to be similar to the previous day. It continued overcast and cold, but there were alternating showers of fine rain and snow. On the *XXXXVIII.PzK* front, the Soviets continued with a number of uncoordinated and weaker assaults, primarily against the eastern front of the *LIX.AK*, and apparently with the intention of reducing the *XXXXVIII.PzK* salient by attacking it from the rear. They met with initial successes, but the whole affair was about to be eclipsed by events further to the south-east where Soviet reconnaissance continued. The *XXXXII.AK* was again subjected to repeated small-scale attacks in anything up to battalion strength, this time supported by tanks, with most of these being made against the centre and left-hand sectors. Meanwhile, German reconnaissance had picked up the arrival of another Russian division from the Kuban; this time the 389th Rifle Division which went into the front north of Stavishche opposite the *8.Panzer-Division*. There were other indications of an impending attack too, particularly since intelligence had not established that any units had been taken out of the frontline. It seemed more likely that these new arrivals were strengthening existing forces. Similarly, there were reports from captured prisoners of war indicating that there were about 200 Soviet tanks parked in the area around the

THE GERMAN SITUATION

Table 7: 4.Panzerarmee Armour Strength at 20 December 1943

Vehicle	Pz I				Pz II				Pz III				Pz IV				Pz V				Pz VI				StuG				PzJg (Sfl.)			
Unit	A	B	C	D	A	B	C	D	A	B	C	D	A	B	C	D	A	B	C	D	A	B	C	D	A	B	C	D	A	B	C	D
1.SS Panzer-Division 'LSSAH'	2	2	0	0	7	3	4	0	10	3	2	5	68	10	49	9	72	6	38	28	20	3	9	8	35	17	18	0	19	4	15	0
1.Panzer-Division	0	0	0	0	3	3	0	0	13	5	3	5	74	22	32	20	47	12	25	10	0	0	0	0	0	0	0	0	19	12	6	1
7.Panzer-Division	0	0	0	0	2	0	0	0	2	1	1	0	48	12	36	0	0	0	0	0	0	0	0	0	0	0	0	0	9	7	2	0
8.Panzer-Division	0	0	0	0	5	3	1	1	10	2	3	5	36	27	4	5	0	0	0	0	0	0	0	0	0	0	0	0	8	5	3	0
19.Panzer-Division	0	0	0	0	0	0	0	0	5	2	3	0	19	14	5	0	0	0	0	0	0	0	0	0	10	7	3	0	11	8	3	0
25.Panzer-Division	0	0	0	0	0	0	0	0	9	8	1	0	61	43	10	8	0	0	0	0	0	0	0	0	12	10	2	0	0	0	0	0
SS Panzer-kampfgruppe 'Das Reich'	0	0	0	0	0	0	0	0	0	0	0	0	22	15	7	0	20	10	10	0	8	4	4	0	0	0	0	0	0	0	0	0
20.Panzergrenadier-Division	0	0	0	0	0	0	0	0	5	1	1	3	0	0	0	0	0	0	0	0	0	0	0	0	10	10	0	0	8	5	0	3
s.Panzer-Abteilung 509	0	0	0	0	0	0	0	0	0	0	0	0	0	0	0	0	0	0	0	0	30	4	26	0	0	0	0	0	0	0	0	0
StuG-Abteilung 202	0	0	0	0	0	0	0	0	0	0	0	0	0	0	0	0	0	0	0	0	0	0	0	0	34	24	8	2	0	0	0	0
StuG-Abteilung 239	0	0	0	0	0	0	0	0	0	0	0	0	0	0	0	0	0	0	0	0	0	0	0	0	22	18	4	0	0	0	0	0
StuG-Abteilung 249	0	0	0	0	0	0	0	0	0	0	0	0	0	0	0	0	0	0	0	0	0	0	0	0	30	5	25	0	0	0	0	0
StuG-Abteilung 276	0	0	0	0	0	0	0	0	0	0	0	0	0	0	0	0	0	0	0	0	0	0	0	0	23	17	6	0	0	0	0	0
StuG-Abteilung 280	0	0	0	0	0	0	0	0	0	0	0	0	0	0	0	0	0	0	0	0	0	0	0	0	28	22	4	2	0	0	0	0
Panzerjäger-Abteilung 559	0	0	0	0	0	0	0	0	0	0	0	0	0	0	0	0	0	0	0	0	0	0	0	0	0	0	0	0	10	5	5	0
Panzerjäger-Abteilung 616	0	0	0	0	0	0	0	0	0	0	0	0	0	0	0	0	0	0	0	0	0	0	0	0	0	0	0	0	22	19	3	0
Panzerjäger-Abteilung 731	0	0	0	0	0	0	0	0	0	0	0	0	0	0	0	0	0	0	0	0	0	0	0	0	0	0	0	0	23	18	5	0
Sturmbataillon PzAOK 4	0	0	0	0	0	0	0	0	1	0	0	1	0	0	0	1	0	0	0	0	0	0	0	0	3	1	0	2	0	0	0	0
Totals	2	2	0	0	17	9	5	3	55	22	14	19	329	143	143	43	139	28	73	38	58	11	39	8	207	131	70	6	129	83	42	4
A. Available	2				17				55				329				139				58				207				129			
B. Operational		2				9				22				143				28				11				131				83		
C. Forward Repair			0				5				14				143				73				39				70				42	
D. Depth Repair				0				3				19				43				38				8				6				4

village of Belka, 20 kilometres north of Stavishche, waiting for an offensive that would begin in a matter of days. In addition there had been a recent increase in the number of artillery units opposite the *Korps* sector, and the *4.Panzerarmee* concluded that a major Soviet offensive would begin in a few days either side of the river Teterev, the objective: the re-capture of Zhitomir.

Part II
The Start of the Soviet Offensive

3

The Initial Breakthrough

Friday 24 December 1943

The night of 23 December passed relatively quietly along the *4.Panzerarmee* front. In the east, with its right flank anchored on the river Dnepr, Nehring's *XXIV.Panzerkorps* reported only local activity.[1] Both sides had sent out reconnaissance patrols along the north-eastern sector, but in contrast to previous nights there had been only negligible disruptive artillery fire laid down by Soviet batteries. There had been a little more activity on the north-western sector where a small-scale Soviet assault had obliged the *I./Infanterie-Regiment 80* of the *34.Infanterie-Division* to pull back its forward positions to a new point about a kilometre north of the main defensive position, although north of Chernyakhov, the Russians had begun to dig in, constructing new positions just 800 metres from the German lines. More positively, a small-scale counterattack by the *82.Infanterie-Division* in the area around and east of the crossroads two kilometres north-west of Chernyakhov had resulted in the capture of three Soviet defensive positions. Later in the night, at about 01.00 hours, the Russians counterattacked again, this time with an estimated 30 or so men in the Makarovka area, but the attempt was unsuccessful. Patrols sent out that night had discovered that Soviet forces had pushed forwards to a point south-east of Hill 190, about four kilometres east of Germanovka, and unlike the sector further east, there was heavy disruptive artillery fire in the area.

Hell's *VII.AK* had passed a quieter night, with none of the three divisions reporting any real difficulty.[2] The *75.Infanterie-Division* had intercepted four Soviet patrols, two on the southern edge of Yatski and two on the division's left wing, but all had been successfully seen off. The *198.Infanterie-Division* reported no activity whatsoever, whilst the previous evening, between 16.00 and 17.00 hours, the *88.Infanterie-Division* had defended two company-sized assaults. Both had been against its left wing, and both had been seen off before they even reached the main defensive line.

The *XXXXII.AK*, as might have been expected in view of the impending assault, had a more troublesome night.[3] There had been considerable activity from both sides, and on the right wing the *25.Panzer-Division* reported having destroyed a Soviet outpost in front of Sushchanka. The *19.Panzer-Division* to its left undertook a small operation to clear the low ground east of Yastreben'ka, and reported killing 70 Russian soldiers and capturing two machine guns. Another counterattack, to clear the Soviet penetration a kilometre north of Yastreben'ka was less successful. Fighting had been severe as the assault ran into a well-organised close defensive system, and no real progress was made against stiff resistance. Casualties had begun to mount, and it had been decided to call off the attack. The assault was begun again at 05.30 hours and was still underway by early morning. In addition to its combat engagements, the division also reported considerable

---

1   *XXIV.PzK.*, Morgenmeldung, 05.45 hours dated 24 Dec 43.
2   *VII.AK*, Morgenmeldung, 05.35 hours dated 24 Dec 43.
3   *XXXXII.AK*, Morgenmeldung, 06.30 hours dated 24 Dec 43.

enemy traffic in the areas around Yastreben'ka, Ranok farm, and Mar'yanovka. To the north, the *8.Panzer-Division* had been attacked on its left wing, with a small Soviet penetration into its main battle positions in the eastern part of Rakovichi. This had been sealed off during the night though, and a counterattack was planned for first light. On the *Korps* left wing, the *SS Panzerkampfgruppe 'Das Reich'* reported the Soviets to be reinforcing the sector opposite its front, in many places pushing forward to as close as 60 metres from its main positions. To add to the general sense of unease, it had been noted that these forward troops were not digging in, and it was clear that the main Soviet positions were now manned in strength. But they were not content with just moving troops forward. A Russian assault by between 80 and 100 men in the area of the Belka stream was thrown back, whilst another on the left wing forced a penetration which had to be sealed off prior to launching a counterattack, with the support of a few panzers, at dawn.

To the north the *XIII.AK* had a peaceful night, with no Soviet activity reported along the whole sector.[4] A combat patrol sent out by the *68.Infanterie-Division* overwhelmed a Soviet outpost east of Krasnoborka, killing 10 Russian soldiers. There was however an exchange of disruptive artillery fire, with the German artillery concentrating on targets in the main Soviet positions.

Balck's *XXXXVIII.PzK* spent a mixed night.[5] On its right, the *7.Panzer-Division* reported nothing of interest, whilst over on the left the *1.Panzer-Division* had begun at 03.00 hours to pull out of the salient north-west of Chopovichi, as ordered. The withdrawal had however apparently been picked up by the enemy, as a Soviet armoured group had forced its way onto the railway near the mill south of Liplyany. The division had been obliged to form a task group to deal with the situation, but the danger remained for the time being. The *1.SS Panzer-Division 'LSSAH'* had meanwhile been involved in its own counterattack. The previous evening, an enemy grouping had advanced westwards along the sand road towards Bolyarka Farm, but a swift strike at about 17.00 hours by the *I./SS Panzergrenadier-Regiment 1* mounted on *Sturmgeschützen* dispersed and threw back the attack. Having achieved this small success, this group then participated in the action to clear the situation near the mill south of Liplyany. Elsewhere the division's sector remained quiet.

On the right of von der Chevallerie's *LIX.AK*, the *291.Infanterie-Division* reported the same Soviet penetration at the railway crossing south of Liplyany.[6] The breach was about 600 metres wide and the attack had fallen right on the boundary between the division and the *1.Panzer-Division* to the right. Soviet reinforcements were reported to be advancing through the gap, with six tanks having been observed up until that time. Things were no better elsewhere. Following a number of assaults, a Soviet attack against the right wing of the *Korps-Abteilung C* finally managed to break into the village of Khotinovka, forcing the *Korps-Abteilung* to pull back its wing, thus re-opening the gap between it and the *291.Infanterie-Division* to the right. A counterattack was set in motion to seal off the breach. Further south, in the Irsha valley, an enemy patrol was seen off in the vicinity of Shershni, but otherwise the Soviets contented themselves with

---

4   *XIII.AK*, Morgenmeldung, 06.00 hours dated 24 Dec 43.
5   *XXXXVIII.PzK*, Morgenmeldung, 05.45 hours dated 24 Dec 43.
6   *LIX.AK*, Morgenmeldung, 06.40 hours dated 24 Dec 43.

digging in on that sector. To the north, the rest of *Korps* front remained quiet throughout the night.

It was still dark on the *XXXXII.AK* sector when the Soviet artillery opened fire at 06.00 hours, heralding the start of the first of the Soviet winter offensives. An hour later the guns began to shift their fire further into the German rear, and the main assault began at 07.00 hours. A light rain was falling when the day dawned, heavy and overcast, as an estimated 10 Soviet rifle divisions hit the *XXXXII.AK* front with heavy artillery and armour support.[7] The assault concentrated on two main sectors; in the south between Divin and the river Zdvizh, and in the north between the main Kiev-Zhitomir road and the river Belka. Despite desperate resistance by elements of the three *panzer-divisions* involved, the Soviets succeeded in achieving major breaches in both sectors. The towns of Divin, Ul'shka, Khomutets, Krakovshchina, Yastreben'ka, Dubrovka and Lazarevka were all lost quickly, forcing the defending units back to the eastern edges of Soloveevka and Brusilov in the south, and the west bank of the Zdvizh just west of Lazarevka. The northern wing of the *25.Panzer-Division* was struck by massed infantry and armoured forces in two places. To the south, Soviet forces broke through the Divin sector and advanced west and south-west as far as the northern end of Turbovka and the southern end of Soloveevka. A little to the north, they broke through the Khomutets area and pushed on westwards, passing Morozovka and reaching Vodoty, 15 kilometres in the rear. An armoured group of the division counterattacked north and south of Divin, reportedly causing the enemy heavy casualties, and although street fighting broke out in Soloveevka, with 18 Russian tanks reported as destroyed, there was little that could be done to stop the Soviet momentum. Another counterattack, this time northwards towards Morozovka, succeeded in knocking out an estimated 15 Soviet tanks, but the situation there remained unclear. To the north, the right wing of the *19.Panzer-Division* was caught by the same assault, and suffered the same result. After heavy fighting, the Soviets, supported by strong armoured forces, broke through the Yastreben'ka sector and advanced through Dubrovka as far as the eastern edge of Brusilov. To the north, another Soviet assault broke through the division's centre, striking up the Zdvizh valley from Malyi Karashin to Lazarevka. The division tried to mount a counterattack to seal off the penetration in the Dubrovka area, but this came to grief under heavy defensive fire. Another blow, this time in the evening towards Krakovshchina in the south, ran into a strong Soviet tank force. In the battle which ensued, the division reported destroying at least 20 tanks, although many more kept moving westwards. About 15 were observed to have entered the village of Vodoty, whilst a further 57 were actually counted just outside the village to the north-east. To its left, the *8.Panzer-Division* was equally hard hit. The division estimated that it had been attacked by at least 150 tanks on its centre and left, and again despite desperate resistance, the result had been deep Soviet penetrations. North-west of Stavishche, enemy armour had rolled through the division's defences and struck out southwards towards the main Kiev-Zhitomir road, capturing Yusefovka[8] before wheeling back onto the main road towards Zhitomir. About six kilometres along the road, some elements then turned southwards at the junction near Penkovatoe, heading for Osovtsy and threatening to roll up the division's right

---

7   *XXXXII.AK*, Tagesmeldung, 20.00 hours dated 24 Dec 43.
8   Yusefovka does not appear on all maps. It was situated on the south side of the main Kiev-Zhitomir road on the crossroads just west of Stavishche.

wing. Over on the left, the division mounted an armoured counterattack in the Belka valley, and succeeded in pushing back the first Soviet wave, only to have them join forces with a group which had broken through near Rakovichi. The combined Russian force then turned once more and advanced south-west of Zabeloch'e towards Kocherov and Potashnya. Kocherov by this time was defended by only alarm units and elements of the *Kampfgruppe* von Mitzlaff, the armoured group from the *8.Panzer-Division*. The Russian penetrations continued, and soon they had reached a line running from the river Belka north of Kocherov to the main Kiev-Zhitomir road. Further counterattacks in the Zabeloch'e area were to no avail. In the central sector alone, the division reported having destroyed at least 20 enemy tanks, but even this could not prevent Soviet forces from pressing on down the main road towards Zhitomir, where street fighting later broke out in Kocherov itself, 15 kilometres in the rear. The *SS Panzerkampfgruppe 'Das Reich'* on the *Korps* left wing reported being attacked on its right-hand and central sectors. Again there had been heavy artillery and tank support, and the *Kampfgruppe* had proved no more able than the other divisions in holding up the Soviet advance. Russian troops had broken through the line near Garborov and pushed on to the south-west to capture Sobolev.[9] From there they moved on to cross, and thus block, the Kocherov–Radomyshl' road whilst the *Kampfgruppe* pulled back its right wing to a line running from a point two kilometres east of Hill 178.7 through a point two kilometres north of the same hill to the bend of the road west of Sobolev. On its left wing, there had only been minor Soviet assaults by comparison, and the local breaches in the area around Garborov were either cleared off or sealed successfully. By the end of the day the *Kampfgruppe* was still holding a line from the north-west edge of Zabeloch'e through Sobolev to Rudnya[10] on the river Teterev where it maintained contact with the right wing of the *XIII.AK*. The *XXXXII.AK* reckoned that it had been attacked by at least 200 tanks in all, of which it reported destroying at least 60, and in all probability even more than that. Despite the weight of the assault though, and the depth of the penetrations, the *Korps* was still unsure as to future Soviet intentions, although it did rule out the possibility of a local encirclement, predicting instead that the southern Russian group would push on west or south-west, while the more northerly would simply continue its drive down the main road to Zhitomir, with Kocherov as its immediate objective.

The sheer scale of the Soviet assault brought a flurry of activity from the *4.Panzerarmee*. At 08.25 hours the chief of staff at the *XXXXII.AK*, *Oberst* Gerhard Franz, rang *PzAOK 4* headquarters to report his situation, and at 09.00 hours Raus held a conference with his chief of staff, *Generalmajor* Fangohr.[11] Fangohr described the situation facing the *XXXXII.AK*, whereupon Raus decided to transfer the *s.Panzer-Abteilung 509 (Tiger)*, currently attached to the *7.Panzer-Division*, back into the main sector. The *Abteilung* was to head for Kocherov where it would be tasked with holding up any further Soviet armoured advance. In addition, the *18.Artillerie-Division*, still on the move, was to remain in close radio contact. The division had begun to move earlier in response to an order from the *Panzerarmee*, and its first elements had started to move

---

9   The tiny settlement of Sobolev is not shown on all maps. It lay just east of the Kocherov–Radomyshl' road on a line drawn between Mar'yanovka and Guta Zabelotskaya.
10 Rudnya was the name given at the time to that part of Radomyshl' which lies south-east of the river Teterev.
11 *PzAOK 4*, Ia Kriegstagebuch entry dated 24 Dec 43.

the previous night.¹² In this, it had been instructed to pull out of its positions with the *VII.AK* and move through Belaya Tserkov', Skvira, Popel'nya and Zhitomir to the area east of Kocherov where it would be subordinated to the *XXXXII.AK*. It was to have been deployed to support the *8.Panzer-Division* and the *SS Panzerkampfgruppe 'Das Reich'*, but the apparent scale of the Soviet offensive now argued against such intentions, and the division was instructed to remain in close contact with the *Panzerarmee* in case either its movement had to be held up to allow other troop movements, or it even had to be redeployed to face the new threat.

Later in the morning Fangohr spoke with *Generalleutnant* Busse, his opposite number at Army Group South, and described the latest situation.¹³ Fangohr voiced the opinion that the assault represented a major Soviet offensive, to which Busse replied that it was probably high time that the two *panzer-divisions* operating around Korosten' were moved to the area east of Zhitomir. Nevertheless, he also pointed out that it was possible that this was precisely what the Soviet command was hoping for. Following the conversation, Fangohr again spoke with Raus, and this time Raus agreed that the *XXXXVIII.PzK* should now shorten its front line as proposed, and thus free the *1.Panzer-Division* and the *1.SS Panzer-Division 'LSSAH'* for operations elsewhere.

At 10.45 hours, *Oberst* Franz called again from *XXXXII.AK* headquarters, informing the *PzAOK 4* that Soviet forces had managed to make further progress through the existing breaches in the sectors held by the *8.* and *25.Panzer-Divisions*. Immediately afterwards, Fangohr instructed the *XIII.AK* to transfer the *Sturmbataillon* of the *20.Panzergrenadier-Division* direct to *Panzerarmee* control, and ordered the battalion to move to the Kocherov area to support the *s.Panzer-Abteilung 509* which had already been ordered there.¹⁴ At about the same time the *4.Panzerarmee* also issued orders to the *XXIV.PzK* to prepare for the transfer of a reinforced regiment from the *168. Infanterie-Division*.¹⁵ The group was to consist of two *grenadier* battalions and the *füsilier* battalion, supported by an *Artillerie-Abteilung*, a *Pionier-Kompanie* and a *Panzerjäger Kompanie*. The move was to begin the same day, with foot elements, together with a few horses and vehicles, loading up in Kagarlyk for transfer to the Popel'nya area by early on 26 December. Once arrived, the *Regimentsgruppe* would be attached to the *XXXXII. AK*, where it would be tasked with relieving the *Panzergrenadier-Regiment 146* on the southern wing of the *25.Panzer-Division*. This regiment would then be assembled in the Kornin-Lipki-Korolevka area at the disposal of the *Panzerarmee*. The order to begin the move was issued later that night, at 22.00 hours.¹⁶ In it, Mattenklott was instructed to move the *Regimentsgruppe* to the Khodorkov area once it had unloaded, and advise the *PzAOK 4* of his intentions thereafter.

At about 11.45 hours, Fangohr again spoke with Raus, this time proposing that the headquarters and two companies of the *Panzer-Zerstörer-Bataillon 473* should be attached to the *1.Panzer-Division* in anticipation of future operations east of Zhitomir. Raus agreed, and orders were issued accordingly.¹⁷ At the same time, it was agreed that

12 *PzAOK 4*, Ia Nr. 6874/43 geh. dated 24 Dec 43.
13 *PzAOK 4*, Ia Kriegstagebuch entry dated 24 Dec 43.
14 *PzAOK 4*, Ia Nr. 6889/43 geh. dated 24 Dec 43.
15 *PzAOK 4*, Ia Nr. 6875/43 geh. dated 24 Dec 43.
16 *PzAOK 4*, Ia Nr. 6904/43 geh. dated 24 Dec 43.
17 *PzAOK 4*, Ia Nr. 6899/43 geh. dated 24 Dec 43.

the nine *Panzer VI 'Tiger'* of the *s.Panzer-Abteilung 509* would also be attached to the same division.

Elsewhere on the *4.Panzerarmee* front, the day was much easier in comparison. On the right wing the *XXIV.Panzerkorps* reported a quieter day.[18] There had been a few small-scale attacks, but generally the Soviets made no real assaults following their territorial gains of the previous days. On the right wing of the *Korps-Abteilung B*, near Bobritsa, an early morning combat patrol had been thrown back at about 05.30 hours, while a more serious development had occurred near Balyko-Shchuchinka later in the day. In this an estimated one or two Soviet rifle companies had assaulted the *34.Infanterie-Division* at about 13.20 hours, and managed to achieve a local breach. A counterattack was launched and fighting continued into the evening. Elsewhere, the division reported no combat activity, although north of Chernyakhov troops of the *82.Infanterie-Division* launched their own counterattack at 10.00 hours, supported by *Sturmgeschützen*. The attack was aimed at Soviet forward positions just 1,000 metres from the division's main defensive line, and following some stiff fighting, they were rooted out and forced to pull back. The attack brought in 51 prisoners, and caused an estimated 80 Russian dead. The division pushed its own forward elements to a point about 1,500 metres in front of the main defences.

To the left, the *VII.AK* reported that there had been no change in the enemy's dispositions since the previous day.[19] There had been some disruptive artillery and mortar fire, but the main point of interest seemed to be the large amount of sled traffic moving east to west in front of the *88.Infanterie-Division*. The division's artillery engaged these troop movements whenever they were observed, as well as laying fire on known Soviet troop positions. In the sector held by the *198.Infanterie-Division*, the only Soviet activity reported was a combat patrol which attacked a forward listening post, suffering one man killed in exchange for the capture of one wounded German.

North of the main Soviet effort against the *XXXXII.AK*, Hauffe's *XIII.AK* had a quiet day.[20] During the afternoon the Soviets had shelled the *68.Infanterie-Division* on the right wing, and in places even moved up closer to the defensive positions, but apart from that they had remained quiet. The *Korps* had, however, instructed the *Sturmbataillon* from the *20.Panzergrenadier-Division* to move to the Kocherov area in accordance with the orders received from *PzAOK 4*, and the battalion had left the *Korps'* command at 12.45 hours.

On the *XXXXVIII.PzK* front, the Soviets were on both the defensive and the offensive.[21] Things were quiet in the *1.SS Panzer-Division 'LSSAH'* sector, but they pursued the withdrawal of the *1.Panzer-Division* relentlessly, attacking the new defensive positions in up to regimental strength with tank support. Despite this close attention, the division succeeded in making an orderly withdrawal whilst Soviet forces seized the railway and sand road south of Liplyany. The enemy attacks continued throughout the day and into the evening as the division settled down in its new positions. By the end of the day, it was established on a line running from the Meleni road through Bolyarka to the railway crossing just to the north-east. The *Kampfgruppe* von Mellenthin had

---

18 *XXIV.PzK*, Tagesmeldung, 18.15 hours dated 24 Dec 43.
19 *VII.AK*, Tagesmeldung, 17.50 hours dated 24 Dec 43.
20 *XIII.AK*, Tagesmeldung, 17.40 hours dated 24 Dec 43.
21 *XXXXVIII.PzK*, Tagesmeldung, 19.10 hours dated 24 Dec 43.

THE INITIAL BREAKTHROUGH   87

meanwhile counterattacked and surprised the Soviet forces north of the railway in the area around and to the west of the mill. Having first cleared Khotinovka,[22] the *Kampfgruppe* moved off at 10.00 hours following a rapid re-grouping in the north-western part of the village. It struck out northwards, destroying Soviet positions on Hill 171.8 before wheeling to the north-west towards Grozino.[23] Having broken down Russian resistance, the *Kampfgruppe* broke into the southern end of that village and then proceeded to fan out to establish contact with the infantry deployed to the north and west. Seven Russian tanks were reported to have been destroyed in this action, much of the success of which was attributed to the general lack of Soviet armour on that sector. By evening the action was over, and troops of the *1.Panzer-Division* were busy relieving those elements of the *Kampfgruppe* which were still deployed in the front line. The *1.SS Panzer-Division 'LSSAH'* meanwhile had completed its withdrawal without enemy interference, and, apart from the usual reconnaissance patrolling west and north-west of Meleni, the Soviets had stayed quiet all day. Over on the *Korps* right wing, the newly attached *7.Panzer-Division* reported no particular activity other than patrolling and artillery fire on both sides. The division had however pulled back its left wing to the south-west, from Zabrannoe to Guta Dobrynskaya, and sent the *s.Panzer-Abteilung 509* on its way towards Zhitomir as instructed.

To the north, on the left wing of the *4.Panzerarmee*, the *LIX.AK* had a relatively hectic day.[24] Despite the lively Soviet disruptive artillery fire over the whole of the *291. Infanterie-Division* sector, the *Korps* confirmed that the breach south of Liplyany farm had been cleared with the support of the *Kampfgruppe* von Mellenthin. Following a renewed Soviet assault at 11.00 hours however, it had been opened once again, but an immediate counterattack had sealed off the new penetration. The *Korps-Abteilung C*, supported by a few panzers from the *XXXXVIII.PzK*, also succeeded in restoring its old front line, clearing the breach north-east of Khotinovka farm of all enemy troops, although a number of Soviet soldiers did manage to escape northwards across the railway through the area of the breach. Several enemy attacks were then made against the right wing of the *Korps-Abteilung*, and whilst most of these were seen off, weak enemy troops did manage to break into the eastern end of Khotinovka. A hastily mounted counterattack threw back these elements, and by midday the old front line had been restored. Further north a group of about 80 Soviet soldiers broke into the village of Voronovo, just north-west of Nemirovka, but this breach had been cleared by the afternoon. Away to the south-west, and deep in the rear, the *Reserve-Grenadier-Bataillon 320* and the *III./Sicherungs-Regiment 375* had meanwhile arrived in Novograd-Volynskii, on 23 and 24 December respectively.

Back at the *PzAOK 4* headquarters, a call had been received just before midday from *General der Panzertruppen* Balck, commanding officer of the *XXXXVIII.PzK*, informing them that the action to clear Grozino had been completed.[25] At 12.20 hours Raus and Fangohr held another conference, this time to discuss the possibilities for Balck's command, during which Fangohr proposed redeploying it to the Zhitomir

---

22 Referred to as Kosinowka in the German records.
23 Situated at the southern end of Singai.
24 *LIX.AK*, Tagesmeldung, 19.05 hours dated 24 Dec 43.
25 *PzAOK 4*, Ia Kriegstagebuch entry, dated 24 Dec 43.

area.[26] There it could co-ordinate the activities of the *1.Panzer-Division* and the *1.SS Panzer-Division 'LSSAH'*, as well as the *18.Artillerie-Division* which was still south of Zhitomir. The *7.Panzer-Division* would remain in its current positions but be transferred to the *XIII.AK*. Raus agreed, and orders were issued accordingly. The *XXXXVIII.PzK* was instructed to hand over its existing sector to the *XIII.AK* and the *LIX.AK* at 18.00 hours that evening, and prepare to move to the area east of Zhitomir where its new task would be to destroy the Soviet forces which had broken through the *XXXXII.AK* front.[27] The new boundary between the two *Korps* remaining would run from Turchinka along the river Irsha and from there straight to Meleni. The *LIX.AK* would thus hold its positions on a line running from Shershni through Meleni farm and the state farm to Khotinovka, and from there along the railway line to north of Khotinovka farm and Grozino. From there, the front line would be as previously. The order instructed Balck to pull back to the 'Green Line', and pull both *panzer divisions* out of the front. The *1.Panzer-Division* was to begin moving towards Zhitomir the same night, heading for the Korostyshev area, some 30 kilometres east of Zhitomir. The *1.SS Panzer-Division 'LSSAH'* was to remain in the area for another day, to act as a 'fire brigade' in the event of any difficulty, but was to begin moving towards Zhitomir the following afternoon. The *7.Panzer-Division* would remain in its current positions and be attached to the *XIII.AK*. The *Panzer-Zerstörer-Bataillon 473*, still in the Berdichev area, would be attached to the *Korps* and would be moving into the Zhitomir area the following day. As additional reinforcement, Raus attached the *18.Artillerie-Division* to Balck's command, but with the proviso that the division should only be deployed as a single entity, and only then once the Soviet breakthroughs had been cleared up.

At 12.50 hours, Raus spoke to Balck and informed him of these instructions, telling him moreover to move his headquarters to somewhere just north of Zhitomir.[28] Raus also asked whether the *'LSSAH'* should remain for the time being with von der Chevallerie's *LIX.AK*, and Balck replied that it should, considering as he did that the Soviets were still planning another offensive from the Chopovichi area. Indeed the *Panzerkorps* commander had already ordered the construction of comprehensive obstacles and roadblocks on that sector. Raus then spoke with Hauffe at the *XIII.AK* regarding the employment of the *7.Panzer-Division*.[29] He informed the *Korps* commander that he was to retain control of the division, but that it would now have to be employed to try and close the gap to the right wing of the *LIX.AK*. He also advised him to prepare as many obstacles as possible in front of his sector.

Meanwhile *Oberst* Franz, chief of staff at the *XXXXII.AK*, had called in at about 16.15 hours, informing the *Panzerarmee* of the latest situation, and advising that the *Korps* would be attempting to fall back during the night to a line running from Luchin in the south through the eastern edge of Soloveevka, Morozovka, Brusilov, Osovtsy, and Kocherov to Garborov in the north.[30] Half an hour later, Raus spoke again with Balck at *XXXXVIII.PzK*, advising him that the leading Soviet elements had already advanced as far as Kocherov, and it was therefore of the utmost importance for the *Korps* to reach

---

26 *PzAOK 4*, Ia Kriegstagebuch entry, dated 24 Dec 43.
27 *PzAOK 4*, Ia Nr. 6888/43 geh. dated 24 Dec 43.
28 *PzAOK 4*, Ia Kriegstagebuch entry, dated 24 Dec 43.
29 *PzAOK 4*, Ia Kriegstagebuch entry, dated 24 Dec 43.
30 *PzAOK 4*, Ia Kriegstagebuch entry, dated 24 Dec 43.

and block the Teterev crossings at Korostyshev as quickly as possible, thus denying them to the enemy armour.[31] Further to his earlier instructions, and countermanding them for the present, Raus then ordered the *18.Artillerie-Division* to move no further than just south of Zhitomir, where its lead elements were to find suitable firing positions[32]. On no account was the division to pass through the city, although further orders would follow. Once it had arrived in the area south of the city, the division would be attached the *XXXXVIII.PzK* rather than the *XXXXII.AK* as originally intended. Raus had considered moving the division's *Sturmgeschütz-Batterie* to the Korostyshev area, but the unit was at the rear of the division's column, still in its original positions, and the idea was dropped.

Just after 17.00 hours, the *4.Panzerarmee* received disturbing news. It had intercepted a radio message sent by the *SS Panzerkampfgruppe 'Das Reich'* to the *68.Infanterie-Division* on its left.[33] The message indicated that the *'Das Reich'* intended to pull back its left wing in the Radomyshl' area. Fangohr called his opposite number at the *XXXXII.AK*, *Oberst* Franz, and advised him that any such manoeuvre should be avoided at all costs. There might otherwise have been the risk of having the *XXXXII.AK* left wing unhinged altogether. This subject was later raised again by *Oberstleutnant* Hermani, the *Ia* at the *XXXXII.AK*, during a conversation with Fangohr, in which Hermani informed the latter that the *'Das Reich'* still wanted to pull back its left wing onto the river Teterev further south. Fangohr again stressed the importance of maintaining the current position, and that any such withdrawal should be avoided at all costs. He ended with a thinly veiled threat. If the order to hold existing positions was not obeyed, the division commander would be held personally responsible.

At 20.15 hours, Mattenklott called to give Raus a personal update on the situation facing the *XXXXII.AK*.[34] He confirmed that, in his estimate, the *Korps* was facing 10 Soviet rifle divisions and about 200 tanks, 60 of which had been destroyed already. He put down the rapid collapse of the *25.Panzer-Division* to a lack of unity and strict control in one of its regiments, although in the circumstances this was, in all probability, a very harsh judgement. Raus, at least, was of the view that the division had been unfortunate, and that had it been able to deploy all its operational panzers, it would undoubtedly have fared better and destroyed more enemy tanks.[35] Mattenklott also advised that the town of Kocherov had fallen during the afternoon, but that the *8.Panzer-Division* had been ordered to recapture it. Earlier in the evening, at 19.35 hours, the *PzAOK 4* had issued the *XXXXII.AK* with new orders for the following day.[36] Using the information supplied earlier in the afternoon by the *XXXXII.AK* chief of staff, Mattenklott was now instructed to hold the Soviet advance to a general line running from Luchin in the south

---

31 *PzAOK 4*, Ia Kriegstagebuch entry, dated 24 Dec 43.
32 *PzAOK 4*, Ia Nr. 6887/43 geh. dated 24 Dec 43.
33 *PzAOK 4*, Ia Kriegstagebuch entry, dated 24 Dec 43.
34 *PzAOK 4*, Ia Kriegstagebuch entry, dated 24 Dec 43.
35 During the previous night the division had been ordered to pass 21 of its 41 Panzer IVs to the *19.Panzer-Division*, leaving it just 20 Panzer IVs of the *II./Panzer-Regiment 9* which were kept in reserve. To make matters worse, the *Panzer-Regiment 9* had no *I.Abteilung*; the *s.Panzer-Abteilung 509 (Tiger)* initially being attached by way of compensation. This unit however was deployed with the *7.Panzer-Division* when the offensive began. Moreover, on the morning of the attack, at 07.30 hours, the division was also ordered by the *XXXXII.AK* to pass its remaining 20 panzers to the *19.Panzer-Division*. The only armour left were the nine Sturmgeschützen of the *Panzerjäger-Abteilung 87*.
36 *PzAOK 4*, Ia Nr. 6899/43 geh. dated 24 Dec 43.

through Turbovka, the eastern edge of Soloveevka, Morozovka, Brusilov, Osovtsy, to Kocherov, and from there along the road to Rudnya. Armoured groups were to conduct continuous mobile operations in an attempt to force the enemy to break off his offensive, and in particular a counterattack was to be launched to close the gap which had opened up between Soloveevka and Brusilov on the boundary between the *19.* and *25.Panzer-Divisions*. It was stressed once more that the *SS Panzerkampfgruppe 'Das Reich'* was to keep its left wing anchored on the Teterev in its existing positions, whilst the artillery of the *XIII.AK* was to support the *Kampfgruppe* from its positions on the left bank of the river north of Radomyshl'.

The day had seen much heavy fighting on the *XXXXII.AK* front. Following the usual heavy artillery barrage, the Soviets had jumped off to the attack either side of the main Kiev-Zhitomir road and the initial impression of the *PzAOK 4* was that the offensive was aimed at re-capturing Zhitomir.[37] There were two main areas of effort; one in the south, in the Divin-Khomutets area, which seemed to be infantry heavy, and one in the north, either side of Rakovichi which seemed to be tank heavy.[38] The more southerly assault was being mounted by the right wing of the Soviet 38th Army with four rifle divisions supported by one or two tank brigades, while north of the Kiev-Zhitomir road, the attack was launched by the 1st Guards Army with about six full-strength rifle divisions supported by at least 150 tanks from the 1st Tank Army. Although intelligence had identified the presence of the 1st Tank Army, it had been unable as yet to spot any of its subordinate units. Three new rifle divisions had been identified in the attack, and the large number of infantry troops on the battlefield suggested that the divisions had all been brought up to full strength. Enemy intentions seemed to be to roll up the front either side of the Kiev-Zhitomir road and then strike south-westwards towards Zhitomir. Further north, the fact that the *XXXXVIII.PzK* had encountered mainly weak infantry forces in clearing the situation south-east of Korosten' suggested that those elements of the Soviet 25th Tank Corps which had been engaged in the area the day before had now been pulled out of the front line. It was possible that these were now being re-grouped in the Chopovichi area prior to a likely drive southwards by the 60th Army towards Zhitomir where it would join up with the main thrust as part of the wider offensive. In the absence of any more concrete ideas with regard to enemy intentions, the *4.Panzerarmee* intended to hold the Soviet advance to the line already indicated, maintaining firm contact between the *XXXXII.AK* and the *XIII.AK*. To support the crumbling front, Raus would concentrate the *XXXXVIII.PzK*, without the *7.Panzer-Division* but including the *1.Panzer-Division*, the *1.SS Panzer-Division 'LSSAH'*, and the *18.Artillerie-Division*, in the area around Zhitomir.[39] In the rear, the *Kommandant Zhitomir* was designated as a full *Kampfkommandant*, with all the requisite authorities and responsibilities.[40] For the time being the *Feldkommandantur 675* would remain as *Kampfkommandant*, being tasked with raising and organising the deployment of alarm units to defend the city. At this stage though, no alarm units were to be committed without the authority of the *Panzerarmee*.

---

37 *PzAOK 4*, Ic Abendmeldung an H.Gr. Süd, 19.00 hours dated 24 Dec 43.
38 *PzAOK 4*, Tagesmeldung an H.Gr. Süd, 21.45 hours dated 24 Dec 43.
39 *PzAOK 4*, Ia Nr. 6902/43 g.Kdos dated 24 Dec 43.
40 *PzAOK 4*, Ia Nr. 6891/43 geh. dated 24 Dec 43.

Saturday 25 December 1943

The first news of the day from the *XXXXII.AK* sector was bad, if not entirely unexpected.[41] Mattenklott had lost all communications with his divisions, and he had no idea as to the events of the night just passed. Later in the morning though, at 09.10 hours, his chief of staff, *Oberst* Franz reported that the *Korps* had been unable to form the new defensive line it had intended.[42] A wide gap of almost 12 kilometres had effectively opened up between Brusilov and the town of Gnilets[43] to the south-west, and strong enemy infantry and armoured forces were pouring through to the west. The leading tanks had been reported as pushing as far forwards as the Brusilov-Khodorkov road, and things were no better on the other wing, where the *SS Panzerkampfgruppe 'Das Reich'* had pulled back over the river Teterev in defiance of its orders. Further to the rear, the *Sturmbataillon* of the *20.Panzergrenadier-Division* had arrived in its new sector around Korostyshev, and reported a quiet night.[44] The *s.Panzer-Abteilung 509* had not yet arrived.

News from the other sectors was less worrying. The *XXIV.PzK* reported little activity for the night, although a small breach south of Shushchinka had been settled by troops of the *Korps-Abteilung B* the previous evening.[45] In the east, there had even been almost no Soviet patrolling, but there had been more on the north-western front, including a very small-scale assault by about 15 men against a forward outpost of the *34.Infanterie-Division* south of Staiki. This had been seen off successfully. The *VII.AK* too reported a generally quiet night, although there had been the usual light disruptive artillery and infantry fire, and a few patrols.[46] Four combat patrols were reported on the *75.Infanterie-Division* sector, one on the left wing of the *198.Infanterie-Division*, and another two on the right wing of the *88.Infanterie-Division*. The *18.Artillerie-Division* meanwhile had continued to move westwards, and the majority of its units had passed out of the *Korps* area at 21.00 hours the previous evening. To the left of the *XXXXII.AK* sector, Hauffe's *XIII.AK* reported the enemy situation to be unchanged.[47] A company-strength assault against the *213.Sicherungs-Division* at about midnight had been beaten off, and a local patrol in the *340.Infanterie-Division* sector had been intercepted. There had been exchanges of artillery and mortar fire throughout the night, during which the *Korps*, particularly the *68.Infanterie-Division*, laid fire on suspected Soviet troop movements. A more worrying report came from the *68.Infanterie-Division*, confirming that its patrols had been unable to make contact with the *SS Panzerkampfgruppe 'Das Reich'* on the right wing of the *XXXXII.AK*. This was the first notice of the unauthorised withdrawal which would later be confirmed by the *XXXXII.AK* itself. Balck's *XXXXVIII.PzK*, having already pulled out of the front south-east of Korosten' and begun moving towards Zhitomir, reported a quiet night in its old sector.[48] The *Reserve-Grenadier-Regiment 212* had, at about 01.00 hours, moved into its new positions as ordered, and the *Pionier-*

---

41 *XXXXII.AK*, Morgenmeldung, 06.00 hours dated 25 Dec 43.
42 *PzAOK 4*, Ia Kriegstagebuch entry, dated 25 Dec 43.
43 Referred to as Dolinovka on more recent Soviet maps.
44 *PzAOK 4*, Nachmeldung zur Morgenmeldung an *Hgr.Süd*, dated 25 Dec 43.
45 *XXIV.PzK*, Morgenmeldung, 05.50 hours dated 25 Dec 43.
46 *VII.AK*, Morgenmeldung, 05.35 hours dated 25 Dec 43.
47 *XIII.AK*, Morgenmeldung, 06.05 hours dated 25 Dec 43.
48 *XXXXVIII.PzK*, Morgenmeldung, 05.15 hours dated 25 Dec 43.

Bataillon 70 had been transferred to the *LIX.AK*. The *LIX.AK* itself meanwhile had a very quiet night, reporting no activity at all.[49]

With all the morning reports received, Raus and Fangohr met at 09.15 hours to discuss the developing situation.[50] Raus was now considering deploying the *XXXXVIII. PzK* to mount two counterattacks into the advancing Soviet forces; one from south of the main Kiev-Zhitomir road through Brusilov to the south-east, and the other using the *1.SS Panzer-Division 'LSSAH'* in an outflanking manoeuvre to the south to attack north-eastwards from the Khodorkov area. In this way, the forward Soviet forces would be caught in a pincer movement and destroyed. He now believed quite clearly that the main direction of the offensive was towards Kazatin and Berdichev.

At about 09.30 hours, Balck reported that the towns of Kocherov, Privorot'e and Vil'nya had all been captured off the march by Soviet forces, and, with the leading enemy elements thus only 15 kilometres away, he did not believe the majority of the *1.Panzer-Division* could be re-assembled in the Korostyshev area much before that evening.[51] Raus described to Balck the situation facing Mattenklott's *Korps*, adding his view that the offensive was being mounted by a total of four Soviet armies, including one tank army. He also mentioned that he was considering authorising a general withdrawal to the *'Siegfriedstellung'*, a line running generally southwards from Rudnya, through Voitashevka,[52] Vil'nya, Ozera, Lipki, Belki, Zhovtnevoe,[53] Savertsy to Taborov, and from there along the river Rostavitsa to the east. It would be the task of the *1.Panzer-Division* to support this withdrawal either side of the Kiev-Zhitomir road, although there was still the possibility that the division could later be employed together with the *1.SS Panzer-Division 'LSSAH'* for a counterattack from Korostyshev to the south. It was also possible that the strike north-eastwards from Khodorkov might still take place, but these were matters for the future.

In the meantime the *PzAOK 4* had reported to *Generalleutnant* Busse at Army Group South during the morning update. Busse mentioned that the *25.Panzer-Division* seemed to be falling back extremely quickly, and also that the division's reporting, through the *XXXXII.AK*, seemed to leave something to be desired.[54] Given the division's particular circumstances and problems, it is perhaps not surprising that it attracted such criticism, however well intentioned. Busse also suggested that scale of the Soviet assault might even be such that this was the major offensive which had been expected; the ultimate objective of which had been predicted to be the river Bug. Raus' intentions for the *XXXXVIII.PzK* were also discussed during the call, but Busse's main comment in response to the ideas of the *Panzerarmee* was that he did not regard it appropriate to deploy the two *panzer divisions* separately on different sectors.

Meanwhile the battle on the *XXXXII.AK* sector raged on. In the early hours of the morning, the Soviets resumed their attacks, this time apparently concentrating on the *Korps* southern wing, the right wing of the already weakened *25.Panzer-Division*.[55]

---

49 *LIX.AK*, Morgenmeldung, 05.00 hours dated 25 Dec 43.
50 PzAOK4, Ia Kriegstagebuch entry, dated 25 Dec 43.
51 *PzAOK 4*, Ia Kriegstagebuch entry, dated 25 Dec 43.
52 Referred to as Kvitnevoe on more recent Soviet maps.
53 Referred to as Shidowzy in German records.
54 *PzAOK 4*, Ia Kriegstagebuch entry, dated 25 Dec 43.
55 *PzAOK 4*, Ia Orientierung, 14.30 hours dated 25 Dec 43.

Mokhnachka was lost as strong motorised infantry troops struck through the main defensive positions south-east of the town, before wheeling westwards along the railway. At 10.10 hours, Mattenklott himself reported this latest development to Raus at the *Panzerarmee*.[56] He was advised in turn that the Army Group had released the rest of the *168.Infanterie-Division*,[57] and that consequently it would be attached to the *XXXXII.AK* forthwith. Raus confirmed this in an order issued later in the day.[58] In this, Mattenklott was instructed to assemble the division south of Pavoloch' on the river Rostavitsa, and use elements of it to secure the Kamenka river crossings west of Paripsy to the north, where it was to make contact with the *Sperrverband*[59] deployed there by the *VII.AK*. During the same conversation, Raus also informed Mattenklott to begin pulling his *Korps* back, step-by-step, into the '*Siegfriedstellung*', taking all its weapons and equipment with it; nothing was to be destroyed or left behind. In any event, contact with the neighbouring *VII.AK* was to be maintained at all costs, and a counterattack to close the gap was to be mounted as soon as possible.

The Soviet offensive meanwhile rolled on through the steady rain, and on the *XXXXII.AK* right wing a group of Soviet tanks advancing from east of Kornin had also outflanked the town to the south, with about another 45 enemy tanks striking past the north-eastern end of the town and advancing towards Krivoe. There were even reports of Soviet tank fire in the town of Kotlyarka, 15 kilometres away to the south-west. North-west of Kornin, Russian tanks occupied Korolevka and Sobolevka, whilst both infantry and tanks were reported in Gnilets. Tanks were similarly reported during the morning to be in the town of Skochishche, 15 kilometres west of Kornin. Further north-west, other Soviet armour captured the villages of Zdvizhka, Vil'nya and Voitashevka. This effectively enclosed the *8.* and *19.Panzer-Divisions* in a loosely drawn pocket, fighting as they still were further east. Elements were still fighting in Karabachin, west of Brusilov, whilst others were reported to be falling back from the Osovtsy area towards Brusilov and the south-east. The *Kampfgruppe* von Mitzlaff had meanwhile re-appeared either side of the Kiev-Zhitomir road just west of Kocherov, where it reported the presence of 10 Soviet tanks on the western edge of the town. To the north, the *SS Panzerkampfgruppe 'Das Reich'* had pulled back its right wing to the line Potashnya-Stavatskaya Sloboda-Mar'yanovka, whilst maintaining its left wing south-west of Rudnya where it claimed to maintain contact with the *XIII.AK*.

Over on the *Panzerarmee* right wing, the situation remained quiet with Nehring's *XXIV.PzK* on the Dnepr.[60] The weather was again poor, with thick cloud cover and steady rain, and in the dreary conditions visibility was necessarily limited. Apart from having to defend against a single combat patrol near Dudari, the *Korps* reported no activity. The patrol itself had consisted of about 25 men, and had been thrown back at about 06.00 hours with no great difficulty.[61] To the left however, the *VII.AK* had finally been caught up in the Soviet offensive.[62] Following an artillery barrage lasting for half

---

56   *PzAOK 4*, Ia Kriegstagebuch entry, dated 25 Dec 43.
57   *Hgr.Süd*, Ia Nr. 4353/43 g.Kdos dated 25 Dec 43.
58   *PzAOK 4*, Ia Nr. 6921/43 geh. dated 25 Dec 43.
59   A blocking unit.
60   *PzAOK 4*, Ia Orientierung, 14.30 hours dated 25 Dec 43.
61   *XXIV.PzK*, Tagesmeldung, 18.15 hours dated 25 Dec 43.
62   *PzAOK 4*, Ia Orientierung, 14.30 hours dated 25 Dec 43.

an hour, enemy forces had assaulted the extreme left wing of the *88.Infanterie-Division* in and to the west of Volitsa. The attack was made with an estimated four rifle battalions and had struck the boundary between the *XXXXII.AK* and the *VII.AK*. Pivni and Koshlyaki both fell, although a swift counterattack managed to recapture the wooded area south of Volitsa. Having occupied Pivni though, the Soviet troops began digging in on the southern edge of the village, having done enough to sever links between the two *Korps*. Elsewhere however, the *Korps* front lay completely quiet.

On the *XIII.AK* sector things were similarly quiet.[63] The right wing of the *68.Infanterie-Division* had seen noticeable enemy reconnaissance activity, and two Soviet troop assemblies had been observed; one east of Malaya Racha and the other further north opposite Krasnoborka. Both had been targeted with artillery fire, but that remained the extent of the combat activity in that sector. The *LIX.AK* too had little to report, spending a comparatively restful day, the only activity being the orderly withdrawal of the *291.Infanterie-Division* to its new positions.[64] Balck's *XXXXVIII. PzK* had meanwhile assumed command of the *8.* and *19.Panzer-Divisions* and the *SS Panzerkampfgruppe 'Das Reich'* at 14.00 hours.[65] *Kampfgruppe* Neumeister, comprising the leading elements of the *1.Panzer-Division*, had arrived in Korostyshev during the morning, but there was no news concerning the rest of the division. The *1.SS Panzer-Division 'LSSAH'* was also underway to its new area of operations.

Late in the morning, Raus had decided to re-organise the composition of his subordinate *Korps*.[66] With the arrival of the *XXXXVIII.PzK* in the Korostyshev area, he had decided to transfer the *8.* and *19.Panzer-Divisions*, and the *SS Panzerkampfgruppe 'Das Reich'*, from the *XXXXII.AK* to Balck's command, leaving just the *25.Panzer-Division* and the newly attached *168.Infanterie-Division* under Mattenklott. In addition, Balck would retain both the *1.Panzer-Division* and the *1.SS Panzer-Division 'LSSAH'*, with the task of first establishing a new defence based on the *'Siegfriedstellung'*, and then, having brought the Soviet advance to a stop, of counterattacking into the enemy flank. The corresponding order was issued during the course of the afternoon under the title *Panzerarmeebefehl Nr.49*.[67] In this, he outlined his intentions to hold the Soviet advance between the Teterev and Kamenka rivers as far east of Zhitomir as possible. This in turn depended upon the *XXXXII.AK* and the *XXXXVIII.PzK* first holding together all those divisions still fighting east of the *'Siegfriedstellung'* and then pulling them back step-by-step, maintaining their cohesion. The *VII.AK* was to shift its main effort on to its left wing to secure and maintain contact with the right wing of the *XXXXII. AK*, by counterattacking if necessary. The *XXXXII.AK*, having handed over the *8.* and *19.Panzer-Divisions* to the *XXXXVIII.PzK*, together with the *SS Panzerkampfgruppe 'Das Reich'*, was to assume responsibility for the newly arriving *168.Infanterie-Division* which was to be assembled in the area around Popel'nya. Its task now was to keep fighting east of the *'Siegfriedstellung'* for as long as possible, making a fighting withdrawal to the new

---

63 *PzAOK 4*, Ia Orientierung, 14.30 hours dated 25 Dec 43.
64 *PzAOK4*, Ia Orientierung, 14.30 hours dated 25 Dec 43.
65 *PzAOK 4*, Ia Orientierung, 14.30 hours dated 25 Dec 43. Although this report indicates that the *Korps* assumed command at 14.45 hours, a message sent by the *XXXXVIII.PzK* to the *19.Panzer-Division* gives the time as 14.00 hours. This is later confirmed in the *XXXXVIII.PzK* Tagesmeldung.
66 *PzAOK 4*, Ia Kriegstagebuch entry, dated 25 Dec 43.
67 *PzAOK 4*, Ia Nr. 6908/43 geh. dated 25 Dec 43.

position only if obliged to do so. This position was then to be held at all costs, with any Soviet armoured breakthroughs being destroyed at a later date. The *18.Artillerie-Division* would remain attached to the *XXXXVIII.PzK*, and its commander, *Generalmajor* Thoholte, was appointed *Kampfkommandant Zhitomir*. The order also confirmed the attachment of the *s.Panzer-Abteilung 509* and the *Panzer-Zerstörer-Bataillon 473* to the *XXXXVIII.PzK*. Its task would be to hinder any rapid advance by Soviet forces towards Zhitomir, by continuing the fight east of the '*Siegfriedstellung*', and only falling back gradually to this line under enemy pressure. Orders regarding the intended counterattack would follow in due course, although the *1.Panzer-Division* was to be assembled in such a way that it could leave a screening force in the Korostyshev area and mount a counterattack from south-east of Zhitomir towards Popel'nya on 26 December.[68] The objective of the attack would be to strike the flank of the enemy grouping advancing southwards over the Kornin-Khodorkov line, and re-establish contact with the left wing of the *VII.AK*. The *XIII.AK* meanwhile was to shift its weight onto its southern wing in order to maintain close contact with the *XXXXVIII.PzK*, whilst at the same time constructing a fallback position along the general line running from Radomyshl' to the north-west along the road to Detinets and Yanovka. New boundaries came with the new *Korps* responsibilities. That between the *VII.AK* and the *XXXXII.AK* was shifted to Pavoloch'-Pochuiki-Pivni-Skragilevka; between the *XXXXII.AK* and the *XXXXVIII. PzK* to Andrushevka-Yaropovichi-Ozera-Vodoty-Morozovka-Khomutets; and between the *XXXXVIII.PzK* and the *XIII.AK* along the course of the river Teterev from south of Zhitomir as far as Radomyshl'. In the rear, the *20.Panzergrenadier-Division* was to speed up its refit, and by midday on 26 December assemble a strong *Kampfgruppe*, including artillery, infantry and anti-tank units, in the Berdichev area, to be ready to be committed at any time thereafter. In this respect, the *Sturmbataillon* attached to the *XXXXVIII. PzK* would be returned to the division. In the meantime, the division's commander, *Generalleutnant* Jauer, was appointed as *Kampfkommandant Berdichev*.

Before the formal issue of this order, at about midday, Balck called *PzAOK 4* headquarters to speak to Raus.[69] He proposed pulling back all those elements of the *8.* and *19.Panzer-Divisions* still fighting in the area bounded by the Kiev-Zhitomir road in the north and the Fastov-Zhitomir railway in the south, to the positions around Gorodskoe, which had recently been established by the *Kampfgruppe* von Mitzlaff of the *8.Panzer-Division*.[70] With the support of the *1.Panzer-Division*, he hoped thereby to bring back the majority of available forces into the '*Siegfriedstellung*' as intact as possible. The gap to the south which would be created as a result would just have to be tolerated. Balck called again at 14.00 hours, this time to propose allowing the *1.SS Panzer-Division 'LSSAH'* to strike south-eastwards of Zhitomir towards Volitsa.[71] Once in that town, the division could then wheel to the north-east and strike towards the *1.Panzer-Division* moving south-east from Korostyshev. The resulting pincer movement

---

68 *PzAOK 4*, Ia Kriegstagebuch entry, dated 25 Dec 43.
69 *PzAOK 4*, Ia Kriegstagebuch entry, dated 25 Dec 43.
70 Gorodskoe is not shown on all maps, but it was situated on the main Kiev-Zhitomir road about 8 kilometres south-west of Kocherov.
71 *PzAOK 4*, Ia Kriegstagebuch entry, dated 25 Dec 43. It should be noted here that there are two towns in this area sharing the name Volitsa. The one already encountered in the *88.Infanterie-Division* sector lies in the Unava valley 10 kilometres south-west of Fastov; this other lies on the main Zhitomir-Popel'nya road, about 35 or so kilometres distant from the former.

would pocket the Soviet forces west of Vil'nya where they could then be destroyed. Raus agreed in principle with these proposals, but argued that the success of any such attack by the *1.Panzer-Division* would depend critically on timing. The attack would have to begin as early as the following morning; otherwise the advancing Soviet forces would simply be too strong. The proposals were put to the Army Group *Ia*, *Oberst* Schulze-Büttger, who considered that it would not be possible to co-ordinate the two separate attacks effectively. He proposed instead waiting for a day in order to be able to deploy the whole of the *XXXXVIII.PzK* against the enemy's southern flank. Raus was informed of the Army Group's views, but he maintained that the *1.Panzer-Division* would still have to be deployed south of the Kiev-Zhitomir road against the Soviet spearheads. The alternative was that Zhitomir would fall in a very short time. He issued a corresponding order, advising the interested *Korps* headquarters that the *1.Panzer-Division* would be undertaking limited attacks either side of the main road.[72] The objective would be to strike the enemy just hard enough to allow the *8.* and *19.Panzer-Divisions*, and the *'Das Reich'*, to fall back in a relatively orderly fashion.

Whilst Raus thus considered his options, the Soviet forces continued to batter his front. But at least there had been some respite. Over in the east, Nehring's *XXIV.PzK* reported that the enemy attacks had died down.[73] The *Korps* expected that the attacks would resume as soon as the weather improved though, and as soon as the Soviet units had had time to absorb replacements for the casualties that had been sustained over the past few days' fighting. It was considered nevertheless, that such attacks would only have limited objectives, such as establishing the nature of German defensive positions and pinning troops on the sector. But apart from the Soviet patrol reported earlier, there had been no combat activity other than a light exchange of artillery fire. The rest of the *168. Infanterie-Division* had meanwhile begun to move, one train having already left, and another one loading. Elements of the *Grenadier-Regiment 417*, together with the *III./Artillerie-Regiment 248*, were already on the road from the Kagarlyk area. The division commander had left for the *XXXXII.AK* earlier that afternoon in the company of a small advance staff.

Hell's *VII.AK* had spent the afternoon struggling with the Soviet breach on its left wing.[74] Following the loss of Pivni and Koshlyaki, the *88.Infanterie-Division* had mounted a counterattack in the area south of Volitsa and managed to recapture two defensive strongpoints. The afternoon had seen renewed Soviet pressure in the area however, and the division had been obliged to pull back once again. A reconnaissance patrol sent out by the division during the afternoon established that Soviet troops had occupied signalmen's houses on the railway three kilometres north-west of Pochuiki and also 1,500 metres further west. The Kazatin-Fastov railway had been cut, and the *Korps* was predicting a renewed Soviet assault for the following day, heading from the Romanovka area to the south-west. In an effort to forestall such an advance, Hell was planning to mount a counterattack the following day, using the division's reserve battalion supported by the *Sturmgeschütz-Abteilung 202*.[75] The objective would be to retake both the high ground south-west of Koshlyaki and the eastern edge of Romanovka. Further

---

72 *PzAOK 4*, Ia Nr. 6908/43 geh. dated 25 Dec 43.
73 *XXIV.PzK*, Tagesmeldung, 18.15 hours dated 25 Dec 43.
74 *VII.AK*, Tagesmeldung, 19.15 hours dated 25 Dec 43.
75 *VII.AK*, Ia Nr. 6052/43 geh. dated 25 Dec 43.

west, there was no news from the *Sperrverband* which was blocking the river Kamenka line on the Pochuiki-Paripsy sector. To the right of the *88.Infanterie-Division*, the *198. Infanterie-Division* reported two separate small-scale assaults against its right wing in the Shevchenkovka area. Both had involved between 30 and 35 men, and both had been thrown back from the southern edge of the village.

To the north-west, the Soviets had resumed their attacks against the *XXXXII.AK* at daylight, now deploying an estimated 13 or 14 rifle divisions and three tank corps.[76] Mattenklott's divisions had fought on, using their last reserves and whatever alarm units could be found, gradually giving ground as they headed back west and south-westwards. The *25.Panzer-Division* reported knocking out a total of 40 Russian tanks, and the *8.Panzer-Division* another 36. The *Korps* total for the day was estimated to be at least 96 tanks. It now appeared likely that the Soviet forces were aiming in two closely linked directions; one for Zhitomir, the other for Berdichev. In the *25.Panzer-Division* sector, the enemy had struck the boundary with the *VII.AK*, capturing first Mokhnachka, and then striking to the west of Dmitrievka, reaching Erchiki on the river Unava by 11.00 hours. Further north, the division had counterattacked from the Gnilets area aiming for Morozovka, but this had quickly run into strong Soviet forces just north of the town, and following a brief firefight, the group had been forced to fall back on Korolevka. At 10.00 hours, the enemy had attacked from Soloveevka towards Lysovka, supported by 40 to 50 tanks, and succeeded in overrunning the defenders in the village, before rolling on southwards past either side of Kornin and over the river Irpen'. At about 13.00 hours, Khodorkov, 15 kilometres further west, was captured by Soviet troops despite a desperate defence by alarm units and dispersed elements of the *19.* and *25.Panzer-Divisions*. Having taken the town, the Russians headed off south-west and south where they ran into other elements of the *25.Panzer-Division* defending Kotlyarka. There had been little news of the *19.Panzer-Division* since the failure of the Morozovka counterattack, but faced with overwhelming Soviet armour, the division continued to fall back to the southwest, reaching the area around Vilen'ka. To the north, the *8.Panzer-Division* had been hit hard again. The elements defending Osovtsy had been assaulted and forced to pull back about 15 kilometres to the south-west, reaching the Vil'nya area. On the Kiev-Zhitomir road, other elements of the division had been engaged on the western end of Kocherov along with troops from the *'Das Reich'*, but these had been forced to pull back along the road to new positions around Gorodskoe. Details were not available, but it was known that Soviet forces had reached the general line between Vil'nya and Voitashevka.

Behind the *XXXXII.AK*, the *XXXXVIII.PzK* had been busy trying to establish a second line of defence.[77] Although it knew that both infantry and armour were advancing either side of the Kiev-Zhitomir road in an as yet undetermined strength, the *Korps* still had no clear idea of Soviet movements and intentions. In the wooded area between the road and the railway further south, there seemed to be only weak advanced elements, including both armoured and infantry units, and for the time being, the main direction seemed to be the south and south-west. Elements of the *19.Panzer-Division*, together with a *Panzergrenadier-Regiment* from the *8.Panzer-Division*, had continued falling back, passing through Vilen'ka between 16.00 and 17.00 hours. Further north, on the Kiev-Zhitomir road, the *Kampfgruppe* von Mitzlaff of the *8.Panzer-Division*, based around

---

76 *XXXXII.AK*, Tagesmeldung, 19.30 hours dated 25 Dec 43.
77 *XXXXVIII.PzK*, Tagesmeldung, 19.45 hours dated 25 Dec 43.

the *Panzeraufklärungs-Abteilung 8* and now supported by the '*Tigers*' of the *s.Panzer-Abteilung 509*, had meanwhile formed a defence in the area of the *Kolkhoz* Gorodskoe. The position had been attacked several times during the day, in battalion strength with tank support, but by evening the position was still held. The *1.Panzer-Division* was still moving up, and by the end of the day the majority of the *Panzergrenadier-Regiment 113*, supported by most of the divisional artillery, the *Panzeraufklärungs-Abteilung 1*, and the *Panzerjäger-Abteilung 37*, had secured a bridgehead over the river Teterev east of Korostyshev. Contact had been made with the *8.Panzer-Division*, and reconnaissance parties sent out to the south, south-east, and east. One such party reached the town of Stepok, over 20 kilometres away to the south, without reporting any enemy contact. There had been no word from the other directions by evening. In the rear, the *18.Artillerie-Division* had all arrived in the Zhitomir area, with the exception of the armoured elements and one heavy howitzer battalion, whilst since midday, the *1.SS Panzer-Division 'LSSAH'* had been moving through Zhitomir on its way towards Volitsa.

The Soviets had meanwhile begun to extend their offensive to the *XIII.AK* sector.[78] Following the earlier increase in reconnaissance activity against the *68.Infanterie-Division*, the Russians now began to assault both the *68.* and the *340.Infanterie-Divisions* in anything up to battalion strength. One was a battalion assault against Lutovka on the extreme right wing of the *68.Infanterie-Division*, just north of Radomyshl'. East of hill 170.2, an estimated one to two Soviet rifle companies were observed forming up, presumably for an attack, and this group was hit with artillery fire and dispersed. To the north, the *213.Sicherungs-Division* repulsed a company strength assault, with the combined defensive fire stalling the attack before it reached the main defensive position. In the *340.Infanterie-Division* sector, a Soviet battalion assault towards Vorsovka was similarly beaten back, while further west, both the *208.Infanterie-Division* and the *7.Panzer-Division* reported only reconnaissance and combat patrolling. In general, the enemy situation facing the *Korps* remained unchanged, although there had been a marked increase in both combat activity and artillery and mortar fire, particularly against the *68.Infanterie-Division* and the *213.Sicherungs-Division*. It all gave the appearance of testing the whole of the *Korps* front. All attacks had been beaten back though, mostly with the assistance of defensive artillery fire, but it still remained to be seen whether this increased activity represented a vigorous attempt to pin the *Korps*, or more seriously, whether it heralded the widening of the general offensive.

Away to the north-west, under cover of a thick mist, the *LIX.AK* completed the withdrawal of the *291.Infanterie-Division* and the *Reserve-Grenadier-Regiment 212* without difficulty, establishing contact to both the left and right.[79] The day had been generally quiet, with the Soviets following up the withdrawal at no great pace, but at about 13.00 hours there had been a small, company-sized assault, supported by three T-34 tanks, against the centre of the *291.Infanterie-Division*. This had been beaten off, but it was followed by a similar attack against the right wing of the *Reserve-Grenadier-Bataillon 316* of the *Reserve-Grenadier-Regiment 212* at about 13.50 hours. This too had been successfully defended. Meanwhile the *Reserve-Grenadier-Regiment 212* had been attached to the *291.Infanterie-Division*, along with the *Pionier-Bataillon 70*, and the boundary between the division and the *Korps-Abteilung C* to the left had been

---

78 *XIII.AK*, Tagesmeldung, 18.30 hours dated 25 Dec 43.
79 *LIX.AK*, Tagesmeldung, 18.45 hours dated 25 Dec 43.

moved slightly to a line running from the road fork north-east of Sobolevka to the windmill south-east of Khotinovka, and from there to the western edge of the *Kolkhoz* Zubovshchina. Earlier that morning, at about 05.15 hours, the *Korps-Abteilung* had been attacked north-west of Bekhi, but the assault was estimated at only company strength, and had been seen off without real difficulty.

Back at *4.Panzerarmee* headquarters, and following the earlier discussions with *Oberst* Schulze-Büttger, a directive had arrived from Army Group South at about 17.00 hours.[80] In this, von Manstein stressed that the main task facing the *4.Panzerarmee* at the moment was to prevent Soviet forces from breaking through to the Kazatin-Berdichev area, as this would sever the main supply lines upon which the right wing of the Army Group depended. He instructed Raus to assemble the *XXXXVIII.PzK*, with the *1.Panzer-Division*, the *1.SS Panzer-Division 'LSSAH'*, the *168.Infanterie-Division* and the *18.Artillerie-Division*, such that it could deliver a decisive counterstroke against the southern flank of the Soviet forces advancing from the Kornin area towards Kazatin and Berdichev. It was important to delay the enemy advance along the Kiev-Zhitomir road as much as possible, but the *1.Panzer-Division* was not to be allowed to get bogged down in such fighting. Having considered the message, Raus called the Army Group at 18.05 hours and spoke with von Manstein.[81] He pointed out that, in addition to the fresh Soviet units already reported to have joined the offensive, the *PzAOK 4* had now identified the presence of the Soviet 8th Guards Mechanised Corps and the 3rd Guards Tank Corps.[82] He also informed von Manstein of his intention to pull back to and hold the '*Siegfriedstellung*', whilst using the *1.Panzer-Division* and the '*LSSAH*' to mount a counterattack from a south-westerly direction against the advancing Soviet forces. Von Manstein pointed out, perhaps unnecessarily, that all means should be employed to prevent the enemy advance from disrupting the redeployment of these troops. Raus also described the increase in Soviet activity opposite the *XIII.AK*, putting forward his view that this represented preparations for an extension of the main offensive. He added moreover that new Soviet armoured units had been detected in the Chopovichi area opposite the boundary between the *XIII.AK* and the *LIX.AK*, and that a major offensive towards Zhitomir could be expected on that sector before much longer.

During the course of the day, it had become apparent to the *PzAOK 4* that not only the whole of the Soviet 38th Army was now engaged but that right wing of the 40th Army had also been committed.[83] Indeed, it had now been established that about 14 rifle divisions were involved in the offensive, as well as at least three tank or mechanised corps. In addition to the drive towards Zhitomir, it now seemed clear that the offensive was also aimed towards Berdichev and Kazatin to the south-west, with the 8th Guards Mechanised Corps and the wrongly-identified 3rd Guards Tank Corps on this sector. What was still not clear though was whether the Russians intended to commit additional armoured reserves from those then refitting in the Kiev area. Other intelligence suggested that the 10th Tank Corps would be arriving some time opposite the left wing, indicating

---

80   *Hgr.Süd*, Ia Nr. 4357/43 g.Kdos. dated 25 Dec 43.
81   *PzAOK 4*, Ia Kriegstagebuch entry, dated 25 Dec 43.
82   The *4.Panzerarmee* was in fact in error here. The 3rd Guards Tank Corps was not deployed in this sector, although the Ic may have confused the unit with either the 6th Guards or 7th Guards Tank Corps, both of which were attached to the 3rd Tank Army.
83   *PzAOK 4*, Ic Abendmeldung an H.Gr. Süd, 19.30 hours dated 25 Dec 43.

again that the Soviets were building another concentration in the Chopovichi area.[84] For the time being though, the day had seen the Soviets apparently shift the main weight of their assault from the Zhitomir direction away to the south. On the southern wing of the *XXXXII.AK* sector, either side of Kornin, the already weakened *25.Panzer-Division* had borne the brunt of the fighting, and had proved completely unable to hold up the enemy attack. The leading Soviet elements had pushed on westwards as far as the area south and south-west of Khodorkov, having advanced almost 30 kilometres during the first two days of the offensive. But at least the change of emphasis and direction now seemed to indicate quite clearly that the operation was directed towards the Berdichev-Kazatin area. With that assumption in mind, Raus could now plan accordingly, and he reported his future intentions to the Army Group later that night.[85] First, he planned to stabilise the situation on the Kiev-Zhitomir road with local counterattacks by the *XXXXVIII. PzK*, whilst the main body of the *Korps* would be re-assembled south-east of Zhitomir on the road to Popel'nya, with forward elements in the area around Ivnitsa-Volitsa. The *168.Infanterie-Division* meanwhile would assemble along the Skvira-Popel'nya road, its leading troops as far north as the river Rostavitsa.

---

84 This seems to have been Soviet disinformation as the 10th Tank Corps had been in the *Stavka* reserve since the beginning of December 1943 and would not be released again until September 1944.
85 *PzAOK 4*, Ia Nr. 6930/43 g.Kdos. dated 25 Dec 43.

4

The Offensive Widens

Sunday 26 December 1943

Following the earlier discussions between Raus and von Manstein regarding the future course of operations, Army Group South issued further instructions to the *PzAOK 4* during the evening of 25 December, although these were not received until the following day.[1] In these, the *PzAOK 4* was formally given the task of securing the deep flank of the Army Group and keeping open the important rail communications through Berdichev and Kazatin. Von Manstein informed Raus that his immediate objective was to bring to a halt the Soviet advance towards Kazatin and Zhitomir at any cost, and at the same time prevent the enemy from rolling up the left flank from the north. All possible resources were to be deployed to halt the Soviet advance, both in the gap between the left wing of the *VII.AK* and the wooded area east of Zhitomir, and on the Kiev-Zhitomir road itself. At the same time, the operations of the *XIII.AK* and *LIX.AK* were to be conducted so as to prevent any enemy strike towards Zhitomir from the north or north-east, and if possible to free troops for the two sectors under most threat. To assist in this seemingly impossible task, the *17.Panzer-Division* would be transferred to the *Panzerarmee* from the area south-east of Kirovograd. It was planned to arrive in the Kazatin area by 31 December.

The night had proved quiet on the right wing of the *Panzerarmee*, particularly so opposite the *XXIV.PzK*.[2] Apart from heavy machine-gun and rifle fire in the vicinity of Kanada, there had been no combat activity at all to report. The main news was the departure of another three trains to the Pavoloch' area, transferring elements of the *168. Infanterie-Division* to its new sector. The *VII.AK* too had passed a relatively undisturbed night, with the only fighting reported being a Soviet combat patrol in the *198.Infanterie-Division* sector.[3] Over on the extreme left wing however, the Russians had not been idle, and heavy engine noises had been heard throughout the night in the Pivni area in the Unava valley. Further south, elements of the *Sperrverband* had meanwhile taken up positions in the village of Novoselitsa, south of Pochuiki.

To the north-west, elements of the retreating *25.Panzer-Division* were trying desperately to establish new defensive positions on the south bank of the river Unava in the Velikaya Lesovtsy-Kotlyarka-Voitovtsy[4] area, despite Soviet tanks already having reached the town of Popel'nya, effectively outflanking the division's right wing and cutting it off from the *VII.AK*.[5] Mattenklott's *XXXXII.AK* had meanwhile lost contact

---

1 *Hgr.Süd*, Ia Nr. 4365/43 g.Kdos. dated 25 Dec 43.
2 *XXIV.PzK*, Morgenmeldung, 05.35 hours dated 26 Dec 43.
3 *VII.AK*, Morgenmeldung, 04.30 hours dated 26 Dec 43.
4 Referred to as Mostovoe in more recent Soviet maps.
5 *PzAOK 4*, Morgenmeldung an *Hgr.Süd*, dated 26 Dec 43.

with the division, and was unaware of developments.[6] There had been no word from the *168.Infanterie-Division*, assembling to the south in the Pavoloch' area.

Over 35 kilometres away to the north-west, the majority of the *1.Panzer-Division*, less the *Panzer-Regiment 1*, had assembled during the night, and by morning it was ready to move off to the attack along the road to Kiev towards the '*Siegfriedstellung*'.[7] The *Kampfgruppe* von Mitzlaff, based around the *Panzergrenadier-Regiment 8* of the *8.Panzer-Division*, had spent the night trying to beat off Soviet attempts to encircle it in its positions around Gorodskoe,[8] whilst the *Kampfgruppe* von Radowitz, formed from the *Panzergrenadier-Regiment 28*, was further south, still desperately trying to fight its way back westwards. At about 22.00 hours the previous evening, it had reported being in the town of Shchegleevka, 15 kilometres south-east of Korostyshev, fighting alongside troops from the *19.Panzer-Division*. The main body of this division had attacked Soviet positions along the Dubovets[9] stream, destroyed a reported 26 enemy tanks, and then, following the collapse of Russian resistance, formed a 'hedgehog' around the villages of Zdvizhka and Vilen'ka.[10] Further south, the *1.SS Panzer-Division 'LSSAH'* had already established its headquarters in Starosel'ye, and had continued to move south-east of Zhitomir towards Volitsa. In the rear, the *18.Artillerie-Division* had completed its assembly in the Zhitomir area, and had just begun its preparations for the construction of '*Festung Zhitomir*'. Over on the left wing of the *XXXXVIII.PzK*, the SS *Panzerkampfgruppe 'Das Reich'* had meanwhile pulled back to the west bank of the Teterev, holding the sector from Gorodsk in the south to the *Kolkhoz* Lenino just south of Radomyshl'. To its left, the *XIII.AK* reported continuous combat and reconnaissance patrolling throughout the night on its sector.[11] Small-scale assaults were also reported, but these had been successfully seen off. The previous evening an estimated Soviet rifle company had broken into Radomyshl' itself, but a counterattack had cleared the situation. There had been another assault later, in the vicinity of the brewery south of the town, and a counterattack, begun in the early hours, was still in progress by morning. A little to the south, the *68.Infanterie-Division* reported that Soviet troops had managed to force a crossing of the Teterev, and set foot on the west bank about 1,500 metres south of the *Kolkhoz* Lenino. The strength of the enemy bridgehead was not known, but a counterattack was being planned for later in the morning in conjunction with the '*Das Reich*'. Meanwhile further north, according to statements taken from prisoners of war, there were strong Soviet forces, including tanks and heavy weapons, assembling in the area north of Malin,[12] whilst over on the left wing, the *7.Panzer-Division* observed much more enemy movement in the Ustinovka area than on previous days. These had been fired upon whenever practicable, but most of the night's artillery fire had been Soviet.

To the north-west, the *LIX.AK* reported enemy forces feeling their way forward on a number of sectors, pushing as far as the main defensive positions in several

---

6 *XXXXII.AK*, Morgenmeldung, 06.00 hours dated 26 Dec 43.
7 *XXXXVIII.PzK*, Morgenmeldung, 06.20 hours dated 26 Dec 43.
8 Referred to as Gorodezkaja in the German records.
9 Referred to as the Wilenka stream in the German records.
10 *PzAOK 4*, Morgenmeldung an *Hgr.Süd*, dated 26 Dec 43.
11 *XIII.AK*, Morgenmeldung, 06.25 hours dated 26 Dec 43.
12 According to the German records, the location was 'east of Morosovka'. This village is no longer shown on more recent Soviet maps, but it was situated just north of Malin on the road to Pirozhki.

instances.¹³ One of these patrols had infiltrated into the southern end of Stariki, on the right wing of the *291.Infanterie-Division*, but this had been spotted and dispersed with a small counterattack. A patrol sent out by the division had meanwhile established that Soviet forces had occupied the village of Zabrannoe, north-east of Guta Dobrynskaya, and that the adjoining elements of the *7.Panzer-Division* had pulled back from their positions a kilometre further south-west, thus causing the *Korps* to lose contact with its neighbour. There had been other signs of an impending assault further north too. Several concentrations of artillery and mortar fire had landed in the area around and to the south of Novaki, on the *Korps-Abteilung C* right wing, and in the same area it also reported observing troop movements and hearing engine noises. On the basis of this, the *Korps* was predicting a tank-supported assault on the sector between Novaki and the nearby *Sovkhoz*.

The day dawned heavy once more; grey and wet, with the continuing drizzle turning to light snow in places as the afternoon turned colder. In the early morning, at about 08.30 hours, the chiefs of staffs from the *XXXXII.AK* and the *XXXXVIII.PzK* both reported that the towns of Volitsa and Andrushevka had been occupied by advancing Soviet forces.¹⁴ In response, Raus ordered the *Kampfgruppe* being assembled in the Berdichev area by the *20.Panzergrenadier-Division* to move north-eastwards towards Chervonoe, to reconnoitre and secure that area. At 09.20 hours, Balck called the *PzAOK 4* to advise Raus that those elements of the *8.* and *19.Panzer-Divisions* still fighting south of the Kiev-Zhitomir road, and also the remaining troops either side of the road, were now heavily engaged with Soviet troops, but for the time being at least, they were managing to hold their ground.¹⁵ Elements of the *1.Panzer-Division* had moved off south-eastwards from Korostyshev, with the objective of enabling the *8.* and *19.Panzer-Divisions* to pull back and join the remaining troops either side of the main road. Further north, Soviet forces had attacked the *SS Panzerkampfgruppe 'Das Reich'* near Lenino, but the situation there was still unclear. Raus, for his part, reminded Balck that the *1.Panzer-Division* would have to be pulled out as soon as possible in accordance with the Army Group's instructions. He also took the opportunity of informing the *Panzerkorps* commander of his future intentions. These included attaching the *25.Panzer-Division* and the *168. Infanterie-Division* to his *Korps*; exchanging the *XXXXII.AK* and the *XXIV.PzK* and attaching the *8.* and *19.Panzer-Divisions*, together with the *'Das Reich'*, to Nehring's command. Army Group South had already given its approval to these proposals, and instructed the *4.Panzerarmee* to use both the *1.Panzer-Division* and the *'LSSAH'* to counterattack towards Khodorkov to bring the Soviet advance there to a halt. Busse had also asked Raus to consider future operations of the *XIII.AK* in the event that the *Korps* was subjected to a major offensive. He was of the opinion himself that the *Korps* would not be able to withstand a strong enemy assault, and would eventually be forced to pull back onto the Radomyshl'-Chernyakhov line. Whether in such desperate circumstances the *LIX.AK* should remain in the Korosten' area, or whether it should be pulled back in order to maintain contact with the left wing of the *XIII.AK*, would be a matter for judgement depending on how the situation developed. Either way there would be further crises to face.

---

13 *LIX.AK*, Morgenmeldung, 06.10 hours dated 26 Dec 43.
14 *PzAOK 4*, Ia Kriegstagebuch entry, dated 26 Dec 43.
15 *PzAOK 4*, Ia Kriegstagebuch entry, dated 26 Dec 43.

A little later, Raus spoke with von Mellenthin at *XXXXVIII.PzK* to discover whether there was any chance of the *Korps* being in a position to launch its planned counterattack from the Volitsa area by the following day.[16] With the *1.Panzer-Division* still heavily engaged against Soviet armour south of Korostyshev, Raus was not convinced that the original idea of a pincer attack to meet the *'LSSAH'* coming up from the south-west was still feasible. The division was just not likely to break through towards Vilen'ka. He was now considering using the two divisions together on a narrow sector to strike from the Volitsa area, through Khodorkov toward Soloveevka, to meet up there with infantry units attacking northwards through Kornin.

At about 11.00 hours that morning, von Manstein arrived at *4.Panzerarmee* headquarters for a conference with Raus and his staff.[17] Raus began the meeting by describing the latest situation, and setting out his intentions. Von Manstein, for his part, agreed that the two *panzer-divisions* had to be committed together whatever the circumstances, but he certainly concurred with the intended strike from Khodorkov to the north-east. If the current strike by the *1.Panzer-Division* to the south-east had not achieved a breakthrough by the end of the day, the attack would have to be delayed by another day, and the *'LSSAH'* would have to use the time to take up screening positions facing north so as to protect the assembly area of the *1.Panzer-Division* when it arrived. Hauffe meanwhile, was to conduct *XIII.AK* operations such that, if attacked in strength, the *Korps* could fall back to the south-west, keeping the *7.Panzer-Division* echeloned to the rear on the left flank. Things on the left wing of the *Panzerarmee* were not so clear cut, and von Manstein agreed that no decision could yet be made as to whether the *LIX.AK* should stand fast around Korosten' or whether it should be allowed to fall back. The only thing for certain was that the *Korps* should concentrate its efforts on its southern wing. The final point raised by the Army Group commander related to increased reconnaissance activity. Before leaving at 11.45 hours, he urged Raus to carry out as much aerial reconnaissance as possible, particularly opposite his left wing where the German picture of Soviet intentions was especially vague. He suggested the areas just west of Kiev, and around both Malin and Chopovichi.

Out in the field, the weather had begun to change. Temperatures had risen during the night and there had been a slight thaw, particularly in the east nearer the Dnepr. The skies were still heavily overcast though, offering a mixture a rain and light snowfall and keeping visibility poor. The roads were beginning to turn to mud, although in general they still remained passable to vehicles, particularly the further west they were. Over on the right wing, the *XXIV.Panzerkorps* reported enemy troop movements from the north towards Pshenichniki opposite the *Korps-Abteilung B*, and a small troop assembly north of Shchuchinka.[18] Nothing further developed however, and the transfer of the *168. Infanterie-Division* continued undisturbed, with one train leaving during the morning and another planned for early afternoon. To its left, Hell's *VII.AK* was still struggling with the Soviet assault south-east of Kornin.[19] Elements of the *88.Infanterie-Division* had recaptured the southern part of Koshlyaki and the high ground to the west, but these had both been lost again following a renewed enemy assault with artillery support.

---

16 *PzAOK 4*, Ia Kriegstagebuch entry, dated 26 Dec 43.
17 *PzAOK 4*, Ia Kriegstagebuch entry, dated 26 Dec 43.
18 *PzAOK 4*, Ia Orientierung, dated 26 Dec 43.
19 *PzAOK 4*, Ia Orientierung, dated 26 Dec 43.

THE OFFENSIVE WIDENS 105

Further south, an estimated two Soviet rifle battalions had attacked Pochuiki, throwing back the weak covering forces, and advancing eastwards south of the Kamenka valley, threatening to roll up the division's left flank. To the west, a force estimated to be a Soviet rifle regiment had already crossed the river Unava, capturing Erchiki and pushing on to the south-west towards Paripsy. Earlier the same morning, four Soviet tanks had already reached the outskirts of that town, but having fired a few rounds into the village, moved away heading to the north-east.

Communications with Mattenklott's *XXXXII.AK* had been lost again during the morning, although the *PzAOK 4* managed to gain some idea of the situation on that sector from an intercepted radio message from the *25.Panzer-Division* to its *Korps* headquarters.[20] The division's right wing had been outflanked by an estimated 45 Soviet tanks, whilst the main front had been held by attacks by both infantry and armour along the whole sector. It first withdrew to its main defensive positions, and then back behind the Kamenka stream between Paripsy and Vasil'evka. In the rear, elements of the *168. Infanterie-Division* continued to assemble in the area south of the river Rostavitsa. One battalion was scheduled to be in Maliye Erchiki by 11.00 hours, and another, together with the divisional headquarters and some of the train, in Skvira by 16.00 hours.

About 30 or so kilometres further north, the retreating elements of the *8.* and *19.Panzer-Divisions* had meanwhile been instructed by the *XXXXVIII.PzK* to try and pull back from the Vilen'ka-Shchegleevka area to the south-west towards the town of Ivnitsa.[21] The original plan, for the divisions to pull back to the north, had been frustrated by the arrival of strong Soviet forces, including 30 or so tanks, in the area, whilst the attack by the *Panzergrenadier-Regiment 1* of the *1.Panzer-Division*, had hit strong Russian forces south of the Korostyshev-Voitashevka road. Of the division's available armour, only eight operational panzers had so far arrived in Korostyshev, with the others still being on the road in the rear. The counterattack had been unable to break through on this sector, and had then been hit by an attack from the north-east which effectively pinned the unit where it was. To the north, in the Teterev valley, the *SS Panzerkampfgruppe 'Das Reich'* had meanwhile struck back, partially recapturing the village of Lenino. The attacking elements had then been isolated themselves in the southern end of the village, and another assault was underway to relieve them. Other than this action, the *'Das Reich'* was, by midday, holding a line running north from Gorodsk as far as the Mika river, although aerial reconnaissance had reported Soviet troops already in the town of Kichkiry in the Mika valley. On the southern wing of the *Panzerkorps*, elements of the *'LSSAH'* had begun to arrive in the Volitsa-Ivnitsa-Starosel'ye area, although the *panzers* were still way back in the column. Further south, the *Regimentsgruppe* from the *20.Panzergrenadier-Division* was busy making its way from Berdichev to Chervonoe.

Away to the north, the full weight of the Soviet offensive had finally struck Hauffe's *XIII.AK*.[22] At about 10.00 hours, the Soviet artillery had opened fire along the whole of the *Korps* front, heralding the start of an extremely heavy artillery and mortar barrage.[23] At about 10.25 hours, Hauffe reported these developments to the *Panzerarmee*, adding

---
20 *PzAOK 4*, Ia Orientierung, dated 26 Dec 43.
21 *PzAOK 4*, Ia Orientierung, dated 26 Dec 43.
22 *PzAOK 4*, Ia Orientierung, dated 26 Dec 43.
23 *XIII.AK*, Tagesmeldung, 20.45 hours dated 26 Dec 43.

that he considered this to be the beginning of a major offensive.[24] Raus wondered whether, in the circumstances, the *XIII.AK* should not begin to pull back that evening into a line running from Verlok through Detinets to Budilovka. Hauffe considered however that his divisions were already in well-constructed defensive positions, and that he should leave them where they were. If they began to fall back, the Soviets would inevitably follow up very closely, and probably prevent the *Korps* from establishing itself in new positions. Under such circumstances it would be more difficult to stop the advance.

Whilst the two men talked, the barrage continued unabated, and throughout the hail of fire, the whole of the *XIII.AK* artillery responded by laying fire on all known troop assembly areas. Despite this desperate measure, the Soviet assault began promptly at 11.00 hours. Superior forces, including a reported 20 tanks, fell on the positions held by the *68.Infanterie-Division* and the right wing of the *213.Sicherungs-Division*, concentrating on the area between Radomyshl' and Mircha, 15 kilometres further north. Between Malaya Racha and Krasnoborka, in the *68.Infanterie-Division* sector, the Soviets managed to achieve a breakthrough in something between battalion and regiment strength, whilst individual tanks were deployed between Malaya Racha and Velikaya Racha.[25] By the end of the morning, the division had organised a counterattack from the area around and to the north of Zabolot', but the centre of the *Korps* front had been badly dented. The front line ran from Radomyshl' in the south to the north-west edge of Malaya Racha, from there it bent backwards to Zabolot', north to Khodory, and from there it turned back north-eastwards to a point two kilometres east of Korolevka. Beyond that it ran unchanged, and both the *340.* and *208.Infanterie-Divisions* had maintained their positions, seeing off a number of company and battalion strength assaults. Over on the *Korps* left wing, the *7.Panzer-Division* reported heavy Soviet traffic in the Ustinovka area, where a few tanks were spotted during the course of the morning.

To the north-west, the *LIX.AK* had also been subjected to attack.[26] The left wing of the *291.Infanterie-Division* had been struck by an unknown force including tanks, either side of the main Malin-Korosten' road, and this assault had resulted in a breakthrough south of the road. Fighting continued into the afternoon. A few kilometres away, the right wing of the *Korps-Abteilung C* had managed to see off a number of reconnaissance probes in the area between Novaki and Shatrishche. Two Soviet tanks had been reported in these actions, but other than these manageable problems, the *Korps-Abteilung* reported no enemy activity.

Back at *4.Panzerarmee* headquarters, at 14.20 hours, Balck reported the difficulties being experienced by the *8.* and *19.Panzer-Divisions* in pulling back to the main Kiev-Zhitomir road.[27] The two divisions had become entangled with an estimated 80 Soviet tanks, and been obliged to reconsider their situation. To make matters worse, a number of Russian tanks had also been reported as having broken through to the main road between Korostyshev and Gorodetskoe. Balck now proposed pulling the troops on the Teterev either side of Korostyshev back southwards. This manoeuvre would include the *1.Panzer-Division*, as well as the *8.* and *19.Panzer-Divisions*. Raus was unsure, and reserved such a decision for himself, pointing out that such a move would prevent

---

24   *PzAOK 4*, Ia Kriegstagebuch entry, dated 26 Dec 43.
25   *PzAOK 4*, Ia Orientierung, dated 26 Dec 43.
26   *PzAOK 4*, Ia Orientierung, dated 26 Dec 43.
27   *PzAOK 4*, Ia Kriegstagebuch entry, dated 26 Dec 43.

the intended counterstroke by the combined forces of the *1.Panzer-Division* and the *'LSSAH'*, an operation upon which von Manstein placed great importance. Raus then discussed the situation with Fangohr, and expressed the view that, given the change in circumstances, it would no longer be practicable to carry out the necessary troop regrouping in order to deal a decisive blow, particularly if it would need at least another three days to complete. Instead, he thought that the *Panzerarmee* stood a greater chance of bringing the Soviet advance to a halt by mobile defensive operations. A little later, Balck made another proposal, this time for the *'LSSAH'* to assume a defensive role and just block the Zhitomir-Volitsa road. Raus turned down the request, pointing out that the task of the *Panzerarmee* was not only to delay the Soviet advance in the Zhitomir area, but also to prevent them from pressing on to the apparent objectives of Berdichev and Kazatin.

Later in the afternoon, at about 16.25 hours, Raus took the opportunity of discussing with Fangohr the whole situation and the future course of operations.[28] On the right flank of the Soviet breakthrough, everything now depended on the *XXXXII.AK* being able to establish a defensive line along the south bank of the river Kamenka, through Pochuiki and Paripsy, and from there north-westwards through Popel'nya to Sokol'cha on the south bank of the river Unava and then westwards along the valley as far as Gorodishche. Its task on that line would be to prevent any further Soviet advance to the south. The *XXXXVIII.PzK* would then block both the Zhitomir-Volitsa road and the Teterev sector as far as Korostyshev, before committing the *1.SS Panzer-Division 'LSSAH'* to an attack from the Starosel'ye area through Zarubintsy to restore contact with the left wing of the *XXXXII.AK*. In case any Soviet forces had already passed south-westwards in that area, the *Regimentsgruppe* from the *20.Panzergrenadier-Division* would move up from Chervonoe to take up covering positions in Arapovka and Lebedintsy. Raus discussed these proposals with von Manstein at 18.50 hours that evening, and obtained the Army Group's approval. Von Manstein did not miss the opportunity to remind Raus that everything would now depend on the *XXXXII.AK* holding its current positions, and on the ability of the *XXXXVIII.PzK* actually to close the gap. When the idea was put to Balck, he suggested instead that, rather than go through Zarubintsy, the advance should be made further south, on the other side of the river Guiva. Raus agreed, and instructed the *18.Artillerie-Division* to move to the Kazatin area. He also ordered the *Kavallerie-Regiment Süd* to move to the Kashperovka area, south of Chervonoe.[29] It was to begin arriving by 04.00 hours on 27 December, and take up defensive positions behind the river Guiva, facing east and north. Formal orders went to the *20.Panzergrenadier-Division* too, instructing it to place the forward *Regimentsgruppe* on the line from Brovki station to Lebedintsy, on the left wing of the *XXXXII.AK*.[30] It was to establish and maintain contact with the left wing of the *25.Panzer-Division* in the vicinity of Brovki station, whilst pushing forward reconnaissance elements as far as the line Gorodishche-Andrushevka.

Nehring's *XXIV.Panzerkorps* had meanwhile passed another easy day, reporting no Soviet attacks along its entire sector.[31] It was still predicting strong attacks in the

---

28 *PzAOK 4*, Ia Kriegstagebuch entry, dated 26 Dec 43.
29 *PzAOK 4*, Ia Nr. 6955/43 geh. dated 26 Dec 43.
30 *PzAOK 4*, Ia Nr. 6954/43 geh. dated 26 Dec 43.
31 *XXIV.PzK*, Tagesmeldung, 18.00 hours dated 26 Dec 43.

near future, but so far, Soviet activity had been limited to continued troop movements. Traffic had been observed in the areas around Pshenichniki, where four guns had been seen, Romashki, and Balyko-Shchuchinka. Two Soviet patrols had been intercepted by troops of the *Korps-Abteilung B* south of Romashki, and thrown back, whilst north of Germanovka a troop assembly had been observed and estimated at battalion strength. There were movements too, with one column, including seven vehicles, being spotted in Germanovka before heading off to the north-east. Another, with sledges, was seen heading north from Germanovka towards Dolina, but this was subjected to artillery fire and forced to take a detour. The *Korps* had meanwhile been transferring units itself. The *I.* and *II./Grenadier-Regiment 417* had arrived in the area north-west of Skvira where it was deployed to screen the arrival of the rest of the *168.Infanterie-Division*. The two battalions, together with the *Füsilier-Bataillon*, the *Aufklärungs-Abteilung 168*, the *Panzerjäger-Kompanie 248* and a *Kompanie* from the *Pionier-Bataillon 248*, had all been transferred to the *XXXXII.AK*. Other elements of the *Grenadier-Regiment 417* had arrived in Belaya Tserkov', together with the *III./Artillerie-Regiment 248*. The *I./Artillerie-Regiment 221* was in Vintsentovka, whilst the *Regimentsgruppe 385* had left Kagarlyk on board five trains, and the *Regimentsgruppe 425* was busy unloading. Most other elements of the division were ready assembled in the Kagarlyk area, awaiting transport, although the *IV./Artillerie-Regiment 248* was still making its way to the assembly area.

Things had been more difficult for Hell as the *VII.AK* continued to battle away on its extreme left wing.[32] The Soviets had continued to strengthen their forces opposite the *88.Infanterie-Division*, bringing in elements of the 74th Rifle Division, and pushing closer and closer towards the main defensive positions. As early as 08.30 hours, Soviet troops had attacked out of Koshlyaki, but this had been met with a counterattack and completely disrupted. Another attack, this time at 13.00 hours, by an estimated two rifle battalions against the village of Dekhtyarka just north of Stavishche, was thrown back, as was another at 15.30 hours in the Trilesy area. Further west though, at about 14.00 hours, the division was obliged to fall back from Koshlyaki and the high ground to the west following heavy pressure from the west and north. All the while the artillery continued to engage Soviet troop assemblies whenever these were spotted, fire being laid upon the villages of Chervonoe and Bortniki on the division's right, and Pivni on the left. By 16.00 hours, the division had taken up new positions, running from Stavishche in the west, along the Kamenka river to Trilesy, and unchanged from there to the east. To the division's left, the *Sperrverband*, comprising the *Pionier-Bataillon 215* supported by a *Sturmgeschütz-Batterie*, had been attacked during the afternoon by an estimated two rifle battalions moving in from the north. Following the assault, it had been forced to give up its positions in Pochuiki, and was unable to prevent the Soviet forces wheeling eastwards into the left flank of the division. At about 15.00 hours, the *Sperrverband* attempted to recapture Pochuiki, counterattacking from the Novoselitsa area with the support of the *Sturmgeschützen*, but there was no news of progress by evening. Further west, Soviet forces estimated to be a rifle regiment had been observed heading south-westwards from Erchiki towards Paripsy at about 13.45 hours, but this was beyond the *Korps* area of responsibility. Elsewhere in the *Korps* sector other Soviet preparations were visible. Opposite the right wing of the *75.Infanterie-Division* there seemed to be

---

32   *VII.AK*, Tagesmeldung, 19.10 hours dated 26 Dec 43.

various traffic and troop assemblies to indicate a renewed attack any time. There was considerable vehicle and foot traffic moving towards Germanovka from the north and north-west, including two T-60 tanks, whilst troop assemblies were observed in the woods south of the town. Many of these units had also been moved up into the front line. Opposite the *198.Infanterie-Division* too, there had been other troop movements, with between 50 and 100 men pulling out of the villages of Bol'shoi Grab, Mar'yanovka and Fastovets and heading westwards. The division was also subjected to small-scale probing though, and three separate platoon-sized patrols were thrown back north of Ol'shanskaya Novoselitsa, Pinchuki, and the *Sovkhoz* west of Ksaverovka. Despite these small actions though, the *Korps* concluded that the Soviets were actually pulling troops out of this particular sector for redeployment elsewhere, presumably to strengthen the attack against the *88.Infanterie-Division*. Further in the Soviet rear, a large column was seen heading south of Velikaya Snetinka towards Fastov.

To the west the *XXXXII.AK* was still struggling to keep itself together.[33] The Soviets continued to press hard with both infantry and armour, particularly in the sector south of Popel'nya. Enemy armoured units threatened to outflank the right wing of the *25.Panzer-Division*, obliging it to pull back southwards behind the river Kamenka. The main assault had begun at about midday when massed infantry and armour had struck the Velikaya Lesovtsy-Sokol'cha sector, whilst an estimated 45 Soviet tanks struck southwards from the Popel'nya area against the division's right wing. Following heavy fighting, it began to pull back behind the Kamenka, completing the move under the cover of darkness. Over on its left wing, Soviet infantry and armour had attacked Voitovtsy at 09.30 hours, forcing the division to pull back on that sector too. By night-time it was established along the Kamenka between Vasil'evka and Paripsy, with reconnaissance patrols probing further west. During the afternoon, both Brovki station and Lebedintsy had been reported as free of enemy troops, although the sound of fighting could be heard from the area around Gorodishche to the north.

It was a similar story for the *XXXXVIII.PzK*.[34] Soviet forces had continued to press the offensive on a broad front, with two objectives seeming to become clearer. First, the strike along the main Kiev-Zhitomir road, where the Soviet 3rd Tank Army had now been identified; and second, the strike to the south-west, by the 1st Tank Army, apparently with Kazatin and Berdichev as its objectives. It could not yet be established however, whether the latter grouping might not also wheel westwards towards the area south of Zhitomir. Meanwhile, the majority of the *1.SS Panzer-Division 'LSSAH'* had now arrived in its assembly area around Volitsa and Starosel'ye, including the two *SS-Panzergrenadier-Regiments*, the *SS Panzer-Aufklärungs-Abteilung 1*, elements of the *SS-Panzer-Regiment 1*, elements of the *SS-Artillerie-Regiment 1*, and a few units from the *SS-Panzer-Pionier-Bataillon 1*. Whilst the division was trying to organise its defensive position, Soviet forces, including about 25 to 30 tanks, made repeated attacks from the north-east and east against Volitsa. The *'LSSAH'* lost two panzers repulsing these attacks, but reported destroying 10 Russian tanks in the process. To the south-east, Soviet troops were seen to be digging in near the bend in the road about four kilometres from Volitsa, whilst later in the afternoon, at about 16.00 hours, a Soviet motorised column, including a number of tanks, was seen heading south-westwards from Yaropovichi

33 *XXXXII.AK*, Tagesmeldung, 20.15 hours dated 26 Dec 43.
34 *XXXXVIII.PzK*, Tagesmeldung, 19.30 hours dated 26 Dec 43.

towards Zarubintsy. To the north, both Stepok and Ivnitsa were both reported lost to the enemy. All in all, the division reported the presence of about 80 Soviet tanks on its sector. The *1.Panzer-Division* meanwhile had launched the *Kampfgruppe* Neumeister, based on the *Panzergrenadier-Regiment 113*, in an attack towards the '*Siegfriedstellung*'. The *Kampfgruppe* had moved out from its assembly area south-east of Gorodetskoe, through the *Kampfgruppe* von Mitzlaff's positions, and struck out through the woods to reach the Dubovets stream near Tsarevka before turning south. The Soviets threw counterattack after counterattack against the *Kampfgruppe*, hitting it with infantry and tanks from both the east and the south, and before long the attack bogged down, and no further progress was possible. The division's other *Panzergrenadier-Regiment*, the *Kampfgruppe* Friedrich, was subjected to an estimated regimental-sized attack in its assembly area about six kilometres east of Korostyshev, and was unable to contribute to the attack, being pinned from both the north and south. It opted instead to fight its way back towards the town. The division's artillery positions east of Korostyshev were also targeted by Soviet attacks, and before long the main road itself was blocked by Russian troops. The *Kampfgruppe* Neumeister called off its attack, and turned around to clear the road to Korostyshev where the *Panzeraufklärungs-Abteilung 1* was still screening the eastern and southern edges of the town. It had reported 20 Soviet tanks as early as 10.00 hours that morning. During the evening, the *Kampfgruppe* struck westwards along the road to Zhitomir, and quickly dislodged the advance Soviet forces, clearing the road once more as it headed west. To the south, the *19.Panzer-Division* and elements of the *8.Panzer-Division*, including the *Panzergrenadier-Regiment 28*, managed to fight their way westwards from Vilen'ka, edging towards relative safety, and by about 13.45 hours the last elements had reached the area around Mashina, a couple of kilometres north of Grabovka. In the north, the *SS Panzerkampfgruppe 'Das Reich'* was attacked a number of times as it tried to defend the Teterev line. The attacks were made in anything up to regimental strength, supported by both tanks and artillery, and Lenino had been lost again. The group isolated in the southern part of the village had been rescued following an armoured counterattack, but by the end of the day, the *Kampfgruppe* was defending on a line running from a point two kilometres east of Gorodsk to the area south-east of Novaya Yurovka. It also had forward positions on the edge of the wood south of Kichkiry, screening the Soviet troops in the town.

The *XIII.AK* had continued its efforts to hold off the Soviet offensive and to some degree had been successful.[35] The *68.Infanterie-Division*, having borne the brunt of the assault, had succeeded in holding the attack to a line running from the west edge of Malaya Racha to a point 1,500 metres east of Zabolot'. Radomyshl' itself however had been evacuated following heavy fighting and the threat of encirclement, and the division's right wing was now positioned on the high ground west of the town. On the left, the counterattack which had begun that morning was still underway as darkness fell. Further north, the *213.Sicherungs-Division*, neither fully equipped nor trained for front line combat, offered what Hauffe described as 'courageous resistance', but was simply unable to stand fast, and pulled back to a line running from Lyski farm to the eastern edge of Khodory. Contributing to the need for this withdrawal had been the poor defensive performance of the *Ost-Reiter-Abteilung 403* and the *Landesschützen-Bataillon*

---

35 *XIII.AK*, Tagesmeldung, 20.45 hours dated 26 Dec 43.

987, with neither unit being suited to front line combat. To the north, the *340.Infanterie-Division* reported a number of strong attacks, but had managed to defend all of these successfully. One had actually penetrated the main defensive positions on the road about two kilometres south of Vorsovka, but this had been cleared in a small counterattack. The *208.Infanterie-Division* reported similar activity and similar success. All attacks had been seen off, and some Soviet troop assemblies had even been disrupted by artillery fire before the attack began moving. Further west, the *7.Panzer-Division* again reported increased Soviet troop movements, with tank and infantry reinforcements arriving not only in the Ustinovka area, but also further south near Staritsa and Zamery, just west of Budilovka.

Things were also beginning to move opposite the *LIX.AK*.[36] The main Soviet assault against the left wing of the *291.Infanterie-Division* had followed an hour-long artillery barrage, and jumped off either side of the Malin-Korosten' road at about 14.15 hours. The attack was made by an estimated two rifle battalions supported by nine tanks, and hit the sector held by the *Grenadier-Regiment 505*. Having made the initial breakthrough, the Soviet forces wheeled southwards as far as the local *Sovkhoz*, rolling up the division's left flank as far as the sector held by the *Reserve-Grenadier-Bataillon 316*. At about that point though, the division managed to seal off the penetration, and was actively engaged in trying to restore the situation. Two Russian tanks were reported destroyed. Elsewhere, Soviet forces began probing the *Korps* front, making individual attacks in anything up to two-battalion strength, sometimes supported by a few tanks. On the right wing of the *291.Infanterie-Division*, on the Stariki-Shershni sector, there was considerable Russian traffic movement and reconnaissance activity, whilst further north large motor and *panje* columns were seen moving north-west from Meleni. The *Pionier-Bataillon 70* saw off a company strength assault during the morning, while the *Reserve-Grenadier-Bataillon 316* threw back a similar but battalion-strength attack. Further north, the *Korps-Abteilung C* reported considerable Soviet patrolling, both combat and reconnaissance, during the night and into the morning. This was followed at 12.25 hours by a battalion assault, supported by two tanks, in the Novaki-Singai area. The attack was met with well-laid artillery fire, causing it to break down before it gained momentum, and forcing the two tanks to wheel off towards Novaki. To the north, continual Soviet troop movements were observed heading from Chernyavka to Bardy, whilst still others were seen around Mikhailovka and Pleshchevka. At 14.50 hours, Soviet forces attacked from the north, either side of the Korosten'-Ignatpol' railway, and forced a small breach west of the line. By evening the *Korps-Abteilung* was taking steps to clear the penetration.

The day had not been a good one for the *4.Panzerarmee*. Its limited counterattacks had amounted to nothing, whilst the Soviets had considerably widened the scope of their offensive. On the southern wing, they had committed additional forces from the 40th Army, whilst troop movements in the area south of Fastov probably indicated that still further troops could be expected to be committed on the sector opposite the left wing of the *VII.AK*.[37] Between the rivers Kamenka and Zdvizh, forces of the 38th Army and the 1st Tank Army continued to strike further south-westwards, with the Russian armour seeming to concentrate on the Popel'nya and Volitsa sectors. Recently identified on the 1st Tank Army's right wing was the 11th Guards Tank Corps. Further north,

---

36 *LIX.AK*, Tagesmeldung, 18.30 hours dated 26 Dec 43.
37 *PzAOK 4*, Ic Abendmeldung an H.Gr. Süd, 20.00 hours dated 26 Dec 43.

between the Zdvizh and the Teterev, the 1st Guards Army and the 3rd Guards Tank Army continued to attack westwards towards Zhitomir, where both the 6th Guards Tank Corps and the 9th Mechanised Corps had been identified in the area east and south-east of Korostyshev. Further north still and west of the Teterev, the Soviets had broadened the offensive and struck the eastern front of the *XIII.AK*, although no new units or strong armour forces had so far been identified on that sector. The *Panzerarmee* concluded that the armour suspected of being in the 60th Army area was being refitted and re-organised prior to being recommitted. This included the 7th Guards Tank Corps, the 4th Guards Tank Corps, the 5th Guards Tank Corps, and the 25th Tank Corps.[38] The 10th Tank Corps was still reported to be somewhere in the region, but there had been no confirmation of the earlier intelligence. South-east of Korosten', Soviet forces had now completed their follow up of the *LIX.AK* withdrawal, and had even started testing and probing the new front line. The remaining problem on that sector was whether the Soviet armour in the vicinity of Chopovichi would be used to renew the attack towards Korosten', or whether it would be deployed to support a southward drive by the 60th Army towards Zhitomir. The answer would presumably depend upon developments west of the Teterev on the *XIII.AK* sector. There was however some better news from Army Group South. Following his visit earlier in the day, von Manstein had decided that the *4.Panzerarmee* needed reinforcement, and during the evening Raus learned that the *1.Panzerarmee* had been instructed to relieve the *17.Panzer-Division* from the front as quickly as possible and transfer it to the Kazatin area by road and rail.[39] The division would then come under *PzAOK 4* control.

Even with this welcome reinforcement, the options left open to Raus were still limited. Proposals were however still being made, and at about 20.55 hours Balck again called *PzAOK 4* headquarters, speaking this time to Fangohr.[40] The *Panzerkorps* commander did not pull any punches. He advised the chief of staff that he considered the *Armee* to be facing one of the worst crises of the war. He perhaps overplayed his hand for effect, but he now put forward the view that the single objective of the Soviet offensive was the destruction of Army Group South. The strike towards Zhitomir might eventually be aimed for L'vov, while the advance through Berdichev could strike directly southwards, deep into the Army Group's rear. Clearly if such were the case, the *4.Panzerarmee* did not have adequate resources with which to meet the assault. Balck proposed drastic measures. The *Panzerarmee* should pull back towards Zhitomir immediately, using the forces in the south to screen the movement, and then, having assembled a force of about 200 panzers, strike deep into the flank of the Soviet forces advancing to the south-west and thus destroy them. Fangohr however was more concerned with his immediate problems, and he responded by reminding Balck of the importance of the local rail network to the supply of the entire Army Group. The priority was to prevent the Soviet advance from reaching the Kazatin-Berdichev area, and thus guaranteeing continued logistic support for the Army Group as a whole.

---

38 It seems this was a reasonably accurate assessment with the exception of the 7th Guards Tank Corps, which was deployed with the 3rd Guards Tank Army on the road to Zhitomir.
39 *Hgr.Süd*, Ia Nr. 4366/43 g.Kdos. dated 26 Dec 43.
40 *PzAOK 4*, Ia Kriegstagebuch entry, dated 26 Dec 43.

Raus' intentions were therefore for the *Panzerarmee* to cover the deep flank of the Army Group and keep open the railway running through Berdichev and Kazatin.[41] The *XXIV.PzK* and the right wing and centre of the *VII.AK* were to remain in their current defensive positions. The left wing of the *VII.AK* was to pull back behind the Kamenka river and hold the Trilesy-Paripsy sector. The appropriate order was issued later that evening, advising the new boundary with the *XXXXII.AK* to be the Skvira-Popel'nya road.[42] The *XXXXII.AK*, to the left of the *VII.AK*, would hold the line of the Kamenka from Paripsy as far as Brovki station, and assemble the *168.Infanterie-Division* south of Pavoloch'. Corresponding orders were issued later that evening, instructing the *XXXXII.AK* to prevent any further Soviet advance southwards on its sector.[43] The *168.Infanterie-Division* was to continue assembling in the area south of Pavoloch', whilst at the same time screening the line of the river between Paripsy and Kamenka to the north. Elements of the *20.Panzergrenadier-Division* were meanwhile to strike from Chervonoe towards Lebedintsy where they were to establish contact with the left wing of the *XXXXII.AK*. The *XXXXVIII.PzK* was to block the Popel'nya road on the line Starosel'ye[44]-Turovetskie Khutora, and use the *1.SS Panzer-Division 'LSSAH'* to strike through Andrushevka and Min'kovtsy to make contact with the *25.Panzer-Division* near Brovki station.[45] On the other wing, elements of the *1.Panzer-Division* were to remain in place and prevent any further Soviet advance towards Zhitomir, whilst the boundary with the *XIII.AK* to the north was to be maintained by the *SS Panzerkampfgruppe 'Das Reich'* at Glinitsa, west of Novaya Yurovka. The new boundary would run from Trokovichi to the line of the Mika stream and from there to the Teterev. The *18.Artillerie-Division*, already instructed to head for Kazatin, was formally ordered to move to take up positions south-east and north-north-west of the town so as to form the backbone of what would become '*Festung Kazatin*' or Fortress Kazatin. With the division leaving Zhitomir, it would be necessary to appoint a new *Kampfkommandant*, and this task was left to Balck.

Further north, the *XIII.AK* received instructions to disengage and fall back later that night.[46] Hauffe was ordered to pull back his *Korps* to a line running north-west from Glinitsa through Chaikovka, Potievka, and Staraya Buda to Guta Dobrynskaya, a withdrawal of about 20 kilometres for some units. Once there it was to form a new defensive position. At the same time, elements of the *7.Panzer-Division* were to be pulled out of the front and assembled behind the left flank of the *Korps*. Raus was also planning for the *XIII.AK* to pull back yet further, to a line running from Korostyshev through Gumenniki to Chernyakhov, as part of which manoeuvre, the whole of the *7.Panzer-Division* would be pulled out of the front.[47] On the left wing, the *LIX.AK* was to continue to hold its present positions, and if necessary constrict the ring around Korosten' in the event of enemy attack.[48] If it looked likely that Korosten' would be fully

---

41 *PzAOK 4*, Ia Nr. 6965/43 geh. dated 26 Dec 43.
42 *PzAOK 4*, Ia Nr. 6951/43 geh. dated 26 Dec 43.
43 *PzAOK 4*, Ia Kriegstagebuch entry, dated 26 Dec 43.
44 Referred to as Staraya Kotel'nya on more recent Soviet maps.
45 *PzAOK 4*, Ia Kriegstagebuch entry, dated 26 Dec 43. Copies of this and the *XXXXII.AK* order are not actually held on the appropriate file.
46 *PzAOK 4*, Ia Nr. 6953/43 geh. dated 26 Dec 43.
47 *PzAOK 4*, Ia Kriegstagebuch entry, dated 26 Dec 43.
48 *PzAOK 4*, Ia Kriegstagebuch entry, dated 26 Dec 43.

encircled, the intention was to give the town up and pull back along the main road to Novograd-Volynskii.

Monday 27 December 1943

The night passed quietly along the eastern wing of the *4.Panzerarmee*, with the *XXIV. PzK* reporting only light artillery exchanges and two Soviet patrols.[49] These had been in the vicinities of Grushev, near the boundary between the *34.Infanterie-Division* and the *Korps-Abteilung B*, and in the *82.Infanterie-Division* sector north of Antonovka. Both had been seen off. In the rear, the *168.Infanterie-Division* continued to pull out, with another six trains leaving and a further one ready to depart in the morning. The *I./Artillerie-Regiment 223* and the *II./Artillerie-Regiment 248* (less two batteries) had both left the *Korps* sector.

Further west, the left wing of the *VII.AK* pulled back behind the river Kamenka, under heavy Soviet pressure in places.[50] Elements of the retreating *88.Infanterie-Division* counterattacked in the Stavishche area, and obtained a local success, killing 80 counted enemy, and capturing a further 26. Further south, the village of Dunaika was also captured, and another 30 Russian dead counted, and four taken prisoner. Enemy reinforcements were seen moving into Pochuiki, where the noise of tank engines was also heard. Further down the Kamenka valley, Soviet forces succeeded in infiltrating into Trilesy, forcing the weak covering troops to pull back to the southern edge of the town. Other Soviet troops forced a crossing of the Kamenka at Kozhanka, and pushed on to take the village of Suvari. By morning, the *Korps* had managed to organise a concerted counterattack to restore the positions in both Suvari and Trilesy, and this continued into the day. Despite his desperate attempts to mount counterattacks, Hell considered that the enemy would continue to put pressure on the Trilesy-Pochuiki sector, hammering away at the *88.Infanterie-Division*. Elsewhere on the *Korps* front, things had remained quiet, although the *75.Infanterie-Division* did report continued heavy Soviet traffic opposite its sector.

To the left of the *88.Infanterie-Division*, the *Grenadier-Regiment 417* of the *168. Infanterie-Division*, in position behind the Rostavitsa between Pavoloch' and Strokov, reported no contact with the enemy.[51] To the south-west, another 10 kilometres further upstream, the division's *Füsilier-Bataillon* moved into positions around the village of Trubeevka, whilst a battalion of the *Divisionsgruppe 223* was also approaching the area following its transfer. Further west, the *25.Panzer-Division* was still struggling to hold itself together. The previous evening, Soviet forces, with tank support, had attacked and captured Voitovtsy, forcing the division to pull back as best it could towards the Kamenka, seven kilometres away to the south. The *Gruppe* Wechmar, based on the *Panzergrenadier-Regiment 147*, had moved into defensive positions either side of Vasil'evka by morning, but there was no news from the rest of the division.

To the left, the leading group of the *20.Panzergrenadier-Division*, moving up from the Chervonoe area, reported a quiet night with no enemy contact.[52] Away to the north though, Balck's *XXXXVIII.PzK* was having a difficult time. Its counterattack had met

---

49 *XXIV.PzK*, Morgenmeldung, 06.25 hours dated 27 Dec 43.
50 *VII.AK*, Morgenmeldung, 06.00 hours dated 27 Dec 43.
51 *XXXXII.AK*, Morgenmeldung, 06.10 hours dated 27 Dec 43.
52 *20.Pz.Gr.Div.*, Morgenmeldung, 05.00 hours dated 27 Dec 43.

with little success, and its withdrawal movements were being bogged down as a result of the deteriorating road conditions.⁵³ The planned strike by the *1.SS Panzer-Division 'LSSAH'* through Gordyshevka, Lesovka, and Andrushevka had come to nothing in the face of determined Soviet resistance. The leading troops had reached no further than the northern edge of Lesovka and the west bank of the river Guiva, before being called back to hold Gordyshevka on the northern edge of Andrushevka. The group was still holding the town by early morning, preparing to fight its way back towards the southern end of Starosel'ye. About 25 kilometres away to the north, the *19.Panzer-Division*, together with the *Panzergrenadier-Regiment 28* of the *8.Panzer-Division*, had been given orders to fight its way back westwards through Smolovka to Levkov on the river Teterev. By 20.15 hours the previous evening, the first elements had reached the village of Trikoptsa, about five kilometres short of Smolovka. To their left, on the other side of the main gap, the *1.Panzer-Division*, supported by elements of the *8.Panzer-Division*, had disengaged from the enemy and had withdrawn behind the river Teterev, where they began constructing new positions between Kosharishcha, Korostyshev and Bobrik.⁵⁴ The Soviets meanwhile had followed up very closely, and by the end of the night they had taken up positions on the main Kiev-Zhitomir road, just east of Korostyshev. The bridge in the town was blown. On the *Korps* left, the *SS Panzerkampfgruppe 'Das Reich'* had been instructed to pull back to a line running from Bobrik to Novaya Yurovka, and hold it.

There was little news from Hauffe's *XIII.AK*, but according to the latest reports the withdrawal of the various divisions seemed to be going as planned.⁵⁵ A battalion strength assault against the *340.Infanterie-Division* in Vorsovka had been thrown back the previous evening, but other than that there seemed to have been little Soviet activity.

Things were livelier opposite the *LIX.AK* front, where enemy reconnaissance and combat patrols had been active throughout the night along the entire *Korps* sector.⁵⁶ There had also been two separate attacks against the sector held by the *291.Infanterie-Division*, one either side of the Meleni-Zlobichi road, and the other south-east of hill 189.5. Both had involved between one and two Soviet rifle companies, and both had been seen off. The division also reported hearing tank noises throughout the night, heading from Meleni back eastwards towards Chopovichi. It also engaged Soviet troop movements observed near the local *Sovkhoz*, using artillery to lay disruptive fire against Russian positions in Meleni and Bolyarka to the north. To the left, the *Korps-Abteilung C* had succeeded in clearing the Soviet penetration west of the Korosten'-Ovruch railway the previous evening. At about 02.30 hours however, a strong Soviet combat patrol advanced from the Grozino farm area and infiltrated through the German positions as far as the railway line. The *Korps-Abteilung* mounted a local counterattack to clear the area, but this continued into the morning. The previous evening a number of Soviet truck columns, some with up to 15 vehicles, had been reported moving into the area north of Bekhi, where various unloading operations had also been seen. Wherever possible, these movements had been engaged with artillery fire. During the course of the night, the *Korps-Abteilung* had also received a welcome reinforcement in the shape of 108 NCOs and 291 other ranks of the *Marschbataillon 183/8*. On the other hand,

---

53 *XXXXVIII.PzK*, Morgenmeldung, 05.50 hours dated 27 Dec 43.
54 The village of Bobrik is not marked on all maps. It was situated just west of Kozievka.
55 *XIII.AK*, Morgenmeldung, 06.20 hours dated 27 Dec 43.
56 *LIX.AK*, Morgenmeldung, 05.30 hours dated 27 Dec 43.

the *291.Infanterie-Division* had lost more heavy weapons; two light field howitzers, as well as a heavy and a medium anti-tank gun. Excluding the self-propelled guns of the *Panzer-Zerstörer-Bataillon 731*, it now deployed just 15 light field howitzers, and three heavy anti-tank guns.

Having received the *XXXXVIII.PzK* morning report, and learned that the *'LSSAH'* had lost Volitsa during the night, Raus decided to speak with the *Korps* to clarify the situation.[57] He called the headquarters at 07.45 hours and informed Balck that he considered the proposed strike into the Soviet flank was no longer likely to be successful. With the *'LSSAH'* pulling back, the gap was now too wide, and the Russians would undoubtedly have used the intervening period to strengthen their flank with anti-tank guns. He therefore ordered the *XXXXVIII.PzK* to leave just weak covering forces on northern flank of this group, in the area around the southern part of Starosel'ye and the area just north of the main road, and use the main body of the *'LSSAH'* to strike southwards to the line Krylovka-Chervonoe.

At about 08.00 hours, *Oberst* Franz, chief of staff at *XXXXII.AK*, called *4.Panzerarmee* headquarters to advise that the *25.Panzer-Division* had pulled back to the south-west under heavy Soviet pressure, but rather than stand and hold the Kamenka line, it would be forced all the way back to the Rostavitsa where it could hold the sector around Pavoloch'.[58] Raus would not give formal authority for such a move, insisting that, if it was under such heavy pressure, the division should instead pull back to the south-west, where at least it should try and prevent the Soviet advance towards Kazatin. Franz was instructed to bring together all available forces and shift them westwards to the Chernorudka area where they could confront the Soviet advance either side of the railway towards Kazatin. Contact was moreover to be established with elements of the *XXXXVIII.PzK* in the areas of Khalaim-Gorodok[59] and Krylovka. In addition, the *18.Artillerie-Division* would be released to the *XXXXII.AK* with a view to it assisting the defence of Kazatin, where it was to be employed as a single unit. Raus now intended to move the *XXXXII.AK* to Kazatin, the *XXXXVIII.PzK* to Berdichev, and the *XIII. AK* to Zhitomir, each headquarters providing the necessary operational support for the respective towns.

Daylight dawned once more under a cover of thick cloud, and the day proved dull and damp again, with a light snowfall scattered across the region. Near the Dnepr, the *XXIV.PzK* was attacked in four different places on the Shchuchinka sector, each time by about one or two Soviet rifle companies.[60] All were successfully seen off, and the activity died down. The *VII.AK* was more heavily engaged, beginning with the *75.Infanterie-Division* which had to defend against two battalion-sized assaults south of Germanovka.[61] On the left wing of the *198.Infanterie-Division*, Soviet forces of about one or two rifle companies attacked German lines in Palenichentsy, just north of Kovalevka, but a well laid defensive fire ensured that the assault never reached the main defensive positions. The *88.Infanterie-Division* meanwhile reported heavy enemy traffic moving from Fastov southwards towards Chervonoe. The same division had also managed to

---

57 *PzAOK 4*, Ia Kriegstagebuch entry, dated 27 Dec 43.
58 *PzAOK 4*, Ia Kriegstagebuch entry, dated 27 Dec 43.
59 Referred to as Gorodkovka on more recent Soviet maps.
60 *PzAOK 4*, O1 Orientierung, dated 27 Dec 43.
61 *PzAOK 4*, O1 Orientierung, dated 27 Dec 43.

score a minor success during a small counterattack which succeeded in breaking into the south-western part of Trilesy. The attack began at 13.00 hours, supported by a few *Sturmgeschützen*, the objective being to relieve elements of the *II./Sicherungs-Regiment 318* which were still hanging on in the town. By the time the action was over, at about 14.30 hours, an estimated 150 Soviet soldiers lay dead whilst seven prisoners from the 797th Rifle Regiment of the 232nd Rifle Division had been taken. The continuing threat of enemy encirclement from the west however, forced the attacking troops to pull back to their start positions. Another counterattack led to the recapture of the *Sovkhoz* Sofievka, just south of Kozhanka. But not all the news was positive. An estimated two Soviet rifle companies had infiltrated through the division's lines and pushed on to the southwestern edge of Yakhny; a counterattack was planned. In another attack, an estimated Soviet rifle battalion captured Dunaika in an encircling attack, whilst the *Sperrverband* over on the left wing in Novoselitsa was forced back at about 13.00 hours, following an enemy assault from the north and north-east. The unit fell back towards Strokov on the Rostavitsa, closely pursued by Soviet forces. By afternoon, a Russian regiment was attacking the village, and the whole area lay under artillery fire.

Contact with Mattenklott's *XXXXII.AK* had meanwhile been lost.[62] According to intercepted radio messages though, the *25.Panzer-Division* was struggling by early afternoon, trying to maintain order as it attempted to pull back behind the river Rostavitsa near Pavoloch'. Other information also indicated that strong Soviet forces, estimated to be a division, were heading south-westwards from Popel'nya along the road to Andrushki. Moving towards this area from the west was the *Regimentsgruppe* of the *20.Panzergrenadier-Division*. The group had already lost four light field howitzers and a 100mm cannon when enemy tank fire in the village of Krasovka, south of Chervonoe, had destroyed the towing vehicles. Despite this setback though, the *Regimentsgruppe* had reached Chernorudka, and by early afternoon it was heading for Vcheraishe where an estimated 200 Russian troops and two tanks had been spotted. Soviet tanks had also been reported in Chervonoe, and the division ordered its armoured reconnaissance units against these.

To the north, on the right wing of the *XXXXVIII.PzK*, elements of the 'LSSAH' had begun to strike south towards Chervonoe, whilst other elements had successfully seen off four Russian tanks trying to force their way along the Volitsa-Zhitomir road during the morning.[63] In the afternoon, these attacks against the division's northern wing were renewed, and by the end of the day it was holding a line from Velikaya Moshkovtsy through the southern edges of Antopol' and Starosel'ye to Turovetskie Khutor. It also posted a forward detachment in Turovets on its left flank. Further north, the *19.Panzer-Division* and elements of the *8.Panzer-Division* succeeded in pulling back across the river Teterev, and were establishing positions on the west bank between Levkov and Kosharishcha. To their left, the *1.Panzer-Division* was also installed along the river, holding the line as far as Korostyshev. During the morning, a Soviet assault crossing had forced a bridgehead over the Teterev, attacking across the river from Kharitonovka towards Strizhevka. Weak enemy troops infiltrated through the division's lines and succeeded in reaching the main Kiev-Zhitomir road east of Strizhevka, threatening to

---

62 *PzAOK 4*, O1 Orientierung, dated 27 Dec 43.
63 *PzAOK 4*, O1 Orientierung, dated 27 Dec 43; *XXXXVIII.PzK*, Tagesmeldung, 18.55 hours dated 27 Dec 43.

cut off the main line of retreat from those troops still in the Korostyshev area. Just southeast of the same village, Soviet tanks forced a breakthrough of the German lines, and the division launched an armoured counterattack which continued into the evening. As the division struggled to contain the breach, the Russians organised the bridgehead quickly, and by 13.10 hours they launched a series of attacks aiming westwards south of the main Kiev-Zhitomir road. Further east, about 2,000 men and 16 tanks were seen assembling in the wooded area just east of Korostyshev, presumably massing for an assault against the town. On the right wing of the *'Das Reich'*, the Soviets launched two separate assaults against Kozievka and Gorodsk, the former involving about 20 tanks, and the latter in about regimental strength. Further north, another attack, involving about 1,000 men and four self-propelled guns, hit the *Kampfgruppe* just south of Novaya Yurovka, and according to reports from the *XIII.AK*, they achieved a deep penetration. Fighting continued into the afternoon. On the southern wing of the *XIII.AK* itself, the *68.Infanterie-Division* was hit by an assault from an estimated division with tank support.[64] It was thrown back violently to a line from Berezovka through Zhuravlinka and Pilipovichi to Chaikovka. On the *Korps* left wing, the *7.Panzer-Division* tried to pull back, but in doing so was infiltrated by Soviet forces which struck through its defences and reached the wooded area south-west of Staraya Buda.

In the *LIX.AK* sector further north, the *291.Infanterie-Division* reported Russian forces, estimated at 200 men and three tanks, to be assembling south of Meleni, preparing to attack.[65] Before this, it had managed to see off a number of regimental strength attacks against its centre, reportedly inflicting heavy casualties on the attackers. The assaults had begun either side of the Meleni-Zlobichi road, with the support of a few tanks, but each had failed under concentrated defensive fire. The *Korps-Abteilung C* meanwhile had been unable to prevent another Soviet breach of its front line, this time on the right wing, but it had at least succeeded in sealing off the penetration prior to mopping up later in the day.

At 13.30 hours Raus spoke with von der Chevallerie at *LIX.AK* to update him on the situation on the other *Korps* sectors.[66] He instructed the *Korps* commander to hold Korosten' if at all possible, concentrating his position around the town if under heavy assault. In the event of real danger of encirclement, he should strengthen his southern wing, and try to break out to the south-west. Von der Chevallerie was also instructed to relieve the *Pionier-Bataillon 70* from the front line, and transfer it to the Berdichev area where it would come under the command of the *XXXXVIII.PzK*; appropriate orders were issued the same day.[67] Later in the afternoon, at about 16.50 hours, *General der Artillerie* Hell, commanding the *VII.AK*, called to give Raus a personal situation report.[68] Hell defended his *Korps'* performance, saying that it had succeeded, by adopting an aggressive posture, in inflicting severe casualties on the attacking Russian forces, although there was no way in which it could have prevented the Soviets from gaining ground. The *Korps* had now constructed a new defensive line running from the southern edge of Trilesy to Malopolovetskoe, but from there to the west there was a gap as far

---

64 *PzAOK 4*, O1 Orientierung, dated 27 Dec 43.
65 *PzAOK 4*, O1 Orientierung, dated 27 Dec 43.
66 *PzAOK 4*, Ia Kriegstagebuch entry, dated 27 Dec 43.
67 *PzAOK 4*, Ia Nr. 6979/43 geh. dated 27 Dec 43.
68 *PzAOK 4*, Ia Kriegstagebuch entry, dated 27 Dec 43.

as Strokov on the Rostavitsa, a gap which the *VII.AK* was in no position to fill. Soviet forces had already begun to move through the gap, and had reached the woods south-east of Strokov. Given these circumstances, Hell was concerned that there was a danger of his right-wing divisions, those still facing north and relatively undisturbed by the fighting, being rolled up from the left flank. He therefore proposed to Raus that the *Korps* be allowed to fall back to the '*Siegfriedstellung*' in order to preserve its strength, but the *Panzerarmee* commander refused any such concession, advising Hell instead that the divisions in question should not pull back at all in the absence of enemy pressure. If, subsequently, there should prove to be a real threat to the flank, they should pull back step-by-step southwards, but always maintaining a north or north-west facing front against the enemy. To compound Hell's problems, Raus also made it quite clear that the *168.Infanterie-Division*, still assembling in the Skvira area, would not in any circumstances, be committed into the gap. It was now earmarked for the defence of the Kazatin area.

The day had passed like so many others for Nehring's *XXIV.Panzerkorps*, anchored with its right wing on the Dnepr.[69] It had been dull and misty, with poor visibility, and some of the snow which had been falling recently had begun to drift. The temperature rose to about freezing, but for the time being the roads remained good, with the exception of the occasional snowdrift. Throughout the day, the Soviets had kept up the pressure with numerous pinning attacks and continuous reconnaissance activity, and things had reached such a pitch that Nehring was now expecting the Russians to begin larger and more threatening attacks in the near future. For the time being though, things went on as they had on previous days. In the north-east, a Soviet troop assembly was spotted at Kanada west of Romashki, and this was dispersed at about 14.30 hours by artillery fire. Following the earlier attacks against the Balyko-Shchuchinka sector, the Soviets re-organised and assaulted twice more during the afternoon. Both ground to a halt under defensive fire, and at 16.30 hours further troop assemblies were seen. Further west at about midday, there had been two battalion-sized assaults south-east of Germanovka, but these had not had the benefit of preparatory artillery fire, and both came to grief in defensive fire about 800 metres in front of the German positions. In the rear, the *168. Infanterie-Division* continued to pull out, with another nine trains leaving during the day. All elements making the move by road had now gone, leaving just the remainder which were to travel by rail.

The weather was much the same further west, where the *VII.AK* reported snowfall during the previous night, and a drizzly, misty day with poor visibility.[70] The *Korps* had had mixed fortunes during the day, standing firm on the major part of its sector, but unable to prevent an enemy breakthrough on the left near Strokov. On the right wing, on the sector held by the *75.Infanterie-Division*, the Soviets renewed their assaults at 14.45 hours and 15.30 hours, striking either side of the main Germanovka-Mirovka road and out of the wooded area south of Germanovka respectively. The assaults were carried out in each case by an estimated one to two rifle battalions, but neither made any progress under concentrated defensive fire, and they ground to a halt about 100 metres in front of the main German positions. Despite the reportedly heavy Soviet losses, the division was predicting further attacks. To the left, the *198.Infanterie-Division* reported

69 *XXIV.PzK*, Tagesmeldung, 18.25 hours dated 27 Dec 43.
70 *VII.AK*, Tagesmeldung, 20.45 hours dated 27 Dec 43.

no further attacks since the earlier assault had been repulsed at about 11.00 hours that morning. There had however, been considerable traffic heading westwards south of Mar'yanovka. The real problems faced by the *VII.AK* lay in the *88.Infanterie-Division* sector. Whilst the northern wing of the division had managed to see off all attacks, the left wing had been unable to prevent Soviet forces from pushing into Yakhny, and capturing Dunaika, Novoselitsa and Strokov. The counterattack planned earlier by the division against Yakhny had been successful, clearing the town of Soviet troops, but the momentum of the strike had not proven sufficient to take Dunaika as well, and the village remained under enemy control. A Russian group trying to strike south-eastwards from Trilesy was meanwhile intercepted about a kilometre south of the town, its troops being either destroyed or dispersed. At about 16.00 hours, an estimated two Soviet rifle battalions attacked from the Suvari and *Sovkhoz* Sofievka areas, leading to a temporary breach in the defences, through which the Soviet forces advanced to capture the north-western part of Malopolovetskoe. Over to the west, the *Sperrverband* was still in trouble. Having been thrown back to Strokov on the river Rostavitsa, it was attached to the *Grenadier-Regiment 417* from the *168.Infanterie-Division*. The regiment itself, attached directly to *Korps* headquarters, having previously deployed north of the river, found itself under heavy attack from three sides, and at 15.45 hours it had retired to the south bank. Having blown the bridge at Strokov, it proceeded to take up defensive positions between Buki and Pavoloch', to defend against the main Soviet drive south along the Paripsy-Skvira road. All in all, the gap on the left wing of the *VII.AK* was growing more unmanageable by the hour, and Hell reported that it could not be closed by the *Korps* transferring units from the as yet untouched northern front, much before midday the following day.

Mattenklott, meanwhile, was still trying to piece together a coherent defence for his *XXXXII.AK* further west.[71] The *168.Infanterie-Division*, having newly assumed responsibility for the sector on the right, became embroiled in the fighting straightaway as Soviet troops attacked Golubyatin and Pavoloch'. Both attacks were successfully defended. Further west, in an effort to extend the lines to the left, the division's *Füsilier-Bataillon* and the battalion from the *Divisionsgruppe 223* were both ordered to head further west, towards the Chernorudka area where the *Regimentsgruppe* from the *20.Panzergrenadier-Division* would be assembling. North of the Rostavitsa, the Soviets continued to batter away at the *25.Panzer-Division*. It had managed to hold its own during most of the morning, but by afternoon it had been forced to pull back to the south-east towards Pavoloch' under heavy enemy pressure. At 17.30 hours, the *Korps* chief of staff called *PzAOK 4* headquarters to inform them of Mattenklott's intention to shift the *25.Panzer-Division* westwards during the night to cover the line Pavoloch'-Moiseevka-Bystreevka-Shpichintsy.[72] The *168.Infanterie-Division*, still arriving, would be moved up from the Ruzhin area to take up positions on the left of the *25.Panzer-Division*, between Chernorudka and Khalaim-Gorodok, to cover the main approach to Kazatin. Three battalions had already begun to move westwards to their new positions. Raus agreed with these proposals, and even promised to send the *s.Panzer-Abteilung 509 (Tiger)*, currently still deployed with the *1.Panzer-Division*, to assist in the defence of Chernorudka. The *Gruppe* Wechmar, already engaged in the vicinity of Vcheraishe,

71 *XXXXII.AK*, Tagesmeldung, 20.30 hours dated 27 Dec 43.
72 *PzAOK 4*, Ia Kriegstagebuch entry, dated 27 Dec 43.

north-west of Shpichintsy, would be attached to the *168.Infanterie-Division*, as would the *Regimentsgruppe* of the *20.Panzergrenadier-Division*. In the same area meanwhile, a motley collection of alarm units under the command of the *Korps* artillery commander, *Arko 107*, was ordered to make a desperate attempt to stand and fight. The *18.Artillerie-Division* was formally transferred to Mattenklott's command during the day, with orders to assemble in the area north-east of Kazatin, between Bol'shaya-Chernyavka[73] and Voitovtsy.[74] The *Sturmgeschütz-Batterie* was scheduled to arrive in Chernorudka by morning, whilst a *Wespe Abteilung* (self-propelled 105mm howitzer) was already in firing positions around Kazatin. The *20.Panzergrenadier-Division* meanwhile reported that its *Regimentsgruppe* had failed in its efforts to capture Vcheraishe.[75] The *Gruppe* had fallen back towards Chernorudka under heavy pressure, and by evening was holding that town, including the railway station. Lack of forces however precluded the posting of any detachments to guard the northern front around Khalaim-Gorodok, as the rest of the division was deployed as reserve under the *Kampkommandant* Berdichev.

Opposite the *XXXXVIII.PzK* sector, the morning had passed relatively quietly, with the Soviets seemingly limiting their operations to reconnaissance activity.[76] The afternoon however had seen a return to the offensive, with the main weight falling against the sectors held by the *1.Panzer-Division* and the *SS Panzerkampfgruppe 'Das Reich'*. It all gave the appearance of the Russians having used the time to consolidate and bring up infantry and heavy weapons, and Balck was predicting a resumption of strong attacks to the south and south-west. On the southern wing, the *1.SS Panzer-Division 'LSSAH'*, striking southwards during the course of the afternoon, had occupied Velikaya Moshkovtsy, Malyi Moshkovtsy, and Chervonoe, at the same time defending against a Soviet tank thrust from Zabara to the south-west. The division had also seen off another attack along the Volitsa-Zhitomir road, this time by an estimated regiment with tank support, but in the main the Soviets contented themselves with increased reconnaissance activity. Further north, the *1.Panzer-Division* was still struggling with the Soviet bridgehead over the Teterev near Strizhevka, whilst the Russian troop assemblies east of Korostyshev had materialised into an assault against the town. During the afternoon this attack achieved a sizeable breach in the defences, and an estimated Soviet rifle battalion pushed into the northern part of the town. The breach was sealed off, but could not be cleared. There were still more Russian forces north of the town, and at about 15.00 hours these broke through the defences near Bobrik. A quickly mounted counterattack cleared this problem, inflicting reportedly heavy casualties on the attackers, including at least 12 tanks. On the left wing, the *SS Panzerkampfgruppe 'Das Reich'* had been badly hit. The two attacks in the morning, at about 10.00 hours, had both turned out to be regimental in size, whilst at the same time Soviet forces had assaulted around the left wing, aiming for Glinitsa and Ivanovka.[77] These latter attacks had been made by an estimated rifle battalion, with support from a few assault guns, and had managed to

---

73 Referred to as Vishnevoe on more recent Soviet maps.
74 Referred to as Rastavitsa on more recent Soviet maps. It should be noted that this village of Voitovtsy is situated just north of Bystrik, about 20 kilometres east of Kazatin. It should not be confused with the town of the same name further north on the river Unava.
75 *20.Pz.Gr.Div.*, Tagesmeldung, 21.00 hours dated 27 Dec 43.
76 *XXXXVIII.PzK*, Tagesmeldung, 18.55 hours dated 27 Dec 43.
77 Referred to as Travnevoe on more recent Soviet maps.

advance as far as the eastern edge of Ivanovka. There was by this time a very real danger of the *Kampfgruppe* being outflanked from the north, and the decision was taken to pull back the left wing and form a new line from Bobrik farm to Mineiki. The *19.Panzer-Division*, back in Levkov, meanwhile continued to re-organise itself behind the Teterev, preparing for the imminent Soviet assaults.

At 16.35 hours, Balck called the *4.Panzerarmee* to acquaint them with his latest situation.[78] Following his report, he proposed pulling back the *1.Panzer-Division* and the *'Das Reich'* to the line Kmitov-Studenitsa, although he admitted that even on this shortened line, it was unlikely that the divisions would be able to put up a prolonged resistance. This view was shared by Raus, who then ordered that the *1.Panzer-Division* was to be relieved during the coming night. In contrast to Balck's thinking though, which foresaw the division being re-deployed on the *Korps* left wing, Raus promptly directed that it be transferred to the *Korps* right wing, where the *Panzerarmee* was trying to establish a concentration of force. Balck, seeming to miss the wider picture, continued to argue against such a move, claiming that the defence of Zhitomir would be severely weakened. Raus could only agree, but pointed out that the situation demanded a concentration of effort in the Berdichev-Kazatin area. If such a move all but guaranteed Soviet success in the Zhitomir area, it would just have to be tolerated. As long as the *7.Panzer-Division* could not be pulled out of the front and transferred to the Berdichev area, it would fall to the *1.Panzer-Division* to form a reserve in that vicinity, from where it could be committed either near Pavoloch' or Chernorudka. Moreover, Raus had now decided to attach the *19.* and *8.Panzer-Divisions* and the *'Das Reich'*, in their existing sectors, to the *XIII.AK*, thus releasing the *XXXXVIII.PzK* for operations in the Berdichev area.

To the north meanwhile, Hauffe's *XIII.AK* had been strongly attacked during the morning on both its wings.[79] The attack against the left wing had been led largely by armoured forces, and it seemed that the concerted assault had been designed to cause the entire *Korps* front to collapse. Despite the constant pressure, the *Korps* had nevertheless been able to pull back as planned, taking up new positions on the Glinitsa-Guta Dobrynskaya line. On the right wing, the *68.Infanterie-Division* had been hit by three Soviet assault groups, each estimated to be a regiment supported with four to six tanks, with the main strike coming either side of the Mika stream. With the division endeavouring to pull back, the attack made good progress before being brought to a halt on the east edge of Berezovka. Further north, breaches were also achieved along the Bystreevka stream, nearer the new defensive positions, in the vicinity of Peremozh'e and east of Pilipovichi, but these were less serious and were sealed off and partially cleared through local counterattacks. Further north, a battalion-sized assault against Chaikovka was thrown back. To the division's left, in the *340.Infanterie-Division* sector, the Soviets attacked with three smaller groups, each about battalion size, but each with tank support. All were successfully defended, as was another similar attack against Gorodishche on the *208.Infanterie-Division* front. In the evening though, a renewed assault against the *208.Infanterie-Division* in Potievka led to a penetration in the new line, and fighting continued on into the night. The *7.Panzer-Division*, trying to maintain a mobile defence on the *Korps* left wing, was struck with a powerful armoured advance

---

78 *PzAOK 4*, Ia Kriegstagebuch entry, dated 27 Dec 43.
79 *XIII.AK*, Tagesmeldung, 19.45 hours dated 27 Dec 43.

heading southwards on the Chopovichi-Fasova road where the Soviet 5th Guards Tank Corps had now been identified in the area. The advance made little progress though, and was brought to a halt near Guta Dobrynskaya, with eight Soviet tanks reported as destroyed.

During the course of the morning, von Hammerstein-Gesmold and von Mellenthin, the respective chiefs of staff of the *XIII.AK* and the *XXXXVIII.PzK*, had spoken regarding the question of the *XIII.AK* withdrawal, and its impact upon the boundary between the two commands.[80] The two men had agreed on a suitable new boundary, and this had then been officially promulgated by *PzAOK 4* headquarters. Somewhat later in the morning, Raus spoke directly with Hauffe and pointed out that the withdrawal to the next defensive line would in all probability be a very large one, but in the interest of the troops, it was one which would have to be made in order to allow them to become established in the new positions. In order to avoid the possibility of Soviet forces interfering in such a withdrawal, the *7.Panzer-Division* was to be employed to ensure that no enemy forces followed the movement too closely. Following the completion of the move, the division was to be committed again on the *Korps* left wing, although if, by that time, the *Korps* was no longer in any danger of being outflanked, the division was to be transferred to the area north of Berdichev. Hauffe was convinced though, even with the *7.Panzer-Division* covering the withdrawal, that the Russians would be able to outflank the *Korps* if they should strike south-westwards from the Guta Dobrynskaya area.

On the right wing of the *LIX.AK*, the *291.Infanterie-Division* had meanwhile been sending out reconnaissance patrols to try and establish contact with the left wing of the *7.Panzer-Division*. This had been done in Dobryn' and Guta Dobrynskaya, and formal contact made, but further north opposite Shershni, it had been noted that the Russians were reinforcing their positions. In the centre of the division's sector, following hard on the heels of their earlier attacks in the morning, the Soviets renewed their efforts against hill 189.5 and in the area west of Bolyarka farm during the afternoon. These were smaller scale assaults, being no more than battalion-sized, although a few tanks were involved, but they succeeded where the others had not. They overran the forward positions, and in places pushed on as far as the artillery emplacements. To the north-west, the *Korps-Abteilung C* reported a quiet day, with no Soviet activity. The *Pionier-Bataillon 70* had meanwhile been extricated from the front line, and passed from the control of the *291. Infanterie-Division*, prior to being transferred to the *XXXXVIII.PzK* in Berdichev. During the course of the evening, *Oberst* Schleusener, chief of staff at the *LIX.AK*, spoke with Fangohr regarding the latest situation.[81] The *291.Infanterie-Division* had been quite badly hit during the day, and having given up the *Pionier-Bataillon 70*, it was no longer in a position to be able to hold its own. He proposed strengthening the southern wing as much as possible, and then wheeling it back north-westwards to a new line running from Ioganovka north-eastwards through Sobolevka to Khotinovka. Raus agreed.

Overall, the day had been relatively successful for the *4.Panzerarmee*, at least compared to previous ones. Over on the right wing, the whole of the *XXIV.PzK*, and the centre and right wing of the *VII.AK*, had seen little more than a series of pinning attacks, none of which had caused any serious problems. The Soviet 50th Rifle Corps under the

---

80 *PzAOK 4*, Ia Kriegstagebuch entry, dated 27 Dec 43.
81 *PzAOK 4*, Ia Kriegstagebuch entry, dated 27 Dec 43.

40th Army continued in its attacks against the left wing of the *VII.AK*, pushing further and further to the south and south-east, but in general it had made only moderate gains.[82] A little to the west, infantry forces in unknown strength were advancing southwards from the Popel'nya area with a few tanks in support. Similarly, pressure had been maintained on the Pavoloch'-Vcheraishe sector, with at least two Soviet rifle divisions and the 3rd Guards Tank Corps in the area,[83] but here the *XXXXII.AK* had at least managed to throw up a covering force, even if it was a weak one. Some kind of line now extended from Pavoloch' through Vcheraishe and Chervonoe to a point west of Ivnitsa. On the direction of what appeared to be the main thrust, towards Berdichev and Kazatin, it appeared as if the Soviets had spent the day closing up to the new German positions where the 11th Guards Tank Corps had been confirmed in the Volitsa area.[84] Otherwise, they had used the time to conduct wide-ranging reconnaissance. Further north, the Soviet 6th Guards Tank Corps and the 9th Mechanised Corps had attacked Korostyshev to try and take this important crossing over the Teterev. They had tried to outflank the German positions either side of the town, but the manoeuvre had not been particularly successful. The *PzAOK 4* assumed that the partial lull indicated that the major armoured units were being re-supplied, and that they would resume the offensive the following day, with the possibility that at least one of the tank corps would be transferred eastwards to support the 40th Army assault in the area between Belaya Tserkov', Skvira and Pavoloch'. West of the Teterev, the Russians had attacked the *XIII.AK* on both wings, each with the support of an estimated tank brigade, but the *Korps* had managed to fall back as planned, and the successful enemy attacks against its southern flank had not badly disrupted the withdrawal. On the *Korps'* left wing, the anticipated attack had not materialised, except for a half-hearted attempt by elements of the 5th Guards Tank Corps. On the *LIX.AK* sector too, there had been small-scale attacks with limited armoured support, and although these had achieved local successes they had not proved critical to the *Korps* situation.

It was against this background, at about 16.00 hours, that Raus issued new instructions to his *Korps* commanders in the shape of '*Panzerarmeebefehl Nr. 50*'.[85] The order summarised enemy intentions, stating that about sixteen rifle divisions and five tank or mechanised corps belonging to the 1st Tank and 3rd Guards Tank Armies were attacking between the Kamenka and Teterev rivers, aiming west and south-west with the immediate objective of capturing Kazatin, Berdichev and Zhitomir. On the southern wing, the Soviet 40th Army had joined the offensive, attacking the left wing of the *VII.AK* to push it back south-eastwards. West of the river Teterev, the Russians were following the withdrawal at an unusually leisurely pace, whilst in the north, increased Soviet traffic indicated the imminence of a major attack on that sector. The task of the *4.Panzerarmee* now was to prevent any further Russian advance, preferably as far to the

---

82 *PzAOK 4*, Ic Abendmeldung an H.Gr. Süd, 20.00 hours dated 27 Dec 43. Intelligence had confirmed the presence of the three Soviet rifle divisions on the sector; the 232nd, the 74th, and the 163rd.
83 As has been stated before, German intelligence appears to have failed to identify this unit correctly. The 3rd Guards Tank Corps was in the *Stavka* reserve at this time, while the 3rd Tank Corps was with the 2nd Tank Army, also in the *Stavka* reserve.
84 The 8th Guards Mechanised Corps had also been identified on this sector.
85 *PzAOK 4*, Ia Nr. Panzerarmeebefehl Nr 50 dated 27 Dec 43.

east and north of Kazatin, Berdichev and Zhitomir as possible, and in particular it was to keep open the railways that ran west and south-west from Kazatin and Berdichev.

In this respect, the task of the *XXIV.PzK* remained unchanged, although it was to release the *Pionier-Bataillon 74* to the *Armee-Pionier-Führer* and make preparations for the release of a grenadier-regiment. The *VII.AK* was to maintain its existing positions on the right and centre of its sector, and, by the ruthless stripping of those quieter sectors if necessary, prevent any further enemy advance to the south or south-west on its left wing. Contact was to be maintained with the neighbouring *XXXXII.AK* on the line of the river Rostavitsa. The *XXXXII.AK* itself was to prevent any further enemy advance towards Kazatin in its sector. To assist it in carrying out this task, the *Korps* was allocated the *25.Panzer-Division*, the *168.Infanterie-Division* (which was to be moved to the Chernorudka area), the *18.Artillerie-Division* (to be deployed in the Kazatin area as a complete unit), and the reinforced *Regimentsgruppe* from the *20.Panzergrenadier-Division* (already counter-attacking in the Vcheraishe – Khalaim-Gorodok area). The *Korps* headquarters was instructed to move to Kazatin. The *XXXXVIII.PzK*, with the *1.SS Panzer-Division 'LSSAH'*, the *1.Panzer-Division* and the *Kavallerie-Regiment Süd*, was to prevent any further enemy advance south-west or westwards over the general line Krylovka-Velikaya Moshkovtsy-Starosel'ye-Korostyshev. Those elements of the *1.Panzer-Division* which could be relieved during the coming night were to be transferred to the new sector further south. The *7.Panzer-Division* meanwhile was to be pulled out of the front line by the *XIII.AK* and assembled in the area north of Zhitomir for transfer to the *XXXXVIII.PzK*. The *Kavallerie-Regiment Süd* was to move to the Chervonoe area, and the *Korps* headquarters was to set up in Berdichev on the following day. To the north, the *XIII.AK* would gain the *19.* and *8.Panzer-Divisions* and the *SS Panzerkampfgruppe 'Das Reich'* with effect from 06.00 hours the following morning. The *Korps* was to assume responsibility that night for the sector either side of Korostyshev, redeploying the *'Das Reich'* to cover those elements of the *XXXXVIII.PzK* which were due to pull out. Moreover, it was to continue falling back, this time to a line running from Korostyshev in the south, through Bobrik, the northern edge of Gumenniki, and the northern edge of Chernyakhov to the northern edge of Novopol'. The headquarters was to move to Zhitomir. The new organisations and tasks required a redefining of the boundaries between the *Korps*, and these were set as follows: between the *VII.AK* and the *XXXXII.AK*, it ran from Ruzhin along the Rostavitsa to western Pavoloch' and from there to Savertsy and Koshlyaki; between the *XXXXII.AK* and the *XXXXVIII.PzK*, it ran from Glukhovtsy through Kashperovka, Khalaim-Gorodok and Min'kovtsy to Khodorkov; between the *XXXXVIII.PzK* and the *XIII.AK* it ran from Troyanov through Peski and Levkov to Korostyshev, and from there along the Teterev.

Sometime after issuing this order though, Raus reconsidered the proposals Balck had made earlier in the day regarding pulling back the left wing of the *XXXXVIII.PzK* to the line Kmitov-Studenitsa, and changed his earlier opinion. However, the orders just issued required the detail of Balck's proposals to be altered somewhat, and Raus instructed the *XXXXVIII.PzK* to pull back the *8.Panzer-Division* and the *'Das Reich'* into the line that same night.[86] As specified in the original order, the two units would still be transferred to the *XIII.AK* at 06.00 hours the next morning, but they were to

---

86 *PzAOK 4*, Ia Nr. 6984/43 geh. dated 27 Dec 43.

be combined with the *19.Panzer-Division* to act as a single group under the division's commanding officer, *Generalmajor* Källner.

By the end of the day then, the intentions of the *4.Panzerarmee* were largely unchanged with a few exceptions.[87] The *8.Panzer-Division* and the *SS Panzerkampfgruppe 'Das Reich'* were now to take up new positions on a line running from either side of Kmitov to Studenitsa, whilst the *1.Panzer-Division* was to be pulled out of the front line and transferred to the area east of Berdichev, leaving just a reserve group east of Zhitomir. On the left wing, the *LIX.AK* was to build a new defensive position on its right along a line running from the southern end of Zlobichi through Sobolevka to the western edge of Khotinovka. Meanwhile there had been further news regarding the *17.Panzer-Division* which had been promised as reinforcement. A signal had been received from Army Group South advising that the *s.Panzer-Abteilung 506 (Tiger)* would be transferred from the *PzAOK 1* along with the promised *Panzer-Division*.[88] The *Abteilung* was to remain attached to the division in every respect, and its transfer would be co-ordinated accordingly. The *1.Panzerarmee* also copied to Raus a message issued regarding the relief of the *17.Panzer-Division* itself.[89] The relief from the front line was due to be completed by early on 29 December, and the division, together with the attached *Sturmgeschütz-Abteilung 249*, was to be transferred to the Kazatin area where it would come under the command of the *PzAOK 4*. All units not already engaged had been instructed to start moving immediately, with combat elements forming up in battle groups for the transfer. Units to be transported by rail would start loading in Kirovograd on 28 December, whilst the units moving by road would use the *DG IV*[90] from Novoukrainka to Vinnitsa. All units were to be fully supplied with fuel before moving. There were also additional reinforcements in the shape of a *Landesschützen-Bataillon*, this being made available for local security of the *18.Artillerie-Division*.

Later that night, the *4.Panzerarmee* received a signal from the Army Group *Oberquartiermeister* regarding the destruction of railway installations.[91] The message acknowledged that the developing situation might well require the temporary evacuation of railway junctions, and it lay down instructions for the demolition of installations east of the stations at Berdichev, Kazatin and Novograd-Volynskii. Any proposals for demolitions were to be agreed first with the Army Group transport officer, and no independent action was to be undertaken in this regard, either by the troops or the various *Kampfkommandanten*. The *Panzerarmee* was, moreover, to advise its various subordinate units precisely which installations were to be regarded as militarily important, and which therefore had to be destroyed. These were defined as those which were of direct benefit to the conduct of operations, and in cases of doubt, the Army Group was to be consulted. Disruption of installations involving foodstuffs, and the agricultural and industrial economies, would be the responsibility of the civil administration, although instructions in this regard were to be agreed with the *Panzerarmee* and its subordinate units. In cases where military supply installations had to be evacuated, goods were only to be destroyed if they could not be moved out and if they would be of immediate use

---

87 *PzAOK 4*, Ia Nr. 6989/43 g.Kdos. dated 27 Dec 43.
88 *Hgr.Süd*, Ia Nr. 4366/43 geh. dated 27 Dec 43.
89 *PzAOK 1*, Ia Nr. 1247/43 g.Kdos. dated 27 Dec 43.
90 The *Durchgangstrasse IV* (or Through Road IV); an all-weather, good quality, metalled road.
91 *Hgr.Süd*, O.Qu./Qu. Nr. F655/43 g.Kdos. dated 27 Dec 43.

to the enemy, such as fuel, rations, captured munitions, and mines. Goods which were not of immediate value to the enemy, such as flour and German munitions, were only to be destroyed if it seemed unlikely that the installation would be recaptured in the foreseeable future.

5

The *4.Panzerarmee* Falls Back

Tuesday 28 December 1943

On the *4.Panzerarmee* right wing, the night again passed quietly on the *XXIV.PzK* sector.[1] Two Soviet patrols had been thrown back by the *34.Infanterie-Division* near Balyko-Shchuchinka, whilst a local breach in the front line south of Gusachevka was cleared in a small-scale counterattack by the *82.Infanterie-Division*, following an assault by an estimated company. A total of three prisoners were taken during the actions. In the Germanovka area, Soviet troops contented themselves with digging in about 300 metres from the main German positions. In the rear, the *168.Infanterie-Division* continued its transfer to the *XXXXII.AK*, and the tenth train left during the course of the night.

The *VII.AK*, to the left, reported heavy truck traffic moving into the Germanovka area from the north-west, and a prisoner taken during the defence of a Soviet patrol confirmed the presence of a new rifle division in the area.[2] It was due to have attacked on 26 December, but no other details were available. The *198.Infanterie-Division* reported little more than the odd enemy reconnaissance patrol, although it had been attacked by a single low-flying aircraft in the Vinnitskiye Stavy area. Opposite the *88.Infanterie-Division* things were different. Soviet forces had maintained their pressure against Malopolovetskoe and Yakhny, and had pushed on into the northern parts of both towns. The division mounted counterattacks against the spearheads, and these continued on into the morning. To the south-west though, reconnaissance parties had found the villages of Rogozna and Krasnyanka already occupied by Russian troops. It was clear that the division was being outflanked. On the *Korps* left wing, Soviet armour had forced its way into Pavoloch' the previous evening, and the defending elements of the *Grenadier-Regiment 417* from the *168.Infanterie-Division* had been obliged to fall back away from the river Rostavitsa to take up new positions on the high ground to the south-east. The Soviet 240th Rifle Division, previously 40th Army reserve, had been newly identified on the sector.

Meanwhile elements of the *XXXXII.AK* pushed warily forwards to try and strengthen the *Korps'* defensive position into a coherent line.[3] The remnants of the *25.Panzer-Division* continued pulling back from the north, with those elements which had crossed the river Rostavitsa at Pavoloch' heading south-westwards and reaching the Ruzhin area by early morning. Two Panzergrenadier battalions were then pushed forwards north of the river again, towards their new positions, one heading for Krylovka and the other for Yaroslavka. The two remaining operational panzers had not yet arrived in the new sector, although one of the division's artillery battalions, the *I./Panzerartillerie-Abteilung 91* was already in firing positions north of Ruzhin. To the left, the *168.Infanterie-Division* moved progressively into its new positions, and as its lead battalion advanced slowly towards

---

1   *XXIV.PzK.*, Morgenmeldung, 05.35 hours dated 28 Dec 43.
2   *VII.AK.*, Morgenmeldung, 05.45 hours dated 28 Dec 43.
3   *XXXXII.AK.*, Morgenmeldung, dated 28 Dec 43.

the Vcheraishe-Spichintsy sector, it encountered Soviet reconnaissance troops heading southwards. Other Russian troops had however already pushed passed this point heading south. Two Soviet tanks had been reported east of Voitovtsy, a few kilometres north-west of Ruzhin, as early as 02.00 hours, and it was only two hours later when, a little to the west, elements of the division's *Grenadier-Regiment 442* first moved north-westwards through Voitovtsy to a point east of Malaya Chernyavka. The division headquarters had meanwhile been set up in Bol'shaya-Chernyavka, and the *III./Artillerie-Regiment 248* had arrived in Ruzhin. To the left of the division, elements of the *Panzergrenadier-Regiment 90* from the *20.Panzergrenadier-Division* had taken up positions in Chernorudka and Khalaim-Gorodok, but not before they had come across Soviet tanks at about 04.00 hours on the road between Kashperovka and Chernorudka.[4] Once in position, in the early hours of the morning, the elements in Chernorudka became involved in another Soviet tank-supported attack, this time from the north and west. Away in the rear, about 20 kilometres to the south-west, the *18.Artillerie-Division* had begun to arrive in the Kazatin area, with the *Artillerie-Regiment 288* and the *Heeres-Flak-Abteilung 280* both having reached the area during the night. The *Artillerie-Regiment 88* was due to arrive later the same morning.

The Soviets had sprung to life again opposite the *XXXXVIII.PzK* to the north-west.[5] The previous evening, the *1.SS Panzer-Division 'LSSAH'* had reported a Russian assault against the southern end of Starosel'ye and this had resulted in a penetration into the eastern part of the town by about 300 Soviet troops and four tanks. The division mounted a counterattack during the night and succeeded in restoring the situation. Further north, other Soviet troops, including 10 tanks and a number of trucks, had attacked the division's left wing, north of Ivnitsa at about 03.00 hours. These broke through and headed off westwards through Turovets towards the main road to Zhitomir. The division mounted another counterattack, but it appeared too late as the Russian tanks had already wheeled off north-westwards along the main road. To the north, the *19.Panzer-Division* had spent the night moving into its new positions, assuming responsibility for its sector on the river Teterev. The remainder of the *8.Panzer-Division* meanwhile continued to fall back in as orderly a fashion as was practicable, and by morning its rearguards were only about two kilometres east of the main defensive line. The *1.Panzer-Division* began to pull out of its front line positions prior to its planned transfer south, and it had passed the main defensive position by about 03.30 hours. However, the withdrawal had been closely followed by the pursuing Soviet forces and this caused some difficulty. The *Panzeraufklärungs-Abteilung* 1, acting as rearguard, had been attacked by the advancing Russian troops, but it was still fighting its way back to Sloboda Selets on the south-eastern outskirts of Zhitomir. On the *Korps* left wing, there was no news from the *SS Panzerkampfgruppe 'Das Reich'*.

The *XIII.AK* had passed a night of mixed fortunes.[6] The previous evening had seen a number of relatively small-scale Soviet assaults against the *340.* and *208.Infanterie-Divisions*, in anything between company and battalion strength, but all these had been successfully seen off. A small penetration had however been made in the Potievka area. At midnight, the divisions of the *Korps* all began the second stage of their major withdrawal,

---

4 PzAOK 4, Morgenmeldung an *Heeresgruppe Süd*, Ia Nr. 6990/43 geh. dated 28 Dec 43.
5 XXXXVIII.PzK., Morgenmeldung, 06.00 hours dated 28 Dec 43.
6 XIII.AK., Morgenmeldung, 06.15 hours dated 28 Dec 43.

leaving only rearguards in the existing positions. By 05.00 hours, the *208.Infanterie-Division* had covered a distance of about nine kilometres, and had reached the area either side of Annopol'. There had been no reports from the other divisions, although it was known that the road conditions had hampered all foot movement, for both men and horses. To the west, the *7.Panzer-Division* reported constant Soviet pressure along its whole front throughout the night. Enemy tanks had been reported in Vikhlya,[7] where the division indicated it had destroyed a Soviet company-sized combat patrol.

On the *Panzerarmee* left wing, the *LIX.AK* reported that the withdrawal of the *291. Infanterie-Division* had been carried out as planned.[8] Up until about 21.00 hours the previous evening, the Soviets had attempted to disrupt the withdrawal, making repeated attacks, particularly in the Graby area just east of Zlobichi, but these had made little impact. The *Sicherungs-Regiment 375* also reported hearing continuous engine noises from about 19.00 hours onwards, apparently indicating a large volume of vehicle traffic heading from south to north. Also during the previous evening, at 19.30 hours, the Soviets had attacked the Khotinovka area on the right wing of the *Korps-Abteilung C*. This had involved about a 150 soldiers, and had been successfully defended. Further Russian troop assemblies, observed in the Novaki area, had been dispersed by defensive artillery fire. On the northern wing, there had been considerable Soviet reconnaissance activity throughout the previous afternoon and evening, although this later extended to the rest of the sector too. Beginning at about 06.00 hours in the morning, very heavy artillery fire began to fall on the main positions of the *Korps-Abteilung* north-east of Korosten', particularly on the Stremigorod-Bekhi sector, but at that stage it was difficult to determine what the fire indicated.[9]

At about 09.35 hours, the chief of staff at the *VII.AK*, *Oberst* Schwatlo-Gesterding, called *4.Panzerarmee* headquarters to discuss the latest situation on his sector.[10] On his right wing, he reported that an attack by a Soviet force estimated to be two rifle battalions had resulted in a breach in the Germanovka area. On the left wing, the Soviets continued to press south and south-east and were well positioned on the left flank of the *88.Infanterie-Division*. Schwatlo-Gesterding requested permission to pull the *Korps* left wing back to a line from Grebenki, through the northern edge of Pologi and Drozdy to Mikhailovka, as had been discussed the previous evening. Raus agreed, on the condition that any forces freed by such a withdrawal would be redeployed to strengthen the hanging left flank. The *VII.AK* was later issued with appropriate formal instructions.[11] In the directive, Hell was ordered to maintain his current positions on the right and centre sectors, and pull back the left wing into a line running through the northern edges of Grebenki, Pologi, Drozdy, and Mikhailovka, and from there to Ruda on the Rostavitsa. Over on the left, the *Grenadier-Regiment 417* was to pull back, keeping its left shoulder pushed against the Rostavitsa.

Meanwhile, the Soviet offensive rolled on relentlessly, under thick clouds and falling temperatures. On the right wing, there was a noticeable increase in the number and strength of the Soviet pinning attacks against both the north-eastern and the north-

---

7   Referred to as Wischja in the German records.
8   *LIX.AK.*, Morgenmeldung, 05.30 hours dated 28 Dec 43.
9   *PzAOK 4*, Morgenmeldung an *Heeresgruppe Süd*, Ia Nr. 6990/43 geh. dated 28 Dec 43.
10 *PzAOK 4*, Ia Kriegstagebuch entry, dated 28 Dec 43.
11 *PzAOK 4*, Ia Nr. 6993/43 geh. dated 28 Dec 43.

western sectors, and during the morning the *PzAOK 4* received a message from Nehring's *XXIV.PzK*.[12] There had been a series of apparently co-ordinated assaults at different locations along the *Korps* sector, and all had begun at about 09.00 hours. Three company strength attacks had been made against the right wing of the *34.Infanterie-Division* in the vicinity of Vedmedevka, and another of the same size to the north-west near Balyko-Shchuchinka. All had been repelled, but by 10.15 hours Balyko-Shchuchinka was under attack again. Other assault preparations had also been spotted, with Soviet troop assemblies of between one and two rifle companies. Either side of Makarovskii, an estimated 900 men were observed by troops of the *82.Infanterie-Division* preparing to make another attack, but this was seen in time and engaged with disruptive artillery fire. On the *Korps* left wing, a more serious attack had developed south-east of Germanovka, where, following a heavy artillery barrage including *Katyushas*, an estimated rifle regiment assaulted German positions, only to be driven off.

The assaults continued in much the same vein throughout the day, and the *Korps* reported a total of eight separate attacks on the Dudari-Ul'yaniki sector alone, striking either side of the boundary between the *Korps-Abteilung B* and the *34.Infanterie-Division*.[13] These ranged in strength between company and battalion size, and achieved no less than five breaches in the front line. All of these except one were eventually cleared by evening, and compared with what the *Korps* described as its own slight losses, the Soviets were reported to have lost an estimated 160 dead, 110 of them counted, 35 wounded and six taken prisoner. On the north-west sector, the *82.Infanterie-Division* reported a total of six attacks between Chernyakhov and Leonovka,[14] each by an estimated two Soviet rifle battalions, but all were seen off. Despite the increased enemy activity on its front, the *XXIV.Panzerkorps* was still under instructions to transfer the *Pionier-Bataillon 74* and a *Grenadier-Regiment* to other commands, and arrangements had been made to fulfil these orders. The *Pionier-Bataillon* had been instructed to move to Komsomolskaya, and was already on the move, whilst the *82.Infanterie-Division* had already taken steps to release the *Grenadier-Regiment 158*. The final transports had left by 10.35 hours that morning, and the regimental headquarters, together with the *II.Bataillon*, was on its way to Belaya Tserkov'.

To the left of the *XXIV.Panzerkorps*, the *75.Infanterie-Division* under the *VII.AK* also reported increased enemy activity.[15] During the course of the afternoon, the Soviets had launched several attacks in anything up to battalion strength, but in general these had all been thrown back. Despite the close attentions of forward Soviet troops, the *198.Infanterie-Division* had pulled back its left wing as authorised by Raus earlier in the day. There had been a series of strong assaults along the whole of the division's front, with elements of three separate rifle divisions having been identified in the fighting. Perhaps fortunately, there had been no Russian armour on the sector. On the left, in the *88.Infanterie-Division* sector, Soviet troops had forced three separate crossings over the river Rostavitsa at Dulitskoe, Buki and Pavoloch', and had subsequently succeeded in breaching the new defensive positions near Maly Lisovtsy. Since 16.00 hours, they had been pushing on to the south-east and Hell reported that, in the event of a concerted

---

12 *XXIV.PzK.*, Ia report, 10.15 hours dated 28 Dec 43.
13 *XXIV.PzK.*, Tagesmeldung, dated 28 Dec 43.
14 Referred to as Iwanowka in the German records.
15 *VII.AK.*, Tagesmeldung, dated 28 Dec 43.

attack, he would no longer be able to hold open the main road running from Belaya Tserkov' through Skvira to Ruzhin. He also reported that although his troops had distinguished themselves during this fighting, they were now exhausted. Although Soviet losses were reported to be high, the casualties of the *VII.AK* had also been not inconsiderable.

In addition to his formal report, Hell also spoke direct with Raus regarding his situation, advising the *Armee* commander that the *Korps* would continue to fall back to the newly authorised line that night. He pointed out though that Soviet occupation of the towns of Malopolovetskoe, Krasnolesy and Dulitskoe constituted a real danger to the flank of the *VII.AK*, although the immediate threat might initially be negated by deploying a *Sperrverband* (blocking unit) between Krasnolesy and Ruda. In this respect, the *Aufklärungs-Abteilung* from the *75.Infanterie-Division* had already been moved to the left wing, and had counterattacked in the Dulitskoe area, throwing back the leading Soviet troops from the southern part of the village. Since the Russians had succeeded in achieving a breakthrough further west, in the Maly Lisovtsy area south of Pavoloch', the *Korps* had been obliged to order the *Regimentsgruppe 417* of the *168.Infanterie-Division* which was covering the sector, to pull back to a line running from Velikaya Erchiki to Trubeevka. In that way, contact could be maintained with the *XXXXII.AK* on the river Rostavitsa, but, Hell believed, the *VII.AK* would no longer be able to prevent the Russians from breaking through along the main road to Skvira. Raus responded by saying that maintaining contact with the *XXXXII.AK* on the Rostavitsa was not as important as facing, and destroying, the Soviet forces on his own sector. The task of the *VII.AK* would therefore have to be to prevent a Russian advance towards the main east-west road between Ruzhin and Belaya Tserkov'; the road was after all of great importance to the *PzAOK 4*, since it provided a good means of transferring forces on a lateral axis behind the front line.

Further west, Mattenklott's *XXXXII.AK* had been in real difficulty as the dismal weather continued.[16] In the drizzle and light snowfall, Soviet forces had continued to press their attacks against the *Korps* centre and left wing, with the main weight falling against the weak left wing. In the centre, a Russian assault during the afternoon against the left wing of the *25.Panzer-Division* had resulted in the loss of Yaroslavka, with an estimated rifle regiment and 10 tanks breaking through the German defences. The division counterattacked during the evening and managed to restore the situation. Over on the left however, the sector under the *168.Infanterie-Division* was attacked in the early morning, resulting in a breakthrough west of Chernorudka. Soviet armour poured through the resulting breach, and between 30 and 40 tanks, with infantry mounted, struck past the *Panzergrenadier-Regiment 90* west of the railway and headed straight for Kazatin. They reached the town and occupied it the same day. In contrast, east of the railway the division escaped relatively unscathed, maintaining its positions between Bol'shaya-Chernyavka and Radzivilovka[17] as the Russians simply bypassed its left wing. In the rear meanwhile, and directly in the path of the advancing Soviet armour, the *18.Artillerie-Division* was completing its assembly and deployment in the Kazatin area. Six of its battalions had arrived during the night, leaving just three still to come, and those which had arrived had been busy trying to deploy into firing positions when the

---

16 *XXXXII.AK.*, Tagesmeldung, 20.30 hours dated 28 Dec 43.
17 Referred to as Velikoe on more recent Soviet maps.

leading Soviet tanks struck. The majority of the division was by that time in the Kazatin-Sestrenovka area, but the confusion caused by the unexpected arrival of the Russian armour prevented it from deploying as planned. To try and eject these Soviet forces from Kazatin, an improvised group of infantry was hurriedly thrown together and pushed into a counterattack. The attack began at about midday, and by evening the alarm units had advanced into the centre of the town, but fighting continued on into the night.

At about 20.10 hours that evening, Mattenklott called *PzAOK 4* headquarters to speak to Raus.[18] He explained that the 30 or so Soviet tanks had broken into Kazatin from the north-west, rather than the north-east as had been expected, thus bypassing the defensive measures adopted on the north-east approach to the town. The attacking tanks had taken the opportunity to destroy a number of vehicles before being engaged by the various alarm units assembled by the *Korps*. Raus reminded Mattenklott of his mobile resources, and pointed out that an advance by Soviet tanks into Kazatin was to be prevented by using the *Sturmgeschützen* attached to the *Artillerie-Division*, together with any other mobile anti-tank means he could find. He also reminded the *Korps* commander that the *25.Panzer-Division* and the *168.Infanterie-Division* were only to pull back if there proved to be a real danger of their being encircled, although he did authorise the transfer of a single battalion from the *25.Panzer-Division* to support the defence of the *Artillerie-Division*. This was in addition to the *Landesschützen-Bataillon 857* which the Army Group had allocated from the *Feldkommandantur* in Vinnitsa, and which was scheduled to arrive the following day.[19] Raus formalised these intentions in an order issued to the *XXXXII.AK* at about 22.00 hours,[20] in which the *Korps* was instructed to hold the line Karabchiev-Krylovka-Malaya Chernyavka with the two divisions, only allowing them to fall back in a fighting withdrawal if they were threatened with destruction. The *18.Artillerie-Division* and the various alarm units were to prevent any further Soviet advance through Kazatin.

The *XXXXVIII.PzK* was meanwhile in trouble too. The *Kampfkommandant* in Berdichev had reported at about 05.00 hours, that Soviet tanks and infantry had been seen in the Belopol'e area, near Kashperovka, and that these were heading westwards along the main road directly towards the city.[21] Upon receiving this news, Fangohr called von Mellenthin at *XXXXVIII.PzK* headquarters and directed him to accelerate the relief of the *1.Panzer-Division*, and re-deploy it further south than originally intended, on the main Berdichev-Kashperovka road rather than in the Maly Moshkovtsy area. The division itself was meanwhile transferring southwards from the sector east of Zhitomir, and by evening, it would begin assembling in the area east of Berdichev. From its new positions, the division was to push south-eastwards to make contact with the left wing of the *XXXXII.AK*. A little to the north, the *1.SS Panzer-Division 'LSSAH'* was having a hard time trying to prevent any further Soviet advance on its sector.[22] On its extreme right wing, the division reported that it had seen about 40 tanks and 300 trucks, each with an estimated 30 men on board, and some with towed anti-tank guns, moving from the Kashperovka area, heading south-west towards Glukhovtsy, about nine kilometres

---

18   *PzAOK 4*, Ia Kriegstagebuch entry, dated 28 Dec 43.
19   *Hgr.Süd*, Ia Nr. 4593/43 geh. dated 28 Dec 43.
20   *PzAOK 4*, Ia Nr. 6991/43 geh. dated 28 Dec 43.
21   *PzAOK 4*, Ia Kriegstagebuch entry, dated 28 Dec 43.
22   *XXXXVIII.PzK.*, Tagesmeldung, dated 28 Dec 43.

north-west of Kazatin. The advance was parallel to the strike further south which captured Kazatin, and indicated a strong Soviet presence in the gap between the left wing of the *XXXXII.AK* and the right wing of the *XXXXVIII.PzK*. On receipt of this news, the *4.Panzerarmee* instructed Balck to deploy the *1.Panzer-Division* on the sector between the Berdichev-Kashperovka road and the Berdichev-Kazatin railway, concentrating the main weight on the right near the railway.[23] The division was then to attack with its right wing, advancing along the railway, through Glukhovtsy to recapture Kazatin. The centre was to maintain its positions, whilst the left wing was to fall back behind the river Guiva. Balck responded by saying that there was no prospect of any advance that night, not only because the night would be completely dark, but also because the troops were badly exhausted and required some rest. Raus agreed.

Meanwhile, the *'LSSAH'* had also been forced out of Krylovka and obliged to fall back westwards towards Chervonoe. An estimated Soviet rifle battalion had then proceeded to attack that town with the support of 12 tanks, but this had been beaten off. On the left wing, another battalion-sized attack had been made from the south-east against the division's positions in the southern end of Starosel'ye, although this too had been unsuccessful. This however was followed by a heavier attack from the north-east involving an estimated two rifle regiments and about 40 to 50 tanks from the Ivnitsa-Volitsa area. A small penetration in the northern part of the town resulted, but this was sealed off. To the north-west, other attacks along the river Guiva followed. An estimated Russian rifle battalion advanced from the north and assaulted the high ground two kilometres north-west of Starosel'ye, and a regimental-sized assault started from the Turovets area heading south. Ivankov was assaulted by about 25 Soviet tanks while Tulin[24] was occupied by Russian troops. Overall, the *'LSSAH'* reported having destroyed a total of 19 Russian tanks during the course of the day, but fighting nonetheless continued into the evening. At 16.45 hours, Balck reported the division's problems to *PzAOK 4* headquarters, pointing out that it had been heavily attacked on its northern wing and in its rear, and that as a result it had been forced to fall back behind the river Guiva.[25] The division was responsible for a sector about 60 kilometres wide, and, with the forces available, it was simply not in the position to withstand a concerted attack. Balck proposed therefore that the *XIII.AK* be allowed to withdraw to a new line running from Levkov through Gadzinka and Trokovichi to Zorokov, thus providing a closer defence of Zhitomir with an arc running from north to east about 15 kilometres in front of the city. This would allow the *XXXXVIII.PzK Sperrverband*, elements of the *1.Panzer-Division*, to be released, and possibly an additional *Infanterie-Division* too. Raus considered the idea, but was not convinced that a full division could be spared from even such a shortened front. Moreover, he thought that such a withdrawal would inevitably lead to another, to a line running from Sloboda Selets[26] through Zhitomir station and Smokovka[27] to Kamenka and Berezovka. The front might be much shorter, but there were no prepared positions, and in any event it was intended that the *SS Panzerkampfgruppe 'Das Reich'* would soon take over the sector currently held by the *Sperrverband*.

---

23 *PzAOK 4*, Ia Nr. 6979/43 geh. dated 28 Dec 43.
24 This is now the part of Leshchin which lies north of the river.
25 *PzAOK 4*, Ia Kriegstagebuch entry, dated 28 Dec 43.
26 On the northern bank of the river Teterev opposite Stanishovka.
27 Referred to as Cheshkaya in the German records.

THE *4.PANZERARMEE* FALLS BACK

Nevertheless, Raus did speak to Hauffe at *XIII.AK* to get the latter's views on Balck's proposals.[28] Hauffe was less than enthusiastic, and suspected that little would be gained from such a withdrawal, suggesting instead that he could remain in his current positions and still allow Balck's *Sperrverband* to be relieved. In this, he echoed Raus' own views. The units of the *XIII.AK* meanwhile continued to fall back as ordered.[29] The Soviets were quick to recognise the withdrawal however, and followed up very closely, particularly on both wings. During the morning, Russian forces attacked both wings, presumably with the objective of causing the whole *Korps* front to collapse. In the south, the assault was led predominantly by infantry with tank support, whilst in the north it was a major armoured strike involving about 90 tanks. By afternoon, the Soviets had also attacked the *Korps* centre, again with tank support. At 06.00 hours that morning, as directed, the *Korps* assumed responsibility for the *19.* and *8.Panzer-Divisions*, and the *SS Panzerkampfgruppe 'Das Reich'*, and as a result it had become involved in the fighting around Korostyshev straightaway. Either side of the main road to Zhitomir, the *Kampfgruppe* Källner, based on the *19.Panzer-Division*, reported three separate attacks.[30] Two had been of battalion size, and the third of regimental size, but all had been repelled. Some attacking troops, including about 13 tanks with infantry support, did however manage to break through and reach the north-eastern part of Studenitsa, but these had then been intercepted by elements of the *'Das Reich'*. Six of the attacking tanks were destroyed, and the *Kampfgruppe* began operations to mop up in the area of the breach. Further north, the *68.Infanterie-Division* was assaulted by strong infantry forces with heavy tank support, and on the right wing a separate battalion-sized attack was beaten back. On the sector held by the *340.Infanterie-Division*, a Soviet force estimated to be a rifle regiment with about 15 tanks in support assaulted just before the division completed its withdrawal. The attack succeeded in breaking into the northern part of Devochki, just east of Chernyakhov. The division launched a counterattack against the penetration, and this carried on into the evening. To the north-west, the *208.Infanterie-Division* managed to complete its withdrawal as planned, without suffering any enemy interference, but the *7.Panzer-Division* to its left was not so fortunate. It had been attacked by strong Soviet armoured forces on the Brazhenka-Toporishche sector, but had been able so far to maintain its defensive integrity, destroying a reported 16 tanks in the process. Now securing the *Korps* left wing, the *213.Sicherungs-Division* moved into positions west of Chernyakhov, on a line running from Kruchenets to Ivanovichi. Many of the division's supporting units were still further west in the Vasilevka- Pulin[31]-Kurnoe area, although a reconnaissance screen had been thrown up along the Pulin-Kurnoe line. During the

---

28 *PzAOK 4*, Ia Kriegstagebuch entry, dated 28 Dec 43.
29 *XIII.AK.*, Tagesmeldung, dated 28 Dec 43.
30 According to a message sent by the *19.Panzer-Division* to the *XXXXVIII.PzK* on this day, the division deployed the following combat strength at this time:
  • *Panzergrenadier-Regiment 73*: 14 Officers, 49 NCOs, 200 Men
  • *Panzergrenadier-Regiment 74*: 10 Officers, 24 NCOs, 155 Men
  • *Panzeraufklärungs-Abteilung 19*: 10 Officers, 33 NCOs, 190 Men
  The regiments therefore were no bigger than full strength companies. To make matters worse, the *Panzer-Regiment 27* had no operational panzers, and only eight in short-term repair. The division had just three heavy anti-tank guns, eight self-propelled anti-tank guns, eleven light field howitzers, two heavy field howitzers, and three 100 mm guns.
31 Shown on more recent Soviet maps as Chervonoarmeisk.

course of their earlier conversation, Raus had advised Hauffe that the *7.Panzer-Division* was to remain committed on the *Korps* northern front in the Chernyakhov area, with the aim of preventing the strong Soviet armoured forces from breaking through the somewhat thinly held front along the Korosten'-Zhitomir road, and breaking into the city itself.[32] Raus later confirmed this intention with *Generalleutnant* Busse at Army Group South, only to learn that the Army Group did not agree with this course of action.[33] Busse not only considered that the *XIII.AK* should hold its current positions, but also that the *7.Panzer-Division* should be pulled out of the front and transferred to the Berdichev-Kazatin area. In reply, Raus pointed out that the main weight of the Soviet offensive was in precisely that area, and that it was questionable whether the planned attack by the *1.Panzer-Division* would make any headway through Glukhovtsy towards Kazatin. On the other hand, pulling the *7.Panzer-Division* out of its current sector would almost inevitably lead to the loss of Zhitomir. Busse's response was only pragmatic, given the lack of resources. If the *Panzerarmee* were to be able to strike the Russians on their own main direction, risks would have to be taken. The Army Group issued Raus with formal instructions in this regard, directing that the *XIII.AK* was to maintain its current positions north and north-east of Zhitomir.[34] There was no question of the front being withdrawn. Moreover, the *Panzerarmee* was ordered to re-group the *7.Panzer-Division* with a view to transferring it to the Berdichev-Kazatin area.

There was little news from the *LIX.AK* on the *Panzerarmee* left flank, although it was known that strong Soviet infantry forces, supported by about 60 tanks, had attacked along the whole of the *Korps* sector.[35] The front had been penetrated in many places, and Russian troops had made deep inroads into the defensive positions. Beyond that, there were few details available. At 13.45 hours, Fangohr called the Army Group and spoke with the *Ia*, *Oberst* Schulze-Büttger, advising him of what details there were of the attack.[36] At 09.00 hours, following a heavy artillery barrage, the positions of the *Korps-Abteilung C* north-east of Korosten' had been attacked near Singai and Bekhi, and by the end of the morning Soviet tanks had broken through the main defensive line and reached many German artillery positions. This new situation raised the old question of whether Korosten' should still be held, as demanded by the earlier *Führerbefehl* from Hitler himself. Schulze-Büttger advised that the order no longer had to be regarded as in force, but that in the event of a strong Russian attack, the defensive ring around Korosten' was to be drawn tighter, and only if there was a real threat of encirclement was the *Korps* to withdraw to the south-west, towards Novograd-Volynskii.[37] All this must have come as something of a relief for Raus, given his orders to the *LIX.AK* the previous day, and he now reminded von der Chevallerie that the town was to be held as long as possible, but that his earlier order would be in full force should there be any danger of encirclement.

---

32 *PzAOK 4*, Ia Kriegstagebuch entry, dated 28 Dec 43.
33 *PzAOK 4*, Ia Kriegstagebuch entry, dated 28 Dec 43.
34 *Hgr.Süd*, Ia N. 4393/43 geh. dated 28 Dec 43.
35 *PzAOK 4*, Tagesmeldung an *Heeresgruppe Süd*, 22.30 hours dated 28 Dec 43.
36 *PzAOK 4*, Ia Kriegstagebuch entry, dated 28 Dec 43.
37 Referred to as Zwiahel in the German records.

THE *4.PANZERARMEE* FALLS BACK   137

Later that evening a signal arrived from von Manstein at Army Group South regarding the employment of Hauffe's *XIII.AK*.[38] The Army Group had clearly reconsidered the position, and admitted that, notwithstanding the necessity of maintaining the current positions, there was every possibility that the future development of the situation would require the *Korps* to pull back step-by-step. In such a case, it was to withdraw to a line running from the railway bend south-east of Zhitomir, through Zhitomir and along the line of the Kamenka river west of the city as far as Vasilevka. This line would have to be held firmly in order to maintain a solid contact with the *XXXXVIII.PzK* and to protect the latter's deep left flank. The *Korps* would have to be supplied from a south-westerly direction, and arrangements to safeguard this were to be put in place by the *PzAOK 4*. Moreover, the *Armee* was to ensure by thorough mining that the Soviets would be unable to make rapid advances along either the Kiev-Zhitomir road or the Korosten'-Zhitomir road.

The Army Group had other good news as well.[39] In addition to the *17.Panzer-Division* and the *s.Panzer-Abteilung 506 (Tiger)*, the *4.Panzerarmee* would be receiving other substantial reinforcements. The *4.Gebirgs-Division* was being transferred in from Army Group A, and the *16.Panzer-Division*, newly equipped with 79 *Panzer V 'Panther'*, was being sent by Army Group Centre. Both divisions would begin arriving on either 30 or 31 December. Army Group South was also sending three *Panzer-Zerstörer-Kompanien*, and a *Feldgendarmerie-Kompanie*, the latter having proved necessary due to the constant traffic problems being experienced by the *Armee* on the road between Zhitomir and Berdichev. The movements of the *'LSSAH'*, the *18.Artillerie-Division* and the *1.Panzer-Division* had all suffered badly over the past few days with the large number of non-combat vehicles using the road. The new *Kompanie* was to ensure that the road was kept free for the movement of combat units. All other vehicles were to be re-routed further south-west.

In contrast to the preceding day then, 28 December had been something of a minor disaster for the *4.Panzerarmee*, particularly with the fall of Kazatin and the resumption of the offensive against the *LIX.AK*. Over on the right wing, the Soviets had increased their pressure on the *XXIV.PzK* and the right wing of the *VII.AK*, mounting heavier and heavier pinning attacks to prevent the *Armee* from transferring troops away from that sector. They had continued to batter away at the left wing of the *VII.AK* with four rifle divisions, pushing it back south and south-east.[40] So far there had been no major Soviet armoured effort on this sector, and the *PzAOK 4* suspected that the main task of the 40th Army was to protect the deep flank of the tank armies which were moving south-west further west. Between Kazatin and Zhitomir, the Russians had continued to advance in three main groups as expected, with strong armour and mobile forces, supported by the closely following rifle divisions. The southern group had headed directly for Kazatin and captured the town from the north-west, while the central group was advancing straight for Berdichev. The northern group was meanwhile seemingly trying to dislodge the *'LSSAH'* from the Starosel'ye -Ivankov area in order to open the road to Zhitomir where the 56th Guards Tank Brigade from the 7th Guards Tank Corps had already been identified in the northern part of Leshchin. The *PzAOK 4* estimated that the Soviets

---

38 *Hgr.Süd*, Ia Nr. 4395/43 g.Kdos. dated 28 Dec 43.
39 *PzAOK 4*, Ia Kriegstagebuch entry, dated 28 Dec 43.
40 *PzAOK 4*, Ic Abendmeldung an H.Gr. Süd, 20.00 hours dated 28 Dec 43

had deployed between 230 and 250 tanks on this sector alone. Further north, west of the Teterev, the Russians had attacked the *XIII.AK* as it tried to pull back, hitting hard against its two wings, and attempting to outflank the left wing, pushing the 5th Guards Tank Corps southwards along the Korosten'-Zhitomir road. There were another 100 to 120 Soviet tanks deployed against this sector, and another 60 to 80 operating further north against the *LIX.AK*. The appearance of this latter group of enemy armour indicated that the Russians were now planning to force the issue on that sector too. The *4.Panzerarmee* front was being torn apart, and prospects for the future looked bleak. With this appreciation, and on the basis of his various discussions during the day, Raus issued his latest orders to the *XXXXVIII.PzK* and the *XIII.AK* during the night.[41] Those given to Balck have already been mentioned, whilst those for Hauffe confirmed what had already been discussed. The *Korps* was to hold its current positions and relieve the *Sperrverband* belonging to the *1.Panzer-Division*, which would then be returned to the *XXXXVIII.PzK*. The *7.Panzer-Division* was to be pulled out of the front the following day, and assembled in the area north of Zhitomir at the disposal of the *Panzerarmee*. Hauffe was to be prepared for the division to be transferred to the Berdichev area, where it would come under the command of the *XXXXVIII.PzK*.

Raus also issued new instructions to Nehring at *XXIV.PzK*.[42] He too was to maintain his existing positions, but in addition he was now to transfer to the *VII.AK* another regimental headquarters and an infantry battalion. The transfer of both was to be carried out in close co-operation with Hell's staff. The intentions of the *4.Panzerarmee* were now therefore as follows. The left wing of the *VII.AK* was to be pulled back to a line running from Grebenki through Pologi, Drozdy, Ruda, and Velikaya Erchiki to Trubeevka, while the *XXXXII.AK* was to hold a line from Trubeevka through Krylovka to Malaya Chernyavka and from there through the centre of Kazatin to the crossroads west of the town. The *XXXXVIII.PzK* was to attack on its right with the *1.Panzer-Division*, through Glukhovtsy to re-capture Kazatin, whilst its left wing held the line of the river Guiva as far as Peski, south-east of Zhitomir. The *XIII.AK* meanwhile was to hold its current positions and assemble the *7.Panzer-Division* north of Zhitomir, while the *LIX.AK* would continue to hold Korosten', falling back south-westwards only in the event of threatened encirclement.[43]

Wednesday 29 December 1943

The evening of 28 December, and the night which followed, saw Nehring's *XXIV. PzK* continue its efforts to clear up the previous day's penetration south of Balyko-Shchuchinka, but without success.[44] The *34.Infanterie-Division* now estimated that it would not be able to clear the area before the afternoon at the earliest, and only then with reinforcements. During the night, on the left wing of the *82.Infanterie-Division*, a Soviet patrol had been intercepted and thrown back south-east of Germanovka, whilst at about 23.00 hours, the *I./Grenadier-Regiment 158* had been relieved by the *I./Grenadier-Regiment 475* (otherwise known as the *Regimentsgruppe 677*) from the *Korps-Abteilung B*. At 03.00 hours, the newly inserted *Regimentsgruppe* had been attacked in unknown

---

41 PzAOK 4, Ia Nr. 6979/43 geh. dated 28 Dec 43.
42 PzAOK 4, Ia Nr. 6995/43 geh. dated 28 Dec 43.
43 PzAOK 4, Ia Nr. 6977/43 geh. dated 28 Dec 43.
44 XXIV.PzK., Morgenmeldung, 06.25 hours dated 29 Dec 43.

strength, and had been unable to prevent a breach of the front line south-east of Germanovka. The *I./Grenadier-Regiment 158* was rushed back to seal off the penetration.

On the right wing of the *VII.AK*, the *75.Infanterie-Division* had concluded a successful mopping up operation the previous evening south of Germanovka, and the division reported Soviet losses on this sector for the previous day to be 462 dead.[45] During the night there had been another two patrols, one combat and one reconnaissance, but both of these had been seen off. Nevertheless, some Russian troops had clearly managed to evade the mopping up, or perhaps even infiltrated the German lines once more, since, by morning, the division was still engaged in clearing the area south of the village. To the left, the withdrawals by the *198.* and *88.Infanterie-Divisions* had been carried out according to plan, although the latter did have to see off a number of Soviet patrols north and north-west of Ruda on the Rostavitsa. By morning though, the left wing of the *VII.AK* had been extended to a point west of Skvira. Reconnaissance patrols had been sent out into the dark beyond the town, but these had not reported in by morning.

Contact with the *XXXXII.AK* had been lost during the night, a critical failure given the events of the previous day, but this would be restored during the morning.[46] For the time being though, Raus remained unaware of developments on the most critical sector of his front, although he did know that elements of the *20.Panzergrenadier-Division* were still holding on in Bol'shaya-Chernyavka.[47]

On the *XXXXVIII.PzK* front, the Soviets had maintained their pressure into the night, attacking the right wing of the *1.SS Panzer-Division 'LSSAH'* on the Chervonoe-Maly Moshkovtsy sector.[48] The attack had been made between 20.00 and 22.00 hours, involving an estimated rifle battalion with tank support, but it had been seen off without too much difficulty. As soon as darkness had fallen, the division had begun to fall back to its new positions, and despite the difficult conditions it had managed to disengage from the enemy. The Russian forces however noticed the movement quite quickly, and followed the withdrawal closely, even to the extent that they had crossed the river Guiva at Leshchin before morning. The *1.Panzer-Division*, except the detached *Sperrverband*, had meanwhile reached its new assembly area south-east of Berdichev, and all elements had spent the night re-organising. Further east, covering the division's assembly, a reconnaissance patrol sent out by the *Kampfkommandant Berdichev* reported continual traffic noises on the north-south road running to Panasovka.

Further north, Hauffe's *XIII.AK* was subjected to further assaults throughout the night.[49] These were made along the whole of the *Korps* front, and many were supported by tanks. On the right, the *Kampfgruppe* Källner threw back a small, company-sized attack against the bridge in Levkov, whilst further north it also managed to clear up a small penetration in Studenitsa. Soviet assault preparations were also seen either side of the main Kiev-Zhitomir road, and these were successfully engaged with artillery fire. To the left, the *68.Infanterie-Division* managed to mount a small counterattack against a Russian force, consisting of about 300 men and a few tanks, which had succeeded in pushing its way into the northern part of Zabrod'e. The attack was successful and

---

45   *VII.AK.*, Morgenmeldung, 06.05 hours dated 29 Dec 43.
46   *PzAOK 4*, Ia Morgenmeldung an *Heeresgruppe Süd*, 07.00 hours dated 29 Dec 43.
47   *PzAOK 4*, Ia Morgenmeldung an *Heeresgruppe Süd*, 07.00 hours dated 29 Dec 43.
48   *XXXXVIII.PzK.*, Morgenmeldung, 05.55 hours dated 29 Dec 43.
49   *XIII.AK.*, Morgenmeldung, 06.45 hours dated 29 Dec 43.

the front line was restored. There were no other assaults against the division's sector, but there had been considerable enemy reconnaissance activity throughout the night. A similar assault had been made against the positions of the *340.Infanterie-Division* in Devochki, south-east of Chernyakhov, and although the exact size of the attack was not yet known, four Russian tanks were reported to have been spotted. The Soviet troops managed to advance into the eastern part of the village during the night, but by morning, the division had launched a counterattack to restore the situation. Chernyakhov itself had been attacked as well, when about 30 Soviet tanks with mounted infantry burst through the lines of the *208.Infanterie-Division* to storm the town at about 04.00 hours. The situation was confused, and was still unclear by morning. The *7.Panzer-Division* meanwhile had passed through Kletishche on the way to its new assembly area in and to the south of Malaya Gorbasha – Zorokov, where its new task was to prevent any Soviet breakthrough from Chernyakhov towards Zhitomir. Over on the *Korps* left wing, the *213.Sicherungs-Division* had taken up new positions north-west of Zhitomir, and reported no enemy contact.

Now almost 50 kilometres away to the north, the *LIX.AK* had pulled out of Korosten' and had passed the night falling back towards Novograd-Volynskii from its earlier positions.[50] It reported no enemy contact.

By about 10.20 hours, the *PzAOK 4* had managed to re-establish contact with the *XXXXII.AK*, and Raus took the opportunity to instruct Mattenklott to transfer a regiment of the *168.Infanterie-Division* to the west as quickly as possible with orders to hold Kazatin.[51] He also emphasised the importance of redeploying a battalion from the *25.Panzer-Division* to secure the *18.Artillerie-Division*. This had already been ordered the previous day, but without it the *Artillerie-Division* could be lost. Later that morning, the *PzAOK 4* chief of staff, Fangohr, spoke to von Mellenthin, his counterpart at the *XXXXVIII.PzK*, to inform him that the *Panzerarmee* no longer believed that the strike by the *1.Panzer-Division* would make any progress towards Glukhovtsy.[52] This prompted a response from Balck to Raus later that afternoon. The *Korps* commander acknowledged that although the attack had not been able to reach its objectives, it had succeeded in capturing the villages of Puzyr'ki and Panasovka in the face of stiff resistance and had managed to destroy 13 Soviet tanks in the process. A price however had been paid, and the screening front put up by the division further north had been unable to prevent Russian forces from taking Singaevka and Sadki as they pushed on towards Berdichev. The *1.SS Panzer-Division 'LSSAH'* too had had mixed fortune. Whilst its right wing had been successful in holding its positions and defending against all attacks, about 20 or so Soviet tanks had broken through the lines north of Antopol'. On the left wing about 40 tanks had crossed the Guiva at Peski and struck out into the rear of the division. A few had even pushed on as far as the area around the railway station north-west of Kodnya and had appeared close to the divisional headquarters. Raus suggested using the *'LSSAH'* panzers to counterattack against these incursions, but Balck stated merely that they were in no position for such an operation. Instead, he fell back once more upon his argument for a new major operational decision, stressing that in his opinion the current situation was simply untenable. He proposed pulling the *XXXXVIII.PzK* back

---

50   *LIX.AK.*, Morgenmeldung, 05.45 hours dated 29 Dec 43.
51   *PzAOK 4*, Ia Kriegstagebuch entry, dated 29 Dec 43.
52   *PzAOK 4*, Ia Kriegstagebuch entry, dated 29 Dec 43.

to a new line running from Kazatin through the crossroads west of the town, and from there through Zhezhelev, Semenovka, Polovetskoe, Kodnya to Pryazhev. The withdrawal of the *'LSSAH'* could be covered by its *Aufklärungs-Abteilung*, whilst the *Kavallerie-Regiment Süd* would screen Berdichev itself. Such a move would allow the *'LSSAH'* to halve its frontage from 35 kilometres to just 18. However, it would also mean that the *XIII.AK* would have to concentrate its front too, pulling back to a narrower defence of Zhitomir, and using the *Kampfgruppe* Källner to close the gap between the two *Korps*. Alternatively, the *7.Panzer-Division* could be attached to the *XXXXVIII.PzK* and used to attack southwards to close the gap, meeting up with a *Panzerkampfgruppe* from the *'LSSAH'* which would attack northwards. This would have the advantage of destroying those enemy troops which had broken through.

Following this conversation, Raus spoke with Fangohr at 15.20 hours to discuss Balck's proposals. They both agreed that the most important thing was for the *Armee* to maintain its cohesion whatever the circumstances, and as a result there was no reason why the *XXXXVIII.PzK* could not pull back as Balck proposed. However, whilst Raus preferred to bring the *XIII.AK* back to the 'middle' line, from Levkov through Gadzinka, Trokovichi, Vil'sk, to Vasilevka, Fangohr tended to the view that the *Korps* should be allowed to fall back to positions on the edge of Zhitomir so as to free troops for the counterattack. Without reaching a decision, Raus spoke to Hauffe at *XIII.AK* headquarters to discuss the matter with him. He advised the *Korps* commander that either the *7.* or the *19.Panzer-Division* would have to be made available for the proposed counterattack to close the gap between his and Balck's *Korps* and destroy the Soviet troops which had infiltrated south of Pryazhev. Moreover, Hauffe was to deploy some armour on his left wing to prevent the Soviets from striking into his western flank. Given these preconditions, Hauffe still believed that the *XIII.AK* could still make a stand on the 'middle' line, where, in the northern sector, elements of the *7.Panzer-Division* had already brought the Russian advance to a standstill between Chernyakhov and Kletishche.

Raus then spoke with Busse at Army Group South to brief him on the situation and inform him of these latest proposals. The Army Group chief of staff pointed out that the *XIII.AK* had been falling back relatively quickly, and it might be more advantageous for it to remain in its positions, particularly as it would have to hold out for another three or four days before reinforcements arrived. As far as the breakthrough in the *VII.AK* area around Skvira was concerned, there seemed to be no other solution than to allow the Soviet forces to continue their drive southwards. Nevertheless, there were still two essential issues which needed to be addressed. First, the left flank of the *VII.AK* was not to be allowed to be hemmed in, and second, measures needed to be taken to ensure that the logistic situation was secured despite the Soviet advance. All this though was just his initial response, and Busse told Raus that he could expect a final decision in due course. This gave Raus the opportunity to implement his plan to concentrate the centre into a single block around Berdichev and Kazatin, and pull back the *168.Infanterie-Division* and the *25.Panzer-Division* further west. In the meantime, he issued orders to the *XIII.AK*, instructing it to relieve the *7.Panzer-Division* with immediate effect and to ensure that it was on its way through Zhitomir to Berdichev by no later than midday.[53] The division was to be transferred to the *XXXXVIII.PzK*.

Far from the relative safety of these discussions though, the battle continued to rage across the Ukrainian countryside. During the course of the morning, and despite its earlier appraisal, the *34.Infanterie-Division*, under the *XXIV.PzK*, had succeeded in clearing the breach in its front line south of Balyko-Shchuchinka.[54] The success only brought renewed assaults from the Soviets though, and this time the attacks resulted in two separate penetrations of the front line in the same area. The division was again obliged to take new measures to deal with the situation. Further west, similar assaults went in against both Makeevka and Germanovka, but the *75.Infanterie-Division* managed to restore the situation following local counterattacks.

On the right wing of the *VII.AK*, the *198.Infanterie-Division* continued to pull back, reporting that the enemy was only following up slowly.[55] Unsuccessful weak Soviet attacks were made against the villages of Mikhailovka and Ruda on the left wing of the *88.Infanterie-Division*, but further west the village of Zolotukha north-east of Skvira was lost. On the same sector, defended by the *Grenadier-Regiment 417* from the *168.Infanterie-Division*, the Soviets launched strong attacks either side of the Pavoloch'-Skvira road, forcing the defenders to pull back through Skvira where they established new defensive positions on the southern edge of the town. Further west, on the road to Ruzhin, Soviet forces had occupied Krivosheintsy, whilst the northern edge of Berezyanka, six kilometres to the south, lay under enemy artillery fire.

Information from the *XXXXII.AK* was still sketchy, and there was, for example, no news from the right wing of the *25.Panzer-Division*.[56] However, on the division's left wing, the Soviets launched a regimental-sized assault at 11.00 hours, aiming for the railway station two kilometres north-west of Belilovka on the river Rostavitsa. The attack though had been beaten off. Six kilometres further north-west though, Russian tanks had broken into the town of Sestrenovka, leaving the defending elements of the *168. Infanterie-Division* holding onto the eastern edge only. A few kilometres further south, and immediately east of Kazatin, other enemy troops occupied Volokhskie[57] during the morning, and a column estimated to be a rifle division was seen heading south-west in the same area. Its leading elements had crossed the Kazatin-Pogrebishche railway near Makharintsy station at about 10.00 hours. On the left wing of the *Korps* meanwhile, elements of the *18.Artillerie-Division* and its supporting units were now in place on a line running from the southern edge of Kazatin, through the western edge of the town, along the road westwards towards Plyakhovaya, and then northwards to a point on the southern edge of the wood south of Glukhovtsy.

Ten kilometres away to the north, elements of the *1.Panzer-Division* had meanwhile attacked south-eastwards from their assembly areas south-east of Berdichev.[58] They struck forwards and, as we have already seen, they captured the villages of Puzyr'ki and Panasovka in the Guiva valley, where they were then subjected to two separate

---

53 *PzAOK 4*, Ia Nr. 6996/43 geh. dated 29 Dec 43.
54 *PzAOK 4*, O1 Orientierung dated 29 Dec 43.
55 *PzAOK 4*, O1 Orientierung, dated 29 Dec 43.
56 *PzAOK 4*, O1 Orientierung, dated 29 Dec 43.
57 Shown on more recent Soviet maps as Makharintsy.
58 *PzAOK 4*, O1 Orientierung, dated 29 Dec 43.

THE *4.PANZERARMEE* FALLS BACK 143

counterattacks by Soviet tanks from the south and east. Both were seen off. On the division's left, Soviet forces continued to attack towards Berdichev itself. A few tanks reached Singaevka and then a battalion-sized assault was launched against a suburb of Berdichev just eight kilometres east of the centre of the town. The *'LSSAH'* meanwhile was subjected to repeated attacks throughout the morning, some of these in anything up to regimental strength with tank support. Although most of the attacks were beaten off, the Russians did succeed in breaking into Novaya Kotel'nya[59] in two different places, forcing the division to pull back to the western edge of the town. Further south, a counterattack was launched to restore the situation in Antopol', whilst to the north, a few kilometres down the valley, Ivankov was lost. Seven kilometres to the north-west, on the division's left wing, other Soviet forces managed to force a bridgehead over the Guiva at Mlinishche before continuing their advance south-westwards. It was a similar story at Peski, further downstream, where the leading Russian elements proceeded to consolidate in Skomorokhi.

Things were just as hectic on the *XIII.AK* sector to the north.[60] Soviet preparations for an assault had been spotted in the eastern part of Levkov, although it had been impossible to determine the scale of the movements in the built-up area. Following a series of heavy, but sporadic, artillery barrages, the *Kampfgruppe* Källner, the *68.* and *340.Infanterie-Divisions* had all been attacked during the morning. The assaults were estimated to have been made generally by regiments and battalions, but the strongest attacks came either side of the main Kiev-Zhitomir road near Kmitov. The attacks lasted all morning, but in general the lines held. Just south-east of Chernyakhov, the village of Devochki was again hotly contested, and following the earlier successful counterattack by the *340.Infanterie-Division*, the Soviets stormed it once more, forcing the division to pull back. The *208.Infanterie-Division* was in even more trouble. It had been attacked by between 40 and 50 Russian tanks north of Chernyakhov, and been forced to pull back southwards, abandoning the town altogether. The Soviet forces captured the town and pressed on southwards, with the *7.Panzer-Division* caught up in the subsequent fighting around Malaya Gorbasha later in the morning. Other Russian troops had meanwhile wheeled to the south-west, and by the end of the morning they were reported to be on the Kletishche-Ivankov road. To make matters worse, small groups of Soviet forces were attempting to infiltrate through the thin lines of the *213.Sicherungs-Division* on the *Korps* left wing, presumably in an effort to outflank Zhitomir from the north-west. Indeed, seven Russian tanks had been reported in the village of Pochta Rudnya,[61] about 30 kilometres north-west of Zhitomir, on the main road to Novograd-Volynskii. The *XIII.AK* was already being outflanked.

The *LIX.AK* had continued with its planned withdrawal, and during the morning it had moved into its new positions west of Korosten' on a line running northwards from Ushomir station through Mogilno[62] and Vygov to Kupishche.[63] In the meantime, the *Korps* had established that Russian troops had already crossed the Zhitomir-Korosten' road further south at a point south-east of Lesovshchina and were heading westwards. In

---

59 Novaya Kotel'nya was that part of Starosel'ye which lay on the western bank of the river.
60 *PzAOK 4*, O1 Orientierung, dated 29 Dec 43.
61 Marked on more recent Soviet maps as Martynovka.
62 Referred to as Polesskoe on more recent Soviet maps.
63 *PzAOK 4*, O1 Orientierung, dated 29 Dec 43.

order to secure his deep right flank, von der Chevallerie therefore formed the *Kampfgruppe Gehrke*[64] and sent it to Ryshavka, nearly 30 kilometres south-west of Korosten'. The Soviets meanwhile had not been slow in following up the *Korps'* withdrawal, and during the morning they mounted a company-strength probing attack against Ushomir on the right wing of the *291.Infanterie-Division*. At this stage though, it was seen off without difficulty.

The day had again been dull and overcast, with temperatures struggling to reach freezing point in the patchy fog and mist, but at least the rain and snow had been holding off. The river Dnepr remained frozen over, even to the extent of bearing the weight of columns of infantry and loaded sledges estimated to weigh something in the region of two tonnes. On the right wing, Nehring reported his general impression of Soviet activity opposite the *XXIV.PzK*.[65] The pinning attacks had continued, ostensibly with the intention of widening the existing breaches in the German defences. There had been a total of eight separate assaults recorded against the positions of the *34.Infanterie-Division* around Balyko-Shchuchinka, and these ranged from company to battalion strength. Five of these had been brought to a fairly quick standstill, and one had been driven off in a counterattack, but two had led to new breaches in the front line totalling 1,500 metres in width. The division had mounted counterattacks against these sectors, but by evening these had met with only partial success. On its north-west front, the *34.Infanterie-Division* reported two enemy troop assemblies east of Verem'e, each estimated to be a company forming up for the attack, whilst repeated battalion-strength assaults had been made against the *82.Infanterie-Division* near Makarovskii and in the area south of Germanovka. Although all these had been seen off or cleared in local counterattacks, there were still problems on the division's right wing where the previous day's breach near Chernyakhov had still not been completely cleared. Nehring also reported that the patchy weather had permitted intermittent enemy air activity, and a few Soviet bombers had carried out ground attacks in the *Korps* area, but without achieving any tangible results. The *XXIV.PzK* also reported the final figures for the previous day's enemy attacks along the Dudari-Ul'yaniki sector either side of the boundary between the *Korps-Abteilung B* and the *34.Infanterie-Division*. They had now counted a total of 290 Soviet enemy dead in their trenches, and estimated that a further 170 lay in front of the main defensive positions. In addition, 35 others had been wounded, 16 taken prisoner, and a single soldier was reported to have deserted. As a result of the current day's fighting, the *82.Infanterie-Division* now added another 316 Russian dead, 75 prisoners (including three officers), and two deserters. It had been a costly two days fighting.

To Nehring's left, the *VII.AK* reported continuing Soviet pressure as it struggled to maintain its positions.[66] Opposite its right wing, there had been a number of attacks in varying strengths of up to regimental size, but these had caused few real problems and all had been successfully defended. In the centre, the pressure eased off a little as the Russians seemed to take time following up the previous day's withdrawal, but they nevertheless managed to force new breaches on the left wing of the *88.Infanterie-Division*

---

64 The *Kampfgruppe* was headed by the headquarters *Divisionsgruppe 217*, and consisted of the *Regimentsgruppe 311*, the *Divisions-Füsilier-Bataillon 217*, a *Batterie* from the *Sturmgeschütz-Abteilung 276*, and a platoon from the *Pionier-Bataillon 219*.
65 *XXIV.PzK.*, Tagesmeldung, 18.30 hours dated 29 Dec 43.
66 *VII.AK.*, Tagesmeldung, 20.45 hours dated 29 Dec 43.

in the area east and north-east of Ruda. A counterattack was mounted, and by evening the division was anticipating a successful conclusion to its action. Over 12 kilometres away to the south-west, a different Soviet group, estimated to be two rifle regiments and a tank brigade, had meanwhile broken into and captured the northern part of Skvira at about 11.30 hours that morning. The *Grenadier-Regiment 417*, holding that sector, had been thrown back out of the town and had been obliged to fall back to the south-east, despite reporting having destroyed eight of the attacking tanks. The *Korps* also confirmed the earlier report that the Soviet forces in the area had orders to strike south-eastwards and block the roads leading south from Kiev and Belaya Tserkov'. Further west, in the gap between it and the *XXXXII.AK*, the *VII.AK* had put out reconnaissance feelers to try and gauge the Russian presence in the area, and this had discovered what was estimated to be a Soviet rifle regiment with artillery support in Krivosheintsy, west of Skvira. At 17.55 hours, Hell informed the *Panzerarmee* that Soviet forces had made a deep and broad penetration on the *VII.AK* left wing in the vicinity of Skvira.[67] According to an intercepted radio message, the Russians intended to block the main north-south running roads which were so critical for the Germans supply and movement, and Hell now reported that the *VII.AK* was simply no longer in position to be able to prevent this. Raus could only endorse the *Korps* commander's assessment, and he agreed that the gap could only be closed with fresh reinforcements. Raus was not convinced though that there was a serious threat to this sector, particularly since the Soviet forces known to be in the area amounted to little more than part of a tank brigade and a weak rifle division. The main task now facing the *VII.AK* was to keep its divisions together in a strong cohesive block, and use all of its skill to pull back its open left flank to prevent it being rolled up, while at the same time maintaining its current positions along the majority of its sector. Overall, Hell's *Korps* had been involved in heavy fighting over the previous three days, and in that time the *88.Infanterie-Division* in particular reported having captured 70 prisoners and killed about 1,000 Russian soldiers, of which 400 had actually been counted. A large number of weapons had also been captured or destroyed. The *Pionier-Bataillon 188*, under *Major* Kranz, was given a special commendation for its efforts. The *75.Infanterie-Division* too had been involved in some stiff fighting, and over the same period, it reported having repulsed a total of 29 separate Soviet attacks, in anything up to regimental strength, bringing in 56 prisoners and accounting for 650 Russian dead. A number of machineguns and anti-tank rifles, and a single anti-tank gun, were also taken.

On the other side of the 30 kilometre gap which had now opened up, the *XXXXII. AK* was still fighting hard to maintain its positions, and it now seemed that an armoured train had fallen into enemy hands, having been unable to escape the disaster which had befallen Kazatin the previous day. Soviet forces, including tanks, were still pushing against the *Korps* right wing and centre, forcing it to fall back southwards despite desperate resistance.[68] It was also noticeable that Russian forces in the Kazatin area were being reinforced, and Mattenklott's intelligence indicated that the Soviets were forming two distinct groupings opposite his front: one on his right wing in the Ruzhin area, with the task of driving straight southwards, and the other on his left wing, around and to the east of Kazatin, with the aim of advancing both south and south-westwards.

---

67 *PzAOK 4*, Ia Kriegstagebuch entry, dated 29 Dec 43.
68 *XXXXII.AK.*, Tagesmeldung, 23.00 hours dated 29 Dec 43.

The *25.Panzer-Division* had been attacked along its right flank for most of the day, and both Ruzhin and Balamutovka[69] had been lost to a two-pronged Soviet attack from the north and east. By the end of the day, the division had been forced back about 12 or so kilometres and had taken up a hasty defensive position on a general line running between Zarudintsy and Belilovka. Beyond the reach of the division's right wing, on the extreme eastern wing of the *Korps*, Soviet reconnaissance troops, including both tanks and infantry, had meanwhile pushed on as far south as Bukhny, just 13 kilometres north of Pogrebishche. Further west, the *168.Infanterie-Division* had been involved in heavy fighting throughout its sector, before it too had been obliged to pull back southwards into new positions. The Russian forces were hard on its heels though, and the division first managed to throw up a coherent defensive line as far south as a line running between Belilovka and Volokhskie. It reported having destroyed six Soviet tanks, but the Russians still pressed on. Several regimental-sized assaults, with tank support, were launched against the sector between Makharintsy and Rastavitsy stations, north-west of Belilovka, but the first of these were seen off, with a further three enemy tanks reported as destroyed. However, Soviet persistence paid off, and at about 14.30 hours they achieved a breakthrough with tanks on the division's left wing, advancing southwards to capture the villages of Korolevka and Sokolets.

The *18.Artillerie-Division* meanwhile had been less troubled than in previous days, and had been limited to undertaking reconnaissance and firing upon observed enemy movements. During the morning, a column of about 5,000 men had been spotted moving along the railway line west of Sestrenovka, heading into Kazatin, and this had been engaged with unknown results. On the other hand, a Russian advance along the railway west of the town had been seen to be disrupted following a quickly laid defensive barrage. The division had also sent out a reconnaissance patrol to establish the position on the *Korps* left wing, and this reported Glukhovtsy to be unoccupied for the moment. Unknown to the patrol though, this situation would not last; Soviet troops were heading in that direction.

Late in the day, Mattenklott called *4.Panzerarmee* headquarters and spoke to Raus.[70] He informed the *Armee* commander that the *XXXII.AK* had been thrown back southwards, with elements of the *25.Panzer-Division* and the *168.Infanterie-Division* having to take up new positions on the south bank of the Sitna stream between Belilovka and Volokhskie. But even these positions had not lasted long as the Soviets pressed forwards, reaching Korolevka and Sokolets. Mattenklott could however report some relief. Although Kazatin had fallen the previous day, the Soviet forces on that sector had apparently spent the day consolidating, probably as a result of casualties caused by the massed artillery fire from the defending *18.Artillerie-Division*. Whatever the reason though, there had been no major thrust southwards on that sector during the day. Things were similarly quiet a few kilometres away to the north-west, where a few Soviet tanks had pushed on to reach the main Berdichev-Vinnitsa road during the evening, but there had been no major thrust. Mattenklott attributed this to the arrival and counterattack of the *1.Panzer-Division*. After discussing the concentration and the amalgamation of the *25.Panzer-Division* with the *168.Infanterie-Division*, Raus now authorised Mattenklott to carry out the measure. The former had been badly mauled during the offensive and

---

69 Referred to as Zarech'e on more recent Soviet maps.
70 *PzAOK 4*, Ia Kriegstagebuch entry, dated 29 Dec 43.

was, for all intents and purposes, no longer able to function effectively as a unit, whilst the latter now found itself cut into two by the Soviet advance. The two men agreed that the headquarters of the *25.Panzer-Division* should be relieved from the front line and its units attached to the *Infanterie-Division*. This would attempt to make good the continued absence of the *Grenadier-Regiment 417* and the division's supply troops, both of which were still fighting on the left wing of the *VII.AK*. The remaining troops of the *25.Panzer-Division* therefore passed under the command of the *168.Infanterie-Division*, now headquartered in Yusefovka,[71] and the now superfluous division staff and *Nachrichten-Abteilung*[72] were instructed to assemble the following day in Leonardovka.[73]

Balck's *XXXXVIII.PzK* further north passed an equally poor day.[74] It had started with an attempt to regain at least some initiative when troops of the *1.Panzer-Division* jumped off to the attack at 07.00 hours. As has already been described, the division moved out from its assembly area around Semenovka, about eight or so kilometres south-east of Berdichev, striking eastwards and capturing both Puzyr'ki and Panasovka, before seeing off a battalion-sized counterattack and destroying about 15 Russian tanks. But Soviet resistance stiffened from that time onwards, and the attack made no further progress. Instead, Russian forces mounted their own co-ordinated attack against both wings of the *Panzerkorps*, apparently with the intention of capturing Berdichev. This involved a tank corps on each wing; one east and south-east of Berdichev, and the other further north near Kodnya station. These forces attacked during the afternoon, and the southern pincer struck either side of the narrow salient newly won by the *1.Panzer-Division*. One group headed south-west and captured Glukhovtsy before moving on to block the main Vinnitsa-Berdichev road east of Brodetskoe, while the other wheeled to the north-west, and headed up the railway line towards Berdichev. North of the salient, a smaller, battalion-sized, force struck west from the Singaevka and Chekhi[75] area, aiming directly towards Berdichev. This group however, was beaten back by the division, which reported destroying 23 of the supporting Soviet tanks.

The *1.SS Panzer-Division 'LSSAH'* was faring no better to the north. It had been involved in heavy fighting throughout the day, although it had managed to keep its hold on Chervonoe despite repeated tank supported attacks up to regimental strength. During the afternoon, the centre of the division's sector was subjected to several attacks as the Soviets attempted to widen their bridgehead over the Guiva. The first of these were made from the Novaya Kotel'nya area against the division's positions around Velikaya Moshkovtsy, to be followed by others from the Ivankov and Leshchin areas with the objective of gaining the high ground south of the river. These were all seen off, although a breach near Novaya Kotel'nya had to be sealed off rather than cleared up. A similar breach near Antopol' was also cleared up, and the existing front line restored. The Russian forces however, maintained their relentless pressure, and a renewed attack south of Antopol', this time supported by 16 tanks, resulted in a breach. Fortunately the

---

71   Referred to as Iosipovka on more recent Soviet maps.
72   The signals battalion.
73   Referred to as Golubevka on more recent Soviet maps.
74   *XXXXVIII.PzK.*, Tagesmeldung, 20.00 hours dated 29 Dec 43. According to this report, the *1.Panzer-Division* deployed the following operational armour at this time: 14 x *Panzer IV*; 17 x *Panzer V 'Panther'*; and 12 *Panzer VI 'Tiger'* of the attached *s. Panzer-Abteilung 509*. It also deployed 12 self-propelled anti-tank guns, and 16 towed heavy anti-tank guns.
75   Referred to Dubovka on more recent Soviet maps.

penetration was not exploited quickly, and the division intercepted the breakthrough forces just 1,500 metres west of the town. Under the weight of the continued pressure though, these defensive successes could not last, and a breach was finally achieved in the Mlinishche area nearer Zhitomir, where Soviet infantry supported by about 10 tanks broke through. Facing no further opposition, this group raced on to reach the small village of Krasny Stepok by around 15.30 hours.[76] From there they wheeled southwestwards and struck out towards Kodnya. A similar breakthrough was achieved further down the Guiva valley, near Peski, where at about midday, Soviet forces crossed the river and headed southwards along the railway line from Zhitomir to Berdichev. By 17.00 hours, a force of about 35 Russian tanks had reached Kodnya station. The *'LSSAH'* began to fall back as quickly as it could, to avoid being cut off altogether, whilst the *Panzerzug 69* was deployed on the line between Zhitomir and Berdichev in an effort to stem the Soviet tide. The division reported having destroyed a total of 36 Soviet tanks during the day, bringing the *Korps* total to 59.[77]

To the north, Hauffe's *XIII.AK* was also heavily attacked, although in general it managed to hold its new positions. The attacks had been supported by armour in places, and although the *Korps* had been assaulted along the whole of its front, the main Russian efforts seemed to have been made against the two wings: either side of the main Kiev-Zhitomir road on the right, and on the Devochki-Chernyakhov sector on the left.[78] The intention seemed to be to pin the *Korps* by fixing its flanks, and presumably to force it to collapse as a result. Despite its exhaustion, the *Korps* managed to put up a stiff resistance and succeeded in beating off most of the attacks. Nevertheless, there were local breaches, but these were cleared up, and despite the close attentions of the Soviet forces, the troops succeeded in remaining in good order. Opposite the right wing, the Soviet artillery barrage began at 09.30 hours, lasting for half an hour, but despite this preparation, the *Kampfgruppe* Källner was able to lay a concentrated defensive fire when the Russian infantry attacked. The assault petered out, leaving the *Kampfgruppe* still holding its positions. The attacks began again later, but these were now weaker affairs, and were more easily seen off. In the Studenitsa area, the *SS Panzerkampfgruppe 'Das Reich'* was hit by heavy regimental-sized attacks with tank support, but with the assistance of the *XIII.AK* artillery, these too were successfully defended. Similar scale assaults were launched against the front held by the *68.Infanterie-Division*, particularly on the Zabrod'e – Vysoko-Cheshskoe[79] sector, but these proved to be no more successful than the others. Later on, the division spotted Soviet troop assemblies in preparation for another assault, but this was engaged with artillery fire and disrupted before it began.

The *340.Infanterie-Division* had meanwhile continued the battle for Devochki, first repulsing a battalion-sized attack in the morning, and later counterattacking to

---

76   Referred to as Chervony Stepok on more recent Soviet maps.
77   For its efforts, the *'LSSAH'* received a special mention in Balck's report of the following day, in which the *Korps* commander recognised the division's achievements under its commanding officer, *Oberführer* Wisch. At that time, it was reported to have distinguished itself in maintaining a defensive front of 35 kilometres in the face of bitter attacks by superior Soviet forces. Despite being encircled and outflanked, and with strong tank forces behind its lines, it succeeded in disengaging during the night and taking up positions in the new positions as instructed. It reported having destroyed 48 Russian tanks in the process.
78   *XIII.AK.*, Tagesmeldung, 20.00 hours dated 29 Dec 43.
79   Referred to as Vysokoe on more recent Soviet maps.

recapture half of the village. The Russians attacked again during the afternoon, and forced the division to fall back on the high ground south of the village where they established new positions on Hill 238.8. The most critical sector however was held by the troops of the *208.Infanterie-Division*, astride the Korosten'-Zhitomir road. Under cover of darkness, Soviet infantry and tanks had forced their way into Chernyakhov, causing confusion and obliging the division to pull back to the southern edge of the town to regroup. There they established new positions, clinging on to the outskirts as long as they could, before being finally dislodged by a renewed Russian tank thrust from the north-west which threatened to strike into the division's rear. They fell back to the south, to a line running from Velikaya Gorbasha to Malaya Gorbasha. The *7.Panzer-Division* meanwhile spent the day helping the *208.Infanterie-Division* to fend off the Soviet drive towards Zhitomir, concentrating against the armoured spearheads, and by evening it was established on a line running from Malaya Gorbasha to Zorokov. According to the reports available at the time, the division had destroyed five Russian tanks. On the *XIII. AK* left wing, the *213.Sicherungs-Division* too was unable to prevent Soviet armour from advancing further southwards, and fell back to a line running from Kletishche through the western edge of the wood south of the town to the northern edge of the wood about six kilometres north-west of Vil'sk. Further to the south-west, on the division's far left flank, the *Ost-Reiter-Abteilungen 403* and *454* pulled back to the south-west towards Pulinka.[80]

On the northern wing, von der Chevallerie's *LIX.AK* was now hopelessly isolated from the rest of the *4.Panzerarmee*, but continued in its efforts to fall back in one piece. The *Korps* had managed to move into its new defensive positions on the line Ushomir-Krasnopol'[81]-Kupishche during the morning, and it had barely settled in when Soviet forces attacked its right wing at about 14.00 hours.[82] The combined Soviet tanks and infantry forced a number of breaches in the positions held by the *291.Infanterie-Division*, and fighting raged on into the night. Elsewhere along the *Korps* front though, all Soviet attacks were successfully seen off. The *Kampfgruppe* Gehrke meanwhile, sent southwards to keep an eye on the vast gap between the *LIX.AK* and the *XIII.AK*, had reached Ryshavka only to discover it free from enemy troops. It had seen no Soviet forces during its travels.

The day had not been a good one for the right wing of the *4.Panzerarmee*. Soviet forces had managed to pin down the *XXIV.PzK*, and smash a large hole between the *VII.AK* and the *XXXXII.AK*, ostensibly with the objective of rolling up the *VII.AK* front to the east. On this sector, the continuing attack by the Soviet 40th Army had pushed back the left wing of the *VII.AK* to the south and south-east, apparently with the support of a tank brigade.[83] Raus simply had no more forces with which to counter this breakthrough. On the central and left-hand sectors too, the Russians had pressed the offensive in undiminished strength, with two new rifle divisions even having been identified. Between Belilovka and Kazatin they were advancing southwards with strong

---

80 Referred to as Ul'yanovka on more recent Soviet maps.
81 Situated just south-east of Vygov.
82 *PzAOK 4, Tagesmeldung an Heeresgruppe Süd*, dated 29 Dec 43.
83 *PzAOK 4, Ic Abendmeldung an H.Gr. Süd*, 19.00 hours dated 28 Dec 43. The *PzAOK 4* was uncertain as to identification of this tank brigade, and still believed it might be part of the 3rd Guards Tank Corps.

armoured forces, and it was expected that the 8th Guards Mechanised Corps would soon attempt to break through the defences either side of Kazatin. It seemed that the initial Russian attempt to break through between Kazatin and Berdichev had been halted by the counterattack by the *1.Panzer-Division*, but in the end this had really come to nothing in the face of stiff resistance and flanking attacks. Soviet tanks had already passed Glukhovtsy to reach the main road between Berdichev and Vinnitsa. To the north, strong infantry forces, supported by four tank brigades, were pushing hard against the '*LSSAH*' south-east of Zhitomir, and elements of two new rifle divisions had also been identified on this sector. Although they had made little progress during the day, it seemed clear that the strong attacks would continue, perhaps with an attempt to outflank the division to the north. Taken together, these two strikes, south-east of Kazatin and south-east of Zhitomir, now posed a very real danger, especially as it was possible that that their objective was the encirclement of the *XXXXVIII.PzK*. It was clear to Raus that if he was to prevent a Soviet breakthrough of his centre, he would not only have to conduct mobile defensive operations with his armour, but he would also have to concentrate his central three *Korps* commands, the *XXXXII.AK*, the *XXXXVIII. PzK*, and the *XIII.AK.*, into one solid block. The story was the same on the left wing, where other Soviet armour seemed to be trying to outflank the *XIII.AK* on both sides, with the 5th Guards Tank Corps and the 9th Guards Mechanised Corps attacking from the north and east respectively. At the same time, smaller groups of Russian tanks were advancing southwards on a broad front west of Chernyakhov, pushing forward to cut the road from Zhitomir to Novograd-Volynskii and threatening to outflank the *Korps* altogether. Overall, the *Panzerarmee* reported having destroyed a total of 72 Russian tanks during this single day, and this is perhaps a measure of the pressure being exerted by the Soviet forces.

With this assessment of the day's events on the table, Raus discussed his intentions for the following day with Fangohr, and decided that, as an initial measure, the *XXXXVIII.PzK* would have to make contact with, and then support, the left wing of the *XXXXII.AK*.[84] Responsibility for the main point of effort for this action would lie with the armoured forces on the *Korps* right flank, the object being to secure the main crossroads just south-east of Brodetskoe. Moreover, the *Panzerkorps* would fall back into the line previously discussed, and close the gap still existing between it and Hauffe's *XIII. AK* to the north, using armoured elements of the *7.Panzer-Division* from the north and the '*LSSAH*' from the south. The *XIII.AK* meanwhile was to fall back into the 'middle' line, pulling the *7.Panzer-Division* out of the front, and transferring the *Kampfgruppe* Källner to its left wing to secure the western flank. The *XXXXII.AK* was to consolidate its positions on the line running from Komsomol'skoe through Kazatin to Belilovka.

During the course of the evening though, new orders arrived from Army Group South.[85] In these, von Manstein instructed Raus that the *XIII.AK* was to hold its existing positions north and north-east of Zhitomir; there was no question of a withdrawal being authorised at this time. The *7.Panzer-Division* meanwhile was to be regrouped immediately and sent to reinforce the units currently in the Kazatin-Berdichev area.

---

84 *PzAOK 4*, Ia Kriegstagebuch entry, dated 29 Dec 43.
85 *PzAOK 4*, Ia Kriegstagebuch entry, dated 29 Dec 43. A copy of the actual order is not held on the appropriate file.

THE *4.PANZERARMEE* FALLS BACK

Later that night, at 21.35 hours, Raus spoke with von Manstein to discuss the situation.[86] He drew the Army Group commander's attention to the three main thrusts now being directed against the *Panzerarmee*; namely that through Skvira to the south, that through Kazatin towards Kalinovka, and that from Chernyakhov to the south. These had just about been brought to a stop for the time being, but at the cost of having to give up considerable ground. In response, von Manstein pointed out that the enemy was now attacking with mainly armour and only fairly weak infantry forces. The artillery, which had so often proved decisive in the past, had so far been unable to bring itself to bear against the new positions as it was still in the process of moving up. It was imperative therefore that the *Panzerarmee*, particularly the *XIII.AK*, use the opportunity to maintain its position, and Raus was instructed to speak to his *Korps* commanders on this subject to make them all aware of the Army Group's views.

However, none of this fundamentally altered the position Raus had adopted, and the orders he issued that night, the *Panzerarmeebefehl Nr.51*, accorded more with his own appreciation than that of the Army Group.[87] In this, Raus described the three main strikes being conducted against the *Panzerarmee*, in response to which its main tasks were to prevent a Soviet breakthrough across the Zhitomir-Berdichev-Vinnitsa road and delay the Soviet advances, both that towards Zhitomir and that heading from Skvira to the south-east. In order to stand any chance of achieving these objectives, it was critical for the various *Korps* groupings to remain solid. The *XXIV.PzK* was to retain its existing mission of holding its current positions. The *VII.AK* was to employ mobile defensive tactics on its left wing to delay the enemy advance from Skvira to the south-east, although it was to fall back behind the river Ros' in the longer term. However, every step of ground was to be contested, and the withdrawal was only to be carried out if Soviet pressure forced such a manoeuvre. The *Grenadier-Regiment 417* would remain attached to the *Korps* for the time being, although it was no longer to try and maintain contact with the right wing of the *XXXII.AK*. The *XXXII.AK* itself was to prevent a Russian breakthrough either side of Kazatin towards the Berdichev-Vinnitsa road. At the same time, it was to begin shifting its strength to the north-west to create its main effort on the left wing, although the other wing was to remain fastened on Belilovka for the time being. The open right flank was to be secured as best as possible by reconnaissance. The *Korps* would be allocated three *Panzer-Zerstörer-Kompanien* being sent by Army Group South; two of these were to be assigned to the *168.Infanterie-Division* and the third to the *18.Artillerie-Division*. The *XXXVIII.PzK* was to engage in mobile defensive operations, concentrating on the right wing, in order to prevent the enemy from crossing the Berdichev-Komsomol'skoe road. Those Russian elements which had already crossed were to be counterattacked and destroyed. The *7.Panzer-Division* was being attached to the *Korps* for this purpose. The *Kampfkommandant Berdichev*, being the headquarters of the *20.Panzergrenadier-Division*, was also now attached to the *Korps*. The *XIII.AK* was meanwhile to draw in its circle around Zhitomir, pulling back step-by-step in a fighting withdrawal to a line from Gadzinka, past a point east of Veresy, through Trokovichi and Vil'sk to Novi Zavod. In order to prevent a Soviet armoured breakthrough in the area, a mobile unit was to be created by the *Korps* and re-grouped behind the left wing. In the meantime the *7.Panzer-Division* was to be relieved immediately and moved southwards

---

86 *PzAOK 4*, Ia Kriegstagebuch entry, dated 29 Dec 43.
87 *PzAOK 4*, Ia Nr. 7019/43 geh. dated 29 Dec 43.

through Zhitomir where it would receive tactical direction from the *XXXXVIII.PzK*. By way of some compensation for the loss of the division, the *SS-Sturm-Brigade 'Langemarck'* would be attached to the *Korps* for incorporation into the *SS Panzerkampfgruppe 'Das Reich'*. A new boundary line between the *XXXXII.AK* and the *XXXXVIII.PzK* was set to run from Khmel'nik through Kustovtsy, Komsomol'skoe, Plyakhovaya, and Nepedovka to Chernorudka, with all towns falling to the *XXXXII.AK* except Nepedovka. Between the *XXXXVIII.PzK* and the *XIII.AK*, the boundary still ran as before, but now began at Chudnov. All supply and support services were to be sent back by the three central *Korps* in a south-westerly direction, together with all vehicles not strictly necessary for combat operations, although all units were to remain within their respective areas. All such traffic was forbidden to use the main north-south Vinnitsa-Berdichev-Zhitomir road, and this was now reserved solely for the use of combat troops. The *Panzerarmee* would be responsible for traffic control between Vinnitsa and the crossroads west of Kazatin, whilst the more northerly sections would remain the responsibility of the respective *Korps* headquarters in whose areas it passed. The two *Feldgendarmerie-Kompanien*[88] stationed in Zhitomir would be attached to the *Korps* to assist.

Although there is no discussion of the proposal in the *4.Panzerarmee* papers, the *Panzerarmeebefehl Nr.51* indicates a planned exchange of *Korps* level headquarters under its command. The implication is that the staffs of Mattenklott's *XXXXII.AK* and Nehring's *XXIV.PzK* simply exchange sectors and responsibilities, leaving behind all units attached to their respective commands, and taking just those which were organisationally part of the *Korps* headquarters, such as the artillery commander and signals units. There is no obvious reason for this transfer, other than to bring in Nehring's greater experience to play in what had already become a very dangerous situation. But there is no confirmation of this view in the records. In any event, the exchange of the *XXXXII.AK* and the *XXIV.PzK* was to be carried out as quickly as possible, and completed by 1 January 44.

In short then, Raus intended to prevent the Soviets from rolling up the left wing of the *VII.AK*, allowing the *Korps* to pull back behind the river Ros' if need be.[89] He wanted to create strongpoints at Kazatin and Berdichev by drawing the *XXXXII.AK* and the *XXXXVIII.PzK* together in the central sector, and pulling the *7.Panzer-Division* out of the front and transferring it to the *XXXXVIII.PzK*. He intended to destroy those Soviet forces which had broken through north-west of Kazatin and south of Zhitomir, and transfer a mobile *Kampfgruppe* to the western wing of the *XIII.AK*. Only time would tell whether his measures would prove effective, although to assist him, as we have already seen, further reinforcements were now on the way. He had been allocated the *SS Sturm-Brigade 'Langemarck'*, a Waffen-SS unit comprising a reinforced *Panzergrenadier* battalion, which was scheduled to arrive (less its *Sturmgeschütz-Batterie*) at Chudnov, some 45 kilometres south-west of Zhitomir, by about midday on 31 December.[90] In view of the problems being experienced on the hanging left flank of the *XIII.AK*, Raus attached the unit to Hauffe's *Korps*, where it was to be incorporated into the *SS Panzerkampfgruppe 'Das*

---

88 Military police companies
89 *PzAOK 4*, Ia Nr. 7017/43 g.Kdos. dated 29 Dec 43.
90 *PzAOK 4*, Ia Kriegstagebuch entry, dated 29 Dec 43. The *'Langemarck'* had been formed on 31 May 1943 from the *Freiwilligen-Legion 'Flandern'*, itself formed from Flemish volunteers in July 1941, and on 15 October 1943, its official title had been changed to the *6.SS-Freiwilligen-Sturm-Brigade 'Langemarck'*.

Reich', a unit with which it had associations.[91] The *Sturmgeschütz-Batterie* meanwhile was due to arrive ahead of the main body, being scheduled to reach Kalinovka that same evening. Raus informed Hauffe that it would be sent on to the *XIII.AK* by way of Khmel'nik and Ivanopol', arriving at Chudnov sometime later.

---

91 *PzAOK 4*, Ia Nr. 7014/43 geh. dated 29 Dec 43.

6

The Front is Split Apart

Thursday 30 December 1943

On the *4.Panzerarmee* right wing, the *XXIV.PzK* had little to report in respect of the night just passed.[1] On the right wing of the *82.Infanterie-Division*, there had been two Soviet assaults north-west of Chernyakhov during the night. These had been in no more than battalion-strength, and while they had caused no real alarm, a forward position had to be given up, forcing the defenders to return to the main defensive position. Despite the retreat, the division reported taking two prisoners of war. Another two prisoners had also been taken during the night by the *34.Infanterie-Division* to the right.

The *VII.AK* had meanwhile seen more activity during the night.[2] The right wing of the *75.Infanterie-Division* had been assaulted in about battalion-strength, and although a local counterattack by the division had managed to bring the attack to a halt, it had not succeeded in recapturing the earlier main defensive positions. The division also reported observing further Russian troop assemblies, so more attacks were expected in that sector. There were other Soviet assaults against the front held by the *198.Infanterie-Division*, and many of these achieved local breaches of the German defences. By morning though, all of these had been cleared except one on the division's left wing in the vicinity of the railway line between Belaya Tserkov' and Ustinovka. On the left wing of the *Korps*, the *88.Infanterie-Division* and the *Grenadier-Regiment 417* both passed quieter nights, reporting only reconnaissance patrols.

On the other side of the widening gap, the situation at the *XXXXII.AK* was far from clear.[3] Following the outflanking of its right wing, the *25.Panzer-Division* spent the night trying to fall back to a line between Sosnovka and Blazhievka.[4] The *18.Artillerie-Division* reported no changes in its situation during the night, and there was no report at all from the *168.Infanterie-Division*. In the meantime, various dispersed units from the *20.Panzergrenadier-Division* were reporting that the main road from Belilovka through Sokolets to Kazatin was crowded with heavy Soviet traffic.

The situation at the *XXXXVIII.PzK* was even less clear, following the loss of contact during the night with both the *7.Panzer-Division* and the *1.SS Panzer-Division 'LSSAH'*.[5] The withdrawal of the *1.Panzer-Division* had meanwhile gone according to plan, although not without difficulty. The roads and paths had become icy overnight, slowing the whole movement down, and the Russian forces had taken advantage of the difficulties and pursued the division as it pulled back. The Soviets had also pressed the *XIII.AK* as it tried to pull back to its new positions.[6] Despite this pressure though, the majority of the

---

1 *XXIV.PzK*, Morgenmeldung, untimed dated 30 Dec 43.
2 *VII.AK*, Morgenmeldung, 05.55 hours dated 30 Dec 43.
3 *XXXXII.AK*, Morgenmeldung, 06.40 hours dated 30 Dec 43.
4 Referred to as Blaschniwka in the German records.
5 *XXXXVIII.PzK*, Morgenmeldung, 05.40 hours dated 30 Dec 43.
6 *XIII.AK*, Morgenmeldung, 06.05 hours dated 30 Dec 43.

Korps had managed to complete the planned withdrawal by morning, and only the *340. Infanterie-Division* had failed to report in. On the northern front though, two Soviet tanks had managed to break through the withdrawing units, and by around midnight they had pushed on into Peschanka where they began to fire on anything that came into view. Countermeasures were undertaken, but the threat had still not been removed by morning. Just a couple of kilometres south-east of Zhitomir, the Russians also launched strong attacks against the defensive positions established by the *Korps* near Stanishovka to protect its right wing. At around midnight, these resulted in a breach in the area of the railway bridge just north of Skomorokhi, and despite a swift counterattack supported by *Sturmgeschützen*, the penetration could not be cleared before morning. The fighting continued. In the meantime, the majority of the *7.Panzer-Division* had managed to pass through Zhitomir heading southwards, while the *SS Panzerkampfgruppe 'Das Reich'* had begun its shift to the west.

To the north, the *LIX.AK* reported only that, between the right wing of the *291. Infanterie-Division* and the *Kampfgruppe* Gehrke, a Soviet column of about 20 tanks and 40 trucks had broken through at about 05.00 hours between Ryshavka and Santarka from where they were heading directly for Belka, over ten kilometres further west.[7]

The new day dawned overcast, with freezing fog and temperatures a few degrees below zero. On the right wing, the Soviet diversionary and pinning attacks continued against the *XXIV.PzK*.[8] On the left wing of the *Korps-Abteilung B*, a company-strength assault near Romashki had been beaten off, but a few kilometres to the west, an assault by about 200 Russians managed to break into the defensive positions of the *34.Infanterie-Division* in Vedmedevka. The division reacted and started to counterattack, but the fighting continued into the evening. To the north-west, the division was also attacked later in the day in the area south of Balyko-Shchuchinka. The strength of this assault was not known at the time, and here too the fighting continued on into the night. Nearer to the town, a separate Russian attack broke into the division's positions, but this was cleared in a local counterattack. On the division's left wing, Soviet forces assaulted the forward German positions west of Staiki and west of Verem'e, and forced these to pull back into the main defensive line. Eight kilometres further west, a similar attack against the sector held by the *82.Infanterie-Division* forced the forward positions to be pulled back near Makarovskii.

Things were quieter immediately to the left where the *75.Infanterie-Division* under the *VII.AK* reported no new attacks throughout the whole day, perhaps as a result of the previous days' heavy fighting.[9] The sector held by the *198.Infanterie-Division* though saw several assaults, many of which again succeeded in breaking into the German positions. Some of these were cleared following counterattacks, but at about 12.30 hours, *Oberst* Schwatlo-Gesterding, the chief of staff at the *VII.AK*, reported to the *PzAOK 4* that Soviet forces estimated to be at least a rifle regiment had broken through the division's defences and were heading southwards either side of the railway line towards Belaya Tserkov'.[10] In addition, reconnaissance had shown that there was heavy Soviet traffic heading southwards beyond the *Korps* left wing. As a result of this situation, he advised

---

7   *LIX.AK*, Morgenmeldung, 06.25 hours dated 30 Dec 43.
8   *PzAOK 4*, Ia Tagesmeldung an *Heeresgruppe Süd*, dated 30 Dec 43.
9   *VII.AK*, Tagesmeldung, 19.00 hours dated 30 Dec 43.
10 *PzAOK 4*, Ia Kriegstagebuch entry dated 30 Dec 43.

Fangohr that the *VII.AK* was no longer able to offer any real resistance in its current positions, and that it was therefore proposing to pull back its left wing to the line of the river Ros' from Malaya Skvirka to Belaya Tserkov'. Fangohr suggested that the new forces moving to support the *VII.AK* left wing would be in a position to strike the extended flank of the Russian troops heading south, and Raus therefore authorised Hell to pull back his left wing to the proposed line. Later that day, strong Soviet forces again attacked the left wing of the *198.Infanterie-Division*, and they succeeded in forcing a breach between Pologi and Drozdy, obliging the division to pull back to new defensive positions. It began the withdrawal at about 16.00 hours that afternoon, and retreated to a line from Pavlovka through Losyatin to the north-western and western edges of Belaya Tserkov'. Despite the move though, heavy fighting continued on into the darkness. The *88.Infanterie-Division* was meanwhile fighting its way back to the line of the river Ros' south of Belaya Tserkov', and was engaged in heavy fighting for most of the day. The Russians launched a regimental-sized assault, supported by about 20 tanks, against the Ruda-Matyushi sector and forced a breach in the front line, temporarily surrounding the defending German units. In the ensuing fighting, the *Sturmgeschütz-Abteilung 202* reported destroying 11 Soviet tanks. Further south, past the *VII.AK* hanging left flank, the town of Pustovarovka was bypassed during the afternoon, and by 15.00 hours the town of Antonov further south had been captured. To the west, heavy enemy motor traffic had also been observed heading south from Skvira as the Soviets exploited the wide gap that had opened up between the *VII.AK* and the *XXXXII.AK* to the west.

Mattenklott's *XXXXII.AK* also had a difficult day, with the Russians continuing to press southwards in the area east of Kazatin.[11] On the far right, the *Korps* had thrown out a reconnaissance screen south-east of Belilovka, along a line running from Kotelyanka through Sakhny to Leshchintsy, but during the course of the evening, this had been obliged to pull back to the south-west as a result of increasing Soviet pressure. Part of this pressure had been exerted in the *25.Panzer-Division* sector, where Russian forces attacked southwards out of Belilovka and, during the afternoon, forced back the *Panzergrenadier-Regiment 146* over the high ground and into Nemirintsy. With the Russian pressure continuing, the regiment wheeled back towards the west and the rest of the *Korps*. Further west, at around 08.00 hours that morning, the Soviets had launched a regimental-sized assault with armour support against the positions of the *168.Infanterie-Division* in Zhurbintsy. This had been successfully defended, but a breach in the northern part of the town needed to be cleared in a counterattack. The positions of the *18.Artillerie-Division* were also attacked throughout the day. South-east of Kazatin, the Soviets made separate assaults in anything up to battalion-strength, striking out from Sokolets against Prushinka to the south. All of these were seen off though. A couple of kilometres to the west, an estimated Soviet rifle battalion managed to break into the northern edge of Kordyshevka, before being thrown back in a counterattack. In the same area, the Russians launched a series of assaults beginning at 08.00 hours, striking the sector from Titusovka to the north. These were made in up to battalion-strength, and all were beaten back. During the morning, the Russians also made several attacks out of Kazatin to the west and south-west. These too were up to battalion-size in strength, and with armour support, they succeeded in breaking through the thin defensive lines

---

11   *XXXXII.AK*, Tagesmeldung, untimed dated 30 Dec 43.

manned by the alarm units to reach the Chubinskii farm and the local *sovkhoz* a short distance to the south-west. Mattenklott discussed the situation with Raus during the day, and confirmed that reconnaissance had shown that Soviet forces were advancing southwards past his right wing.[12] In general, the *XXXXII.AK* had managed to hold its positions with the benefit of effective support from the artillery, but Mattenklott was concerned about the situation developing north-west of Pikovets where the alarm units were struggling. Raus advised the *Korps* commander that the *XXXXVIII.PzK* had already been given instructions to deal with this problem, and that a *Kampfgruppe* from the *1.Panzer-Division* had orders to attack and destroy this Russian grouping. It was critical now for the two *Korps* headquarters to co-operate closely in this area and ensure that the *18.Artillerie-Division* was not drawn into the fighting any more than necessary. Kazatin was to remain Mattenklott's priority, and his task was to maintain his positions.

Further north, the *XXXXVIII.PzK* had seen a series of apparently un-coordinated attacks along the whole of its front as the Soviet 3rd Guards Tank Army pressed forwards.[13] The attacks seemed to Balck as if they had degenerated into individual assaults, and although they were still made in up to regimental-strength, and often with tank support, they seemed to lack an overall common objective. It appeared instead that, following their losses of the previous day, the Russians were restricting their operations against the centre and right wing of the *Korps* to reconnaissance activity, although on the left, the continued attacks did suggest that the main offensive was still ongoing. In the south, the *1.Panzer-Division* took up its new positions in the front line south-east of Berdichev, and immediately ran into Soviet forces around Zhezhelev. It attacked and broke down Russian resistance before pressing on to reach the main crossroads about four kilometres west of Plyakhovaya where it made contact with a *Flak* unit of the *18.Artillerie-Division*. These lead elements then wheeled to the east along the road to Kazatin and pushed on into Plyakhovaya, driving out the advancing Russians and relieving some of the pressure on the defending *Flak* units. Behind this advance, the Soviets continued to press towards Berdichev. They attacked Khazhin, just eight kilometres south-east of the town, striking from the south-east with 46 tanks. To the north, on the Kazatin-Berdichev railway line, they attacked from Ivankovtsy towards Semenovka with an estimated battalion supported by six tanks. Further north still, they made a similar sized assault, also supported by six tanks, advancing westwards along the main road from the Sadki-Singaevka area. This attack was thrown back, but at about 14.15 hours, around 15 Russian tanks broke into Zhezhelev behind the leading elements of the *1.Panzer-Division*. The division reacted quickly, and by 17.00 hours the same evening the situation had been restored, with six Soviet tanks reported to have been put out of action. On the other side of Berdichev, the *1.SS Panzer-Division 'LSSAH'* was also subjected to a series of attacks. Following a battalion-sized assault, the division was forced to pull back its forward positions from Zhurbintsy, a few kilometres north-east

---

12 *PzAOK 4*, Ia Kriegstagebuch entry dated 30 Dec 43.
13 *XXXXVIII.PzK*, Tagesmeldung, 19.40 hours dated 30 Dec 43. By this time, the *Korps* had identified the 11th Guards Tank Corps, the 6th Guards Tank Corps, and the 9th Mechanised Corps operating on its sector, as well as between eight and ten rifle divisions. This intelligence was not completely accurate though, as the 11th Guards Tank Corps was actually attached to the Soviet 1st Tank Army, whereas the 7th Guards Tank Corps formed part of the 3rd Guards Tank Army. The rifle divisions were actually attached to other Armies too.

of Berdichev, while other Russian troops were observed assembling in the wooded area east of the village. Further north, the Soviets sent forward a reconnaissance probe from Novy Solotvin towards Stary Solotvin, but this was repulsed by defensive tank fire. Later on, the Russians attacked again on this sector, this time with an estimated regiment supported by six tanks, and succeeded in breaking into Stary Solotvin before being forced to withdraw following a counterattack. There were further assaults to the north in the Kodnya area. One of these was made in battalion-strength with a few tanks, and struck south-westwards from the town before being intercepted and halted. A separate tank attack was launched towards the railway crossing west of the town, but this too was brought to a halt by the division, and two Soviet tanks which had broken through were found and destroyed. In the meantime, the division launched its own counterattack, striking out of Kodnya towards the railway station to the north-west. The attack jumped off at 11.00 hours and captured the station before pushing on towards Dvorets on the main road to Zhitomir. By 16.00 hours, the lead elements were still caught up in fighting south of the town and along the railway embankment to the east. Between them, the units of the *XXXXVIII.PzK* reported having destroyed at least 37 Russian tanks during the course of the day. At 16.20 hours, Balck briefed Raus on his situation, confirming that the pressure against his front had eased a little with the Russians generally limiting their activities during the day to reconnaissance probes.[14] On the basis of intercepted radio messages, Balck believed that the Soviet commanders were growing concerned about the exposed flanks and rear of their forces, and were currently acting cautiously as a result. Raus responded by suggesting that the important thing was to wear down the Russian forces, and if this meant that a withdrawal would have to take place, this should be done towards the south-west. Raus informed Balck of the situation developing in the other sectors, and told him that his task was to maintain his positions if possible, and to keep counterattacking using his mobile forces. Later that evening, at around 21.00 hours, Balck again called *PzAOK 4* headquarters, this time to advise them that Soviet forces had broken through between the *XXXXVIII.PzK* and the *XXXXII.AK* and pushed on to the south-west, reaching the main Berdichev-Vinnitsa road at Peremoga.[15] Following this news, Raus ordered a small *Kampfgruppe* to be formed under the command of the *XXXXII.AK* to deal with the threat. The group was to be based around an armoured *Panzergrenadier* battalion from the *XXXXII.AK* and a group from the *XXXXVIII.PzK*, and once assembled it was to set off in the early hours of the morning with the objective of destroying the Russian units which had broken through. With the recent loss of Kazatin, it was essential that the Soviets should be prevented from breaking through to the railway junction at Kalinovka, north of Vinnitsa. Following this decision though, it appears that Raus had been misinformed regarding some of the details of the Soviet breakthrough. After clearing up a misunderstanding, presumably regarding the precise location of the breach, Raus decided instead to give responsibility for the counterattack to the *XXXXVIII.PzK*. He did however stress that if Balck had not clearly concentrated his effort on the relevant sector by morning, he would transfer the *1.Panzer-Division* to the *XXXXII.AK*.

---

14 *PzAOK 4*, Ia Kriegstagebuch entry dated 30 Dec 43.
15 Referred to as Wuina in the German records.

Away to the north, around Zhitomir, Hauffe's *XIII.AK* was meanwhile under heavy pressure.[16] Throughout the whole day, it had been under attack by what it reported to be superior Soviet infantry and armoured forces. These now appeared to be concentrating against the left wing and flank of the *Korps*, presumably with the intention of rolling up the front from the west and north-west. The *Kampfgruppe* Källner counterattacked during the morning in the area east of Stavishche,[17] and, supported by the *Sturmgeschütz-Abteilung 280* and the *Panzerjäger-Abteilung 559*, it managed to push back the Soviet forces in the area and force them to withdraw eastwards. The *Kampfgruppe* reported 200 Russian dead and a further 30 captured. The Soviets had also undertaken a number of battalion-sized assaults against the sector held by the *68.Infanterie-Division*. Two of these had failed to make any progress, despite the benefit of armour support, but a third was more successful and led to the capture of Veresy, 11 kilometres north-east of Zhitomir. The Russian troops turned south and pressed forwards along the road towards the town, but a hastily assembled armoured *Kampfgruppe* from the *8.Panzer-Division* counterattacked and forced them to pull back to Veresy. The *340.Infanterie-Division* meanwhile found itself in real difficulty. Whilst conducting its withdrawal along the main Zhitomir-Korosten' road, a large part of the division ran into a Russian roadblock in the form of 22 tanks. Despite this obstruction, the division managed to force its way through southwards, destroying five of the Soviet tanks in the process. By afternoon, it had taken up its new positions as instructed, and was able to defend renewed attacks striking south from the Zorokov and Peschanka areas. To the left, the right wing of the *208.Infanterie-Division* had meanwhile been attacked by strong infantry forces, but despite this it had managed to hold its positions as night fell. On the left wing though, things had been very different, and the division had been attacked by Soviet armoured units either side of Vil'sk. Despite the support of the *1.Batterie* of the *Sturmgeschütz-Abteilung 280* which reported having destroyed five Soviet tanks, it was unable to withstand the weight of the attack, and an estimated 50 Russian tanks broke through the defences, forcing the left wing to pull back. The situation was serious enough for Hauffe to call the *PzAOK 4* during the late morning when he had learned a little more.[18] He told the *Armee* that 41 Soviet tanks had broken through around Vil'sk, and another 22 were currently in position on the main road west of Berezovka. Given this situation, Hauffe asked for permission to pull back to the edge of Zhitomir, but Raus would not agree. The *XIII.AK*, he said, would have to maintain its current positions, and would not be allowed to withdraw unless forced to do so by Russian pressure; even then, it would only be allowed to pull back step-by-step provided the *Panzerarmee* had given its prior approval. This may have seemed inflexible for its own sake, but, as Raus pointed out, any sudden withdrawal to Zhitomir at that time would have created traffic problems for the supply and movement of both combat troops and rear echelons. He was also hoping that the situation on the left wing would soon be stabilised following the arrival of the *SS Panzerkampfgruppe 'Das Reich'* and the *SS-Sturm-Brigade 'Langemarck'*. In this respect, Raus had received confirmation from Army Group South that the *'Langemarck'* was now headed towards Shepetovka and would be attached to the *PzAOK 4* on arrival.[19]

---

16 *XIII.AK*, Tagesmeldung, 20.20 hours dated 30 Dec 43.
17 I have not been able to identify this location, but it may be that Stanishovka was intended.
18 *PzAOK 4*, Ia Kriegstagebuch entry dated 30 Dec 43.
19 *Hgr.Süd*, Ia Nr. 4399/43 g.Kdos. dated 30 Dec 43.

The *Panzerarmee* would therefore be responsible for handling it as soon as it arrived, although permission was granted to commit the unit as soon as the situation allowed. On the *Korps* left wing, the *213.Sicherungs-Division* proved incapable of offering any real resistance to the Soviet advance, given the poor quality of its troops and its lack of anti-tank weapons. About 20 Russian tanks were reported to have broken though in the Dubovets area and along the main road into Zhitomir, and the division could do little more than pull back to a line between Berezovka and a point south of Vasilevka, north of Ul'yanovka. The *SS Panzerkampfgruppe 'Das Reich'*, having re-assembled most of its forces by 14.00 hours, was rushed to support the division, and began to counterattack in the Dubovets area by late afternoon where the fighting lasted well into the evening. Despite this rearguard action, Soviet armour had already outflanked the *Korps* left wing, and by late evening, tanks had been reported in Denishi and Buki in the Teterev valley, over 20 kilometres south-west of Zhitomir.[20] West of this lay a wide gap beyond the left flank of the *4.Panzerarmee*, and according to what the *Korps* recorded as reliable sources, the town of Stary Maidan, about 30 kilometres away to the north-west, had already been occupied by Soviet forces. Despite its predicament, the *XIII.AK* reported destroying a total of 25 Russian tanks during the day.

On the extreme left flank of the *Panzerarmee*, the *LIX.AK* was also in a precarious situation, detached and isolated from the main body of the *Armee* in the area west of Korosten'.[21] It had been attacked throughout the day by strong infantry and armoured forces along the whole of its narrow front, and been forced to pull back from both Krasnopol' and Kupishche. To make matters worse, the *Korps* was also aware that it had already been outflanked to the south, where Russian armour had struck out westwards to Belka and Yablonets, from which position they could easily block the most obvious route of escape. At 13.15 hours, von der Chevallerie called the *PzAOK 4* to provide an update of his situation.[22] As a result of the discussion, Raus considered whether it might be more sensible for the *LIX.AK* to pull back more to the south-west, aiming for Kurnoe on the main Zhitomir-Novograd-Volynskii road, where it might be able to establish contact with the *XIII.AK*.

At 14.20 hours, von Manstein paid a visit to the *4.Panzerarmee* headquarters in Gushchintsy, 13 kilometres west of Kalinovka. Raus briefed him on the current situation and gave a rather optimistic view of his intentions.[23] His general plan was, he said, to try and hold his forces together, even though they had already been split into three separate blocks, and maintain them in their current positions for as long as possible. This would allow him both to concentrate his mobile forces in the central block, which he then planned to use to defeat the Soviet forces facing him, and also to commit the newly arriving reinforcements in an organized manner. Von Manstein believed that the Soviet forces had two main objectives. The first was to destroy the *4.Panzerarmee*, and the second was to seize the important railway junction at Zhmerinka, south-west of Vinnitsa. With Korosten' and Kazatin already lost, and Zhitomir and Berdichev currently under threat, the Army Group's rail supply lines had already been severely restricted, and the additional loss of Kalinovka and Zhmerinka would effectively result in a logistical crisis.

---

20 *PzAOK 4*, Tagesmeldung an *Heeresgruppe Süd*, 23.00 hours dated 30 Dec 43.
21 *PzAOK 4*, Tagesmeldung an *Heeresgruppe Süd*, 23.00 hours dated 30 Dec 43.
22 *PzAOK 4*, Ia Kriegstagebuch entry dated 30 Dec 43.
23 *PzAOK 4*, Ia Kriegstagebuch entry dated 30 Dec 43.

In short, the future of Army Group South as a whole was under grave threat. It was therefore Raus' task to ensure that the *4.Panzerarmee* remained intact, with his main point of effort being concentrated around Kazatin and Berdichev as before. With the loss of the rail junction at Korosten', Zhitomir no longer had any particular significance, and it was not especially important whether ground was lost on that sector through continuous withdrawal. The crucial thing was that the Soviet forces were to be weakened through appropriate action. The *XIII.AK* was therefore not to be allowed to be encircled, but was to be pulled back to the south-west to prevent the entire *Panzerarmee* front from being rolled up. In concentrating his main effort on the Kazatin sector, Raus was to prevent any further Russian advance to the south and keep his forces at a level of combat readiness to allow them to co-operate closely with the *1.Panzerarmee* and the *XXXXVI. PzK* which were due to be transferred into the area. Before he left at 15.00 hours, von Manstein agreed to Raus' proposals to transfer the *1.Panzer-Division* further south; to pull back the *XIII.AK* to positions on the edge of Zhitomir; and to withdraw the *LIX. AK* to a point where it could re-establish contact with the *XIII.AK*.

A little later, at 15.35 hours, Hauffe spoke again with the *PzAOK* headquarters.[24] He briefed them on the situation which had developed in the Veresy area, where about two Soviet rifle regiments and 20 tanks, had broken through the *68.Infanterie-Division*, and also provided an update on the progress of the *SS Panzerkampfgruppe 'Das Reich'* on the Berezovka sector and the presence of Soviet tanks in Stary Maidan. In the light of his discussion with von Manstein, Raus now re-considered his earlier decision. He thought it would be better for the *XIII.AK* to be prepared to disengage on all sectors and fall back when pressed hard. In such an event, the withdrawal was to be towards the south-west, and it was essential that firm contact was maintained with the left wing of the *XXXXVIII.PzK* throughout. The *Korps* was to transfer as many mobile forces as possible from the right wing to the left wing to prevent its flank being rolled up. In pulling back to the edge of the city, as many armoured units as possible in particular were to be freed up. If a further withdrawal should prove necessary, the *Korps* was to evacuate Zhitomir altogether and fall back to a line south-west of the city, running from Troyanov through Denishi to Novy Zavod. If possible, the *Korps* was also to consider whether it might not be able to maintain an intermediate position on a line running along the west bank of the river Kamenka and the south bank of the Teterev. As a fallback, the *XIII.AK* was to withdraw further to the south-west and establish a new position on a line between Sosnovka, Godykha and Mar'yanovka. In the meantime, the most important thing was to ensure that the *Korps* left wing was reinforced as much as possible, and that any units not necessary for the defence of the city and the subsequent withdrawal were to be evacuated to the south-west through Troyanov straightaway.

Overall then, Soviet forces had continued to push back the left wing of the *VII.AK*, and it now seemed clear that they intended to advance from the Skvira area to the south and south-east where they had already reached Antonov. The distance between the *VII. AK* and the *XXXXII.AK* was now around 70 kilometres, and the gap was simply too wide for the *PzAOK 4* to have any real idea as what was happening there. In the centre of the *Panzerarmee* front, things had stabilised a little with the *XXXXII.AK* having been able to see off most of the Soviet attacks south-east of Kazatin. South-west of the town

---

24 *PzAOK 4*, Ia Kriegstagebuch entry dated 30 Dec 43.

though, the Russians had been able to break through the German defences and the situation was still unclear at the end of the day.[25] To the north, intelligence indicated that the Soviet forces were still closing up and bringing up their heavy weapons, allowing the *XXXXVIII.PzK* to hold the line of the road between Berdichev and Zhitomir against weaker infantry attacks supported by a few tanks here and there. The lull was not expected to last however, and the *PzAOK 4* was anticipating strong attacks the following day as the Russians tried to capture Berdichev and gain the Zhitomir-Berdichev-Vinnitsa road. The situation around Zhitomir was now precarious, with the *XIII.AK* being assaulted along the whole of its front as the Soviets continued to reinforce the sector, with two new rifle divisions having been identified east of Zhitomir.[26] On the left wing, the presence of the Soviet 7th Guards Tank Corps had been established as strong armoured forces broke through the defensive positions to threaten the *Korps* flank and rear. There was now a very real danger that the *Korps* front would simply be rolled up, and the *PzAOK 4* was expecting these forces to wheel eastwards into Zhitomir. Beyond the left wing, there were reports that unknown Soviet forces had already crossed the Zhitomir-Novograd-Volynskii road to reach Stary Maidan. Out on the left wing of the army, the *LIX.AK* was also in danger of being outflanked as Soviet armour had concentrated beyond its southern flank and had advanced through Belka to cut the main Korosten'-Novograd-Volynskii road behind its main positions.

It was against this background, and in the light of the afternoon's discussion with von Manstein, that Raus issued his new instructions.[27] These set out his main intention to stop the Soviets in the Berdichev-Kazatin area, and delay their advance against both his wings. The overall objective was to protect the northern flank of Army Group South and cover the arrival and assembly of reinforcements, and in this context it was important for the *Panzerarmee* to hold its existing positions as long as possible, and to inflict as much damage as possible on the Russian forces. The *XXIV.PzK* was to continue with its current task, while the *VII.AK* was to pull back its left wing to avoid it being rolled up. It was to withdraw to a general line running from Stepanovka through the northern edge of Belaya Tserkov' and then south along the line of the river Ros' as far as Malaya Skvirka. In addition, it was to ensure that the main supply road from Zvenigorodka through Tarashcha to Belaya Tserkov' was kept open for as long as possible. The orders also contained advanced notice that both these *Korps* would be transferred to a new *Armee* headquarters in the next few days. The *XXXXII.AK* meanwhile was instructed to hold its existing positions, and concentrate its efforts on its left wing. Any proposals for a further withdrawal would need to ensure that the left wing was pulled back in close co-operation with the *XXXXVIII.PzK*, and would in any case require the prior approval of the *Panzerarmee*. With the main effort on the left, the open right flank would simply have to be covered by a mobile screen. The *XXXXVIII.PzK* was to conduct mobile operations to prevent Soviet forces from crossing the Zhitomir-Berdichev road for as long as possible, although here too, if there was any need to pull back, it was imperative that contact be maintained with the *XXXXII.AK* to the south. Any withdrawal on this sector would also need to be approved by the *Panzerarmee*, and in both cases, only a measured, fighting retreat would be permitted. The *XXXXVIII.PzK* also received

---

25 *PzAOK 4*, Ic Abendmeldung an *Heeresgruppe Süd*, 19.00 hours dated 30 Dec 43.
26 The 304th and the 395th Rifle Divisions.
27 *PzAOK 4*, Ia Nr. 7037/43 g.Kdos. dated 30 Dec 43.

separate orders to deal with the Soviet forces which had broken through in the area west of Kazatin.²⁸ According to these it was to strike the blow with concentrated forces, and, as additional assistance in the operation, it would receive as reinforcement the armoured *Panzergrenadier* battalion from the *25.Panzer-Division* which was then deployed just south of the breach in Pikovets. During the coming night, the *XIII.AK* was to pull back to positions on the edge of Zhitomir and from there along the general line of the railway to Novograd-Volynskii but arching back to the south-west to the bend in the road north of Vasilevka. In doing so, it was to transfer another mobile unit to its left wing, this being the *8.Panzer-Division*.²⁹ The *Korps* was instructed to hold this new position for as long as possible to allow the smooth evacuation of Zhitomir in order to prevent any forces being trapped in the city. The *LIX.AK* was meanwhile to fight its way back slowly towards Novograd-Volynskii, but be prepared instead to breakout towards Kurnoe on the Zhitomir-Novograd-Volynskii road if ordered to do so.

As reinforcement for the *PzAOK 4*, Army Group South had managed to secure an undertaking from the *Luftflotte 4* to make available a *Flak-Division* to provide additional anti-tank and artillery support on its right wing.³⁰ This would be the *Flak-Division 17*, comprising three motorised *Flak* regiments, each of two mixed and one light *Flak* battalions. The division was to be assembled in the area around Uman' south of the *VII. AK*, and was only to be committed as a complete unit.

Friday 31 December 1943

There was no news during the night from the *Panzerarmee* right wing where contact had been lost with the *XXIV.PzK*.³¹ The *VII.AK* nevertheless continued with its planned withdrawal during the night, heading for the new line either side of Belaya Tserkov'.³² The *198.Infanterie-Division* succeeded in pulling back in an orderly fashion, despite being put under heavy pressure from the pursuing Soviet forces on its north-western wing, and managed to beat off all attacks. The *88.Infanterie-Division* also spent the night withdrawing to the line of the river Ros' south of Belaya Tserkov', only to be attacked in the early morning by Russian troops in about company-strength assaulting the Pilipcha-Gorodishche sector. The attack was however successfully seen off. There was

---

28 *PzAOK 4*, Ia Nr. 7046/43 geh. dated 30 Dec 43.
29 *PzAOK 4*, Ia Nr. 7043/43 g.Kdos. dated 30 Dec 43.
30 *Hgr.Süd*, Ia Nr. 4405/43 g.Kdos. dated 29 Dec 43. The division was established as follows:
  • *Flak-Regiment (mot.) 99*
    ♦ *Flak-Abteilung II./38*
    ♦ *Flak-Abteilung I./25*
    ♦ *Leichte Flak-Abteilung 81*
  • *Flak-Regiment (mot.) 17*
    ♦ *Flak-Abteilung I./4*
    ♦ *Flak-Abteilung I./5*
    ♦ *Leichte Flak-Abteilung 861*
  • *Flak-Regiment (mot.) 153*
    ♦ *Flak-Abteilung I./7*
    ♦ *Flak-Abteilung I./32*
    ♦ *Leichte Flak-Abteilung 91*
31 *PzAOK 4*, Ia Tagesmeldung an *Heeresgruppe Süd*, dated 31 Dec 43.
32 *VII.AK*, Morgenmeldung, 05.35 hours dated 31 Dec 43.

no news from the rest of the division, although there were reports of Soviet artillery fire on Ol'shanka to the rear.

On the other side of the gap, the sector held by the *XXXXII.AK* remained quiet for most of the night, with combat activity only being reported on the right wing.[33] At around 23.00 hours the previous evening, Soviet troops in unknown strength had attacked units of the *168.Infanterie-Division* and forced their way into Blazhievka. By morning, the fighting was still continuing as the division attempted to restore the situation. There had been no activity reported by the *18.Artillerie-Division* in its positions around Kazatin, and the headquarters and signals battalion of the *25.Panzer-Division* had arrived in Leonardovka behind the front line. On the left wing, the *1.Panzer-Division* confirmed that Komsomol'skoe had been occupied by Russian troops during the night.

Things had been less quiet on the *XXXXVIII.PzK* front.[34] The *Panzeraufklärungs-Abteilung 1* was still screening the eastern side of Berdichev, either side of the road to Chernorudka, and had been attacked during the night on the sector between Semenovka and Velikaya Nizgortsy. The Soviet assault had been conducted by strong infantry and armoured forces, and managed to break through the defensive screen, forcing the *Abteilung* to pull back to the main position east of Berdichev to avoid being outflanked. To the north-west, another Russian tank assault succeeding in breaking into the positions of the *1.Panzer-Division* around the workers' settlement Komnesamovka,[35] but a local counterattack by elements of the *Panzeraufklärungs-Abteilung 1* managed to seal the breach and restore the situation. By the end of the night, four Soviet tanks had been destroyed, and the main defensive position was back in the division's hands. Despite this, a few Russian tanks were still operating in the area north-east of the main railway station in Berdichev, and fighting was continuing there into the morning. To the south, Soviet forces had also attacked Zhezhelev, but this time without success. Further north, the positions of the *1.SS Panzer-Division 'LSSAH'* in Solotvin had been assaulted at midnight. The attack had been made by an estimated rifle battalion with tank support, but had been beaten back. Later in the night, the division also observed six tanks assembling on the edge of the wood south-east of Solotvin, and engaged these with artillery and rocket fire, causing them to disperse. Having taken up its new positions just south of Zhitomir, the *7.Panzer-Division* had also been attacked. At around midnight, Soviet infantry and tanks had assaulted Singuri and Volitsa, and managed to capture both villages before wheeling southwards towards Dvorets. The Russians pressed their attack through the night, but the division managed to bring the assault to a halt before it reached Dvorets.

To the north, the *XIII.AK* pressed ahead in its withdrawal and succeeded in pulling back its forces without major incident.[36] Hauffe was fortunate that the Soviets followed up his movement only slowly and with relatively weak forces, but the reason for this was less comforting. The Russians had conducted a reconnaissance in force against the *Korps* left wing, indicating that the main Soviet effort was being transferred to the west. In this respect, the *SS Panzerkampfgruppe 'Das Reich'* reported that about 50 Soviet tanks, with infantry mounted on them, had again been spotted in the Bolyarka area, on the

---

33 *XXXXII.AK*, Morgenmeldung, 04.55 hours dated 31 Dec 43.
34 *XXXXVIII.PzK*, Morgenmeldung, 06.10 hours dated 31 Dec 43.
35 This is now a suburb of Berdichev on the north-eastern side of the town.
36 *XIII.AK*, Morgenmeldung, 06.00 hours dated 31 Dec 43.

bend in the main road to Novograd-Volynskii. These were observed heading off to the south-west, while further south, another 11 Russian tanks with infantry had been seen approaching the Teterev valley north-west of Buki. It all appeared to confirm the Soviet intention to outflank and encircle the *Korps* position around Zhitomir.

Away on the left wing, the *LIX.AK* had spent the night pulling back quickly.[37] Soviet forces had assaulted its positions with infantry and tanks forces, and succeeded in breaking through its defences and achieving a deep penetration. The *Korps* fell back as best it could, withdrawing over 15 kilometres to the Gulyanka-Okhotovka-Leonovka line, but strong Russian forces had already bypassed its southern flank, advancing along the main Korosten'-Novograd-Volynskii road. By the end of the night, they had reached the Yablonets-Semakovka-Verovka area to the south-west, forcing the *LIX.AK* to the north-west and away from its intention to withdraw to the south-west.

The weather on the new day was unchanged, being overcast with temperatures just below freezing and light snowfall in places. On the *XXIV.PzK* front, the Soviets continued with their customary pinning attacks.[38] There were three separate battalion-strength assaults out of the Bukrin bridgehead against the *Korps-Abteilung B*, and another two against the *82.Infanterie-Division* north-west of Chernyakhov. All of these had been successfully seen off, but an attack against the *34.Infanterie-Division* south of Shchuchinka had managed to break into the German positions, and the fighting continued into the evening. The division also reported observing assault preparations on the other side of the Dnepr opposite Rzhishchev where the river was just about passable for infantry troops. It was expecting the Russians to attack in the near future.

On the *VII.AK* sector, the Soviets continued to attack towards Belaya Tserkov'.[39] Assaults against the town from the north and the north-west were all thrown back by the *198.Infanterie-Division*, but to the south the *88.Infanterie-Division* had been unable to prevent the Russians from forcing a breach. The fighting continued into the evening. Away to the south-west, Soviet forces continued to outflank the left wing of the *Korps*, where armoured units crossed the river Ros' at Shcherbaki and drove forward to take Fastovka off the march, cutting the main Volodarka-Belaya Tserkov' road. During the early afternoon, *Oberst* Schwatlo-Gesterding, the *Korps* chief of staff, called the *4.Panzerarmee* to report the breach in the *88.Infanterie-Division* sector.[40] He pointed out again that the *VII.AK* had no forces available with which to prevent the Russian strike against its flank and rear, and asked for appropriate measures to be taken by the *Armee*. Fangohr reminded him that the *PzAOK 4* had asked for permission to pull back both the *VII.AK* and the *XXIV.PzK* three days before, but that this had been refused. Nevertheless, after discussing the situation, and bearing in mind von Manstein's earlier concerns about the Soviet drive towards Vinnitsa and Zhmerinka, Raus decided to approach Army Group South again. He would ask for authority to pull back the two *Korps* to a line running from Kanev on the Dnepr along the river Rossava through Kagarlyk to Belaya Tserkov', and would seek the release of both the *17.Panzer-Division* and the *4.Gebirgs-Division*. In the meantime, he would make arrangements to allocate the *17.Panzer-Division* to the *Korps*, and transfer the *Sturmgeschütz-Abteilung 239* to it

---

37 *PzAOK 4*, Ia Tagesmeldung an *Heeresgruppe Süd*, dated 31 Dec 43.
38 *XXIV.PzK*, Tagesmeldung, 18.45 hours dated 31 Dec 43.
39 *PzAOK 4*, Ia Tagesmeldung an *Heeresgruppe Süd*, dated 31 Dec 43.
40 *PzAOK 4*, Ia Kriegstagebuch entry dated 31 Dec 43.

from the *XXIV.PzK*.[41] Von Manstein though was not ready to authorise the proposed withdrawal, but after hearing Raus's plans for the *17.Panzer-Division* and the *4.Gebirgs-Division*, he released them both to the *4.Panzerarmee*. But there were conditions. The *17.Panzer-Division* was first to establish the nature and direction of Soviet movements south-west of the Kashperovka-Pogrebishche line, and was to assemble in the Lipovets-Rososha area such that, depending on the circumstances, it could either fall on the flank of any Russian advance from Vakhnovka towards Vinnitsa, or meet head on any southwards advance from the Ocheretnya area. The *4.Gebirgs-Division* meanwhile was to deploy north-east of Vinnitsa in the Sverdlovka[42]-Priluka area, so that it could first prevent any Soviet advance towards Vinnitsa and then, once it had completed its troop assembly, be ready to go over to the counterattack. Raus issued corresponding orders later that day.[43] These reflected von Manstein's conditions, but added that should the *17.Panzer-Division* actually encounter any leading Soviet elements, it should attack and destroy these with an armoured *Kampfgruppe*. The order also set out the detail of the instructions given to the *4.Gebirgs-Division*. It was to reconnoitre in front of the line Turbov-Priluka-Kotyuzhintsy as far as Ovsyaniki-Samgorodok using the *Aufklärungs-Abteilung 94*, while the rest of the division assembled behind the Priluka-Sverdlovka line such that it could prevent any Soviet advance from Vakhnovka on Vinnitsa. Having assembled all it units, the division was to be prepared to counterattack towards either the east or north-east.

The *17.Panzer-Division* itself meanwhile had begun to arrive from the Kirovograd area, and had started to deploy into the gap between the *VII.AK* and the *XXXXII.AK*.[44] It established its headquarters in Berezovka on the southern edge of Lipovets, from where it supervised the unloading of its units. It reported that this was on schedule, with the lead elements de-training at Andrusovo station, only 18 kilometres south-west of Pogrebishche, while others were meanwhile unloading further down the line at Lipovets station and Oratov station.[45] The *Panzeraufklärungs-Abteilung 17* meanwhile had advanced northwards into the gap, and reported that Soviet forces had already occupied the town of Pogrebishche, 25 kilometres south of Ruzhin, and taken up positions in the woods to the south of the town. Russian forward elements had then pushed on further in several columns, reaching the large wooded area north of Adamovka from where they began to direct anti-tank and mortar fire onto the forward German positions. During the course of the afternoon, these Soviet forces attacked the *Abteilung*, launching two separate battalion-strength assaults in the area north of Pogrebishche station. Both

---

41 *PzAOK 4*, Ia Nr. 7055/43 geh. dated 31 Dec 43. According to this order, the *Abteilung* was to begin moving at 03.30 hours on 1 January 1944, and was initially to head for the *VII.AK* headquarters in Rakitno.
42 The place name is actually given in the War Diary as 'Sdwerra' (which would be transliterated into English as 'Zdvera'), but the later order confirms that Sverdlovka was meant.
43 *PzAOK 4*, Ia Nr. 7050/43 geh. dated 31 Dec 43.
44 *17.Pz.Div*, Tagesmeldung, 19.35 hours dated 31 Dec 43.
45 By evening on 31 December, the situation was as follows: The advance guard, comprising one *Kompanie* of the *Panzer-Pionier-Bataillon 27* and the *I./Panzerartillerie-Regiment 27*, was in Adamovka and nearby Pogrebishche station. The *Panzers* and *Sturmgeschützen* were deployed further to the rear in Dolzhok, next to Andrusovo Station, to protect the immediate area around the station. The *Panzer-Pionier-Bataillon 27* was in Pliskov with one *Kompanie* and was reconnoitring to the north-east towards Raskopanoe. Both *Panzergrenadier-Regiments* were still underway, and were expected to unload during the coming night.

these were beaten back with the reported loss of between 70 and 80 Soviet killed, and a number of *panje* wagons destroyed.

To the north-west, the planned transfer of *Korps* headquarters was beginning to take place, and the *XXIV.PzK* had started the process of taking over the sector previously held by the *XXXXII.AK*. Nehring was straight into the action as Soviet forces pressed their attacks against the *Korps* centre and left wing.[46] On the right flank, elements of the *25.Panzer-Division* had established a reconnaissance screen on the river Desna sector, while in the rear, the division headquarters and signals battalion which had been regrouping in Leonardovka, were formed into the *Sperrverband* Tröger together with other dispersed elements from the division. This was then deployed a little further west to counter any Soviet advance towards Vinnitsa along the main road from Berdichev. The *168.Infanterie-Division* had meanwhile been involved in heavy fighting throughout the day south-east of Kazatin. The Soviets made a total of four separate attacks against Blazhievka, Zhurbintsy, and Kordyshevka in the strength of anything up to two rifle battalions, but the division managed to hold its positions. In the evening though, a new assault from Korolevka managed to break into the defences in Prushinka, and new Russian troop assemblies were observed north of Kordyshevka. Reconnaissance in the area had also spotted new units arriving in Korolevka and Sokolets, assessing these to be a rifle regiment with a heavy artillery battery. Having unloaded, these new units marched off to the south-west towards Kordyshevka. To the left, the *18.Artillerie-Division* had also been attacked throughout the day. Five Soviet assaults in up to battalion-strength, and with tank support, had been made against Pikovets and the positions on either side. These had been successfully defended, with ten Russian tanks reported as destroyed. In the midst of all this, the *Korps* managed to pull together a small armoured *Kampfgruppe* in Pikovets to counterattack towards the north-west to establish contact with the *1.Panzer-Division*.[47] This ran into trouble almost as soon as it started though, striking into the flank of Russian troops heading to the south-west, and the counterattack ground to a halt as fighting continued on into the night. Later that evening, the Soviets launched a new assault against Pikovets, this time with the support of between 20 and 30 tanks. The attack was successful, breaking through the front line and penetrating through to the artillery positions, reaching Kumanevka. The defending troops pulled back and prepared to counterattack the following morning. At around 19.00 hours, *Oberst* Franz, the *XXXXII.AK* chief of staff, reported this latest development to the *PzAOK 4*, and also added that the Russians were now trying to get at the *Korps* right wing by outflanking it.[48] He therefore suggested that the *Korps* should pull back to line running from Samgorodok through Mikhailin and Kumanevka to Peremoga. Raus agreed and issued orders to that effect later that day.[49] According to these, the new boundary between the two *Korps* was to lie on a line running from Gushchintsy through Gulevtsy,[50] Nemirintsy and Peremoga to the north-western edge of Kazatin.

---

46 *XXIV.PzK*, Tagesmeldung vom 31.12.43, 10.30 hours dated 1 Jan 44.
47 *PzAOK 4*, Ia Tagesmeldung an *Heeresgruppe Süd*, dated 31 Dec 43.
48 *PzAOK 4*, Ia Kriegstagebuch entry dated 31 Dec 43.
49 *PzAOK 4*, Ia Nr. 7052/43 geh. dated 31 Dec 43.
50 Referred to as Kommunarovka on more recent Soviet maps.

The *XXXXVIII.PzK* meanwhile had also been hard-pressed during the day, with the Soviets making repeated assaults against both wings and also the area east of Berdichev.[51] The attacks had been in anything up to regimental strength, with both armour and artillery support, and in the *1.Panzer-Division* sector these had concentrated on two main areas; against Berdichev itself and against the main crossroads north of Komsomol'skoe. In the sector held by the *1.SS Panzer-Division 'LSSAH'* on the *Korps* left, the attacks had been concentrated between Solotvin and Kodnya station. Despite the Russian tank and artillery support, the *Korps* had initially been able to defend all of these sectors, and reported heavy casualties for the Soviet troops involved. Nevertheless, at some point during the morning, the Russians had forced their way into Komsomol'skoe, and a local counterattack by elements of the *1.Panzer-Division* only managed to advance as far the centre of the town. The fighting continued on through the afternoon and into the evening. To the north, the *'LSSAH'* also lost ground before midday when strong Soviet forces captured Kodnya station. The situation grew worse when Russian troops, including about 25 tanks, advanced north-westwards from the Volitsa-Singuri area and pressed on to take the village of Shumsk.[52] Aware of the problem, the *7.Panzer-Division*, which was still in the area, pulled together a small armoured *Kampfgruppe* to deal with the situation. At about 13.30 hours, von Mellenthin, Balck's chief of staff, spoke to Fangohr at *PzAOK 4* headquarters.[53] He advised the *Panzerarmee* chief of staff that the *Korps* had not yet been able to establish any firm contact with the *XXXXII.AK*, and that the *7.Panzer-Division* had been unable to progress any further south towards Berdichev. He told him that the division had instead become entangled in heavy fighting in the Volitsa area, where Soviet armour had broken through to Shumsk. Fangohr was of the view that the *7.Panzer-Division* should remain in its current position, rather than risk having to pull back the *Korps* left wing to the Troyanov area before the *XIII.AK* had reached its new positions. Later on, Raus spoke direct with Balck who said that he thought his troops had achieved a defensive success that day, having destroyed 55 Soviet tanks. Balck now believed that the Russian forces opposite his *Korps* were formed into four distinct groups. The first deployed around 50 tanks in the Glukhovtsy area north-west of Kazatin, while the second had about the same number but was east of Berdichev. Further north, the third group was the largest, deploying about 100 tanks on the Kodnya-Solotvin sector, while a fourth, just south of Zhitomir in the Volitsa area, had about another 50. With all this armour moving up, he was anticipating a renewed Soviet offensive during the coming night, and thought the situation to be critical as his infantry forces were not sufficient to deal with such an attack. Raus stressed that a Soviet breakthrough to the west had to be prevented with all available means, and the *7.Panzer-Division* should therefore be used to cover the flank of the *XIII.AK* to enable it to pull back to its new positions unimpeded. Balck suggested pulling the *1.SS Panzer-Division 'LSSAH'* towards Troyanov to free up the *7.Panzer-Division* for a strike north-eastwards towards the right wing of the *XIII.AK*. Raus therefore agreed that the division should strike towards Perlyavka in the Teterev valley, essentially following the Soviet tanks that had advanced on Shumsk earlier. Having reached the village, it was to make contact with the *XIII.AK* and prevent any Russian forces from crossing the river on that sector. Then,

---

51 *PzAOK 4*, Ia Tagesmeldung an *Heeresgruppe Süd*, dated 31 Dec 43.
52 The village of Shumsk is no longer shown on more recent Soviet maps.
53 *PzAOK 4*, Ia Kriegstagebuch entry dated 31 Dec 43.

THE FRONT IS SPLIT APART

once the *XIII.AK* had successfully taken up its new positions, the *XXXXVIII.PzK* would be allowed to pull back to the eastern edge of Berdichev to free up additional forces. Any such forces must then be used to support the *XIII.AK* though. Given the apparent Soviet intention to continue their drive to the south-west in the Kazatin area, Balck also intended to form a *Kampfgruppe* as a reserve behind his right wing, ready to counter any Russian moves against the boundary between the two *Korps*.

The *PzAOK 4* issued formal instruction later in the day to cover all these concerns.[54] These confirmed that the *XXXXVIII.PzK* was to pull back its right wing behind the river Gnilopyat' and ensure that contact with the *XXXXII.AK* was maintained near Peremoga. Berdichev itself was to be held for as long as possible, but Balck was given permission to pull back his northern wing to a line running from Troyanov to the north-west edge of Grishkovtsy near Berdichev, and use the *7.Panzer-Division* to support the withdrawal of the *XIII.AK*.

Meanwhile, the Russians continued their attacks against the *XIII.AK* around Zhitomir.[55] During the morning they had launched a concerted assault against the sector held by the *340.Infanterie-Division* north of the town. Two regimental-sized groups attacked simultaneously from the north and north-west, and succeeded in breaking through the division's defences and advancing to the outskirts of the city. With Russian armour already on both flanks and in the *Korps* rear area, and now faced with a major breach of his front line, Hauffe decided to pull back out of the city, fight his way along the Zhitomir- Vysokaya Pech' road, and establish a new defensive position on the line from Troyanov through Denishi to Ul'yanovka. With Soviet forces already on the river Teterev at Buki, the encirclement of Zhitomir was effectively complete, and Hauffe's decision could not have been left much later. Even as things stood, the troops of the *XIII.AK* would have to continue to fight their way out of the encirclement through the night. Raus later confirmed his agreement to this course of action, and advised Hauffe that the *7.Panzer-Division* had been instructed to support the withdrawal by conducting mobile operations on his southern wing.[56] He also added that, behind the new *XIII.AK* defensive line, the *SS Sturm-Brigade 'Langemarck'* had been ordered to keep the Denishi-Chudnov road open.

Further north, the *LIX.AK* was in trouble.[57] Although the Russians made no attempt during the morning to assault the new defensive position on the Gulyanka-Okhotovka-Leonovka line, they were known to be reinforcing their positions south-west of the right wing in the Semakovka and Verovka areas. The troops deployed by the *Korps* on flank security in the Verovka area had been pushed back, and were now falling back to the north-west towards Emil'chino. The main road to Novograd-Volynskii was now completely in Soviet hands, and it was clear that they were determined to keep the *Korps* isolated from the rest of the *4.Panzerarmee*. During the morning, von der Chevallerie reported his situation to the *PzAOK 4* headquarters, and advised them that, due to a lack of proper infantry forces and the extreme exhaustion of his troops, he believed the *LIX.AK* would no longer have the strength to break out towards the south. Raus had little alternative but to agree, and he ordered the *Korps* to keep its forces closely concentrated

---

54 *PzAOK 4*, Ia Nr. 7053/43 geh. dated 31 Dec 43.
55 *PzAOK 4*, Ia Tagesmeldung an *Heeresgruppe Süd*, dated 31 Dec 43.
56 *PzAOK 4*, Ia Nr. 7061/43 geh. dated 31 Dec 43.
57 *PzAOK 4*, Ia Tagesmeldung an *Heeresgruppe Süd*, dated 31 Dec 43.

and aim instead for Novograd-Volynskii to the south-west, rather than allowing itself to be forced out to the west.[58] He also suggested that in the event the *Korps* could not force its way along the main road to Novograd-Volynskii, it should take the longer route through Emil'chino.[59] In any event, Raus issued instructions to the *Kampfkommandant Zwiahel* in Novograd-Volynskii, advising him that the *LIX.AK* was now trying to fight its way back towards him.[60] The *Kampfkommandant* was ordered to begin reconnaissance north-east, east and south-east of the town in an effort to gain a clearer picture of the situation, and thereby help von der Chevallerie's troops as they pulled back. Earlier in the day, the *Kampfkommandant* had provided a report stating that of the Soviet tanks which had first been reported on the Zhitomir-Novograd-Volynskii road on 29 December, three had recently been established in Sokolov, about 36 kilometres south-east of Novograd-Volynskii.[61] From this position, they now effectively blocked all traffic along the road, although it did seem that they were running short of ammunition, having used anti-tank rounds to attack a soft column. The tanks were not alone either, as a German patrol in the same area had encountered a group of partisans equipped with mortars and anti-tank guns. Apart from these two encounters though, reconnaissance had yielded nothing so far.

The day had therefore been characterised by continued Soviet efforts to press the offensive on all fronts.[62] The course of events suggested to the *PzAOK 4* that the Soviets were attempting to encircle and destroy its different groupings as they tried to maintain their positions, and thereby tear open a breach in the front line which would be beyond repair and use this to facilitate the advance to the south-west.[63] The left wing of the *VII.AK* was still being hammered in order to open up the rear of both that *Korps* and the *XXIV.PzK*, with Belaya Tserkov' being attacked from the north and north-west in unknown strength while Russian tanks had already reached the road between Belaya Tserkov' and Volodarka further south. In the gap between the *VII.AK* and the *XXXXII.AK*, strong Soviet infantry forces, estimated by the *PzAOK 4* to be two rifle divisions, were advancing south-westwards towards Pogrebishche, and according to aerial reconnaissance the lead elements had already reached a general line from Pogrebishche through Ordyntsy to Monchin and Sopin. Armoured reconnaissance units had even been spotted as far forward as Britskoe. The *XXXXII.AK* had been involved in continual heavy fighting throughout the day, with the Soviets having closed up with the previously identified four rifle divisions supported by individual groups of tanks.[64] It was suspected that a concentration of forces was being formed in the Kazatin area. The *XXXXVIII.PzK* front had also been assaulted for much of the day, but by and large it had been able to maintain its positions, and reported having destroyed a total of 55 Soviet tanks in doing so. The *Korps* now suspected that it was facing more than one major Russian armoured group, having observed about 40 tanks opposite its right wing, a further 50 east of Berdichev, another 40 or so opposite the right wing of the *1.SS Panzer-Division 'LSSAH'*,

---

58 *PzAOK 4*, Ia Unreferenced order dated 31 Dec 43.
59 *PzAOK 4*, Ia Unreferenced order dated 31 Dec 43. Though also without a reference number, this was a different order to the earlier one.
60 *PzAOK 4*, Ia Nr. 7049/43 geh. dated 31 Dec 43.
61 *Kampfkommandant Zwiahel*, Ia Nr. 16385/43 dated 31 Dec 43.
62 *PzAOK 4*, Ia Nr. 7062/43 geh., Tagesmeldung an *Heeresgruppe Süd*, dated 31 Dec 43.
63 *PzAOK 4*, Ic Abendmeldung an *Heeresgruppe Süd*, 19.30 hours dated 31 Dec 43.
64 The 100th, 211th, 241st, and 68th Guards Rifle Divisions.

and 50 more south of Zhitomir facing the left wing of the *'LSSAH'* and the *7.Panzer-Division*. It appeared likely that the Soviets would be making a concerted effort to take Berdichev the following day, while simultaneously trying to outflank the *XXXXVIII.PzK* on both wings. It was a different story for the *XIII.AK* as it struggled to defend the Zhitomir area. The Soviets had managed to achieve a number of breaches on the northern and north-western sectors, forcing the *Korps* to abandon the city and pull back south-westwards to the line Troyanov-Denishi-Ul'yanovka. This line too was already under threat as aerial reconnaissance had shown that Russian motorised infantry and tank forces were moving west of Vysokaya Pech', advancing on the Godykha-Chudnov axis. With Zhitomir now lost, and Berdichev under serious threat, Raus was in desperate need of reinforcement. The *4.Panzerarmee* had been torn apart into three distinct groups and he had no means of either bringing the Soviet offensive to a halt or pulling his disparate forces together. Nevertheless, reinforcements were now beginning to arrive, and further to the news received on 28 December, the first trains bringing the *16.Panzer-Division* and the *4.Gebirgs-Division* had begun to arrive in the *PzAOK 4* area. A total of 19 trains appeared from the former, including eight bringing the *I./Panzer-Regiment 2* with the new 'Panthers', and seven from the latter. Seven more trains also arrived with elements of the *SS Sturm-Brigade 'Langemarck'*, and another five had also arrived with more units from the *17.Panzer-Division*.[65] Raus also received a message from Army Group South on the subject of reinforcements, this time advising him that a new *Korps* headquarters, the *XXXXVI.PzK*, together with its *Korpstruppen*, was now being transferred south from Army Group Centre and would be arriving soon in Proskurov.[66]

Saturday 1 January 1944

The night had passed relatively quietly on the front held by the *XXXXII.AK*, where two Soviet patrols against the right wing of the *82.Infanterie-Division* in Chernyakhov had been thrown back without too much difficulty.[67] Other than these two incidents, the *Korps* reported no activity.

Things had not been quite so easy for Hell's *VII.AK*.[68] Although the situation remained quiet on both wings, the central sector around Belaya Tserkov' had been worrying. On the right, the *75.Infanterie-Division* reported a Soviet reconnaissance patrol near Makeevka and a combat patrol north-west of Pavlovka, but it had managed to see off both. On the left, the sector held by the *88.Infanterie-Division* saw no combat activity at all. In contrast, the *198.Infanterie-Division* reported several Russian assaults before midnight along the whole of its front, with the main point of effort being towards Belaya Tserkov' itself. The division succeeded in seeing off all these attacks, although not

---

65 PzAOK 4, 'Stand der Bewegungen am 31.Dezember 1943, 16 Uhr'. According to this document, the *'Langemarck'* was loaded onto a total of nine trains and was arriving in the Polonnoe-Stary Miropol'-Chudnov area. The *I./Panzer-Regiment 2* was being transported on 11 trains, with seven *Panthers* on each. Six of the eight trains had arrived in Chudnov, with the other two going to Berdichev and Shepetovka instead. The *16.Panzer-Division* required a total of 74 trains to transport it, and the majority of the trains that had arrived so far had unloaded their units at different stations along the stretch between Shepetovka and Chudnov. The *4.Gebirgs-Division* on the other hand had unloaded further south-east, with all of the trains so far unloading in either Kalinovka or Vinnitsa.
66 Hgr. Süd, Ia Nr. 4426/43 g.Kdos dated 31 Dec 43. The town of Proskurov is now known as Khmel'nitskii.
67 *XXXXII.AK*, Morgenmeldung, untimed dated 1 Jan 44.
68 *VII.AK*, Morgenmeldung, 06.20 hours dated 1 Jan 44.

before one had first forced a breach in its defences. The assaults began again in the early hours of the morning, and the Soviets forced two breaches north and south-west of the town, each in between battalion and regiment-strength. The division had been obliged to commit its last reserves to try and restore the situation, and the fighting continued on into the morning.

Away to the south-west, the *17.Panzer-Division* was still attempting to establish some kind of defensive position in the gap between the *VII.AK* and the *XXIV.PzK*.[69] Forward security had been established by elements of the *Panzer-Pionier-Bataillon 27* in Pliskov, while troops of the *Panzergrenadier-Regiment 63* were now on their way towards Spichintsy to the north-west, while elements of the *Panzergrenadier-Regiment 40* were heading towards Zozov in the west. Though there had been no combat activity during the night, the division reported large Soviet troop assemblies in the area north of Pogrebishche station, west of Adamovka.

The *XXIV.PzK* had meanwhile spent the night continuing its withdrawal to the new line between Samgorodok and Peremoga.[70] This had gone according to plan without intervention from the enemy, although contact with the *18.Artillerie-Division* on the left wing had been lost following disruption of the communications network.

In the *XXXXVIII.PzK* sector though, the Soviets continued to press their attacks during the night.[71] The positions held by the *1.Panzer-Division* in Berdichev, Zhezhelev and Khazhin had all been assaulted by Russian infantry, supported by artillery and tanks. These had only been partially successful, with limited infiltrations into Zhezhelev and Khazhin and a local breach in Berdichev. The division counterattacked the Soviet penetration in Berdichev, and managed to restore the situation before the end of the night. The *1.SS Panzer-Division 'LSSAH'*, with its headquarters now in Shvaikovka, was more fortunate and managed to conduct its planned withdrawal without interference from the Russians. The *7.Panzer-Division* too had succeeded in disengaging during the night and re-assembling west of the river Gnilopyat', ready to begin its counterattack to the north at 06.15 hours.

The situation was not much quieter further north, where the *XIII.AK* was continuing to pull back south-west of Zhitomir but had run into difficulties.[72] The main road out of the town to the south-west had not been fully cleared of Soviet forces, and the withdrawal had been delayed as a result of traffic congestion in the area around Vysokaya Pech'.

On the northern wing, the *LIX.AK* reported Russian attacks against the right wing of the *291.Infanterie-Division* west of Bondarevka.[73] These had been made in unknown strength and continued through the night until daylight. It was a similar situation in the centre of the *Korps* sector, while on the northern wing Russian forces had managed to achieve a deep penetration. In the *Korps* rear to the south-west, the *Kampfkommandant* in Novograd-Volynskii had already reported the appearance of several Soviet tanks in Chizhovka, just eight kilometres north of the town.

Over towards the Dnepr, the new day dawned clear and bright. Visibility remained average and although the temperature remained below freezing, the sun made the day feel

---

69 *17.Pz.Div*, Morgenmeldung, 06.30 hours dated 1 Jan 44.
70 *XXIV.PzK*, Morgenmeldung, 06.45 hours dated 1 Jan 44.
71 *XXXXVIII.PzK*, Morgenmeldung, 06.00 hours dated 1 Jan 44.
72 *PzAOK 4*, Ia Morgenmeldung an *Heeresgruppe Süd*, 07.20 hours dated 1 Jan 44.
73 *PzAOK 4*, Ia Morgenmeldung an *Heeresgruppe Süd*, 07.20 hours dated 1 Jan 44.

warmer. Later though, the clouds returned, but the roads remained frozen for the most part, leaving mobility still good. The *XXXXII.AK*, having now assumed responsibility for the easternmost sector of the *PzAOK 4*, reported a relatively quiet day.[74] Opposite the Bukrin bridgehead, the Soviets had attacked the *Korps-Abteilung B* sector near Glincha and succeeded in achieving a breach with an estimated rifle company. This had eventually been sealed off and cleared, with a total of 23 counted Russian dead found in the German trenches. A further three were taken prisoner. Another three prisoners were also brought in when a combat patrol was sent out by the *Korps-Abteilung* east of Chernyshi which managed to break into the Russian defensive system there and rolled up a section of the trench. On the *34.Infanterie-Division* sector to the north-west, a weak Soviet patrol was thrown back near Ul'yaniki, while other Russian troops were observed heading westwards from Khodorov. On the north-western front, the *82.Infanterie-Division* intercepted a platoon-sized patrol near Verem'e, throwing it back from the forward positions. A little to the west, the division also spotted two separate Russian troop assemblies north of Chernyakhov, one of which involved about 200 men,[75] and engaged these with artillery fire, dispersing both. With the improvement in the weather, the *VII.AK* reported an increase in Soviet air activity, with several waves of bombers, each of up to 15 aircraft with fighter cover, flying over the *Korps* sector. As instructed, Mattenklott had also given up the *Sturmgeschütz-Abteilung 239*, transferring it during the day to the *VII.AK* to his left.

Hell's *Korps* had meanwhile been struggling. Although the Russians had discontinued their attacks against the *75.Infanterie-Division* on his right wing, seemingly limiting their activities instead to transferring forces to the west, the *198.Infanterie-Division* either side of Belaya Tserkov' was under almost constant assault.[76] Initially, it had been able to seal off and clear different breaches either side of the town, but renewed Soviet assaults gave rise to fresh penetrations in Losyatin to north-east of the town, and Glybochka to the south-west. The division was forced to commit its last reserves just to seal these off and restore the situation. Further south, more than 15 kilometres from the *VII.AK* left wing, other Russian forces had already captured Volodarka, while over 35 kilometres away, Soviet troops estimated to be a rifle division had been observed in the area around and to the north-west of Kashperovka on the river Ros'ka. At around 21.10 hours that evening, Schwatlo-Gesterding called Fangohr from the *VII.AK* headquarters to give him a short briefing on the situation.[77] With the success of their attack in the Losyatin area, it now seemed likely that the Russians would concentrate on encircling Belaya Tserkov' from the east. The *Korps* no longer believed that it would be able to maintain its current positions for much longer, particularly as the *198.Infanterie-Division* was incurring serious casualties as a result of the heavy Soviet artillery fire. He therefore requested permission to pull the *VII.AK* back to the 'Siegfriedstellung' in order to free up at least a division. As an example, Schwatlo-Gesterding suggested that a strong assault by the Russians against the *75.Infanterie-Division* would probably cause the division to break and run, but if allowed to do so now, it would be able to pull back in good order without suffering any casualties. Fangohr responded by saying that he did not consider the threat

---

74 *XXXXII.AK*, Tagesmeldung, 18.30 hours dated 1 Jan 44.
75 *PzAOK 4*, Ia Tagesmeldung an *Heeresgruppe Süd*, 22.00 hours dated 1 Jan 44.
76 *PzAOK 4*, Ia Tagesmeldung an *Heeresgruppe Süd*, 22.00 hours dated 1 Jan 44.
77 *PzAOK 4*, Ia Kriegstagebuch entry dated 1 Jan 44.

to the *VII.AK* left flank to be all that serious, although he did undertake to raise the question of withdrawal once more.

Over 25 kilometres to the west, the *17.Panzer-Division* reported lively Soviet traffic opposite its sector, leading it to believe that the Russians were not only conducting reconnaissance in the area but also reinforcing their leading elements.[78] A few *panje* wagons had been seen on the eastern edge of the wood north-east of Adamovka, heading southwards towards Raskopanoe. To find out more, the division sent out a reconnaissance patrol to collect more information. Further west, in the Ros' valley, the village of Pedosy had already been occupied by about 60 Soviet troops accompanied by roughly 20 horse-drawn vehicles. Further west again, two different columns of about 50 *panje* wagons each had been seen pushing south and south-west from Cheremoshnoe and Malinki. None of these movements had made contact with the forward elements of the division, although they had been engaged with artillery fire. To the south-east, the *Panzer-Pionier-Bataillon 27*, supported by a few self-propelled artillery guns, had now established defensive positions north-east of Pliskov, while further north the leading elements of the *Panzeraufklärungs-Abteilung 17* were deployed in the area around Pogrebishche station. On this sector, Soviet units had pushed far enough forward to engage the division, and during the course of the day, there were several occasions where mortar and anti-tank fire were received. As darkness fell though, the Russians attacked in earnest. A unit of about battalion-strength began the assault at 17.15 hours, and the fighting continued on into the night. The *Panzergrenadier-Regiment 63* meanwhile had not reached Spichintsy but had instead moved into position around Dolzhok where it secured the exits to the town, and sent reconnaissance patrols forward towards Bulai. The village was found to be weakly held by a partisan unit. The *Panzergrenadier-Regiment 40* had meanwhile pressed on westwards and deployed around the northern end of Zozovka, with forward detachments sent out to Britskoe and the crossroads a couple of kilometres north of Zozovka. It was now about 20 kilometres south of the right wing of the *XXIV.PzK* in Samgorodok. With the exception of the attached *Flak* troops, the *HQ Kompanie* and a few elements which had fallen out during the journey, all the combat troops of the *17.Panzer-Division* had by this time arrived and deployed.[79]

While the *17.Panzer-Division* was taking up its new positions in relative peace, the *XXIV.PzK* south-west of Kazatin was being attacked on its right wing and in the centre either side of the Vinnitsa-Kazatin railway line.[80] The *168.Infanterie-Division* reported a lot of Soviet traffic opposite the right wing, as well as being assaulted several times throughout the day. The Russians made four separate battalion-sized assaults against the division's positions in Samgorodok, Shirokaya Greblya,[81] and Mikhailin, but all of these were seen off successfully. As the daylight faded, the Russians attacked again, this time striking southwards from Florianovka, and the fighting here continued on into the night. Meanwhile the *4.Gebirgs-Division* was moving into position to the right of the *168.Infanterie-Division*, with the *Aufklärungs-Abteilung 94* being deployed in the

---

78 *17.Pz.Div*, Tagesmeldung, 19.25 hours dated 1 Jan 44.
79 This good news was somewhat tempered by the lack of operational armour deployed by the division. According to the same report, it possessed just 25 operational tanks: nine *StuGs*, four *Panzer III lg*, four *Panzer IV lg*, six *Panzer V*, and two command tanks.
80 *XXIV.PzK*, Tagesmeldung, 17.45 hours dated 1 Jan 44.
81 Located south-west of Yusefovka.

Konstantinovka area.[82] During the afternoon, this had established that both Ovsyaniki and Sopin were free of Soviet troops at 16.00 hours, at which time, there were barely eight kilometres separating them from the leading elements of the *17.Panzer-Division* in Britskoe. With the arrival of the *4.Gebirgs-Division*, the *168.Infanterie-Division* felt able to pull back its mobile reserve, the *Panzergrenadier-Regiment 146* from the *25.Panzer-Division*, from Novaya Greblya on its southern wing. The regiment was transferred northwards to the Lopatin area, where it could be deployed to support the defence around Mikhailin where the Russians were pressing hard. In addition to this reserve, the *XXXXVIII.PzK* was instructed to pull the *s.Panzer-Abteilung 509* out of the front line, and transfer it to the command of the *XXIV.PzK*.[83] To the left of the *168.Infanterie-Division*, the *18.Artillerie-Division*, with the *I./Flak-Regiment 231* attached once more, had also had a difficult day.[84] There had been series of infantry and armour attacks north-east of Velikaya Step' during the morning, but all of these had been driven back. To the north-west, the southern part of Kumanevka had been cleared of the Russian troops that had broken through the previous day, and the counterattack continued on into the night to try and clear the northern part of the village as well. Elements of the division had also come across a Soviet motorised artillery battery just north of Peremoga during the day and managed to destroy it. Later in the day though, the Soviets mounted a major assault with about 40 tanks in support,[85] hitting the division's positions either side of the Kazatin-Vinnitsa railway. This assault succeeded in breaking through the defence, and although a local counterattack was launched, the situation had become unclear by the end of the day. It seemed from the nature of the attack that the Soviets were now trying to break through and strike along the railway line towards Vinnitsa. The headquarters of the *25.Panzer-Division* had meanwhile assembled its scattered units and, together with the *Landesschützen-Bataillon 857*, was now holding a sector of nearly 20 kilometres to screen the left flank of the *Korps* on a line running south-west from Peremoga through Nemirintsy and Napadovka to Pisarevka. The division reported no contact with Soviet forces during the day.

The *XXXXVIII.PzK* also suffered a number of assaults during the course of the day. Most of these came in against the centre and right wing, but they appeared to be largely uncoordinated.[86] In the *1.Panzer-Division* sector, the Russians continued with their efforts to take Zhezhelev and Khazhin, assaulting both villages repeatedly throughout the day. Most of the assaults were made in battalion-strength with the support of a few tanks, but all were beaten back. To the south-east, the Soviets were seen bringing up fresh forces into Glukhovtsy, and the division reported Russian troop assemblies in the wooded area south-west of the village. For the time being though, Komsomol'skoe remained free of Soviet troops. Further north, an attack by between 25 and 30 Soviet tanks with mounted infantry attacked the north-eastern part of Berdichev and succeeded in breaking into the suburbs. The division organised a local counterattack, and by

---

82 *PzAOK 4*, Ia Tagesmeldung an *Heeresgruppe Süd*, 22.00 hours dated 1 Jan 44.
83 *PzAOK 4*, Ia Nr. 17/44 geh. dated 1 Jan 44.
84 According to the same report, in the five days between 28 December and 1 January, the *18.Artillerie-Division* had destroyed a total of 44 Soviet tanks, immobilised three others, and destroyed a motorised artillery battery.
85 *PzAOK 4*, Ia Tagesmeldung an *Heeresgruppe Süd*, 22.00 hours dated 1 Jan 44.
86 *XXXXVIII.PzK*, Tagesmeldung, 20.30 hours dated 1 Jan 44.

late evening a total of 23 Russian tanks were reported to have been knocked out. The fighting continued on into the night. The positions held by the *1.SS Panzer-Division 'LSSAH'* were also assaulted in different places throughout the day, while the Soviets undertook reconnaissance along the whole sector. At 10.30 hours, the Russians attacked out of Polovetskoe with an estimated regiment, and this was followed by others against Gvozdava and Troyanov. All of these were seen off, but Soviet armour was also seen advancing in the area around Tartarinovka,[87] with 20 tanks heading into the village itself while another 17 were spotted heading southwards towards Gvozdava. By late evening, around 20.00 hours, the Russians assaulted the division's positions in Troyanov again, this time from the north with an estimated rifle regiment with tank support. The fighting continued into the night, with the division reporting having destroyed 19 Soviet tanks by 20.30 hours. To the left, the *7.Panzer-Division* had launched its counterattack at 06.15 hours that morning, striking out from the area west of Troyanov to the north. By 09.45 hours it had advanced more than ten kilometres to capture the strongly-held village of Perlyavka in the Teterev valley. Other elements had meanwhile moved off westwards, and taken up positions on the bend in the road 2½ kilometres west of Rudnya Gorodishche. The *Panzeraufklärungs-Abteilung 7* was in position in the hamlet of Gruska,[88] while those elements which had been in Zheleznyaki[89] in the valley south-west of Golovenka had been forced back towards Troyanov, following a Soviet assault. Following this withdrawal, the armoured *Kampfgruppe* that had captured Perlyavka was ordered to turn around and attack into the rear of those Russian units attacking Troyanov. During the course of the day, the division reported knocking out six Soviet tanks. The clearer weather had seen an increase in air operations on both sides, with German bombers and dive bombers supporting the *Korps'* defensive fighting, and Soviet fighters appearing in groups of anything up to 40 aircraft. As the day came to an end, the Russians renewed their offensive pressure, and at 16.30 hours, they launched a co-ordinated assault against the left wing of the *XXXXVIII.PzK*, striking it with strong infantry and armoured forces on a broad front. The fighting carried on into the night.

The *XIII.AK* meanwhile had conducted its fighting withdrawal with the support of the *7.Panzer-Division*, and had reached a line either side of the river Teterev from Troyanov through Denishi to Ul'yanovka.[90] The *Korps'* mobile units, the *8.Panzer-Division* and the *SS Panzerkampfgruppe 'Das Reich'*, had for the moment taken up positions further west to try and protect the deep left flank of the withdrawal. By the end of the day, they were engaged in the area around Vila[91] and Tartak trying to see off Soviet armoured attacks from the north. The *19.Panzer-Division* was still pulling back behind the *Korps* left wing, and by evening it was assembling in the Vysokaya Pech' area. The overall withdrawal had gone quite smoothly, and with the exception of the single breach in the sector held by the *68.Infanterie-Division* north of Troyanov, the *Korps* had managed to beat off all the attacks made by the pursuing Soviet forces. At 19.00 hours,

---

87 Referred to as Ozeryanka on more recent Soviet maps.
88 Gruska is no longer shown on more recent Soviet maps. It lay west of the Gnilopyat' about two kilometres north of Zheleznyaki.
89 Referred to as Zalizny on more recent Soviet maps. It was located on both sides of the Gnilopyat' just upstream from Golovenka in the large bend in the river.
90 *PzAOK 4*, Ia Tagesmeldung an *Heeresgruppe Süd*, 22.00 hours dated 1 Jan 44.
91 Vila is not marked on all maps, but it was situated at the top end of the lake north-west of Tartak.

von Hammerstein-Gesmold, the chief of staff, reported in to confirm that the *Korps* had now taken up its new positions on the Troyanov-Ul'yanovka line, and to advise the *Panzerarmee* of the Soviet breach in Zaliznya, north of Troyanov.[92] As a result of this penetration, the *Korps* requested permission to pull back further to a line running from Rudnya Gorodishche to Vila. Raus agreed and issued orders accordingly.[93] At the same time, the *XXXXVIII.PzK* was instructed to pull back its left wing to maintain contact with the *XIII.AK*. At 22.30 hours, Hauffe reported back to the *PzAOK 4* that, despite the exhaustion of his men and the superior strength of the Soviet forces, he had managed to get most of his troops out of Zhitomir with the help of the *XXXXVIII. PzK*.[94] The supply and support troops had also played their part in the withdrawal, helping to delay the Soviet armour advancing against the left flank, despite suffering significant losses. Despite defending the city as late as the previous evening, the *68., 340.* and *208.Infanterie-Divisions* had succeeded in conducting a fighting withdrawal back to the Troyanov-Denishi line, sometimes in heaving fighting with the pursuing Russian forces. Contact had been established with the *XXXXVIII.PzK* on the right wing, while over on the left the *Korps* had been able to beat off Soviet tank attacks against the Korchevka[95]-Ul'yanovka sector. The deep left flank in this area was held by the *Kampfgruppe* Frölich, comprising the *8.Panzer-Division* and the *SS Panzerkampfgruppe 'Das Reich'*, screening a line from Karvinovka in the south to Vysokaya Pech'. Despite its position, the *Kampfgruppe* had already been involved in the fighting, and had been obliged to defend against advancing Russian armour. Further west, Soviet tanks were also seen striking south-westwards from the area around Tartak, and up to four tanks had been spotted as far south of Siryaki and Serbinovka.[96] There had even been reports of Russian tank fire on the northern outskirts of Chudnov. Hauffe intended to move the *19.Panzer-Division* to bolster the defence of the town, but apart from that he now planned to try and hold his new defensive positions.

Over 60 kilometres away to the north-west, a new front had opened when advancing Russian troops closed in on Novograd-Volynskii from all sides and captured the railway station on the western edge of the town.[97] *Generalleutnant* Otto Matterstock, commanding officer of the *147.Reserve-Division*, had recently been appointed as the town's *Kampfkommandant* and was now responsible for its defence. At about 17.30 hours, he reported that the town was largely encircled by Soviet forces and all the main roads leading out had already been blocked by Russian tanks, including about 30 on the road west to Rovno.[98] The Soviet troops that had captured the railway station had then forced their way into the town, and the whole area lay under artillery fire. Fangohr discussed the matter with Raus, and the two of them agreed that the loss of Novograd-Volynskii would cause great difficulty for the *LIX.AK* as it tried to pull back. They therefore discussed the possibility of relieving the town, and in this respect they saw only two options. The first of these was to use the forces already available, and the second was to use the

---

92 *PzAOK 4*, Ia Kriegstagebuch entry dated 1 Jan 44.
93 *PzAOK 4*, Ia Nr. 18/44 geh. dated 1 Jan 44.
94 *XIII.AK*, unreferenced Funkspruch, 22.30 hours dated 1 Jan 44.
95 Referred to as Pokostovka on more recent Soviet maps.
96 Referred to as Yagodinka and Budichany respectively on more recent Soviet maps.
97 *PzAOK 4*, Ia Tagesmeldung an *Heeresgruppe Süd*, 22.00 hours dated 1 Jan 44.
98 *PzAOK 4*, Ia Kriegstagebuch entry dated 1 Jan 44.

newly-arriving *16.Panzer-Division*. They ruled out the latter option as the division had not yet fully assembled, and in any event it would probably need to be committed on a different sector where the situation was even more serious. They also considered using the *7.Panzer-Division*, but did not believe it was strong enough for the proposed task, a view also held by Balck at the *XXXXVIII.PzK*. There were other considerations too. The *Panzerarmee* needed to concentrate its main effort in the Kazatin-Berdichev area where Soviet preparations for a renewed assault had been observed, and there was also the question of the intentions and whereabouts of the recently arrived Russian motorised columns in the Zhitomir area. These may have been nothing more than supply columns, but equally they may have been fresh combat units being moved up. In the end, Fangohr suggested a compromise. He proposed that the *7.Panzer-Division* might initially be pulled out of the front and sent westwards to advance to the north from Dzerzhinsk as far as the main crossroads at Ludvikovka.[99] From there, it would send out reconnaissance patrols to the north-west in the general direction of Novograd-Volynskii, while also reconnoitring the roads to the south in case it had to transfer quickly to the Berdichev area. Raus agreed, and cleared the proposal with Army Group South which stressed that although Novograd-Volynskii was still to be held, the *PzAOK 4* was nevertheless to keep its main effort in the Berdichev-Kazatin area. Orders were issued later that day.[100] These instructed Balck to relieve the *7.Panzer-Division* and transfer it through Chudnov to the Dzerzhinsk-Stolbov-Romanovka area, where it was to begin reconnaissance north of the Ludvikovka-Baranovka line. To ensure it could be transferred quickly to support the fighting south of Kazatin, it was also to reconnoitre to the south to check the situation on the major routes.

Matterstock spoke again with Raus and Fangohr later that evening, advising them that the situation was growing more serious with more Soviet reinforcements arriving all the time. He did not believe that the *LIX.AK* would now be able to fight its way back to Novograd-Volynskii, but would instead be pushed away westwards north of the town. Raus was not yet convinced, and preferred to wait for a couple of days to see how the situation developed. He therefore issued instructions that the town was to be held at least until the end of the following day,[101] although he did suggest that Matterstock may receive some assistance from forces to the south-west of his position.

The *LIX.AK* was meanwhile still more than 50 kilometres away to the north-east, trying to fight its way back towards Novograd-Volynskii. Generally, the Soviets had not pressed the *Korps* too hard, although the fighting had been quite heavy on the Bondarevka sector.[102] In the rear, the *Korps* mobile group was south of Emil'chino and had been attacked by Russian armour in Kuliki. The attack had been beaten back and two Russian tanks were reported as destroyed. The isolation of the *Korps* now meant that it needed supplies from the air, and the day saw the Luftwaffe making the first re-supply drop. At 10.55 hours, the *PzAOK 4* sent a message to von der Chevallerie, advising him that Zhitomir had been given up and that the northern wing of the *XIII.AK* would be in the Ul'yanovka-Novy Zavod area.[103] The note also informed him though that 36

---

99 Referred to as Zaluzhnoe on more recent Soviet maps.
100 *PzAOK 4*, Ia Nr. 20/44 geh. dated 1 Jan 44.
101 *PzAOK 4*, Ia Nr. 19/44 geh. dated 1 Jan 44.
102 *PzAOK 4*, Ia Tagesmeldung an *Heeresgruppe Süd*, 22.00 hours dated 1 Jan 44.
103 Unreferenced note, 10.55 hours dated 1 Jan 44.

Soviet tanks had already been observed near Novy Zavod heading north-westwards, and that the Zhitomir-Novograd-Volynskii road had already been blocked by Russian troops south of Sokolov.

Meanwhile, reinforcements continued to arrive.[104] Eight of nine trains carrying the *SS Sturm-Brigade 'Langemarck'* had now arrived, with the last train close behind. Ten out of eleven trains with the *I./Panzer-Regiment 2* had also arrived, with the final train due soon. Eighteen trains of the *16.Panzer-Division* had arrived, and sixteen of the *4.Gebirgs-Division*, with a further ten underway. Ten trains carrying the *17.Panzer-Division* had already arrived and another three were on their way, including 13 *Panzer VI 'Tiger'* from the *s.Panzer-Abteilung 506*. The first train carrying the *6.Panzer-Division* had also arrived, and as far as the *PzAOK 4* knew, this was carrying 26 *Panzer IVs* belonging to the *Panzer-Regiment 11*. With the *16.Panzer-Division* beginning to arrive in strength, the *4.Panzerarmee* issued instructions for its deployment.[105] The order began by setting out the current situation, stating that the Soviets had succeeded in taking Zhitomir and were advancing north-west along the road to Novograd-Volynskii, while other forces were advancing south-westwards from the Korosten' area.[106] Faced with this situation, the *16.Panzer-Division* was ordered to assemble in the area either side of the Berdichev-Shepetovka railway line, with its forward elements around Polonnoe. Those elements which had already unloaded east of Polonnoe were to be pulled back. It was to be responsible for its own security while de-training, and was to establish a screen to the east and north-east running along the river Sluch', from Lyubar in the south through Miropol' and Vil'kha, and then bending back to Dubrovka. From that forward position, the division was to conduct aggressive reconnaissance as far east and north as a line running from Godykha through Stary Maidan and a point west of Kurnoe to Novograd-Volynskii. The important thing was to prevent a surprise attack by the Russians into the division's assembly area. The *I./Panzer-Regiment 2* was to remain with the division for the time being, and those elements already in Ivanopol' were to be moved back to Polonnoe. In terms of other potential reinforcements available to the *4.Panzerarmee* at this time, there were also a number of units of lower combat value in the region, comprising Hungarian troops employed mainly on railway security and reserve units on training duties.[107] While looking out for potential reinforcements for itself, the *PzAOK 4*

---

104 *PzAOK 4*, 'Stand der Bewegungen am 1.Januar 1944, 16 Uhr'.
105 *PzAOK 4*, Ia Nr. 1/44 geh. dated 1 Jan 44.
106 The order identified the 6th Guards Tank Corps south of Zhitomir, the 9th Mechanised Corps east of the town, and the 5th Guards and elements of the 7th Guards Tank Corps to the north. These mobile units were supported by infantry forces from the 18th and 1st Guards Armies, together with elements of the 60th Army. The 13th Army was identified in the Korosten' area, where it was supported by the 4th Guards Tank Corps. The 25th Tank Corps was meanwhile attempting to cut of the retreating *LIX.AK* from the south.
107 *PzAOK 4*, Ia Nr. 7044/43 geh. dated 1 Jan 44. According to this report, the following troops were deployed east of a general line running from Bar in the south through Proskurov and Shepetovka to Novograd-Volynskii:
Kampfkommandant Zwiahel:
- HQ *147.Reserve-Division*
- HQ *Reserve-Regiment 268* with its regimental troops
- *Reserve-Grenadier-Bataillon 488*
- *Reserve-Grenadier-Bataillon 27*
- *Reserve-Pionier-Bataillon 27*

was also concerned with the possibility that the recently abandoned areas might prove a fertile ground for recruiting into the advancing Red Army. Orders were therefore issued to all the subordinate *Korps* commanders to evacuate all men capable of bearing arms found within the combat zone up to 30 kilometres behind the front line.[108] The order applied to all men between the ages of 15 and 65, and those affected were to be handled and processed as normal prisoners of war.

Overall, the day had seen the Soviets maintaining their offensive pressure on the different sectors on the *4.Panzerarmee* front. They had pressed ahead with their attempts to bypass the southern wing of the *VII.AK*, and, although they had met with little success in actually pushing back the German defences, they had continued to push hard either side of Belaya Tserkov'. Troop transfers opposite the sector held by the *75.Infanterie-Division* also seemed to indicate that additional forces would be fed in to reinforce the penetration achieved near Losyatin. Between the *VII.AK* and the *XXIV.PzK*, the Russians had advanced with infantry forces as far as the line of the rivers Ros' and Ros'ka between Volodarka and Kashperovka, where German intelligence estimated that at least three Soviet rifle divisions were currently in the general area between Volodarka, Kashperovka and Pogrebishche. The concern at *PzAOK 4* headquarters was that these forces could now turn east or west to strike either the *VII.AK* or the *XXIV.PzK*. On the *XXIV.PzK* sector itself, strong Soviet armoured units tried again to break through the German defences either side of the railway between Kazatin and Kalinovka to the southwest, and the situation facing the *Korps* was now precarious, particularly as there was a shortage of infantry and anti-tank forces on the sector. Although the Soviet assaults against the *XXXXVIII.PzK* had been largely seen off, there now seemed to be a distinct possibility that the Russians were planning to try and encircle the German positions around Berdichev, especially as they appeared to be reinforcing the sector opposite the *Korps* right wing. On the other hand, the *XIII.AK* had managed to extricate all its units out of the encirclement of Zhitomir, and, other than a Russian breach north of Troyanov, had also succeeded in beating off all the attacks made against it. Nevertheless, weak Soviet armoured units had already advanced to the area west of Godykha, while others had been reported passing through Novy Zavod, although it was not known whether these were heading south or west. The *Korps* was therefore still in danger of being outflanked. The previous night, large motorised Soviet columns had been spotted by German aerial reconnaissance heading towards Zhitomir from Kiev, and although these had not appeared at the front during the day, it did suggest that the Russians were

---

- I./Hungarian Infantry Regiment 42 (deployed along the Shepetovka-Novograd-Volynskii railway)

Kampfkommandant Shepetovka:
- HQ Hungarian 21st Infantry Division
- HQ Hungarian Infantry Regiment 42
- II./Hungarian Infantry Regiment 42 (deployed along the Shepetovka-Polonnoe railway)
- 23rd Hungarian Hussar Squadron

Kampfkommandant Polonnoe:
- II./ Hungarian Infantry Regiment 40 (deployed along the Polonnoe-Miropol' railway)

Kampfkommandant Proskurov:
- HQ Hungarian Infantry Regiment 44

Kampfkommandant Staro Konstantinov:
- HQ 201st Hungarian Infantry Division

108 III./ Hungarian Infantry Regiment 44 (deployed along the Proskurov-Zhmerinka railway). *PzAOK 4*, O.Qu./Qu.2 Nr. 1/44 geh. dated 1 Jan 44.

bringing up fresh mobile forces from the 1st Ukrainian Front reserves.[109] These vehicles seemed to be concentrating in the Zhitomir area for the time being and, although it seemed likely that they would soon be moving through Zhitomir to the west towards Novy Zavod, the *PzAOK 4* was unable to ascertain whether the Russians intended to use these to reinforce the drive to the south-west on the left wing of the *XIII.AK*, or whether they might be planning to use them to drive further west. Away to the north-west, Soviet forces estimated to be one or two rifle divisions were advancing on Novograd-Volynskii from the south-east and had reached a point about 25 kilometres from the town. Meanwhile, other Russian forces including about 30 tanks had advanced on the town from the north-east, and surrounded it deep in the rear of the retreating *LIX.AK*.

In response to this situation, the *PzAOK 4* intended to seek approval from Army Group South to pull back the *XXXXII.AK* and *VII.AK* to the '*Siegfriedstellung*' to free up two divisions for operations on the hanging west flank of the *VII.AK*. It also planned to continue the reconnaissance activities by the *17.Panzer-Division* and the *4.Gebirgs-Division* to gain a clearer picture of Soviet activities in the main gap. Further north, the left wing of the *XXXXVIII.PzK* was to be pulled back to Rudnya Gorodishche, while the *XIII.AK* was to withdraw to a line from Rudnya Gorodishche through Vysokaya Pech' to Vila, screening its open left flank with mobile troops. The *7.Panzer-Division* was meanwhile to be pulled out of the front and transferred westwards to the Stolbov-Dzerzhinsk-Romanovka area at the disposal of the *Panzerarmee*.

---

109 *PzAOK 4*, Ic Abendmeldung an *Heeresgruppe Süd*, 19.00 hours dated 1 Jan 44. According to this report, Soviet casualties and losses for the month of December 1943 included:
- 6,694 prisoners, including 59 deserters
- 11,707 counted dead
- 10,615 estimated dead
- 828 tanks destroyed
- 11 tanks immobilised
- 267 artillery pieces
- 23 rocket launchers
- 887 anti-tank guns.

Part III
The Arrival of the *1.Panzerarmee*

7

Hube Assumes Command

Sunday 2 January 1944

It was 19.45 hours on the evening of 2 January when von Manstein at Army Group South issued formal orders to *General der Panzertruppen* Hans-Valentin Hube, commanding officer of the *1.Panzerarmee*, instructing him to move his headquarters to the area previously held by the right wing of the *PzAOK 4*.[1] The order directed him to take command of the *XXXXII.AK* and the *VII.AK*, as well as the *17.Panzer-Division* and a few miscellaneous forces assembling in the Tsybulev area. The order was to take effect at 21.00 hours that evening, and effectively gave Hube control of seven divisions, these being the *Korps-Abteilung B*, the *34.* and *82.Infanterie-Divisions* under the *XXXXII.AK*, the *75.*, *198.*, and *88.Infanterie-Divisions* under the *VII.AK*, and the *17.Panzer-Division* assembling in the rear.

In anticipation of the formal order, Hube had already begun to move his staff earlier that day, setting off as early as 06.30 hours. It was still dark therefore when the first elements began their long journey under heavy skies and in thick fog, but despite the poor weather the majority of the *Führungsabteilung* managed to reach Uman' the same afternoon. They were led by Hube's chief of staff, *Generalmajor* Walter Wenck, and when they arrived they found much of the town in ruins following earlier bombing, and suitable accommodation proved difficult to find. Initially they had to be accommodated in cramped conditions until an understanding could be reached with the locally based units of the *Luftwaffe*. The men of the *I.Flak-Korps* and *Luftflotte 4* were apparently reluctant to accommodate their comrades, and it was only after Army Group South designated Hube as *Territorialbefehlshaber* in Uman' that the problem was solved, the *Panzerarmee* commander then having the necessary authority in the town.

Despite these initial difficulties, the *PzAOK 1* assumed command of the *XXXXII. AK*, the *VII.AK*, and the *III.PzK* (consisting at the time of the *6.* and *17.Panzer-Divisions*, with further forces in the process of being brought up) at 21.00 hours that evening. As Hube assumed responsibility for these forces, the northern front of his new sector remained quiet. Further west though, opposite the centre and left wing of the *VII.AK*, Soviet troops were concentrating their efforts to break through the *Korps* sector in an attempt to wheel back eastwards and roll up the front from the south. If successful, this manoeuvre would widen the existing gap to the *PzAOK 4* still further. In the actual area of the breach meanwhile, the *PzAOK 1* estimated that the Russians were continuing to push southwards with about five rifle divisions, supported by a few tanks, and by midday on 2 January, the lead elements of these troops had reached the line of the river Ros' between Fastovka and Kashperovka. Elsewhere, other Soviet forces had also pushed on, and a number of units had reached as far as the Kalinovka-Andrusovo railway line. On the basis of this intelligence, the *PzAOK 1* assumed that the Russians were

---

1 *H.Gr.Süd*, Ia Nr.18/44 dated 2 Jan 44.

still trying to pursue two separate objectives. First, to widen the penetration they had already achieved, either by continuing the attack against the *VII.AK* or by bypassing the *Korps'* southern flank towards the east and south-east, and second, to advance directly southwards into the breach. Hube was therefore faced with a number of immediate tasks, including continuing to hold his right wing, preventing any further widening of the existing breach, intercepting and stopping the Soviet advance in the area of the breach, and creating the necessary conditions for a counterattack.

His first order was issued later that evening, setting out the respective missions for the subordinate *Korps* headquarters, and giving them their first instructions.[2] The *XXXXII.AK* on the right wing was to maintain its current positions, whilst the *VII.AK* was to prevent any further enemy breakthroughs and seal off existing breaches. If Soviet pressure proved heavy enough though, it was permitted to fall back to a line running from Vasilevo through Yankovka, Ostriiki, Novo-Yanovka, Biryuki, and Cherkasy to Yezerno. This line, though, was to be held at all costs. In addition, the *Korps* was to begin reconnaissance in the area of its open southern flank as far as the river Ros'. Hell's left hand boundary line with the *III.PzK* was to run on the line Stavishche and Volodarka, with both placed in the latter's sector. Meanwhile, the newly-arriving *III.PzK*, under *General der Panzertruppen* Hermann Breith, was to clarify the situation in the area of the breakthrough by continuous reconnaissance, with the subsequent objective of bringing the advance to a halt, using a series of small-scale counter attacks with limited objectives. The *Korps* was also to secure the unloading and assembly areas designated for the arrival of the additional forces, and in that respect it was to prevent the Russians from crossing a line running through Yanishevka-Pyatigori-Novozhivotov-Medovka-Rososha-Vakhnovka. Since the *III.PzK* was not due to assume command of this sector until the following day, these orders were issued directly to the *6.* and *17.Panzer-Divisions*. The former was to reconnoitre the breach area as far as the line Volodarka-Kashperovka-Verbovka, and concentrate its forces that evening in the Tsybulev area, ready to begin offensive operations under the *III.PzK* on 4 January.[3] The *17.Panzer-Division* meanwhile was given similar instructions, and ordered to conduct limited counterattacks towards Chernyavka, against the right flank of the advancing Soviet forces. In addition, the division was to prevent the enemy from pushing over the Medovka-Rososha-Vakhnovka line, and push out reconnaissance as far as the limit allocated to the *6.Panzer-Division*.

Monday 3 January 1944

The night had passed fairly quietly in the *XXXXII.AK* sector.[4] A combat patrol sent out by the *Korps-Abteilung B* had overwhelmed a Soviet outpost in the bridgehead north-west of Dudari, killing three men and capturing a machine gun. The troop movements from the sector between Khodorov and Balyko-Shchuchinka area to the north-west, reported by the *Korps* the previous afternoon, had apparently continued since there had been continuous traffic noises throughout the night, and Mattenklott concluded that the Russians were withdrawing a number of infantry units from the front. On the *Korps'* northern front, there had been little combat activity, although the sector held by the

---

2   PzAOK 1, Ia Nr.1/44 g.Kdos dated 2 Jan 44.
3   As it arrived in Monastyrishche, the *6.Panzer-Division* deployed 21 operational *Panzer IVs* and 5 operational *Panzer IIIs*. See Wolfgang Paul, *Brennpunkte*, p.346.
4   XXXXII.AK., Morgenmeldung, 05.30 hours dated 3 Jan 44.

34.Infanterie-Division had been subjected to disruptive artillery fire. Reconnaissance patrols had also established that Staiki was still firmly held by Russian troops, and in doing so they had killed two men and captured a machine gun.

Things had been livelier on the *VII.AK* front, where, following a quiet night, the Russians had attacked the sector held by the *75.Infanterie-Division* with a force estimated to be a battalion.[5] The attack had come suddenly and had managed to break into the German positions north-west of Oleinikova Sloboda. The division instigated countermeasures, but the situation was still not settled at the time of the report. Further west, the Soviets had broken off their attacks against the left wing of the *198.Infanterie-Division*, and by morning there was only artillery fire being reported. Several barrages were reported by the *Grenadier-Regiment 323* in the area around Belaya Tserkov'. Despite this easing of pressure, the division had still managed to intercept and destroy a Russian patrol, but in general the front had remained quieter than hitherto. On the left wing of the *Korps* though, the *88.Infanterie-Division* had been involved in bitter street fighting in Ol'shanka. The fighting had lasted for several hours, but by the time it had all died down, the division had managed to master the situation and clear the town of enemy troops. The Russians were reported to have suffered heavy casualties, and the units which fell back were considered to be close to exhaustion.[6]

In the area of the breach on the left wing of the *1.Panzerarmee*, the two *Panzer-Divisions* were moving into position. Things had been quiet in the sector held by the *6.Panzer-Division*, where nothing of importance was reported at all,[7] whereas the *17.Panzer-Division* had made contact with advancing Soviet troops. During the night, the division's right wing had completed the move into its new positions without enemy interference, and by morning it held a line running from Ochitkov through Lyulintsy, Parievka, Ocheretnya and Zozov to the crossroads north-west of Zozovka and on to Britskoe.[8] However, whilst the Russians had remained relatively quiet on the right and in the centre, they had managed to bring up fresh troops into the northern and north-eastern parts of Zozov. In response, the division had undertaken a limited counterattack in the early hours of the morning, and succeeded in regaining the whole village.

The new day dawned much the same as the previous one, with dark cloudy skies, and temperatures hovering around the freezing mark. The thaw was continuing. There were a number of snow and rain showers throughout the course of the day, but for the time being the roads remained passable for wheeled vehicles. At 10.15 hours that morning, Hube issued instructions informing the three subordinate *Korps* headquarters of the new boundaries the *PzAOK 1* would share with its neighbours.[9] These would come into force with effect from midday the same day. On the right, the boundary with the *8.Armee* would run on the line Gaivoron-Uman'-Zhizhintsy-Ivanovka-Bobritsa-Piryatin, whilst on the left, the boundary with the *4.Panzerarmee* would run on the line Voronovitsa-Vakhnovka-Ruzhin-Pavoloch'. Meanwhile, as the fighting progressed, the situation on the hanging left flank of the *VII.AK* began to cause Hube real concern. The units deployed there, on the northern flank of the breach, had suffered considerable

---

5 *VII.AK.*, Morgenmeldung, 06.30 hours dated 3 Jan 44.
6 The 78th Rifle Regiment of the Soviet 74th Rifle Division was one of the units involved in this fighting.
7 *6.PzDiv.*, Morgenmeldung, 05.45 hours dated 3 Jan 44.
8 *17.PzDiv.*, Morgenmeldung, 05.10 hours dated 3 Jan 44.
9 *PzAOK 1*, Ia Nr.2/44 g.Kdos dated 3 Jan 44.

casualties over the past few days, and their strength was dwindling in the face of continued Soviet pressure. He therefore decided to pull the *34.Infanterie-Division* out of the *XXXXII.AK* sector, and transfer it south-west to the Tarashcha-Luka area where its immediate task would be to support the *VII.AK* hanging flank. In the longer term, the division was to be prepared to join with fresh, mobile reinforcements in a counterattack to destroy the Soviet forces between the left wing of the *VII.AK* and the *6.Panzer-Division* further west.[10] Hube issued the appropriate orders himself, using the radio just before midday. The division would pass to the *VII.AK* once radio contact had been established between the two commands, although in the meantime certain elements would be transferred to the new *Korps* almost immediately. These were formed into a small *Kampfgruppe* comprising the *I./Grenadier-Regiment 475* and the *Füsilier-Bataillon 34*, with the *II./Artillerie-Regiment 64* attached for support. Its immediate mission was to secure the *Korps'* deep flank on a line running from Potievka through Ostraya-Mogila and Yanyshevka to Stavishche. The rest of the division would then transfer in due course and assemble unhindered behind this screen. The *Kampfgruppe* would be returned to the control of the division once the staff were in place, scheduled to be by 12.00 hours on 4 January. In an effort to strengthen his position, Hube had also sought direct support from the *Flak* units deployed in the area, requesting the *I.Flak-Korps* to instruct the *10.Flak-Division*, currently arriving in the Tsybulev-Monastyrishche area, to work in close co-operation with the *6.Panzer-Division*.[11]

The fighting continued throughout the day in the *XXXXII.AK* sector on the northern wing, although no particular trouble was reported.[12] The Soviets had continued to move troops along the Khodorov-Shchuchinka road, apparently confirming the *Korps'* earlier impressions that a withdrawal was underway. To cover the movement, the Russians had even undertaken four distinct low-key assaults further north striking the *34.Infanterie-Division* on the Staiki-Verem'e sector. The largest of these had been undertaken by an estimated two companies, but all had been repulsed without great difficulty by troops in the forward positions. Nevertheless, it had been noted that towards evening the Soviets had begun to pull units into the sector south of Staiki. The *82.Infanterie-Division* had undertaken a limited counterattack during the course of the day, assaulting the Soviet positions between Chernyakhov and Germanovka. This small attack achieved a moderate success, with two companies breaking into the Russian defences about two kilometres north-west of the latter village, whilst another achieved a similar result four kilometres east of the village. The action brought in a total of 17 prisoners, 13 machine guns, and even a 45 mm anti-tank gun. The Russians were not about to pull back though, and a patrol sent out later in the day to occupy hill 190.0 just east of Germanovka established Soviet positions about 600 metres further north.

In the centre, the *VII.AK* had passed a day of mixed activity.[13] On its northern front, in the areas east of Belaya Tserkov' and north-east of Losyatin, Soviet forces had undertaken only two battalion-strength assaults all day. Both of these had gone in against

---

10 *PzAOK 1*,Ia Kriegstagebuch entry, dated 3 Jan 44. The *3.Panzer-Division* and the *Panzergrenadier-Division "Grossdeutschland"* were both earmarked as possible reinforcements for the *PzAOK 1* at this time.
11 *PzAOK 1*, Ia Nr.3/44 g.Kdos dated 3 Jan 44.
12 *XXXXII.AK*, Tagesmeldung, 18.00 hours dated 3 Jan 44.
13 *VII.AK*, Tagesmeldung, 19.30 hours dated 3 Jan 44.

the *198.Infanterie-Division* and made little progress, and by afternoon they had been discontinued. Further south though, against the left wing of the *Korps*, the Russians continued to attack in great strength on the Ol'shanka-Pertsovka sector.[14] There were seven separate regimental-size assaults against this sector during the course of the day, and some of these were supported by armoured units. Nevertheless, the *88.Infanterie-Division*, together with the attached *Grenadier-Regiment 417*, managed to hold its ground and see off the attacks, sometimes using small-scale local counterattacks. Over on the division's left wing there were other assaults, with the Russians making three battalion-size attacks out of Yezerno. These too were successfully thrown back, with elements of the division even following up the retreating Soviet troops and re-capturing the village itself. The *Grenadier-Regiment 417*, together with the *Sturmgeschütz-Abteilung 202* and the *Pionier-Bataillon 88*, received Hube's personal thanks for their efforts in these actions. Other Soviet troops were caught pushing forwards on the Rozhki-Potievka sector, and were intercepted in the eastern part of the latter village. All told, Hell's *VII.AK* reported for the day a total of 220 counted Soviet dead, 50 prisoners, seven T-34 tanks knocked out, and a quantity of other equipment destroyed or captured.

At 16.00 hours, over on the left wing of the *PzAOK 1*, Breith's *III.PzK* in Sarny assumed command of the 6. and *17.Panzer-Divisions* as instructed.[15] The *6.Panzer-Division*, with its headquarters based in Monastyrishche, had completed its assembly around Tsybulev and had begun reconnoitring to the north-west, the north, and the north-east. It had established that Soviet forces had not yet reached northern Skibino, Gorodishche, Krivchunka, Vysokoe, Stadnitsa, or Sitnivtsy, although there were Russian troops in the Oratov and Rostovka areas. At 10.15 hours that morning, the division had spotted a large Soviet column moving from Novozhivotov towards Oratov, containing about 1,200 infantry, which by the afternoon had occupied the latter town. The poor weather conditions had precluded any further reconnaissance effort. The *17.Panzer-Division* on the left had meanwhile set up headquarters in Gaisin and set about its assigned tasks. During the night a Soviet group had managed to infiltrate to a point about two kilometres west of Andrusovo station, west of Andrushevka, and the division's first job was to clear the penetration. It attacked the group and destroyed it, taking about 50 prisoners and leaving another 100 Russians dead on the battlefield. That completed, the division in turn had to defend against Soviet assaults from the Pliskov-Andrushevka area. The Russians, supported by between 20 and 25 tanks, succeeded in making a penetration south of Pliskov in about battalion strength before the division was able to restore the front line, reportedly destroying 14 of the attacking tanks. Towards the end of the day the division began another local offensive operation towards Kruglik, and this continued into the evening. All the while, the Soviets were reported to be reinforcing the areas south of Bulai and around Belyanki, including armoured units, and the *17.Panzer-Division* concluded that they must be concentrating on that sector. In addition, Soviet

---

14 *PzAOK 1* intelligence had picked up the presence of the 42nd Guards Rifle Division on the sector, together with support from an as yet unidentified armoured unit.
15 *III.PzK*, Tagesmeldung, 18.50 hours dated 3 Jan 44. According to the report, the *Korps* deployed the following operational armour:
  • *6.Panzer-Division*: 2 *PzIII lg*; 14 *PzIV lg*; 2 *Flammpanzer*
  • *17.Panzer-Division*: 2 *PzIII lg*; 5 *PzIV*
  • *Panzer-Abteilung 506*: 11 *PzVI*
  • *Sturmgeschütz-Abteilung 249*: 8 *StuG*

forces estimated to be a regiment had been observed moving out of the Skala-Chernyavka area heading south. In the evening the *III.PzK* received instructions from the *PzAOK 1*, advising it which *Heerestruppen* were to be assigned to its command.[16] These included the *s.Panzer-Abteilung 506 (Tiger)* and the *Sturmgeschütz-Abteilung 249*, both of which were already attached to the *17.Panzer-Division*, the *II./Artillerie-Regiment 67*, already attached to the *6.Panzer-Division*, and the *s.Artillerie-Abteilung 629 (Mörser)* which was still in the process of moving up. Also still in process of arriving was the *Werfer-Regiment 54*, with the *I.* and *II.Abteilungen*, the *I./Werfer-Regiment 52*, and a *Panzer-Werfer-Batterie* attached.

By this time, the picture was beginning to clear for Hube. On his right wing, the Soviets seemed to be pulling forces out of the front opposite the *XXXXII.AK*, as suggested by the continued troop movements from the Khodorov area to the north-west. There had, moreover, been little combat activity on that sector apart from a few reconnaissance probes. On the other hand, whilst there had been only limited attacks east of Belaya Tserkov', the southern flank of the *VII.AK* had been subjected to repeated fierce and heavy assaults. Ol'shanka had been attacked in strength with about 20 Soviet tanks in support, and a new division, tentatively identified as the 42nd Guards Rifle Division, had been observed in the Ol'shanka-Yezerno area.[17] Some troops had pushed on to reach Potievka, and intelligence suggested that they were heading for Severinovka and Rozhki. According to other reports, the Soviet 240th Rifle Division had already pressed on to reach Yanyshevka just north of Stavishche. Intercepted radio traffic meanwhile indicated that the Russians believed the German forces were in general retreat towards Zhashkov and Uman'. Reconnaissance had shown that Zhashkov, Stadnitsa and Golod'ki were all still free of Soviet troops, but further south-west the town of Oratov had been occupied since at least 13.00 hours, probably by the column of about 1,200 men seen earlier in the day. Rostovka had already been occupied by Russian forces, and a group of tanks which had appeared in Lyulintsy near Ochitkov had been engaged, resulting in the reported destruction of 14 of them. These were believed to be from an independent tank brigade, but this had not been confirmed.[18] Overall, it appeared as though the Soviets were stripping out their front opposite the army right wing, and Hube was expecting the attacks south of Belaya Tserkov' to continue pressing to the east and south-east. This continual pressure against the left wing and deep flank of the *VII.AK* was, not surprisingly, a source of great concern to the *PzAOK 1*, particularly since the units fighting there had lost much of their strength in the course of operations over the past few days. Hube was worried that, without outside assistance, these divisions might not be able to hold their own for much longer, and it was for this reason that he had ordered the *34.Infanterie-Division* to move to that sector. In connection with this shift, Hube decided to change the boundary between the two *Korps* commands involved.[19] The new line would run from Ol'shanitsa through Vintsentovka and Bendyugovka to Germanovka. Hube followed these orders

---

16 *PzAOK 1*, Ia Nr.4/44 geh., dated 3 Jan 44.
17 *PzAOK 1*, Ic Abendmeldung, 24.00 hours dated 3 Jan 44. The 42nd Guards Rifle Division had recently been released from the 1st Ukrainian Front's reserves, and had arrived south of Belaya Tserkov' the day before, having previously been deployed on the Kiev-Zhitomir road.
18 *PzAOK 1* intelligence thought these might belong to the 3rd Guards Tank Corps, but was not sure. This was in any case impossible, as the corps was still held in the *Stavka* reserve at the time.
19 *PzAOK 1*, Ia Nr.5/44 geh., dated 3 Jan 44.

with his main instructions for the following day.[20] The *PzAOK 1* was still hoping to receive additional mobile units to assist the *Panzer-Divisions* in the area of the main breach, but in the meantime, the tasks for the three *Generalkommandos* were as follows. The *XXXXII.AK* retained the same basic mission as before, although now it also had to complete the withdrawal of the *34.Infanterie-Division* by 5 January at the latest. The division was to be assembled in the Tarashcha-Luka area at the disposal of the *Armee*. The *VII.AK* also kept its previous basic task, and in addition it was now to screen its open southern flank with the newly arriving *Kampfgruppe* from the *34.Infanterie-Division*. This *Kampfgruppe* was to come under the direct control of the *Korps* headquarters and was to protect the assembly of the rest of the division when it followed along. The *III. PzK* was likewise to carry on with its existing mission, although the *6.Panzer-Division* was to complete the destruction of the Soviet grouping around Oratov and Rostovka the following day. This was particularly important since the group was now threatening the railway line north-west of Uman', an essential part of the supply line on the left wing of the *PzAOK 1*. Following this, the division was also to prepare for an attack northwards on 5 January. In addition, Breith was instructed to undertake reconnaissance further east on the Bashtechki-Okhmatov-Yatskovitsa-Knyazh'ya Krinitsa sector, to establish the conditions of the roads and crossing points over the Gorny Tikich river, as the area was being considered for a possible assembly and jump off area for the mobile reinforcements still expected.

Later that evening, Hube received word from Army Group South that the *96.* and *254.Infanterie-Divisions* had been released from Army Group North for employment in the Ukraine.[21] The divisions would begin their long moves southwards on 6 January and assemble in the Shepetovka area under the *4.Panzerarmee*. Shortly afterwards, the *PzAOK 1* also learned of additional reinforcements on their way, this time from the *Luftwaffe*. In response to Hube's earlier request, the *Luftflotte 4* had instructed the *10.Flak-Division*, then assembling in the area north-west of Uman', to co-operate closely with the *Panzerarmee*.[22] The division would be ready for operations on 7 January and the only stipulation placed upon its employment was that it should be deployed as a complete unit rather than be split up piecemeal. To complete the good news regarding reinforcements, Hube received another message from Army Group South regarding the *3.Panzer-Division*.[23] The division had begun its withdrawal from the front line earlier that evening, and the main body would soon be moved by the *8.Armee* by road through Novomirgorod and Yampol' to Tsybulev. Those elements required more urgently would be transported by rail and the *PzAOK 1* would be responsible for the division once it passed Yampol'. Hube was reminded that the *Panzergrenadier-Division 'Grossdeutschland'* was also on the move, and that this had been assigned to the main through route, the *DG IV*. Although co-ordinating the arriving reinforcements might prove complex, Hube at least knew that he could expect his command to grow considerably in strength over the coming days. Events were conspiring against him however, and although he could not know it, he was destined to make do with what he had.

---

20 *PzAOK 1*, Ia Nr.4/44 g.Kdos dated 3 Jan 44.
21 Hgr. Süd, Ia Nr.28/44 g.Kdos dated 3 Jan 44.
22 *Lfl.Kdo 4 Führ.Abt.*, Ia Nr.22/44 g.Kdos dated 3 Jan 44.
23 Hgr. Süd, Ia Nr.37/44 g.Kdos dated 3 Jan 44.

Tuesday 4 January 1944

The night passed in much the same way as previous nights had.[24] On the northern wing, the *XXXXII.AK* had been subjected to the usual disruptive artillery and mortar fire, although a German patrol from the *82.Infanterie-Division* had also taken small arms fire from the Soviet positions three kilometres east of Germanovka. There was no other combat activity though, and the *Korps* was able to concentrate on continuing the relief of the *34.Infanterie-Division*. The relief itself was being hampered by the poor state of the roads, but both the *Regimentsgruppe 677* and the *Füsilier-Bataillon 34* had left the *Korps* area by morning and had passed from under its command. The Russians had proved just as quiet to the south-west where the *VII.AK* had met with no serious problems during the night whilst falling back to its new positions. Meanwhile, over on the left wing of the *Panzerarmee*, the *III.PzK* pressed ahead with its reconnaissance tasks. The *6.Panzer-Division* had reported Sitnivtsy to be clear of Russian forces the previous evening, although rifle and machine-gun fire had been heard further south-west in the vicinity of Gonoratka. There were also unconfirmed reports that Zhashkov had now been occupied by Soviet troops, numbering about 300 men and three tanks. Further west, elements of the *17.Panzer-Division* had meanwhile reported Ochitkov to be occupied by enemy troops, whilst contact had been made with infiltrating Soviet units in the north-eastern part of Lyulintsy. This followed a similar action earlier in the night when the division encountered a Soviet group which had forced its way into Ocheretnya. This had initially been driven back, but the Russians had attacked again at about 23.00 hours, forcing another penetration. The division mounted another counterattack and surrounded the assaulting forces, cutting them off from their lines of communication. Further west, the Russians pressed on with their advance, mounting a two-company assault against Britskoe, and pushing the Germans back to the southern edge of the village. Apart from noticing the presence of strong artillery and anti-tank forces in the area west of Belaya[25] though, the *Korps'* picture of enemy intentions remained unchanged. Later that morning, at 09.45 hours, the *PzAOK 1* issued orders attaching the newly allocated *10.Flak-Division* to Breith's *III.PzK*, advising the *Korps* commander that the unit was still assembling north of Uman' and would not be ready for operations until 7 January. The order also made it clear that any proposal to commit any of its units before the whole division was assembled would require the prior approval of the *Armee*.[26]

When the new day broke, the weather had shown signs of clearing, and although temperatures remained about the same, the morning proved to be a little brighter than previous days. It was not to last though, and the cloud returned as the day wore on, and the roads in general stayed icy. Over on the right wing, the *XXXXII.AK* had been subjected to a couple of assaults.[27] Although the *Korps-Abteilung B* on the extreme right, and anchored on the river Dnepr, had escaped unscathed, Russian forces had attacked the positions of the *82.Infanterie-Division* on the *Korps'* left wing. An estimated 400-600 Russian troops had pushed forwards, forcing their way as far as the defensive line south-east of Germanovka, obliging the forward troops to fall back onto the main defensive positions. Things were no easier on the southern wing where forward elements of the

---

24 *PzAOK 1*, Summary of Morgenmeldungen, 05.00 hours dated 4 Jan 44.
25 Referred to as Bila in the German records.
26 *PzAOK 1*, Ia Nr.5/44 g.Kdos dated 4 Jan 44.
27 *XXXXII.AK*, Tagesmeldung, 19.25 hours dated 4 Jan 44.

34.Infanterie-Division reported contact with advancing Soviet troops in the Tarashcha area. These units had already taken Lesovichi with the support of between 15 and 20 tanks, so the division decided against leaving troops in the Luka area, and chose instead to assemble the entire force in the Tarashcha-Ol'shanitsa area. Mattenklott, the *Korps* commander, now considered that the Soviets would drive directly eastwards towards Boguslav on the river Ros', straight in the *Korps* rear area. Indeed, Hube received a disturbing message from the *XXXXII.AK* later that afternoon, stating that a supply column had been overrun by three Russian tanks at Malaya Berezyanka about 12 kilometres south of Tarashcha. The column had been dispersed as the tanks headed off eastwards, seemingly confirming the Soviet intention to strike into the deep flank of the *VII.AK*. This was also confirmed by events on the *VII.AK* sector itself where 30 Soviet tanks were reported in the south-western part of Tarashcha.[28] These had been engaged and fighting continued into the evening. Elsewhere the *Korps* was still attacking and succeeded in regaining Potievka and Chupira, whilst Chernin and Lesovichi were now occupied by Soviet troops. Later that evening the *Korps* commander, Hell, informed *PzAOK 1* that the Soviet troops opposite Potievka had now moved off, bypassing the town and heading off to the south-east. Meanwhile, fresh Russian units had been identified in Tarashcha as the next elements of the *34.Infanterie-Division* just completed their unloading in Ol'shanitsa about 15 kilometres further north-east.

On the *Panzerarmee* left, the *III.PzK* had mixed fortunes.[29] It had been unable to prevent the Soviet advance to the south-east, and was aware that a major Russian force, involving about 500 motor vehicles and between 10 and 15 tanks, had moved off from the Volodarka area into the gap between it and the *VII.AK* to the right. By evening, this grouping had advanced some 40 kilometres, passing to the south-east of Zhashkov to reach a line running from Bagva through Mariika to Litvinovka. Nevertheless, the *6.Panzer-Division* further west had managed to complete its local operation against the Soviet group in the Oratovka-Oratov area. Using a *Panzerkampfgruppe*, it had fought its way north-westwards from Sabarovka through Oratovka, destroying the Russian troops there, before pushing on into Oratov to meet up with another *Kampfgruppe* which had moved up from the south. The division believed it had destroyed the major part of two Soviet rifle battalions in the action, and captured much equipment. Further to the north-east though, the Soviets had occupied Pyatigori, Nenadikha, Denikhovka, Dubina, and the *Sovkhoz* Dorotka, and to complicate matters further, the area directly to the south of these villages was now under the partial control of local partisan forces. The *6.Panzer-Division* therefore achieved some little success on the day, but the *17.Panzer-Division* to its left had been less fortunate. A *Kampfgruppe* from the division had attempted to destroy a group of Soviet forces around Velikaya Rostovka, but had made little progress in the face of determined defensive fire, particularly flanking fire from the wooded area east of Mervin. The division had been obliged to break off the attack after reaching hill 291.1, and then, after destroying a ski column on the road east of Mervin, it had to pull back to its starting positions around Oratov station. To the north-west, at 15.00 hours, the Soviets had attacked, moving against Parievka from Andrushevka, deploying an estimated battalion supported by about 15 tanks. The assault had been driven back, leaving the division still holding the northern edge of the village having knocked out at

---

28   *PzAOK 1*, Tagesmeldung an *Heeresgruppe Süd*, 21.35 hours dated 4 Jan 44.
29   *III.PzK*, Tagesmeldung, 19.15 hours dated 4 Jan 44.

least six of the attacking tanks, and possibly a further two. Two hours later the Russians attacked again, this time against Andrusovo station, north-east of Ocheretnya, but with only five tanks in support. Fighting continued into the evening. Elsewhere on the front, some nine kilometres away to the south-east, Soviet troops had also occupied Kozhanka and were beginning to probe out to the west, threatening the division's positions around Andrushevka. The centre of its sector had also been subjected to a number of attacks, and south of Ocheretnya elements of the division had been forced to pull back to the high ground around Napadovka. Despite the difficulty of their respective positions though, both the *6.* and the *17.Panzer-Divisions* were on the offensive by evening; the former towards Zhashkov, and the latter towards Rostovka.[30]

On the northern wing of the *1.Panzerarmee* then, the day had again passed without serious incident, whilst the Soviets concentrated their effort in bypassing the southern flank of the *VII.AK* to strike deep into the *Korps'* rear area. They had nevertheless tried to break through the right wing of the *VII.AK* too, in what seemed to be an attempt to encircle Belaya Tserkov', but all the attacks on this sector had been unsuccessful. South of the town, Russian troops were advancing north-eastwards from Ol'shanka towards Shkarovka behind Belaya Tserkov', and seemed to showing signs of success.[31] The Soviets had been forced out of Potievka, but had simply bypassed the town to advance through Chernin and the woods to the east to reach Ulashevka on the western outskirts of Tarashcha. The leading elements of these had pushed on to cross the main Tarashcha-Belaya Tserkov' road just north of the town. To the south another group had struck out from Rozhki to seize Vladimirovka and Lesovichi where two Russian battalions were thought to be operating, while about 30 tanks had already attacked the south-western edge of Tarashcha, forcing the weak German covering force back into the town. Further south, Malaya Berezyanka had already been occupied, with three tanks being seen in the village in the early afternoon, and groups moving out of Stavishche had already captured Zhuravlikha and Geisikha. Further south again, Soviet forces had now spread out in a wide arc south of Zhashkov, occupying Razumnitsa, Teterevka, Mariika, Ol'shanka and Zhitniki. Behind these leading elements, the results of aerial reconnaissance had again showed substantial Soviet forces moving into the area of the breach, including this time an estimated 500-700 horse-drawn and motor vehicles and 30-50 tanks, all heading towards the Zhashkov area. The *PzAOK 1* concluded that this column represented either one or maybe even two major mobile units. The earlier indications that the Russians were trying to outflank the left wing of the *VII.AK* were growing clearer as they pressed eastward towards Tarashcha with strong armour support. To date, the 42nd Guards and the 240th Rifle Divisions had already identified on this sector, and it now appeared as if elements of the 163rd Rifle Division had also arrived in the Chupira area. The identity of the armoured unit was not yet clear. Away to the west, an enemy rifle regiment had been badly disrupted and several anti-tank guns captured north of Oratov, while to the west other Soviet troops, thought to be from the 211th Rifle Division, were advancing southwards from Rostovka towards Oratov station. On the left wing, about 20 Soviet tanks had been seen in Andrushevka, of which ten had already pushed forwards into Parievka. Here too the Russians were increasing the pressure and deploying additional

---

30 *III.PzK*, Ia Nr.12/44 g.Kdos dated 4 Jan 44.
31 *PzAOK 1*, Ic Abendmeldung, 24.00 hours dated 4 Jan 44.

armour, with the 40th Guards Tank Brigade from the 11th Guards Tank Corps being identified on the sector.

The Soviet advance on the left wing of the *VII.AK* was now critical for Hube as his intended screening force, the *34.Infanterie-Division*, was still a long time from completing its re-assembly following its relief from the *XXXXII.AK*. Moreover, the *PzAOK 1* fully expected the Soviet advance to continue on both fronts; that is, southwards towards Uman', and south-eastwards towards Tarashcha and on to Zvenigorodka. Such an advance would paralyse the lines of supply and communication in its right-hand sector, and consequently Hube authorised Hell to pull back the left wing of the *VII.AK* to the line Vasilevo-Ostriiki-Tomilovka-Yezerno, thus giving up the town of Belaya Tserkov'. Over the course of a number of telephone conversations with the *Korps* commanders, both Wenck and his *Ia* emphasised this appraisal of Soviet intentions and stressed the importance of assembling the *34.Infanterie-Division* as quickly as possible. Hube issued his orders for the following day at 19.20 hours that evening.[32] According to these, the *XXXXII.AK* was to accelerate the movement of the *34.Infanterie-Division* to the Tarashcha area, and in addition it was to assign all its anti-tank means to the division. The number of weapons involved was to be reported back to the *Armee*. The *VII.AK* retained its existing mission, although the *34.Infanterie-Division* was now formally transferred to the *Korps*, which was to ensure that it was assembled as quickly as possible.[33] The *III.PzK* was to continue with its attacks. The *6.Panzer-Division* was to advance in the general direction of Zhashkov, with the objective of destroying the Soviet forces deployed south of the town. This would have the effect of delaying, for a time at least, the Soviet advance towards Uman'. The *17.Panzer-Division* meanwhile was to wipe out the Russian grouping in the Rostovka area and then cover the sector further west with a view to re-establishing contact with the right wing of the *4.Panzerarmee*.

The *PzAOK 1* also advised the *III.PzK* that the *10.Flak-Division*, then assembling in the *Korps* area, had been ordered to co-operate directly with the *Generalkommando*.[34] Hube had authorised the division to be deployed with the *6.Panzer-Division*, although this did not stretch to using the *Flak* troops in the forthcoming attack. However, the news from Army Group South in respect of other reinforcements was not good. Hube was not now going to receive the *3.Panzer-Division* as had been promised earlier, as the situation in the *8.Armee* sector had deteriorated considerably following the Soviet offensive in the Kirovograd area. Wenck made repeated efforts to try and convince the Army Group that the threat posed by the Soviet forces between the *VII.AK* and the *III.PzK* was such that the *1.Panzerarmee* would need an additional major mobile unit over and above the only one now remaining, the *Panzergrenadier-Division 'Grossdeutschland'*. To make matters worse, the results of aerial reconnaissance had indicated that the *17.Panzer-Division* on the left wing of the *Panzerarmee* could also be expected to be subjected to numerous strong and tank-supported assaults within the next few days. The Army Group chief of staff, Busse, replied that both he and von Manstein were fully aware of the problems, but the situation around Kirovograd necessitated the *3.Panzer-Division* staying where it was. Wenck's only response was that the primary task of the *PzAOK 1*, that of driving into the

---

32 *PzAOK 1*, Ia Nr.5/44 g.Kdos dated 4 Jan 44.
33 In this respect, the *XXXXII.AK* chief of staff, *Oberst* Gerhard Franz, believed that if the requisite rail and road transport means were made available, the division could complete its transfer by 5 January.
34 *PzAOK 1*, Ia Nr.9/44 geh. dated 4 Jan 44.

flank of the Soviet forces attacking the *4.Panzerarmee* to the west, would be questionable under such circumstances. The *1.Panzerarmee* would be forced to limit itself to defending its current positions and hope thereby to hold up any further Russian advance. When Hube submitted his evening report to von Manstein, he again emphasised the strength of the Soviet troops heading south and south-east from the Volodarka area, estimating them to include over 1,000 vehicles and about 50 tanks.[35] He stressed his view that the Russians would continue to press the advance, forcing the *VII.AK* and the *III.PzK* further and further apart as they struck out for the railway north of Uman'.

Meanwhile the bad news continued to arrive from the front. The *XXXXII.AK* reported that Soviet troops had again attacked out of Germanovka, beginning at 20.30 hours and advancing either side of the road towards Mirovka. Fighting continued on into the night. Just over an hour later, the *VII.AK* reported that Russian forces had crossed the main road north-west of Tarashcha, and that it had, of necessity, ordered the *88.Infanterie-Division* to conduct a fighting withdrawal to the Pugachevka-Nastashka-Salikha line, a retreat of over 15 kilometres. Indeed, later the same night, Hell reported that he was moving his headquarters out of Rakitnoe to a safer location, and from 07.30 hours the following morning, it would be located in Teleshovka about 12 kilometres to the north-east.

Wednesday 5 January 1944

The night on the northern front of the *Panzerarmee* passed much the same as the previous one.[36] The Soviets had sent out many patrols and subjected the *Korps-Abteilung B* sector to considerable artillery fire, but other than that there had been little combat activity. On the *Korps*' left, the attack against the left wing of the *82.Infanterie-Division* had proved to be no more than a battalion-sized assault, and had eventually been seen off. In response to the earlier request from *PzAOK 1*, Mattenklott advised Hube at midnight that he had managed to send a total of nine heavy anti-tank guns to assist the *34.Infanterie-Division* in its new task south-east of Belaya Tserkov'. Three of these had been sent to the main body, and six had been instructed to join the advance *Sperrverband* on the river Ros'.

To the left, the *VII.AK* had suffered a much more difficult night.[37] On the right, the sectors held by the *75.* and *198.Infanterie-Divisions* had been subjected to a total of eight separate assaults. All of these had, however, been thrown back eventually, some as a result of locally organised counterattacks. Over on the left meanwhile, the *88.Infanterie-Division* had been busy trying to establish some kind of cohesion on the open southern front, by piecing together a line of sorts. The fighting was still raging on in Tarashcha, and away to the south-east, the *34.Infanterie-Division* still had two battalions in Luka. Nevertheless, Hube reported to von Manstein that morning that Soviet forces had captured Tarashcha the previous evening, and were now on the main road north-west of the town, whilst the left wing of the *88.Infanterie-Division* was undertaking the planned fighting withdrawal to the line Pugachevka-Nastashka-Salikha.[38] In the *III. PzK* sector, Zeleny Rog had fallen to the advancing Russian forces, and the *6.Panzer-*

---

35 *PzAOK 1*, Tagesmeldung an *Heeresgruppe Süd*, 21.35 hours dated 4 Jan 44.
36 *XXXXII.AK*, Morgenmeldung, 06.00 hours dated 5 Jan 44.
37 *VII.AK*, Morgenmeldung, 06.45 hours dated 5 Jan 44.
38 *PzAOK 1*, Morgenmeldung an *Heeresgruppe Süd*, 07.00 hours dated 5 Jan 44.

Division was organising appropriate counter-measures.³⁹ Further west, on the *17.Panzer-Division* sector, about 20 Soviet tanks had pushed southwards along the road from Bulai to Lipovets, heading towards Ganovka, and had also penetrated the division's lines near Parievka, a few kilometres to the east. The division managed to clear the area of the breach before pulling back southwards to the high ground either side of Napadovka.

In the morning, the day broke cloudy again, and, with the warmer weather continuing, the local thaw showed no signs of coming to an end, with the roads by this time becoming more and more slippery. During the morning, Hube received further news concerning his reinforcements. The *I.Flak-Korps* had now formally instructed the *10.Flak-Division* to co-operate with the *III.PzK*, its task being to support the troops of the *Generalkommando* as both artillery and anti-tank assets in both offensive and defensive operations.⁴⁰ In another message, at midday, the *Kommandeur der Nebeltruppe 3* informed Hube that the second rail transport carrying the *Werfer-Regiment 52* had now arrived in Monastyrishche, and that the regiment's commander was expected to report to the *III.PzK* headquarters later the same day.⁴¹ The remaining transport had completed its loading in Kirovograd, along with the *s.Artillerie-Abteilung 628*, and although this final train was ready to leave, there had been no news regarding the planned time of departure. The wheeled elements of the regiment were due to arrive in Monastyrishche over the next few days, with the *II./Werfer-Regiment 54* expected during 5 January, the *I./Werfer-Regiment 54* and the *I./Werfer-Regiment 52* during 6 January, and the *21.(Pz.) Werfer-Batterie/Werfer-Regiment 54* during 7 January.

As the morning wore on, Hube discussed with both Hell and Mattenklott the possibility of making some form of general withdrawal. No major reinforcements were now expected to arrive in the immediate future, and he did not believe the *Panzerarmee* could afford to wait and do nothing in the meantime. If reinforcements could not be found from outside the *Armee* area, they would have to be found from within it, if need be by pulling back to shorten the existing front line. Following these discussions, Hube issued appropriate instructions to the two *Korps* commanders just before 14.00 hours, informing them both to begin pulling back, and a later message from the *PzAOK 1* indicates the *XXXXII.AK* falling back to a line running from the northern edge of Vedmedevka through Kagarlyk to the southern end of Stavy.⁴²

Meanwhile, the fighting continued through the day, although with less intensity than the past few days. The *XXXXII.AK* had been subjected to a number of small-scale local assaults along the whole of its front, with none of these being carried out by any unit larger than a company.⁴³ All of these had been seen off eventually, but a penetration in the area around Germanovka in the sector held by the *82.Infanterie-Division* had involved particularly heavy fighting. In the *VII.AK* sector, the sudden withdrawal seemed to have thrown the Soviet forces off balance for a while.⁴⁴ Things remained pretty much unchanged opposite the right wing and centre, with both the *75.* and *198.Infanterie-Divisions* reporting the Russians doing little more than combat patrolling and following

---

39   Ibid.
40   *I.Flak-Korps*, Ia Nr.14/44 g.Kdos dated 5 Jan 44.
41   *Kommandeur der Nebeltruppe 3*, Ia unreferenced report dated 5 Jan 44.
42   *PzAOK 1*, radio message to "Landsknecht 6 für Einsatzstab Knapp", 21.45 hours dated 5 Jan 44.
43   *PzAOK 1*, Tagesmeldung an *Heeresgruppe Süd*, 21.45 hours dated 5 Jan 44.
44   Ibid.

up the withdrawal. On the left too, there had been only half-hearted attempts to follow up the *88.Infanterie-Division* as it fell back. Despite this though, Soviet infantry, with about 8-10 tanks in support, were still reported to have entered the south-eastern part of Nastashka. The lead elements of the *34.Infanterie-Division* meanwhile took advantage of the quieter situation to undertake reconnaissance in the area around Tarashcha, finding not only tanks in the town itself, but also other Soviet troops in the villages of Malaya and Velikaya Berezyanka further south. The wood south-east of Lesovichi was also occupied.

Over on the left, the Soviet forces opposite the *III.PzK* seemed to have shifted their main effort westwards.[45] The Russian units which had pushed forwards into the area south of Zhashkov the previous day had apparently been pulled back to the north, and the attack by the *6.Panzer-Division* consequently met with almost no resistance at all. According to the local population, the Soviets had pulled out during the night before, leaving the area either side of Zhashkov and transferring further westwards. Consequently, the villages of Poboinaya,[46] Bashtechki, Tynovka, Skibino, Tikhi Khutor, Krivchunka, Tarasovka and Osichnaya were all left defended by no more than weak rearguards. Further west, a small Soviet force of about two rifle companies armed with anti-tank weapons had probed forwards through Oratov, coming in from the north-west and heading off to the south-east. By evening they were deployed on hill 259.1, about two kilometres south of the town. In contrast, the Soviets had stepped up the pressure on the sector to the left, where the *17.Panzer-Division* estimated that there were now at least two mobile corps and three rifle divisions operating in that area.[47] The night before, Russian forces had followed the division's withdrawal closely, and the leading units had established themselves on a wide arc around Lipovets, running from Strizhakov, near Oratov station in the south-east, north-westwards to Ochitkov and Bogdanovka and then turning to the west to run south of Ocheretnya and Zozov to a point about two kilometres north-west of Lipovets. From the centre of this position Soviet armour had then launched an attack from Ocheretnya towards Ganovka, but this had been intercepted and brought to a halt by elements of the *17.Panzer-Division* which reported destroying a total of 23 Russian tanks. The division then mounted a counterattack to try and regain Oratov station on its right wing, but this met with no success despite initial progress. The attack started well, destroying a Soviet column near the village of Mervin, and then going on to capture the village off the march, but as the assault drew nearer to its objective, it faced an increasingly stubborn armour and anti-tank defence, and it had to be called off without taking the station. The division fell back to positions around Mervin, but a renewed assault by the Russians during the afternoon retook the village. Back on the division's northern front again, the Soviets continued their attacks against the Ochitkov-Bogdanovka sector, but these all proved unsuccessful by the end of the day, with three Soviet tanks and two anti-tank guns being reported as destroyed. More serious however was the regimental-sized attack against the Zozov-Zozovka sector over on the division's left wing. The assault, supported by 14 tanks, came in from the north and struck the weak screening force stationed by the division to cover the area, forcing the forward units to pull back to the southern edge of Zozov. Even further west,

---

45   *III.PzK*, Tagesmeldung, 20.45 hours dated 5 Jan 44.
46   Referred to as Poboika in the German records.
47   According to German intelligence, the two mobile corps involved were the 11th Guards Tank Corps and the 8th Guards Mechanised Corps under the 1st Tank Army.

another armoured assault, this time with about eight tanks, struck south-eastwards from Vakhnovka through Yasenki before wheeling to the east and advancing to a point about one kilometre north-west of Lipovets from which position it brought the Lipovets-Zozov road under fire. Slowly but surely, the *17.Panzer-Division* was being outflanked on both wings, and to make matters worse, the *III.PzK* was convinced that the Soviet attacks would only grow stronger, particularly against the right flank.[48]

As expected then, the Soviet command had continued to press its attacks against the southern wing and deep flank of the *VII.AK*, although the identity of the Russian armour had still not been established.[49] Although they had initially been pushed back out of Nastashka, the Russians seemed to be in no great hurry to follow up the withdrawal of the *88.Infanterie-Division*, although patrols sent out by the division later in the afternoon had found assault preparations underway in the area north and north-west of Nastashka. Similarly, although the Soviets had been unable to capture the northern end of Tarashcha from elements of the *34.Infanterie-Division*, further south they had advanced to take Stanishovka and Velikaya Berezyanka. The pressure of the advance was now such that the *34.Infanterie-Division*, transferring to the area, had proved unable to assemble for an immediate counterattack. Nevertheless, the results of aerial reconnaissance in the gap between the *VII.AK* and the *III.PzK* to the south-west had actually showed little Soviet movement in the area between the two *Korps*. Hube now suspected that the Russian forces which had previously pushed towards Zhashkov had been pulled back northwards during the night, and this was apparently confirmed not only by statements taken from the local population, but also by reports from the *6.Panzer-Division* which had met with little resistance during the course of its attack between Okhmatov and Shulyaki. On the other hand, both aerial and ground reconnaissance opposite the *17.Panzer-Division* further west had established major Soviet troop concentrations on that sector, and it appeared that a shift in emphasis was underway. Between 30 and 50 tanks had been spotted in Kozhanka, and intelligence suggested that these were planning to strike south-eastwards through Medovka and Rostovka towards Oratov station. Further west, another 20 Soviet tanks had been reported south of Ocheretnya, while both Zozov and Vakhnovka had been occupied by Russian troops. This armour seemed to form the main thrust of the Soviet 1st Tank Army as, according to information received, the 8th Guards Mechanised Corps was now in the area north of Pliskov station while the 11th Guards Tank Corps was in the area around Verbovka.

Notwithstanding the apparent shift to the west, it seemed clear that the Russians would renew their attempt to outflank the *VII.AK* the following day, and with the situation growing more serious by the hour, Hube decided that the matter would have to be settled by a strong counterattack. Since he could not rely on receiving forces from outside, he was obliged to find the necessary troops from his existing resources. To enable him to do this, he proposed to Army Group South that he pull back the *XXXXII. AK* on his right wing to a shorter line. Von Manstein on this occasion agreed. Hube

---

48 At this stage, the *17.Panzer-Division's* armour strength was down to just 5 operational *Panzer V "Panthers"*. For support it also deployed the 5 *Panzer VI "Tigers"* remaining to the *s.Panzer-Abteilung 506*, and the 4 *StuGs* of the *Sturmgeschütz-Abteilung 249*. The division reported having destroyed over 40 Soviet tanks since 3 January.

49 *PzAOK 1*, Ic Abendmeldung, 22.30 hours dated 5 Jan 44.

lost no time and issued revised orders at 18.50 hours that same evening.⁵⁰ According to these, the main task now facing the *PzAOK 1* was to prevent any further attempts by Soviet forces to encircle its right wing, and consequently it would be pulled back to a line running from Vedmedevka through Kagarlyk and Vintsentovka, and from there southwards along the Gorokhovatka stream to Koshevatoye, south-east of Tarashcha. The units freed by this withdrawal, the *34.* and *198.Infanterie-Divisions*, were then to be re-deployed on the left wing of the *VII.AK* where they would participate in a counterattack into the area of the Soviet breakthrough. In particular, the *XXXXII.AK* was to pull back its left wing during the coming night to the line running from north of Vedmedevka through Kagarlyk to the southern end of Stavy, while the *VII.AK* was to pull back at the same time to the line running from the northern end of Vintsentovka through Rakitnoe to Salikha. The hanging southern flank was to be secured by the *34.Infanterie-Division* on the Tarashcha-Koshevatoye-Luka line.

Mattenklott confirmed the intentions of the *XXXXII.AK* later that evening, advising the *Panzerarmee* that he would pull back as ordered, with each battalion leaving behind a reinforced company as rearguard.⁵¹ These would only pull back under heavy enemy pressure. The *Korps* was also planning to establish its own reserve, using two infantry and one artillery battalions from the *82.Infanterie-Division*. The second stage of the withdrawal, to the line of Gorokhovatka as far as Koshevatoye, would follow on the subsequent night. The *198.Infanterie-Division* would need to complete its relief from the front line by early on 7 January, and its various units would be deployed behind the *VII.AK* left flank as they were relieved, helping to strengthen and extend the line to the south. The division was to be re-deployed in such a way that it could go over to the offensive quickly and smoothly once all its constituent elements had arrived. As part of this new internal transfer, the boundary between the *VII.AK* and the *XXXXII.AK* was shifted again, and with effect from midnight on 6 January, it would run from Karapyshi through Stavy to Mirovka.

During the course of the evening, Hube received bad news from the *8.Armee*. Army Group South had ordered the *Panzergrenadier-Division 'Grossdeutschland'* to turn around, and instead of moving towards the *PzAOK 1*, it was now to re-assemble around Losovatka, south-west of Kirovograd.⁵² Wenck, the chief of staff at the *Panzerarmee*, subsequently spoke with the operations officer at von Manstein's headquarters and advised him that the absence of this division would have a considerable adverse effect on the overall situation, particularly in view of the heavy Soviet pressure now being exerted against both wings of the *Panzerarmee*. Given that the *3.Panzer-Division* had already been withheld, despite earlier promises, the loss of the *'Grossdeutschland'* now meant that the *PzAOK 1* had no real idea as to how the existing gaps in the front line might be filled. In response, the Army Group chief of staff, Busse, admitted that the final decision regarding the deployment of the division had not yet been made, and depended, amongst other things, on how the situation of the *AOK 8* around Kirovograd might develop by the following morning. News of other reinforcements included the attachment of the

---

50 *PzAOK 1*, Ia Nr.6/44 g.Kdos dated 5 Jan 44.
51 *XXXXII.AK*, Ia Nr.18/44 geh. dated 5 Jan 44.
52 *PzAOK 1*, Ia Kriegstagebuch entry for 5 Jan 44. At 06.45 hours that morning, troops of the Soviet 2nd Ukrainian Front had launched a major offensive either side of Kirovograd, threatening to make a serious breakthrough in the AOK 8 sector.

101.Jäger-Division, then beginning to arrive in the Vinnitsa-Zhmerinka area, along with the *4.Gebirgs-Division* under the *4.Panzerarmee*, although by this time only three trains had arrived as yet.[53] There was also news of troops in the rear area, with a report being received from the *Ortskommandant* in Gaisin behind the left wing of the *17.Panzer-Division*. Although of dubious combat efficiency, being previously used to no more than guarding stretches of railway, the *Ortskommandant* deployed the *Transport-Sicherungs-Bataillon 896*, the *2.Kompanie/Transport-Sicherungs-Bataillon 361*, and *4./Kompanie/Transport-Sicherungs-Bataillon 594*, a total of just over 1,000 officers and men armed with little more than rifles and machine-guns. There were other units in the town in addition to these, but the *Kommandant* had not been able to establish whether these formed part of the garrison, or were simply billeted there whilst passing through.

---

53 *PzAOK 1*, Tagesmeldung an *Heeresgruppe Süd*, 21.45 hours dated 5 Jan 44; BvTO beim *PzAOK 1*, Tätigkeitsbericht für das 1.Halbjahr 1944, page 1.

8

The *1.Panzerarmee* Splits into Three

Thursday 6 January 1944

It was 01.00 hours in the morning when Hell, his headquarters now established in Pustovity, south of Kagarlyk, sent Hube a message outlining his intentions in respect of the latest instructions from the *Panzerarmee*.[1] During the course of the night the main body of the *VII.AK* would fall back to the Vintsentovka-Rakitnoe-Salikha line, whilst the *198.Infanterie-Division* was to assemble in the Teleshovka area, with a *Regimentsgruppe* from the *34.Infanterie-Division* assembling in the Savarka-Stepok area, south of Ol'shanitsa. The following day, he intended to send out a combat patrol to establish the position in Tarashcha, and begin the transfer of the *198.Infanterie-Division* to the Savarka-Stepok-Lyutari area. At the same time, a second *Regimentsgruppe* from the *34.Infanterie-Division* would be moved to the Luk'yanovka area, whilst the final *Regimentsgruppe* would be assembled in Dybintsy further east.[2] Hell also outlined his intentions for the following night, in which he would pull his *Korps* back to the line Vintsentovka-Ol'shanitsa-Stepok-Luk'yanovka, and assemble the entire *34.Infanterie-Division* in the Luk'yanovka-Branoe Pole area. In this way, Hell planned to have two *Regimentsgruppen* of the *34.Infanterie-Division* ready for offensive operations early on 7 January, and the entire division, plus perhaps two thirds of the *198.Infanterie-Division*, the day after that.

The fighting meanwhile continued unabated as the *PzAOK 1* right wing pulled back under cover of darkness.[3] In the *XXXXII.AK* sector, the withdrawal went according to plan despite a number of minor attacks against the rearguards on the left wing. On the *Korps-Abteilung B* front, Soviet troops had attacked at about 01.30 hours and had made a small penetration near hill 118.2, but this had been cleared up in some close fighting. The Russian traffic from Khodorov to the west continued throughout the night as it had done on previous nights. On the left, the *82.Infanterie-Division* had been subjected to two separate assaults, one at about 22.00 hours the previous evening, and another at about 03.15 hours in the morning. The attacks had been made against the division's left wing and the area around Leonovka, with no more two Russian rifle companies involved in each. Both had been beaten off without too much difficulty. There was only incomplete information regarding the situation at the *VII.AK*, but according to what news had been received, the withdrawal was proceeding as planned.[4] On the southern wing, the sector held by the *6.Panzer-Division* had been relatively quiet, although a few Soviet elements had managed to push forwards near Balabanovka and occupy Budenovka about two

---

1 *VII.AK*, Ia Nr.111/43 [sic] geh. dated 6 Jan 44.
2 Referred to as Dybnizy in the German records.
3 *PzAOK 1*, Summary of Morgenmeldungen, 05.20 hours dated 6 Jan 44.
4 Ibid.

kilometres north-west of the village. Sabarovka, about three kilometres north-east of Balabanovka, was also suspected as being occupied by enemy forces. Further west, the division also reported having heard tank track noises in the vicinity of Oratov station for about an hour the previous evening, and these seemed to have approached the area from the west. Reconnaissance patrols also reported hearing other noises coming from the southern part of Oratov. The *17.Panzer-Division* meanwhile had fallen back under heavy pressure, and was now established on a line running from Vladimirovka through Skitka, Vitsentovka, Ul'yanovka, and Slavnaya to Yasenki. The Russian forces facing its left wing seemed to have received continual reinforcement throughout the night, and the division's commander was expecting serious Soviet assaults in that area at some point during the coming day.

The day brought both good and bad news for Hube in respect of reinforcements. A message arrived from Army Group South to say that the *Panzerzug 62*[5] had been transferred to him from Army Group A, and that it should be arriving in the Khristinovka area later the same day. There was also an update on the progress of the arrival of the *Nebelwerfer* troops from the *Kommandeur der Nebeltruppe 3*.[6] The *6./Werfer-Regiment 54* was now attached to the *6.Panzer-Division*, while the *II./Werfer-Regiment 54* would have two batteries operational by 7 January, its third battery still being stuck in transit near Kirovograd. The *I./Werfer-Regiment 54* and the *Panzer-Werfer-Batterie* were both expected to be available by 8 January, as was the *I./Werfer-Regiment 52*. Despite the welcome nature of this support, the effectiveness of the *Nebelwerfer* units was highly dependent upon the continued availability of suitable transport means, and at the moment these were unfortunately in short supply with the *Panzerarmee 1*.

Later the same day, Hube learned from Army Group South that he would be responsible for the arrival and assembly of the *371.Infanterie-Division*, currently underway from the *PzAOK 2* in the Balkans.[7] The division was planned to arrive in the Zhmerinka area on either 7 or 8 January, and although the *PzAOK 1* was to oversee its assembly, it would remain at the disposal of the Army Group for the time being. Less welcome news arrived a little later. Von Manstein had decided to assemble the *Panzergrenadier-Division 'Grossdeutschland'* behind the *AOK 8* sector near Losovatka in the area south-west of Kirovograd.[8] Nevertheless, no firm decision had yet been made regarding its final employment, and it was ordered to stand ready either to intervene in the Kirovograd fighting or move out to the *PzAOK 1* through Novoukrainka. In fact, the *AOK 8* had been given strict instructions not to allow any elements of the division to become embroiled in the fighting around Kirovograd. Von Manstein's chief of staff, Busse, had already given Wenck advance notice of this decision during the morning situation report, and Wenck had again taken the opportunity of stressing

---

5 Armoured Train 62. During the offensive stage of the war, the *Wehrmacht* used armoured trains to seize and hold key railway installations, such as stations and bridges, but their role had changed by this time, and they were chiefly deployed to patrol and keep open railways in areas of partisan operations. Typically they would remain under Army Group control, and would comprise, in addition to the locomotive itself in the middle of the train, two armoured gun trucks, two armoured anti-aircraft trucks, and two armoured infantry trucks.
6 *Kommandeur der Nebeltruppe 3*, unreferenced report dated 6 Jan 44.
7 Hgr. Süd, Ia Nr.77/44 g.Kdos dated 6 Jan 44.
8 Hgr. Süd, Ia Nr.81/44 g.Kdos dated 6 Jan 44.

that the *Panzerarmee* had no idea how it was expected to master the situation without reinforcement from such mobile units.

In the continuing absence of such reinforcement however, Hube had apparently been combing out his rear area in an effort to try and redress the balance. A message issued by the *Waffen-Schule PzAOK 1* at 17.15 hours that evening confirmed that the *Panzer-Zerstörer-Bataillon (mot.) 471* had left its command the day before, and was expected to arrive in Uman' on 7 January.[9] On the other hand, the *Waffen-Schule* also reported that neither it nor the *Lehr-Batterie*, nor the *Sturm-Bataillon*, would be able to move from their current positions. They simply had no means of transport available, and despite repeated requests to the *BvTO* at *AOK 6*, none had been allocated. However, the news was not all bad, and a report from the *101.Jäger-Division* at 17.35 hours indicated that the first forces had now arrived in the area, including the *I./Jäger-Regiment 228*, the *III./Artillerie-Regiment 85*, the *1.Batterie/II./Artillerie-Regiment 85*, and reduced staffs from the headquarters of both the *Jäger-Regiment 228* and the *Artillerie-Regiment 85*.

In the meantime though, Hube was still faced with the problem of trying to make do with what he had. In a conference held earlier that morning, with both Wenck and the *Ia*, he decided to pull back the whole of the right wing of his *Armee* as far as was necessary to enable him to prevent the Soviets from exploiting the two main problem areas; namely, the potential breakthrough between the *VII.AK* and the *III.PzK*, and the actual breakthrough between the *III.PzK* and the *XXIV.PzK* under the *PzAOK 4* further west. He therefore decided to extend his existing planning beyond the initial counterattack already envisaged. With the forces freed by a withdrawal of its right wing, the *PzAOK 1* would now begin its counterstroke by attacking from the left wing of the *VII.AK* to regain contact with the *III.PzK*. With a new front thus established, the assault forces would then go on to strike the left flank of the Soviet troops facing the *PzAOK 4*. Wenck passed on details of the plan to Busse at Army Group South, only to be told that the idea stood little chance of being authorised. Hube decided to speak direct to von Manstein. He made a direct request for approval to pull back his right wing, explaining again that he needed to free forces to lengthen the left wing of the *VII.AK* which would then, in conjunction with the *6.Panzer-Division*, strike a blow against the eastern flank of the Russian forces which had broken through towards Morozovka. Von Manstein pointed out that he was unable to give such approval himself, since instructions had already been received 'from above' that the current positions were to be held at all costs. Nevertheless, despite the discussions between the two commanders, the reality was that part of the right wing of the *PzAOK 1* was still falling back, and just before midday, Hube actually authorised Hell to pull back the *VII.AK* in the second stage of the withdrawal.[10] The *Korps* was to take up new positions on the line of the Gorokhovatka as far south as Koshevataya, although close contact was to be maintained with the *XXXXII.AK* in the southern end of Stavy. A little later, Hell reported that the towns of Isaiki, Medvin, and Poberezhka were all still clear of Soviet troops at 12.35 hours.

---

9 *Waffen-Schule PzAOK 1*, Ia Nr.18/44 geh. dated 6 Jan 44. The *Waffen-Schule* was a Weapons School operated by the *Panzerarmee* for training in specialised weapons. The *Panzer-Zerstörer-Bataillon (mot.) 471* (a tank destroyer battalion) had been formed by the *1.Panzerarmee* during December 1943 using elements of anti-tank units from divisions which had been disbanded.

10 *PzAOK 1*, Ia Nr.7/44 g.Kdos dated 6 Jan 44.

THE *1.PANZERARMEE* SPLITS INTO THREE

In contrast with previous days, the morning had broken clear and sunny, leaving an early ground frost and good visibility. But it was not to last, and later in the day signs of cloud cover began to re-appear. As the day progressed, it became clear that the Soviets were not completely ignoring the right wing of the *PzAOK 1*, and at 14.45 hours, the *XXXXII.AK* reported an air attack against positions around the rail junction at Mironovka, deep in the rear area. Moreover, at about midday, the *82.Infanterie-Division* reported seeing Soviet troops moving southwards from Gorokhovatka[11] towards Pereselenie, just north of Kagarlyk. Further west, and later in the afternoon, at 16.00 hours, the *VII.AK* also reported Soviet movements. This time, Russian forces had been seen moving from the north-east towards Tarashcha, and 20 or so tanks had already been spotted in the woods to the south-east of the town. Despite this advance though, the *Korps* continued to hold positions in the northern part of the town.

Mattenklott had by this time moved the *XXXXII.AK* headquarters to Maslovka, but despite the increasing Soviet activity in his sector, little of consequence had actually occurred.[12] The Russians had shown no inclination during the morning to push hard on the heels of the *Korps'* withdrawal, although this changed somewhat in the afternoon when a much closer pursuit was reported, particularly opposite the left wing. A number of motorised units had even been observed in the area. In the sector held by the *Korps-Abteilung B*, Russian infantry and sledges had been seen moving towards Selishche and Studanets opposite the right wing, presumably with the intention of reinforcing the Soviet positions there. On the other wing, the rearguards left by the *Korps-Abteilung* had been obliged to pull back as early as 09.00 hours that morning in the face of persistent pressure, and had taken up new positions on the high ground either side of Lipovy Rog. Soviet artillery had meanwhile already begun to register on the new defensive positions around Vedmedevka. Even with this increased activity though, the *Korps-Abteilung* reported no particular incidence of traffic moving in the Russian rear area, so things remained relatively quiet. Opposite the *82.Infanterie-Division* though, there had been much more traffic, where the troop movements reported earlier in the day had turned out to be quite extensive. These had started from the area north of Mirovka, moving eastwards along the embankment towards Yanovka, but by afternoon the troops involved had moved up against the division's left wing. About two battalions had advanced from Gorokhovatka to Pereselenie, and another regiment had moved in from the north towards Stavy where five troop-carrying trucks and three tanks had been seen. Meanwhile, a smaller force of about two companies had also moved up towards Kagarlyk. The whole day had seen considerable air activity over the entire division sector, with roads and villages being the main targets for both bombing and strafing. Mattenklott meanwhile took advantage of the relative quiet, forming up a reserve of his own in the Mironovka-Lipovets area, using elements of the *82.Infanterie-Division*. This comprised the *I./Grenadier-Regiment 158*, the headquarters of the *I./Artillerie-Regiment 182*, the *II./Artillerie-Regiment 182*; and the *11./Artillerie-Regiment 182*.

Whilst there had been little news from the *VII.AK* earlier in the day, the evening report submitted by Hell detailed events since the previous night.[13] The screen deployed

---

11 Referred to as Kasimirowka in the German records.
12 *XXXXII.AK.*, Tagesmeldung, 18.30 hours dated 6 Jan 44.
13 *VII.AK.*, Tagesmeldung, 19.00 hours dated 6 Jan 44. The report gave the operational armour strength for the two attached *Sturmgeschütz-Abteilungen* as follows:

on the *Korps* left flank by the newly arrived elements of the *34.Infanterie-Division* had enjoyed no respite, and had been quickly attacked by the leading Soviet troops. Six Russian tanks, with mounted infantry riding on top of them, had assaulted the new positions in the Bolkun area at 02.30 hours, and this had been followed by another attack, this time by about four tanks, in the area of Tarashcha station. Both attacks had been beaten back. However, the Soviet forces regrouped and attacked around Bolkun again, this time with more success. About ten tanks, with infantry clinging to their backs, began the assault in the early hours of the morning at about 07.00 hours, and pushed forward into the village before losing four of their number to defensive fire. They pulled back again, this time into the woods to the west of the village. Despite this limited defensive success, the road between Tarashcha and Bolkun remained under heavy Soviet fire whilst the Russians regrouped for another attack. This came at about 10.00 hours, with between 200 and 300 Soviet infantry trying to find a way through further south, near Luk'yanovka, but it too met with no success. Around and east of Tarashcha itself, there were repeated attacks, but despite the support of an estimated 20 or so tanks, the Russian infantry were unable to make any real headway. The attacks had not been without result though. Having been involved in all this fighting, the *VII. AK* had been unable to send out reconnaissance patrols to try and establish whether the Soviets were still pressing their attempts to outflank the *Korps* left wing to the south-east. Over on the right wing meanwhile, the *75.Infanterie-Division* had been attacked during the late afternoon near Vintsentovka, where Soviet troops had managed to break their way into the defensive positions on the northern and southern edges of the village. The fighting continued for some time, and raged on into the darkness. Further south-west, a company-sized assault north-west of Bakumovka had been seen off without great difficulty before it penetrated into the main defensive position, but to the west, the Russians had succeeded in forcing a breach in the north-western part of Rakitnoe. The division finally succeeded in bringing the attack to a halt though, and the hole was sealed off. By late afternoon, at around 16.15 hours, Soviet troops were again attacking east of Tarashcha, this time towards the southern edge of Stepok and supported by about ten tanks. Another 14 or so had also been counted in the Luk'yanovka area. Meanwhile, the Russians kept on moving, and the *Korps* reported considerable traffic heading from Tarashcha towards Tsakyanovka, including about 100 vehicles, many of which were motorised. As with the *XXXXII.AK* sector further north, the improved weather conditions had also seen an increase in Soviet air activity over the *VII.AK*. Hell reported a number of bombing attacks, primarily against villages and supply lines, but he also recorded the shooting down of two Russian aircraft. Later in the evening, the *VII.AK* reported its intentions for the following day.[14] The line would be held as already ordered, and a *Kampfgruppe* would be thrown forwards towards Stanishovka south of Tarashcha. In the rear, the *34.* and *198.Infanterie-Divisions* would complete their respective assemblies with a view to beginning the attack to close the gap to the *III. PzK* away to the south-west.

- *Sturmgeschütz-Abteilung 202*: 15 *StuGs*
- *Sturmgeschütz-Abteilung 239*: 10 *StuGs*.

14   *VII.AK.*, Ia Nr.115/44 geh. dated 6 Jan 44.

THE *1.PANZERARMEE* SPLITS INTO THREE

Over on the left wing of the *PzAOK 1*, the contrast between the sectors held by the *6.* and *17.Panzer-Divisions* continued.¹⁵ The right wing of the *6.Panzer-Division* had now established a screening force to cover the crossings over the Gorny Tikich at Poboinaya, Okhmatov, Buzovka, and Shulyaki, and this had seen no Soviet activity at all. No new Russian troops had been observed in the area between the sugar factory and Zhashkov, although further west some troop movement had been seen involving battalion-sized units heading through Klyuki and Khmelevka towards Lukashovka. On the left though, a *Kampfgruppe* from the division made no progress in its assault from the Oratovka-Gonoratka area to the north-west. The group had completed its assembly by the middle of the day, and at 13.00 hours it crossed the Sabarovka-Balabanovka line heading to the north-west. The right-hand group managed to capture the high ground about four kilometres south-east of Oratov off the march, and struck out for the eastern part of the town, destroying four Soviet anti-tank guns on the way. Another group reached the high ground about two kilometres north of Gonoratka and pressed on towards the southern edge of Oratov. Other elements fighting on the southern end of Kazimirovka then received flanking fire from Soviet troops in Zarud'e, and the attack began to grind to a halt. At 17.00 hours, on orders from the *III.PzK*, the assault was called off. It seemed the Russians had built up a strong anti-tank and artillery defence in the area to screen their main advance against the *17.Panzer-Division* further west. In the *17.Panzer-Division* sector itself, the Soviets had attacked during the morning with strong armoured forces from the 1st Tank Army.¹⁶ The attack had involved somewhere between 40 and 50 tanks moving off southwards from the Rososha area towards Morozovka. They captured the town in quick time and pressed on, despite a local counterattack mounted by elements of the division converging from the north and east. Results of both ground and aerial reconnaissance indicated meanwhile that further reinforcements were heading south from Rososha, and it was clear by midday that this advance represented a fairly major effort, involving anything up to 150 tanks in total. During the afternoon, the Russians pressed on southwards, pushing a few tanks over the river Sob at Ilyntsy before heading into the wooded area to the south to establish contact with a local partisan group; something the *17.Panzer-Division* viewed as particularly serious, especially with regard to its future defensive prospects in the area. Elsewhere other Soviet armour broke through the division's thin screen, pushing southwards from the Ganovka-Zozov area, and eastwards from near Yasenki. The division continued to fall back, being forced to give up its positions by the relentless Russian advance, and it considered that the attacks would continue still further. Leaving a few armoured rearguards in contact with the leading Soviet elements, it therefore began to fall back on the line of the river Sob, some 15 kilometres to the south. A later message from Breith indicated that the two *Panzer-Divisions* had been instructed to strike the flanks of this Soviet advance and attack towards each other to establish a firm contact on their inner wings.¹⁷ The *6.Panzer-Division* was to continue screening the Gorny Tikich in the east, but would now attack

---

15 *III.PzK.*, Tagesmeldung, 19.50 hours dated 6 Jan 44.
16 *PzAOK 1* intelligence had by this time established the presence of the 11th Guards Tank Corps, the 10th Tank Corps and the 8th Guards Mechanised Corps, all operating in the area. It is not clear which formation the Germans had identified as the 10th Tank Corps, as this unit had been in the *Stavka* reserve since December the previous year, and it was not operating in this sector.
17 *III.PzK.*, Ia Nr.28/44 geh. dated 6 Jan 44.

westwards on its left wing, moving through Koshlany and Dubrovintsy towards Ilyntsy, whilst the *17.Panzer-Division* was to establish a screen along the river Sob and strike eastwards towards the crossing at Ilyntsy.

At about the same time, Hube learned that Army Group South had finally decided to commit the *Panzergrenadier-Division 'Grossdeutschland'* in the Kirovograd area, and that it had now been attached to the *AOK 8*.[18] The *PzAOK 1* had now been deprived of both major mobile units it had been promised, and it was a serious blow. Nevertheless, the *101.Jäger-Division* was now beginning to arrive in strength, and at 21.05 hours, Hube issued its first orders.[19] Beginning the following day, the division was to assemble south-east of Vinnitsa in the Voronovitsa-Pisarevka-Malye Khutora[20]- Parpurovtsy-Tsvizhin area, although it was not to use the *DG IV* at this time.[21] It was not to cross the road to the north-east, but it did have to provide its own defensive screen to protect the assembly from that direction. The primary anti-tank screen was to be concentrated around the road fork three kilometres north-east of Gumennoe station, blocking the main Lipovets-Vinnitsa route.

The day's developments left Hube with considerable problems. Over on the right, there had been little combat activity although the Soviets did eventually follow up the withdrawal of the *XXXXII.AK*. On the *VII.AK* sector, they assaulted Rakitnoe with little success, but with tank support they managed to press the advance as far as Bolkun east of Tarashcha. They had been unable to dislodge the defenders from Tarashcha itself though, and had also been checked at Luk'yanovka to the south. There was every sign that they were still pressing hard on this sector, threatening to outflank the left wing of the *VII.AK*. In the centre, there seemed to have been little reinforcement and in the area from west of Tarashcha through Zhashkov to Oratov, there were relatively few Soviet troops, estimated to be two rifle divisions, although local strongpoints appeared to have been created around Goroshkov and Stadnitsa. On the left, the Soviet 1st Tank Army had achieved a major breakthrough either side of and along the main Ochitkov-Ilyntsy road with troops of the 8th Guards Mechanised Corps and the 11th Guards Tank Corps, pushing on in a wide arc as far as and over the river Sob. A battalion-strength assault had gone in against Yablonovitsa and a regimental-sized attack had been launched southward from Oratov station. There had been tank combat around Rososha, and Soviet armour from the 11th Guards Tank Corps had broken through to reach Lipovets, leaving a large column of tanks and motorised vehicles strung out along the road back to Rososha. Further west, there had been a strong tank-supported assault on Lukashovka, and according to the results of ground and aerial reconnaissance, there were now estimated to be between 130 and 150 Russian tanks in the Ocheretnya-Rososha-Lipovets area. Further mobile forces were also thought to be arriving. To screen the eastern flank of this fresh advance, the Russians had apparently built a strong defensive position along the river Zhiva either side of Oratov, implying that their intention was to breakthrough

---

18 Hgr. Süd, Ia Nr.81/44 geh. dated 6 Jan 44.
19 *PzAOK 1*, Ia. Nr.10/44 geh. dated 6 Jan 44.
20 Now part of the south-eastern suburbs of Vinnitsa.
21 The DG IV, *Durchgangsstrasse IV*, was an important through route or highway, heading through Vinnitsa on its way to Uman' to the south-east and it was in great demand from vehicles of all kinds. The *PzAOK 1* obviously did not want the normal logistics traffic disrupted by the assembly of the *101. Jäger-Division*.

all the way to the *DG IV* and establish contact with the partisan group much further south in the wooded area north-east of Bratslav on the Southern Bug river. It was also possible that elements of the advancing forces would wheel off westwards and aim for Vinnitsa, an important road and rail junction. The Russians were showing no sign of easing the pressure and, until Hube was able to complete the re-deployment of the *34.* and *198.Infanterie-Divisions*, he was faced with trying to conduct the battle in such a way that not only avoided his divisions being destroyed piecemeal, but also prevented the *III.PzK* from being irretrievably separated from the rest of the *Panzerarmee*. For the time being therefore, these two aspects were his main task, and his orders for the following day reflect these priorities.[22] In general, the tasks given to the *XXXXII.AK* and the *VII.AK* remained unchanged, although on the hanging southern flank the *VII. AK* was now to push troops to the line Stanishovka-Velikaya Berezyanka with a view to creating the necessary preconditions for an attack by the *34.Infanterie-Division* and elements of the *198.Infanterie-Division* on 8 January. The *III.PzK* meanwhile was to prevent the *17.Panzer-Division* from being pushed any further to the south-west, away from the left wing of the *6.Panzer-Division*. The Soviet forces which had broken through past Ilyntsy to the south and west, and had split the divisions from each other, were to be attacked by the *6.Panzer-Division* in the area north of the river Sob in an effort to stem the tide of Russian reinforcements on that sector. The *17.Panzer-Division* itself was to fall back behind the line of the river Sibok under cover of its counterattack against Ilyntsy. It was crucial for the continued operations of the *PzAOK 1* for the two *Panzer-Divisions* to regain contact, and thus prevent the advancing Soviet troops from crossing the *DG IV*. Hube was also taking precautions on the other wing though, and in a later order, Mattenklott and Hell were both instructed to carry out reconnaissance of rearward positions. The position was to be divided into three sections, with the first of these, codenamed 'Rosa', running along the southern bank of the river Rossava as far as Mironovka. The position would then divide, with one arm ('Meta') continuing along the river as far as Karapyshi, and from there south-westwards to Koshevatoye, and the other ('Olga') running from Mironovka station through Yukhni and the high ground north-west of Boguslav to the hills west of Medvin. If a withdrawal to the 'Rosa' line was subsequently authorised, it was intended that the *82.Infanterie-Division* would be made available to the *Armee* for re-deployment on the southern wing of the *VII.AK*. The *XXXXII.AK* would then assume responsibility for the sector of the front from the Dnepr to the area west of Medvin, deploying just the *Korps-Abteilung B* and the *75.Infanterie-Division* for that purpose. This would then release the *VII.AK*, with the *34.*, *82.*, and *198.Infanterie-Divisions*, for offensive operations to the south-west.

Friday 7 January 1944

The night to 7 January passed fairly quietly in the *XXXXII.AK* sector.[23] The previous evening there had been light artillery fire on the *Korps-Abteilung B* front at about 16.00 hours as the rearguards in the Balyko-Shchuchinka area began to fall back to the high ground north and north-west of Pevtsy. Despite this though, the Russians made no attempt to interfere with the withdrawal itself. Further west, combat patrols had established that the villages of Velikaya Pritski and Sloboda were already occupied

22 *PzAOK 1*, Ia Nr.19/44 g.Kdos dated 6 Jan 44.
23 *XXXXII.AK.*, Morgenmeldung, 06.20 hours dated 7 Jan 44.

by Soviet troops, and at 15.30 hours the previous afternoon, the *82.Infanterie-Division* had observed five Russian trucks with guns in tow in the area two kilometres north of Kagarlyk. Following this, at about 17.00 hours, between 150 and 200 Soviet soldiers had attacked out of the Pereselenie area, but the assault came to grief in the division's defensive fire as the attackers withdrew leaving about 50 dead behind. The final event of the night took place at about 21.40 hours when a brief firefight occurred in the vicinity of the southern end of Sloboda. Behind the fighting in this sector, the Soviets had continued their movements throughout the previous evening, perhaps indicating the on-going transfer of forces further south.

To the left, the withdrawal movements planned by the *VII.AK* were carried out according to plan, despite a number of small-scale Soviet assaults.[24] In the *75.Infanterie-Division* sector a total of three Russian combat patrols, each involving between 25 and 30 men, were thrown back during the night, and a patrol sent out by the division stumbled across a Soviet unit assembling near Vintsentovka. The patrol attacked the assembly, surprising the Russians who quickly dispersed, leaving about 45 dead behind. Meanwhile, the *198.Infanterie-Division* had started to move to its new sector, and the *Grenadier-Regiment 308* was now south of the Ros' river in the Dybintsy-Raskopantsy area. The *Grenadier-Regiment 305* had also nearly completed its move, and was assembling further north-west in the Alexeyevka-Borodani-Lyutari area. The *Grenadier-Regiment 326*, due to assemble further west near Bolkun and Stepok, had not yet reported in, so was presumably still on the move. Immediately to the south-west of the division's new assembly area, Soviet troops with tank support had meanwhile been attacking the villages of Koshevatoye, Luka and Branoe Pole during the night. Although these had initially been thrown back, the Russians managed to break into the defensive positions in Luka at about midnight, forcing the defenders to fall back towards Branoe Pole and Dybintsy. By morning, a new defensive position was being constructed about two kilometres south-west of the latter village.

Over on the left flank of the *Panzerarmee*, the right wing of the *6.Panzer-Division* received a sudden jolt at about 01.30 hours in the morning.[25] This had come in the form of a battalion-sized assault from the Russians, supported by heavy weapons, heading for Shulyaki on the Gorny Tikich. The area had been only lightly screened as the division was echeloned for its forthcoming attack to the west towards the *17.Panzer-Division*, and the weak detachments soon fell back from the village. A counterattack was quickly organised in the darkness, and by 04.00 hours this had jumped off to recapture the village. Further west, the Soviets had earlier seemed to take advantage of the division's new orientation, and moved to occupy Sabarovka as the main strike force headed off westwards. Another counterattack had been put together, and by midnight the village had been re-captured after finally rooting out some determined resistance. In contrast, the situation over on the left had been comparatively quiet, and the *17.Panzer-Division* had completed its withdrawal behind the river Sob as planned, taking up its new positions as instructed.

---

24 *VII.AK.*, Morgenmeldung, 07.00 hours dated 7 Jan 44.
25 *III.PzK.*, Morgenmeldung, 05.40 hours dated 7 Jan 44.

The previous evening, Hube had received a new directive from Army Group South, outlining the intended future course of operations.[26] This had been issued by the Army Group to both the *PzAOK 1* and the *PzAOK 4*, and in it von Manstein set out his view that the 1st Ukrainian Front posed two main threats. First, it could try and encircle the main body of the *PzAOK 4*, and second, it could try and force two deep drives, one towards Rovno and Shepetovka in the west, and the other towards Zhmerinka in the south-west. All of these towns were important rail junctions. Von Manstein believed the latter option was the more probable, but in any case thought it would not be possible to counter both strikes at once. He therefore ordered the two armies to concentrate on dealing with the southward thrust of the Soviet 1st Tank Army and 40th Army. The first task was for Hube to use the *III.PzK* to counterattack against the 40th Army advance, and to enable him to do this, he would have to pull back the *VII.AK* and the *XXXXII. AK*. Once this had been completed, von Manstein envisaged the second stage beginning about eight days later, with the *III.PzK* driving westwards into the extended flank of the Soviet 1st Tank Army, whilst the *XXXXVI.PzK* under the *4.Panzerarmee*, having shifted southwards, would undertake a corresponding drive into the Tank Army's right flank. In the meantime though, Hube's two right-hand *Korps* were to withdraw to the line of the river Ros' in conjunction with the left wing of the *8.Armee* to the east, thus freeing the forces required to conduct the offensive to close the gap to the *III.PzK*. At about 10.30 hours on 7 January, on the basis of this instruction, Hube issued the codewords 'Karla' and 'Meta' to the *XXXXII.AK* and the *VII.AK*, instructing them to begin pulling back. Not long afterwards though, the *PzAOK 1* received another communication from von Manstein, informing it that the *OKH* had not actually authorised the withdrawals yet, and that the matter was still under consideration. In the meantime, Hube was to make sure that the current positions were maintained. Wenck repeated the view of the *Armee* that only by pulling back to the river Ros', and thereby freeing the *82.* and *75.Infanterie-Divisions*, would the *PzAOK 1* stand any chance of re-gaining the upper hand over the situation of the left wing of the *VII.AK*. The Army Group supported the line, but could offer little more than moral support. At about 14.00 hours, orders arrived stating that withdrawals of any kind had been expressly forbidden. Given this directive, it may be worth re-stating the situation facing Hube at this very point in time. On his right, the Soviets were managing to pin down the majority of the *XXXXII.AK* and the *VII.AK* with relatively weak forces, whilst outflanking the southern wing of the *VII.AK* with a much stronger drive. Russian armour, thought to be a tank regiment or other major mobile unit, had been reported deep in the area of the breakthrough, threatening the rear of both *Korps*. At the very least, the main lines of supply of both *Korps*, running northwards from Zvenigorodka, were in very real danger of being cut. Between the open southern wing of the *VII.AK* and the easternmost units of the *III.PzK* to the west around Okhmatov, there was now a gap of about 50 kilometres in which there were no German units other than a few radio posts[27] and some rear area installations belonging to the *8.Armee*. No clear picture was available of Soviet movements in the

---

26 A copy of this directive is not actually included in the *PzAOK 1* papers, but mention is made of it in the war diary on 7 Jan 44. A copy is however held in the *PzAOK 4* papers where the reference is given as Hgr. Süd, Ia Nr. 0748/44 dated 6 Jan 44.

27 These were *Dezimeter-Funkstellen*, whose function seems to have been as switching and relay stations for radio traffic.

sector, and it could only be over-watched by air, and only then on fine days. To the left of this gap, the two *Panzer-Divisions* of Breith's *III.PzK* were covering a sector of 110 kilometres against increasing Soviet pressure. The right wing of the *Korps* was coming under renewed attack, presumably to keep it away from the *VII.AK*, whilst over on the left a massive Russian offensive was underway, with strong mobile and infantry forces threatening a breakthrough, either to the south and the *DG IV*, or more likely to the south-west and Vinnitsa. With the *XXXXII.AK* and *VII.AK* locked into their existing positions, the *PzAOK 1* simply had no forces available to defend against the Soviet outflanking manoeuvre south of the *VII.AK*, still less mount a counterattack in the same area with a view to closing the gap. Von Manstein's latest instructions, to use the *III.PzK* to attack north-westwards towards the right wing of the *PzAOK 4*, seemed to Hube to be based on a complete mis-appreciation of the situation further east. In other words, it seemed the Army Group believed the Soviet forces facing the right wing of the *PzAOK 1* no longer possessed any freedom of action. This situation and the lack of promised reinforcements, the *3.Panzer-Division* and the *Panzergrenadier-Division 'Grossdeutschland'*, left Hube facing an almost impossible predicament. The only way he stood any chance of stemming the Soviet advance was to deploy additional forces, and the only way he could do that was by pulling back and shortening his existing front line. His last remaining solution had thus been denied him. The *PzAOK 1* war diary records the deep disappointment of the *Armee*, from Hube down to the last soldier on the front line, at the decision to forbid any withdrawal. The effect of the order was that the *Armee* would be fighting with its hands tied behind its back, leaving the Russians to capitalise on their freedom of movement. To make matters worse, it was clear that every day that passed would make it more difficult to carry out a withdrawal if approval were finally to be given at a later date, and this in turn was likely to have a decisive effect upon the rest of the *PzAOK 1* front. Nevertheless, Hube accepted his instructions, and the measures already undertaken with the withdrawal were cancelled. The war diary records that the *Armee* did so with 'heavy hearts'.

Meanwhile, the fighting continued unabated. The clear weather continued and the morning broke with a deep frost, blue skies and good visibility. Under such conditions the temperature necessarily remained cold, never rising above -6°C, and there was a strong south-easterly wind to make it feel colder still. In the *XXXXII.AK* sector, the Soviets had undertaken a number of battalion-strength assaults against both the *Korps-Abteilung B* and the *82.Infanterie-Division*.[28] With the continuing clearer weather, there had also been an increase in Russian air activity, with reconnaissance sorties, and bombing and strafing attacks being reported throughout the whole *Korps* area, but particularly against the lines of supply and rear areas. The main targets had been Mironovka, Lipovets, and Maslovka. The ground attacks meanwhile had met with varied success. A few had been broken up by fire even before the Soviet units had finished assembling, but on at least one occasion, the attack had led to a breach in the defensive positions. Opposite the right wing of the *Korps-Abteilung B* there had been little combat activity, with the Russians concentrating instead on troop and materiel movements. There had been a lot of sledge traffic, and Soviet troops had even been observed moving up timber materials near Kanev on the Dnepr. Nevertheless, in the centre of the sector, the Russians had

---

28 XXXXII.AK., Tagesmeldung, 19.00 hours dated 7 Jan 44.

mounted a couple of assaults at about midday against the forward detachments around Lipovy Rog. Both these had been seen off without too much difficulty, leaving about 50 Russian dead on the field of battle. The attack was repeated at 16.00 hours, but with no more success. Over on the right, there had been another attack, at about 15.30 hours, this time north-east of Chernyshi. This had been carried out by an estimated two companies and was more serious, resulting in a penetration of the main defensive position. Fighting continued on into the evening when the *Korps-Abteilung B* mounted a counter-attack. Earlier in the day, at about 06.00 hours, on the *82.Infanterie-Division* sector further west, the Russians had attacked along the Rossavka valley east of Stavy, but the division had mounted a swift counterattack, throwing back the assault and taking a single prisoner. A few hours later, the Russians attacked again, this time on the Kagarlyk sector at about 09.00 hours. The assault, conducted by at least a battalion, managed to force a breach near the hospital, but fighting continued on through the day. By evening, the division had sealed off the penetration in a counterattack, taking another three prisoners. Deep in the rear area, in what amounted to the *Korps'* southern flank, the *Sperrverband* Boguslav[29] had meanwhile reported no contact with the enemy as at 13.00 hours, although it felt it necessary to make an urgent request for either flak support or fighter cover.

The *VII.AK* had meanwhile continued to pull back into its new positions, closely followed by the Russians along the whole front.[30] The enemy troops who had forced their way into Luka during the night remained generally quiet although there had been a few small-scale attacks. On the basis of captured documents and observation reports, Hell now suspected that the Soviet 1st Guards Cavalry Corps had been committed in the area and given the task of striking past the *Korps'* left flank by overtaking the withdrawal. Air reconnaissance over the area between the *VII.AK* and the *III.PzK* had discovered considerable horse-drawn traffic moving southwards from Satonskoe. In the *75.Infanterie-Division* sector, the Russians had brought up fresh forces and widened the breach they had created either side of Teleshovka, and with no troops available in the area, the division had been unable to mount any kind of counterattack. It had therefore started planning an attack against the penetration for the following day. Over on the right wing, there had been two other attacks, mounted by either one or two companies, but these had been seen off by the division. Nevertheless, reports indicated that the Russians were continuing to reinforce the area, particularly opposite the boundary with the *XXXII.AK*. The *88.Infanterie-Division* meanwhile had spent an easier day, with no combat activity other than disruptive artillery and mortar fire. Nevertheless, although they had not pressed the attack, the Russian troops had used the time to advance their forward detachments closer to the German positions. In the area now held by the *198. Infanterie-Division* on the southern flank, Soviet forces had attacked out of the Stepok area at about 13.00 hours following a heavy artillery bombardment, but the assault had been successfully defended. The Russians had then re-grouped, brought up fresh forces including six tanks, and renewed the attack a little further south towards the northern

---

29 The *PzAOK 1* papers do not seem to contain any reference to the creation of this clearly *ad-hoc* unit, which appears to have been formed to occupy and defend the area around the town of Boguslav on the river Ros'. Its task was presumably to hold the river crossing in the town, and prevent any Soviet forces from crossing the river and pushing northwards into the rear of the *Korps* area.

30 *VII.AK.*, Tagesmeldung, 19.30 hours dated 7 Jan 44.

end of Buda and Kislovka,[31] but this too met with no success. Further south, the Soviet armoured unit that had attacked Tarashcha the day before, struck out during the night and ran straight into the *34.Infanterie-Division* as it was still assembling. At about 02.00 hours, a force comprising around 30 tanks with mounted infantry, supported by other motorized infantry, made a two-wave assault against Luka and forced the division to pull back with considerable losses among the artillery units. The attack pressed on towards Dybintsy and was finally brought to a halt about 2½ kilometres south-west of the village, following the destruction of seven tanks by elements of the *III./Artillerie-Regiment 34*. Renewed attacks during the morning against Luk'yanovka, Koshevatoye, and Branoe Pole were all thrown back. In total, the division reported accounting for 13 Soviet tanks either destroyed or immobilized. By mid-afternoon, the division had mounted a counter-attack to re-capture Luka, using three battalions supported by the *Sturmgeschütz-Abteilungen 202* and *239*, but this made slow progress, owing to the poor road conditions, and continued on into the evening. Those elements assembling southeast of Branoe Pole meanwhile had reported no enemy contact at all, even though they were just a few kilometres away.

Breith's *III.PzK* had also had a difficult day.[32] During the course of the day, the Russians had moved up an estimated two additional rifle divisions opposite the *Korps'* right wing, closing with the forward German positions. The withdrawal of the *17.Panzer-Division*, with its headquarters now located in Potoki, west of Zhornishche, had been closely followed by strong infantry and armoured forces, with over 1,000 infantry and 60 tanks south of Lipovets in the Troshcha-Gordievka area alone. The *Korps'* attempt to close the gap between the two divisions had made progress, although Breith was now expecting the following day to bring a concerted Soviet attack, not only against the respective lead units, but also against the Troshcha-Gordievka area. On the right wing, in the sector held by the *6.Panzer-Division*, Soviet forces estimated at battalion-strength had advanced from the north through Adamovka towards Zarubintsy, crossing the marshy valley of the Gorny Tikich before capturing the northern end of the village. The division had thrown its last available troops into the counter-attack, and this continued on into the evening. At the same time, other Russian troops had attacked the positions around Shulyaki and forced the Germans to pull back across the river where they took up new positions on the high ground to the south. Further west, south of Oratov, another Soviet grouping of about two companies moved into the wood about two kilometres east of Gonoratka, only to be engaged by concentrated defensive fire. Meanwhile, the *Panzergruppe* of the *6.Panzer-Division* had moved off to the attack at 09.00 hours that morning, moving out from Gonoratka towards Koshlany and taking by surprise a Soviet force including tanks which was assembling in the woods to the south-west. The *Panzergruppe* dispersed the assembling troops, destroying four tanks, before heading off towards Koshlany at about 13.00 hours. By 15.00 hours, the lead elements had reached the town and began to take up positions in it in preparation for continuing the attack.

Opposite the *17.Panzer-Division*, the Russians had continued to reinforce the Ilyntsy area, and movements which had been spotted in the woods east of Borisovka to the south had been subjected to artillery fire. By about midday, Soviet forces had occupied the whole of the northern bank of the Sob between Ilyntsy and Gordievka and

---

31 Both of which were situated just north of Koshevatoye.
32 *III.PzK.*, Tagesmeldung, 19.15 hours dated 7 Jan 44.

were bringing up reinforcements of at least one rifle division from the Khorosha area. During the late afternoon, a massed attack by Russian troops in the Troshcha-Gordievka area against the division's weak covering force had forced a breach in the area of the low ground south-west of Troshcha. The division mounted a hasty counter-attack using tanks, *panzergrenadiers* and artillery, and this ran on into the evening. The division's own attack, supported by 'Tigers' from the *s.Panzer-Abteilung 506*, was meanwhile making only slow progress due mainly to poor terrain conditions, but by 16.00 hours the lead units had reached the southern church in Borisovka after first having taken Ulanova off the march and crossed the intervening high ground. Later in the evening, the division wheeled northwards and pressed the counter-attack into the centre of Ilyntsy during which it succeeded in re-taking the bridge over the river Sob. South of the action, the *III.PzK* reported Lysaya Gora and Krasnen'koe to be clear of enemy troops, as were all other villages as far south as the *DG IV*.

Overall, the Russians had continued in their efforts to roll up the left wing of the *VII.AK*, and intelligence had now picked up the presence of the 5th Guards Tank Corps on this sector. On the northern front, there had been local breaches in the Teleshovka area, while further south Kislovka had been assaulted from the north-west. Aerial reconnaissance had meanwhile spotted about 120 vehicles moving along the road from Belaya Tserkov' towards Tarashcha and heavy traffic had also been seen moving from Tarashcha towards Stavishche. A group of about 30 to 40 Soviet tanks had tried to force their way into Dybintsy from Luka, but had been checked and thrown back to the edge of the woods to the south-west.[33] No prisoners had been taken so it was not certain what unit these tanks belonged to. Further south it now seemed as though the Soviets were pushing forward into the gap between the *VII.AK* and the *III.PzK*, with aerial reconnaissance spotting units in the Tinovka area. On the right wing of the *III.PzK*, there were strong Russian troops in Shulyaki, and a battalion-sized assault had been made against Zarubintsy. Further west, the 155th Rifle Division had been identified in the Oratovka area, while a group of about 15 to 20 Soviet tanks had been disrupted in Koshlany by troops from the *6.Panzer-Division*. The line of the river Sob was now firmly held by strong Russian infantry between Ilyntsy and Berezovka, with the main concentration in the centre between Gordievka and Troshcha where a full rifle division was believed to hold the line. About 85 tanks had also been seen on the sector between Ilyntsy and Troshcha. The arrival of the new division suggested that the infantry formations were now closing up to the Shulyaki-Oratov-Ilyntsy-Vakhnovka line, and this, together with the assembly of a large number of tanks in the Ilyntsy area, probably indicated that the 1st Tank Army had now completed its current advance.

Elsewhere, the *101.Jäger-Division* was still arriving, and at 20.00 hours the *PzAOK 1* issued the division with its instructions for the following day.[34] The lead elements were to reach the area north-east of Bratslav where they were to secure the crossings over the Southern Bug between Nizhnaya Krapivna and Bratslav. Reconnaissance was meanwhile to be conducted in the wooded areas to the north-east, north and north-west, and contact was to be established with the anti-tank line set up by the *10.Flak-Division* in the Alexandrovka-Ometintsy area. In addition, the division was also to press further

---
33 German intelligence had identified the 1462nd Self-Propelled Artillery Regiment in this sector, and it was this that indicated the presence of the 5th Guards Tank Corps of which it was a part.
34 *PzAOK 1*, Ia Nr.40/44 geh. dated 7 Jan 44.

north and establish contact with the *17.Panzer-Division* towards Ilyntsy, although for the time being it would remain under the direct control of the *PzAOK 1* and not be released to the *III.PzK*.

Hube issued no further orders to either the *XXXXII.AK* or the *III.PzK* on 7 January, but he gave new instructions to Hell's *VII.AK* at 20.05 hours.[35] In these he directed the *Korps* to clear the Russian penetration in Luka, push its left wing forward to the high ground east of Krutye Gorby, and undertake wide-ranging reconnaissance-in-force in the gap to the *III.PzK*. Hell confirmed receipt of these orders later in the evening and additionally stated his intention to extend his left wing as far as the major road junction south-west of Isaiki and push forward his lines to Zakutintsy. In his report to Army Group South later that evening, Hube made brief mention of the air situation, referring to the considerable activity of the Russian air force, particularly against his supply routes and dumps, with the main target seeming to be Mironovka.[36] For its part the Luftwaffe had supported the *III.PzK* attack, in particular the *17.Panzer-Division*, with its efforts being recorded as 'indefatigable'.

Saturday 8 January 1944

Over on the right wing of the *PzAOK 1*, the *XXXXII.AK* had spent a busy night.[37] The *Korps-Abteilung B* had counterattacked during the previous evening, assaulting the Soviet penetration north of Chernyshi and succeeding in clearing the breach, killing 12 enemy soldiers and capturing a machine-gun. The Russians too had not been idle and had launched a number of assaults against the German forward positions around Lipovy Rog, leading to another breach in the area north of Pii. The *Korps-Abteilung* had counter-attacked almost immediately and by midnight the area had been cleared following heavy fighting. At that point, the troops manning the forward positions were pulled back to the main defence line. Further west too, in the area north of Kadomka, the Russians had undertaken several company-strength assaults beginning at 21.00 hours the previous evening, supported for the first time on this sector by cavalry troops, but all these had been seen off with reported heavy Soviet casualties. In the *82.Infanterie-Division* sector, there had been considerable Russian reconnaissance activity against the right wing, with motor noises being heard from the Sloboda area and a few other movements observed east of Stavy. Meanwhile the enemy penetration into the northern part of Kagarlyk had been cleared, resulting in 42 counted Russian dead, and the capture of four prisoners, a small calibre anti-tank gun, eight machine-guns and a quantity of small arms.

Opposite the northern sector of the *VII.AK*, the Soviets had limited their operations during the night to patrolling and light disruptive artillery fire, but east and south-east of Stepok and west of Buda they pushed ahead with their attacks. In the north, the *75.Infanterie-Division* had first sealed off and then cleared a breach in Teleshovka, capturing a small amount of light equipment. At 23.40 hours the previous day, the *198.Infanterie-Division* had similarly cleared up another penetration south of Stepok in a counter-attack, whilst the *34.Infanterie-Division* had re-captured Luka the same evening, destroying two Russian tanks in the process. A different breach by an estimated 150 enemy troops north of Buda was also cleared up by about 22.00 hours the previous

---

35 *PzAOK 1*, Ia Nr.41/44 geh. dated 7 Jan 44.
36 *PzAOK 1*, Tagesmeldung, Ia an *Heeresgruppe Süd*, 22.00 hours dated 7 Jan 44.
37 *PzAOK 1*, Morgenmeldung, 05.30 hours dated 8 Jan 44.

evening, although by early morning there were new reports of Soviet armour being moved up towards the German positions in Branoe Pole, with at least nine tanks having been counted.

Further south, in the *III.PzK* sector, Soviet forces spent the entire night assaulting the whole length of the positions held by the *6.Panzer-Division* along the Gorny Tikich with the sole exception of Zarubintsy. A battalion-strength assault against Buzovka on the right had begun at about 23.00 hours, but this had come to grief in the German defensive artillery fire. Further west though, Russian troops had successfully pushed forward into the northern end of Knyazh'ya Krinitsa, before being engaged by German flak units operating in the ground role. However, the main weight of the night assault lay on the left wing in the area around Gonoratka where an initial attack from the north at about 22.30 hours had been beaten back. An hour later the Russians renewed their attacks, this time with a pincer movement from both the north and east and involving at least two battalions. The fighting continued through the night, and by early morning the *6.Panzer-Division* was preparing to counter-attack. Further west, the *17.Panzer-Division* had tried to blow the bridge in Ilyntsy, but had failed owing to direct enemy action, and on the left its withdrawal movement had been struck by advancing Soviet armour either side of Popovka. For some time during the night, contact with the division was lost during the ongoing fighting, but it was restored by morning. To the west of Ilyntsy, the Russians had launched heavy attacks against the German positions on the Sibok river in Ulanovka, but despite the weight of the assault, the division held its positions.[38] Further upstream, the bridge over the Sibok at Yakubovka had been secured by elements of the *Pionier-Bataillon*, whilst to the north ten Russian tanks had been intercepted by the weakened *Panzergrenadier-Regiment 63* supported by four Panthers. To the west, 16 Soviet tanks with accompanying infantry had moved against Pesochin, no doubt trying to seize a bridge somewhere over the river, but despite the difficulties brought about by the piling snowdrifts, the weak defence managed to hold its positions, destroy five of the attacking tanks, and inflict considerable casualties on the infantry too.

At 07.30 hours, Hube passed his report to von Manstein, advising the Army Group that according to reports from the *III.PzK* at 04.50 that morning, between 50 and 60 Soviet tanks had been observed heading west on the Ilyntsy-Obodnoe road just north of Ivan'ki.[39] The *Armee* had also informed the *PzAOK 4* of this development. The report led Hube to issue revised orders to the *101.Jäger-Division*, and these were sent out at 09.00 hours.[40] The division's earlier instructions were superseded as there was now a very real possibility that this Russian column might push on westwards through Obodnoe and head straight for the town of Vinnitsa. This town was an important road and rail junction, and its loss would have given the Germans significant logistical problems. The *101.Jäger-Division* was therefore ordered to secure the unloading area in Vinnitsa and prevent any Soviet breakthrough towards the town in the area either side of the main road fork north of Komarov, namely between the left wing of the *17.Panzer-Division* and the right wing of the *4.Gebirgs-Division* under the *PzAOK 4* to the north. As part of this task, the division was also to reconnoitre eastwards as far as the Korolevka-Obodnoe road and try to establish contact with the *4.Gebirgs-Division* in the area around Lozovataya, some

---

38 *III.PzK.*, Nachmeldung, 07.45 hours dated 8 Jan 44.
39 *PzAOK 1*, Tagesmeldung, Ia an *Heeresgruppe Süd*, 07.30 hours dated 8 Jan 44.
40 *PzAOK 1*, Ia Nr.27/44 geh. dated 8 Jan 44.

12 kilometres north of Obodnoe. Army Group South confirmed this change in orders later in the morning.⁴¹ At the same time, von Manstein instructed Hube to prevent any breakthrough, particularly by enemy armoured forces, to both Vinnitsa and its airfield, by concentrating the *101.Jäger-Division* in the area around the railway junction east of Pisarevka, namely around Gumennoe station. Later that afternoon, the *101.Jäger-Division* informed the *PzAOK 1* that, following a forced landing, a reconnaissance pilot had said he had seen about 60 Soviet tanks moving along the main road from Berestovka⁴² towards Gumennoe, only 15 kilometres away from Vinnitsa. Other ground reconnaissance reports indicated that about 15 tanks, with an estimated rifle company in support, were moving from Obodnoe to Stepanovka, whilst another similar-sized unit was heading south-west to Bairakovka.

Meanwhile, following overnight snowfall of about five centimetres, the day had broken sunny and clear with temperatures rising as high as -2°C. If the sunshine brought some relief, the recent snow had also created problems, with roads in some areas being blocked by drifting. If his left wing was causing Hube some consternation, he also had other worries away on his right where the Russians continued to batter against the boundary between the *XXXXII.AK* and the *VII.AK*. At about midday, *Oberst* Franz, the chief of staff at the *XXXXII.AK*, had informed the *PzAOK 1* of the latest situation regarding the breach between the two *Korps*, and stressed the very real danger of them being torn wide apart. Shortly afterwards, Hube ordered both Hell and Mattenklott to make preparations for a withdrawal of their respective inner wings during the coming night to a position where they could again establish contact. The new position was codenamed 'Anna' and was to run on a line from Krasnopolka to the northern tip of Zemlyanka to Ol'shanitsa. As part of this withdrawal, the *VII.AK* was also to prepare an attack group behind its right wing such that it could also be deployed easily on the left wing of the *XXXXII.AK* if needs be. The order to execute 'Anna' went out shortly before 14.00 hours once it became all too obvious that the existing breach could not be cleared using the troops currently available. The Soviets meanwhile continued to attack throughout the afternoon.⁴³ Supported by a few tanks, they had succeeded in creating a large breach in the German defensive positions. The fighting continued into the evening and the situation remained unclear for some time, although Mattenklott reported that further assaults against the new 'Anna' line could be expected, with the main effort on the left. The *Korps-Abteilung B* had thrown back company-strength attacks north of Vedmedevka and south of Pevtsy, leaving 30 dead enemy on the field, whilst artillery had been used to disrupt other Soviet assembly areas around Lipovy Rog. During the morning, the *82.Infanterie-Division* had managed to clear up a small penetration by an estimated rifle battalion in the area of hill 177.2, and disperse a separate troop assembly around hill 183.3. Things had become more difficult in the afternoon though, and a serious breach occurred south and east of Stavy where individual tanks had broken through towards Ternovka, but the situation was still unclear by evening. Once again, there had been almost continuous Soviet air strikes throughout the *Korps* area, with most of the activity being directed against supply routes and installations, particularly Mironovka, Ivanovka and Boguslav.

41 Hgr. Süd, Ia Nr.112/44 g.Kdos. dated 8 Jan 44.
42 Referred to as Felixowka in the German records.
43 *XXXXII.AK.*, Tagesmeldung, 19.30 hours dated 8 Jan 44.

The *VII.AK* had also had a difficult day. It too had been subject to lively air activity over the whole *Korps* area following the clearing skies, and the Soviets had reinforced their assaults against the right wing at the boundary with the *XXXII.AK*. This had resulted in a new breach in the front line in addition to the widening of the existing penetration in Teleshovka. Reconnaissance in front of the southern wing of the *Korps* had indicated that a Soviet armoured unit, probably the 5th Guards Tank Corps, was now heading towards Medvin from which position it could roll up the *Korps'* flank. In the *75.Infanterie-Division* sector, the counter-attack had failed to clear the breach in Teleshovka although the heavy fighting, with considerable casualties on both sides, seemed to have prevented any serious widening of the existing penetration. As a result of the major breach in the area of the *82.Infanterie-Division* to its right, the division was obliged at 13.30 hours to issue orders to pull back its right wing to the line Leshchinka-Teleshovka, and it started moving back to the 'Anna' line at about 17.00 hours that evening. In comparison, the *88.Infanterie-Division* had a relatively quiet day, having to defend a single battalion assault in the Prussy area. The *198.Infanterie-Division* meanwhile had to deal with a couple of minor incursions, seeing off an enemy patrol against the Sech bridgehead during the morning, and defending a larger assault of between 150 and 200 Soviet infantry against Buda. The division also reported enemy movements opposite its left wing. Reconnaissance in the *34.Infanterie-Division* sector near Krutye Gorby, and in the gap further east, had indicated that both Sofiyevka and Krasnogorodka were already occupied by Russian troops. According to statements given by members of the local population, there were eight Soviet tanks with accompanying infantry in Sofiyevka, making a total of 15 tanks that had been observed opposite the division's front during the day. The division had set the time for its counter-attack against Krutye Gorby for 19.00 hours, but no news of its progress arrived at the *PzAOK 1* that evening. There was likewise no news of the assault by the *Sturmgeschützen* against the high ground west of Medvin. Despite this lack of information, Hell still reported his intentions for the following day at about 19.45 hours that evening.[44] He would continue with the *34.Infanterie-Division* counter-attack, deploying a *Regimentsgruppe* against each of Krutye Gorby and Zakutintsy, with the objective of destroying the Soviet forces advancing towards Medvin.

On the front held by the *III.PzK*, the Russians had continued their attacks against the German positions along the Gorny Tikich.[45] On the right an estimated three rifle divisions had assaulted the *6.Panzer-Division* on a broad front heading south, and succeeded in forcing crossings over the river in several places. Sabadash and Buzovka had both been taken, whilst the division's counter-attack to recapture the northern end of Zarubintsy had been called off at about midday after making good initial progress. The majority of the troops involved in the counter-attack were pulled back to support the position in Tsybulev to the south-west, where Russian units had succeeded in breaking into the northern edge of the town against the defending flak units. On the division's left wing, Soviet forces had also managed to break through the defences around Knyazh'ya Krinitsa and Frontovka, and the defending flak troops were pulled back to the high ground further south. The *6.Panzer-Division* reacted swiftly, and a rapid counter-attack

---

44 *VII.AK.*, Ia Nr.131/44 geh. dated 8 Jan 44. According to this report the *Sturmgeschütz-Abteilungen 202* and *239* now deployed just 11 and 9 assault guns respectively.

45 *III.PzK.*, Tagesmeldung, 19.20 hours dated 8 Jan 44.

caught the Russians in Frontovka by surprise and they were effectively wiped out as a fighting force, with 100 counted dead and 70 taken prisoner. Gonoratka, to the north-west, was abandoned following an overwhelming Soviet assault, and the battalion deployed there fell back to a line running from hill 274.8 to the workhouse. Other assaults in the area, including a pincer attack from the south-west and north-east against Koshlany, were all thrown back, but the division in any case pulled its wing back to a line running from Frontovka through Kantelina to Zhadany where it was tasked with establishing contact with the *17.Panzer-Division*.

On the left, the Soviet 1st Tank Army had probably wheeled its main force westwards, leaving only elements to attack the positions held by the *17.Panzer-Division*. This had allowed Breith a certain freedom of manoeuvre, and he was currently trying to contain the Soviet bridgehead by establishing a new defensive position on the line Zhadany-Vasilevka-Lysaya Gora-Krasnen'koe-Zhornishche. He was also using the opportunity to try and close the gap between his two divisions. Having failed to blow the bridge in Ilyntsy the previous night, the *17.Panzer-Division*, with its headquarters now in Ometintsy 15 kilometres to the south, was now obliged to give up its positions on the river Sob. It had tried to attack to recapture the bridge and destroy it, but the effort had come to nothing in the face of determined Russian counter-attacks. With its *Panzergrenadier* strength considerably reduced as a result of the previous days' fighting, it now fell back southwards under continued Soviet pressure. Rearguards were left to fend off further enemy advances while the rest of the division pulled back in an orderly fashion, leaving forward detachments north of Zhornishche and in the area around Bondurovka. The division reported heavy concentrations of Soviet armour, up to 50 tanks, west of its left wing in the Potoki-Voitovtsy-Ferdinandovka area, from which it foresaw a continued enemy advance either to the south-east or the south-west, striking either further into the gap or rolling up the *Korps'* left flank.

For Hube then, the day had passed much the same as previous ones. The *XXXXII. AK* had been attacked on a broad front for much of the day, but in all probability these were no more than pinning attacks to assist the Soviet attempts to outflank the southern wing of the *VII.AK*. In addition to these attacks, the Russians had persisted in their efforts to outflank the left wing of the *VII.AK*, with the presence of the 5th Guards Tank Corps now being confirmed following the establishment of the 22nd Guards Tank Brigade around Bolkun.[46] A captured map suggested that the corps was aiming eastward towards Boguslav and Mironovka station. To the south, some troops had pushed forward to northern edge of Medvin, while others had occupied Sofiyevka with a few tanks and other vehicles. Further south still, the Soviets were also beginning to push units through the gap towards Zhashkov and Tsybulev, and were increasing the pressure along the line of the Gorny Tikich, occupying Poboinaya, assaulting Buzovka from the north, and forcing their way into Sharnopol' from Zarubintsy. They had also broken into the northern edges of Tsybulev and Knyazh'ya-Krinitsa, while attacking Balabanovka, Frontovka and Gonoratka further west. It all suggested that the Russians were stepping up the pressure towards the *DG IV* east of Gaisin. Further west, the towns of Zhadany, Zhornishche and Ferdinandovka had all fallen, and between 50 and 60 Russian tanks had been spotted heading westwards from Ilyntsy, with an advanced guard of about

---

46 *PzAOK 1*, Ic Abendmeldung, 21.30 hours dated 8 Jan 44.

15 having reached Stepanovka. Another group of about 60 had also been seen near Schastlivaya just after midday. According to aerial reconnaissance at least two tanks had already pressed on as far as Gumennoe, while three others had already blocked the *DG IV* south of Voronovitsa. Thus, while the infantry pressure against the right wing of the *III.PzK* was beginning to grow, the Russians had wheeled the armoured units of the 1st Tank Army away from Ilyntsy and started to move to the west into the gap between the *III.PzK* and the *4.Gebirgs-Division* on the right wing of the *PzAOK 4*. The 8th Guards Mechanised Corps was now suspected of being in the Volovodovka-Obodnoe-Stepanovka area, with the 11th Guards Tank Corps to its right. It was therefore anticipated that the Russians were now trying to take Vinnitsa from the south-east while forcing back the forward elements of the *III.PzK*. The *Panzerarmee* was expecting a breakthrough towards Vinnitsa the following day, and in light of this appraisal, Hube issued new orders at 19.55 hours that evening.[47] The *XXXXII.AK* and the *VII.AK* received confirmation that they were to pull back during the night to the 'Anna' position, with the *VII.AK* being reminded of the need to assemble an assault group behind its right wing. The *III.PzK* was to prevent any Soviet breakthrough towards the *DG IV* between Uman' and Gaisin. If the situation required, it was to fall back westwards behind the river Sob, screen the area between Novaya Dashev and Gaisin and prepare to re-deploy the *17.Panzer-Division* to attack south of the Buzovka-Tsybulev-Balabanovka line. The *Korps* was also to secure the bridges over the river Bug in Semenki, Bratslav and Pechera, and prevent any Soviet interference in those areas. The *101.Jäger-Division* was meanwhile to continue securing the unloading area and airfield in Vinnitsa, and prevent a Russian breakthrough east of the town over the line Voronovitsa-Komarov-Telepen'ki. The division was to send out patrols to establish and maintain contact with the *4.Gebirgs-Division* on its left, and carry out continuous reconnaissance of the area south-east of Nemirov towards the left wing of the *III.PzK*.

At 19.45 hours that evening, Hube also issued orders to the *371.Infanterie-Division*, which was then newly arriving from the Balkans.[48] The division was to remain initially at the disposal of Army Group South and assemble south-west of Vinnitsa in the area between Zhmerinka and Gnivan' bounded by a line running from Gnivan' though Vitava, Voroshilovka and Potoki to the Gnivan'-Zhmerinka railway line. In addition it was to secure the bridge over the river Bug at Gnivan' as well as putting out reconnaissance and security detachments to the east and north-east, namely towards Vinnitsa and the positions of the *101.Jäger-Division*.

Meanwhile, reinforcements continued to trickle in, and at 18.30 hours Hube informed Breith that the *Panzer-Zerstörer-Bataillon (mot.) 471* would be attached to the *III.PzK* on its arrival, with the lead elements being expected later the same day.[49] About half an hour later a message arrived from Army Group South informing Hube that the *6.Armee* was finally releasing the remaining units of the *s.Panzer-Abteilung 506*, comprising seven operational and four damaged 'Tigers' from the Krivoi Rog area together with the workshop platoon, and a further three operational 'Tigers' from Nikolayev.[50]

---

47 PzAOK 1, Ia Nr.18/44 g.Kdos dated 8 Jan 44.
48 PzAOK 1, Ia Nr.42/44 geh. dated 8 Jan 44.
49 PzAOK 1, Ia Nr.45/44 geh. dated 8 Jan 44.
50 Hgr. Süd, Ia Nr.116/44 geh. dated 8 Jan 44.

During the course of the evening, Hube telephoned von Manstein personally to describe the situation facing Breith's *III.PzK* with its two weakened *Panzer-Divisions*. After pointing out the poor state of both divisions, Hube asked von Manstein not to allow the *Korps* to become split up, suggesting instead that the *17.Panzer-Division* leave weak covering forces in its previous positions and be allowed to fall back eastwards over the river Sob, rather than westwards, so that it could join forces again with the *6.Panzer-Division*. Hube believed the risk associated with such a move would be manageable, given the counterattack which was then being planned by the *PzAOK 4* for 11 January in the Vinnitsa area. Von Manstein agreed, but insisted that the Bug bridges in Semenki, Bratslav and Pechera still be guarded. Hube also made another attempt to obtain approval to withdraw his right wing to free two divisions for operations on the southern wing of the *VII.AK*. Now that the Soviet 5th Guards Tank Corps had been identified on the *Korps'* left wing, Hube no longer knew how to give the *Korps* any further assistance in the face of the continuing threat, particularly as the *Panzerarmee* had already transferred all available forces to lengthen its southern wing at the expense of weakening its northern front. He pointed out that since such a withdrawal would have to be carried out sooner or later as a result of the general situation, the current delay was only costing men and materiel which he could not afford to lose. Von Manstein replied that he was well aware of all that, and promised to see what might be done.

Sunday 9 January 1944

By early the next morning, the *PzAOK 1* had summarised the night's reports from its subordinate units.[51] In the *XXXXII.AK* sector, Russian troops noticed the *Korps* withdrawal and followed up closely behind. There had been a few attempts by Soviet forces to break into the new positions, but these had all been broken up, some following local counterattacks. In the *Korps-Abteilung B* area, the Russians had undertaken a company-strength assault north of Pii and also sent forward a combat patrol in the same area. Both of these had been thrown back by the forward positions east of Pevtsy. There had also been disruptive artillery fire throughout the area, but apart from that there had been no activity of any significance. On the left wing of the *82.Infanterie-Division*, the earlier Soviet penetration into the centre of Rossavka had been sealed off and two Russian tanks immobilised in the process. After that, things quietened down, and the Soviet troops made no further effort to push forward. However, as the division began to pull back, the Russians pursued closely and managed to take advantage of the movement to achieve a breakthrough with about 150 men in the area three kilometres west of Yanovka. The German troops reacted quickly and by 02.00 hours the penetration had been cleared and the main defensive position restored. The counterattack brought in a single prisoner and a quantity of equipment, and had accounted for 86 Russian dead. The division had taken up its new positions by 02.00 hours.

---

51 *PzAOK 1*, Tagesmeldung 05.30 hours dated 9 Jan 44. A report early the same morning from the *III.PzK* gave the *Korps'* armoured strength as:
  • *6.Panzer-Division*: 6 *Panzer IV lg*; 1 Command vehicle
  • *17.Panzer-Division*: 5 *Panzer V*; 1 Command vehicle
  • *Panzer-Abteilung 506*: 7 *Panzer VI*
  • *Sturmgeschütz-Abteilung 249*: 5 StuGs.

Meanwhile, in the *VII.AK* sector to the west, the *75.Infanterie-Division* had fallen back and occupied its new defensive positions only to be immediately attacked by an estimated two Soviet rifle companies in the Zemlyanka area. The division managed to hold its own however, and the new positions were maintained. In contrast, both the *88.* and the *198.Infanterie-Division* had spent quiet nights, but away on the hanging southern flank the *34.Infanterie-Division* had been subjected to a surprise attack including artillery and tanks in the Buda and Luk'yanovka sectors a few kilometres south-east of Tarashcha. Despite stiff resistance from the defending Soviet troops, the division's own night attack had resulted in the capture of Krutye Gorby eight or so kilometres further south.

In the *III.PzK* sector, the *6.Panzer-Division* had meanwhile demolished the bridge over the Gorny Tikich in Buzovka, south of Zhashkov, after the village had been occupied in strength by Soviet troops. Unfortunately, this did not actually prevent some of the Russian troops from managing to cross to the southern bank. Soviet attacks against the village of Ostrozhany just to the west had by and large been repulsed, although some Russian elements had managed to secure a foothold between the two places. In Tsybulev, a few kilometres further west again, the division had managed to maintain the line envisaged, although some Soviet troops had forced their way over the Gniloi Tikich and occupied the wooded area to the west of the town and north of Antonina. The division acknowledged that it would need to undertake some action to seal off the breach. Twelve kilometres further west, the village of Korytnya had also been captured by Russian forces, and to the left Soviet elements had also infiltrated through the *Flak* positions south of Stupki, between Balabanovka and Novoselka. On its left wing, the *6.Panzer-Division* had taken up new positions as ordered, although here too, the withdrawal had been closely followed up by weak Russian elements such that north of Dashev, the village of Zhadany had been occupied by Soviet forces. In the *17.Panzer-Division* area, strong Russian forces had attacked during the night from both east and west, and had broken into the division's defensive positions as far as the centre of Krasnen'koe, ten kilometres south of Ilyntsy. In the event, the local *Flak* units had been unable to provide effective support for the division's defence as they had run very low on ammunition. The division organised a counter-attack with *Panzers* and *StuGs*, and this was still underway by early morning. Because the Soviet advance had interfered with the planned routes of retreat, the division began to withdraw during the night to a line running from the north-west edge of the wood two kilometres south of Krasnen'koe to northern Ometintsy. Meanwhile, east of Vinnitsa, the *101.Jäger-Division* had thrown back a Soviet armoured assault at about 19.00 hours the previous evening. The attack had come in from the Gumennoe station area heading westwards, and had been turned back largely due to effective anti-tank fire. Being unable to press on into Vinnitsa, about 30 Russian tanks, with mounted infantry, had then wheeled away to the south, overrunning the divisions' positions in Komarov before making two separate assaults on the town of Voronovitsa further south. The division counterattacked, heading north along the road to Komarov, forcing the Russians to withdraw and pull back into the ravine just north of the village. The fighting however continued.

The new day dawned sunny again and proved to be even warmer than previous days, though fortunately the condition of the roads remained unchanged. Over on the river Dnepr, the *XXXXII.AK* had managed to hold its own throughout the day.[52] On the *Korps-Abteilung B* front, Russian forces had attacked the area north of Vedmedevka in the morning, resulting in three separate breaches in the defensive positions. Counterattacks had been launched and all three penetrations sealed off and cleared. In a separate incident, a Soviet combat patrol with about 30 men was intercepted north of Shadovka, and during the ensuing fire fight about 15 of them had been killed. Meanwhile, the *82.Infanterie-Division* had moved its headquarters to Zelen'ki south of Kagarlyk, whilst elements of the division had thrown back an initial Soviet assault north of Krasnopolka, before a renewed attack in battalion strength finally led to a penetration of the defensive position. By midday though, the division had successfully mounted a counterattack and cleared the area. Two other assaults were also made by the Russians in company strength against the north-western part of Yanovka, but these were thrown back. South-west of Kagarlyk, artillery fire had been directed onto a column of an estimated 300 Russian troops moving across the high ground three kilometres north-east of Ternovka, whilst during the afternoon in the same area a battalion column including motor vehicles was observed moving south-east from Vintsentovka towards Leshchinka. In total some 20 prisoners had been brought in, along with a quantity of machineguns and small arms, and the *Korps* reported a total of 122 counted Russian dead. In addition, there were now unconfirmed reports of about 30 Soviet tanks in the area north of Vedmedevka. Mattenklott was therefore reckoning on the pinning attacks continuing in the days to come, although the *Korps* did report that the Russians were reinforcing the sector opposite its left wing.

Little of significance occurred in the sector held by Hell's *VII.AK*.[53] There had been no major Soviet assaults along the *Korps* front, although on the southern wing, south-east of Tarashcha, German troops had re-taken the villages of Krutye Gorby, Sofiyevka and Poberezhka, destroying two T-34 tanks, two assault guns and a self-propelled gun during the action. Further south-east though, Mitaevka and Pisarevka had both been occupied by Russian troops, and, according to statements from local inhabitants, a Soviet armoured unit with about 30 tanks had set off early on 9 January, heading from Krasnogorodka towards Zvenigorodka. In response, Hube issued orders at 19.10 hours transferring the *Sperrverband* of the *XXXXII.AK* on the river Ros' to Hell's *VII.AK* with immediate effect so that it could be deployed to lengthen the hanging southern flank. This was followed by a further instruction to both *Korps* commanders concerning operations for the following day.[54] The orders stated that a number of Soviet tanks had been reported west of Zvenigorodka, with a presumed intention of outflanking the *VII.AK* south of Medvin, and that the *VII.AK* should carry out an attack on 10 January heading southwards for Boyarka, about halfway between Tarashcha and Zvenigorodka on the Gniloi Tikich river. The intention of the attack was twofold: to prevent any attempted encirclement by the Russians moving northwards into the *Korps* rear area, and to pin Soviet forces in the area to prevent any further advance to the south-east.

---

52 *XXXXII.AK* Tagesmeldung, 22.00 hours dated 9 Jan 44.
53 Unreferenced teletype message timed 20.05 hours dated 9 Jan 44.
54 *PzAOK 1*, Ia Nr. 52/44 geh. dated 9 Jan 44.

THE *1.PANZERARMEE* SPLITS INTO THREE

Over on the left wing of the *Panzerarmee*, Breith's *III.PzK* had passed another difficult day.[55] In the east, following considerable Russian pressure, the *6.Panzer-Division* had been obliged to give up its positions in Buzovka, where the main road from Zhashkov to Uman' crossed the Gorny Tikich, and it had fallen back on Konela about five kilometres further south. A few kilometres to the west, the division was again outflanked by Soviet forces, and it pulled back its units once more, this time to the northern edge of Knyazhiki and Vladislavchik. Soviet troops meanwhile continued to expand their bridgehead over the Gorny Tikich and occupied Konelski wood and Konel'skie Khutora itself, before wheeling to the west to take part in a two-pronged attack against Vladislavchik from the Zyubrikha and Sharnopol' areas. The division successfully repelled all these attacks. Further west though, Tsybulev had been lost during the course of the morning, threatening to outflank the troops in Vladislavchik, but the division mounted a quick counterattack and managed to regain the southern half of the town. At about 15.00 hours, the Russians had renewed their assaults and forced the defending *Flak* troops to retreat again to the southern edge of the town. The division began building new defensive positions on the northern edge of the wooded area to the south. On the western edge of the same wood, the division laid down heavy artillery fire on the village of Antonina, forcing the majority of Soviet troops to withdraw to Knyazh'ya Krinitsa. Further west, another Russian force of about two battalions advanced during the afternoon, heading south-west from Korytnya and crossing the railway line, despite the resistance put up by the local *Flak* units. The division started a counterattack to try and clear the penetration. As part of the same drive, Soviet troops put in a concentrated assault against Rossokhovata, and managed to push into the village before a counterattack managed to recapture and clear the southern part.

In the sector held by the *17.Panzer-Division*, the right wing had been relatively quiet, although the breakthrough made by Soviet forces the previous night either side of Krasnen'koe had led to the encirclement of the *Flak-Abteilung* in that town. The division, with its headquarters now in Nosovtsy to the south-east of Sitkovtsy, had then launched a counterattack and recaptured the town, relieving the encircled *Flak* troops, and accounting for a reported nine Soviet anti-tank guns destroyed and a large number of Russian soldiers killed. A separate action, this time against a Soviet column of about battalion strength marching from the north-east towards the town, resulted in the destruction of a further seven anti-tank guns and reported heavy losses for the Russian troops. Overall, the division reported having killed an estimated 250 Russian soldiers during the day. With the onset of darkness, it began to wheel anti-clockwise as authorised by the *III.PzK*, and pulled back its left wing to take up new positions on a line facing east running from Lysaya Gora through Ometintsy to Semenki, and from there along the line of the river Bug westwards to Bratslav and Pechera.

The sector further west was no longer Hube's responsibility. At 12.40 hours the *PzAOK 1* had received a call from Army Group South informing it that the *101.Jäger-*

---

55 *III.PzK* Tagesmeldung, 19.30 hours dated 9 Jan 44. The report indicated the *Korps'* operational armoured strength as:
- *17.Panzer-Division:* 2 Panzer V;
- *Panzer-Abteilung 506:* 6 Panzer VI
- *Sturmgeschütz-Abteilung 249:* 6 StuGs.

Division was to be transferred to the *PzAOK 4* with immediate effect,[56] and this message was passed to the division later that afternoon. At the same time, Hube asked the division for its latest situation, and the reply arrived shortly before 18.30 hours that evening, confirming the worst.[57] The Russian tanks had now broken through Komarov and had pushed on westwards as far as Tyut'ki station, south of Vinnitsa. The *Jäger-Regiment 228*, supported by an *Artillerie-Abteilung*, was still holding its positions in Voronovitsa despite now being surrounded, and the division was organising a counter-attack from Sokirintsy to relieve the encircled troops. Elsewhere, the division's front had been quiet. Later in the day, Hube also learned he had lost his second major unit when a telegram arrived from Army Group South instructing the *PzAOK 1* to transfer the *371.Infanterie-Division* to the *PzAOK 4* as well.[58] This transfer was also to take place immediately, although it was more than likely that the division would remain at the disposal of the Army Group for the time being. In the meantime, it was made responsible for securing its own assembly area, particularly the important rail junction at Zhmerinka, whilst the Army Group planned to attach to it both the *II./Panzer-Regiment 23* and the *s.Panzer-Abteilung 503*, with a view to clearing the southern bank of the river Bug of Soviet armoured and motorised forces.

And as if the problems facing Hube were not already bad enough, a new issue now raised its head to compound his already considerable difficulties. Deep in the rear area, in the wooded area north-east of Uman', a partisan group armed with machineguns and mortars had seemingly come to life and had taken the town of Man'kovka about 24 or so kilometres north of Uman', wresting it from a weak German garrison. They had then proceeded to head south where they occupied Potash station, cutting the Potash-Leshchinovka railway line and causing considerable confusion. A few trains had been attacked subsequently, and the *BvTO* had been requested to move the *Panzerzug 62* to the area the following morning to try and assist in restoring the situation. Unfortunately for Hube, there were no longer any German troops north of the railway line between Tal'noe and Leshchinovka, although the airfield south-west of Tal'noe was still held by a small garrison. In desperation, Hube turned to whatever forces he could, and issued instructions to the *Armee-Pionier-Führer*, *Oberst* Luschnig, and the *Artillerie-Division z.b.V. 311* to tackle the problem.[59] Luschnig was instructed to secure the roads from Man'kovka through Krasnopolka to Uman' around Potash station. For the task, he was to be assigned two 'G-Wagen' from the *BvTO* in the Potash station area, and use them to establish contact between the various patrols deployed by the *Artillerie-Division z.b.V. 311* along the line of the railway.[60] In turn, the *Artillerie-Division z.b.V. 311*[61] was to begin patrolling all the roads which crossed the railway between Rogi in the east and Pobodnaya in the west. Both units were to maintain close contact and report the results of all reconnaissance, both to the *Panzerarmee*, and also to *Generalmajor* Kittel, the *Kampfkommandant* in Uman'.

---

56 Hgr. Süd, Ia Nr.12/44 geh. dated 9 Jan 44.
57 Radio message from *101.Jäger-Division* to *PzAOK 1*; 18.28 hours dated 9 Jan 44.
58 Hgr. Süd, Ia Nr.140/44 g.Kdos dated 9 Jan 44.
59 *PzAOK 1*, Ia Nr.56/44 geh. dated 9 Jan 44.
60 The G-Wagen (or *Gelände-Wagen*) was a light, wheeled, four-wheel drive, all–terrain vehicle.
61 This formidable-sounding unit was actually no more than a headquarters for artillery. Until 24 November 1943, it had been designated the *Höherer Artillerie-Kommandeur 311*.

THE *1.PANZERARMEE* SPLITS INTO THREE   227

The day had been much the same again for the *PzAOK 1*. The Soviets were still trying to outflank the southern wing of the *VII.AK*, and intelligence received now indicated that the 5th Guards Tank Corps had been committed to the area for that purpose.[62] Two brigades had been established at the front, with a third still hanging back north of Rakitnoe. The 22nd Guards Tank Brigade had been given the task of capturing Medvin, presumably to open the road to Zvenigorodka, although it was already known that some tanks had broken through earlier and had opened fire on the town from the high ground to the west. Meanwhile it had been established that elements of the 240th Rifle Division had been drawn off from the Zhashkov area with orders to take Zarubintsy to the south-west, and continuing troop movements from Zhashkov towards Korytnya suggested that a new formation had been committed in the area, possibly having been transferred from the northern front of the *VII.AK*. Having crossed the Gorny Tikich, Soviet infantry had pushed into Konel'skie Khutora and Vladislavchik, and had advanced into the southern end of Tsybulev. Further west, a force of about two battalions had also attacked southwards out of Korytnya in an attempt to take Rossokhovata, while the fighting still raged for Podvysokoe. Further west, the Soviets maintained their southward pressure against the forward positions of the *III.PzK* with infantry forces, although the 17 anti-tank guns captured in the counterattack around Krasnen'koe indicated that they were still expecting German armour on that sector.

Later that evening, Hube made his report to von Manstein at Army Group South.[63] In it he summarised the day's events, adding that Zvenigorodka had now been taken under fire by Soviet armoured units, probably the 22nd Guards Tank Brigade of the 5th Guards Tank Corps, which had taken up position on the high ground west of the town. He was also able to update the Army Group commander on the partisan situation north of Uman', and reported that the initial *Pionier* operations had proved fruitless. The continuing large Soviet movements into the area of the breach between the *VII.AK* and the *III.PzK*, and the ever-increasing pressure against the latter's right wing, was causing real concern at Hube's headquarters. There were now Russian tanks as far east as Zvenigorodka, and, it seemed, as far south as the Leshchinka-Potash railway north of Uman'. Even if these were only forward detachments supported by local partisans, the situation still demanded serious consideration. Hube believed that his *Armee* was no longer able to prevent this Soviet advance as long as his right wing was held fast in its positions by 'orders from above'. There was now no way in which he could prevent the Russians from blocking the railway line upon which not only his own right wing, but also the neighbouring *8.Armee*, depended so heavily. With some justification, the *Panzerarmee* pointed out that it had foreseen the possibility of such a development, and repeatedly drawn attention to the danger it posed, but all requests to draw back from what was called the 'balcony' had been denied. In response, Army Group South issued new orders to the *PzAOK 1*.[64] These indicated that von Manstein was still more concerned with the gap between Hube and the *PzAOK 4* away to the north-west and the threat posed by the Soviet 1st Tank Army south of Vinnitsa. The new orders instructed Hube to concentrate the two *Panzer-Divisionen* of the *III.PzK* on their inner wings, and use them to attack on 11 January, initially striking northwards through the Soviet

---

62   *PzAOK 1*, Ic Abendmeldung, 22.30 hours dated 9 Jan 44.
63   *PzAOK 1* Tagesmeldung an *Heeresgruppe Süd*, 22.00 hours dated 9 Jan 44.
64   Hgr. Süd, Ia Nr.142/44 g.Kdos, 23.15 hours dated 9 Jan 44.

divisions in front of them. Without worrying about their own flank security, they were then to wheel north-westwards between the Uman'-Kalinovka railway on the right and the river Sob on the left, heading roughly towards Lipovets and the *XXXXVI.PzK* under the *PzAOK 4*. The Army Group was of the opinion that the current Soviet deployment and the nature of the local terrain conditions indicated that the attack would stand its best chance of success in that sector, starting out from a line between Podvysokoe-Kupchintsy, north-east of Dashev.

Still later, the *PzAOK 1* received a call from *Hauptmann* Hansen, the *Feldkommandantur* in Zvenigorodka.[65] In the fading light between 16.30 hours and 18.30 hours, ten Soviet tanks, escorted by partisans dressed in civilian clothing and armed to some degree with captured German weapons, had carried out an assault towards the town from the west. In the darkness, Hansen had been unable to assess the strength of this force with any accuracy, but he did report the destruction of one Russian tank, the immobilisation of another, and ten Soviet dead. He had lost one dead and three wounded in the action. By late evening, the situation had quietened down as the Russian troops withdrew to the north and no further attacks were made. Hansen though was expecting the assaults to be renewed soon, probably from the north-east. The successful defence of the town now depended on the few troops he had, comprising only non-mobile units supported by an attached *Kampfgruppe* with heavy weapons, including *Flak* and anti-tank troops together with a few *panzers*. With these, Hansen organised an all-round defence to cover all possible avenues of attack, and confirmed he would attempt to hold the town as instructed.

---

65 Lage in Zvenigorodka, Fernmeldung, Durchgabe *Hptm*. Hansen, 23.00 hours dated 9 Jan 44. The *Feldkommandantur* was formally attached to the *AOK 8*.

Part IV

The *4.Panzerarmee* Front Begins to Stabilise

9

The Offensive Slows

Sunday 2 January 1944

The day before Hube assumed command of the right wing of the *4.Panzerarmee*, the night had passed quietly in the *XXXXII.AK* sector.[1] A Soviet patrol north-east of Lipovy Rog was intercepted by troops of the *34.Infanterie-Division* and forced to withdraw, that being the only reported enemy activity during the night. The *Korps* itself undertook a number of reconnaissance missions in front of its north-western sector, but otherwise there had been no activity at all. In the *VII.AK* sector further west, things had been a little more hectic. The *75.Infanterie-Division* had been involved in heavy fighting in the Makeevka area where a Soviet attack had managed to break into the defensive positions.[2] There had been fierce fighting, and the division had been forced to commit its last reserves before regaining control of the situation. The previous evening the *198. Infanterie-Division* further west had also become embroiled in a number of Russian assaults. Two small-scale but separate attacks had been made against Losyatin and both had been successfully defended. More seriously, several company and battalion strength assaults had been made during the night north of Belaya Tserkov', but the division had likewise managed to see these off. Ominously, it also reported increasingly heavy Soviet artillery fire against its centre and left-hand sectors. South-west of Belaya Tserkov', on the right wing of the *88.Infanterie-Division*, Soviet troops were reported to have infiltrated through the division's defences in unknown strength, and to be heading eastwards from Glybochka into the wooded area east of the main Ol'shanka-Belaya Tserkov' road. The division was planning to counterattack at daybreak, using *Sturmgeschützen* to support a strike from south to north to close the gap.

Far away to the south-west, the *17.Panzer-Division* had managed the previous evening to see off the initial Soviet attacks.[3] The first assaults had begun at about 17.30 hours, but these had been beaten back and fallen off by 20.00 hours, with the Russians reported to have suffered considerable losses. Just half an hour later though, the Soviets renewed their assaults, this time with stronger forces, and the *Panzeraufklärungs-Abteilung 17* was obliged to fall back to new positions about four kilometres north of Pliskov. It reached these by about 01.00 hours, having destroyed two Soviet anti-tank guns in the process. West of Pliskov, other Russian forces were reported heading southwards through Andrushevka, whilst further east, elements of the division's *Panzer-Pionier-Bataillon 27* had conducted reconnaissance in the Gannovka area, only to discover that the town was now occupied by Soviet troops deploying machineguns and an anti-tank gun. Elsewhere in the sector, things remained relatively quiet.

Further west, in the gap to the right wing of the *XXIV.PzK*, the *4.Gebirgs-Division* was continuing its assembly in the area about 20 kilometres north-east of Vinnitsa.

---

1   *XXXXII.AK.*, Morgenmeldung, 05.45 hours dated 2 Jan 44.
2   *VII.AK.*, Morgenmeldung, 06.30 hours dated 2 Jan 44.
3   *17.Pz.Div.*, Morgenmeldung, 05.15 hours dated 2 Jan 44.

By morning, a number of units had arrived including the *Gebirgsjäger-Bataillon 99*, the *Aufklärungs-Abteilung 94*, and the *Panzerjäger-Abteilung 94*. In addition, elements of the *Gebirgsjäger-Regiments 13* and *91* had also arrived, together with the artillery, including the *I.*, *II.*, and *IV.Gebirgsartillerie-Regiment 94*.[4] To the north, the *XXIV.PzK* front had remained fairly quiet throughout the night, with only light reconnaissance being reported opposite the right wing.[5] The previous evening however, it had been somewhat different. The *168.Infanterie-Division* had been subjected to several different assaults, the more serious of these having been two attacks made on the left wing, each in estimated battalion strength. Both of these achieved local breaches in the division's defences, but these had been cleared following swiftly mounted counterattacks. Two smaller, company strength attacks, had also been made on the right wing against Mikhailin and Shirokaya Greblya (on the south-western edge of Yusefovka), but these too had been successfully seen off. At about 22.00 hours, the Soviets launched another assault near the brickworks at Shirokaya Greblya, again in about company strength, but this too came to grief in the combined defensive artillery and small arms fire. Following this failure, the Soviets withdrew before continuing to lay disruptive artillery and mortar fire along the division's sector. To its left, the *18.Artillerie-Division* managed to complete its withdrawal from Kumanevka without too much difficulty, whilst at the same time moving the *Panzergrenadier-Regiment 146* from the *25.Panzer-Division* into the front line. The withdrawal had not gone unnoticed however, and the Soviets followed up quickly, moving into Velikaya Step' by morning. The rest of the *25.Panzer-Division* meanwhile continued to regroup in the rear, receiving the *Landesschützen-Bataillon 857* as welcome reinforcement the previous evening.

To the north, the sector held by the *1.Panzer-Division* under the *XXXXVIII.PzK* remained relatively quiet throughout the night, and there was little more than Soviet reconnaissance activity along the whole of the front.[6] On its right wing, the division spent the night assembling a small force for the recapture of Komsomol'skoe, but other than that, the only activity reported was the Soviet shelling of Berdichev. To its left, the *1.SS Panzer-Division 'LSSAH'* had a more difficult time. Soviet infantry and armour had assaulted the Ekaterinovka-Gvozdava sector and penetrated the division's defences. A counterattack was planned for the morning. Over on its left, the division continued to pull back, with the Soviet forces following up closely behind. In contrast, the *7.Panzer-Division* had managed to pull out of the front line, apparently unnoticed, and by morning, it was busy re-assembling behind the left wing of the *Korps*. Further north, on the left wing of the *Panzerarmee*, the situation remained unclear. Contact had been lost with both the *XIII.AK* and the *LIX.AK*, and neither headquarters had been able to submit reports.

In the east, the second dawn of the New Year rose over the Dnepr under a cover of cloud. The skies would begin to clear by midday, but the morning saw a light snowfall across the countryside. The front held by the *XXXXII.AK* remained quiet for most of the day, with the *Korps-Abteilung B* even reporting that Russian artillery was being withdrawn to the Khodorov area on the banks of the Dnepr.[7] However, further to the

---

4 *4.Geb.Div.*, Morgenmeldung, 05.55 hours dated 2 Jan 44.
5 *XXIV.PzK.*, Morgenmeldung, 05.40 hours dated 2 Jan 44.
6 *XXXXVIII.PzK.*, Morgenmeldung, 06.10 hours dated 2 Jan 44.
7 *XXXXII.AK.*, Tagesmeldung, 19.55 hours dated 2 Jan 44.

north-west, reconnaissance conducted by the *34.Infanterie-Division* showed the situation in that sector to be unchanged, indicating that Soviet intentions in the area remained the same. Further west, a Soviet patrol west of Chernyakhov was intercepted by troops of the *82.Infanterie-Division* and forced to pull back. The division's own patrolling likewise indicated there had been no real change in Soviet deployments opposite the sector. Nevertheless, the division did report that the Russians seemed to be digging in, building trenches about two kilometres north-west of Chernyakhov.

Further west however, on the *VII.AK* sector, things were less quiet as the Germans endeavoured to maintain their hold on Belaya Tserkov'.[8] The battle continued to rage with undiminished ferocity, although the Soviets did eventually break off their assault on the town, apparently as a result of continuing high losses. Instead they began to lay heavy artillery fire in the vicinity of the town, and concentrated their efforts elsewhere. To the east, the Soviet 180th Rifle Division attacked on a front of just four kilometres and succeeded in breaching the forward defences of the *198.Infanterie-Division*. The defenders, being hampered by a shortage of ammunition, were obliged to fall back, and despite mounting casualties the division was established by evening on a new defensive position north of Oleinikova.[9] Away to the south-west, on the other side of Belaya Tserkov', the counterattack of the *88.Infanterie-Division* in the Glybochka area had managed to seal off the gap caused by the Soviet infiltration the night before. Further south, another smaller Soviet penetration into the woods north-west of Sorokotyagi had also been cleared. To the south-east, over on the division's extreme left wing, a Soviet force of about two to three battalions had meanwhile wrested control of the village of Korzhevka away from the weak garrison there, forming a dangerous base from which they threatened to outflank the division, attacking northwards towards both Sorokotyagi and Ol'shanka. The threat to this latter town was deemed to be the more serious, lying as it does on the main road running south from Belaya Tserkov', and the division began to pull back north-eastwards from Sorokotyagi and the woods, using the forces gained to bolster the new defences. The fighting for the Ol'shanka area itself continued unabated, whilst a group of Soviet troops who had managed to infiltrate through the division's lines further north as far as Shkarovka were intercepted and largely destroyed. Only a few succeeded in reaching Soviet lines again. The division had by this time been involved in continuous heavy fighting since the start of the Soviet offensive, and given the losses it had incurred over the previous eight days, Hell was now seriously concerned as to whether it would even be able to continue the battle. Particularly worrying was its ability to prevent the Soviets from outflanking the *Korps* by attacking north-eastwards from the Yezerno area. But for the time being, he had little option but to leave it where it was.

Meanwhile, over 70 kilometres away to the south-west, the *17.Panzer-Division* was still struggling as it completed its assembly.[10] The Soviets began to step up the pressure

---

8   *VII.AK.*, Tagesmeldung, 20.15 hours dated 2 Jan 44.
9   The *I./Grenadier-Regiment 305*, for example, was reported at this time as having a combat strength of just 50 men.
10 *17.Pz.Div.*, Tagesmeldung, 19.40 hours dated 2 Jan 44. This report gave the division's operational panzer strength as follows:
   • *Panzer III lg.*: 3
   • *Panzer IV lg.*: 1
   • *Panzer V* : 5
   • *Panzer VI* : 11 (from the newly-arrived *Panzer-Abteilung 506*)

against the lone division, particularly opposite its two wings; in the Chernyavka-Gannovka area on the right, and the Bulai-Monchin-Shenderovka area on the left. This increased pressure was felt right away when, during the afternoon at about 15.00 hours, a Soviet attack from the Chernyavka-Gannovka area, estimated to be in regimental strength, forced the division to pull back out of Pliskov. On the other wing though, it had a limited success, and a counterattack north of Zozovka, launched at 14.45 hours, succeeded in breaking up Soviet troop assemblies and bringing in about 40 prisoners. A total of 15 Russian dead were counted, and two anti-tank guns were also captured. The dispersed Soviet forces withdrew northwards in disorder.

Fifteen kilometres further north-west, elements of the *III./Gebirgsjäger-Regiment 13* from the *4.Gebirgs-Division* had meanwhile arrived in Novaya Greblya and taken up screening positions facing east.[11] The battalion was under instructions to make contact on both its flanks, with troops in Germanovka and Konstantinovka, whilst the rest of the division was still assembling as quickly as the transport situation would allow. Other troops from the division were meanwhile being pushed forwards towards Novaya Greblya, whilst behind this position the town of Kotyuzhintsy was reinforced with anti-tank means against the possibility of a Soviet armoured breakthrough. The *II./Gebirgsjäger-Regiment 13* meanwhile was still stuck back in Kalinovka, where problems with the railhead had delayed its unloading. Nevertheless, the battalion had been ordered to head south-east as quickly as possible and make for Priluka, some ten or so kilometres south-west of Novaya Greblya. There was some good news however, since despite the transport problems, all the division's artillery had finally arrived.

To the north, the Soviets kept up the pressure against the whole of the *XXIV.PzK* sector.[12] Many of the attacks had been supported by armour, and on the right, in the *168. Infanterie-Division* sector, they managed to achieve a penetration between Samgorodok and Lopatin. The assault had been made by an estimated regiment, supported by almost 40 tanks, and had exploited its success to a depth of several kilometres. The division reported having destroyed eight of the tanks, and disabled a further two, but it had been unable to prevent the advance south-westwards to a point west of Samgorodok. Four other smaller, battalion-sized, assaults had also been made against the division's front during the day, particularly against the two wings, but these had all been successfully defended. To its left, the *18.Artillerie-Division* had also been attacked, but less severely. A couple of limited assaults in the Velikaya Step' area had been thrown back, but these proved to be the only serious Soviet activity on that sector. The division did however report a number of Soviet troop movements in the rear, these being observed heading south-east from Mshanets (just to the north-east of Peremoga) and also from Markovtsy to the south-west.

- *Sturmgeschützen*: 8.
11 *4.Geb.Div.*, Tagesmeldung, 19.55 hours dated 2 Jan 44. According to this report, the following units arrived on 2 January:
    - *III./Gebirgs-Artillerie-Rgt. 94;*
    - Elements *III./Gebirgsjäger-Rgt. 13;*
    - Main body *II./Gebirgsjäger-Rgt. 13;*
    - Elements *Gebirgs-Pionier-Btl. 94;* and
    - *Fla.Kp./Gebirgsjäger.Rgt. 91.*
12 *XXIV.PzK.*, Tagesmeldung, 20.10 hours dated 2 Jan 44.

The *XXXXVIII.PzK* to the north meanwhile had formed the impression that the Russians were moving up fresh forces to the Berdichev area, presumably to make good their losses.[13] It had been noticeable, for example, that throughout the day the Soviets had deployed their tanks only for fire support, perhaps indicating a lack of any armour reserves as a result of losses from the previous days. Nevertheless, it was to be expected that any such losses would be made good quickly, and the *Korps* foresaw the possibility that the Soviets would soon resume their efforts to capture Berdichev, perhaps in the next few days, and perhaps by a double envelopment. On the *Korps* right wing, troops of the *1.Panzer-Division*, having completed their assembly, began their attack against the town of Komsomol'skoe at daybreak. The assault went in from the north against a determined resistance, and the fighting lasted all day. Nevertheless, by evening, the western part of the town was in German hands, although resistance still continued, with the defending Soviet troops proving extremely stubborn in clinging to the south-eastern edge of the town. Indeed they launched a counterattack from the north-east, using an estimated rifle battalion with armour support, but this was seen off without too much difficulty. To the south-west however, the village of Markovtsy had been occupied by Soviet troops infiltrating on the division's extreme right wing, and threatening to undermine its recent gains in Komsomol'skoe. Further north too, Soviet forces in battalion strength had attacked both Zhezhelev and Khazhin in the Gnilopyat' valley, but these had been successfully defended. Over on the division's left wing, Berdichev itself had been subjected to unremitting assaults throughout the whole day. These had come in the shapes of various sized attacks from the north and east, ranging in anything up to regimental strength with tank support. In the end though all were repulsed, and the town remained in German hands for the time being. On the eastern and south-eastern outskirts though, the division reported fresh troop concentrations in the area north-east of Semenovka. The fighting was going to continue. North of Berdichev, the *1.SS Panzer-Division 'LSSAH'* was meanwhile engaged in its own desperate struggle. At about midday, an estimated Soviet rifle regiment had struck the division's right wing just south-east of Osykovo, about five kilometres from the northern outskirts of Berdichev. In heavy fighting, the assault was thrown back, and the front line stabilised. The division had also cleared up the earlier breach, made the night before in the Ekaterinovka-Gvozdava area, and reported having destroyed six Soviet tanks in the process. Russian troop assemblies observed during the day in the area around the village of Reya a few kilometres further east seemed to indicate that the Soviets had not yet lost interest in this sector. Further north, on the division's left wing, the Soviets continued to apply pressure with repeated attacks in the Troyanov area, but all these were seen off. The division was therefore being subjected to heavy attacks on both wings, and these continued not only through the day but also into the evening. On the right, a renewed battalion-sized assault went in against the railway crossing south-east of Osykovo, whilst on the left the Troyanov sector saw repeated tank attacks. None were successful. Behind all this frantic activity the *7.Panzer-Division* had meanwhile completed its assembly in the rear, and it now passed from the command of the *Panzerkorps*.

The division was now attached to the *XIII.AK*, and having finished assembling in the Pilipovka-Pyatka area north-west of Berdichev, it had been rushed westwards to the

---

13   XXXXVIII.PzK., Tagesmeldung, 19.20 hours dated 2 Jan 44. The 17th Mechanised Brigade and the 389th Rifle Division had been newly identified.

left flank of its new *Korps*, hurrying along the main Berdichev-Polonnoe road through Chudnov.[14] By evening, its leading elements had reached the area of Romanovka, and begun to wheel northwards into the *Korps'* hanging left flank. Meanwhile the rest of the *Korps* had passed a somewhat easier day, with Soviet forces doing little more than edging their way forwards against the hanging left flank. The only serious Soviet advance was made by an armoured unit heading southwards down the Teterev valley towards Chudnov, but this had been intercepted and brought to a halt by elements of the *19.Panzer-Division* and the *SS Panzerkampfgruppe 'Das Reich'*. Nevertheless the overall situation required some form of action, and during the evening, the *PzAOK 4* issued instructions for the *Korps* to pull back between 12 and 15 kilometres the following day, to a line running from Pilipovka through Glubochok to Karvinovka.[15] Once established on that line, the *Korps* was to hold it. Its mobile units, comprising elements of the *19.Panzer-Division* and the *SS Panzerkampfgruppe 'Das Reich'*, were meanwhile to go over to the offensive west of the Teterev valley, and, attacking northwards, push the Soviet forces back to the line Sadki-Karvinovka. The *7.Panzer-Division*, operating on the *XIII.AK* extreme left flank, was similarly to attack northwards; its mission being to capture and hold the town of Dzerzhinsk about six kilometres west of Sadki.

Meanwhile, over 50 kilometres away to the north-west, the *Kampfkommandant* Zwiahel in Novograd-Volynskii reported a stream of tank supported attacks against the town, particularly the western districts. The situation grew increasingly serious as the attacks continued to make deep inroads in to the defensive positions, but despite destroying a reported eight enemy tanks, the defending units of the *454.Sicherungs-Division* proved unable to clear the breaches. To the south, the *16.Panzer-Division* continued to assemble behind its own screen, and, having pushed out its reconnaissance, established that both Orepy, south of Novograd-Volynskii, and Baranovka, lying in the Sluch' valley 24 kilometres further south-east, were now occupied by Soviet forces. That evening, orders arrived from the *PzAOK 4*, instructing the division to block the Novograd-Volynskii-Shepetovka road at Dormanka, and the Novograd-Volynskii-Polonnoe road at Glubochek, south of Baranovka.[16] It was also to assemble a reserve group in the vicinity of Polonnoe itself, comprising most of the available panzers.

By the end of the day it was clear that the Soviets were trying to encircle the central body of the *4.Panzerarmee* from both sides, and this view was echoed by the Army Group chief of staff during the morning situation report.[17] Indeed, the Army Group even considered the possibility that the recent slowing down of the enemy advance might have indicated that the Soviet command believed it had already achieved this objective. There could be no doubt that the arrival of fresh forces, currently being brought up from the Soviet rear, would have a major impact on future operations, particularly if deployed in the *XXIV.PzK* sector north-east of Vinnitsa. The Army Group considered that in such circumstances it would eventually be necessary for Nehring's *Panzerkorps* to give up Pavlovka and for the *XXXXVIII.PzK* to the north to pull back its centre and right wing. This would allow the *1.SS Panzer-Division 'LSSAH'* to be pulled out of the front line and transferred to support the southern flank. Fangohr, however, was not

---

14 *PzAOK 4*, Tagesmeldung an *Heeresgruppe Süd*, dated 2 Jan 44.
15 *PzAOK 4*, Ia Kriegstagebuch entry, dated 2 Jan 44.
16 *PzAOK 4*, Ia Kriegstagebuch entry, dated 2 Jan 44.
17 *PzAOK 4*, Ia Kriegstagebuch entry, dated 2 Jan 44.

convinced that a full division could be pulled out of the front in this way, but accepted that such a proposal lay somewhere in the future anyway. For the time being, the main Soviet effort lay opposite the northern wing of the *Panzerarmee*, where the continuous arrival of further mobile forces seemed to indicate that it would remain there for the foreseeable future. The *VIII.Fliegerkorps* had reported just after midday that there had been very heavy traffic along the main Kiev-Novograd-Volynskii road either side of Zhitomir, and the majority of this had been observed turning southwards just northwest of Kurnoe, about 50 kilometres north-west of Zhitomir. Moreover, there had been heavy traffic on all roads leading southwards from the main road between Kurnoe and Novograd-Volynskii, either side of the Sluch' valley. As had already been established by the *16.Panzer-Division*, these advance elements had reached Orepy and Baranovka, whilst further east they had already occupied Dzerzhinsk, towards which the *7.Panzer-Division* was already striking. These routes were taking the Soviets into an area from which they could strike directly at the hanging left flank of the *XIII.AK*, or even bypass it altogether and head straight into the assembly area of the *16.Panzer-Division*. But while the Soviets appeared to be concentrating their main effort on the northern flank of the *4.Panzerarmee*, they seemed to be content to pin the southern sector, using mainly infantry forces and attacking on a broad front, moving southwards from the Pogrebishche area further into the gap between the *VII.AK* and the *XXXXII.AK*. By 2 January, these forces, estimated to be three or four rifle divisions, had reached a general line running from Stavishche in the east through Kashperovka and Pliskov to Britskoe and had cut the Kalinovka-Uman railway.[18] Having reached that area though, they seemed to split into two separate groups. The larger of these wheeled south-westwards towards the area south of Vinnitsa, whilst the other turned to the south-east towards Zhashkov. They were apparently trying to roll up both hanging flanks; that of the *VII.AK* in the east, and that of the *XXIV.PzK* in the west. South-west of Kazatin, elements of the Soviet 8th Guards Mechanised Corps had tried to break through the *XXIV.PzK* sector east of the railway, and the *PzAOK 4* was aware that the 31st Tank Corps might also be committed on this sector. Further north, aerial reconnaissance had shown around 600 motorised vehicles heading along the road from Korostyshev towards Zhitomir, suggesting that two mobile units were being moved forward to the Zhitomir area.[19] Beyond the left wing of the *XIII.AK*, Russian infantry forces were advancing towards Chudnov, supported by tanks from 12th Guards Tank Brigade of the 4th Guards Tank Corps, and were still threatening to outflank the *Korps* as it fell back. The situation was also serious on the far left flank, where the position of the *LIX.AK* was still unclear, despite reports having been received that the town of Novograd-Volynskii had been attacked from all sides by mixed armour-infantry forces. The garrison, consisting mainly of reserve units from the *454.Sicherungs-Division*, had proved unable to hold up the Soviet advance, and nearly the entire town had been lost. The Russians also seemed to be reinforcing the sector. Recognising the hopelessness of the situation, and concerned about the possibility of seeing the garrison isolated and destroyed, Fangohr, the *PzAOK 4* chief of staff, radioed direct to the *Kampfkommandant* Zwiahel in the town, advising him to pull back south-westwards to the Dubrovka area if it looked likely that Novograd-Volynskii could no longer be held. Later that evening,

---

18 *PzAOK 4*, Ic Abendmeldung an *Heeresgruppe Süd*, 20.00 hours dated 2 Jan 44.
19 It is not clear which units these may have been, particularly as the main body of the 3rd Guards Tank Army was by this time operating south of Zhitomir.

at 18.45 hours, Fangohr again spoke to the *Kampfkommandant*, this time instructing him to pull back southwards to an interim position on a line running between Kiyanka and Orepy. The *Kampfkommandant* for his part made a desperate plea for air support to cover his movement.

With effect from 21.00 hours that evening though, Raus would have fewer problems to worry about. At that time the *1.Panzerarmee* formally assumed control of the right wing; namely the *XXXXII.AK*, the *VII.AK*, and the *17.Panzer-Division*. Fangohr duly informed Hube's chief of staff, *Generalmajor* Wenck, of the concerns and proposals for withdrawal submitted by Hell's *VII.AK*, but added that the *PzAOK 4* could not agree with them. The *Korps* had no alternative but to hold out as long as possible in its current positions, particularly as it was not likely to find such well-constructed defensive works anywhere else. Moreover, Army Group South had withheld its agreement on operational grounds, insisting that the positions be held as long as possible, particularly since the Soviets had not deployed noticeably strong forces on that sector. In particular, there had been no armour reported in the area. As one of his last instructions to the *VII.AK*, Raus ordered Hell at 18.00 hours to seal off existing Soviet penetrations and maintain his current positions. Hell argued once more, but to no avail. He was now ordered to recapture Ol'shanka, using the available *Sturmgeschützen* in support, and then hold the line running from Belaya Tserkov' through Glybochka to Ol'shanka. He was also to throw out screening troops to the south-east as far as Yezerno. At this point, the intentions of the *4.Panzerarmee* were for the *VII.AK* to clear the Soviet penetration around Losyatin and restore the situation around Ol'shanka. In the Vinnitsa area, the *4.Gebirgs-Division* was to continue assembling in the designated area and engage any Soviet forces attempting to advance into the area, while the *XXIV.PzK* was to fall back onto the line Novaya Greblya-Gerasimovka-Tucha-Peremoga. North of Berdichev, the *XXXXVIII.PzK* was to pull back its left wing in conjunction with the *XIII.AK* to a general line running from the northern edge of Berdichev, along the line of the river Gnilopyat' to the area east of Pilipovka. Berdichev itself was still to be held. The *XIII.AK* was to fall back to the line Pilipovka-Glubochok-Karvinovka and extend its left wing westwards as far as Sadki by attacking northwards west of the Teterev, while the *7.Panzer-Division* was to occupy the Dzerzhinsk area and prevent any further Soviet advance southwards. Further west, the *16.Panzer-Division* was to block the Novograd-Volynskii-Shepetovka road at Dormanka and the Novograd-Volynskii-Polonnoe road at Glubochek. The division was also to form an armoured reserve in the Polonnoe area. To the north, the *Kampfkommandant* Zwiahel in Novograd-Volynskii was to break out of his encirclement and move southwards to hold the line Orepy-Kiyanka, while the *LIX.AK* was to continue fighting its way back to the river Sluch' in the vicinity of Kurchitsa.

Monday 3 January 1944

On the *XXIV.PzK* front, Soviet forces maintained the pressure during the night.[20] They struck through the right wing of the *168.Infanterie-Division* as it was withdrawing, and captured both Novaya Greblya and Bol'shoi Chernyatin. The division organised a local counterattack, and this was still underway before daybreak. A few kilometres further south-west, in an effort to intercept any further advance by Soviet armour, the

---

20 *XXIV.PzK*, Morgenmeldung, 06.35 hours dated 3 Jan 44.

Panzerjäger-Abteilung 94 of the *4.Gebirgs-Division* had completed the establishment of an anti-tank line between Polevaya Lysievka and the wood north-west of Kotyuzhintsy. To the south-east, the rest of the division reported no enemy contact. To the north though, in the area south-west of Kazatin, strong enemy motorised forces were seen heading south from Pikovets, while reconnaissance further west established that Markovtsy and Khutor Lutsianovka, west of Peremoga, were both free of Soviet troops, despite the fact that Markovtsy had been occupied as late as 17.00 hours the previous evening.

To the left, things had been no easier on the *XXXXVIII.PzK* front.[21] The previous evening had seen continuous attacks against Zhezhelev and Khazhin in the *1.Panzer-Division* sector, with artillery and mortar support. The Russians had achieved local breaches in the division's defences, but these had all eventually been intercepted and thrown back, and the main positions restored. No assault was launched against Berdichev itself, though the town was subjected to disruptive artillery fire during the night. In the *1.SS Panzer-Division 'LSSAH'* sector, the planned withdrawal had been made more difficult by a Soviet attack from the Troyanov area, where attacking infantry and tanks hit the division's left wing as it tried to pull back. Despite this, the new positions had been taken up by about 03.00 hours in the morning. Things were unclear as to events on the left wing where the *7.Panzer-Division* had been given the task of securing Dzerzhinsk, and the only report received indicated that the division's lead elements had reached Korchevka, a few kilometres south of Dzerzhinsk, while screening forces had been sent west as far as the eastern edge of Miropol'.[22]

The *XIII.AK* had meanwhile been able to pull back to its new positions without serious interference.[23] The main thrust of the Soviet advance lay against the centre and left wing of the *Korps*, particularly along the main road heading south-westwards from Zhitomir towards Chudnov. In places the Russians followed the *Korps* withdrawal very closely, and during the night they even managed to break through the defensive lines north of Knyazhin, and by morning countermeasures were still being prepared. Further north, where the main body of the *SS Panzerkampfgruppe 'Das Reich'* was now deployed, a Soviet assault against Karvinovka was successfully repelled. To the south-west, the *19.Panzer-Division*, reinforced with elements of the *'Das Reich'* and the *8.Panzer-Division*, had launched a counterattack the previous evening, capturing Lutai and, after bitter fighting, Stolbov as well. During the course of the fighting, the division established the presence of strong enemy forces in the area, including the 12th Guards Tank Brigade and the 206th Rife Division. The rest of the *8.Panzer-Division* was meanwhile still assembling in its new area. Further west, the *16.Panzer-Division* had been forced to interrupt its detraining near Polonnoe following the disruption of the rail movement by track demolitions. Its forward elements were deployed to the north about six kilometres south of Baranovka, and during the night these had been assaulted by Russian forces.[24] This placed the division in a difficult position, and clearly the Army Group was concerned. At 11.45 hours that morning, it issued instructions to the *4.Panzerarmee* to make sure that whatever happened, it was to ensure that the division

---

21 *XXXXVIII.PzK*, Morgenmeldung, 05.45 hours dated 3 Jan 44.
22 *PzAOK 4*, Morgenmeldung an *Heeresgruppe Süd*, 07.45 hours dated 3 Jan 44.
23 *XIII.AK*, Morgenmeldung, 07.15 hours dated 3 Jan 44.
24 *PzAOK 4*, Morgenmeldung an *Heeresgruppe Süd*, 07.45 hours dated 3 Jan 44.

was not committed to combat too soon.[25] In the event that Soviet pressure in the area grew too strong, the detraining and assembly of the division was to be shifted away to the south-west as far as need be to make sure it did not become embroiled in the fighting.

On the *4.Panzerarmee* left wing, the *LIX.AK* continued with its withdrawal.[26] The *291.Infanterie-Division* had passed over the river Sluch' at Gorodnitsa and was moving to take up positions in bridgeheads over the river Korchik in Korets, Kobylya, and Storozhev. The *Korps-Abteilung C* meanwhile covered the southern flank of the withdrawal as the Germans pulled back south-westwards from Emil'chino from the line Taiki-Medvedevo, with the intention of being able to cross the river Sluch' and then turn to face eastwards again from the area around and to the north of Korets.

When the new day dawned, the temperature climbed enough for a small thaw to set in, leaving the roads icy and slippery on the surface. The weather also had an adverse effect on air operations, and the day saw little activity from either side in this respect. On the southern front of the *4.Panzerarmee*, the *XXIV.PzK* spent a quiet day.[27] The whole front had remained peaceful, although Soviet movements had been observed near Bol'shoi Chernyatin involving both infantry and trucks. Nineteen tanks had been counted near Golendry station, with another ten being counted in Leonardovka a little to the south-east. To the left, in the *XXXXVIII.PzK* sector west of Kazatin, the *1.Panzer-Division* spent much of the day mopping up in the eastern part of Komsomol'skoe as Soviet troops continued to infiltrate into the town.[28] By evening, the situation had still not been cleared, and the division was planning to conduct a night assault to try and resolve things. To the north of Berdichev, Soviet troops launched a battalion-strength assault out of Polovetskoe, but this had been seen off by the division. Since 09.00 hours that morning, Russian forces had also been attacking southwards towards Grishkovtsy either side of the main Zhitomir-Berdichev road, with a supporting attack from the north-west. This supporting assault succeeded in breaking into the north-western part of the town, and the division was obliged to organise a local counterattack to try and dislodge the attackers. This continued on into the evening, by which time Berdichev was pretty much being attacked from all sides. To the north, opposite the *1.SS Panzer-Division 'LSSAH'*, Soviet forces spent the day moving up closer to the main German defensive position along the whole sector, attacking in places. In the Gnilopyat' valley, north-east of Pyatka, the Russians launched a battalion-strength assault from the north against Sosnovka[29] with 15 tanks in support, but this was repulsed, with the division reporting three T-34 tanks destroyed in the action. This first assault was followed by repeated Soviet attacks in the same area, each being made in about battalion-strength, each having the benefit of tank support, and each coming in from either the north or the north-east. Finally, following one of these assaults, Soviet troops managed to break into the north-west part of Sosnovka and force a breach in the German defensive positions to the north-east of the village, obliging the *'LSSAH'* to take appropriate countermeasures. Further west, the *7.Panzer-Division* had moved off to the attack at daybreak, with Dzerzhinsk as its objective. It destroyed eight enemy anti-tank guns as it moved forward, and by

---

25　Hgr. Süd, Ia Nr. 34/44 geh. dated 3 Jan 44.
26　*PzAOK 4*, Morgenmeldung an *Heeresgruppe Süd*, 07.45 hours dated 3 Jan 44.
27　*PzAOK 4*, Ia Orientierung, dated 3 Jan 44.
28　*XXXXVIII.PzK*, Tagesmeldung, 18.45 hours dated 3 Jan 44.
29　Referred to as Wilschanka in the German records.

10.00 hours it had taken the town. In pressing forward so quickly though, the division had bypassed Soviet forces deployed either side of the main road, and it now turned its attention to these. It deployed troops to head back south-east where they attacked Ratsi and pushed back the Russian screening forces. To the west, reconnaissance troops sent out from Dzerzhinsk discovered that the village of Velikaya Kozara[30] was also enemy-occupied, but these were not attacked. The Soviets though were not prepared to give up Dzerzhinsk without a fight, and at 16.25 hours the inevitable counterattack against the town began. This was launched from the east and it continued on into the evening until finally the division decided to pull back to avoid being surrounded.[31] Overall then on the *XXXXVIII.PzK* sector, Soviet forces had generally limited themselves to reconnaissance activity against the right wing, but had kept up the pressure against not only Berdichev but also the left wing of the *1.SS Panzer-Division 'LSSAH'*. Balck believed that the relatively successful defence of the Berdichev area to date had led the Soviets to shift their main point of effort away from the town itself and on to the wings, where the *XXIV.PzK* in the south and the *XIII.AK* in the north-west were now the main targets. He reckoned that these assaults would continue, both in order to pin his existing troops but also to capture Berdichev itself.

On the *XIII.AK* front, the day passed a little quieter than previously.[32] It was not clear though whether this was due to the casualties suffered by the advancing Russian forces, or whether it simply meant that the Soviets were transferring forces to the sector west of the river Teterev. Nevertheless, there were still attacks to be dealt with. On the right wing of the *68.Infanterie-Division* the Russians made two separate assaults against the boundary with the *'LSSAH'*. One of these was in battalion-strength, the other in about regimental-strength, and both enjoyed tank support. With the help of the neighbouring troops though, both assaults were beaten back, with 14 enemy tanks being reported as destroyed. On the division's left, there were no attacks, but Soviet troop assemblies were observed and engaged with disruptive artillery fire. To the left, the *340.Infanterie-Division* had also been attacked. There were several assaults in up to battalion-strength, and some of these had led to breaches in the forward positions. The division launched a number of counterattacks during the day, and by evening all the penetrations had been sealed off and cleared with the exception of one north of Knyazhin. Here the fighting continued into the night. Opposite the *SS Panzerkampfgruppe 'Das Reich'* meanwhile, the Russians passed the day closing up towards the German positions, and were seen to be taking the opportunity to reinforce the sector. Considerable Soviet troop movements had been observed in the wooded area north-east of Karvinovka and around Siryaki, and this, together with the heavy artillery fire along the front throughout the day, all seemed to reinforce the feeling that the enemy offensive would be resumed shortly. Russian infantry, with tank support, had already tried to infiltrate through to Serbinovka north-west of Chudnov, but this had been seen off with the loss of a couple of tanks.[33] To

---

30 Referred to as Kosari in the German records.
31 *PzAOK 4*, Tagesmeldung an *Heeresgruppe Süd*, dated 3 Jan 44.
32 *XIII.AK*, Tagesmeldung, 19.35 hours dated 3 Jan 44. According to this report, the *XIII.AK* had, in the period 25 December to 2 January, captured or destroyed 187 tanks, 18 anti-tank guns, 14 artillery pieces and numerous other weapons. It had also brought in a total of 796 prisoners, and estimated that the Russians suffered about 4,800 killed, of whom 1,935 had actually been counted.
33 *PzAOK 4*, Ia Orientierung, dated 3 Jan 44.

the left, the reinforced *19.Panzer-Division* managed to take Stolbov, just north-west of Chudnov, but any further advance proved impossible in the face of heavy defensive fire. Having had a little time to review the withdrawal from Zhitomir, Hauffe noted in this report that due to the efforts of the troops concerned, and despite the considerable difficulties involved, almost all of the divisional and *Korps* artillery had been brought safely out of the potential encirclement of the city.

Meanwhile, the *16.Panzer-Division* continued de-training in the Shepetovka area, and sent the *Panzergrenadier-Regiment 64*, supported by elements of the *Panzer-Regiment 2*, northwards to provide a screen in the Dubrovka area behind which the rest of the division could assemble without disruption.[34] From this point, reconnaissance was sent forwards towards Novograd-Volynskii and reached a point within seven kilometres of the town from which position they were able to establish that the place was occupied in strength by the Russians, with infantry, armour, and anti-tank units. A little to the south-west though, the town of Yarun' was still unoccupied. On the other side of the road, a reconnaissance in force towards Baranovka in the Sluch' valley ran into stiff resistance from suspected partisans in the village of Svinobychi, while to the south of Baranovka the division's *Panzeraufklärungs-Abteilung* encountered resistance in Markovka,[35] north of Glubochek, destroying two guns and two anti-tank guns before going on the capture the village. Further south, a *Panzer-Abteilung* of the *Panzer-Regiment 2* withdrew into Polonnoe given the threatened advance of Soviet units, but left a rearguard holding Poninka a few kilometres to the north.

There had been little contact during the day with von der Chevallerie's *LIX.AK*, and the only report received indicated that the *Korps'* intended movements were going according to plan,[36] although it was later reported that the *291.Infanterie-Division* had been delayed in crossing the river Korchik owing to the thaw conditions.[37] Nevertheless, Emil'chino had been attacked the previous day by Russian troops early in the morning at 07.25 hours, with assaults coming in from three areas, Stepanovka, Kuliki and Seredy. These covered an arc running from east to south-west, and effectively left just two roads available for the withdrawal, the one running west to Medvedovo and the other longer route running north-west to Podluby. The Soviet troops pressed their assault into the southern part of Emil'chino, and by 09.15 hours, the defenders had been forced to blow the bridge in the centre of town. The rest of the day saw the *Korps-Abteilung C* and the *291.Infanterie-Division* pulling back towards and over the river Sluch', with the former acting as the rearguard and looking to take up new positions on a line east of Gorodnitsa running from Kurchitsa to Dubniki. The Soviets pursued the withdrawal closely and made a number of attacks throughout the day, but none of these seriously disrupted the *Korps'* movements.

Overall, the day had passed somewhat more quietly than recently for the *4.Panzerarmee*, and the only significant enemy offensive action came on the *XIII.AK* sector where the 3rd Guards Tank Army continued to attack between the Gnilopyat' and the Teterev.[38] Further south, the 1st Tank Army appeared to be heading southwards across

---

34 *16.Pz.Div.*, Tagesmeldung, 19.00 hours dated 3 Jan 44.
35 Referred to as Pershotravensk on some maps.
36 *PzAOK 4*, Ia Orientierung, dated 3 Jan 44.
37 *PzAOK 4*, Tagesmeldung an *Heeresgruppe Süd*, dated 3 Jan 44.
38 *PzAOK 4*, Ic Abendmeldung an *Heeresgruppe Süd*, 19.00 hours dated 3 Jan 44.

the front of the *XXIV.PzK*, perhaps trying to feel its way around the right flank towards Vinnitsa. In any event, the *PzAOK 4* was expecting a resumption of the Soviet offensive by both tank armies around Berdichev and Vinnitsa. At the same time, intelligence indicated that the 60th Army opposite the left wing of the *XIII.AK* was being reinforced with the 1st Guards Cavalry Corps and the 25th Tank Corps, presumably with the objective of trying to encircle the German forces in the area. As far as Raus could ascertain therefore, the Soviet intention to encircle the *4.Panzerarmee* on both sides had now been confirmed. What was not so clear was whether the Russians were currently concentrating on closing up to the new defensive positions, or whether they were waiting for fresh forces to arrive. In any event, it seemed that the main points of effort would fall against the *XXIV.PzK* in the south, in the area around Chernyatin and Chervonaya Step', and against the boundary between the *XIII.AK* and the *XXXXVIII.PzK* in the north near Chudnov. The worrying thing for Raus though was that he had lost track of the mobile forces that had been reported in the Zhitomir area the day before.

Earlier that morning, Raus had received new instructions from von Manstein at Army Group South.[39] These ordered the *PzAOK 4* to assemble an armoured force west of the river Teterev as quickly as possible, and in doing so bring together the 7., 8., and *19.Panzer-Divisions*, as well as the *SS Panzerkampfgruppe 'Das Reich'*, under Balck's *XXXXVIII.PzK*.[40] The *1.SS Panzer-Division 'LSSAH'* was also to be pulled out of the front line and held as reserve by the *Panzerarmee*, while the *XIII.AK* was to pull back to a line running from Berdichev to Korochenki, just south-east of Chudnov. During the course of the day, Raus discussed the relief of the *'LSSAH'* with Fangohr, his chief of staff, who suggested that the division might be pulled out the day after tomorrow. Raus agreed. It fell to Balck's *XXXXVIII.PzK* to organise the relief while at the same time stretching the *1.Panzer-Division* sector as far as Raiki. Recognising that holding Berdichev would demand the commitment of troops essential for the occupation of the new sector, Balck proposed that the city be given up and a new defensive position established to the west. The suggestion was approved by the Army Group, but only on the condition that a strong rearguard was to be left east of the city with instructions only to pull back if pressed hard by the enemy. By the end of the day, the *PzAOK 4* had completed its planning, and Raus issued his new instructions that evening.[41] In this, he summarised Soviet intentions, stating that the enemy was attempting to surround the *Panzerarmee* on both sides, with the main point of effort being made against the northern wing where strong motorised and armoured forces had been established. In contrast, the southern wing of the encirclement was being attempted mainly by infantry forces. In

---

39 *PzAOK 4*, Ia Kriegstagebuch entry dated 3 Jan 44.
40 According to an unreferenced report, the operational armour strength of the *PzAOK 4* on 3 January was follows:
 - *1.SS Panzer-Division 'LSSAH'*: 10 *Panzer IV lg*; 6 *Panzer V*; 8 *StuGs*
 - *1.Panzer-Division*: 14 *Panzer IV lg*; 22 *Panzer V*
 - *s.Panzer-Abteilung 509*: 8 *Panzer VI*
 - *18.Artillerie-Division*: 5 *StuGs*
 - *19.Panzer-Division*: 2 *Panzer IV lg*
 - *Panzerkampfgruppe 'Das Reich'*: 6 *Panzer IV lg*
 - *8.Panzer-Division*: 5 *Panzer IV lg*
 - *Sturmgeschütz-Abteilung 280*: 10 *StuGs*
41 *PzAOK 4*, Ia Nr.54/44 geh. dated 3 Jan 44. The order was titled '*Panzerarmee*befehl Nr 53'.

response to this threat, Raus's intentions were now to prevent any further enemy advance to the south-west over a line running from Vakhnovka through Berdichev and Chudnov. On the northern wing, this was to be achieved through a mobile defence so that the *Panzerarmee* could provide a degree of protection for the deep flank of the Army Group as a whole, and in particular ensuring that the vital stretch of railway between L'vov and Vinnitsa was secured. To achieve this objective, the subordinate *Korps* headquarters were given their respective tasks. The *XXIV.PzK* was to maintain its current positions, concentrating on its southern wing. From 16.00 hours the same day, it was to assume command of the *1.Panzer-Division* and withdraw from Berdichev during the coming night, leaving only a rearguard in place. The following night, from 4 to 5 January, it was to pull the *1.SS Panzer-Division 'LSSAH'* out of the front, after which it was to be transferred north to the *XIII.AK*. To assist in its defensive mission, the *Korps* was given extra reinforcements. These included the *s.Panzer-Abteilung 509 (Tiger)*, three *Panzer-Zerstörer* companies, the *Armee-Panzerjäger-Abteilung 731* (less one company), and the *Granatwerfer-Bataillon 9* which was due to arrive on the following day. Having given up the two divisions, the *XXXXVIII.PzK* was meanwhile to begin the withdrawal of the remaining elements of the *1.Panzer-Division* from Berdichev and pull them back to the west bank of the Gnilopyat' during the coming night. North of the city, those elements of the *'LSSAH'* deployed along the river between Skraglevka and a point two kilometres north of Raiki were to be relieved during the night to 5 January. These were all preparatory measures though, and Balck was instructed to leave strong screening forces in the eastern part of the city with orders to defend their positions and only pull back to the west bank in the event an overwhelming assault from Soviet forces was likely to result in their destruction. With effect from 06.00 hours the following morning, the *XXXXVIII.PzK* was to assume control of the *7.*, *8.*, and *19.Panzer-Divisions* as well as the *SS Panzerkampfgruppe 'Das Reich'*. The *Korps* would then be transferred to the north-west where its new task was to prevent Soviet forces from pushing south- and south-eastwards across a line from Rudnya Gorodishche through Dzerzhinsk to Malaya Kozara, and in doing so it was to concentrate its main efforts in conducting a mobile defence west of the river Teterev. The *XIII.AK* was instructed simply to hold its current positions and take control of the *'LSSAH'* with effect from 16.00 hours that afternoon. Hauffe was also ordered to make preparations for a more general withdrawal to a line running from Shvaikovka through Pyatka to Gorodishche, whilst making arrangements for the relief of those elements of the *'LSSAH'* which were still in the front south of Shvaikovka. These arrangements were to be prepared for the night to 5 January, and were to be such that by early on 5 January all elements of the division had been relieved and the rest of the *Korps* was fully deployed in its new main defensive position. Following its withdrawal, the *'LSSAH'* was to be moved to the area between Ivanopol',[42] Ulanov and the main crossroads south-east of Ivanopol', where it was to remain for the time being as the *Panzerarmee* reserve. The newly arrived *XXXXVI.PzK* under *General der Infanterie* Hans Gollnick was meanwhile to assume command of all those elements of the *16.Panzer-Division* and the *1.Infanterie-Division* which had arrived so far, and ensure that their assembly was secured by screening the line Glubochek-Dormanka-Slavuta.[43]

---

42 Referred to as Januschpil in the German records.
43 The record actually states Belavuta, but appears to have been a transcription error. Ten trains carrying elements of the *16.Panzer-Division* had arrived during the day, with only two trains from the

Reconnaissance was to be undertaken to the north-east as far as the main road between Novograd-Volynskii and Zhitomir, and to the north-west as far as Korets where elements of the retreating *LIX.AK* were expected early on 4 January. In response to the point made earlier by Army Group South, Raus instructed Gollnick to ensure that if Soviet pressure in the area increased, the unloading of the new divisions was to be moved south-west, to the area south of Shepetovka and south of the main road between Gritsev and Belogorodka. This was not to be taken as a general approval for falling back though, and it was made clear that any weak Russian forces that assaulted the covering forces were to be attacked and destroyed. Over on the right wing of the *4.Panzerarmee*, the *4.Gebirgs-Division* was to continue assembling in its current area. A screen was to be thrown out to a line running from Britskoe through Konstantinovka to Novaya Greblya, but only using the forces already committed. No other troops were to be deployed this far forward, and indeed the division was to make preparations for shifting its assembly area westwards behind the railway line between Gumennoe and Kalinovka in case strong Soviet pressure made this necessary. Here too, Raus stressed the importance of the division not being committed to action before it had completed its assembly and preparations. As a result of all these changes, it was necessary to shift the boundaries between the *Korps* commands. On the very right, the boundary with the *1.Panzerarmee* would run on the line Voronovitsa-Vakhnovka-Ruzhin. With effect from 05.00 hours on 4 January, the new boundary between the *XXIV.PzK* and the *XIII.AK* would move to the line Ulanov-Buryaki-Demchin-Malaya Tartarovka-Shvaikovka-Gvozdava, while at the same time, the boundary between the *XIII.AK* and the *XXXXVIII.PzK* would shift to Motovilovka-Troshcha-Gorodishche-Vysokaya-Pech'. Until that time, the boundary would lie along the river Teterev. Further west, the river Sluch' would serve as the boundary between the *XXXXVIII.PzK* and the *XXXXVI.PzK*. Raus meanwhile planned to move his headquarters to Letichev with effect from 10.00 hours.

Tuesday 4 January 1944

On the southern wing of the *4.Panzerarmee*, Soviet forces had continued to apply pressure throughout the night against the forward positions of the *4.Gebirgs-Division* held by the *Aufklärungs-Abteilung 94*.[44] Following a company strength assault, the covering force in the Konyushevka area fell back to the road fork just south-east of Konstantinovka, while in the early hours of the morning a separate assault involving an estimated two companies attacked Petrovka from the north-east again obliging the covering troops to fall back. Thereafter, Konstantinovka was subjected to continuous Soviet mortar fire. Further south, a patrol sent out by the division came under fire whilst passing through Vakhnovka, and it was thought that this had come from a unit of partisans about 30 men strong. On the left wing, there were repeated reconnaissance patrols towards Novaya Greblya, one of which involved two enemy tanks feeling their way forwards out of Germanovka. Both were reported as destroyed. Novaya Greblya had also been subjected to mortar and light artillery fire throughout the night. The Russians were now reported to be bringing up reinforcements into the area, and the previous afternoon alone, a column of about 80 sledges and 1,200 men had been observed moving south-westwards from Lozovka to Ovechache.

1.Infanterie-Division.
44 *4.Geb.Div.*, Morgenmeldung dated 4 Jan 44.

Things had been quieter on the front held by the *XXIV.PzK* to the left.[45] The previous evening, the Russians had been able to force a breach in the defences in Komsomol'skoe, but after this had been cleared up in a counterattack there was no further combat during the night. To the south, the *18.Artillerie-Division* noted that Soviet forces were beginning to dig in along the sector running five kilometres north of Golendry station.

On the *XIII.AK* sector too, the Soviets had not really pressed further during the night.[46] There had been just a single breach along the front, and this had fallen in the area north of Slobodishche on the sector held by the *1.SS Panzer-Division 'LSSAH'*. By morning, the division was still trying to deal with the problem. The *68.Infanterie-Division* had meanwhile taken advantage of the lull to try and improve its positions. With support from elements of the *'LSSAH'* it had attacked and captured the north-eastern end of Pilipovka and reported destroying a number of Russian tanks in the process. The *340.Infanterie-Division* was also planning to tackle the remaining breach in its defensive lines north of Knyazhin, and was due to start early that morning with the support of a few *panzers*. There had been disruptive artillery fire during the night from both sides, but nothing more serious than this.

To the left, the Soviets had also remained quiet opposite the *XXXXVIII.PzK*.[47] The *19.Panzer-Division* reported only enemy artillery and mortar fire against Stolbov and Serbinovka throughout the night, although this included repeated rocket fire too. North of Siryaki, combat patrols observed lively truck traffic moving in both directions, whilst north of Stolbov, motor and track noises were heard in the vicinity of Dreniki. The *7.Panzer-Division* meanwhile, having pulled out of Dzerzhinsk, had taken up new positions in Vrublevka, Korchevka and the northern part of Romanovka, but there had been no report from the *SS Panzerkampfgruppe 'Das Reich'*. To the west, the *16.Panzer-Division* reported a quiet night, with no incidents worthy of mention,[48] whilst things remained unclear regarding the *LIX.AK* which was still trying to fight its way back towards the Korets area.[49]

The new day was rainy and overcast, and this, together with the warmer temperatures, began to turn the ground softer. Despite this, some of the roads were still ice-bound, particularly in the north, so for the time being, the majority of the network was still usable. On the right wing, the *XXIV.PzK* had a relatively quiet day.[50] The *168.Infanterie-Division* had just a single contact with Soviet forces when it intercepted and threw back a company-strength reconnaissance patrol near Gerasimovka. The *18.Artillerie-Division* reported an assault against Peremoga by an estimated two rifle companies, but this too had been successfully repulsed. Given the lack of serious pressure against his right wing, Nehring had the impression that the Russians were pulling forces out of the front line and moving them to the south. However, the attacks were stronger and more persistent further north in the sector held by the *1.Panzer-Division*, where a series of assaults in up to battalion-strength against Komsomol'skoe were all successfully defended. Further north, the Soviets appeared to follow up the withdrawal from the Zhezhelev-Khazhin

---

45 *XXIV.PzK*, Morgenmeldung, 05.45 hours dated 4 Jan 44.
46 *XIII.AK*, Morgenmeldung, 06.05 hours dated 4 Jan 44.
47 *XXXXVIII.PzK*, Morgenmeldung, 05.35 hours dated 4 Jan 44.
48 *16.Pz.Div.*, Morgenmeldung, 05.55 hours dated 4 Jan 44.
49 *PzAOK 4*, Morgenmeldung an *Heeresgruppe Süd*, dated 4 Jan 44.
50 *XXIV.PzK*, Tagesmeldung, 19.30 hours dated 4 Jan 44.

line only slowly, although at 14.00 hours they attacked the new positions in the latter village, but without success. In and to the north of Berdichev however, the Russians were more active and pressed the German defences harder. They succeeded in forcing a breach at Skraglevka and forged a bridgehead over the river Gnilopyat' in about battalion-strength. By evening, the breach had been sealed off, but the Soviet pressure continued as before. During the morning briefing between Fangohr and Busse at Army Group South, the question arose of how best to employ the newly attached *4.Gebirgs-Division*, particularly as there was no real doubt in their minds that the Soviets had moved new troops into the area around Rososha and Zozovka and were currently re-grouping their forces. Busse suggested that the division might be used in conjunction with the *1.SS Panzer-Division 'LSSAH'* to strike into the flank of the Soviet 1st Tank Army which was at that moment advancing further to the south in the area. Later the same evening, Busse spoke again with the *4.Panzerarmee* and advised that the main body of the *4.Gebirgs-Division* was to be assembled in the Britskoe area with a view to it being used to attack north or north-westwards. Fangohr subsequently spoke with *Oberstleutnant* Giese, Nehring's chief of staff, and let him know that with effect from midnight the division would be attached to the *XXIV.PzK*.[51] Formal instructions followed, making it clear that the *4.Gebirgs-Division* was being attached to the *Korps* for the purpose of covering the southern flank of the *4.Panzerarmee*.[52] The main body of the division was to advance and occupy the Britskoe-Konyushevka-Petrovka area, and from there be prepared to launch an attack towards either the north or the north-west. Other elements of the division were meanwhile to ensure that the boundary to the *1.Panzerarmee* to the right was secured.

On the *XIII.AK* front, the Soviets renewed their offensive in strength, attacking the whole sector with an estimated eight rifle divisions and several tank brigades.[53] The attack had begun at 08.00 hours that morning, and the *Korps* had identified the two main axes of attack as being in the Pilipovka-Pyatka and Knyazhin areas. Overall, the main assault appeared to be aimed at achieving a breakthrough to the south-west, with subsidiary assaults aimed at rolling up the *Korps* flanks on either side, towards Chudnov on the left and Berdichev on the right. The assault was preceded by a heavy artillery barrage and quickly broke through the thinly-held front line in several places. South-west of Knyazhin, strong Soviet forces, supported by tanks, broke through the defensive positions around Tyutyunniki and seized the village, while another enemy assault group succeeded in breaking through all the way to Mikhailenki, just west of Korovintsy. A counterattack against this grouping was launched by elements of the *208.Infanterie-Division* from the Rachki area to try and prevent any further breakthrough, and the resulting losses were reported to be high for the Russians and considerable for the division too. Overall, the situation was becoming critical, particularly as the defensive capability of the *XIII.AK* was now adversely impacted by a lack of ammunition. To make matters worse, the *Korps* reported that in its view these attacks would continue. At about midday, *Oberst* von Hammerstein-Gesmold, Hauffe's chief of staff, called Fangohr at *PzAOK 4* headquarters and advised him of the situation.[54] Fangohr wanted to know whether in the new circumstances the *1.SS Panzer-Division 'LSSAH'* could still be pulled out of

---

51 *PzAOK 4*, Ia Kriegstagebuch entry dated 4 Jan 44.
52 *PzAOK 4*, Ia Nr. 99/44 geh. dated 4 Jan 44.
53 *XIII.AK*, Tagesmeldung, 19.00 hours dated 4 Jan 44.
54 *PzAOK 4*, Ia Kriegstagebuch entry dated 4 Jan 44.

the line as had previously been instructed. Perhaps unsurprisingly, von Hammerstein-Gesmold thought not. Given the new situation, the Army Group raised no objection to the division remaining with the *XIII.AK*, so during the afternoon Hauffe was given fresh instructions. He was to proceed with the withdrawal during the coming night, but instead of those elements being transferred to the *PzAOK 4* reserve, the *Korps* was to use them to close the gaps that had been newly opened up in the front line and create a new defensive position on a line running from Pyatka to Korochenki. At 18.00 hours, Fangohr spoke to Busse at Army Group South and briefed him on the latest situation. The bad news was that Balck, who had been present on the field of battle, believed that the *XIII.AK* was in the process of falling apart, and that this was probably attributable to the enormous efforts and fatigue of the troops involved. Balck was extremely concerned about the possible effect of this on the morale of the remaining troops, so Fangohr proposed to the Army Group that the *XIII.AK* be withdrawn from the front, particularly as the divisions involved now had a front line strength of between 150 and 300 men each.[55] Busse believed that this would not be possible, and instead asked the *Panzerarmee* to speak direct with Hauffe to get his opinion on the state of his troops. Raus therefore spoke with Hauffe at 18.20 hours, and was told that the condition of the *68.* and *208. Infanterie-Divisions* was still the same as had been reported the previous evening. It was the *340.Infanterie-Division* which had borne the brunt of the day's fighting, but even in this case, Hauffe thought it was probably going too far to say that the division was actually falling apart. That said, he did stress that his whole *Korps* now possessed the infantry strength of no more than a weak regiment and that it was no longer in a position to put up any kind of durable defence. Notwithstanding the good condition of the artillery units therefore, Hauffe believed that a withdrawal of the '*LSSAH*' would inevitably lead to a collapse of his whole front. Raus therefore advised him that the division would stay with the *XIII.AK*, and that the *XXXXVIII.PzK* had been ordered to provide him with support in his effort to re-establish the front line. After this discussion, the *PzAOK 4* again contacted Busse who considered that all available means should be used to intercept the Soviet breakthrough, and that the proposed new defensive positions were to be held at all costs.

To the left, the Soviet attacks against the *XXXXVIII.PzK* continued, with the main point of effort being against the right wing, which was caught up in the main Russian assault against the *XIII.AK*.[56] In response, an armoured group from the *SS Panzerkampfgruppe 'Das Reich'* attacked out of the area north of Kikhti at 09.00 hours. The assault initially headed south-east, but after Soviet forces had broken through the left wing of the neighbouring *XIII.AK*, the group was wheeled to the south towards Gorodishche in an attempt to prevent the Russians from driving into the *Korps* right flank. A little to the north-west, Soviet troops estimated to be a battalion attacked southwards along the Teterev valley, and two separate assaults against Dryglov were beaten back. On the western bank of the Teterev, there had been continual artillery and rocket fire against the sector held by the *19.Panzer-Division*, with the heaviest fire falling on Stolbov and Serbinovka. Lutai was attacked during the morning by an estimated two Russian companies coming out of Siryaki, but the assault had been seen off. To

---

55 The numbers given referred to *Grabenstärke*. This comprised those personnel in the line forward of battalion headquarters, including company headquarters personnel, but excluding stretcher-bearers.
56 *XXXXVIII.PzK*, Tagesmeldung, 20.00 hours dated 4 Jan 44.

the left, another Soviet assault, this time made by an estimated battalion, moved south from Dreniki towards Stolbov, but this was deflected and forced to wheel to the west. In response, the division organised a local counterattack by an armoured group towards Dreniki and this advanced northwards through the woods west of Stolbov. Here it ran into a large Russian assembly area, and despite a strong anti-tank defence, it managed to inflict severe casualties on the enemy troops including the destruction of three tanks. In a separate action, the division also pushed some of its *panzergrenadiers* westwards out of Stolbov to take possession of the same woods. To the north-west, elements of the *7.Panzer-Division* meanwhile managed to see off a battalion-strength assault from the east and south-east against the northern part of Romanovka. Things were not so successful to the north where the defensive position in Korchevka was attacked repeatedly throughout the early part of the morning, with the assaults coming in from both the north-east and the north-west. The attacks were all beaten back initially, and a local counterattack was even reported to have caused heavy losses to the Soviet forces. However, a renewed assault by the Russians at 10.00 hours, this time with armour support, succeeded in forcing the defending Germans out of the village, and at that point the defence seemed to collapse. The Soviet advance pressed south-westwards to take Vrublevka off the march before continuing on, wheeling to the west as it moved. North of Vrublevka though, the Russians seemed to have gone over to the defensive, and were seen to be digging in along the sector between Dzerzhinsk and Velikaya Kozara. Further west, later reconnaissance patrols sent out by the division established that the Soviets were in the area in force, with Kamen', Buldychev, Malaya Kozara, and Erasimovka to the north[57] all now being strongly held by Russian troops. South-west of Kamen', the division had made contact with elements of the *16.Panzer-Division* in Pechanovka.

Further elements of this division had meanwhile continued to arrive, including the *Panzer-Pionier-Bataillon 16*, the *Panzergrenadier-Regiment 79* (less the heavy weapons companies), the headquarters of the *Panzer-Artillerie-Regiment 16* (with the *I.Abteilung* and the 5. and *7.Batterien*), and the *3./Panzer-Flak-Abteilung 16*.[58] To secure the assembly areas for those elements still arriving, the division had meanwhile been undertaking reconnaissance as ordered. On its left wing, it had sent a patrol out along the road from Shepetovka towards Korets, and just after midday it reached Mukharev, about eight kilometres south of the town. At that point, the village was still unoccupied by Russian troops, but contact with the patrol had been lost after that. Further east, in the area south of Novograd-Volynskii, Soviet forces had occupied Smoldyrev at about 02.00 hours the previous night, and had spent most of the day reinforcing the area. By evening it seemed clear to the division that they would be making this area the main point of effort for future operations. At about midday, other Russian troops also occupied Orepy about eight kilometres south of Novograd-Volynskii on the main road to Shepetovka. Further south, the division established that although the village of Glubochek had not yet been occupied by Russian troops, the eastern bank of the river Sluch' in that area was held by partisan units as far as the edge of the woods north of Miropol'. According to statements taken from prisoners, these were under the control of

---

57 Referred to as Promin' on more recent Soviet maps. The village is not marked on all maps, but was situated 4 kilometres north of Pilipo-Koshara.
58 *16.Pz.Div.*, Tagesmeldung, 18.15 hours dated 4 Jan 44. According to this report, the division deployed the following operational armour: 22 *Panzer IV lg*; 63 *Panzer V*; 4 command tanks, and 17 *StuGs*.

a regimental headquarters located in Ul'kha. To the east, the division had made contact with elements of the *Sicherungs-Regiment 177* in the northern part of Miropol', and with elements of the *7.Panzer-Division* south of Romanovka.[59] By the end of the afternoon, at 17.15 hours, there had been Soviet mortar fire reported in the northern end of Miropol', and there were reports of Russian tanks advancing southwards from Kamen' over the main road between Chudnov and Miropol'. At some point during the day, the division also reported that *Generalleutnant* Matterstock, commander of the *147.Reserve-Division* and former *Kampfkommandant* in Novograd-Volynskii, had arrived in Dubrovka on the main road to Shepetovka, together with about 1,000 men. They had been forced to withdraw in heavy fighting, and most of the group's heavy weapons had been lost along the way.[60] The *LIX.AK* meanwhile continued with its planned withdrawal on the far left wing, and the *291.Infanterie-Division* took up new positions in a bridgehead on the river Korchik between east of Korets through Kobylya to Zastava, opposite Storozhev.[61] It had also sent out reconnaissance patrols to the east towards Novograd-Volynskii, and reported the presence of enemy armoured cars in the vicinity of Pilipovichi. To the division's left, the *Korps-Abteilung C* was meanwhile screening the northern flank and was still falling back to a line from Storozhev through Budki-Ushienskie to the southern end of Bel'chaki on the river Sluch'. During the course of the evening, von der Chevallerie received orders to assemble his troops around and west of Korets and hold them in readiness to advance towards Novograd-Volynskii. In the meantime, he was to push out screening forces as far as possible to the east, north-east and north.

In the rear, the headquarters of the newly-arrived *XXXXVI.PzK* made contact with the *16.Panzer-Division*, and was informed during the evening that, in addition to the *1.Infanterie-Division*, it was also due to receive the *254.Infanterie-Division* as reinforcement.[62] The new division was currently underway and was planned to arrive in the Shepetovka area behind the *1.Infanterie-Division*. To give it the benefit of some armour support, the *Sturmgeschütz-Abteilung 300* was being unloaded in Starokonstantinov, and Gollnick was given the responsibility of moving the new unit to the *254.Infanterie-Division* as soon as the latter arrived. The *XXXXVI.PzK* was however forbidden to deploy the new units before they had fully assembled.

Overall then, the assault against the southern wing which the *4.Panzerarmee* had anticipated had not actually occurred, and there were now signs that, following their unsuccessful attack either side of the Kazatin-Vinnitsa railway, the Soviets opposite the *XXIV.PzK* were actually transferring the mobile troops of the 1st Tank Army away to the south-east.[63] That notwithstanding, the *PzAOK 4* was still expecting renewed enemy pressure against the Novaya Greblya-Konstantinovka sector on the right wing of the *XXIV.PzK*. In contrast, the major offensive against the northern wing between Berdichev and Dzerzhinsk had succeeded in opening a serious breach in the centre of the sector held by the *XIII.AK*. The attack had been launched either side of the Teterev,

---

59 Although the *7.Panzer-Division* reported this to have taken place in Pechanovka, a few kilometres further west.
60 *PzAOK 4*, Tagesmeldung an *Heeresgruppe Süd*, dated 4 Jan 44
61 *PzAOK 4*, Ia Kriegstagebuch entry dated 4 Jan 44. The location is actually given as Rastava, but this is a transcription error since the village is shown on German maps as Zastava.
62 *PzAOK 4*, Ia Nr. 98/44 geh. dated 4 Jan 44.
63 *PzAOK 4*, Ia Kriegstagebuch entry dated 4 Jan 44. *PzAOK 4*, Ic Abendmeldung an *Heeresgruppe Süd*, 20.00 hours dated 4 Jan 44.

in the east by the 1st Guards Army supported by the 6th Guards Tank Corps from the 3rd Guards Tank Army and in the west by the 60th Army supported by the 4th Guards Tank Corps.[64] In the west, the attack had generally been thrown back, but east of the river Teterev Soviet armour had broken through the defences to reach the Zhitomir-Shepetovka railway at Mikhalenki. Indeed it had been reported that a few enemy tanks had even pushed on over the railway line to reach a point only six kilometres north of Ivanopol'. By the end of the day, the *PzAOK 4* had not identified any new units involved in the offensive, and, with the weather hindering comprehensive aerial reconnaissance, the army had only been able to form a sketchy picture of Russian reserves in the Zhitomir-Novograd-Volynskii area. This showed a large Soviet presence in the areas around Novograd-Volynskii-Pilipovichi, the woods west of Novy Zavod, and north of Dzerzhinsk where an extensive encampment was observed. If greater detail was lacking, it nonetheless indicated that the Russians still maintained considerable uncommitted forces in the region, which they could use against either the *XIII.AK* or the *XXXXVIII. PzK* if they wished. However, in the more immediate future, the *PzAOK 4* anticipated that the rest of the 3rd Guards Tank Army would also be thrown into the attack east of the Teterev, meaning that they expected both the 7th Guards Tank Corps and the 9th Mechanised Corps to be committed soon. Further west, the Germans also expected the 60th Army assault to be reinforced by the 5th Guards Tank Corps and the 25th Tank Corps to help drive the advance forwards to the south-west.

It was against this background that the *4.Panzerarmee* issued its instructions for the following day.[65] According to these, the *XXIV.PzK* was to maintain its current positions under any circumstances and transfer elements of the *1.SS Panzer-Division 'LSSAH'* to the *XIII.AK*. The *XIII.AK* in turn, with those new elements attached, was to counterattack and close the gaps that had opened up in the front line between the *68.* and *340.Infanterie-Divisionen*, and establish a new defensive line between Pyatka and Korochenki. The *XXXXVIII.PzK* was meanwhile to pull back the *SS Panzerkampfgruppe 'Das Reich'* on its right wing to the line Gorodishche-Dubishche and form an armoured *Kampfgruppe* to support the fighting on the left wing of the *XIII.AK*. In the centre, the *Korps* was to hold its positions and continue with its mobile operations on the left wing, maintaining contact with the *16.Panzer-Division* to the west. In addition to these new measures, the *PzAOK 4* also intended that the *XXXXVI.PzK* was to continue assembling its forces in its allotted area, while establishing a screening force to the north and north-east.[66] The *LIX.AK* was to assemble in the area around Korets, with screening forces to the north, north-east and east, and at the same time collect together those elements of the *147.Reserve-Division* which had escaped from Novograd-Volynskii prior to moving them to Starokonstantinov where transport would be arranged to take them out of the area to the *Wehrmachtbefehlshaber Ukraine*. By this time, Raus had grown concerned about the condition of his armour, noting to his *Korps* commanders that the number of operational vehicles had dropped off sharply over the previous few days.[67] Whilst he recognised the difficulties then faced by the repair workshops, he still felt obliged to

---

64 The 7th Guards Tank Corps also took part in the attack, but German intelligence had not identified it at this stage.
65 *PzAOK 4*, Ia Nr. 90/44 geh. dated 4 Jan 44.
66 *PzAOK 4*, Ia Nr. 101/44 geh. dated 4 Jan 44.
67 *PzAOK 4*, Ia Nr. 100/44 geh. dated 4 Jan 44.

ask his subordinates to keep a close eye on the repair activities to ensure that these were conducted as quickly as possible.

Wednesday 5 January 1944

The night to 5 January passed quietly enough for most of the *4.Panzerarmee*, with the exception of the *XIII.AK*. On the right wing, the *XXIV.PzK* had extended its sector to the north-west of Berdichev and assumed control of the *4.Gebirgs-Division* as instructed.[68] The positions of the division's *Aufklärungs-Abteilung* in Konstantinovka had been assaulted at 20.00 hours the previous night, but despite support from two enemy tanks, the attack had been driven back. On the sector held by the *168.Infanterie-Division*, both sides had conducted reconnaissance patrols, and there had been heavy Soviet artillery fire against the small wood south of Maly Chernyatin. On the left wing of the *18.Artillerie-Division*, the village of Peremoga had been occupied by Russian troops, whilst north of Berdichev the relief of the *1.SS Panzer-Division 'LSSAH'* by elements of the *1.Panzer-Division* had been complicated by Soviet assaults against Raiki. As a result, the withdrawal was still not complete by morning.

Things had not been as quiet in the sector held by the *XIII.AK*.[69] The strong Soviet pressure had continued across the whole front throughout the night, and the Russians were reportedly bringing up continuous fresh reinforcements to the Malye Korovintsy area. They had widened the existing breach and pushed forward to capture Velikaya Korovintsy, before advancing further southwards.[70] So far 40 enemy tanks had been observed, together with anti-tank weapons and strong infantry forces, including a column of about 1,000 men. Further south, Russian tanks had been firing on Ivanopol' throughout the night, and it appeared as though the Soviets were preparing for an armoured assault against the town. During the night the *Korps* had managed to destroy only two enemy tanks. The advance towards Ivanopol' was already blocking the German supply routes north of the town, including in the area around Medvedikha. Hauffe confirmed that the relief of the right-hand units of the *'LSSAH'* had not yet been completed, as these were still waiting for the relieving forces to arrive.

With the Russians concentrating their efforts against the *XIII.AK*, the *XXXXVIII.PzK* to its left had been able to complete the withdrawal of the *19.Panzer-Division* to a line running from the northern edge of Chudnov through the high ground to the west and then north to Serbinovka. Apart from an artillery barrage at around 19.30 hours the previous evening in the Stolbov area, there had been no combat activity to report. To the right, things were less clear as contact had been lost with the *SS Panzerkampfgruppe 'Das Reich'*, but on the left the *7.Panzer-Division* had taken up new positions on a line running from the northern end of Romanovka to Gordeevka.

Away to the north-west, the *LIX.AK* had pushed out reconnaissance east of Korets on a wide front and had reached a line running from Bol'shoi Pravutin in the south, through Dedovichi (east of Pishchev) on the main road to Novograd-Volynskii, to Krasilovka (west of Bogolyubovka) in the north. Behind this screen, the first units of the *291.Infanterie-Division* had begun to arrive in the Korets area, whilst behind it, all

---

68 *XXIV.PzK*, Morgenmeldung, 06.15 hours dated 5 Jan 44.
69 *XIII.AK*, Morgenmeldung, 07.40 hours dated 5 Jan 44.
70 *PzAOK 4*, Morgenmeldung an *Heeresgruppe Süd*, dated 5 Jan 44.

elements of the *Korps-Abteilung C* had now crossed to the southern bank of the river Sluch'.

The weather meanwhile had changed little. Despite the cloud cover, the temperature remained around the freezing point, leaving a light frost and ice in places on the roads. On the southern wing of the *Panzerarmee*, the *4.Gebirgs-Division* had been unable to complete its mission due in part to the late arrival of some units but also due in part to enemy resistance encountered.[71] Nevertheless, by the end of the day, it had made progress to the south-east, and both Zhurava and the southern part of Vakhnovka were in German hands, although the division had been unable to force the Russian troops from the northern part of the town. Partisan units were reported in the wooded area south-west of Vakhnovka, and to the north, the village of Petrovka was strongly held by Soviet forces. On its left wing, the division had been obliged to delay regrouping following a successful counterattack against an estimated two Soviet battalions east of Chervonaya Tribunovka, although by evening, it could at least report that all its combat units had now arrived. To the north, the Russians had launched four separate assaults during the morning against the positions held by the *168.Infanterie-Division* in Maly Chernyatin and Gerasimovka. These had been made in company or battalion strength, but all of them had been seen off. The division also reported enemy movements, with a column of about 60 sledges being observed on the road between Chernyatin and Leonardovka. The *18.Artillerie-Division* had been subjected to a larger number of assaults, suffering nine in total. These had been made against a wide front stretching from Zalivanshchina in the south to Peremoga in the north, and had ranged from small-scale assaults by no more than individual platoons, up to full scale regimental attacks. A little to the north, the Russians were also seen to be reinforcing the area around Mshanets just north of Peremoga, and the division concluded that further attacks were to be expected. To the left, the *1.Panzer-Division* had also been assaulted. On its right, Soviet attacks in about battalion strength against Komsomol'skoe had been driven off, while further north stronger assaults in up to regimental strength on both the Zhezhelev and Khazhin sectors had also been successfully defended. On the Berdichev sector though, the Soviets seemed to have made a determined effort to secure the town. At 13.30 hours, there had been a major assault along the whole front between Berdichev and Malaya Tartarovka, and this had succeeded in achieving four separate breaches in the German defences. The first of these was south of Berdichev near Bystrik, the second west of the town itself, the third south of Skraglevka, and the last near Raiki. As a result of these breakthroughs, the Russians were able take possession of the western part of Berdichev and complete the liberation of the town.[72] The *Panzeraufklärungs-Abteilung 1* had nevertheless managed to seal off some of these penetrations with the support of 12 *panzers*, but it seemed likely that further enemy troops were being brought into the area as a considerable amount of Soviet movement had been observed opposite the sector. The division's situation was not

---

71 *XXIV.PzK*, Tagesmeldung, 18.45 hours dated 5 Jan 44.
72 The papers of the *PzAOK 4* are curiously reticent on the question of the withdrawal from Berdichev. The report from the *XXIV.PzK* contains no reference at all to the fact that the town had been given up, and even suggests that the situation had been brought back under control following the reported breakthroughs. It was left to the *Panzerarmee* to report that the Russians had been able to take the western part of the town, and, given this lack of consistency in reporting, it may be possible that the local commanders had agreed that the town should be evacuated, but that the record should show no official sanction of the fact.

being helped by having to provide a screen on the left flank against the Soviet breach in the *XIII.AK* sector, and by the delay to the relief of *1.SS Panzer-Division 'LSSAH'*. This had not been completed owing to some elements having already moved out of their positions, but the relieving infantry units were finally helped into position with the assistance of a reinforced *Kompanie* from the *Panzeraufklärungs-Abteilung 1*.

The main Soviet effort though continued against the *XIII.AK*.[73] The attacks persisted throughout the whole day and the *Korps* estimated between eight and ten rifle divisions were involved, supported by maybe two tank corps.[74] The majority of these were regiment and battalion strength assaults, and together they resulted in the widening of the breach in the Korovintsy area. The enemy advance continued to the south, where Soviet tanks with mounted infantry reached the southern edge of the wooded area a few kilometres north of Ivanopol'. According to both ground and aerial reconnaissance, these forward units were continually being reinforced by additional troops, so it appeared likely that the advance here would be continued in strength. On the *Korps* right, the *1.SS Panzer-Division 'LSSAH'* had proved relatively successful in defending its sector. A regimental-sized assault against Malaya Tartarovka was driven off, and another group which had forced its way into the northern end of Rachki with the support of a few tanks, was forced back northwards in a local counterattack. To its left the *68.Infanterie-Division* started the day by having to attack just to clear its main defensive positions. Its left wing was attacked in force, and was obliged to fall back on to the northern edge of the woods south of Korovintsy. Meanwhile, the *Korps* launched its counterattack to try and seal the breach around Mikhailenki. The *208.Infanterie-Division*, starting in the Rachki area, had struggled to make any progress in the absence of the armoured *Kampfgruppe* which had been expected from the *'LSSAH'*, but which had been tied up counter-attacking the Soviet advance into Rachki. On the other side of the breach, the *340.Infanterie-Division* moved out from the Tyutyunniki area, supported by a *Batterie* from the *Sturmgeschütz-Abteilung 280* and an armoured group from the *SS Panzerkampfgruppe 'Das Reich'*. The attack succeeded in capturing Mikhailenki and the northern end of Korovintsy,

---

73 In response to the concerns raised the previous day regarding the combat strength of the *XIII.AK*, the *PzAOK 4* collated data regarding the *Grabenstärke* of the three infantry divisions. These were reported as follows:
- *68.Infanterie-Division*:
  - *Grenadier-Regiment 169:* 85
  - *Grenadier-Regiment 188:* 100
  - *Grenadier-Regiment 196:* 80
  - *Grenadier-Regiment 172:* 54
  - *Grenadier-Regiment 245:* 41
  - *Panzerjäger-; Pionier- and Fusilier-Bataillon (in total):* 96
- *208. Infanterie-Division*:
  - *Grenadier-Regiment 337:* 72
  - *Grenadier-Regiment 338:* 55
  - *Panzerjäger-; Pionier- and Fusilier-Bataillon (in total):* 88
- *340.Infanterie-Division*
  - *Grenadier-Regiment 695:* 152
  - *Grenadier-Regiment 769:* 84
  - *Panzerjäger-; Pionier- and Feldersatz-Bataillon (in total):* 83

By comparison, a full strength infantry company in an *Infanterie-Division n.A. 1944* had a total establishment of 142 men.

74 *XIII.AK*, Tagesmeldung, 18.00 hours dated 5 Jan 44.

destroying six enemy tanks in the action, and by the end of the day it had reached a line running through the eastern edges of Malye Korovintsy, Korovintsy and Mikhailenki. Nevertheless, due to the stiff resistance offered by Soviet forces, the attack had not been wholly successful and the breach could only be reduced rather than sealed off completely. While the attack had the benefit of close air support, particularly in the Korovintsy area itself, the *Korps'* combat ability was beginning to suffer owing to lack of supplies, especially ammunition but also to a lesser extent fuel. Not only was this affecting the immediate operations, but it also meant the *Korps* had been unable to direct artillery fire on to known enemy assembly areas, and the majority of the 100mm cannons and heavy field howitzers had instead been pulled back to the rear because they had run out of ammunition.

The Russians also continued their assault against the front held by the *XXXXVIII. PzK*.[75] The positions of the *SS Panzerkampfgruppe 'Das Reich'* in Korochenki were attacked twice from Gorodishche during the morning by Soviet forces estimated to be a battalion, but the assaults had been seen off. During the afternoon, in the area north-east of Chudnov, the Russians pushed forwards an estimated rifle regiment from the north and north-east, moving closer the *Kampfgruppe's* main defensive positions. Opposite its left wing, the afternoon also saw mortar and rocket fire, while a little further north, Soviet infantry and tank forces were observed assembling in the Siryaki area. The *19.Panzer-Division* too had been attacked during the morning, with a battalion-strength assault being made against Stolbov. Though this was driven off, a renewed assault was made with tank support, and this was brought to a halt under a defensive artillery barrage. Preparations for still further assaults seemed underway, as north of Serbinovka Soviet troops moved forward to within 200 to 400 metres of the division's main defensive positions. The *7.Panzer-Division* to the left was also in the action. The Russians had put in two battalion-strength assaults against the northern part of Romanovka, but these had been successfully defended with two enemy tanks reported as destroyed. Meanwhile other Soviet forces attacked Romanovka from the north-west, coming out of Vrublevka, but this too was beaten back. During the afternoon, 20 Soviet tanks struck southwards out of Vrublevka, with some of these wheeling to the south-west, and by the end of the day Razino station and the northern part of Gordeevka had been lost. The division's positions in Romanovka had been outflanked. Overall, Balck's impression was that the Russians were reinforcing opposite the whole of his sector, but with particular emphasis on the two wings. Troop assemblies had been spotted in the area north and north-west of Chudnov, including both infantry and armoured forces, and according to the results of aerial reconnaissance, fresh Soviet forces were also being brought up into the Knyazhin and Malye Korovintsy areas. In total, around 2,000 vehicles of various types had been observed in the area. Balck considered that Russian intentions were now to widen the breach in the Rachki-Korovintsy area to the west, thereby making the drive southwards more secure, while a second group including the 4th Guards Tank Corps continued to try and get around the left flank of his *Korps*. At *PzAOK 4* headquarters, the situation seemed to be developing adversely, and as a result Raus authorised Balck to pull back his left wing to avoid being rolled up.[76]

---

75 *XXXXVIII.PzK*, Tagesmeldung, 19.15 hours dated 5 Jan 44.
76 *PzAOK 4*, Ia Kriegstagebuch entry dated 5 Jan 44.

On the left wing, the *XXXXVI.PzK* was still consolidating its position. The *16.Panzer-Division* had formed a small *Kampfgruppe* to try and secure the flank facing the *XXXXVIII.PzK*, and this had struck out from Miropol' to the east where it succeeded in defeating an estimated two Soviet companies before returning to its starting positions.[77] Reconnaissance had shown that Glubochek was still unoccupied, while further north two Soviet tanks had been seen in Baranovka. Further north again, the village of Klimental had been occupied by Russian units since about 15.00 hours, while a few kilometres further west, Zeremlya was still unoccupied. Meanwhile, on the left wing, other elements of the division had struck northwards from Kozhushki and taken Orepy, south of Novograd-Volynskii, but to prevent them being isolated, they had later been brought back to their starting positions. A little further to the north-west, the town of Yarun' was strongly held by Soviet forces, but the division had been able to establish some form of contact with the *LIX.AK* through reconnaissance patrols. In the rear, the elements of the new divisions which were still arriving were re-directed to the new assembly areas to avoid being too close to the front line. In general, the Soviets had made no real effort to push against this sector of the *4.Panzerarmee*, where the *Korps* had been able to deploy screening forces to protect the assembly of the new reinforcements. The Russians had occupied Klimental again and sent forward weak cavalry units west of Baranovka, but neither of these gave any real indication of whether and how they intended to advance west of the river Sluch'. As a result, Gollnick thought it might still be possible for the *XXXXVI.PzK* to maintain the line already taken up by the screening forces.

In the *LIX.AK* sector, the bulk of the *291.Infanterie-Division* was now in the area around and to the north of Korets, with screening forces pushed out eastwards to a line running from Pishchev to the north.[78] Behind it, the *Korps-Abteilung C* was following on from the Bel'chaki area, leaving rearguards to watch the crossings over the river Sluch'.

Overall, the picture remained similar to the previous day. On the southern wing of the *PzAOK 4* south of Berdichev, the Soviets had limited themselves to pinning attacks and reconnaissance patrolling where they had pushed forward to the tiny hamlet of Yasenetskoe,[79] between Yasenki and Vakhnovka. They also seemed to be continuing to draw off forces to the south-east.[80] Similarly, on the northern wing, in the sector held by the *XXXXVIII.PzK*, the attacks had eased a little, although there was concern now that the Soviets were shifting forces to the west in an outflanking manoeuvre, striking south or south-east from the Kamen'-Buldychev area. In the centre on the other hand, and especially north-west of Berdichev, the Russians had continued with their major offensive, with the apparent objective of breaking through the *XIII.AK*. There were clear indications that considerable enemy reinforcements were also being moved up in the region, with aerial reconnaissance reporting around 2,000 motor vehicles in the Maly Korovintsy-Knyazhin-Dubishche area. A further 500-800 vehicles were also observed north-west of Korovintsy heading southwards towards Ivanopol', presumably with the objective of striking directly into the rear of the army. The presence of the Soviet 7th Guards Tank Corps and the 9th Mechanised Corps had now been confirmed on this

---

77 *XXXXVI.PzK*, Tagesmeldung, 19.45 hours dated 5 Jan 44.
78 *PzAOK 4*, Ia Tagesmeldung an *Heeresgruppe Süd*, dated 5 Jan 44.
79 Referred to as Romanowka in the German records.
80 *PzAOK 4*, Ic Abendmeldung an *Heeresgruppe Süd*, 19.00 hours dated 5 Jan 44.

sector, with between 60-70 tanks being observed in the area between Rachki and Maly Korovintsy. In the circumstances, Raus believed that if the *PzAOK 4* were to have any chance of being able to close the gap that had opened up west of Berdichev, it needed to be handled by a single command.[81] During the morning therefore, he spoke with Balck at the *XXXXVIII.PzK* and discussed with him the possibility of transferring all the *XIII.AK* units to his command. The two men agreed, and Raus subsequently instructed Balck to take over all the relevant forces and direct the counterattack accordingly. It is indicative of the weakness of the infantry units attached to the *XIII.AK* at this stage that Raus even thought about re-organising all the remaining units into single *Korps-Abteilung*. Later that evening, Balck called Raus to brief him on progress. He believed the whole situation was now critical, and pointed out that Soviet forces thought to be at least a rifle regiment and a tank brigade were already in the wooded area south of Korovintsy, although he estimated that these had been reduced to half strength through a combination of air strikes and ground action. That notwithstanding, the *XXXXVIII. PzK* would attack at 10.00 hours the following morning to try and close the gap. The attack would be conducted by the *1.SS Panzer-Division 'LSSAH'* from the east, and the *SS Panzerkampfgruppe 'Das Reich'* from the west. Arrangements had been made with the *Luftwaffe* for ground support, and it was hoped that this would be a decisive factor in the operation. Stiff resistance was to be expected from the defending Russian units, but Balck was optimistic that the operation would be successful.

During the course of the day, the *XXIV.PzK* had asked the question as to how in the current circumstances contact was to be made with the neighbouring *1.Panzerarmee*. Raus discussed the issue with Fangohr, and they considered there were two possibilities.[82] The first was to take Britskoe and establish contact in that area, and the second was to extend the right wing to the south and block the road to Vinnitsa. Fangohr later discussed the issue with *Generalmajor* Wenck, his counterpart at the *PzAOK 1*, and suggested that, since there were already strong Soviet forces including armour in Yasenetskoe, they drop the first option to take Britskoe, and try instead to close the gap by concentrating all available forces to strike south-eastwards. Wenck recognised the situation to be critical, particularly where the Russians were pressing the *17.Panzer-Division* hard from the north with what was assumed to be the entire 1st Tank Army. Given that the division had already extended its forward positions as far as possible to the west in reaching Vyselki, just north-west of Nartsizovka, Wenck was of the opinion that any further advance in that direction was not really possible. He therefore asked whether the *PzAOK 4* would be in a position to close the gap by attacking eastwards towards it. Raus discussed the possibility with Nehring, and came to the conclusion that the *XXIV.PzK* was not really strong enough to achieve this on its own. He did however ask Nehring whether he might not be able to carry out a short sharp strike in the Yasenki area to force the Soviets to stop their advance, but without holding on to the area once this had been achieved. Nehring thought that this would also be difficult, particularly as Vakhnovka was already held by strong Russian forces. Raus therefore decided that the *XXIV.PzK* should first undertake a specific reconnaissance in the Yasenki area with a view to establishing the precise strength of enemy forces in the region and how best they might be attacked. The *1.Panzerarmee* was informed of his decision.

---

81 *PzAOK 4*, Ia Kriegstagebuch entry dated 5 Jan 44.
82 *PzAOK 4*, Ia Kriegstagebuch entry dated 5 Jan 44.

Meanwhile, the same concerns seem to have been worrying Army Group South, and in the early hours of the morning von Manstein had sent Raus new orders for the deployment of Gollnick's *XXXXVI.PzK* which was then still assembling in the Shepetovka area.[83] In a significant change from his previous instructions, Raus was now ordered to transfer the *Korps*, together with the *16.Panzer-Division*, the *1.* and *254. Infanterie-Divisions* to the area north-west of Vinnitsa, where it was to re-assemble either side of the Khmel'nik-Kalinovka railway, in the Kalinovka-Gulevtsy-Pikov-Khmel'nik-Bruslinov area. The transfer was to begin immediately, although transport during the daylight hours was only to be allowed provided there was no chance of enemy air activity. The tracked elements were to move by rail as far as possible, and even the infantry were to be moved by truck to reduce fatigue. To fill the hole that would be left by the *Korps*' departure, the *LIX.AK* was to drop southwards to the Shepetovka area where it would assume responsibility for the *96.Infanterie-Division*, newly arriving from Army Group North. In the meantime, those elements of the *XXXXVI.PzK* which had previously been pushed out to screen the unloading activities were to remain in position to keep open the railway network around Shepetovka and provide cover for the *LIX.AK* as it pulled back into its new positions. The *4.Panzerarmee* called Gollnick straightaway to inform him of the change of plans, and to make sure that those trains still arriving could be re-directed to their new destinations. The call was followed in the early afternoon by formal instructions.[84] These set out the timetable and the routes to be taken by the *16.Panzer-Division* and the *1.Infanterie-Division*, with both units scheduled to arrive in their new assembly areas west of Vinnitsa during the night to 7 January. Those elements of both divisions which had not yet arrived were to be diverted directly to the new areas, and to assist in the move, the *PzAOK 4* allotted 400 tonnes of its own truck capacity to the *Korps*, with the *XXXXVIII.PzK* ordered to provide a further 60 tonnes. Given the Army Group's earlier concerns about enemy aerial reconnaissance, Raus instructed Gollnick to ensure that all movement only took place at night, although the orders did permit empty trucks to be returned during daylight hours. New orders also went out to von der Chevallerie at *LIX.AK*.[85] These instructed him to pull back to the south to cover the Shepetovka-Polonnoe-Slavuta sector, and take up new positions either side of the river Korchik on a line running from Glubochek through Zamorochen'e[86] and Khutor to Yanushevka. The *Korps* was to relieve the remaining elements of the *XXXXVI.PzK* as quickly as possible and then concentrate the defence on its eastern sector, ensuring the railway line to Shepetovka was kept open. In the meantime though, the *454.Sicherungs-Division*, temporarily known as the *Kampfgruppe* Korets, was to remain behind in Korets and block the main road running from Novograd-Volynskii to Rovno. Specific orders were given that it was not be permitted to pull back southwards with the rest of the *Korps*. A later order advised von der Chevallerie of those elements of the *XXXXVI.PzK* which were still holding their screening positions, and which would therefore need to be relieved.[87] On the right wing, these included units of the *Panzeraufklärungs-Abteilung 16*, which deployed its headquarters and armoured elements in Polonnoe, and a reinforced

---

83 Hgr. Süd, Ia Nr. 61/44 geh.Kdos. dated 5 Jan 44.
84 *PzAOK 4*, Ia Nr. 107/44 g.Kdos. dated 5 Jan 44.
85 *PzAOK 4*, Ia Nr. 110/44 geh. dated 5 Jan 44.
86 Situated on the main road between Gorodnyavka and Dormanka.
87 *PzAOK 4*, Ia Nr. 113/44 geh. dated 5 Jan 44.

Kompanie in each of Miropol' and Glubochek. In the centre, the *I./Panzergrenadier-Regiment 64* had its headquarters in Dubrovka, with units in Serednya, Suyemtsy, Orepy and Zhelobnoe, while on the left, a battalion from the *1.Infanterie-Division* was still holding its positions on a line running from Khutor through Peremyshel' to Baran'e, north-west of Slavuta. During the evening, *Oberst* Schleusener, the *LIX.AK* chief of staff, called the *PzAOK 4* headquarters, and confirmed to Fangohr that the withdrawal would begin the following morning with the intention of relieving the remaining elements of the *16.Panzer-Division*.

Finally, Raus issued his instructions for the remainder of the *4.Panzerarmee*.[88] His intention was now to hold his current positions south of Berdichev and pull back the northern wing to a line running along the railway from Berdichev to Polonnoe whilst closing the gap in the Korovintsy area. The *XXIV.PzK* was ordered to establish new defensive positions on a line running north from a point west of Bystrik passing west of Berdichev and then along the road and railway from there to Demchin. It was to make contact with the right wing of the *XIII.AK* on the western edge of nearby Golod'ki. The *XIII.AK* was to be subordinated to the *XXXXVIII.PzK* for the time being, while this *Korps* in turn was to pull back to the railway line running from Demchin through Ol'shanka and Gordeevka to Pechanovka. At the same time, it was to free up whatever forces it could from the sector west of the river Teterev and also from the *1.SS Panzer-Division 'LSSAH'* so that it could continue the counterattack to close the gap in the front line. The *Luftwaffe*, in the form of the *VIII.Fliegerkorps*, was to provide all possible support to the attempt to close the breach, and the *XXXXVIII.PzK* was instructed to make the necessary arrangements direct.

---

88 *PzAOK 4*, Ia Nr. 115/44 geh. dated 5 Jan 44.

10

Preparing the Counterstrike

Thursday 6 January 1944

The night to January 6 passed quietly on the southern wing of the *4.Panzerarmee*. On the *XXIV.PzK* sector, reconnaissance patrols had been sent out by both sides, while the *4.Gebirgs-Division* had finished mopping up in southern Vakhnovka and had started to clear the northern part of the town.[1] The *168.Infanterie-Division* had confirmed that Bol'shoi Chernyatin was still held in strength by Russian forces, and the *18.Artillerie-Division* reported observing Soviet reinforcements moving into its sector. The *1.Panzer-Division* had meanwhile completed its planned withdrawal, despite having to defend a battalion-strength assault by the Russians west of Khazhin.[2] There had been more activity further north where the *XXXXVIII.PzK* was now responsible for the breach around Korovintsy.[3] The *1.SS Panzer-Division 'LSSAH'* had sealed off a number of breaches near Malaya Tartarovka, and launched a local counterattack against Russian troops who had struck out from the Rachki area against the division's flank. At 02.45 hours, it had also begun the task of clearing Malaya Tartarovka itself. To the left, the planned withdrawals by the *SS Panzerkampfgruppe 'Das Reich'* and the *19.* and *7.Panzer-Divisions* all took place without serious incident, although the *Kampfgruppe* reported seeing the unloading of enemy infantry opposite its right wing. In the rear, a few Soviet tanks had pushed on into the northern parts of Ivanopol', and the defending German units had been obliged to pull back to the south-western part of the town.[4] North-west of Ivanopol' meanwhile, the situation in Malaya Volitsa and Galievka remained unclear. There was no report from Hauffe's *XIII.AK*, but this was of little consequence since it had effectively been removed from the chain of command the day before. There had been no activity of significance on the *Panzerarmee* western wing, where neither the *XXXXVI.PzK* nor the *LIX.AK* reported anything particular during the night.

The new day dawned colder than of late. There was a mixture of clearing skies and cloud with temperatures falling again to -5°C, leaving the roads in a reasonable condition. In the south, fighting had erupted again on the *XXIV.PzK* sector following the quiet night.[5] About 150 Soviet troops supported by tanks had attacked the positions of the *4.Gebirgs-Division* in southern Vakhnovka, but these had been seen off with all six tanks reported as having been destroyed. The Russians attacked again, this time with about 200 troops, but this too had been successfully defended. A few kilometres to the south, the division assaulted and captured the hamlet of Yasenetskoe at about 15.00 hours, while nearby a Soviet battalion-strength attack against Yasenki was thrown

---

1 *XXIV.PzK*, Morgenmeldung, 06.30 hours dated 6 Jan 44.
2 *PzAOK 4*, Morgenmeldung an *Heeresgruppe Süd*, 07.30 hours dated 6 Jan 44. The report is mistakenly dated as 5 Jan 44.
3 *XXXXVIII.PzK*, Morgenmeldung, 06.00 hours dated 6 Jan 44.
4 *PzAOK 4*, Morgenmeldung an *Heeresgruppe Süd*, 07.30 hours dated 6 Jan 44.
5 *XXIV.PzK*, Tagesmeldung, untimed dated 6 Jan 44.

back. Further north, at 14.30 hours, a company-strength assault out of Petrovka was also driven back by the division, while enemy tanks, rocket launchers and artillery were all observed in the area. On the division's left wing, in the Desna valley, there had been considerable Russian troop movements spotted in the Ovechache area, east of Novaya Greblya. Overall, it seemed as if the Soviets were maintaining the heavy pressure against the division in order to allow them to keep open the route for continuing the advance to the south, and they appeared already to be exploiting the situation as much of the 1st Tank Army had effectively bypassed the hanging right flank of the *Korps*. Further north, the right wing of the *168.Infanterie-Division* had been attacked at Maly Chernyatin by an estimated two rifle companies. To the left, a Soviet reconnaissance patrol near Gerasimovka had been intercepted and thrown back. Things had been quieter in the sector held by the *18.Artillerie-Division* with no combat being reported, and apart from troop movements the Russians had remained fairly inactive. In contrast, the *1.Panzer-Division* had been repeatedly assaulted by strong enemy forces throughout the day across its sector. On its right wing, Soviet troops had attacked Komsomol'skoe, and in the centre they had struck out of Zhezhelev and Khazhin, but all of these had been seen off. Around Berdichev though, things had been more difficult.[6] To the south, Russian forces had attacked out of the Bystrik area and had broken through the division's defences heading to the west. In the hours that followed, the fighting was hard and confused, but by the end of the day the advance had made only a little progress and it was finally brought to a halt on the outskirts of Zhitintsy. North-west of the city, Soviet troops had attacked either side of Skraglevka on a wide front, and following desperate fighting threw the division back to a line running from Radyanskoe to the eastern part of Gardyshevka. The attacks were continued against Gardyshevka from the north and north-east, but despite the strength of these, the division managed to hold its positions throughout the afternoon. These renewed attacks seemed to be attempting to take advantage of the breach achieved north of Ivanopol', and therefore constituted a risk of encirclement not only for elements of the division, but for the *'LSSAH'* as well.

    The fighting continued on the *XXXXVIII.PzK* front too.[7] On the right wing, the *1.SS Panzer-Division 'LSSAH'*, with elements of the *208.* and *68.Infanterie-Divisions* attached, had been subject to heavy Soviet attacks throughout the whole day. These had come in from three sides, the east, north and west, and had generally been made in about battalion strength, sometimes with tank support. Overall, most of the attacks had been beaten off, and though some had achieved local success in the defences around Rachki, the division had been able to seal these off and clear them. It meant though that the planned counterattack to seal the breach had not taken place, and at 10.25 hours Balck called the *PzAOK 4* to explain the situation.[8] He found no sympathy though, and Raus instructed him to start the attack without any further delay as otherwise it was not likely to succeed. Nevertheless, Raus did discuss the situation further with

---

6   *PzAOK 4*, Tagesmeldung an *Heeresgruppe Süd*, untimed dated 6 Jan 44.
7   *XXXXVIII.PzK*, Tagesmeldung, 22.25 hours dated 6 Jan 44. According to this report, the operational armour deployed by the *Korps* was now:
- *7.Panzer-Division*: 5 Panzer IV lg
- *1.SS Panzer-Division 'LSSAH'*: 4 Panzer IV lg; 7 Panzer V; 6 StuGs (the report referred to 5 January).
- SS Panzerkampfgruppe 'Das Reich': 1 Panzer IV lg; 5 StuGs.
There was no report available for the *19.Panzer-Division*.
8   *PzAOK 4*, Ia Kriegstagebuch, entry dated 6 Jan 44.

Fangohr, and between them they agreed upon a new defensive position which should be taken up in the event the attack was not successful. Meanwhile behind the front line, the supply route running south from Demchin to Ozadovka came under fire during the afternoon from Soviet tanks holding the wooded area to the west. The division's situation deteriorated still further when the Soviets achieved a breach in the line held by elements of the *20.Panzergrenadier-Division* south-east of Golod'ki.[9] This now presented a threat of encirclement, as an estimated Soviet tank brigade with 40 tanks, together with a rifle division, had already broken through to the west into the area bounded by the woods north-east of Ivanopol' and the villages of Lesovaya Slobodka and Chervonoe. The *'LSSAH'* and the attached units therefore found themselves in an exposed salient, and the division ordered a withdrawal to avoid being cut off. Balck spoke with Raus again and pointed out that due to this threat of encirclement, it would no longer be possible to press ahead with the operation to close the breach, and even pulling back the *'LSSAH'* at this late stage was likely to run into difficulties.[10] Raus therefore approved a withdrawal of the *XXXXVIII.PzK* to a line he had agreed with Balck that morning during his visit to the *Korps* headquarters. The new defensive position would run from Buryaki in the east, over the high ground south of Ivanopol', through the northern edges of Dubrovka and Troshcha to Tsetselevka, Velikaya Bratalov and Goropai. In agreeing to this withdrawal, Raus stressed that it was essential for the *'LSSAH'* to secure the valley in the Ozadovka area, and ensure that it was kept free until the withdrawal was complete.

Given this development, Raus then spoke with Nehring at the *XXIV.PzK* at about 15.10 hours the same afternoon.[11] He informed the *Korps* commander of the Soviet breach near Golod'ki, and told him that the *1.SS Panzer-Division 'LSSAH'* was now in an extremely difficult position. Its attack to close the breach had failed, and there was the possibility that the Russian troops in the Lesovaya Slobodka area would strike eastwards into its rear. The *XXXXVIII.PzK* was therefore going to pull back its right wing, and as a result the *XXIV.PzK* would have to pull back its left wing too. It was important though that this movement was not carried out before the *'LSSAH'* reached Ozadovka, and it was also crucial that all available anti-tank weapons were to be concentrated on this wing to stop the enemy armour from advancing south-eastwards and disrupting the *Korps'* withdrawal. The *XXIV.PzK* was now to pull back to new positions on a line running from Markovtsy through Volchinets, Fridrovo, and Andreyashevka to Buryaki where it would join with the left wing of the *XXXXVIII.PzK*.

The *SS Panzerkampfgruppe 'Das Reich'* meanwhile, with the *Kampfgruppe 340. Infanterie-Division* attached, managed to get its counterattack towards Korovintsy underway. The assault began at 11.00 hours but immediately ran into stiff resistance, and in the face of increasing anti-tank and artillery fire the attack came to a halt about 500 metres west of the town. To the west, Soviet forces attacked Mikhailenki and Tyutyunniki in about battalion strength and managed to achieve a local breach near the former village. Both attacks were eventually beaten back though, and the defensive positions maintained. To the left of the *Kampfgruppe*, in the sector held by the *19.Panzer-Division*, the Russians made a series of attacks in the Chudnov area. These began with an assault from Chudnov to the south in about battalion strength, and a company strength

---

9   Referred to as Miroslavka on more recent Soviet maps.
10 *PzAOK 4* Ia, Kriegstagebuch entry dated 6 Jan 44.
11 *PzAOK 4* Ia, Kriegstagebuch entry dated 6 Jan 44.

attack west of the river Teterev. Both of these were driven off, but they were followed by a larger operation involving an estimated two rifle regiments. This also began in Chudnov but it headed instead towards the south-west where it came to a halt in the face of concentrated defensive fire, never having reached the division's main defensive positions. During the afternoon, the division spotted a Soviet column moving westwards from Stolbov, but it had been unable to estimate its strength. Throughout the whole day then, the entire front held by the *XXXXVIII.PzK*, except the left wing, had been attacked by what was reported to be strong armoured and infantry forces, with the main point of effort being made against the right wing where between 30 and 40 enemy tanks had been seen in the area around and north of Ivanopol'. Balck reported that Soviet intentions still appeared to be to exploit the existing breakthrough and continue the advance to the south. On the left wing though, the Russians seemed to have gone over to the defence opposite the *7.Panzer-Division*, where, having reached the Berdichev-Polonnoe railway line, they appeared to be replacing armoured units by infantry, and regrouping the mobile units in the Romanovka-Buldychev area, possibly for a renewed advance to the west.

Further to the west meanwhile, Gollnick's *XXXXVI.PzK* was concentrating on the transport arrangements for moving to the Vinnitsa area.[12] Novy Miropol' had been evacuated during the previous night after the rearguards of the *16.Panzer-Division* had been attacked by strong forces which threatened to encircle them. During the course of the day, the Soviets established a bridgehead over the river Sluch' in Kamenka, and by nightfall this was estimated to be held by a rifle battalion. Once firmly established, the Russians began to put out reconnaissance feelers with mounted units moving both towards the north-west and towards the division's new positions in Dertka.[13] During the day, Gollnick had issued instructions to designate the headquarters of the *Grenadier-Regiment 1* as *Kampfkommandant Shepetovka*, placing it in command of the forces ordered to remain behind to screen the withdrawal. Assigned to the new *Kampfkommandant* were the *Panzeraufklärungs-Abteilung 16*, the *I./Panzergrenadier-Regiment 64* and the *II./Grenadier-Regiment 1*. Apart from the attack against Novy Miropol' though, the Soviets remained relatively quiet, allowing the *Korps* to begin the troop transfers. Elements of both the *16.Panzer-Division* and the *1.Infanterie-Division* had already got underway, and by morning the other two battalions of the *Panzergrenadier-Regiment 64* together with the *III./Panzerartillerie-Regiment 16* were already in Proskurov. The *Panzergrenadier-Regiment 79* and the *I./Panzerartillerie-Regiment 16* were even further ahead, having reached Khmel'nik, while the *I./Panzer-Regiment 2* had begun loading its 'Panther' tanks at the railway station in Shepetovka.

Covering the left flank of the *4.Panzerarmee*, the *LIX.AK* pressed ahead with its planned withdrawal.[14] The *Korps-Abteilung C* had fallen back in an orderly fashion and taken up new positions on a line running from Tokarev northwards to Pishchev and then bending back north-westwards through Polchino, Morozovka and Kazak to Rechki.

---

12   *XXXXVI.PzK*, Tagesmeldung, 19.10 hours dated 6 Jan 44. The *Korps* reported the following operational armour:
   • *16.Panzer-Division*: 33 Panzer IV lg; 62 Panzer V; 5 command tanks; 21 StuGs.
   • *1.Infanterie-Division*: 14 StuGs
13   PzAOK 4, Tagesmeldung an *Heeresgruppe Süd*, untimed dated 6 Jan 44
14   *LIX.AK*, Tagesmeldung, 19.40 hours dated 6 Jan 44.

There had been no contact with enemy forces throughout the withdrawal, although contact had been made with the *II./Panzergrenadier-Regiment 64* in Zhelobnoe, south-east of Tokarev. Nevertheless, there had been considerable Soviet reconnaissance activity further east along the road to Novograd-Volynskii, where armoured cars had been seen in the Dedovichi-Pilipovichi-Yurkovshchina area. To the south-west, the *291.Infanterie-Division* had by 15.00 hours reached the Kutki-Chernokaly-Mukharev-Pechivody area without incident. Despite the poor weather and road conditions, von der Chevallerie had finally brought his *Korps* through 14 days of a difficult defensive withdrawal operation without any significant loss of artillery or anti-tank assets, meaning it was still in a condition in which it could take its place again on the left wing of the *4.Panzerarmee*.[15] During the evening, he received new instructions from the *PzAOK 4*.[16] According to these, the *LIX.AK* was now to prevent any further Soviet advance either to the west or the south-west. To this end, the *Korps-Abteilung C* was to be deployed either side of Korets to block any westward advance by the Soviets along the main road from Novograd-Volynskii to Korets. It was to place its forward units as far east as possible, and cover its northern flank in the area around Velikaya Kletska. The *291.Infanterie-Division* was to be moved to the south-east where it was to deploy either side of the main Shepetovka-Novograd-Volynskii road to block any Russian moves to the south-west. The division was to be ready to counterattack to the east, the north-east or the north, and was to place its forward troops on a line running from Kamenka through Poninka, Burtin and Zamorochen'e to Khorovets. The *XXXXVIII.PzK* had been given the task of making contact with it in the Kamenka area. Those elements of the *16.Panzer-Division* and the *1.Infanterie-Division* were meanwhile to be relieved as soon as possible and returned to their parent units. All those units belonging to the *454.Sicherungs-Division* which were currently deployed in the *LIX.AK* area were now placed under its command and given instructions to assemble in the Korets area. Finally, the *Korps* was also informed that the *96.Infanterie-Division* would be arriving soon following its transfer from Army Group North, and was to be assembled on the right wing in the Polonnoe area.

Overall, the Soviets had continued their pinning attacks on the eastern front of the *PzAOK 4* as far north as Berdichev.[17] Just north of the town though, the troops of the 18th and 1st Guards Army, supported by the 3rd Guards Tank Army, had pressed ahead with the assault either side of Skraglevka, striking south-westwards towards the left wing of the main offensive which was heading south-east from the Malaya Tartarovka-Rachki-Korovintsy sector. The main effort however had been to widen the breach either side of Korovintsy, and Russian forces had managed to push this out to the southern end of Rachki and Lesovaya Slobodka in the east, and Dubrovka and Galievka in the west.[18] In the centre, Raus estimated that a Soviet rifle division, supported by about 35-40 tanks, had already reached Ivanopol'. Further west, the assault had not been as strong, although troops of the 60th Army had been testing their way forward between Chudnov and Stolbov, trying to push to the south and south-west. Although elements of the 4th Guards Tank Corps had been identified assembling in the area east and south-east of Miropol', the Russians seemed to have made no serious attempt to outflank the

---

15 *PzAOK 4*, Tagesmeldung an *Heeresgruppe Süd*, untimed dated 6 Jan 44.
16 *PzAOK 4*, Ia Nr. 131/44 geh. dated 6 Jan 44; *PzAOK 4*, Ia Nr. 157/44 geh. dated 6 Jan 44.
17 *PzAOK 4*, Ia, Kriegstagebuch entry dated 6 Jan 44.
18 *PzAOK 4*, Ic, Abendmeldung dated 6 Jan 44.

XXXXVIII.PzK on its left, and the *Korps* had by and large been able to maintain its cohesion. Opposite this sector, Soviet forces were reported to be digging in on a line from Razino station through Gordeevka to Privitov, and were bringing up artillery support. According to information received, the armour of the Soviet 4th Guards Tank Corps was now busy re-grouping behind this new line, in the Romanovka-Buldychev area. Raus was of the opinion that this Corps, together with the Soviet 60th Army, was now planning to renew the advance to the south-west. It seemed to him less likely that it would be transferred eastwards to support the main breakthrough near Korovintsy. Further north though, there were no signs as yet that the Soviet forces were planning to advance any further west and south-west, and the results of aerial reconnaissance had shown that there was no real Russian troop movement on the major roads in that area.

Faced with this situation, Raus issued new orders.[19] In these, he confirmed that the northern wing of the *Panzerarmee* was to pull back to a general line running from Brodetskoe on the river Gnilopyat', through Fridrovo and Buryaki, passing over the high ground south of Ivanopol' before running on through Troshcha and Velikaya Bratalov to Goropai. The *XXIV.PzK* was to occupy this new line as far west as Buryaki, but was to delay its withdrawal for as long as necessary to give the *1.SS Panzer-Division 'LSSAH'* time to pull back through Gardyshevka to the south-west. As part of the withdrawal the *SS Panzer-Aufklärungs-Abteilung 1* was to be returned to the division. Once in its new positions the *Korps* was to concentrate the defence on its left wing. The *XXXXVIII.PzK* was to occupy the new line from Buryaki to Goropai, and was to patrol its western flank with reinforced reconnaissance units and thereby maintain contact with the forward detachments of the *LIX.AK* towards Kamenka.

Earlier in the day, between 12.30 hours to 13.30 hours, von Manstein had paid a visit to the *PzAOK 4* headquarters in Letichev.[20] During the visit, Raus had briefed him on the situation facing the *Panzerarmee*, and after this, von Manstein had acknowledged that Raus' position was difficult, recognising in particular that the situation facing both wings of the *PzAOK 4* was dangerous. He informed the meeting that he had originally intended to use the *1.Panzerarmee* to strike the Soviets forces east of Vinnitsa, and the *XXXXVI.PzK* to strike those heading towards Shepetovka, hoping thereby to stabilise the situation on both wings at the same time. In order to find the necessary forces however, it would have been necessary to shorten the front lines in other sectors, and this had been forbidden to him. He had therefore decided to assemble all available forces north of Vinnitsa and use these to strike into the flank and rear of the Soviet 1st Tank Army to destroy it. The northern wing of the *Panzerarmee* would just have to hold up any further Russian advance to the south and south-west for as long as possible with the forces already at its disposal. Von Manstein explained that the counterattack from the area north of Vinnitsa would probably jump off from the sector held by the *18.Artillerie-Division* and strike out towards Pogrebishche, but depending on the situation it might have to start from somewhere further south and aim more to the south-south-east. Although he planned to begin the strike as soon as possible, it would still have to wait until the *XXXXVI.PzK* had completed its troop assemblies, with the exception of the *254.Infanterie-Division*, which could arrive later. Raus was of the opinion that the *1.Infanterie-Division* would not begin to arrive in its new area before 9 January, simply

19 *PzAOK 4*, Ia Nr. 135/44 geh. dated 6 Jan 44.
20 *PzAOK 4*, Ia, Kriegstagebuch entry dated 6 Jan 44.

because the available transport means were not adequate. The horse-drawn elements, in particular some of the artillery units, would have to be waited for. On this basis, it seemed that 10 January was the earliest practicable date for the start of the offensive. During the course of the visit, Army Group South informed the *PzAOK 4* that further reinforcements for the planned strike could be expected in the near future.[21] This would be the *371.Infanterie-Division*, which was being transferred from the Balkan theatre, and was due to arrive by rail in Zhmerinka beginning either 7 or 8 January. However, it was due be attached to Hube's *1.Panzerarmee*, rather than the *PzAOK 4*.

Raus was also concerned with the future of the *XIII.AK*, and at 17.35 hours that evening, he spoke with Hauffe about von Manstein's agreement that the *Korps* could split up for tactical reasons.[22] It was now decided that the *Korps* should re-assemble in the Ulanov area, taking all of its *Korpstruppen* that could be spared, together with the headquarters of the *68.* and *340.Infanterie-Divisions*, and the whole of the *208.Infanterie-Division* except its artillery. In conjunction with the respective division commanders, Hauffe was then to create three new *Regimentsgruppen* from the remnants of the divisions and bring these together to form a new *Korps-Abteilung*. The superfluous supply and service units of the divisions were to be combed out to produce additional combat personnel, and further manpower would also be provided from newly arriving replacements. In the meantime, the task of supplying the affected units would remain the responsibility of the *Korps* and the respective division headquarters.

Following von Manstein's visit, Army Group South issued formal instructions requesting proposals for implementing the counterattack which had been discussed during the briefing.[23] These summarised the situation, stating that the Soviets had called a halt to their offensive opposite the central sector, where the Russian 38th Army was believed to hold the front from Berdichev south-east to Germanovka, and transferred their main effort onto the wings. The Soviet 1st Tank Army, with the 11th Guards Tank Corps, the 8th Guards Mechanised Corps, and about four or five rifle divisions, was meanwhile attempting to strike southwards from the Pogrebishche area through Lipovets and Ilyntsy. The intention seemed to be either to outflank and encircle the southern wing of the *PzAOK 4* or to drive even further south to cut the Zhmerinka-Odessa railway. To the east, this drive was being screened with relatively weak infantry forces facing south in the area around and to the west of Zhashkov, while the Soviet 40th Army was at the same time trying to outflank the western wing of the *VII.AK*. On the northern wing of the *4.Panzerarmee*, the Russians had brought together the forces of the 18th and 1st Guards Army, as well as the 3rd Guards Tank Army, to try and overrun the sector between Berdichev and the river Teterev. Further west, the Russian 60th Army was meanwhile trying to outflank this wing between the rivers Teterev and Sluch', while the 13th Army seemed to be covering the manoeuvre from the north and north-west. It was still not clear whether this army would strike westwards towards Rovno, or turn to the south-west towards Shepetovka. Faced with this situation, von Manstein intended to conduct a stiff and mobile defence on the outer wings of the *1.* and the *4.Panzerarmee*, whilst simultaneously attacking and destroying the Soviet 1st Tank Army with all the forces that could be made available. This would then allow Raus

---

21 Hgr. Süd, Ia Nr. 77/44 g.Kdos dated 6 Jan 44.
22 *PzAOK 4*, Ia, Kriegstagebuch entry dated 6 Jan 44; *PzAOK 4*, Ia Nr. 135/44 geh. dated 6 Jan 44.
23 Hgr. Süd, Ia Nr. 0748/44 geh. dated 6 Jan 44.

and Hube to concentrate upon their respective wings and restore the situation there too. Raus was advised that the *1.Panzerarmee* would be tasked to bring the outflanking manoeuvre against the *VII.AK* to a halt, close the gap between the *VII.AK* and the *III. PzK* by counterattacking towards Stavishche and Zhashkov, and prevent any further advance by the Soviet 40th Army towards Uman' and Khristinovka. The *PzAOK 4* meanwhile was to prepare a counterattack from the area east of Kalinovka to strike into the flank and rear of the advancing 1st Tank Army. This was to be conducted by the *XXXXVI.PzK*, with the *16.Panzer-Division*, the *4.Gebirgs-Division* and the *1.* and *254. Infanterie-Divisions*, although the actual direction of the strike, as well as the precise start positions, would depend on how the situation developed over the next few days. It was important though that the attack had the benefit of the support of the strongest possible elements of the *18.Artillerie-Division*. In the meantime, the northern wing of the *Panzerarmee* was to conduct defensive operations to prevent any Soviet breakthrough on the broad front between the Berdichev-Vinnitsa road and the river Sluch', and if necessary the *XXXXVIII.PzK* was to pull back further and anchor its left wing on the Sluch' at Lyubar. The *LIX.AK* was to continue covering the left wing of the *PzAOK 4* to ensure it was not outflanked west of the Sluch', and was to concentrate on the sector between Polonnoe and the Novograd-Volynskii-Shepetovka road. Other forces were to block the Novograd-Volynskii-Rovno road as well, and the *Korps* was to create a mobile reserve as soon as possible to conduct long-range reconnaissance missions. Raus and Hube were instructed to prepare proposals to implement this counterattack, and to report these to Army Group South.

Friday 7 January 1944

Behind the southern wing of the *4.Panzerarmee*, the *XXXXVI.PzK* spent the night to 7 January moving towards its new assembly area,[24] while to its left the *XXIV.PzK* was still struggling to maintain its positions. The Soviets maintained their pressure against the *4.Gebirgs-Division*, and after several hours of heavy fighting it had pulled back from Romanovka.[25] By early morning, an estimated two or three Russian rifle companies also attacked the division's positions south-east of Konstantinovka, and the fighting here continued into the morning. At around 19.00 hours the previous evening, the *168.Infanterie-Division* had been assaulted by about two Soviet companies in the Maly Chernyatin area, but these, together with a reconnaissance patrol, had been successfully defended. On the left wing of the *18.Artillerie-Division*, the Russians had mounted a combat patrol just north of Tucha, but this had been intercepted and beaten back. Late in the night, a few kilometres to the north-west, they launched an assault against the division's positions near Markovtsy, and the fighting went on into the daylight. On the left wing of the *Korps*, the *1.Panzer-Division* had begun pulling back to the new line between Markovtsy and Buryaki at 21.30 hours the previous evening, and spent most of the night moving. It reported nonetheless that the Russians maintained their pressure and continued to make heavy attacks throughout the night.

The *XXXXVIII.PzK* also spent much of the night pulling back to its new positions.[26] The *1.SS Panzer-Division 'LSSAH'* ran into problems almost straightaway, finding the

---

24 *XXXXVI.PzK*, Morgenmeldung, 05.30 hours dated 7 Jan 44.
25 *XXIV.PzK*, Morgenmeldung, untimed dated 7 Jan 44.
26 *XXXXVIII.PzK*, Morgenmeldung, 05.50 hours dated 7 Jan 44.

route of withdrawal blocked in several places by Soviet armour, but after breaking the Russian resistance, it managed to fight its way through. By 23.30 hours, most of the division had passed through Ozadovka, and by midnight the armoured rearguard had also pulled back out of the town. The *SS Panzerkampfgruppe 'Das Reich'* had things a little easier. Although Soviet forces had assaulted its positions before it began to withdraw, it successfully defended these and then managed to disengage following local counterattacks. After that, it pulled back without interference, and by morning the majority of the *Kampfgruppe* was in its new positions. The *19.Panzer-Division* had also been assaulted during the previous evening, but counterattacked to try and give itself some breathing space to disengage. In doing so, it succeeded in capturing a quantity of prisoners and material, leaving an estimated 250 Soviet dead on the field. The tactic proved successful, and the division immediately began to pull back, although it does not appear as though it had managed to take up its new positions by morning. The *7.Panzer-Division* on the other hand had been able to withdraw unmolested, and was already in its new positions by 01.00 hours. On the north wing of the *Panzerarmee*, the *LIX.AK* passed a quiet night, reporting nothing of significance.[27]

The weather was largely unchanged as the new day dawned. It remained dry, with varied amounts of cloud cover ranging from overcast to broken, and the temperature was still hovering a few degrees below zero. Gollnick's *XXXXVI.PzK* continued to assemble its units behind the right wing of the *Panzerarmee*, and by the end of the day, the headquarters of the *16.Panzer-Division* had set up in Vinnitsa, and all of the division had arrived in the area north-west of the town except the *Panzer-Regiment 2* and the *II./Panzerartillerie-Regiment 16*.[28] One train carrying troops belonging to the *I./Panzer-Regiment 2* had set out, but the loading of the remainder of the battalion had been delayed as a result of Soviet air attacks on the loading area. In total, there had been three Russian bombing raids during the previous night against the railway station in Zhmerinka. These were followed during the day by a surprise attack against the railway station in Shepetovka, where Soviet bombers caused a lot of damage by using the low cloud ceiling to good effect.[29] Nevertheless, 31 tanks had already arrived in the new assembly area, together with five command vehicles, with a further 63 still underway. In addition, four battalions of the *1.Infanterie-Division* had arrived in their new assembly area west of Kalinovka, together with 14 *Sturmgeschützen*, while the forward headquarters of the *254.Infanterie-Division*, now attached to the *Korps*, had also arrived in Litin. To the right, south-east of Vinnitsa, the *1.Panzerarmee* was assembling the newly-arriving *101.Jäger-Division* in the Voronovitsa-Pisarevka area behind the *DG IV*.[30] The division was responsible for securing its own assembly area to the north-east, and was ordered to create a strong anti-tank line west of the main road junction three kilometres west of Gumennoe station. So as not to interfere with other troop movements in the area, the division was, for the moment, forbidden either to use the main road or cross it to the north-east.

---

27 *LIX.AK*, Morgenmeldung, 06.00 hours dated 7 Jan 44.
28 *XXXXVI.PzK*, Tagesmeldung, 18.50 hours dated 7 Jan 44.
29 According to the *PzAOK 4* Ia war diary, this bombing raid destroyed or damaged several hundred railway wagons as well as causing severe damage to the railway lines themselves. The transfer of the remaining elements of the *16.Panzer-Division* was delayed as a result.
30 *PzAOK 1*, Ia Nr. 10/44 geh. dated 6 Jan 44.

Meanwhile, as the *XXXXVI.PzK* was assembling behind the front, the Soviets had maintained their pressure against the *XXIV.PzK*. Russian armour continued to threaten both wings of the *Korps*, particularly the left wing where the withdrawal of the *1.Panzer-Division* was followed up very closely, while the centre was also subjected to repeated pinning attacks.[31] In the south, on the extreme right wing of the *4.Gebirgs-Division*, Lozovataya was subjected to platoon and company-strength assaults, but all these had been seen off. In the same area, prisoners captured by the division indicated that about 800 Soviet soldiers were assembling in the area north of Yasenki, and that about 20 to 30 Russian tanks were currently moving south from the Britskoe area. Despite these Soviet movements, the division had managed to capture the northern end of Vakhnovka from Russian forces estimated to be a rifle battalion. The Soviets counterattacked beginning at about 16.15 hours, with six tanks in support, and the fighting continued on into the darkness. Further north, in the area south and east of Konstantinovka, Russian troops attacked again in up to company-strength, but the division managed to defend these assaults successfully. North of the village and in Novaya Greblya, the division pulled back its forward troops to the main defensive position, and these were followed closely by the pursuing Soviet troops. Before 14.00 hours, there had been a number of Russian assaults, but all these had been beaten back. To the left, the positions of the *168.Infanterie-Division* right wing near Kirovka were assaulted, but the attack proved unsuccessful with two Russian trucks and three anti-tanks guns reported as destroyed. At 09.45 hours, the division was attacked again, this time by an estimated battalion in the Maly Chernyatin area, but this too was thrown back. The left wing of the *18.Artillerie-Division* was assaulted three times during the day and all on the same sector. These were company-sized attacks striking westwards from Mshanets towards Markovtsy, but each of them had been beaten off. The sector had been relatively quiet apart from this area, although the division reported heavy Soviet traffic, including artillery, heading southwards from Velikaya Step' towards Golendry station. The day had started quietly for the *1.Panzer-Division*, and it had been able to complete its withdrawal to the new positions during the morning. Here too, the Russians followed up quickly and closely, and by 13.00 hours they struck south from Terekhovo in battalion-strength against the division's new positions. This was seen off though, as was a separate company-sized assault from Kikishevka towards Polichintsy. On the division's left wing, the Soviets launched an early attack from the Martynovka area towards Raigorodok at about 08.00 hours, but despite the support of around 15 tanks, the assault was beaten back with the reported loss of six tanks. By 11.00 hours, the division was desperately trying to make contact with the *1.SS Panzer-Division 'LSSAH'*.[32] The *Kavallerie-Regiment Süd* was deployed around the north-west edge of Buryaki but had been unable to establish contact with its left-hand neighbour. To make matters worse, the Soviets attacked the division's left wing during the afternoon, and this time the assault was more successful. A Russian force estimated at two to three battalions, with 13 tanks in support, succeeded in capturing the town of Buryaki. The division organised a local counterattack by an armoured *Kampfgruppe*, and this had succeeded in re-taking the town before 21.00 hours that evening, destroying a reported six Soviet tanks in the process.[33] The clearing

---

31 *XXIV.PzK*, Tagesmeldung, 19.20 hours dated 7 Jan 44.
32 *XXIV.PzK*, Ia unreferenced message to *PzAOK 4*, 11.00 hours dated 7 Jan 44.
33 *PzAOK 4*, Tagesmeldung an *Heeresgruppe Süd*, 21.00 hours dated 7 Jan 44.

skies had seen an increase in Soviet air activity over the *Korps* front during the morning, particularly against the left wing, where Fridrovo, Andreyashevka and Buryaki had all been attacked by between 15 and 20 bombers. Behind the front line, Yurovka had also been attacked but not as strongly.

The Soviets had also followed up closely behind the withdrawal of the *XXXXVIII. PzK* to the north, but they had undertaken no major assaults, limiting their activity in the main to reconnaissance activity.[34] The *1.SS Panzer-Division 'LSSAH'* had moved into its new positions as ordered, and was trying to establish contact with the *SS Panzerkampfgruppe 'Das Reich'* to its left. During its withdrawal, the division estimated that between 60 and 80 Soviet tanks were deployed opposite its sector, as well as a full rifle corps. It had destroyed nine of those tanks, including three which had advanced out of the area south-west of Ivanopol'. To the north-west, a Soviet reconnaissance group had moved south against Dubrovka, but this had been intercepted and thrown back. On the division's left wing, a group of Russian infantry with anti-tank guns infiltrated into the woods south-east of Troshcha after dark, and countermeasures were started straightaway. To the left, the *SS Panzerkampfgruppe 'Das Reich'* reported that there was increasing mortar fire against its positions on the northern and north-eastern edges of Troshcha, and more worryingly that behind its main positions, the Burkovtsy-Troshcha road was already under Russian anti-tank fire. In the *19.Panzer-Division* sector, the Russians seized the town of Krasnoselka at around 11.00 hours with an estimated battalion, before striking out south-westwards down the road towards Lyubar. By 14.30 hours that afternoon, the *Panzeraufklärungs-Abteilung 19*, acting as the division's rearguard, was assaulted in Mikhailovka by about a regiment, but managed to hold its positions before later pulling back to Vishchikusy. The Soviets followed up quickly, and renewed fighting had broken out by evening. To the left, the positions of the *7.Panzer-Division* were assaulted by Russian infantry accompanied by about seven tanks that struck south and south-east from Lipno towards Kutyshche. All seven tanks were knocked out by defensive fire, including two by troops of the *19.Panzer-Division*, and following the loss of their armour support, the Soviet infantry pulled back. Further west, the town of Korostki in the Sluch' valley, some six kilometres north of Lyubar, was occupied by Russian troops, including a few tanks. Further north along the valley, the division's reconnaissance had established that the towns of Novaya Chertoriya, Tiranovka and Dertka were all occupied by Soviet forces. Dertka had been held earlier during the day by elements of the *Panzeraufklärungs-Abteilung 16*, but following a regimental-sized assault, it had pulled back to new positions just east of Polonnoe.[35] In contrast to the *XXIV.PzK*, the *XXXXVIII.PzK* reported no Russian air activity over its sector during the day, although the better weather had allowed the *Luftwaffe* to provide close support to

---

34 *XXXXVIII.PzK*, Tagesmeldung, untimed dated 7 Jan 44. According to this report, the *Korps* deployed the following operational armour:
 • *7.Panzer-Division*: 8 Panzer IV lg.
 • *19.Panzer-Division*: 2 Panzer IV lg.; 6 SP anti-tank guns
 • *SS Panzerkampfgruppe 'Das Reich'*: 1 Panzer IV lg., 6 StuGs
 • *1.SS Panzer-Division 'LSSAH'*: 6 Panzer IV lg., 11 Panzer V; 2 Panzer VI; 7 StuGs; 3 SP anti-tank guns
 In contrast, the *'LSSAH'* reported having knocked out twelve Russian tanks, with the *19.Panzer-Division* and the *7.Panzer-Division* reporting two and seven destroyed respectively. The *Korps* was also allocated the *Kavallerie-Regiment Süd* with effect from this day.
35 *PzAOK 4*, Tagesmeldung an *Heeresgruppe Süd*, 21.00 hours dated 7 Jan 44.

the ground troops, accounting for another seven Soviet tanks and several anti-tank guns to add to the total of 11 tanks the previous day. During the course of the day, the *Korps* had established the presence of the Russian 7th Guards Tank Corps in the area around Ivanopol', and was aware that, following ground and air reconnaissance, the Soviets were also moving up fresh forces opposite the left wing where they were striking out to the south-west. These were believed to include the Soviet 6th Guards Tank Corps. Despite the absence of any major combat activity during the day therefore, the presence of the two major armoured units suggested to Balck that the Russian offensive would begin again soon in these sectors.

On the left wing of the *PzAOK 4*, the *LIX.AK* reported no real combat activity.[36] The *291.Infanterie-Division* was still pulling back though, and was anticipated to be in its new positions between Novograd-Volynskii and Shepetovka, on the line Svinobychi-Radulin-Zhelobnoe by late evening.

In the rear area, the *XIII.AK*, which had earlier been withdrawn from the front line, was given the task of reconnoitring an alternative defensive position north of the Southern Bug river.[37] This was to run on a line running westwards from Kalinovka, heading over Hill 313 north of Pavlovka and then through Ivanov, Kolybabintsy, Voitovtsy, Paplintsy, Misyurovka, and Deserovka to Svinnaya, at which point it turned to the north-west to include Starokonstantinov before running on through Kapustin to Zelentsy. With the more northerly lines now lost, the stretch of railway between Kalinovka and Starokonstantinov began to assume a greater significance for the movement of both troops and supplies, and this was now reflected in the increasing threat from the partisan units operating in the area of the Southern Bug. Things had already become so bad that the stretch could now only be used safely during daylight hours.[38] Things were also difficult south of the river, where a number of partisan groups were known to be based in the woods about 30 kilometres west of Vinnitsa. These presented a threat to any German traffic using the Vinnitsa-Proskurov road during the night. To try and counter the threat to the railway, the *PzAOK 4* ordered the *Feld-Ersatz-Bataillon 9* to take over responsibility for the stretch of railway between Kalinovka and Khmel'nik, and the *3./Landesschützen-Bataillon 987*, together with the *II./Ost-Reiter-Abteilung 403*, to secure the stretch between Spichintsy and Starokonstantinov. The previous day had seen an assault by about 100 partisans against a German traffic column about five kilometres east of Dyakovtsy.[39] The partisans were reported to have deployed four light machine-guns against the half-tracks, but there were no details of casualties on either side.

The day had been different then for the two wings of the *4.Panzerarmee*. On the eastern wing, the Soviets eased off the pressure and limited their offensive activity to a number of relatively weak reconnaissance probes. The movements which had been observed, including the 30 or so tanks seen heading south from Britskoe, seemed to indicate that the Russians were re-grouping their forces with the intention of outflanking the southern wing. In contrast, the northern wing of the *Panzerarmee* had seen a number of attacks in the areas around Polichintsy, Buryaki, west of Ivanopol', and Lipno. However, these too had not been as strong as in recent days, and it seemed that the main

---

36 *PzAOK 4*, Tagesmeldung an *Heeresgruppe Süd*, 21.00 hours dated 7 Jan 44.
37 *PzAOK 4*, Ia Nr. 156/44 geh. dated 7 Jan 44.
38 *PzAOK 4*, Tagesmeldung an *Heeresgruppe Süd*, 21.00 hours dated 7 Jan 44.
39 *PzAOK 4*, Ia Nr. 157/44 geh. dated 7 Jan 44.

Soviet forces had been held back. Nevertheless, opposite the *PzAOK 4* left wing, the Russians had forced bridgeheads over the river Sluch' east of Polonnoe, at Tiranovka and at Dertka, and were also feeling their way forwards slowly towards Shepetovka along the road from Novograd-Volynskii. At this point though, there had been only infantry forces reported on that sector. Away to the north, aerial reconnaissance had, for the first time, picked up Soviet forces moving through the area north of Korosten' as well as others heading south and west on the southern wing of the *2.Armee* under Army Group Centre. These all now indicated that the Russians were advancing westwards along the southern edge of the Pripyat' marshes, threatening not only the deep left flank of Army Group South but also the deep right flank of Army Group Centre. Picking up on this concern, von Manstein issued a notice to Raus advising him of the measures Army Group South was putting in place to avoid any surprises from this area.[40] The *Luftflotte 4* had been requested to fly continuous reconnaissance missions over the area as far as the weather would allow, and keep an eye in particular on the roads, railways and junctions. In this respect, a boundary between it and the *Luftflotte 6* in the Army Group Centre area would have to be agreed, and the results of the reconnaissance would be shared between the two Army Groups. Von Manstein was also going to increase the use of agents in the area to obtain early notice of Soviet deployments, as was Army Group Centre. The *Wehrmachtbefehlshaber Ukraine, General der Flieger* Karl Kitzinger, would be given orders to establish a screen between the northern wing of the *LIX.AK* and the boundary with Army Group Centre, running along the line of the Sluch' and Goryn' rivers. The two stretches of railway running from Kovel' to Rovno and Kovel' to Sarny were to be given special priority in terms of security. With the screen in place, the *WBU* was also to begin reconnaissance along the whole front to the east. Raus was therefore instructed to make and keep contact with both the *WBU* and the *2.Armee* in order to ensure that the results of all this reconnaissance were properly shared between the interested parties. For its part, Army Group Centre already had a number of security units deployed in the area of the Pripyat' and Goryn' rivers, and it undertook to try and push these as far to the south-east as possible to make contact with the forces of the *WBU*. It was planning to use the *Kavallerie-Regiment Mitte* and the *1.Ski-Brigade* for the purpose.

    Given the developments of the day, Raus saw no reason to alter his current intentions and, apart from continuing to pull together Gollnick's *XXXXVI.PzK*, and instructing the *LIX.AK* to relieve the remaining elements of the *16.Panzer-Division* from the area east and north-east of Shepetovka, the *Korps* headquarters all retained their existing instructions. He did nevertheless see the need to re-shuffle some of his forces to strengthen the *XXXXVIII.PzK* where the main Soviet effort now seemed to be concentrated. He therefore issued instructions for the *XXXXVIII.PzK Korps-Begleit-Kompanie*[41] to be returned by the *XXIV.PzK* to its parent *Korps*, and for the *Kavallerie-Regiment Süd* to be pulled out of the *XXIV.PzK* front and likewise transferred to Balck.[42] The units of the *Panzer-Zerstörer-Bataillon 473* were also to be brought back together, and to be assembled in the Stetkovtsy area, south-east of Lyubar, before being transferred to the *'LSSAH'*. By way of compensation, all the elements of the *18.Artillerie-Division* which

---

40 Hgr. Süd, Ia Nr. 75/44 g.Kdos. dated 7 Jan 44.
41 This was an escort company whose main function was to protect the headquarters and staff of the *Korps*.
42 *PzAOK 4*, Ia Nr. 146/44 geh. dated 7 Jan 44.

had been deployed piecemeal in both *Korps* sector were now to be pulled out of the front and returned to their parent division.

Nevertheless, although the immediate intentions of the *4.Panzerarmee* were largely unchanged, Gollnick submitted proposals in response to von Manstein's instructions of the previous day regarding a counterattack in the Vinnitsa area. The operation was to be known as '*Winterreise*'.[43] In these proposals, Gollnick set out how he intended to conduct the operation, provided there were no significant changes in Soviet deployment in the meantime. The assaulting divisions would move into their starting positions during the night of 10 January so that they would be ready to move off at 04.00 hours on 11 January. To be able to support the offensive effectively, the artillery of the divisions would have to be moved into position the night before. Whether the infantry or *panzers* of the *16.Panzer-Division* would be used to achieve the initial breakthrough would depend upon the results of terrain reconnaissance and the actual Soviet troop dispositions on the day before the attack. Whatever the decision might prove to be, the intended assembly of the 'Panther' tanks of the *I./Panzer-Abteilung 2* in the Staraya Priluka area would require a 40 tonne bridge to be built over the river Desna. This, and the need for other heavy bridges in the assault sector, required a *Heeres-Pionier-Bataillon* to be attached to the *Korps*, and Gollnick requested one accordingly. The assault was to be conducted by three divisions, with one held in reserve. The *4.Gebirgs-Division* was to place its main effort in striking out of Chuprinovka, north-east of Turbov, towards the high ground south-east of Petrovka before pushing on to take the high ground east of Shenderovka. Gollnick had considered deploying the division further south, in the positions then held by the *Gebirgsjäger-Regiment 91*, but had rejected the option on the grounds that artillery support in that sector would be limited and that it would in any case be more difficult to exploit the anticipated success of the *16.Panzer-Division*. In concentrating the attack further north, a number of the division's units on the right wing would need to be relieved by the *PzAOK 1* by no later than the evening of 9 January. These included the *Gebirgsjäger-Bataillon 94*,[44] and the *I.* and *III./ Gebirgsjäger-Regiment 91*, all of which needed to be in their respective assembly area south-east of Chuprinovka by early on 11 January. In addition, the *II./Gebirgsjäger-Regiment 13* would be returned to the division at an appropriate time by the *16.Panzer-Division* to assist in developing the attack. In order to provide the required impetus, both in the initial stage of the attack and also as it developed over the Britskoe-Shenderovka line, Gollnick requested that the *Sturmgeschütz-Abteilung 300* be attached to the division.

In the centre, the *16.Panzer-Division* would be tasked with attacking along the Priluka-Pogrebishche road without worrying about the progress of its neighbours or the threats to its flanks. It was to break through the forward Soviet defences and strike in one bound to take the high ground south of Levkovka, an advance of over 20 kilometres. To assist in this drive, the *XXXXVI.PzK* would arrange the artillery and air assets such that there would always be a concentration of support available to the lead elements. Having achieved its initial objective, the division could either continue the drive eastwards or turn to the south-east, but according to Gollnick it was neither possible nor desirable to make that decision at this stage. In making its preparations, the division would not be

---

43 XXXXVI.PzK, Ia Nr. 8/44 g.Kdos dated 7 Jan 44. '*Winterreise*' translates as 'winter journey'.
44 Formerly the division's *Feld-Ersatz-Bataillon 94*.

able to avoid placing a *Panzergrenadier-Bataillon* in the front line, as this was needed to relieve the *II./Gebirgsjäger-Regiment 13* for return to the *4.Gebirgs-Division*.

On the left wing of the advance, the *1.Infanterie-Division* would provide flank security for the *16.Panzer-Division*, and initially prevent the Russian troops either side of Novaya Greblya from attacking the advancing *panzers*. To do this, the division would be allocated assaults sectors either side of the river Desna with the aim of securing the bridges in and to the north of Ovechache. From there, it was to transfer its main effort over to its right wing and advance to the area around Ovsyaniki. As the attack developed, the northern flank was to be pushed out, and was planned to be held on a line from Lozovka through Stanilovka to Belashki, just north-west of Pogrebishche. In this respect, one of its *Grenadier-Regiments* would initially be tasked with gaining the high ground south of Samgorodok, but would be relieved by elements of the *168. Infanterie-Division* which would then hold a line between Germanovka and Krasnoe, east of Chernyatin. The *Grenadier-Regiment* thus freed would then form a new reserve for the *1.Infanterie-Division* for the fighting expected east of the Desna.

With these three divisions leading the attack, the *XXXXVI.PzK* planned to keep the *254.Infanterie-Division* in reserve. The intention was to assemble it between Vinnitsa and Kalinovka, in the Sosonka-Sal'nik-Medvedka area, by no later than the day before the attack, so that it would be available for commitment the day after the attack began. At that point, it could be used either to strengthen the assault of the *4.Gebirgs-Division* or provide additional screening for the northern flank. Gollnick also planned to make arrangements for air support from the *Luftwaffe*, with preliminary bombing attacks against the villages in the Desna valley and in the area north-east of Vakhnovka. This would be followed by close air support provided by *Stukas* once the attack got underway. The dive bombers would be under the direction of specially appointed officers, and were to concentrate on Soviet artillery and tank units.

Saturday 8 January 1944

The Russian attacks continued through the night along the whole of the *4.Panzerarmee* front. On the southern wing, the *XXIV.PzK* reported a number of uncoordinated assaults.[45] On the extreme right, a Soviet cavalry troop was observed by the *4.Gebirgs-Division* reconnoitring around Belozerovka, while further north Vakhnovka was subjected to a series of attacks. About 150 men supported by two tanks assaulted the northern end of the town, while a number of company-strength attacks with three or four tanks were directed against the southern end. All were beaten back, with two Russian tanks reported as destroyed. To the left, a separate company-strength attack against Konyushevka was similarly seen off, while a few kilometres further north, the division reported Soviet reinforcements in the Konstantinovka area. In contrast, the sector held by the *168.Infanterie-Division* remained quiet throughout the night, and the only Russian activity reported was traffic in the Leonardovka and Chernyatin areas. The *18.Artillerie-Division* also reported Russian traffic movements in the Lopatin and Mshanets areas, while the division's left wing was also attacked. Following three unsuccessful assaults against Markovtsy from the north and north-east, Soviet troops finally managed to outflank the defenders and break into the northern and central parts of the village by

---

45 *XXIV.PzK*, Morgenmeldung, 06.00 hours dated 8 Jan 44.

PREPARING THE COUNTERSTRIKE 275

morning, and the fighting continued on into the day. On the left wing of the *Korps*, the *1.Panzer-Division* reported the Soviets reinforcing their troops opposite its sector. On its right wing, the Russians attacked Volchinets in about battalion-strength, but this had been seen off. On the left wing, another assault managed to break into Buryaki, and although this penetration was initially sealed off, renewed pressure after midnight led to the loss of the northern part of the village. Behind the right flank of the *XXIV.PzK*, the *XXXXVI.PzK* spent the night continuing to pull together its troops, and by morning, the majority of the *16.Panzer-Division* had arrived.[46]

The *XXXXVIII.PzK* had also been attacked during the night and had been unable to maintain its positions.[47] At around midnight, the *1.SS Panzer-Division 'LSSAH'* had been assaulted from the north and north-east, being struck by at least 32 Russian tanks which had advanced from the area around Ivanopol'. These managed to break through the division's defences and force their way into Zherebki where fighting continued into the morning. In contrast, the situation on its left wing, between Dubrovka and Troshcha, was not clear. In the sector held by the *SS Panzerkampfgruppe 'Das Reich'* too, the Soviets had attacked during the night and succeeded in forcing their way into Troshcha. The *Kampfgruppe* initiated countermeasures, but these had not cleared the situation before morning. It was a similar situation with the *19.Panzer-Division* where the Russians managed to break into Kutyshche, just north-east of Lyubar, in about battalion strength. A counterattack was underway, but the fighting continued. A few kilometres to the east, a Soviet company-strength assault either side of the road from Vishchikusy to the south towards Filintsy achieved another breakthrough, but here the division had been able to counterattack and restore the situation. On the *Korps* left, the *7.Panzer-Division* reported Russian pressure, particularly on both wings. On the left wing, this led to another penetration in unknown numbers, but this had been sealed off and countermeasures were being introduced to recapture the main defensive positions.

The *LIX.AK* passed a quieter night and reported no contact with the Russians at all, and reconnaissance conducted the previous evening by the *Korps-Abteilung C* had shown that Dedovichi and the area a few kilometres north of Pishchev were both clear of Soviet troops at that time.[48] The *291.Infanterie-Division* had meanwhile reached its new positions by 21.00 hours the previous evening, and the planned relief of the *I./Panzergrenadier-Regiment 64* was expected to be complete early that morning.

Although there had been light snowfall in places during the night, the skies began to clear during the day, keeping it cold with temperatures no higher than -3°C. The roads therefore stayed hard, and visibility remained good, allowing air operations to continue. On the *XXIV.PzK* front, the Soviets kept up the pressure along the whole sector throughout the new day.[49] In the south, strong tank forces of the Russian 11th

---

46 *XXXXVI.PzK*, Morgenmeldung, 05.00 hours dated 8 Jan 44.
47 *XXXXVIII.PzK*, Morgenmeldung, 06.30 hours dated 8 Jan 44.
48 *LIX.AK*, Morgenmeldungen, 04.20 and 05.15 hours dated 8 Jan 44.
49 *XXIV.PzK*, Tagesmeldung, untimed dated 8 Jan 44. According to this report, the *Korps* deployed the following operational armour and anti-tank assets:
  - *1.Panzer-Division*: 3 *Panzer IV lg*; 8 *Panzer V*; 26 SP anti-tank guns; 22 heavy anti-tank guns
  - *25.Panzer-Division*: 1 *Panzer IV lg*; 1 *StuG*
  - *18.Artillerie-Division*: 10 *StuGs*; 1 heavy anti-tank gun
  - *4.Gebirgs-Division*: 9 heavy anti-tank guns
  - *168.Infanterie-Division*: 10 heavy anti-tank guns

Guards Tank Corps were attempting to outflank the deep right flank of the *Korps* and drive towards Vinnitsa. In the centre, there was heavy fighting around Markovtsy and renewed Soviet assault preparations east of Peremoga, whilst on the left, the attempt to break though the German lines had achieved partial success again.

In the south, the *4.Gebirgs-Division* had managed to hold its positions throughout the day, despite a number of Soviet assaults. One of these had been made in about battalion strength against the forward positions on its extreme right wing in Velikaya Krushlintsy, but this had been beaten back. There were also a number of assaults again against Vakhnovka, also in about battalion strength, but these too had been successfully defended. Despite these attacks, it was noticeable that the Russians were transferring motorised and infantry forces to the south and towards the hanging flank. To the left, the *168.Infanterie-Division* reported no major combat. Although there had been lively artillery and mortar fire across the sector, the only contact had been as a result of Soviet combat and reconnaissance patrolling, all of which had been intercepted and seen off, leaving a reported 26 dead on the field. It was a similar situation with the *18.Artillerie-Division*, where the Russians launched just a single company-strength assault in and to the south of Tucha. This was beaten back, but the division reported major Soviet attack preparations opposite its left wing as well as a lot of troop movements across the whole sector. On the left of the *XXIV.PzK* though, the *1.Panzer-Division* was in trouble. The day had started well enough when it had been able to push the remaining Soviet troops out of the northern end of Markovtsy, but at 15.00 hours the Russians started a major assault against the village with an estimated 1,000 men. To the northwest, they also attacked Volchinets where a Soviet rifle company succeeded in breaking through the defensive positions before the situation was eventually restored. Northwest of Brodetskoe, an estimated Russian rifle battalion was seen finalising its attack preparations, while at about 15.00 hours in the centre of the sector, the southern part of Polichintsy was captured by Soviet troops in about regimental strength. The defenders fell back to a line from Volchinets to Malaya Klitenka.[50] About two Russian battalions had also broken into Fridrovo from the north and north-west, while on the far side of the Berdichev-Ulanov road, Buryaki had been given up following heavy Soviet pressure. The fighting here had moved back and forth, with two Soviet tanks reported as knocked out, before the defenders finally pulled back during the afternoon to take up new positions on the high ground to the south.[51] Following the withdrawal, an estimated Russian regiment, with about 15 tanks as support, was seen regrouping in the area, and there were other troop assemblies spotted not only near Raigorodok and Buryaki, but also further east near Kikishevka. The *Korps* reported having destroyed a total of 14 Russian tanks during the day, but the situation on the left wing of the *1.Panzer-Division* was now serious.

During the course of the evening, Nehring called Raus to discuss his situation.[52] He was concerned that the troops holding the northern sector of the *1.Panzer-Division* front would not be able to withstand any further Soviet attacks as their combat effectiveness

- *s.Panzer-Abteilung 509*: 9 Panzer VI
- *Panzerjäger-Abteilung 739*: 18 SP anti-tank guns

50 *PzAOK 4*, Tagesmeldung an *Heeresgruppe Süd*, 21.00 hours dated 8 Jan 44.
51 *PzAOK 4*, Tagesmeldung an *Heeresgruppe Süd*, 21.00 hours dated 8 Jan 44.
52 *PzAOK 4*, Ia Kriegstagebuch entry dated 8 Jan 44.

had been reduced. The sector was now held by a *Kampfgruppe* formed around the *Kavallerie-Regiment Süd*, and this was showing clear signs of falling apart.[53] It had been thrown together as an emergency measure and consequently had no real unit cohesion. The troops felt themselves to be in a hopeless position, facing what they thought was about five Soviet divisions with armoured support. On the previous day, a number of soldiers had even been shot by their own officers as they tried to flee, and on this day the regiment had collapsed again, even though some officers had taken up positions in the rear to try and stop the men running away, using their machine-pistols in an effort to stem the tide. The regiment was reportedly down to a strength of only 32 men, and had lost both its commanding officer and his deputy. The division had already deployed the *Panzeraufklärungs-Abteilung 1* to the sector in an effort to strengthen the defence, and it reported having destroyed 11 Soviet tanks already, but that was the last of the reserves committed. Despite the seriousness of the situation, the *XXIV.PzK* simply had no other forces available to support this sector, particularly as the troops on the right wing had also become intermixed and found themselves under persistent attack. In the circumstances, Nehring was obliged to report that his *Korps* might not be able to maintain its northern front much longer if the Russians continued with their heavy attacks. Raus could offer little assistance though, and agreed that the most severe measures should be employed where necessary, although he did acknowledge that where the situation allowed, men should be allowed to return to their parent units.

Behind the front line in the south, the *Kampfkommandant* in Vinnitsa reported that the planned defensive position on the eastern edge of the city had now been occupied, and that Soviet tanks and infantry had been observed in Gumennoe just 15 kilometres to the east. A further 16 Russian tanks had also been seen in Zhabelevka a few kilometres further east. More worrying still, three Soviet tanks were reported to have blocked the *DG IV* near Luka, about 30 kilometres south-east of Vinnitsa, and midway between Voronovitsa and Nemirov. The main troops in the eastern part of Vinnitsa were elements of the newly-arrived *16.Panzer-Division*.[54] In particular, the *II./Panzergrenadier-Regiment 64* had been deployed on the eastern edge of the city, where it was being held as reserve for the planned counterattack, and where it was currently supported by the *Panzer-Regiment 2* (less the *I.Abteilung*) which was also in the eastern part of Vinnitsa. The *I.Abteilung* was still underway following the disruption caused by the Soviet air raid in Shepetovka, and although none of the Panthers had yet arrived, a total of 40 had been loaded by this time, ready for transport. Much of the *1.Infanterie-Division* had also arrived by this time, including the *Füsilier-Regiment 22*, the *Grenadier-Regiment 43*, the *Pionier-Bataillon 1*, the *I./Artillerie-Regiment 1*, the *I./Artillerie-Regiment 37*,[55]

---

53 This grouping had been formed around the *Kavallerie-Regiment Süd*, and included troops from the *20.Panzergrenadier-Division* (including men belonging to the *Grenadier-Regiments (mot.) 76* and *90* who were returning from leave or who had been dispersed, the *Aufklärungs-Abteilung 120*, and the *Divisions-Begleit-Kompanie*), a parachute replacement battalion, the light *Flak-Abteilung 299*, and various alarm units.

54 XXXXVI.PzK, Tagesmeldung, untimed dated 8 Jan 44. According to this report, the *Korps* deployed the following operational armour and anti-tank assets in the new area:
 • *16.Panzer-Division*: 21 *Panzer IV lg.*; 14 *StuGs*; 14 heavy anti-tank guns
 • *1.Infanterie-Division*: 13 *StuGs*; 13 heavy anti-tank guns.

55 The *I./Artillerie-Regiment 37* was a slightly unusual unit, being one of two battalions of the heavy *Artillerie-Regiment 37*, itself only a paper regiment with no headquarters and just two battalions. The

and the *Panzerjäger-Abteilung 1*. The *II./Grenadier-Regiment 1* had been pulled out of its previous deployment north of Shepetovka, and was now on the march towards the new assembly area. In response to the request for additional engineer support under the proposals for Operation '*Winterreise*', the *Pionier-Bataillon (mot.) 48* and the *Pionier-Bau-Bataillon 523* were also now attached to the *XXXXVI.PzK*.[56] In the meantime, Gollnick confirmed the report received from the *Kampfkommandant* in Vinnitsa that Soviet troops were already in Gumennoe, stating that these were the units that had been seen in the early morning heading westwards.[57] There had initially been about 50 tanks in this group, of which about 20 occupied Gumennoe with a rifle battalion as support. The remainder had wheeled off southwards, heading for Stepanovka and the area to the south-east. Further east, there were also reports of lively Soviet traffic in the area west and south-west of Lipovets. Raus needed to address this problem on his extreme right wing while the final preparations for Operation '*Winterreise*' were completed. In order not to disrupt these preparations therefore, Army Group South issued instructions to the *1.Panzerarmee* ordering the *101.Jäger-Division* to prevent any further Soviet advance towards Vinnitsa and Vinnitsa airfield by blocking the area around the railway crossing east of Pisarevka.[58] The division was to establish a defensive line running from Voronovitsa through Komarov to a point west of Gumennoe, and make contact with the right wing of the *4.Gebirgs-Division* to the north.[59] The *16.Panzer-Division* was meanwhile instructed to begin armoured reconnaissance in the Gumennoe-Sverdlovka-Maliye Krushlintsy area. In addition, the *XXXXVI.PzK* was to maintain an armoured reserve from the *16.Panzer-Division* just east of Vinnitsa, and also to transfer a *Panzerjäger-Kompanie* to the northern wing of the *101.Jäger-Division* in order to provide additional anti-tank means on that sector.[60] Raus discussed the possible employment of this armoured reserve with Army Group South, and received von Manstein's approval to use it, if needed, to attack any Russian troops moving west or north-west from Gumennoe towards the city. It was essential that the two airfields east and south-east of Vinnitsa did not fall into Soviet hands.

To the left of the *XXIV.PzK*, the *XXXXVIII.PzK* had barely managed to hold its own.[61] The main thrust of the Russian assault had fallen in the Ivanopol' area in the sector held by the *1.SS Panzer-Division 'LSSAH'*. The Soviets broke their way through the division's defensive positions and headed for Zherebki, continuing their advance southwards with about 32 tanks and assault guns. In the heavy fighting which followed, the defenders managed to regain control of the situation in a decisive counterattack, destroying 27 tanks and five assault guns, and forcing the Russians to withdraw back northwards. To the north-west, the Russians also achieved breaches in the Dubrovka and Troshcha areas, and although these had been largely cleared by evening, the division was still counterattacking in the wooded area between the two villages to try to mop up Russian forces which had infiltrated into the area. On the extreme left wing of the *SS*

I./Abteilung was in effect permanently attached to the *1.Infanterie-Division*, while the *II./Abteilung* remained an independent unit.
56   *PzAOK 4*, Tagesmeldung an *Heeresgruppe Süd*, 21.00 hours dated 8 Jan 44.
57   *PzAOK 4*, Tagesmeldung an *Heeresgruppe Süd*, 21.00 hours dated 8 Jan 44.
58   Hgr. Süd, Ia Nr. 112/44 g.Kdos. dated 8 Jan 44.
59   *PzAOK 4*, Ia Kriegstagebuch entry dated 8 Jan 44.
60   *PzAOK 4*, Ia Nr. 186/44 geh. dated 8 Jan 44.
61   *PzAOK 4*, Tagesmeldung an *Heeresgruppe Süd*, 21.00 hours dated 8 Jan 44.

Panzerkampfgruppe 'Das Reich', a Soviet assault east of Verbka[62] had seen the attackers break into the German defences, and a counterattack to restore the situation was still underway by late evening. There had also been a series of assaults further west against the sector held by the *19.Panzer-Division*. Most of these had been in about battalion strength, and all had been successfully defended, some by local counterattacks. On the far left of the *7.Panzer-Division*, Russian troops, having crossed the river Sluch' further north, attempted to advance southwards towards Lyubar, but these had been intercepted and thrown back towards Glezno. Despite the relative success of the defence, it seemed clear that the Soviets were preparing to continue their offensive, and during the afternoon, further Russian troop assemblies were seen in the Vishchikusy and Lipno areas, opposite the *19.* and *7.Panzer-Divisions*. During the evening, Balck called *PzAOK 4* headquarters and spoke with Raus.[63] He believed his *Korps* had achieved a major defensive success during the day, particularly with the *'LSSAH'* destroying all those Soviet tanks that had broken through to the Zherebki area. He attributed the success to the close cooperation between the *panzers* and the air support provided by the *Luftwaffe*. Having discussed the situation further, Balck received orders to keep a reserve in the Lyubar area in order to be able to counter any Russian advance to the south or south-east between the rivers Sluch' and Khomora. Raus also suggested that reconnaissance should be undertaken in the area to establish whether the majority of Soviet forces were heading west towards Polonnoe or south towards the deep flank of the *Korps*.

In the meantime, the Soviets continued to expand their bridgehead over the Sluch' in the Miropol' area. The *LIX.AK*, with its headquarters now in Plesnya, about six kilometres south-west of Shepetovka, reported that the *Panzeraufklärungs-Abteilung 16* had been forced back to the west as Russian troops, supported by heavy weapons, pressed on with their advance from the Dertka area.[64] The defending troops were pressed back into the centre of Polonnoe, as the Soviets occupied Kotelyanka and Novoselitsa near the river Khomora. To the north-west, things remained quiet, with neither the *291. Infanterie-Division* nor the *Korps-Abteilung C* reporting any particular combat activity. During the day, von der Chevallerie and Raus discussed the situation facing the *Korps*.[65] The Soviet intentions in the area were still not clear, and Raus instructed the *Korps* commander to conduct reconnaissance to establish whether the Russians planned to advance to the west or to the south. At the same time, von der Chevallerie was ordered to close the gap between his *Korps* and the *XXXXVIII.PzK* by transferring additional troops to his right wing, and then to maintain close contact until such time as new forces could arrive. For his part, von der Chevallerie believed that, on the basis of reports received from reliable sources, the main body of Soviet forces was heading westwards. He was trying to hold up this advance, but lacked the means to do so. He therefore asked Raus if the *Panzeraufklärungs-Abteilung 16* could remain in the Polonnoe sector for the time being, but Raus would not commit to this. Given the continuing uncertainty as to Soviet intentions, von der Chevallerie was ordered to prevent any further Russian advance to the west and south-west, and if necessary weaken his forces north-east of Shepetovka to

---

62 The tiny village of Verbka is no longer shown on more recent Soviet maps. It was located on the Lyubar-Troshcha road, north of Motrunki.
63 *PzAOK 4*, Ia Kriegstagebuch entry dated 8 Jan 44.
64 *PzAOK 4*, Tagesmeldung an *Heeresgruppe Süd*, 21.00 hours dated 8 Jan 44.
65 *PzAOK 4*, Ia Kriegstagebuch entry dated 8 Jan 44.

do so. Nevertheless, with contact now established between the *XXXXVIII.PzK* and the *LIX.AK*, Raus wrote to von der Chevallerie to acknowledge the accomplishments of the *Korps*.[66] It had been separated from the main body of the *Panzerarmee* three times since September 1943, and been forced to conduct defensive operations on its own through difficult terrain occupied by partisan forces. Despite the weak condition of its troops, it had succeeded in fighting its way back, frustrating Soviet intentions, and carrying out the tasks assigned to it.

By and large, the *4.Panzerarmee* had been able to maintain its positions throughout the day, and reported destroying a total of 41 Soviet tanks in the process.[67] It still seemed to Raus as though the Russians were trying to encircle his army, with the 1st Tank Army on his right and the 60th Army on his left. In the south, his prospects appeared to be deteriorating. Although the Russians had previously limited their operations here to reconnaissance missions, they now seemed to be advancing in strength westwards along and to the south of the Lipovets-Vinnitsa road, bypassing the southern flank of the *XXIV. PzK*. The leading elements of the 1st Tank Army had already reached Gumennoe, east of Vinnitsa, and there were signs that troops from the 38th Army were being brought in from the north to support this drive.[68] Further north, there had been little combat activity on the eastern front, and even on the northern front, where there had been a number of attacks of varying intensity, the front line had generally been maintained. The heaviest fighting had taken place in the Ivanopol' area, where the Soviet 7th Guards Tank Corps tried to exploit its previous gains but without success. However, a number of Soviet troop assemblies had also been observed, suggesting that further assaults were imminent, probably during the coming night. On the left wing of the *XXXXVIII.PzK*, the anticipated Russian attempt to outflank the *Korps* with mobile troops had not actually happened, although weak infantry forces had pushed out of the Miropol' bridgehead and advanced south towards Lyubar. There had been no news of the Soviet 4th Guards Tank Corps, and it was assumed that it had maintained radio silence throughout the day. Despite all this, Balck was still expecting the Soviets to resume their offensive in this area, and the *PzAOK 4* was of the same opinion.

It was against this background that Raus issued his new orders.[69] In these, he acknowledged that Soviet forces had already crossed the river Sluch' and were now feeling their way forward to the west and south-west in the area south and east of Polonnoe. It was therefore probable that they intended to screen off their southern front and continue their drive westwards to capture the important railway junction at Shepetovka. The *LIX. AK* was therefore ordered to prevent any further southward and westward advance by Soviet forces, while maintaining close contact with the *XXXXVIII.PzK* to its right. It was also to continue reconnaissance in the area around and to the north-east of Polonnoe. In case the Russians intended instead to drive southwards, the *XXXXVIII.PzK* was meanwhile to keep a mobile reserve in the area around Lyubar and be ready to intercept any Soviet advance between the rivers Sluch' and Khomora. To give early notice of any such advance, the *Korps* was to conduct continuous reconnaissance in force between the two rivers as far north as the Kamenka-Polonnoe railway. The boundary between

---

66 *PzAOK 4*, Ia unreferenced paper dated 8 Jan 44.
67 *PzAOK 4*, Tagesmeldung an *Heeresgruppe Süd*, 21.00 hours dated 8 Jan 44.
68 *PzAOK 4*, Ic, Abendmeldung dated 8 Jan 44.
69 *PzAOK 4*, Ia Nr. 184/44 geh. dated 8 Jan 44.

the two *Korps* was moved slightly north-west to a line running from Gritsev through Novolabun' and Novoselitsa to Kamenka, with all places falling to the *LIX.AK*.

In the meantime, Gollnick had been pressing ahead with his preparations for Operation '*Winterreise*'. Following repeated requests from the *4.Panzerarmee*, he had finally confirmed during the night of 7/8 January that it would be possible to bring the start date forward by a day. Although the intention still remained to begin the attack on 11 January if possible, Gollnick issued orders in case the operation needed to begin a day early.[70] The order summarised the current situation, stating that against expectations, Soviets forces believed to be the 1st Tank Army had begun an attack towards Vinnitsa and the area to the south. The lead elements of this offensive had already reached the line Gumennoe-Dubovchik,[71] just east of Luka, and it was to be expected that the advance would continue to the west on 9 January. The *101.Jäger-Division* had already been given instructions to build a defensive line west of Gumennoe, and the gap between it and the *4.Gebirgs-Division* to the north had been filled with weak elements of the *16.Panzer-Division* on a general line from Gavrishovka to Velikaya Krushlintsy. In the event the situation became critical during the following day, the *XXXXVI.PzK* would begin its attack on 10 January with whatever forces were by then available. The *16.Panzer-Division* was to assemble either side of Turbov, in the area Kobyl'nya-Novaya Priluka-Chuprinovka-the woods west of Vakhnovka, and be prepared to advance either south or eastwards depending on how the situation developed during 9 January. The *1.Infanterie-Division* was to form up to the left in the area bounded by Hill 288, a point south of Kholyavintsy, Gorlovka and Polevaya Lysievka. It was recognised that the division would not be able to move as quickly as the *16.Panzer-Division*, but it was ordered nonetheless to ensure that as many combat elements as possible were in position and ready to attack by early on 10 January. It too was to deploy to allow it to advance either to the south or to the east. The *254.Infanterie-Division* was initially to assemble all its arriving elements just west of Vinnitsa, but be ready to transfer out of this area on the evening of 9 January, either to the north or north-east. In the event the *XXXXVI.PzK* was obliged to begin its attack on 10 January, Gollnick instructed his units as follows. The *16.Panzer-Division* was to follow one of two possible routes. Either it would advance directly to the south from its assembly area, passing to the west of Vakhnovka to strike into the flank of those Soviet forces attacking towards Vinnitsa, or it would bypass Vakhnovka to the north before wheeling south towards Yasenki. The *1.Infanterie-Division* was also given two possible options. In the event the *16.Panzer-Division* struck directly southwards, it was to follow the advance with whatever troops it had assembled by then. If on the other hand, the *16.Panzer-Division* struck eastwards, it was also to move in the same direction, covering the left flank of the armour by advancing on Belaya. If required, the *254.Infanterie-Division* would support the *101.Jäger-Division* in the event it was pushed back into a bridgehead south of Vinnitsa, the objective being to enable it to prepare for a counterattack out of any such bridgehead, either on 11 or 12 January. To the north, the *4.Gebirgs-Division* would be attached to the *XXXXVI.PzK* with effect from 06.00 hours on 9 January, and would be tasked with securing the assembly areas of both the *16.Panzer-Division* and the *1.Infanterie-Division*. If the *16.Panzer-Division* were to strike southwards, those elements of the division in and to the west of Lozovataya

---

70 *XXXXVI.PzK*, Ia Nr. 11/44 g.Kdos. dated 8 Jan 44.
71 Referred to as Dubmaslovka on more recent Soviet maps.

were to protect its eastern flank by occupying a line running from the high ground northwards as far as Zhurava. If the *16.Panzer-Division* struck eastwards instead, the division was to secure its north-eastern flank by occupying a line between Zozov and Konyushevka, using all elements then deployed south of the Ol'shanka. To support the attack, the *Arko 101*[72] was to ensure that all the available guns of the *16.Panzer-Division* could be brought to bear on the assault sector, together with those belonging to the *18.Artillerie-Division* and the *4.Gebirgs-Division*. He was also to ensure that any artillery units of the *254.Infanterie-Division* that had arrived could be ready for employment in the defence of Vinnitsa. An important element of the attack was establishing precisely where the Russian forces were and where they were heading. The *16.Panzer-Division* was therefore instructed to push out reconnaissance towards the south and south-east to find out not only where the Soviets were and in which direction they were moving, but also how strong they were. The *254.Infanterie-Division* was also ordered to conduct specific reconnaissance, and was told to feel forwards to the south and south-east to try and find out how far the Russians had advanced and where their northern wing was. In the event the attack was to start on the 11 January as originally intended, the original orders remained unchanged, but as we shall see these would be overtaken by events.

Sunday 9 January 1944

The night passed relatively quietly on the southern wing of the *4.Panzerarmee* where the *XXIV.PzK* reported little combat activity but a lot of Soviet movement.[73] On its right, the *4.Gebirgs-Division* had made contact with the *101.Jäger-Division* in the southern end of Gavrishovka, and late in the night there had been a regimental-sized Russian assault in Lozovataya. This was beaten back in heavy fighting, and by 04.20 hours the whole village had been cleared of Soviet troops. Elsewhere in the division's sector, there had been heavy Russian traffic all through the previous evening and night, involving columns of different kinds, including trucks and sledges as well as a few tanks. Some of these had been heading south from Britskoe, while others were moving west from Alexandrovka towards Gumennoe. Further north, a Soviet combat patrol had been thrown back near Konstantinovka the previous evening, while there was also lively traffic reported in Petrovka nearby. Opposite its left wing too, a continuous stream of Russian troops had been moving into the Novaya Greblya area from the north since about 17.00 hours the previous evening, and it seemed clear the Soviets were preparing an assault against the boundary between the division and the *168.Infanterie-Division* to its left. The suspicion was later confirmed in an intercepted radio message. The *168.Infanterie-Division* meanwhile reported light artillery and lively mortar fire, and the appearance of a few Russian night bombers which dropped flares and bombs, none of which seem to have had any major impact. In the *18.Artillerie-Division* sector, the Soviets continued their assaults against Markovtsy without success, while the *1.Panzer-Division* reported just a single battalion-strength assault against Andreyashevka. This began at midnight and managed to break into the division's defensive positions before a counterattack was put in place. This had been the only direct contact during the night however, and the only other Russian activity was artillery and mortar fire.

---

72 The *Artillerie-Kommandeur 101*, a staff subordinate to the *XXXXVI.PzK* and responsible for co-ordinating its artillery operations.
73 *XXIV.PzK*, Morgenmeldung, 06.00 hours dated 9 Jan 44.

PREPARING THE COUNTERSTRIKE

Behind the *XXIV.PzK*, the *XXXXVI.PzK* continued with its troop assemblies and attack preparations, and reported nothing of significance.[74] Further north, the *XXXXVIII. PzK* spent a more difficult night.[75] The Soviets attacked the right wing of the *1.SS Panzer-Division 'LSSAH'* and succeeded in breaking into the main defensive position, before a local counterattack restored the situation. In the centre, the division had taken up its new positions on a line running from a point two kilometres south of Ivanopol' to the road junction three kilometres west-north-west of the town, while opposite the left wing, Soviet forces were reported to be assembling in the large wooded area south-west of Dubrovka. To the left, it was a similar story from the *SS Panzerkampfgruppe 'Das Reich'* where Russian troops had broken through the defences near Troshcha only for the assault to be brought to a halt in a counterattack. The previous evening had also seen Soviet rocket fire laid down on the positions of the *Kampfgruppe*, some using phosphorous rounds. At 22.00 hours, the *'Das Reich'* had begun to pull back to its new positions, and although details were lacking, the withdrawal seemed to have been carried out in an orderly manner. The *19.Panzer-Division* had also been attacked the previous evening, with the assault being made against the boundary between it and the *7.Panzer-Division* to the left. The attack began at 19.00 hours, and again had achieved a degree of success before a counterattack sealed off the breach and cleared the area. Although no further combat took place, the Russians maintained a lively artillery and mortar fire throughout the whole night, against both the left wing and the Filintsy sector. The Soviets were clearly trying to concentrate on the boundary though, and the division reported between 300 and 400 Soviet soldiers in the low ground east of Kutyshche where they were very close to the German positions. The *7.Panzer-Division* meanwhile had succeeded in sealing off the earlier penetration by Soviet troops in its centre, but had been unable to prevent the Russians from reinforcing the breach, including tanks. On the right wing, three Russian tanks forced their way into Kutyshche, while another eight broke into a group of houses 1,500 metres to the west. A *Panzer-Kompanie* attached from the *'LSSAH'* was dispatched to try and deal with the threat.

To the north-west, on the left wing of the *Panzerarmee*, the *LIX.AK* passed a relatively quiet night.[76] The *Panzeraufklärungs-Abteilung 16* had finally been relieved from the front line by about 05.00 hours, being replaced by elements of the *291. Infanterie-Division* which took up positions either side of the road about three kilometres west of Polonnoe. On the right wing of the *Korps-Abteilung C*, the Soviets forced their way into Zhelobnoe the previous evening with about 200 men and two tanks, while the nearby villages of Malaya Gorbasha and Velikaya Gorbasha had both been occupied by Russian troops. Over on the northern wing, statements taken from partisans suggested that there were regular Soviet troops, including tanks, advancing against the *Korps'* left flank, heading southwards towards Velikaya Kletska and the positions held by the *454. Sicherungs-Division*.

When the new day broke, the weather was largely unchanged, with the skies partly cloudy and partly clear. The temperature remained below freezing, leaving the roads still frozen and usable, although a stronger wind in places caused a few light snowdrifts.

---

74 *XXXXVI.PzK*, Morgenmeldung, 06.05 hours dated 9 Jan 44.
75 *XXXXVIII.PzK*, Morgenmeldung, 06.30 hours dated 9 Jan 44.
76 *LIX.AK*, Morgenmeldung, 07.25 hours dated 9 Jan 44.

On the southern wing, the *101.Jäger-Division* had run into difficulty.[77] During the previous night, the *Jäger-Regiment 228* had attacked from the north towards Komarov and succeeded in pushing on through the town into Voronovitsa in the face of armoured resistance. Later though, the Soviets pushed west again north of Komarov, and effectively cut the regiment off from the rest of the division. Given the difficulties, Raus requested that the division be attached instead to the *PzAOK 4*, and it was formally transferred with effect from midday.[78] The original intention of pulling the division back to the edge of Vinnitsa was abandoned immediately, so as not to open the way for Soviets forces to advance directly on Zhmerinka. Instead, it was tasked with preventing just such an advance, first by freeing the trapped regiment in Voronovitsa and then, if placed under sufficient enemy pressure, by withdrawing westwards through Trostyanets.[79] In considering how best to prevent the Russian advance towards Zhmerinka, Raus contemplated transferring strong elements of the *16.Panzer-Division* to assist the *101. Jäger-Division*, but in the end this option was dropped as it would have called into question its use in Operation '*Winterreise*' due to begin the following day. During the afternoon, the isolated regiment was attacked by Russian tanks but managed to beat back the assault and hold its positions. At around the same time, to the north, other elements of the division engaged Soviet infantry and vehicle columns moving along the Yelenovka-Gumennoe road with artillery fire, reportedly to good effect. At 15.00 hours that afternoon, the division launched the planned counterattack from the Sokirintsy area towards Voronovitsa. The attack was made by a battalion, with a *Sturmgeschütz-Batterie* in support, with the intention of allowing the encircled *Jäger-Regiment 228* to pull back to the north-east into a line running from Ivanovka through Tsvizhin to the southern part of Soloviyevka. The action continued on into the evening, and by late evening ten Soviet tanks had already been reported as destroyed.

Meanwhile, Gollnick's *XXXXVI.PzK* reported that the Russians seemed to have picked up the movements of the *16.Panzer-Division* in the area west of Sverdlovka.[80] They had wheeled weak infantry and armoured forces to face them, and it appeared likely that they would be constructing new positions on a line running from Maliye Krushlintsy through Lozovataya to Romanovka.[81] Opposite the *Korps* front, Soviet motorised and horse-drawn forces had been advancing from the east throughout the whole day, passing through Lozovataya and Schastlivaya to the south and south-west. Other Russian troops, estimated to be a battalion with six tanks in support, meanwhile launched an assault from Lozovataya against the positions of the *4.Gebirgs-Division*

---

77   *101.Jäger-Division*, Tagesmeldung, 19.25 hours dated 9 Jan 44.
78   Hgr. Süd, Ia Nr. 126/44 geh. dated 9 Jan 44.
79   PzAOK 4, Ia Nr. 206/44 geh. dated 9 Jan 44.
80   *XXXXVI.PzK*, Tagesmeldung, untimed dated 9 Jan 44. The *4.Gebirgs-Division* had been formally transferred to Gollnick's command with effect from 06.00 hours that day. According to this report, the *Korps* deployed the following operational armour and anti-tank means:
   • *16.Panzer-Division*: 17 *Panzer IV lg*; 4 command vehicles; 9 *StuGs*; 12 heavy motorised anti-tank guns.
   • *1.Infanterie-Division*: 12 *StuGs*; 12 heavy motorised anti-tank guns.
   • *4.Gebirgs-Division*: 9 heavy motorised anti-tank guns.
   In addition, a total of 31 *Panzer V* from the *I./Panzer-Regiment 2* had already arrived in the unloading area.
81   Romanovka does not appears on all maps. It lay on the high ground about three kilometres north-east of Lozovataya.

in Sverdlovka, but this had been successfully defended. In the evening, there was another battalion-sized assault, this time with 18 tanks in support, striking the front line between Velikaya Krushlintsy and Sverdlovka. The fighting continued on into the night, and the situation remained unclear. Behind the fighting, the *16.Panzer-Division* and elements of the *4.Gebirgs-Division* spent the day moving into their assembly areas, while the *1.Infanterie-Division* was a little behind and still on the march. The *Füsilier-Regiment 22* was planned to relieve the left wing of the *4.Gebirgs-Division* during the night. There were considerable elements which had still not arrived though, including the *Panzeraufklärungs-Abteilung 16* and the *I./Panzergrenadier-Regiment 64* from the *16.Panzer-Division*, and the *Grenadier-Regiment 1* and the horse-drawn units of the *Grenadier-Regiment 43* from the *1.Infanterie-Division*. In the Vinnitsa area, the units of the *254.Infanterie-Division* were beginning to arrive, including the *Grenadier-Regiment 454*, the *I./Grenadier-Regiment 484*, the *Pionier-Bataillon 254*, as well as the *II.* and *III./Artillerie-Regiment 254*. During the course of the afternoon, Raus discussed the forthcoming attack with Gollnick, and stressed that success depended on keeping the forces concentrated, and being able to bring up those elements still arriving as soon as possible. As he had insufficient forces available to maintain a proper flank guard as the attack developed, Gollnick requested that he be relieved of responsibility for the sector then held by the *4.Gebirgs-Division*.[82] Raus refused the request on the grounds that he had no other troops available to take over the sector. However, a compromise was reached. At Fangohr's suggestion, Raus ordered the *XXIV.PzK* to assume responsibility for the sector of the division's left-hand regiment by extending the front held by the *168.Infanterie-Division*, so that the regiment could be relieved and would be available as a reserve for the *XXXXVI.PzK*. Fangohr also proposed an alternative approach, in which the *1.Infanterie-Division* would replace the *4.Gebirgs-Division* in advancing to the rear and left of the *16.Panzer-Division*. Raus rejected this however, on the grounds that the *4.Gebirgs-Division* was more mobile and manoeuvrable. He was also of the opinion that in providing flank security, the *1.Infanterie-Division* must not be allowed to be torn apart. The idea was not that the flank should be guarded by establishing a 'string of pearls', but rather that the main body of the division should be held together as a single body and secure the flank through offensive action behind a thin forward screening line. It was also essential that those elements of the *4.Gebirgs-Division* which were to provide initial flank security should be relieved as soon as possible by the arriving *1.Infanterie-Division* to free them up to join the *16.Panzer-Division* in the offensive. Around midday, von Manstein paid a visit to the headquarters of the *4.Panzerarmee*, and during the course of this, the forthcoming operation was discussed.[83] The Army Group commander's contribution to the discussion was limited, and the record only shows that he thought the attack needed to be conducted towards the south-east.

North of Vinnitsa meanwhile, the *XXIV.PzK* had a mixed day.[84] As on recent days, the eastern front remained quiet, while the northern front was subjected to repeated assaults. In the south though, where Nehring was now responsible for the *Kampfkommandant* in Vinnitsa, there was the impression that the Soviets were screening off the city while driving further south-west towards Zhmerinka. The *Kampfkommandant* reported that

---

82 *PzAOK 4*, Ia Kriegstagebuch entry dated 9 Jan 44.
83 *PzAOK 4*, Ia Kriegstagebuch entry dated 9 Jan 44.
84 *XXIV.PzK*, Tagesmeldung, 19.15 hours dated 9 Jan 44.

while there had been no contact on the eastern edge of the city, the results of aerial reconnaissance around midday had shown about 30 Russian tanks in the vicinity of Tsvizhin, some 12 kilometres to the south-east. The armour was reported to be heading westwards, and three Soviet tanks had already been spotted in Ivanovka, three kilometres further on. Meanwhile, south-west of Vinnitsa, at around 13.00 hours, a railway engine had been fired upon near Selishche and burst into flames, and by 15.00 hours, the railway track just north of Tyut'ki station, some eight kilometres south of Vinnitsa, had been blown up. A train in the area, with a number of *Sturmgeschützen* loaded on board, was also attacked and set on fire.[85] Details were unclear, but the *Kampfkommandant* was aware the Soviet tanks had reached the Southern Bug river south of the city. By evening, it was known that the lead Russian elements had reached the river at Voroshilovka, about 24 kilometres south of Vinnitsa, and occupied parts of nearby Vitava too.[86] North of the city, the *168.Infanterie-Division* reported having conducted a successful combat patrol towards Sokolovka,[87] and having spotted and thrown back about 150 Soviet troops approaching the defensive positions near Maly Chernyatin. To the left, the *18.Artillerie-Division* reported no combat activity at all, although to support the forthcoming Operation '*Winterreise*', it had transferred three of its artillery battalions to the *XXXXVI.PzK*.[88] Further north-west, the *1.Panzer-Division* again had a difficult day. On the right wing, there was heavy fighting once more around Markovtsy, while in the centre a company-strength assault against Malaya Klitenka was also thrown back. Further west, a Russian assault of regimental-strength succeeded in pushing the defenders out of Andreyashevka, and a strong anti-tank defence prevented the division's counterattack from making any headway in recovering the village. On the division's left wing, the situation was even worse. East of Podorozhnaya, seven Soviet tanks with mounted infantry had managed to break through the division's defences near the main crossroads, and were advancing south and south-east on Krapivna and Klitenka. At 17.40 hours, Raus spoke with Nehring to discuss the situation.[89] In view of the difficulties being experienced by the *1.Panzer-Division*, Raus informed the *Korps* commander that the division could pull back to the south-west to a new line running from Peremoga through Osichna, Vishenka, and Stupnik to the high ground north of Petrikovtsy where it was to maintain contact with the *XXXXVIII.PzK* to the left. In authorising this withdrawal though, Raus asked Nehring to make it clear to the commanders involved that this new line was to be held come what may. Meanwhile, the harsh face of partisan warfare had showed itself in the rear area, with the villages of Uladovka and Ivanopol' being cleared and burned to the ground, and with 13 partisans being shot in Yatskovski.

In the *XXXXVIII.PzK* sector to the west, Balck reported that the main Soviet effort was being directed against the two wings of his *Korps*.[90] On the right, the Russians had

---

85 According to the report from the *101.Jäger-Division*, this incident took place at 14.30 hours and involved four Soviet tanks firing on two trains as they tried to unload.
86 *PzAOK 4*, Ia Kriegstagebuch entry dated 9 Jan 44.
87 There is no such place opposite the sector held by the division, so it is not possible to know precisely where this small action took place. There seems to be no obvious candidate in terms of spelling mistakes.
88 These were the *II.* and *III./Artillerie-Regiment 288* and the *III./Artillerie-Regiment 388*, all under the command of the headquarters of the *Artillerie-Regiment 288*.
89 *PzAOK 4*, Ia Kriegstagebuch entry dated 9 Jan 44.
90 *XXXXVIII.PzK*, Tagesmeldung, 18.50 hours dated 9 Jan 44.

brought up the 9th Mechanised Corps into the area around Ivanopol', and on the left they had discovered the open left flank and begun to exploit the weakness. During the morning, the *1.SS Panzer-Division 'LSSAH'* had been attacked on its right wing by an estimated regiment with tank support. The Soviet troops succeeded in breaking into the division's defences before a counterattack cleared the breach, destroying a reported 12 Russian tanks in the process. Around midday, the Soviets attacked again, this time advancing southwards out of Ivanopol' with infantry and between 20 and 25 tanks. The assault was directed against the division's positions between Zherebki and Zelentsy farm, about two kilometres west of Buryaki, and managed to effect a breach in the defences between Zherebki and the main crossroads. Soviet tanks pushed forwards into Zherebki itself, but the division counterattacked and managed to seal off the breach, destroying seven enemy tanks and forcing the Russians to withdraw back to the north. About 30 *Katyusha* rocket launchers were observed in the area south-east of Ivanopol', and new Soviet troop assemblies were seen in the woods south-west of Dubrovka, including armoured units. The fighting had been hard for the *SS Panzerkampfgruppe 'Das Reich'* too. A Soviet assault in about battalion-strength had been launched from the area south-east of Mikhailovka against the front about four kilometres east of Verbka. The attack had been supported by an estimated 12 artillery batteries, and again succeeded in breaking into the German defences. The *Kampfgruppe* responded immediately and counterattacked with an armoured group, clearing the breach and restoring the situation. The fighting continued though, and the main defensive position along the northern edge of the woods east of Filintsy changed a number of times during the day. By evening, it was in German hands again. A little to the east, six Russian tanks were seen in the wooded area three kilometres north-west of Troshcha. Left of the *'Das Reich'*, the *19.Panzer-Division* came under repeated assault either side of Vishchikusy, but despite the support of artillery and rocket launchers, the Soviet troops proved unable to make any progress. On the left wing of the *Korps*, the *7.Panzer-Division* continued in its efforts to clear the previous night's breach west of Kutyshche and finally succeeded in doing so by around 15.00 hours. At about midday, the Soviets launched a major attack along the west bank of the river Sluch', advancing from the north towards Lyubar. The assault involved about 1,000 men with 25 tanks in support, and succeeded in pushing back the division's screening troops to a small bridgehead in the town. An armoured *Kampfgruppe* was sent over the river to counterattack, and managed to destroy six Russian tanks before being pulled back to the east bank as darkness fell. With the bridgehead evacuated, Soviet forces proceeded to occupy the western part of Lyubar. In all, the *XXXXVIII.PzK* reported having destroyed a total of 33 Soviet tanks during the day's fighting. During the late afternoon, Balck called the *PzAOK 4* headquarters.[91] He pointed out that during the past couple of days his *Korps* had been involved in heavy defensive fighting, and the recent failure of the *7.Panzer-Division* counterattack in the Lyubar area on the left wing meant that the current positions would soon be untenable. He therefore proposed pulling back to a general line from the high ground north of Petrikovtsy through Smela, the high ground north of Nosovka, Stetkovtsy and Maliye Bratalov to Grinovtsy on the river Sluch', south of Lyubar. Raus agreed, with the proviso that the *7.Panzer-Division* be pulled out of the front line and transferred to the left bank

---

91 *PzAOK 4, Ia Kriegstagebuch* entry dated 9 Jan 44.

of the Sluch'. The new task of the division was to cover the left flank of the *XXXXVIII. PzK* through aggressive action and to establish contact with the *LIX.AK* to the left in the area just west of Polonnoe. Here too, Raus stressed that the new lines would have to be held at all costs in order not to jeopardise the prospects of the forthcoming Operation '*Winterreise*' on the opposite wing. The *4.Panzerarmee* later issued orders to both the *XXIV.PzK* and the *XXXXVIII.PzK* confirming the withdrawal and the transfer of the *7.Panzer-Division*, and instructing both *Korps* to ensure that rearguards were to be left in the current positions for as long as possible.[92] These orders were only later reported to Army Group South, at which point von Manstein rejected the proposition. Whether Raus had deliberately delayed passing the information to the Army Group is not clear, but von Manstein was obliged to agree to the withdrawal after it was explained to him that the movements had already begun.

With the left flank of the *XXXXVIII.PzK* now seriously threatened, there was again the danger that the *LIX.AK* would become isolated from the rest of the *4.Panzerarmee*. It appeared though as if the Soviets were concentrating for the time being on driving southwards down the Sluch' valley against the sector held by the *7.Panzer-Division*, and the forward detachments of the *291.Infanterie-Division* deployed about three kilometres west of Polonnoe reported no contact with Russian troops throughout the day. Pushing forward, they also found the western part of the town free of Soviet forces. Further north though, Russian troops estimated at one or two companies with several tanks in support, assaulted the division's positions in Burtin and drove the defenders out of the town, forcing them to pull back about three kilometres into the woods. According to reports received from aerial reconnaissance, there was lively Soviet traffic on the road running from Burtin towards Polonnoe, presumably including some anti-aircraft units as the pilot also reported coming under heavy fire. Further north, other Soviet units forced the division's forward elements to pull back out of Derevishchina, west of Zhary, and the division was planning a counterattack for the following day. On the left wing of the *Korps*, in the sectors held by the *Korps-Abteilung C* and the *454.Sicherungs-Division*, there had been active reconnaissance undertaken by both sides, but little heavy fighting. Away to the north, over 20 kilometres from Korets, the *454.Sicherungs-Division* reported the sound of track noises coming from the area around Marinin on the river Sluch', indicating that Russian armoured units might be in the vicinity. Given the threat of renewed separation of the *LIX.AK* from the main body of the *Panzerarmee*, Raus spoke with von der Chevallerie during the course of the evening to instruct him to conduct more reconnaissance to the south-east and to ensure that contact was maintained with the *XXXXVIII.PzK*.[93] It was probably an unnecessary piece of advice, but it indicates the concern to make sure the *LIX.AK* did not become separated again.

The situation had therefore changed little for the *4.Panzerarmee* during 9 January.[94] It was still being attacked on both wings by infantry and armoured forces, although in the south, strong forces of the Soviet 1st Tank Army[95] had now broken through the *101. Jäger-Division* and advanced to the eastern bank of the Southern Bug river. The main body of the 11th Guards Tank Corps was known to be in the Komarov-Voronovitsa

---

92 *PzAOK 4*, Ia Nr. 218/44 geh. dated 9 Jan 44.
93 *PzAOK 4*, Ia Kriegstagebuch entry dated 9 Jan 44.
94 *PzAOK 4*, Tagesmeldung an *Heeresgruppe Süd*, 21.00 hours dated 9 Jan 44.
95 The 11th Guards Tank Corps had been correctly identified in the area.

PREPARING THE COUNTERSTRIKE

area, with its leading elements already as far south-west as Sutiski.[96] Troops from the 8th Guards Mechanised Corps were already in the Dubovets-Bairakovka area, although elements of the Corps were known to be still moving up. On the northern wing, the 3rd Guards Tank Army continued its attacks either side of Ivanopol' with the support of the rifle units of the 18th and 1st Guards Armies, and the appearance of further troop assemblies south-west of Berdichev and around Ivanopol' itself suggested that further attacks could be expected still.[97] The situation was also difficult further west where elements of the 4th Guards Tank Corps had crossed the river Sluch' and captured the northern part of Lyubar, despite a counterattack by the *7.Panzer-Division*, while other elements were attacking southwards from the Kutyshche area. Meanwhile, beyond the left flank and beyond the ability of the *PzAOK 4* to do anything about it, the Russian 13th Army continued to advance with several rifle divisions through the marshes and forests either side of Sarny. In all, the *PzAOK 4* reported having destroyed 43 Russian tanks during the day, 33 of which were claimed by the *XXXXVIII.PzK*. At 18.30 hours, the chief of staff at Army Group South, Busse, called the *PzAOK 4* to inform them that the newly arriving *371.Infanterie-Division* would be attached to the *4.Panzerarmee*, rather than the *PzAOK 1* as had originally been intended.[98] The division had already unloaded its leading elements in the Zhmerinka area, and it was to be given instructions to hold the town. The Army Group confirmed this later that evening with formal instructions, subordinating the division to the *PzAOK 4* with immediate effect.[99] In these instructions, the Army Group also authorised the release of two armoured battalions which were then refitting in the Zhmerinka area, the *s.Panzer-Abteilung 503* and the *I./Panzer-Regiment 23*, although they were only to be employed for clearing the southern bank of the river Bug of Soviet armoured and motorised forces. In no circumstances was the refitting of either battalion to be jeopardised. Following the receipt of these orders, Fangohr proposed that the *371.Infanterie-Division*, together with the *s.Panzer-Abteilung 503*, should be deployed to block the crossing over the Southern Bug at Voroshilovka and form a bridgehead on the northern bank at Gnivan'. He also proposed that that these units, together with the *101.Jäger-Division*, be attached to Hauffe's *XIII.AK* which was still quartered in Zhmerinka without any front line responsibility. Raus agreed to both proposals, and orders were issued accordingly.[100] These noted that Soviet forces, correctly identifying the 11th Guards Tank Corps, had broken through the *101.Jäger-Division* at Komarov and had reached both Voroshilovka and Ivanovka with leading armoured elements. The *XIII.AK* was instructed to take command of the *101.Jäger-Division* and the arriving *371.Infanterie-Division* with effect from noon the following day, with the task of blocking any Russian advance over the Southern Bug river at Voroshilovka and forming a bridgehead around Gnivan'. The *101.Jäger-Division* was to ensure that the railway line between Gnivan' and Vinnitsa remained open, and was only to withdraw towards the railway itself if placed under heavy Soviet pressure. If forced to pull back, it was to do so step-by-step, and hold the line of the railway as a last resort. To help

---

96 *PzAOK 4*, Ic, Abendmeldung dated 9 Jan 44.
97 German intelligence had also identified the 9th Guards Mechanised Corps in the area, although this was in fact not a Guards unit.
98 *PzAOK 4*, Ia Kriegstagebuch entry dated 9 Jan 44.
99 Hgr. Sud, Ia Nr. 140/44 g.Kdos dated 9 Jan 44.
100 *PzAOK 4*, Ia 222/44 geh. dated 9 Jan 44.

achieve this, those of its units still east of Vinnitsa would be relieved by elements of the *254.Infanterie-Division* and transferred south. Both the *s.Panzer-Abteilung 503* and the *I./Panzer-Regiment 23* were also attached to the *Korps* with the proviso that they were only to be committed to clearing the area as far as the Southern Bug. As if to reinforce the point, both units would remain attached to Army Group South insofar as their continuing refit was concerned. To provide additional infantry manpower, a couple of Rumanian units then based in Zhmerinka were also attached to the *371. Infanterie-Division*, including the 8th Infantry Regiment and the 715th Independent Battalion. Hauffe was also to appoint a *Kampfkommandant* for Zhmerinka itself, and pass responsibility for the continuing refit of the former units of the *XIII.AK* to the commanding officer of the *208.Infanterie-Division*.[101]

Following von Manstein's earlier visit to the *PzAOK 4* headquarters, formal orders were issued for Operation 'Winterreise' on the basis of an attack towards the south-east.[102] According to these, the Soviet 1st Tank Army had moved from the Berdichev-Kazatin sector and been re-grouped in the area south-west of Pogrebishche. It had started to advance on 8 January, driving forward with the 11th Guards Tank Corps from the Lipovets area towards Vinnitsa and reaching the Gumennoe area already. The deployment of the 8th Guards Mechanised Corps to outflank the southern wing of the *Panzerarmee* could also be counted on. The 38th Army was also believed to be holding a wide front between Tsybulev and a point south of Berdichev with 13 rifle divisions, elements of which would be providing support to the new drive by the 1st Tank Army. Troop movements observed opposite the *PzAOK 4* right wing indicated that a number of rifle divisions were being transferred from the area south of Berdichev to the area north of Vakhnovka. The 135th Rifle Division had already been confirmed in the Oratov area, the 100th Rifle Division in Troshcha, the 241st Rifle Division in Zozov, the 211th Rifle Division south of Novaya Greblya, the 237th Rifle Division in Kirovka, the 68th Guards Rifle Division in Leonardovka, and the 107th Rifle Division in Peremoga. The existence of local reserves had not been established, but the *PzAOK 4* was expecting some to be deployed, particularly resting armour or mechanised units. The primary objective of 'Winterreise' was therefore the defeat of the Russian 1st Tank Army by an attack into its flank and rear. Gollnick's *XXXXVI.PzK* was to undertake the main attack with the *16.Panzer-Division*, the *4.Gebirgs-Division* and the *254.* and *1.Infanterie-Divisions*. The *Korps* was to break through the Soviet front in and to the north of Vakhnovka, and then, having concentrated its forces, drive south-eastwards into the rear of the 1st Tank Army west of the river Sob. In the event Russians forces made good ground towards the west in the meantime, the *XXXXVI.PzK* was to re-direct the assault such that the *16.Panzer-Division* and the *4.Gebirgs-Division* attacked directly southwards towards Stepanovka. These two divisions were to assemble in the Vakhnovka-Konstantinovka-Priluka area during the night, and be ready to start the attack as early as possible following a short artillery barrage. The *254.* and *1.Infanterie-Divisions* were meanwhile to complete their troop assemblies as quickly as possible, so that the former could counterattack against any Soviet forces trying to head north-westwards from Stepanovka, while the latter advanced either south-east or east to gain ground to cover the flank of the attacking divisions. The *XXIV.PzK* meanwhile was to support the attack with all available guns

---

101 These included the *68.*, *208.*, and *340.Infanterie-Divisions*.
102 *PzAOK 4*, Ia Nr. 229/44 g.Kdos dated 9 Jan 44.

of the *168.Infanterie-Division* and the *18.Artillerie-Division*, even to the extent that all the participating units were to be re-grouped in co-operation with the *XXXXVI.PzK* to ensure that they were all in their new positions ready to fire by daybreak. Nevertheless, this support was expected to be limited to the initial breakthrough, and there were no plans for these artillery units to follow the advance. Instead, they were to be returned to the *18.Artillerie-Division* at the earliest opportunity for use by the *XXIV.PzK*. The *168. Infanterie-Division* was also to be prepared to undertake its own attack, both to exploit the success of the main assault and also to provide flank security for the *XXXXVI.PzK*. If required then, the division was to push forward its right wing and attack to the north-east to reach the Lozovka[103]-Chernyatin line. The boundary between the two *Korps* would move to a line running from Pavlovka to Polevaya Lysievka, along the river Desna to Novaya Greblya, and from there to Ovsyaniki. As previously notified, the *XXXXVI. PzK* was to be allocated additional engineer support in the form of the *Pionier-Bataillon (mot.) 48* and the *Bau-Pionier-Bataillon 523*. Air support was also requested from the *VIII.Fliegerkorps*, with the main effort being to provide direct close air support to the leading attack elements, as well as keeping watch over the flanks.

The tasks facing the *4.Panzerarmee* for the following day were therefore quite simple in concept. In the south, Zhmerinka was to be held by the *XIII.AK*, while the *XXXXVI. PzK* launched its counterattack against the Soviet 1st Tank Army east of Vinnitsa. Further north, the *XXIV.PzK* was to maintain its positions along the eastern front and pull back the northern front along with the *XXXXVIII.PzK* to its left, while the *LIX. AK* on the left wing retained in existing mission. Beyond the left wing, the situation was still unclear, and with the *PzAOK 4* unable to assist, von Manstein issued orders to the *Wehrmachtbefehlshaber Ukraine, General der Flieger* Karl Kitzinger, following his earlier notice a couple of days previously, and confirming his earlier thoughts.[104] The orders recognised that elements of the Soviet 13th Army were driving westwards along and to the north of the Novograd-Volynskii-Rovno road as part of conducting aggressive flank security for the main operation directed against the *4.Panzerarmee*. The task of these elements was probably to prevent the Germans from bringing up fresh forces against the west flank of the 1st Ukrainian Front, but it was also likely that in the event of no more than weak resistance they would try to cut the Rovno-Sarny railway and push on as far west as possible in the Rovno-Kovel' direction. Kitzinger was now instructed to concentrate all his efforts on two main tasks. First, he was secure the rail network throughout the region and ensure it was kept open, and second, he was to form a screening line along the rivers Sluch' and Goryn' between the left wing of the *LIX.AK* and the Army Group boundary. He was then to conduct reconnaissance from this line eastwards as far as he was able, using all available means to obtain an early picture of Soviet movements and plans. Rather optimistically, the orders added that any Russian attacks against the screening line were to be beaten back by concentrating the available forces at points where the Soviets were known to be focussing. Despite the need for all available manpower, Kitzinger was not given a free hand with regard to the units of the 7th Hungarian Corps stationed in his area, and for the time being the movement of any

---

103 Referred to as Gubin in the German records. This was the part of Lozovka which lay to the north of the stream which divides the village.
104 Hgr. Süd, Ia Nr. 127/44 geh. dated 9 Jan 44.

of these would require prior orders from the Army Group. The *OKH* had nevertheless been requested to make the necessary arrangements with the Hungarian General Staff.

☆

January 9 proved in many ways to be the high water mark of the Soviet Zhitomir-Berdichev offensive. On the right wing and in the centre, Vatutin had largely achieved his objectives, with only the sector between Lyubar and Vinnitsa falling somewhat short of the original plan. In the north, the 13th Army had reached its objective and was continuing to advance westwards in the absence of any effective opposition. The 60th Army too had achieved its objective of reaching the river Sluch', and had already crossed to the west bank in a number of places and was advancing slowly towards Shepetovka. On the right of the central sector, the town of Lyubar was all but taken, while on the left, Soviet forces were already operating on the eastern edge and to the south and south-west of Vinnitsa. Between these two wings though, the front was still held by the *4.Panzerarmee* in an arc facing to the north-east, effectively preventing the 1st Ukrainian Front from achieving its objectives in that region. Against this background, Vatutin, together with Zhukov, the *Stavka* representative attached to his headquarters, prepared a set of proposals for the further conduct of the operation, and they submitted these to the *Stavka* at 00.50 hours on 9 January.[105] According to these, the immediate task of the 1st Ukrainian Front was to complete all the aims of the original plan, even though it had achieved many of its initial objectives already. On the right wing, this would involve continuing the advance to the line of the Goryn' and Sluch' rivers, and capturing the towns of Dubrovitsa and Sarny. In the centre and on the left wing, the task remained to defeat the German forces around Zhmerinka and Uman', to capture Luka Barskaya, Vinnitsa, Zhmerinka, and Uman', and subsequently to advance to the line running from Lyubar though Khmel'nik, Luka Barskaya, and Murafa (Zhdanovo) to Tul'chin and Uman'. Vatutin set out how he intended to achieve this. The 13th Army was to complete the Sarny operation in accordance with existing plans, after which the 25th Tank Corps was to be placed in army reserve in the Novograd-Volynskii area. The 60th Army, having already achieved its main objective, would maintain its positions on the line it had reached, and would complete its re-grouping and re-organising, while continuing to conduct reconnaissance in depth towards Shepetovka. The 4th Guards Tank Corps was to be transferred to army reserve in the Lyubar area where it was to re-group. If required, the 60th Army would be available to assist the 1st Guards Army in completing its mission. The 1st Guards Army itself meanwhile was to continue the advance and reach the line Lyubar-Khmel'nik by 12 January, at which point it was to halt and prepare for the next stage of the offensive. Further south, the 18th and 38th Armies, supported by the 3rd Guards and 1st Tank Armies, were to complete the defeat of the German forces around Vinnitsa and Zhmerinka and capture both towns, as well as Luka Barskaya. Thereafter, the 18th Army was to advance to the line Khmel'nik-Luka Barskaya-Mateikovo, with the 38th Army[106] to its left reaching a line from Mateikovo to

---

105 TsAMO. F. 236. Op. 2712. D. 56. L. 40—50. Quoted in Russkii arkhiv: *Velikaya Otechestvennaya. Stavka VKG: Dokumenty i Materialy 1944-1945* (Moscow: TERRA, 1999) p. 260.

106 Interestingly, the proposal actually states that it is the 1st Guards Army which is to occupy this line, but this must be a mistake, particularly as the task allotted to the 1st Guards Army had already been

Murafa. To assist in the development of this operation, presumably after the 1st Guards Army had moved to within striking distance of Khmel'nik, the 3rd Guards Tank Army, having received 200 tanks as replacements, and following the arrival of the 31st Tank Corps,[107] was to attack from the Khmel'nik area towards Luka Barskaya to seize the latter town, cut the Zhmerinka-Lvov railway, and hold the area until the arrival of the main forces of the 18th and 1st Guards Armies. The 1st Tank Army was meanwhile to capture the Zhmerinka area and hold it until the arrival of the main forces of the 38th Army. On the left wing, the 40th and 27th Armies, with the 5th Guards Tank Corps[108] in support, would continue trying to defeat the German forces around Uman', leaving the 40th Army on a line from Murafa though Tul'chin to Olyanitsa, and the 27th Army, with the 5th Guards Tank Corps, on a line from Olyanitsa to Uman'. The time foreseen to carry out these tasks and complete the initial operation was estimated at between 10 and 12 days.

In addition to setting out how he intended to fulfil his original mission, Vatutin also offered proposals for the next stage of the operation. In order not to prevent the Germans from establishing a firm defence on the general line of the Goryn' and Zbruch rivers, he suggested a new operation beginning on or about 20 January to advance the 1st Ukrainian Front to a line from the Ozhekhovskii canal in the north, through Kovel', Lutsk, Dubno, Kremenets, Volochisk, Gusyatin, Kamenets-Podol'skii, and along the line of the river Dnestr from Khotin through Mogilev-Podol'skii to Soroki. The intention was to complete this operation by 5-10 February. The main strike would aim from the Luka Barskaya area towards Kamenets-Podol'skii, and be undertaken by forces of the 1st Guards, 18th and 38th Armies, together with the newly arrived 31st Tank Corps and the 5th Mechanised Corps,[109] as well as the 3rd, 13th, and 17th Artillery Divisions and the 3rd Guards Mortar Division[110] in support. According to these new proposals, the 1st Guards Army would advance on the Starokonstantinov-Volochisk axis to capture Starokonstantinov and Proskurov before moving on to concentrate its main forces in the Volochisk area. The 18th Army was to advance on its left through Derazhnya towards Gusyatin, where it was to concentrate its main forces. The 38th Army would meanwhile advance from the Zhmerinka area through Struga to Kamenets-Podol'skii, seizing both Kamenets-Podol'skii and Khotin and reaching a line running from Skala-Podol'skaya through Kamenets-Podol'skii and Khotin to Kalyus. On the right wing of the 1st Ukrainian Front, the forces of the 13th and 60th Armies, reinforced by the 1st and 6th Guards Cavalry Corps, as well as the 4th Guards and 25th Tank Corps,[111] would be tasked with the destruction of the German forces in the Rovno-Shepetovka area. The 13th Army, with the two cavalry corps and the 25th Tank Corps, was to advance towards Rovno and Lutsk with the intention of reaching a line from Kovel' in the north through Lutsk and Dubno to Rovno. Specifically, the 25th Tank Corps was initially to advance towards Ostrog and then wheel to the north-west to capture Rovno after bypassing

---

outlined.
107 Released from the *Stavka* reserve.
108 Released from the 1st Ukrainian Front reserve.
109 Released from the Moscow Military District (MVO).
110 From the 7th Artillery Breakthrough Corps.
111 The 6th Guards Cavalry Corps had recently been transferred from the Belorussian Front, and the 4th Guards Tank Corps had already been released from the 1st Ukrainian Front reserve.

it from the south and the south-west. It was then to press on and take Lutsk. The 1st Guards and 6th Guards Cavalry Corps were to head westwards from the Sarny area, moving between the rivers Goryn' and Styr' towards Lutsk and Dubno with the object of striking the German forces in the Rovno area from the north-west and west. The 60th Army, with the 4th Guards Tank Corps, would advance through Shepetovka and Izyaslav before pressing on to reach a line from Dubno to Kremenets. On the left wing of the Front, the 27th and 40th Armies would meanwhile press on with their existing offensive to link up with forces of the 2nd Ukrainian Front. The 40th Army was to advance on the Gaisin-Tul'chin-Vapnyarka axis to seize Mogilev-Podol'skii on the river Dnestr, and establish a front along the river from Kalyus through Mogilev-Podol'skii to Soroki. The 27th Army, with the 5th Guards Tank Corps, was meanwhile to advance to a line running from Soroki through Verbka and Gaivoron to Uman', with the task of maintaining contact with the right wing of the 2nd Ukrainian Front. The 3rd Guards Tank Army would initially be re-grouped and re-fitted, but would later be deployed to support the drive towards Kamenets-Podol'skii, with the 1st Tank Army advancing on its left to support the attack towards Mogilev-Podol'skii. The proposal also includes mention of the 2nd Tank Army, which at the time was still held in the *Stavka* reserve since being placed there on three September 1943.[112] It is not clear whether the army had been previously offered by the *Stavka*, or whether Vatutin was making a request for its release, but in any event it was then being foreseen as a major mobile reinforcement for the continuation of the 1st Ukrainian Front's operations. The proposal suggests that the army would be concentrated in the Zhitomir area, where presumably it would take initial command of the 31st Tank Corps, which was to concentrate in the Kazatin area, and the 5th Mechanised Corps, which was to concentrate in the Berdichev area. The *Stavka* approved Vatutin's proposals at 21.00 hours the same day.[113]

Interestingly, the proposals seem to give no indication that there had been any change in the balance of forces, and appear to assume that the Germans had not deployed any significant reinforcements. There is moreover no mention of any possibility that the Germans might be preparing a counterattack. Whether this oversight was attributable to a failure of intelligence, an over-optimistic appreciation of the situation, or some other reason, falls outside the scope of this book, but it is nonetheless interesting in view of what would happen during the rest of January. The following day, 10 January, the Germans would begin the first of a series of counterattacks against different sectors held by the 1st Ukrainian Front. Over the course of the following three weeks, these would bring the Russian advance to a standstill, push the Soviet forces back in places, and restore at least a semblance of a cohesive and continuous front line for the German forces. In response to these counterattacks, the *Stavka* would later abandon Vatutin's proposals of 9 January, and on 14 January it would formally bring the Zhitomir-Berdichev offensive to a close. Before doing so however, it tacitly recognised that the offensive had not achieved all its goals, acknowledging that the German salient on the Dnepr was restricting the potential development of operations by both the 1st and 2nd Ukrainian Fronts and delaying their advance to the Southern Bug river. On 12 January 1944 therefore, it would issue instructions to both Fronts to surround and destroy the

---

112 In the event, the 2nd Tank Army would finally be released to the 1st Ukrainian Front on 18 January.
113 TsAMO. F. 148a. Op. 3763. D. 166. L. 6. Quoted in Russkii arkhiv: *Velikaya Otechestvennaya. Stavka VKG: Dokumenty i Materialy 1944-1945* (Moscow: TERRA, 1999) p. 30.

German forces in the Zvenigorodka-Mironovka-Smela area in what would become the Korsun'-Shevchenkovskii operation, the Korsun' pocket.[114]

---

114 TsAMO. F. 148a. Op. 3763. D. 166. L. 8, 9. Quoted in Russkii arkhiv: *Velikaya Otechestvennaya. Stavka VKG: Dokumenty i Materialy 1944-1945* (Moscow: TERRA, 1999) p. 31.

Photographs of Commanders

German

Generalfeldmarschall Erich von Manstein, commander of Army Group South (left) in conversation with *Generalleutnant* Theodor Busse, Chief of Staff of Army Group South (centre). Photo taken in summer 1943. (Bundesarchiv, Bild 101I-219-0579A-21)

Generaloberst Erhard Raus, commander of the *4.Panzerarmee*. (Bundesarchiv, Bild 146-1984-019-28, photographer: Wolff/Altvater)

General der Panzertruppen Hans-Valentin Hube, commander of the *1.Panzerarmee*. (Bundesarchiv, Bild 146-2009-0114, photographer: Hoffmann)

PHOTOGRAPHS OF COMMANDERS

Soviet

L: Lieutenant-General Ivan Chernyakhovskii, commander of the 60th Army.

R: Major-General of Artillery Kirill Moskalenko, commander of the 38th Army.

L: Colonel-General Andrei Grechko, commander of the 1st Guards Army.

R: Colonel-General of Tank Forces Pavel Rybalko, commander of the 3rd Guards Tank Army.

L: Lieutenant-General of Tank Forces Mikhail Katukov, commander of the 1st Tank Army.

R: Army General Nikolai Vatutin, commander of the 1st Ukrainian Front.

L: Colonel-General Konstantin Leselidze, commander of the 18th Army.

R: Lieutenant-General Fillip Zhmachenko, commander of the 40th Army.

Index

Index of People

Balck, Hermann, *General der Panzertruppen*, 60-61, 82, 87-88, 91-92, 94-95, 103, 106-107, 112-114, 116, 121-122, 125, 134-135, 138, 140-141, 147-148, 157-158, 168-169, 178, 241, 243-244, 248, 255, 257, 261-263, 271-272, 279-280, 286-287

Beukemann, Helmuth, *Generalleutnant*, 48-49

Breith, Hermann, *General der Panzertruppen*, 186, 189, 191-192, 207, 212, 214, 220-222, 225

Busse, Theodor, *Generalleutnant*, 4, 43, 85, 92, 103, 136, 141, 195, 200, 203-204, 247-248, 289, 296

Canaris, Wilhelm, Admiral, 60

Chernyakhovskii, Ivan, Lieutenant-General, 4, 31, 297

von der Chevallerie, Kurt, *General der Infanterie*, 65, 82, 88, 118, 136, 144, 149, 160, 169-170, 178, 242, 250, 258, 264, 279-280, 288

Chibisov, Nikandr, Lieutenant-General, 35-36

Ehrig, Werner, *Oberst*, 59

Fangohr, Friedrich, *Generalmajor*, 16, 44, 84-85, 87, 89, 92, 107, 112, 123, 133, 136, 140-141, 150, 155-156, 165, 168, 173, 177-178, 236-238, 243, 247-248, 257, 259, 261-262, 285, 289

Frölich, Gottfried, *Generalmajor*, 53, 177

Franz, Gerhard, *Oberst*, 50, 84-85, 88-89, 91, 116, 167, 195, 218

Giese, Karl, *Oberstleutnant*, 45, 247

Goeschen, Alex, *Generalleutnant*, 58

Gollnick, Hans, *General der Infanterie*, 244-245, 250, 256, 258, 263, 268, 272-274, 278, 281, 284-285, 290

Golubovskii, Vasilii, Lieutenant-General, 25-26

Göritz, Werner, *Generalleutnant*, 66

Grechko, Andrei, Colonel-General, 4, 32-33, 297

Guderian, Heinz, *Generaloberst*, 45, 48

von Hammerstein-Gesmold, *Oberst*, 123, 177, 247-248

Hansen, *Hauptmann*, 228

Hauffe, Arthur, *General der Infanterie*, 56, 86, 88, 91, 104-106, 110, 113, 115, 122-123, 135-139, 141, 148, 150, 152-153, 159, 161, 164, 169, 177, 242, 244, 247-248, 252, 260, 266, 289-290

Hell, Ernst-Eberhard, *General der Artillerie*, 48, 81, 96, 104, 108, 114, 118-120, 130-132, 138, 145, 156, 171, 173, 186, 189, 193, 195-197, 202, 204-206, 209, 213, 216, 218-219, 224, 233, 238

Hermani, *Oberstleutnant*, 89

Heyne, Walter, *Generalleutnant*, 47

Hitler, Adolf, Führer, 44, 62-63, 74, 136

Hochbaum, Friedrich, *Generalleutnant*, 46

von Horn, Hans-Joachim, *Generalleutnant*, 49

Hoth, Hermann, *Generaloberst*, 44

Hube, Hans-Valentin, *General der Panzertruppen*, iii, 4, 185-191, 193, 195-197, 199-200, 202-204, 208-209, 211-212, 216-218, 220-222, 224-227, 231, 238, 266-267, 296

Jauer, Georg, *Generalleutnant*, 55, 95

Källner, Hans, *Generalmajor*, 52-53, 126, 135, 139, 141, 143, 148, 150, 159

Katukov, Mikhail, Lieutenant-General of Tank Forces, 4, 21, 27-28, 37-38, 297

Khozin, General, 37

Kittel, Heinrich, *Generalmajor*, 226

Kitzinger, Karl, *General der Flieger*, 272, 291

Koch, Hellmuth, *Generalleutnant*, 69

Koll, Richard, *Generalmajor*, 64

Kranz, *Major*, 145

Krüger, Walter, *Generalleutnant*, 69

Kuznetsov, Vasilii, Colonel-General, 32

Lammerding, Heinz, *SS Oberführer*, 54-55

Lange, Wolfgang, *Generalleutnant*, 67

Leselidze, Konstantin, Colonel-General, 4, 21, 34, 297

von Lewinski, Erich, *Generalfeldmarschall* - see von Manstein

Lieb, Theobald, *Generalleutnant*, 46

Luschnig, *Oberst*, 226

von Manstein, Erich, *Generalfeldmarschall*, 4, 43, 74-75, 99, 101, 104, 107, 112, 137, 150-151, 160-162, 165-166, 185, 195-196, 199-200, 203-204, 211-212, 217-218, 222, 227, 243, 258, 265-266, 272-273, 278, 285, 288, 290-291, 296

von Manteuffel, Hasso, *Generalmajor*, 52-53, 61

Mattenklott, Franz, *General der Infanterie*, 50-51, 85, 89, 91-94, 97, 101, 105, 117, 120-121, 132-133, 140,

145-146, 152, 156-157, 173, 186, 193, 196-197, 200, 205, 209, 218, 224
Matterstock, Otto, *Generalleutnant*, 68-69, 177-178, 250
von Mellenthin, Friedrich, *Oberst*, 86-87, 104, 123, 133, 140, 168
Moskalenko, Kirill, Major-General of Artillery, 4, 23-27, 36, 297
Müller, *Oberst*, 44

Nehring, Walther, *General der Panzertruppen,* 45, 81, 93, 96, 103, 107, 119, 131, 138, 144, 152, 167, 236, 246-247, 257, 262, 276-277, 285-286

Piekenbrock, Hans, *Generalmajor*, 59-60
Pukhov, Nikolai, Lieutenant General, 4, 30

von Radowitz, Josef, *Oberst*, 102
Raus, Erhard, *Generaloberst*, 4, 44, 75, 84-85, 87-90, 92-96, 99-101, 103-104, 106-107, 112-113, 116, 118-120, 122-126, 130-136, 138-141, 145-146, 149-153, 156-162, 165-171, 177-178, 238, 243-245, 248, 251, 255, 257-259, 261-262, 264-267, 272, 276-280, 284-289, 296
von Rittberg, Graf, *Oberst*, 49
Rommel, Erwin, *Generaloberst*, 45, 53
Rybalko, Pavel, Colonel-General of Tank Forces, 4, 35, 297

von Schell, Adolf, *Generalleutnant*, 51
Scheuerpflug, Paul, *Oberst*, 57
Schleusener, *Oberst*, 123, 259
Schmidt-Hammer, Werner, *Generalmajor*, 47
Schulz, Adalbert, *Oberst*, 61-63
Schulze- Büttger, *Oberst*, 43, 96, 99, 136
Schwatlo-Gesterding, *Oberst*, 130, 155, 165, 173
Sommer, *SS Obersturmbannführer*, 54
Stalin, Joesef, 21, 32

Thoholte, Karl, *Generalmajor*, 50, 95
Trofimenko, Sergei, Colonel-General, 4, 39
Tröger, Hans, *Generalmajor*, 51-52, 167

Vasilevsky, A M, Marshal, 21, 42
Vatutin, Nikolai, Lieutenant-General, 4, 21-24, 27, 29, 292-294, 297

Wenck, Walter, *Generalmajor*, 185, 195, 200, 203-204, 211, 238, 257
Wisch, Theodor, *SS Oberführer*, 62-63, 148

Zhmachenko, Fillip, Lieutenant-General, 4, 38-39, 297
Zhukov, Georgy, Marshal, 21, 25, 292

Index of Places

Adamovka, 166, 172, 174, 214
Akhtyrka, 38,
Alexandrovka, 282
Alexeyevka, 210
Andreyashevka, 262, 270, 282, 286
Andrushevka, 103, 113, 115, 189, 193-194, 231
Andrushki, 117
Andrusovo, 166, 189, 194
Andrusovo Station, 166, 189, 194
Annopol, 130
Antonina, 223, 225
Antonov, 156, 161
Antonovka, 114
Antopol, 117, 140, 143, 147
Antwerp, 59
Arapovka, 107
Armavir, 33
Augsburg, 67
Austria, 54

Bagva, 193
Bahnhof Tschepowitschi, *see* Tschepowitschi, Bahnhof
Bairakovka, 218
Bakhmach, 66
Bakumovka, 206
Balabanovka, 202-203, 220, 223
Balamutovka, 146
Balkans, 48, 54, 63, 203, 221
Balyko-Shchuchinka, 86, 108, 119, 128, 131, 138, 142, 144, 155, 186, 209
Bamberg, 58
Bar, 179
Baran'e, 259
Baranovka, 236-237, 239, 242, 256
Bardy, 111
Barskaya, 292-293
Barvenkovo, 32
Bashtechki, 198
Bekhi, 67, 99, 115, 136
Bel'chaki, 250, 256
Belashki, 274
Belavuta, 244
Belaya, 13, 22-23, 48-49, 85, 108, 124, 131-132, 145, 154-156, 162-163, 165, 170-171, 173, 180, 187-188, 190, 192, 194-196, 215, 231, 233, 238, 281

Belaya Tserkov, 13, 22-23, 48-49, 85, 108, 124, 131-132, 145, 154-156, 162-163, 165, 170-171, 173, 180, 187-188, 190, 194-196, 215, 231, 233, 238
Belgium, 46, 62-63, 65
Belgorod, 21, 28, 36, 38-39, 47
Belilovka, 142, 146, 149-151, 154, 156
Belka, 53-54, 76, 78, 82-84, 155, 160, 162
Belki, 92
Belogorodka, 245
Belokorovichi, 68
Belopol, 133
Belozerovka, 274
Belyanki, 189
Bendyugovka, 190
Berdichev, 13, 23, 55, 88, 92, 95, 97, 99, 101, 103, 105, 107, 109, 112-113, 116, 118, 121-126, 133, 137-143, 147-148, 150-152, 157-158, 160-162, 164, 167-172, 175, 178, 180, 232, 235, 238-241, 243-244, 247, 250, 252-253, 256-257, 259, 261, 264, 266, 289-290, 294
Berestovka, 218
Berezina, 29
Berezino, 59, 61
Berezovka, 118, 122, 134, 159-161, 166, 215
Berezyanka, 142, 193-194, 198-199, 209
Bila, 192
Biryuki, 186
Black Sea, 33, 43
Blaschniwka, 154
Blazhievka, 154, 164, 167
Bobrik, 115, 121-122, 125
Bobritsa, 86
Bogdanovk, 198
Bogolyubovka, 252
Boguslav, 193, 209, 213, 218, 220
Bol'shaya-Chernyavka, 121, 129, 132, 139
Bol'shoi Chernyatin, 238, 240, 260
Bol'shoi Pravutin, 252
Bolkhov, 59
Bolkun, 206, 208, 210, 220
Bol'shoi Grab, 109
Bolyarka, 62, 82, 86, 115, 123, 164
Bolyarka Farm, 82, 123
Bondarevka, 172, 178
Bondurovka, 220
Borisov, 29
Borisovka, 214-215
Borodani, 210
Borodyanka, 22, 68
Bortniki, 108

Bovsuny, 69
Boyarka, 224
Branoe Pole, 210, 214, 217
Bratslav, 209, 215, 221-222, 225
Brazhenka, 135
Britskoe, 170, 174-175, 187, 192, 237, 245, 247, 257, 269, 271, 282
Brittany, 51, 59
Brodetskoe, 147, 150, 265, 276
Brovki, 24, 107, 109, 113
Brusilov, 13, 22-25, 34-36, 43, 83, 88, 90-93
Bryansk, 28-30, 34-35, 38-39, 66
Buda, 113, 118, 213-214, 216, 219, 223
Budenovka, 202
Budichany, 177
Budilovka, 61, 106, 111
Budki-Ushienskie, 250
Bukhny, 146
Buki, 120, 131, 160, 165, 169
Bukrin, 23, 35, 38-39, 165, 173
Bulai, 174, 189, 197
Buldychev, 249
Bulgaria, 62
Burkovtsy, 270
Burtin, 264, 288
Buryaki, 262, 265, 267, 269-271, 275-276, 287
Buzovka, 207, 217, 219-220, 223, 225
Byshev, 22, 27
Bystreevka, 122
Bystrik, 121, 253, 259, 261

Caucasus, 33-34, 40, 49, 57
Chaikovka, 113, 118, 122
Chekhi, 147
Cheremoshnoe, 174
Cherkasy, 186
Chernigov, 30
Chernin, 193-194
Chernogorodka, 22,
Chernokaly, 264
Chernorudka, 116-117, 120-122, 125, 129, 132, 152, 164
Chernovtsy, 33
Chernyakhov, 46-47, 81, 86, 113, 125, 131, 135-136, 140-141, 143-144, 149-151, 154, 165, 171, 173, 188, 233
Chernyatin, 238, 240, 243, 252-253, 260-261, 267, 269, 274, 286
Chernyavka, 111, 129, 133, 138, 186
Chernyshi, 173, 213, 216
Chervonaya Step, 243

Chervonaya Tribunovka, 253
Chervonoarmeisk, 135
Chervonoe, 103, 105, 107-108, 113-114, 116-117, 121, 124-125, 134, 147, 262
Chervony Stepok, 148
Cheshkaya, 134
China, 35
Chizhovka, 172
Chopovichi, 31, 43, 64, 75-76, 82, 88, 90, 99-100, 104, 112, 115
Chubinskii, 156-157
Chudnov, 152-153, 171, 177-178, 236-237, 239, 241-244, 247, 250, 252, 255, 262-264
Chupira, 193-194
Chuprinovka, 273
Crete, 48
Crimea, 34, 40, 43, 51
Czechoslovakia, 62, 68

Dashev, 221, 223, 228
Dedovichi, 252, 275
Dekhtyarka, 108
Demchin, 259, 262
Demyansk, 37, 39, 55
Denikhovka, 193
Denishi, 160-161, 169, 176
Denmark, 48-49
Derazhnya, 293
Derevishchina, 288
Dertka, 263, 270, 272, 279
Deserovka, 271
Desna, river, 29, 167, 261, 273-274, 291
Detinets, 95, 106
Devochki, 135, 140, 143, 148
Divin, 24, 51, 83
Dmitrievka , 49, 51, 97
Dnestr, river, 293-294
Dobryn, 61, 123
Dolina, 108
Dolinovka, 91
Dolzhok, 166, 174
Don, river, 31, 37-38, 43-44, 46, 48, 52, 60
Donbas, 32-33
Donets, river, 57, 60, 62
Dormanka, 236, 238, 258
Dortmund, 63
Dreniki, 246, 249
Dresden, 59
Drozdy, 130, 138, 156
Dryglov, 248

Dubina, 193
Dubishche, 251, 256
Dubmaslovka, 281
Dubniki, 242
Dubno, 37, 67, 263-291
Dubovchik, 281
Dubovets, 102, 110, 160
Dubovka, 147
Dubrova, 62
Dubrovintsy, 208
Dubrovitsa, 292
Dubrovka, 83, 179, 237, 242, 250, 259, 262, 264, 270, 275, 278, 283, 287
Dudari, 93, 186
Dulitskoe, 131-132
Dunaika, 114, 117, 120
Dunkirk, 59
Dvorets, 158, 164
Dyakovtsy, 271
Dybintsy, 202, 210, 214-215
Dybnizy, 202
Dymer, 31
Dzerzhinsk, 178, 236-241, 244, 246, 249-251

East Prussia, 63-65
Eifel, 63
Ekaterinovka, 232, 235
El'sk, 43
Elevka, 59
Eltigena, 34
Emil'chino, 169-170, 178, 240, 242
Erasimovka, 249
Erchiki, 97, 105, 108, 132, 138

Fasova, 123
Fastov, 13, 22, 35, 49, 95, 109, 111, 116
Fastovets, 109
Fastovka, 165, 185
Felixowka, 218
Ferdinandovka, 220
Filintsy, 275, 283, 287
Florianovka, 174
Fortress Kazatin, 113
Fortunatovka, 61
France, 44, 48-51, 53-55, 58-59, 61-65, 69
Fridrovo, 262, 265, 270, 276
Frontovka, 219-220

Gadyach, 38
Gadzinka, 134, 141, 151

Gaisin, 189, 201, 220-221
Gaivoron, 294
Galievka, 260, 264
Gannovka, 231
Ganovka, 197-198
Garborov, 84, 88
Gardyshevka, 261, 265
Gavrishovka, 281-282
Geisikha, 194
Georgia, 34
Gerasimovka, 246, 253, 261
Germanovka, 47-48, 81, 108-109, 116, 119, 128, 130-131, 138-139, 142, 144, 188, 190, 192, 196-197, 234, 245, 266, 274
Germany, 10, 14, 17, 45-46, 51-56, 61, 63-65, 67
Glatz, 69
Glezno, 279
Glincha, 173
Glinitsa, 113, 121
Glubochek, 236, 238, 242, 249, 256, 258-259
Glubochok, 236
Glukhov, 31
Glukhova, 69
Glukhovtsy, 125, 133-134, 136, 138, 140, 142, 146-147, 150, 168, 175
Glybochka, 173, 231, 233, 238
Gnidovka, 75
Gnilets, 91, 93, 97
Gnilopyat', river , 169, 172, 176, 235, 238, 240, 242, 244, 247, 265
Gnivan, 221, 289
Godykha, 161, 179-180
Golendry, 240, 246, 269
Golod'ki, 190, 259, 262
Golovenka, 176
Golubevka, 147
Golubovskii, 25-26
Golubyatin, 120
Gomel, 39
Gonoratka, 192, 207, 214, 217, 220
Gordeevka, 252, 255, 259, 265
Gordievka, 214-215
Gordyshevka, 115
Gorlovka, 281
Gorny Tikich, river, 191, 207, 210, 214, 217, 219-220, 223-225, 227
Gorodetskoe, 106, 110
Gorodezkaja, 102
Gorodishche, 107, 109, 122, 176-177, 181, 189, 244, 248, 255

Gorodkovka, 116
Gorodnitsa, 240, 242
Gorodnyavka, 258
Gorodsk, 102, 105, 118
Gorodskoe, 95, 97-98, 102
Gorokhovatka, 200, 204-205
Goropai, 262, 265
Goroshkov, 208
Goryn', river, 272, 291-294
Gostomel, 22
Grabovka, 110
Graby, 62, 130
Grebenki, 43, 49-50, 130, 138
Greece, 62-63
Grinovtsy, 287
Grishkovtsy, 169, 240
Gritsev, 245, 281
Grozino, 67, 87-88, 115
Grushev, 114
Gruska, 176
Gruzkoe, 27
Gubin, 291
Guiva, 107, 115, 134, 138-140, 142-143, 147-148
Gulevtsy, 167
Gulyanka, 165, 169
Gumenniki, 113, 125
Gumennoe, 208, 218, 221, 223, 245, 268, 277-278, 280-282, 290
Gusachevka, 128
Gushchintsy, 160, 167
Gusyatin, 293
Guta Potievka, 61
Guta Dobrynskaya, 87, 103, 113, 123
Guta Zabelotskaya, 84
Gvozdava, 176
Gzhatsk, 39, 66

Ignatpol, 67
Ilyntsy, 207-209, 214-217, 220-221, 223, 266
Ioganovka, 123
Iosipovka, 147
Irpen', river, 27, 35, 38, 76, 97
Irsha, river, 13, 43, 75-76, 82, 88
Isaiki, 204, 216
Italy, 59-60, 62-63
Ivankov, 134, 143, 147
Ivankovtsy, 157
Ivanopol, 153, 179, 244, 251-252, 254, 256, 260-265, 270-271, 275, 278, 280, 283, 286-287, 289
Ivanov, 271

INDEX

Ivanovichi, 135
Ivanovka, 121-122, 218, 284, 286, 289
Ivnitsa, 105, 110, 124, 129
Iwanowka, 131
Izyaslav, 294
Izyum, 61

Januschpil, 244

Kadomka, 216
Kagarlyk, 85, 96, 108, 165, 197, 200, 202, 205, 210, 213, 216, 224
Kalinovka, 151, 153, 158, 160, 171, 180, 234, 245, 267-268, 271, 274
Kalyus, 293-294
Kamen', 249-250, 256
Kamenets-Podol'skii, 293-294
Kamenka, 49, 93-94, 97, 105, 107-109, 111, 113-114, 116, 124, 134, 137, 161, 263-265, 281
Kanada, 101, 119
Kanev, 22, 39, 43, 46, 165, 212
Kantelina, 220
Kapustin, 271
Karabachin, 93
Karabchiev, 133
Karapyshi, 200, 209
Karvinovka, 177, 236, 239, 241
Kashperovka, 107, 125, 129, 133, 173, 180, 185, 237
Kasimirowka, 205
Kastornoe, 31, 47
Kazak, 263
Kazatin, 23, 27, 92, 99, 101, 107, 109, 112-113, 116, 119-121, 124-126, 129, 132-134, 136-138, 140-142, 145-146, 149-152, 154, 156-158, 160-161, 163-164, 167-170, 174, 178, 180, 237, 239-240, 294
Festung Kazatin, 113
Kazimirovka, 207
Kerch, 34
Khalaim-Gorodok, 116, 120-121, 125, 129
Kharitonovka, 117
Khar'kov, 28, 30-33, 35-39, 44, 47, 49, 51, 61-62
Khazhin, 157, 172, 175, 235, 239, 253, 260-261
Khmel'nik, 152-153, 263, 271, 292-293
Khmel'nitskii, 171
Khmelevka, 207
Khodorkov, 25, 27, 85, 92, 97, 100, 103-104, 125
Khodorov, 173, 186, 190, 202, 232
Khodory, 106, 110
Kholyavintsy, 281
Khomora, 279-280

Khomutets, 83
Khorosha, 215
Khorovets, 264
Khotin, 293
Khotinovka, 66, 82, 87-88, 99, 123, 126, 130
Khristinovka, 22, 203, 267
Khutor, 117, 198, 239, 258-259
Khutor Lutsianovka, 239
Khutora, 113, 208, 225, 227
Kichkiry, 105, 110
Kiev, i, 13, 21-24, 28-40, 47, 49, 51-54, 57-58, 60-65, 68-69, 99, 102, 104, 145, 180
Kikhti, 248
Kikishevka, 269, 276
Kirovka, 269, 290
Kirovograd, 43, 51, 62-63, 101, 126, 166, 195, 197, 200, 203, 208
Kislovka, 213-215
Kiyanka, 238
Kletishche, 140-141, 149
Klimental, 256
Klin, 61
Klitenka, 276, 286
Klyuki, 207
Kmitov, 126, 143
Knyazh'ya Krinitsa, 191, 217, 219, 220, 225
Knyazhiki, 225
Knyazhin, 239, 241, 246-247, 255
Kobyl, 281
Kobylya, 240, 250
Kocherov, 84-86, 88-90, 92-93, 95, 97
Kodnya, 140-141, 147-148, 158, 168
Kolkhoz Gorodskoe, 98
Kolkhoz Kollektivnoe, 11
Kolkhoz Lenino, 102
Kolkhoz Zubovshchina, 99
Kolpny, 30
Kolybabintsy, 271
Komarov, 217, 223, 226, 278, 284, 289
Kommunarovka, 167
Komnesamovka, 164
Komsomol'skoe, 150, 152, 164, 168, 175, 232, 235, 240, 246, 253, 261
Komsomolskaya, 131
Konel'skie, 225, 227
Konela, 225
Konelski, 225
Konotop, 31-32, 38
Konstantinovka, 174-175, 234, 245, 252, 267, 269, 274, 282

Konyushevka, 245, 274, 282
Kopys, 29
Korchevka, 177, 239, 246, 249
Korchik, 240, 242, 250, 258
Kordyshevka, 156, 167
Korenevo, 36
Korets, 68, 240, 245-246, 249-252, 256, 258, 264, 288
Kornin, 23-25, 43, 93, 97, 99-100, 104
Korochenki, 243, 248, 251, 255
Korolevka, 93, 97, 106, 146, 167
Korosten, 13, 22-23, 29, 31, 37, 43, 64-66, 68, 75, 85, 90-91, 103-104, 111-113, 115, 118, 130, 136-138, 140, 143-144, 149, 160-162, 165, 179, 272
Korostki, 270
Korostyshev, 88-89, 91-92, 94-95, 98, 102-107, 110, 112-113, 115, 117-118, 121, 124-125, 135, 237
Korovintsy, 247, 252, 254-257, 259-260, 262, 264-265
Korsun, 13-14, 295
Korytnya, 223, 225, 227
Korzhevka, 233
Kosari, 241
Kosharishcha, 115, 117
Koshevataya, 204
Koshevatoye, 200, 209-210, 214
Koshlany, 208, 214-215, 220
Koshlyaki, 94, 96, 104, 108, 125
Kosinowka, 87
Kotelyanka, 156, 279
Kotlyarka, 93, 97
Kotyuzhintsy, 234, 239
Kovalevka, 116
Kovel, 272, 293
Kozhanka, 114, 117, 194, 199
Kozhushki, 256
Kozievka, 115, 118
Krakovshchina, 83
Krapivna, 215, 286
Krasilovka, 252
Krasnen'koe, 215, 223, 225, 227
Krasnoborka, 57, 82, 94, 106
Krasnodar, 33
Krasnoe, 274
Krasnogorodka, 219, 224
Krasnolesy, 132
Krasnopol, 160
Krasnopolka, 218, 224, 226
Krasnoselka, 57-58, 270
Krasny Stepok, 148
Krasnyanka, 128
Krasovka, 117

Kremenets, 293-294
Kreta, 48
Krinitsa, 191, 217, 219, 225
Krivchunka, 189, 198
Krivoe, 24, 27, 93
Krivoi Rog, 221
Krivosheintsy, 142, 145
Kruchenets, 135
Kruglik, 189
Krutye Gorby, 216, 219, 223-224
Krylovka, 116, 128, 134, 138
Ksaverovka, 109
Kuban, 33, 49, 57, 76
Kuliki, 178, 242
Kumanevka, 167, 175, 232
Kupchintsy, 228
Kupishche, 143,160
Kurchitsa, 238, 242
Kurnoe, 160, 163, 179, 237
Kursk, 28, 30-31, 34-39, 45, 47, 49, 51, 53-54, 57-59, 61-63, 65, 317
Kustovtsy, 152
Kutki, 264
Kutyshche, 270, 275, 283, 287, 289
Kvitnevoe, 92

Ladoga, Lake, 40
Lazarevka, 83
Lebedintsy, 107, 109, 113
Leningrad, 43, 63, 65
Lenino, 102-103, 105, 110
Leonardovka, 147, 164, 167, 240, 253, 274, 290
Leonovka, 131, 202
Leshchin, 134, 137, 139, 147
Leshchinka, 224
Leshchinovka, 226
Leshchintsy, 156
Lesovaya Slobodka, 262, 264
Lesovichi, 193-194, 198
Lesovka, 115
Lesovshchina, 143
Letichev, 245, 265
Levkov, 115, 117, 122, 125, 134, 139, 141, 143
Levkovka, 273
Lipki, 92
Liplyany, 82, 86-87
Lipno, 270-271, 279
Lipovets, 22, 166, 197-199, 208, 212, 214, 228, 266, 278, 290
Lipovy Rog, 205, 213, 216, 218, 231

Litin, 268
Litvinovka, 193
Livny, 30
Lopatin, 175, 234, 274
Losovatka, 200, 203
Losyatin, 156, 180, 188, 231, 238
Lovat, river, 39
Lozovataya, 217, 269, 281-282, 284
Lozovaya, 32
Lozovka, 245, 274, 291
Luchin, 51, 88-89
Ludvikovka, 178
Luginy, 69
Luk'yanovka, 202, 206, 208, 214, 223
Luka, 193, 196, 210, 213-216, 277, 281, 292-293
Luka Barskaya, 292-293
Lukashovka, 207-208
Lutai, 239, 248
Lutovka, 57, 98
Lutsk, 37, 293-294
Luxembourg, 63
L'vov, 112, 244
Lysaya Gora, 215, 225
Lyski, 110
Lysovka, 97
Lyubar, 22, 179, 267, 270, 272, 275, 279-280, 287, 289, 292
Lyulintsy, 187, 190, 192
Lyutari, 202, 210
Lyutezh, 13, 28, 35, 57

Maikop, 33
Makarovka, 81
Makarovskii, 131, 144, 155
Makeevka, 142, 171, 231
Makharintsy, 142, 146
Malaya Berezyanka, 193-194
Malaya Chernyavka, 129, 138
Malaya Gorbasha, 140, 143, 149, 283
Malaya Klitenka, 276, 286
Malaya Kozara, 244, 249
Malaya Racha, 57, 94, 106, 110
Malaya Skvirka, 156, 162
Malaya Tartarovka, 253-254, 260
Malaya Volitsa, 260
Maliye Bratalov, 287
Malin, 13, 22, 24, 29, 31, 43, 58, 61, 64, 68, 75, 102, 104
Malinki, 174
Maliye Erchiki, 105

Maliye Krushlintsy, 284
Maloarkhangel'sk, 30
Malopolovetskoe, 118, 120, 128, 132
Maly Chernyatin, 252-253, 261, 267, 269, 286
Maly Korovintsy, 257
Maly Lisovtsy, 131-132
Maly Moshkovtsy, 133
Malye Khutora, 208
Malye Korovintsy, 252, 255
Malyi Karashin, 83
Malyi Moshkovtsy, 121
Mar'yanovka, 82, 84, 109, 120, 161
Mariika, 193-194
Marinin, 288
Mariupol', 62
Markovka, 242
Markovtsy , 234-235, 239, 262, 267, 269, 274, 276, 282, 286
Martynovka, 143, 269
Mashina, 110
Maslovka, 205, 212
Maslovo, 29
Massel'sk, 40
Mateikovo, 292
Matyushi, 156
Medovka, 199
Medvedikha, 252
Medvedovo, 242
Medvezh'egorsk, 40
Medvin, 204, 209, 219-220, 224, 227
Meleni, 62, 68, 86-88, 111, 115, 118
Melitopol', 33, 57
Mervin, 193, 198
Mestechko, 52
Metz, 51
Mika, river, 105
Mikhailenki, 247, 251, 254-255, 262
Mikhailin, 167, 174-175, 232
Mikhailovka, 111, 130, 142, 270, 287
Mineiki, 122
Minsk, 29
Mircha, 58, 106
Mironovka, 205, 209, 212, 216, 218, 220
Miropol', 171, 179, 239, 249-250, 256, 258-259, 263-264, 279-280
Miroslavka, 262
Mirovka, 196, 200, 205
Misyurovka, 271
Mitaevka, 224
Mius, river, 33, 57, 62,

Mlinishche, 143, 148
Mogilev, 37
Mogilev-Podol'skii, 293-294
Mogilno, 143
Moiseevka, 120
Mokhnachka, , 24, 51, 92-93, 97
Monastyrishche, 186, 189, 197
Monchin, 170
Morosovka, 102
Morozovka, 83, 88, 90, 97, 204, 207, 263
Moscow, 21-23, 27-30, 32, 34, 37, 40, 61, 63-64, 66, 292-295
Mosel, river, 63
Mostovoe, 101
Motovilovka, 245
Motrunki, 279
Motyzhin, 27
Mukharev, 249
Murafa, 292-293

Napadovka, 175, 194, 197
Nartsizovka, 257
Nastashka, 198-199
Negrebovka, 23, 32, 34, 53-54
Nemirintsy, 156, 167, 175
Nemirov, 221, 277
Nemirovka, 67, 87
Nenadikha, 193
Nepedovka, 152
Netherlands, 47, 54, 59, 62, 65
Nezhin, 31
Nikolayev, 221
Nizhnaya Krapivna, 215
Normandy, 317
Norway, 51
Nosovka, 287
Nosovtsy, 225
Novaki, 103, 106, 111, 130
Novaya Chertoriya, 270
Novaya Dashev, 221
Novaya Greblya, 175, 234, 238, 245, 261, 269, 274, 282, 290-291
Novaya Kotel'nya, 143, 147
Novaya Yurovka, 110, 113, 115, 118
Novi Zavod, 151
Novo-Yanovka, 186
Novograd-Volynskii, 22, 67-68, 87, 114, 126, 136, 140, 143, 150, 163-165, 169-170, 172, 177-179, 181, 236-238, 242, 245, 249-252, 256, 258, 264, 271-272, 292

Novolabun', 281
Novomirgorod, 191
Novo-Petrovtsy, 36
Novopol', 125
Novorossiisk, 33-34
Novoselitsa, 101, 108-109, 117, 120, 279, 281
Novoselka, 223
Novosil', 34
Novoukrainka, 126, 203
Novozhivotov, 189
Novy Miropol', 263
Novy Solotvin, 158
Novy Zavod, 161, 179-181, 251
Novyi Bykhov, 29

Obodnoe, 217-218
Oboyan, 26
Ocheretnya, 166, 187, 192, 194, 198-199
Ochitkov, 187, 190, 192, 198
Odessa, 31, 36
Ohrdruf, 52
Okhmatov, 199, 207, 211
Okhotovka, 165, 169
Ol'shanitsa, 190, 193, 202, 218
Ol'shanka, 164, 187, 190, 194, 233, 238, 259, 282
Ol'shanskaya Novoselitsa, 109
Oleinikova, 187, 233
Oleinikova Sloboda, 187
Olevsk, 22, 68
Olyanitsa, 293
Ometintsy, 220, 223, 225
Onega, Lake, 40
Oratov, 166, 189-191, 193-194, 198-199, 203, 207-208, 214, 290
Oratovka, 193, 215
Ordyntsy, 170
Orel, 30, 34, 39, 59
Orepy, 236-238, 249, 256, 259
Orsha, 29
Osichna, 286
Osichnaya, 198
Osovtsy, 83, 88, 90, 93, 97
Ostraya-Mogila, 188
Ostriiki, 186
Ostrog, 293
Ostrogozhsk, 38
Ostrozhany, 223
Osykovo, 235
Ovechache, 245, 261, 274
Ovruch, 115

Ovsyaniki, 175, 274, 291
Ozadovka, 262, 268
Ozera, 24, 92
Ozeryanka, 176
Ozhekhovskii, 293

Palenichentsy, 116
Panasovka, 139-140
Paplintsy, 142, 147
Parievka, 271
Parievka, 187, 193-194, 197
Paripsy, 93, 105, 107-109, 113
Paris, 66
Pavlovka, 156, 171, 236, 271, 291
Pavoloch', 93, 95, 101-102, 113-114, 116-117, 120, 122, 124-125, 128, 131-132, 142
Pechanovka, 249-250, 259
Pechera, 221-222, 225
Pechivody, 264
Pedosy, 174
Peloponnese, 63
Penkovatoe, 83
Peremoga, 158, 167, 169, 172, 175, 234, 239, 246, 252-253, 276, 286, 290
Peremozh'e, 122
Peremyshel, 259
Pereselenie, 205, 210
Perlyavka, 168, 176
Pershotravensk, 242
Peschanka, 155, 159
Peski, 125, 138, 140, 143, 148
Peskovka, 22
Pesochin, 217
Petrikovtsy, 286-287
Petrovka, 245, 253, 261, 273, 282
Pevtsy, 209, 218, 222
Pii, 216, 222
Pikov, 258
Pikovets, 157, 163, 167, 239
Pilipcha, 163
Pilipo-Koshara, 249
Pilipovichi, 118, 122, 250
Pilipovka, 236, 238, 246
Pinchuki, 109
Pirozhki, 102
Piryatin, 187
Pisarevka, 175, 218, 224, 278
Pishchev, 252, 256, 263, 275
Pivni, 94, 96, 101, 108
Pleshchevka, 111

Plesnya, 279
Pliskov, 166, 172, 174, 189, 199, 231, 234, 237
Plyakhovaya, 142, 152, 157
Poberezhka, 204, 224
Pobodnaya, 226
Poboika, 198
Poboinaya, 198, 207, 220
Pochta Rudnya, 143
Pochuiki, 96, 101, 105, 107-108, 114
Podluby, 242
Podvysokoe, 227
Pogrebishche, 146, 166, 170, 172, 174, 180, 237, 265-266, 274, 290
Pokostovka, 177
Poland, 32, 34-35, 40, 47-48, 50, 56, 62-64, 66, 69
Polchino, 263
Polesskoe, 143
Polevaya Lysievka, 239, 281, 291
Polichintsy, 269, 271, 276
Pologi, 130, 138, 156
Polonnoe, 179, 236, 238-239, 242, 258-259, 264, 267, 270, 272, 279-280, 283, 288
Polovetskoe, 141, 176, 240
Poltava, 28-29
Poninka, 242, 264
Popel'nya, 85, 94-95, 100-101, 107, 109, 111, 113, 117, 124
Popovka, 217
Potash, 226
Potashnya, 84
Potievka, 61, 113, 122, 129, 188, 190, 193-194
Potoki, 214, 221
Pravutin, 252
Priluka, 234, 273
Priluki, 36
Pripyat', river, 30, 43, 272
Pristantsionnoe, 64
Privitov, 265
Privorot'e, 92
Prokhorovka, 36, 317
Promin, 249
Proskurov, 171, 179, 263, 293
Prushinka, 156, 167
Prussy, 219
Prut', river, 33
Pryazhev, 141
Psel, river, 36
Pshenichniki, 104, 108
Pugachevka, 196
Pulin, 135

Pulinka, 149
Pustovarovka, 156
Pustovity, 202
Puzyr'ki, 140, 142, 147
Pyatigori, 193
Pyatka, 240, 244, 248, 251

Rachki, 247, 254, 257, 260-261, 264
Radomyshl', 13, 22-23, 31-32, 43, 54, 57, 76, 84, 89-90, 95, 98, 102-103, 106, 110
Radulin, 271
Radyanskoe, 261
Radzivilovka, 132
Raigorodok, 269, 276
Raiki, 243-244, 252-253
Rakitno, 166
Rakitnoe, 196, 200, 206, 208, 227
Rakovichi, 53, 82, 84, 90
Ranok, 82
Raskopanoe, 166, 174
Raskopantsy, 167, 210
Rastava, 250
Rastavitsa, 121
Rastavitsy, 146
Ratsi, 241
Razino, 255, 265
Razumnitsa, 194
Rechki, 263
Reya, 235
Rhine, river, 59, 63
Rivne, 17
Rogachev, 39
Rogachov, 22
Rogi, 226
Rogozna, 128
Romania, 62
Romanovka, 96, 236, 246, 249-250, 252, 255, 267, 284
Romanowka, 256
Romashki, 108, 119, 155
Romny, 36
Ros', river, 210
Rosa, 209
Rososha, 207-208, 247
Rossava, 165, 209
Rossavka, 213, 222
Rossiya, 40
Rossokhovata, 225, 227
Rossosh, 28, 37-38
Rostavitsa, river, 92-93, 100, 105, 114, 116, 117, 119-120, 125, 128, 130-132, 139, 142

Rostov, 33
Rostovka, 189-191, 193-195, 199
Rovno, 17, 177, 211, 258, 266, 272, 293-294
Rowne, 17
Rozhdestkvenskoe, 30
Rozhki, 190, 194
Ruda, 130, 132, 138-139, 142, 144-145
Rudnya, 84, 90, 92-93, 143, 176-177, 181, 244
Rudnya Gorodishche, 176-177, 181, 244
Rumania, 49, 56
Ruzhin, 120, 125, 128-129, 132, 142, 145-146, 166
Ryl'sk, 31, 36, 58
Ryshavka, 144, 149, 155
Rzhev, 54, 61, 63-64
Rzhishchev, 38, 43, 46, 165

Sabadash, 219
Sabarovka, 193, 203, 210
Sadki, 140, 236, 238
Sakhny, 156
Salikha, 200
Sal'nik, 274
Samgorodok, 167, 172, 174, 234, 274
Santarka, 155
Sarny, 189, 272, 289, 292, 294
Satonskoe, 213
Savarka, 202
Savertsy, 92, 125
Schastlivaya, 221, 284
Sech, river, 219
Sedan, 60
Seim, river, 31
Selishche, 205, 286
Semakovka, 169
Semenki, 221-222, 225
Semenovka, 141, 147, 157, 164, 235
Serbinovka, 177, 241, 246, 248, 252, 255
Serednya, 259
Seredy, 242
Sestrenovka, 142, 146
Severinovka, 190
Shadovka, 224
Sharnopol', 220, 225
Shatrishche, 106
Shchegleevka, 102
Shcherbaki, 165
Shchuchinka, 104, 116, 165
Shenderovka, 273

Shepetovka, 159, 171, 179, 191, 211, 242, 245, 249-250, 258, 263, 265-266, 268, 271-272, 277-280, 292, 294
Shershni, 61-62, 82, 88, 123
Shevchenkovka, 97
Shidowzy, 92
Shirokaya Greblya,, 174, 232
Shkarovka, 194, 233
Shpichintsy, 121
Shulyaki, 199, 207, 210, 214-215
Shumsk, 168
Shushchinka, 91
Shvaikovka, 172, 244
Sibok, 209, 217
Singaevka, 140, 143, 147
Singai, 75, 87, 136
Singuri, 164
Siryaki, 177, 241, 246, 248, 255
Sitkovtsy, 225
Sitna, 146
Sitnivtsy, 189, 192
Skala, 190, 293
Skala-Podol'skaya, 293
Skibino, 189, 198
Skitka, 203
Skochishche, 93
Skomorokhi, 143, 155
Skorodnoe, 30
Skraglevka, 244, 247, 253, 261, 264
Skvira, 85, 105, 108, 119, 124, 132, 139, 141-142, 145, 151, 156, 161
Slavnaya, 203
Slavuta, 259
Sloboda, 129, 134, 187, 209-210, 216
Sloboda Selets, 129, 134
Slobodishche, 246
Slobodka, 75, 262, 264
Sluch', river, 22, 179, 236-238, 240, 242, 245, 249-250, 253, 256, 263, 266-267, 270, 272, 279-280, 287-289, 292
Smela, 287
Smokovka, 134
Smoldyrev, 249
Smolensk, 29, 317
Smolovka, 115
Sob, river, 22, 207-210, 214-215, 220-222, 228, 290
Sobolev, 84
Sobolevka, 93, 99, 123, 126
Sofiyevka, 219-220, 224
Sokirintsy, 226, 284

Sokol'cha, 107
Sokolets, 146, 154, 156, 167
Sokolov, 170, 179
Sokolovka, 286
Solotvin, 158, 164, 168
Soloveevka, 24-25, 83, 88, 90, 97, 104
Soloviyevka, 284
Solovy, 67, 69
Sopin, 170, 175
Soroki, 293-294
Sorokotyagi, 233
Sosnovka, 154, 161, 240
Sosonka, 274
Southern Bug, river, 21, 209, 271, 286, 288-289, 294
Soviet Union, 10-12, 44-50, 52-57, 60-65, 69-70
Sovkhoz Dorotka, 193
Sovkhoz Sofievka, 117, 120
Sovkhoz Sovetskoe, 12
Sozh, river, 29
Spas-Demensk, 66
Spichintsy, 172, 174, 271
St Petersburg, 37
Staiki, 38, 91, 155, 187-188
Stalingrad, 28, 30-33, 35, 37, 43-46, 49, 52-54, 57-58, 61, 67
Stanilovka, 274
Stanishovka, 134, 155, 159, 199, 206
Staraya Buda, 113, 118
Staraya Kotel'nya, 113
Staraya Priluka, 273
Staraya Russa, 39
Stariki, 103
Staritsa, 111
Staritskoe, 52
Starokonstantinov, 250-251, 271, 293
Starosel'ye, 102, 107, 109, 113, 115-117, 129, 134, 137, 143
Stary Maidan, 160-162, 179
Stary Solotvin, 158
Stary Oskol, 38
Stavatskaya Sloboda, 93
Stavishche, 23, 53, 76, 78, 83, 108, 114, 159, 186, 188, 190, 194, 215, 237, 267
Stavy, 128, 197, 200, 204-205, 213, 216, 218
Stepanovka, 48-49, 162, 218, 220-221, 242, 278, 290
Stepok, 98, 110, 148, 206, 210, 213, 216
Stetkovtsy, 272, 287
Stolbov, 239, 242, 246, 248-249, 252, 255, 263-264
Storozhev, 240, 250
Strakholes'e, 31

Stremigorod, 64
Strizhakov, 198
Strizhevka, 117, 121
Strokov, 114, 117-120
Struga, 293
Studanets, 205
Studenitsa, 126, 135, 139, 148
Stupki, 223
Stupnik, 286
Styr', river, 294
Sudost', river, 29
Sumy, 28, 36, 48, 57
Sushchanka, 23, 35, 81
Sutiski, 289
Suvari, 114, 120
Suyemtsy, 259
Sverdlovka, 166, 284-285
Svinnaya, 271
Svinobychi, 242
Svir, river, 40
Svyatoshino, 22
Sychevka, 38

Taborov, 92
Taiki, 240
Tal'noe, 226
Taman, 34
Tarashcha, 162, 193-196, 198-200, 202, 205-206, 208, 214-215, 223-224
Tarasovka, 198
Tartak, 176-177
Tartarinovka, 176
Telepen'ki, 221
Teleshovka, 196, 202, 213, 215-216, 219
Terekhovo, 269
Ternovka, 218, 224
Teterev, river,13, 22, 32, 43, 54, 57, 76, 78, 84, 89-91, 94-95, 98, 102, 112, 115, 117, 121, 124, 129, 134, 138, 160, 169, 176, 236, 238, 241-245, 248, 250-251, 259, 263, 266
Teterevka,
Tiflis, 34
Tikhi Khutor, 198
Tim, 29. 36, 38
Tinovka, 215
Tiranovka, 270, 272
Titusovka, 156
Tokarev, 263-264
Tomilovka, 195
Tonezh, 22

Toporishche, 135
Transcaucasia, 34
Travnevoe, 121
Trikoptsa, 115
Trilesy, 43, 49, 108, 114, 117-118, 120
Trokovichi, 113, 134, 141, 151
Troshcha, 215, 262, 265, 270, 275, 278, 283, 287, 290
Trostyanets, 284
Troyanov, 125, 161, 168-169, 176-177, 180, 235, 239
Trubeevka, 114, 132, 138
Tsakyanovka, 206
Tsarevka, 110
Tschepowitschi, Bahnhof, 64
Tsetselevka, 262
Tsvizhin, 284, 286
Tsybulev, 185-186, 189, 191, 219-220, 223, 225, 227, 290
Tuapse, 33
Tucha, 267, 276
Tul'chin, 292-293
Tula, 34
Tulin, 134
Tunisia, 45
Turbov, 273, 281
Turbovka, 83, 89-90
Turchinka, 88
Turovets, 117, 129, 134
Turovetskie Khutor, 117
Tynovka, 198
Tyut'ki, 226, 286
Tyutyunniki, 247, 254, 262

Ukraine, ii, 12, 14-15, 21, 31-33, 35-36, 38, 43-45, 48-49, 52, 56, 58, 62, 67, 191, 251, 272, 291
Ul'kha, 249-250
Ul'shka, 83
Ul'yaniki, 173
Ul'yanovka, 149, 160, 169, 176, 203
Uladovka, 286
Ulanov, 244, 266
Ulanova, 215
Ulanovka, 217
Ulashevka, 194
Uman', 163, 185, 190-192, 195-196, 204, 208, 221, 225-228, 267, 292-294
Unava, 95, 97, 101, 105, 107, 121
Ushomir, 143-144
USSR, 21, 23, 27-28
Ustinovka, 102, 106, 111, 154
Uzh, river, 67

INDEX

Vakhmach, 31
Vakhnovka, 166, 199, 244-245, 253, 256-257, 260, 269, 274, 276, 281, 290
Vasilevka, 137, 141, 160, 163
Vasil'evka, 105, 109, 114
Vasilevo, 186
Vasil'kov, 38-39
Vcheraishe, 117, 120-121, 124-125
Vedmedevka, 46, 131, 155, 197, 200, 205, 218, 224
Velikaya Berezyanka, 198-199
Velikaya Gorbasha, 149, 283
Velikaya Kletska, 264, 283
Velikaya Kozara, 241, 249
Velikaya Racha, 106
Velikaya Rostovka, 193
Velikaya Snetinka, 109
Velikaya Step', 175, 232, 234, 269
Velikiye Luki, 65
Velikii Bukrin, 35
Velikaye Bratalov, 262, 265, 287
Velikaye Erchiki, 132, 138
Velikaye Krushlintsy, 276, 278, 281, 285
Velikaye Lesovtsy, 101, 109
Velikaye Moshkovtsy, 117, 121, 125, 147
Velikaye Nizgortsy, 164
Velikaye Pritski, 209
Velikoe, 132
Velizh, 55, 65
Verbka, 279, 287, 294
Verbovka, 199
Verem'e, 144, 155, 173
Veresy, 151, 159, 161
Verlok, 106
Verovka, 169
Vikhlya, 130
Vila, 176-177, 181
Vilen'ka, 97, 102, 104, 110
Vil'kha, 179
Vil'nya, 92-93, 95-97
Vil'shka, 51-51
Vil'sk, 141, 149, 151, 159
Vinnitsa, 13, 22, 126, 133, 150, 152, 158, 160, 165-167, 171, 175, 208-209, 212, 217-218, 221-223, 226-227, 231, 236-238, 243-244, 257-258, 263, 265, 268, 271, 273-274, 276-278, 280-282, 284-286, 289-292
Vinnitskiye Stavy, 128
Vintsentovka, 108, 190, 200, 206, 210, 224
Vishchikusy, 270, 275, 279, 287

Vishenka, 286
Vishnevoe, 121
Vitava, 221, 286
Vitsentovka, 203
Vladimirovka, 194, 203
Vladislavchik, 225, 227
Vodoty, 25, 83
Voitashevka, 92-93, 97
Voitovtsy, 109, 114, 121, 129, 271
Volchinets, 262, 275-276
Volitsa, 49, 94-96, 98, 102-104, 109, 111, 116, 124, 164, 168, 260
Volitsa Station, 49
Volkhov, 65-66
Volochisk, 293
Volodarka, 170, 173, 180, 186, 193, 196
Volokhskie, 142, 146
Volokolamsk, 37
Volovo, 30
Volovodovka, 221
Voronezh, 28-31, 33-39, 47-48, 57-58
Voronovitsa, 221, 223, 226, 277-278, 284
Voronovo, 87
Voroshilovgrad, 33
Voroshilovka, 221, 286, 289
Vorsovka, 59, 98, 111, 115
Voznya, 59
Vrublevka, 246, 249, 255
Vyazovoe, 36
Vygov, 143, 149
Vyselki, 257
Vysokaya Pech', 171-172, 176-177, 181
Vysoko-Cheshskoe, 148
Vysokoe, 52-53, 148, 189

Wilenka, 102
Wilschanka, 240
Wischja, 130
Wuina, 158
Würzburg, 68

Yablonets, 160
Yablonovitsa, 208
Yagodinka, 177
Yakhny, 117, 120, 128
Yakubovka, 217
Yampol', 191
Yanishevka, 186
Yankovka, 186

Yanovka, 82, 84, 93, 95, 109, 120, 149, 160-161, 169, 171, 176-177, 202-203, 205-206, 208, 214, 222-224
Yanushevka, 258
Yanyshevka, 188, 190
Yaropovichi, 109
Yaroslavka, 128, 132
Yarun', 242, 256
Yasenetskoe, 256-257, 260
Yasenki, 199, 203, 207, 256-257, 260, 269, 281
Yasnogorodka, 31
Yastreben'ka, 23, 52, 81-83
Yatski, 81
Yatskovitsa, 191
Yatskovski, 286
Yefremov, 30
Yelenovka, 234
Yelets, 30
Yezerno, 186, 189, 233, 238
Yugoslavia, 53, 62, 69
Yukhni, 209
Yurkovshchina, 264
Yurovka, 110, 113, 115, 118, 270
Yusefovka, 83, 147, 174, 232
Yushki, 46

Zabara, 121
Zabeloch'e, 84
Zabolot', 106
Zabrannoe, 110
Zabrod'e, 61, 87, 103
Zakutintsy, 139, 184
Zalivanshchina, 216, 219
Zaliznya, 253
Zaluzhnoe, 176-177
Zamery, 178
Zamorochen'e, 111
Zaporozh'e, 258, 264
Zarech'e, 49
Zarubintsy, 146
Zarud'e, 107, 109-110, 214-215, 217, 219-220, 27
Zarudintsy, 207
Zastava, 146
Zauryad'e, 22
Zbruch, river, 293
Zdvera, 166
Zdvizh, 83, 111-112
Zdvizhka, 93, 102
Zelen'ki, 224
Zelentsy, 271, 287

Zeleny Rog, 196
Zemlyanka, 218, 223
Zeremlya, 256
Zhabelevka, 277
Zhadany, 220, 223
Zhary, 288
Zhashkov, 190, 192-195, 198-199, 207-208, 220, 223, 225, 227, 237, 266-267
Zhdanovo, 292
Zheleznyaki, 176
Zhelobnoe, 259, 264, 283
Zherebki, 275, 278-279, 287
Zhezhelev, 141, 157, 164, 172, 175, 235, 239, 253, 261
Zhitintsy, 261
Zhitniki, 194
Zhitomir, 13, 23, 36, 40, 54, 61, 63, 78, 83-85, 87-91, 94-102, 107, 109-110, 112-113, 116, 122, 124-126, 129, 133-138, 140-143, 148-152, 155, 158-165, 168-169, 171-172, 177-181, 237, 239, 242-243, 245, 294
Festung Zhitomir, 102
Zhiva, 208
Zhizhdra, 59
Zhizhintsy, 187
Zhlobin, 39
Zhmerinka, 160, 165, 203, 211, 221, 226, 266, 268, 284-285, 289-293
Zhornishche, 214, 220
Zhovtnevoe, 92
Zhukhovskii, 29
Zhulyany, 22
Zhurava, 253, 282
Zhuravlikha, 194
Zhuravlinka, 118
Zhurbintsy, 156-157, 167
Zlobichi, 85, 126, 130
Zolotukha, 142
Zorokov, 134, 140, 149, 159
Zozov, 172, 187, 198-199, 282, 290
Zozovka, 174, 187, 234, 247
Zusha, 39
Zvenigorodka, 163, 195, 211, 224, 227-228
Zwiahel, 136, 170, 179, 236-238
Zybin, 59
Zyubrikha, 225

Index of German Military Units

Army Groups (*Heeresgruppen*):
    Army Group A, 43, 47, 112, 137, 203, 244
    Army Group B, 30, 45, 57-58

INDEX

Army Group C, 48, 67
Army Group Centre, 4, 43, 46-48, 50, 52-56, 59, 64-66, 137, 171, 272, 296
Army Group Don, 43-44, 46, 52
Army Group North, 43, 46, 50, 53, 55, 63, 65-66, 191, 258, 264
Army Group South, 4, 14, 29, 32, 43, 46-49, 51, 56, 58-59, 62, 65-66, 69, 74, 85, 91-93, 99, 101-103, 112, 126, 133, 136-137, 141, 150-151, 159, 161-163, 165, 171, 178, 181, 185, 191, 195, 199-200, 203-204, 208, 211, 216, 218, 221, 225-227, 238, 240, 243, 245, 247-248, 258, 266-267, 272, 278, 284, 288-291, 296

Armies:
   1.Panzerarmee, iii, 4, 9, 14, 43, 52, 57, 72-74, 112, 126, 161, 183, 185-197, 199-205, 207-209, 211-213, 215-222, 224-228, 238, 245, 247, 257, 265-268, 273, 278, 289, 296
   2.Armee, 57-58, 272
   2.Panzerarmee, 54, 56, 59, 66
   3.Panzerarmee, 55, 65
   4.Armee, 50-51
   4.Panzerarmee, iii, 4, 9, 13-17, 29-31, 35-36, 40-41, 43-46, 48-49, 51-59, 61, 63-67, 69-78, 81, 84-96, 99-107, 111-114, 116-118, 120, 122-126, 128-140, 142-143, 145-146, 149-153, 154-155, 157-163, 165-173, 175-181, 185, 187, 191, 195-196, 201, 204, 211-212, 217, 221-222, 225-229, 231, 236-243, 245-248, 250-274, 276, 278-282, 284-292, 296
   6.Armee, 47, 50-51, 56-57, 59, 65, 204, 221
   8.Armee, 43-44, 49, 51, 54-55, 61, 74, 187, 191, 195, 200, 203, 208, 211, 227-228
   11.Armee, 11, 43, 51
   15.Armee, 54, 59, 67
   16.Armee, 55
   17.Armee, 56-57
   18.Armee, 59, 65

Corps:
   Korps-Abteilung A, 46
   Korps-Abteilung B, 45-46, 73, 86, 91, 104, 108, 114, 131, 138, 144, 155, 165, 173, 185-186, 192, 196, 202, 205, 209, 212-213, 216, 218, 222, 224, 232
   Korps-Abteilung C, 46, 66-67, 69, 71, 72, 82, 87, 98-99, 103, 106, 111, 115, 118, 123, 130,

136, 240, 242, 250, 253, 256, 263-264, 275, 279, 283, 288
I.Armeekorps, 57
I.Flak-Korps, 185, 188, 197
II.SS Panzerkorps, 55
III.Panzerkorps, 7-8, 185-186, 189-199, 204, 206-207, 209-217, 219, 221-223, 225, 227, 267
IV.SS Panzerkorps, 54
IV.Fliegerkorps, 41
VII.Armeekorps, 5-8, 48-51, 55, 57-59, 81, 85-86, 91, 93-97, 101, 104, 108, 111, 113-114, 116, 118-120, 123-125, 128, 130-132, 137-139, 141-142, 144-145, 147, 149, 151-152, 154-156, 161-163, 165-166, 170-174, 180-181, 185-197, 199-200, 202, 204-206, 208-213, 215-216, 218-224, 227, 231, 233, 237-238, 266-267
VIII.Fliegerkorps, 41, 237, 259, 291
X.Armeekorps, 49
XI.Armeekorps, 44
XII.Armeekorps, 49
XIII.Armeekorps, 5-7, 56-60, 66, 76, 82, 84-86, 88, 90-91, 93-95, 98-99, 101-106, 110, 112-113, 115-116, 118, 122-125, 129, 134-139, 141, 143, 148-154, 159-164, 168-169, 171-172, 176-178, 180-181, 232, 235-239, 241-248, 250-252, 254, 256-257, 259-260, 266, 271, 289-291
XIV.Panzerkorps, 60
XIX.Armeekorps, 45
XIX.Panzerkorps, 63
XXIV.Panzerkorps, 5-8, 45-48, 81, 85-86, 91, 93, 96, 101, 103-104, 107, 113-114, 116, 119, 123, 125, 128, 131, 137-138, 142, 144, 149, 151-152, 154-155, 162-163, 165-167, 170, 172, 174-175, 180, 204, 231-232, 234, 236-238, 240-247, 250-253, 257, 259-260, 262, 265, 267, 269-270, 272, 274-278, 280, 282-283, 285, 288, 290-291, 295
XXV.Armeekorps, 56
XXXVII.Armeekorps, 56
XXXVIII.Armeekorps, 67
XXXX.Panzerkorps, 60
XXXXII.Armeekorps, 5-8, 50-53, 55-56, 69, 76, 81, 83-86, 88-97, 100-103, 105, 107-109, 113-114, 116-117, 120, 124-125, 128, 132-134, 138-140, 142, 145-146, 149-152, 154, 156-158, 161-162, 164, 166-171, 173, 181, 185-186, 188, 190-193, 195-197, 199-200, 202, 204-206, 208-209, 211-213, 216, 218-222, 224, 231-232, 237-238

XXXXII.Armeekorps, 50
XXXXVI. Panzerkorps, 8, 161, 171, 211, 228, 244-245, 250-251, 256, 258, 260, 263, 265, 267-269, 272-275, 277-278, 281-286, 290-291
XXXXVII. Panzerkorps, 44
XXXXVIII.Panzerkorps, 5-8, 13, 24, 31, 55, 60-62, 64, 66, 68, 75-76, 82, 85-92, 94-97, 99-100, 102-105, 107, 109, 113-118, 121-123, 125, 129, 133-135, 137-142, 147, 150-152, 154, 157-158, 161-162, 164, 168-172, 175-178, 180-181, 232, 235-236, 238-241, 243-246, 248, 251-252, 255-265, 267, 270, 272, 275, 278-280, 283, 286-289, 291
LVIII.Reserve-Panzerkorps, 64
LIX.Armeekorps, 5-8, 64-66, 69, 75-76, 82, 87-88, 91-92, 94, 98-99, 101-104, 106, 111-113, 115, 118, 123-124, 126, 130, 136-138, 140, 143, 149, 155, 160-163, 165, 169-170, 172, 177-179, 181, 232, 237-238, 240, 242, 245-246, 250-252, 256, 258-260, 263-265, 267-268, 271-272, 275, 279-281, 283, 288, 291
LXII.Reservekorps, 67
LXXXVII.Armeekorps, 59

Divisions:
Infanterie-Division (mot.) Grossdeutschland, 56
Panzergrenadier-Division 'Grossdeutschland', 188, 191, 195, 200, 203, 208, 212
1.Infanterie-Division, 72, 244, 250, 258-259, 263-265, 268, 274, 277, 281, 284-285
1.leichte Division, 53, 64
1.Panzer-Division, 60, 62-64, 68, 71-72, 77, 82, 85-88, 90, 92, 94-96, 98-99, 102-107, 109-110, 113, 115, 117, 120-122, 125-126, 129, 133-134, 136-140, 142, 146-147, 150, 154, 157-158, 161, 164, 167-168, 170, 172, 175-176, 232, 235-236, 239-241, 243-244, 246-247, 251-254, 257, 259-262, 265, 267, 269-270, 275-276, 278, 282-283, 286-287
1.Ski-Division, 53
1.SS Panzer-Division 'LSSAH', 62-63, 68, 71-72, 77, 82, 85-88, 90, 92, 94-95, 98-99, 102, 107, 109, 113, 115-117, 121, 125, 129, 133-134, 137, 139-141, 143, 147-148, 150, 154, 157, 164, 168, 170-172, 176, 232, 235-236, 239-241, 243-244, 246-248, 251-252, 254, 257, 259-262, 265, 267, 269-270, 275, 275, 278-279, 283, 287
2.Fallschirmjäger-Division, 71
2.leichte Division, 61

2.Panzer-Division, 53-54, 60, 71
2.SS Panzer-Division 'Das Reich', 22-23, 53-55, 57, 62, 71, 77, 82, 84-85, 89-91, 93-94, 96-97, 102-103, 105, 110, 113, 115, 118, 121-122, 125-126, 129, 134-135, 148, 152, 155, 159-161, 164, 176-177, 236, 239, 241, 243-244, 246, 248, 251-252, 254-255, 257, 260-262, 268, 270, 275, 278-279, 283, 287
3.leichte-Division, 53
3.Panzer-Division, 51, 188, 191, 195, 200, 212
3.SS Panzergrenadier-Division 'Totenkopf', 55
4.Gebirgs-Division, 72, 137, 165-166, 171, 174-175, 179, 181, 201, 217, 221, 231-232, 234, 238-239, 245, 247, 252-253, 260, 267, 269, 273-276, 278, 281-282, 284-285, 290
6.Panzer-Division, 6-7, 44, 53, 64, 73, 179, 186-193, 195-196, 198-199, 202-204, 207, 209-210, 214-215, 217, 219, 222-223, 225
7. Panzer-Division, 49, 52-53, 59, 61, 63, 68, 71-72, 75-77, 82, 84, 87-90, 98, 102-104, 106, 111, 113, 118, 122-123, 125, 130, 135-136, 138, 140-141, 143, 149-152, 154-155, 164, 168-169, 171-172, 176, 178, 181, 232, 235-240, 246, 249-250, 252, 255, 261, 263, 268, 270, 275, 279, 283, 287-289
8.Panzer-Division, 53, 71, 76-77, 82-85, 89, 95, 97-98, 102, 110, 115, 117, 125-126, 129, 159, 163, 176-177, 239, 243
9.Infanterie-Division, 57
10.Flak-Division, 188, 191-192, 195, 197, 215
11.Infanterie-Division, 50
11.Panzer-Division, 60-61
14.Panzer-Division, 52
16.Panzer-Division, 6-7, 45, 72, 137, 171, 177-179, 236-239, 242, 244, 246, 249-251, 256, 258-259, 263-264, 267-268, 272-275, 277-278, 281-282, 284-285, 290
17.Panzer-Division, 6-7, 73, 101, 112, 126, 137, 165-166, 171-172, 174-175, 179, 181, 185-187, 189-190, 192-193, 195, 197-199, 201, 203, 207-210, 214, 216-217, 220-223, 225, 231, 233, 238, 257
Flak-Division 17, 163
18.Artillerie-Division, 50, 72, 84, 88-91, 95, 98-99, 102, 107, 113, 116, 121, 125-126, 129, 132-133, 137, 140, 142, 146, 151, 154, 156-157, 164, 167, 172, 175, 232, 234, 243, 246, 252-253, 260-261, 265, 267, 269, 272, 274-276, 282, 286, 291
18.Panzer-Division, 45, 50

INDEX

19.Infanterie-Division, 52
19. Panzer-Division, 52-54, 71-72, 77, 81, 83, 89, 94, 97, 102, 110, 115, 117, 122, 125-126, 129, 135, 141, 176-177, 236, 239, 242-243, 246, 248, 252, 255, 261-262, 268, 270, 275, 279, 283, 287
20.Panzergrenadier-Division, 55, 72, 77, 85-86, 91, 95, 103, 105, 107, 113-114, 117, 120-121, 125, 129, 139, 151, 154, 262, 277
22.Infanterie-Division, 59
25.Panzer-Division, 51-52, 54, 71-72, 77, 81, 83, 85, 89, 92, 94, 97, 100-101, 103, 105, 107, 109, 113-114, 116-117, 120, 125, 128, 132-133, 140-142, 146-147, 154, 156, 163-164, 167, 175, 232, 275
29.Infanterie-Division, 56
34.Infanterie-Division, 45-46, 71, 73, 81, 86, 91, 114, 128, 131, 138, 142, 144, 154-155, 165, 173, 186-188, 190-193, 195-196, 198-200, 202, 206, 209, 214, 216, 219, 223, 231, 233
35.Infanterie-Division, 57
36.Infanterie-Division, 50, 53
44.Infanterie-Division, 66, 186, 192
65.Infanterie-Division, 67
68.Infanterie-Division, 56-58, 71, 82, 86, 89, 91, 94, 98, 102, 106, 110, 118, 122, 135, 139, 148, 159, 161, 176, 241, 246, 254
72.Infanterie-Division, 50
75.Infanterie-Division, 48, 71, 73, 81, 91, 108, 114, 116, 119, 131-132, 139, 142, 145, 154-155, 171, 173, 180, 187, 206, 209-210, 213, 216, 219, 223, 231
82.Infanterie-Division, 45, 47, 49, 71, 73, 81, 86, 114, 128, 131, 138, 144, 154-155, 165, 171, 173, 188, 192, 196-197, 200, 202, 205, 209-210, 212-213, 216, 218-219, 222, 224, 233
83.Infanterie-Division, 65
86.Infanterie-Division, 46, 59
88.Infanterie-Division, 49-51, 71, 73, 81, 86, 91, 94-97, 104, 108-109, 114, 116, 120, 128, 130-131, 142, 144-145, 154, 156, 163, 165, 171, 187, 189, 196, 198-199, 213, 219, 231, 233, 254
96.Infanterie-Division, 254, 258, 264
99.leichte Infanterie-Division, 65
101.Jäger-Division, 200-201, 204, 208, 215, 217-218, 221, 223, 225-226, 268, 278, 281-282, 284, 286, 288-289
112.Infanterie-Division, 46, 71
147.Reserve-Division, 67, 69, 177, 179, 250-251
163.Infanterie-Division, 51
164.Infanterie-Division, 48, 59
168.Infanterie-Division, 47, 71-72, 85, 93-94, 96, 99-105, 108, 113-114, 119-121, 125, 128, 132-133, 140-142, 146-147, 151, 154, 156, 164, 167, 174-175, 232, 234, 238, 246, 252-253, 260-261, 267, 269, 274-276, 282, 285-286, 290-291
170.Infanterie-Division, 58
183.Infanterie-Division, 66, 68
198.Infanterie-Division, 49-50, 71, 73, 81, 86, 91, 97, 101, 109, 116, 119, 128, 131, 142, 154-156, 163, 165, 171, 173, 187-189, 200, 202, 209-210, 213, 216, 219, 223, 231, 233
208.Infanterie-Division, 59-61, 71, 98, 111, 122, 130, 135, 140, 143, 149, 159, 247, 254, 266, 290
213.Infanterie-Division, 57
213.Sicherungs-Division, 57-58, 71-72, 91, 98, 106, 110, 135, 140, 143, 149, 160
217.Infanterie-Division, 66
221.Infanterie-Division, 69
223.Infanterie-Division, 47
Divisionsgruppe 223, 114, 120
256.Infanterie-Division, 47
269.Infanterie-Division, 48
290.Infanterie-Division, 58
291.Infanterie-Division, 64-66, 71-72, 82, 87, 94, 98, 103, 106, 111, 115-116, 118, 123, 130, 144, 149, 155, 172, 240, 242, 250, 252, 256, 264, 271, 275, 279, 283, 288
305.Infanterie-Division, 67
Artillerie-Division z.b.V. 311, 226
320.Infanterie-Division, 58
332.Infanterie-Division, 46
339.Infanterie-Division, 66-67
340.Infanterie-Division, 58-59, 71, 91, 98, 111, 115, 122, 135, 140, 143, 148, 155, 159, 169, 241, 246, 248, 254, 262
371.Infanterie-Division, 203, 221, 226, 266, 289-290
454.Sicherungs-Division, 69, 72, 236-237, 258, 264, 283, 288
716.Infanterie-Division, 69

Brigades:
SS Sturm-Brigade 'Langemarck', 152, 159, 171, 179
1.Ski-Brigade, 272
2.Panzer-Brigade, 60, 64
Schützen-Brigade 6, 44

Panzergrenadier-Brigade 19, 52

Kampfgruppen:
    Kampfgruppe 168, 47
    Kampfgruppe Källner, 135, 139, 141, 143, 148, 150, 159
    Kampfgruppe 340. Infanterie-Division, 262
    Kampfgruppe Friedrich, 110
    Kampfgruppe Gehrke, 144, 149, 155
    Kampfgruppe von Mitzlaff, 84, 93, 95, 102, 110
    Kampfgruppe von Mellenthin, 86-87
    Kampfgruppe von Radowitz, 102
    Kampfgruppe Neumeister, 94, 110
    Kampfgruppe Frölich, 177
    Kampfgruppe Korets, 258
    Panzerkampfgruppe SS 'Das Reich', 22-23, 53-55, 57, 82, 84-85, 89-91, 93-94, 102-103, 105, 110, 113, 115, 121, 125-126, 129, 134-135, 148, 152, 155, 159-161, 164, 176-177, 236, 239, 241, 243-244, 246, 248, 251-252, 254-255, 257, 260-262, 268, 270, 275, 278-279, 283, 287

Regiments:
    Artillerie-Regiment Grossdeutschland, 56
    Kavallerie-Regiment Süd, 107, 125, 141, 269-270, 272, 277
    Grenadier-Regiment 1, 263, 278, 285
    Panzer-Regiment 1, 102
    Schützen-Regiment 1, 60
    SS-Artillerie-Regiment 1, 109
    SS Panzergrenadier-Regiment 1, 82
    Grenadier-Regiment 2, 50
    Infanterie-Regiment 2 'Leibstandarte-SS-Adolf Hitler', 63
    Panzer-Regiment 2, 171, 179, 242, 263, 268, 277, 284
    Reiter-Regiment 2, 58
    Polizei-Regiment 6, 58
    Panzergrenadier-Regiment 8, 102
    Panzer-Regiment 9, 89
    SS Infanterie-Regiment 9 'Thule', 55
    Panzer-Regiment 10, 53
    Panzer-Regiment 11, 64, 179
    Gebirgsjäger-Regiment 13, 234, 273-274
    Panzerartillerie-Regiment 16, 249, 263, 268
    Füsilier-Regiment 22, 277, 285
    Panzer-Regiment 23, 226, 289, 290
    Panzer-Regiment 25, 61
    Panzerartillerie-Regiment 27, 166

Panzergrenadier-Regiment 28, 102, 110, 115
Artillerie-Regiment 34, 214
Artillerie-Regiment 36, 50
Artillerie-Regiment 37, 277
Panzergrenadier-Regiment 40, 172, 174
Grenadier-Regiment 43, 277, 285
Werfer-Regiment 52, 190, 197, 203
Werfer-Regiment 54, 190, 197, 203
Artillerie-Regiment 64, 188
Panzergrenadier-Regiment 63, 172, 174, 217
Panzergrenadier-Regiment 64, 242, 259, 263-264, 275, 277, 285
Panzergrenadier-Regiment 73, 52, 135
Panzergrenadier-Regiment 74, 135
Panzerartillerie-Regiment 78, 53
Panzergrenadier-Regiment 79, 249, 263
Infanterie-Regiment 80, 81
Infanterie-Regiment 84, 69
Artillerie-Regiment 85, 204
Artillerie-Regiment 88, 50, 129
Panzergrenadier-Regiment 90, 129, 132
Gebirgsjäger-Regiment 91, 234, 273
Gebirgs-Artillerie-Rgt. 94, 232, 234
Schützen-Regiment 103, 52
Infanterie-Regiment 108, 59
Panzergrenadier-Regiment 113, 98, 110
Infanterie-Regiment 116, 57
Infanterie-Regiment 134, 66
Infanterie-Regiment 145, 67
Panzergrenadier-Regiment 146, 85, 156, 175, 232
Panzergrenadier-Regiment 147, 114
Grenadier-Regiment 158, 131, 138-139, 205
Grenadier-Regiment 169, 254
Infanterie-Regiment 171, 56
Grenadier-Regiment 172, 254
Infanterie-Sicherungs-Regiment 177, 57-58, 250
Artillerie-Regiment 182, 47, 205
Grenadier-Regiment 188, 254
Grenadier-Regiment 196, 254
Reserve-Grenadier-Regiment 212, 62, 68, 91, 98
Infanterie-Regiment 216, 59
Artillerie-Regiment 221, 108
Artillerie-Regiment 223, 114
Jäger-Regiment 228, 204, 226, 284
Flak-Regiment 231, 175
Artillerie-Regiment 248, 96, 108, 114, 129
Infanterie-Regiment 253, 46
Artillerie-Regiment 254, 285
Reserve-Grenadier-Regiment 268, 68, 179
Artillerie-Regiment 288, 50, 129, 286

Grenadier-Regiment 305, 210, 233
Grenadier-Regiment 308, 210
Regimentsgruppe 311, 144
Infanterie-Regiment 318, 57
Sicherungs-Regiment 318, 58, 117
Grenadier-Regiment 323, 187
Infanterie-Regiment 330, 68
Grenadier-Regiment 337, 254
Grenadier-Regiment 338, 254
Infanterie-Regiment 350, 69
Sicherungs-Regiment 360, 69
Infanterie-Regiment 375, 69
Sicherungs-Regiment 375, 69, 87, 130
Infanterie-Regiment 382, 48
Regimentsgruppe 385, 108
Artillerie-Regiment 388, 50, 286
Grenadier-Regiment 417, 96, 108, 114, 120, 128, 130, 142, 145, 147, 151, 154, 189
Infanterie-Regiment 417, 47
Regimentsgruppe 417, 132
Regimentsgruppe 425, 108
Grenadier-Regiment 442, 129
Grenadier-Regiment 454, 285
Ost-Reiter-Regiment 454, 69
Infanterie-Regiment 456, 47
Grenadier-Regiment 475, 138, 188
Grenadier-Regiment 484, 285
Grenadier-Regiment 505, 111
Regimentsgruppe 677, 138, 192
Grenadier-Regiment 695, 254
Grenadier-Regiment 769, 254
Grenadier-Regiment 880, 67

Abteilungen/Bataillone:
    Panzer-Abteilung 'Das Reich', 54
    Panzeraufklärungs-Abteilung 1, 98, 110, 129, 164, 253-254, 277
    Panzerjäger-Abteilung 1, 277-278
    Pionier-Bataillon 1, 277
    SS Panzer-Aufklärungs-Abteilung 1, 109, 265
    SS-Panzerpionier-Bataillon 1, 109
    Panzer-Abteilung 2, 273
    Panzer-Abteilung 8, 55, 243
    Panzeraufklärungs-Abteilung 8, 97-98
    Feld-Ersatz-Bataillon 9, 271
    Aufklärungs-Abteilung 11, 52
    Panzeraufklärungs-Abteilung 16, 258, 263, 270, 279, 283, 285
    Panzer-Flak-Abteilung 16, 249
    Panzer-Pionier-Bataillon 16, 249

Panzeraufklärungs-Abteilung 25, 54
Panzerpionier-Bataillon 27, 166, 172, 174, 231
Reserve-Artillerie-Abteilung 27, 68
Reserve-Grenadier-Bataillon 27, 179
Reserve-Pionier-Bataillon 27, 68, 179
Füsilier-Bataillon 34, 188, 192
Panzerjäger-Abteilung 37, 98
Pionier-Bataillon (mot.) 48, 278, 291
Reserve-Grenadier-Bataillon 63, 68
Pionier-Bataillon 70, 91, 98, 111, 118, 123
Infanterie-Ersatz-Bataillon 73, 68
Pionier-Bataillon 74, 125, 131
Panzerjäger-Abteilung 87, 89
Pionier-Bataillon 88, 189
Schützen-Abteilung 88, 50
Reserve-Grenadier-Bataillon 91, 68
Aufklärungs-Abteilung 94, 166, 174, 232, 245
Gebirgs-Pionier-Bataillon 94, 234
Panzerjäger-Abteilung 94, 232, 238-239
Gebirgsjäger-Bataillon 99, 232
Aufklärungs-Abteilung 168, 108
Marschbataillon 183/8, 115
Sturmgeschütz-Abteilung 202, 96, 156, 189, 205, 214, 219
Kosaken-Abteilung 213, 58
Panzer-Abteilung 214, 51
Pionier-Bataillon 215, 108
Sturmgeschütz-Abteilung 239, 165, 173, 206
Pionier-Bataillon 248, 108
Sturmgeschütz-Abteilung 249, 126, 189-190, 199, 222, 225
Pionier-Bataillon 254, 285
Heeres-Flak-Abteilung 280, 50, 129
Sturmgeschütz-Abteilung 280, 159, 243, 254
Heeres-Flak-Abteilung 284, 55
Sturmgeschütz-Abteilung 300, 250, 273
Reserve-Grenadier-Bataillon 316, 68, 98, 111
Reserve-Grenadier-Bataillon 320, 68, 87
Transport-Sicherungs-Bataillon 361, 201
Ost-Reiter-Abteilung 403, 110, 271
Reserve-Grenadier-Bataillon 423, 68
Artillerie-Abteilung 454, 69
Ost-Pionier-Bataillon 454, 69
Reserve-Grenadier-Bataillon 468, 68
Panzer-Zerstörer-Bataillon (mot.) 471, 204, 221
Panzer-Zerstörer-Bataillon 473, 85, 88, 95, 272
Reserve-Grenadier-Bataillon 488, 68, 179
schwere-Panzer-Abteilung 503, 226, 289-290
schwere-Panzer-Abteilung 506, 126, 137, 179, 189-190, 199, 215, 221-222, 225, 233

schwere Panzer-Abteilung 509, 77, 84-87, 89, 91, 95, 98, 120, 147, 175, 243-244, 275
Bau-Pionier-Bataillon 523, 291
Pionier-Bau-Bataillon 523, 278
Panzerjäger-Abteilung 559, 159
Transport-Sicherungs-Bataillon 594, 201
schwere-Artillerie-Abteilung 628, 197
schwere-Artillerie-Abteilung 629, 190
Panzerjäger-Abteilung 731, 244
Panzer-Zerstörer-Bataillon 731, 116
Panzerjäger-Abteilung 739, 275
Sturmgeschütz-Batterie 741, 50
Landesschützen-Bataillon 857, 133, 175, 232
Transport-Sicherungs- Bataillon 896, 201
Landesschützen-Bataillon 987, 271

Miscellaneous/Other:
Gruppe Wechmar, 114, 120
Panzergruppe 1, 62
Waffen-Schule PzAOK 1, 204
Ausbildungs-Leiter 2, 69
Panzergruppe 2, 45, 48, 56
Nebeltruppe 3, 197, 203
Panzergruppe 3, 29, 52, 55, 61, 63
Luftflotte 4, 41, 163, 185, 191, 272
Panzergruppe 4, 53, 63-64
Wehrkreis VII, 67
Höheres Kommando z.b.V. LIX, 65
Panzerzug 62, 203, 226
Artillerie-Kommandeur 101, 50, 282
Panzerjäger-Kompanie 248, 108
Hohe-Artillerie-Kommandeur 301, 50
Höherer Artillerie-Kommandeur 311, 226
Feldkommandantur 675, 90

Index of Hungarian Military Units
2nd Army, 38
7th Corps, 291
21st Infantry Division, 179
201st Infantry Division, 179
Infantry Regiment 40, 180
Infantry Regiment 42, 179-180
Infantry Regiment 44, 179-180
23rd Hussar Squadron, 179

Index of Rumanian Military Units
8th Infantry Regiment, 290
715th Independent Battalion, 290

Index of Soviet Military Units
Fronts:
   1st Ukrainian Front, 4, 9, 14, 21, 23, 28, 30, 32, 34-35, 37-41, 72, 181, 190, 211, 291-294, 297
   2nd Ukrainian Front, 21-22, 200, 294
   3rd Ukrainian Front, 32

Armies:
   1st Guards Army, 4, 22, 32-34, 37, 90, 112, 251, 264, 266, 292-293, 297
   1st Tank Army, 4, 21-24, 26-28, 37-38, 76, 90, 109, 111, 157, 198-199, 207-208, 211, 215, 220-221, 227, 242, 247, 250, 257, 261, 265-267, 280-281, 288, 290-291, 293-294, 297
   2nd Air Army, 21-22
   3rd Guards Tank Army, 4, 13, 22-24, 34-36, 112, 157, 237, 242, 251, 264, 266, 289, 293-294, 297
   4th Reserve Army, 32, 35
   5th Army, 35-38, 40
   5th Tank Army, 35
   6th Army, 28, 36
   7th Army, 40
   8th Army, 38
   12th Army, 33
   13th Army, 4, 22-23, 29-31, 36, 179, 266, 289, 291-293
   18th Army, 4, 21-22, 24, 26, 33-35, 292-293, 297
   21st Army, 39
   22nd Army, 37
   27th Army, 4, 22, 39-40, 293-294
   32nd Army, 40
   38th Army, 4, 22-27, 34-38, 90, 99, 111, 266, 280, 290, 292-293, 297
   40th Army, 4, 22, 24, 37-39, 99, 111, 123-124, 128, 137, 149, 211, 266-267, 293-294, 297
   46th Army, 32, 34
   47th Army, 33-34, 39
   50th Army, 34
   51st Army, 40
   56th Army, 33
   60th Army, 4, 22, 31-32, 90, 112, 179, 243, 251, 264-266, 280, 292, 294, 297
   69th Army, 36
   70th Army, 30

Corps:
   1st Guards Cavalry Corps, 22, 76, 213, 243
   2nd Mechanised Corps, 36
   3rd Guards Tank Corps, 99, 124, 149, 190

INDEX

3rd Mechanised Corps, 37
3rd Rifle Corps, 34
4th Guards Tank Corps, 22, 75-76, 112, 179, 237, 251, 255, 264-265, 280, 289, 292-294
5th Guards Tank Corps, 22, 112, 123-124, 138, 150, 215, 219-220, 222, 227, 251, 293-294
5th Mechanised Corps, 293-294
6th Guards Cavalry Corps, 36, 293-294
6th Guards Tank Corps, 99, 112, 124, 157, 179, 251, 271
7th Guards Tank Corps, 99, 112, 137, 157, 162, 179, 251, 256, 271, 280
8th Guards Mechanised Corps, 27, 99, 124, 150, 198-199, 207-208, 221, 237, 266, 289-290
9th Guards Mechanised Corps, 150, 289
9th Mechanised Corps, 37, 112, 124, 150, 157, 179, 251, 256, 286-287, 289
10th Tank Corps, 99-100, 112, 207
11th Guards Tank Corps, 27, 111, 124, 157, 195, 198-199, 207-208, 221, 266, 275, 288-290
17th Guards Rifle Corps, 26
18th Independent Rifle Corps, 38
18th Tank Corps, 32
21st Rifle Corps, 26
25th Tank Corps, 21-22, 75-76, 90, 112, 179, 243, 251, 292-293
31st Tank Corps, 237, 293-294
50th Rifle Corps, 123
52nd Rifle Corps, 26
67th Rifle Corps, 39
74th Rifle Corps, 26
94th Rifle Corps, 32
107th Rifle Corps, 32

Divisions:
2nd Guards Airborne Division, 75
8th Guards Fighter Division, 27
11th Cavalry Division, 32
17th Artillery Division, 293
20th Tank Division, 37
28th Tank Division, 31
42nd Guards Rifle Division, 189-190, 194
51st Rifle Division, 36
61st Rifle Division, 39
68th Guards Rifle Division, 290
74th Rifle Division, 108, 187
92nd Rifle Division, 39
107th Rifle Division, 290
129th Guards Rifle Division, 76
135th Rifle Division, 290

143rd Rifle Division, 76
155th Rifle Division, 215
163rd Rifle Division, 194
206th Rifle Division, 239
211th Rifle Division, 194, 290
232nd Rifle Division, 117
237th Rifle Division, 290
240th Rifle Division, 128, 190, 227
241st Rifle Division, 32, 290
291st Ground Attack Division, 27
389th Rifle Division, 76, 235

Brigades:
1st Czechoslovak Infantry Brigade, 22
1st Guards Tank Brigade, 37
1st Motorised Anti-tank Artillery Brigade, 36
4th Tank Brigade, 37
19th Guards Mechanised Brigade, 27
12th Guards Tank Brigade, 237, 239
22nd Guards Tank Brigade, 220, 227
23rd Mechanised Brigade, 36
40th Guards Tank Brigade, 195
44th Guards Tank Brigade, 27
64th Guards Tank Brigade, 27
133rd Mechanised Brigade, 36
248th Rifle Brigade, 76

Regiments:
797th Rifle Regiment, 117
79th Guards Mortar Regiment, 27
1462nd Self-Propelled Artillery Regiment, 215

Battalions:
81st Motorcycle Battalion, 27

Related titles published by Helion & Company

Demolishing the Myth. The Tank Battle at Prokhorovka, Kursk, July 1943: An Operational Narrative
Valeriy Zamulin (edited & translated by Stuart Britton)
672 pages   Hardback
ISBN 978-1-906033-89-7

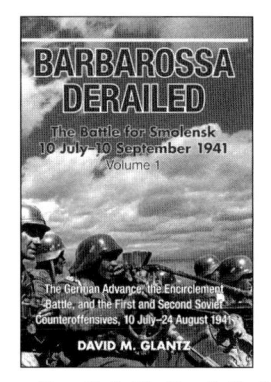

Barbarossa Derailed: The Battle for Smolensk 10 July-10 September 1941 Volume 1: The German Advance, The Encirclement Battle, and the First and Second Soviet Counteroffensives, 10 July-24 August 1941
David M. Glantz
624 pages   Hardback
ISBN 978-1-906033-72-9

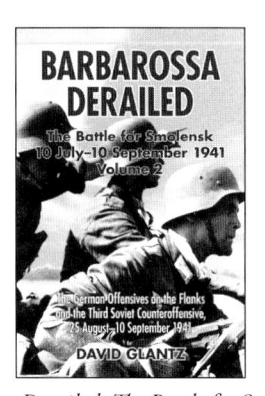

Barbarossa Derailed: The Battle for Smolensk 10 July-10 September 1941 Volume 2: The German Offensives on the Flanks and the Third Soviet Counteroffensive, 25 August-10 September 1941
David M. Glantz
624 pages   Hardback
ISBN 978-1-906033-90-3

Waffen-SS Armour in Normandy. The Combat History of SS Panzer Regiment 12 and SS Panzerjäger Abteilung 12, Normandy 1944, based on their original war diaries
Norbert Számvéber
304 pages   Hardback
ISBN 978-1-907677-24-3

HELION & COMPANY

26 Willow Road, Solihull, West Midlands B91 1UE, England
Telephone 0121 705 3393   Fax 0121 711 4075
Website: http://www.helion.co.uk